THE PAPERS

of

JOHN C. CALHOUN

CALHOUN

Final resting place, St. Philips Churchyard, Charleston
Photography by Michael Givens

THE PAPERS

of

JOHN C. CALHOUN

◫

Volume XXVII, 1849–1850
With Supplement

Edited by

CLYDE N. WILSON

and SHIRLEY BRIGHT COOK

Alexander Moore, *Associate Editor*

UNIVERSITY OF SOUTH CAROLINA PRESS, 2003

CONTENTS

◫

PREFACE

◫

The book in hand is the last volume of the published edition of Calhoun papers, except for a volume that will contain definitive texts of Calhoun's *A Disquisition on Government* and *A Discourse on the Constitution and Government of the United States.* "Papers" have been broadly defined and the edition is as complete as it can be made except for minor administrative correspondence.

The edition represents the labor of many people over a half century. Its production has required the skills of interpretive and synthesizing historian, researcher, manuscript editor, literary textual critic, typist, typographer, printer, publisher, copyreader, proofreader, indexer, fundraiser, grant administrator, librarian, archivist, publicist, and bureaucratic infighter.

Many good people have worked with the editors (Robert L. Meriwether, W. Edwin Hemphill, Shirley A. Cook, and the undersigned) one or two at a time for varying periods, the most recent being Timothy Manning, Jr. For decades the editors have engaged in daily, painstaking, persevering, intense hands-on-labor. This has been made possible by the institutions that have supported us. The support of the National Historical Publications and Records Commission has been continuing and indispensable, as has that of the University of South Carolina. The National Endowment for the Humanities aided us for a time. The University South Caroliniana Society and the Bostick Charitable Trust have come to our aid at critical times.

Robert L. Meriwether, in the Preface to the first volume, published in 1959, indicated a hope to correct superficial and partisan interpretations of Calhoun which had persisted from the controversies of his time. This would assist the larger purpose of understanding "Southern history, which is subject to the defects of interpretation usually attendant on causes involved in defeat and continuing controversy." Some headway has been made toward these goals, and the existence of this edition will make possible further improvement in the future. Because, rarely among publications,

Calhoun is here allowed to speak for himself rather than be judged by prefabricated conventions.

Has it been worth it? The answer is given by the pioneer American professional historian J. Franklin Jameson, in the 1900 preface to the first edition of Calhoun correspondence. He announced that the value of his work was in "having made better known to American readers—to the readers of documents, at least, a small but potent audience—the character and career of one of the greatest and most elevated of American statesmen." Substitute "international" for the first "American" and we rest our case.

CLYDE N. WILSON

Columbia, Summer 2000

OVERVIEW OF THE PAPERS
OF JOHN C. CALHOUN, Vols. 1–27

Ⅲ

There has never been any compelling reason or available leisure to count the materials collected in the preparation and publishing of the twenty-seven volumes of this edition. The late W. Edwin Hemphill, editor of Volumes II–IX, once estimated that 50,000 items (including multiple versions and collateral documents) in various forms of reproduction had been gathered. Many more have been added since that estimate was made.

About two-thirds of these documents relate to the more than seven years of Calhoun's energetic administration of the far-flung War Department, 1817–1825. About a fifth of the extant documents for that period have been published.[1] There have been also some omissions of less important items related to the offices of Vice-President and Secretary of State, as explained in Volume XI:vii–viii and Volume XXI:xv–xix. Otherwise, the presentation is complete either in transcription or in carefully constructed editorial abstracts that are somewhat more than calendar entries.

The Search for Documents

We believe our searching has been as thorough as is humanly possible. We have searched out manuscripts in every possible nook and cranny, a task greatly aided by the previous collecting efforts of J. Franklin Jameson and Robert L. Meriwether, but which we have continued to pursue to the last moment. We have, besides, been through many hundreds of microfilm reels of Record Groups in the National Archives. We have even worked through the manuscript records of the U.S. Senate. (Historians have erroneously assumed

---

[1] For the War Department period there was a preference for the selection of previously unpublished material, so that it may still be necessary to consult the relevant series of *American State Papers* and John Spencer Bassett's edition of Andrew Jackson correspondence to get a detailed picture of Calhoun's administrative work and of some of the major events of the period.

that the published Congressional documents contain all the useful material.) This involved carefully untieing and re-tieing pink ribbons (the origins of the term government "red tape") confining bundles of documents that had not been disturbed since Clerks put them away a century and a half before.

We have also searched extensive files of several hundred newspapers and journals for stray documents. Calhoun did not keep copies of his outgoing letters except in rare cases. We have found in newspapers, sometimes obscure ones, public letters not otherwise known. These were an important part of the political discourse of the time and often contain thoughts that are not elsewhere recorded or amplify the understanding of those that are.

We have also made exhaustive study and textual criticism of the records of Calhoun's speeches, mostly in Congress, though sometimes outside. We have found numbers of differing versions to be compared and published or cited herein, often clarifying or adding to the understanding of notable occasions. And we have made as complete as possible a collection of his brief remarks in Congress on occasions not notable. This has resulted in a substantial contribution to the understanding of neglected aspects of Calhoun's thought and its consistency and wholeness. After all, it is as a political thinker that Calhoun will be of most interest to posterity. These brief remarks contain many gems of overlooked insights.[2]

It is likely that not every historical figure deserves as exhaustive an edition of speeches as we have tried to make. But Calhoun, unlike any other American statesman of his time or later, is a figure in intellectual history as well as political history, and the public utterances are a vital part of his documentary record.

Giants' Shoulders

Calhoun had told his family that his longtime friend, the Virginian Richard Kenner Crallé, should be the editor of his literary remains. Crallé (which seems to have been pronounced "Crawlee") in this capacity gave the world the *Disquisition* and *Discourse*. His publications in 1851 are the earliest known texts from which all others are derived. He worked from Calhoun's manuscript, probably the uncorrected fair copy made a few weeks before his death, which can no longer be found.

Crallé produced five further volumes of *The Works of John C.*

---

[2] I made good use of many of these in *The Essential Calhoun* (New Brunswick, N.J.: Transaction, 1992, 2000).

Calhoun, published between 1853 and 1858, three of speeches and two of public papers, the publication being handsomely subsidized by the State of South Carolina. His selection of documents for importance was impeccable.

There is an extensive correspondence relating to the *Works* among Crallé, Calhoun's sons, and other persons, in the Calhoun Papers at Clemson and Crallé's papers at the University of Virginia. Unfortunately these letters are not very informative for a documentary editor in search of manuscripts. All we have to go on are the brief prefaces ("Advertisements") in the *Works*, volumes 2, 5, and 6, and sparse other notes. It would appear that Crallé had the drafts of some important public documents. Of Calhoun's speeches he said, in part:

> The collection of the Speeches of Mr. Calhoun, here offered to the public, includes, it is believed, all delivered by him in Congress of any general interest—or rather, all, of which any reliable reports have been preserved. Many, no doubt, especially during the War of 1812, through carelessness and the want of competent reporters in the House of Representatives, have been lost . . . .
> Of the Speeches delivered in the Senate, between the years 1833 and 1850, a much larger number has been preserved. They are, for the most part, better reported; and not a few were published in pamphlet form at the time, under his own inspection. Still, so constant and pressing were his engagements—so incessant the demands on his time, that it is impossible he could have bestowed much attention, except on those connected with the more important subjects of discussion. Many were left to be drawn out by the reporters; and his peculiar position, in regard to the two great contending parties of the country, was any thing but favorable to fulness and fidelity. Not a few (and among them some on questions of much interest) were never reported at all, or otherwise so mangled and garbled,—to serve a temporary purpose,—as to render them unworthy of this collection.[3]

J. Franklin Jameson, one of the most energetic and perceptive of the first generation of American professional historians, began in the late 19th century to repair what he considered a great lacunae in published historical documents: Calhoun's correspondence.

Available for this purpose and still the most important Calhoun archive was the collection of papers from Fort Hill that were then (and now) in the keeping of Clemson College. Partly through the good offices of Senator Benjamin R. Tillman, Jameson was allowed

---

[3] Crallé, ed., *Works*, 2:v–vi. Writing Calhoun on 2/2/1849, Crallé indicated that he had carefully preserved Calhoun's speeches (probably the pamphlet versions). *Papers of John C. Calhoun*, 26:268.

to take this massive collection to Johns Hopkins to work on.[4] This was fortunate, because, according to tradition, there was a serious fire in the Clemson library during the time.

The Clemson collection was rich in letters to Calhoun during the latter part of his life. At different points in his life Calhoun seemed to take different actions in regard to his incoming correspondence. That received while he was in Washington was, we know from passing references, packed in trunks, sometimes carried home, sometimes left in Washington, and on a few occasions discarded. Most of the letters received seem to have survived for his last twenty years, except for the last four months when the incoming letters would be extremely valuable for public opinion on the 1850 crisis. These seem to have been lost in the period after his death.

To find the letters that Calhoun wrote to others, except for those to family members that survived in the Clemson collection, it was necessary to cast a wide net—and this Jameson did. His papers in the Library of Congress provide a full record of his pursuit of the descendants of important Calhoun correspondents.

He was quite successful in this, finding a great many valuable letters written by Calhoun, including some which, like those in possession of Duff Green's grandson on the West Coast, have since disappeared. He had a good nose for such a pursuit and enlisted the help of other historians and influential people. The survival rate of manuscripts was limited seriously by the fire and pillage of the federal armies' terrorism campaign against civilians in the conflict of 1861–1865. Much was destroyed and occasionally souvenir letters appeared in Northern homes and auction houses that had been pilfered during the war. Certainly lost in this way were many Calhoun letters to John M. Berrien, Langdon Cheves, William Lowndes, James L. Orr, and Robert Barnwell Rhett.

Because of the dynamism and anonymity of New York City, or for other reasons, many letters to Northerners were lost. It is heartbreaking to Calhoun's editor that his letters to the sympathetic New Yorkers Fitzwilliam Byrdsall and Charles Augustus Davis have vanished without a trace. And Pennsylvanians are under-represented as well. Samuel D. Ingham destroyed his papers before his death. And the daughter of Francis Wharton, the Philadelphia legal scholar who

---

[4] The description of Jameson's collecting which follows is made from the extensive correspondence in his papers at the Library of Congress. See also Alexander Moore, "Present at the Creation: John Franklin Jameson and the Development of Humanistic Scholarship in America," in *Documentary Editing*, vol. 16, no. 3 (September, 1994), pp. 57–60.

was close to Calhoun, was apparently a victim of the bloody-shirt mentality, unwilling to release papers that would disclose her kin's relation to the arch-traitor Calhoun.

Jameson was able to publish an excellent collection of letters by Calhoun and a judicious selection of letters to him in 1900. The latter type of correspondence was supplemented from the Clemson collection by the Boucher and Brooks publication in 1929.

Robert L. Meriwether began preparing *The Papers of John C. Calhoun* in the 1950s after founding the University South Caroliniana Society and the South Caroliniana Library. Working often against the hostility or indifference of administrators and with volunteer labor, and using his contacts among prominent families of South Carolina, he extended Jameson's work of collecting and produced the first volume of *The Papers of John C. Calhoun*. He acquired by purchase or loan as many uncollected Calhoun documents as could be found.

Meriwether's successor W. Edwin Hemphill was forced to grapple with the immense amount of material related to Calhoun's seven-plus years as Secretary of War that had begun to come to light due to searches supported by the National Historical Publications Commission in the National Archives. The original plan had been to devote two volumes to that period, but the abundance of material led to eight volumes, though only about one fifth or less of the known materials were published and many of them in summary rather than transcription.

Searching for all periods of Calhoun's life has continued until the last moment and new documents have steadily come to light alone or in small batches.

It was hoped that Crallé would produce a biography of Calhoun with his unique knowledge of circumstances. Crallé died in 1864 and, after the failed War for Southern Independence, Robert M.T. Hunter was urged to take up the project. The impoverished conditions of the postbellum South limited what could be accomplished. Among Crallé's papers at the Library of Congress and Hunter's at the Library of Virginia are substantial fragments of compositions, hardly touched by historians, that seem to represent what is left of these efforts.

The task was later taken up by William Pinkney Starke. Starke had had extraordinary educational opportunities and was intimate with the Calhoun/Clemson family, actually living at Fort Hill for some years. His writing was a truly unfortunate combination of romanticism and pedantry and is of little value except for the occasional information acquired orally from Calhoun relatives that is not otherwise known. The complete ms. is at Clemson.

Questionable Documents

Calhoun was not infrequently charged with having written documents that appeared over the names of others. Perhaps, most notably, he was accused, falsely, of having ghostwritten his own biography. (See Volume XVII:xvi–xvii.)

In such cases we have pursued the evidence as far as it could go (which was often not very far) in hopes of finding a new Calhoun document. In two notable cases his authorship *was* anonymous. One is the report of June 3, 1812, of the House Committee on Foreign Relations that accompanied the declaration of war. Calhoun had no bad motive in not claiming authorship, but two good ones—deference to the chairman of the committee and reluctance to seek personal credit for an act of the people.

The second notable case is that of the *South Carolina Exposition* of 1828. The belated disclosure of Calhoun's drafting of this document was, as usual, attributed to low political motives. But consider that the paper was officially a production of a committee of the South Carolina General Assembly. If Calhoun's role had been broadcast, the occasion would have been reduced in the minds of many to an incident of presidential politics rather than a solemn act of the State (which is what happened when it was known). For the same reason, Jefferson never publicly acknowledged his drafting of the Kentucky Resolutions.

One can put the charges of clandestine Calhoun authorship in perspective by reflecting that they generally came from jealous rivals within Southern ranks or from Van Buren Democrats. Both groups hoped to chip away at the granite block of Calhoun's reputation for genius and virtue by spreading the caricature of a scheming conspirator pulling the strings to which others danced in the interests of his hidden ambitions.

Such a caricature managed to convince many at the time and later, perhaps because, as Calhoun several times observed, some people are unable to conceive of motives higher than what they themselves experience. One suspects that few people would have come to the politicians who made these charges for inspiration and help in regard to principles and issues, but many would have come for assistance in obfuscating and straddling issues that threatened to disrupt their pursuit of patronage.

What seems reasonable to assume is, that when approached, as he often was, by allies, or in council with them, Calhoun, senior in talent and service, made suggestions and recommendations as to moves and sketched out or rough drafted lines of argument to be pursued, and that these were carried forward by others. This understanding is in keeping with what is known of his character and manner of leadership.

In a number of cases, it is simply not possible to establish whether or to what degree Calhoun may have been involved in drafting public documents that did not appear in his name. It was thought by some that he wrote contemporarily famous reports by Richard M. Johnson in the House of Representatives and Senate in 1829 and 1830. While Calhoun probably agreed with Johnson's effort to quash the demand by some Northern religious denominations to forbid movement of the mails on Sundays, the documents don't at all resemble his style.

Another document attributed to Calhoun was the report made to the House of Representatives on January 24, 1831, by Warren R. Davis of South Carolina, calling for repeal of the 25th section of the Judiciary Act of 1789. Since the document was an important move in the interposition controversy and since Davis represented Calhoun's home district, it can be assumed that he had some involvement in the matter. However, Davis himself was an able lawyer and the style and some of the content do not sound like Calhoun. (*Register of Debates*, 21st Cong., 2nd Sess., Appendix, pp. lxxvii–lxxxi.)

Methods

The methods used for rendering handwriting into type in this edition are straightforward, literal, and as consistent as possible with work done over nearly a half a century by many different people. It has all been checked, and rechecked, and rechecked.

Two silent emendations ought to be stated for the record. Where the initial letter of a word cannot be clearly distinguished as a capital or lower case, as is a frequent occurrence in Calhoun's script, we have tended to render as upper case such words as "State" (when referring to a State of the Union) and "Constitution" (when referring to the Constitution of the U.S. and not another or generic constitution).

We have also, for the sake of clarity in text and index, consistently rendered the names of Calhoun's in-laws as "Colhoun," even though they sometimes wrote themselves or were written to as

"Calhoun." Both branches pronounced the name as something like "Culhoon," with equal emphasis on both syllables.

Readers will also note that beginning with Volume II, symbols used to identify repositories were based on Library of Congress Union Catalog abbreviations. Some of these have since changed and they are no longer much in use, but we have continued to use them for consistency. They are easily deciphered by reference to the symbols list in each volume. With somewhat more difficulty the artificial numbers for series in the National Archives used in Volumes II–XI may be deciphered in the same way.

At this writing there are no plans to make a cumulative index, for several reasons, in addition to the exhaustion of energy and resources. The construction of the indices has varied under different editors over a period of forty years and each book stands alone for its period. Indexing is very much an art and not a science. Reflection on the task of creating many indices has led us to the understanding that our books are not reference works—they are collections of primary sources for research. For that reason we have made our index entries fairly broad, the only feature of the series that has been criticized in reviews, as far as I recall.

To subdivide references into numerous subentries, as is suitable in a discursive work, is to make artificial and misleading divisions, because in a volume of primary sources, it cannot be anticipated what needs and interests the researcher will bring to it. To provide highly detailed indexes would, we fear, encourage the practice of some historians (including distinguished ones) to clip quotations rather than to study contexts. The form of our indexes and the lack of a cumulative one will, we hope lead to more serious research into the too-often superficially dealt-with Calhoun.

Nearly all of Calhoun's significant correspondents, and many of lesser significance, are well identified somewhere in the notes to the letters. We have not repeated such identification, once made, in subsequent volumes.

Calhoun's Library

Curiosity about Calhoun's library and reading is natural but can never be fully satisfied. Unlike some orators, he did not stud his speeches (or letters) with literary allusions. Calhoun was a parliamentary debater, not a ceremonial orator or stump speaker. Some description of his early reading was given in the 1843 *Life of John C. Calhoun*, the writer of that work doubtless having word from Calhoun himself of the authors most remembered and valued. Charles M. Wiltse cites some circulation records in the Library of Congress.[5]

The Fort Hill library seems to have been auctioned off in dispersed lots at the death of Andrew Pickens Calhoun. *De Bow's Review* reported such in 1869, and correctly commented:

> The limited collection of works may be accounted for by the fact that Mr. Calhoun had always the best public libraries at his service, but more especially, we think, that he was a great original thinker . . . . Mr. Calhoun was as little indebted to the authority of others as any man who ever lived, and we do not remember ever to have seen a quotation used by him.[6]

There is thought to have been an inventory of the Calhouns' library at Clemson College which was lost in a fire around 1900. The records of the Pendleton Library Society are at Clemson University but have no significant reference to Calhoun.

In the correspondence of the South Carolina historian Yates Snowden at the South Caroliniana Library of the University of South Carolina is a letter from a Connecticut dealer, William Todd, dated March 30 [1931], listing 27 pamphlets that had belonged to Calhoun then in Todd's possession. Todd remarked that he purchased the items from the "Calhoun Mansion" on Meeting Street in Charleston from "young J.C. Calhoun" (evidently the son of Calhoun's grandson Patrick). They had been found in the attic and were the few library items in the house that had not belonged to other members of the family. In the same year of 1931, Dartmouth College bought a collection of about 100 pamphlets that had belonged to Calhoun, mostly presentation copies from the authors. All of the Dartmouth pamphlets are dated 1828 or earlier.[7]

To place Calhoun in intellectual history requires a good deal of subtlety, and would not be advanced by a too literal-minded reference to his reading matter. It is done well in two 1998 dissertations cited in footnote 23 to the Introduction of Volume 26.

[5] See *The Papers of John C. Calhoun,* 17:7–9; Wiltse, *John C. Calhoun,* 1:441, note 16.

[6] "The Library of John C. Calhoun," *De Bow's Review,* new series, vol. VI, no. 1 (July 1869), p. 594. Even during Reconstruction the sale of Calhoun's library seems to have been news since it was reported as far away as the *Olympia Register* in Washington Territory, March 28, 1868.

[7] See Robert D. Jaccaud, "The Calhoun Collection of Pamphlets and the Presidential Election of 1824," *Dartmouth College Library Bulletin,* new series, vol. XIII, no. 1 (November 1972), pp. 48–58, which describes the collection and lists 21 items related to the 1824 election.

The Permanent Collection

The materials accumulated in the half century of work on the Calhoun edition are expected to become a permanent collection in the South Caroliniana Library of the University of South Carolina. These include:

Photocopies (in various forms, chiefly photostat and microfilm) of documents collected by the project.

Finding aids to the above—chronological, alphabetical, and by repository.

Alphabetical file of transcriptions and abstracts created by the project.

Chronological file of transcriptions and abstracts omitted from publication.

Set of the published volumes with annotations of minor addenda and errata.

Correspondence of the project.

Search records.

Large file of notes and copies of primary and secondary materials accumulated in the course of work, including materials for possible updating of *John C. Calhoun: A Bibliography* (1990).

File of materials related to Calhoun art and photography.

THE PAPERS

of

JOHN C. CALHOUN

Ⅲ

Volume XXVII

AUGUST 1–DECEMBER 2, 1849

〖

Calhoun, of course, could not know that he was spending his last time at Fort Hill, superintending his last harvest and the preparations for winter.

His letters concerned the need for a convention to concert Southern action. Long after he was gone from the scene, there would be argument over whether his promotion of this convention was a step toward secession. At any rate, when it gathered in Nashville after his death, the mood was compromise. Meanwhile, an encouraging sign in politics was the rise of forces in Missouri that could unseat the execrable, to Calhoun, Thomas H. Benton.

His next-to-youngest son, James, was about to graduate from South Carolina College and the youngest, Willie, was making his way through the same institution. Their father wrote on October 27: "You both will soon be on the stage of life, &, I trust, well prepared to act your parts. You will both enter on it, at a most eventful period." "The next step," he wrote on November 11, "will take you into the most important of all, & for which the preceding is but preperation, the business of life . . . ."

Calhoun took a little more time than usual making his way to Washington for the new session of Congress, doubtless to confer with influential men along the way about united Southern action. He stayed overnight in Edgefield on November 23, and arrived at Charleston on the train from Hamburg two days later. On November 28, accompanied by several members from the lower South, he took the boat to Wilmington and from there the train north (on a railroad line that in little more than a decade would be fought over by massive armies). He was in his seat when the session of the Senate opened on December 3. (Edgefield, S.C., Advertiser, November 28, 1849; Charleston, S.C., Courier, November 27 and 29, 1849.)

〖

From Tho[ma]s G. Clemson

Brussels, August 1[s]t 1849

My dear Sir, We are once more comfortably fixed in this city. We have taken furnished lodgings for a month or two, which will give us time to look around us and select a house, which we intend to furnish. That once done we shall be able to live more agreably on my salary. The only difficulty that I foresee in furnishing a house is the first outlay, and if I can possibly arrange that my expenses will be less than they were when I lived here before which I was obliged to do, in furnished lodgings, which are always more expensive. Our pay is so small relatively speaking that I do think the time is come when a change is necessary. The grade of Chargé d'Affaires is now becoming throughout Europe almost obsolete. At this Court all those, save one, who were Chargés have been advanced to Ministers & their salary increased. I find myself at the bottom of the list of the Diplomatic agents. I hope that something will be done at the next session. The fact of it is if I had money I would not trouble myself much about retaining the place. We are all well, notwithstanding the Cholera is not only in Brussels, but every where in Belgium & I may say in the North of Europe. In Antwerp it is very bad, as also in Liege. It has been worse in Brussels than at present, & the deaths have mainly been confined to the lower classes. Still however persons in high position have been swept away. One of the Queens maids of honour died the other day in Liege after a short illness. As yet there is no cause for great alarm, particularly with attention. One thing appears to characterise this visitation throughout Europe. That which took place in 1832 was severe but rapid; it did its work & disappeared. At St. Petersburg where the disease first made its appearance upwards of a year ago, it still continues to make victims & the same may be said of its visitation every where.

As to the political state of this country, it is perfectly tranquil & no change here has been anticipated or feared. The people are perfectly satisfied & determined to mantain tranquility. The king [Leopold I] is become popular, the public securities, which had fallen are gradually rising & without foreign interference, Belgium will pursue her course without commotion of any kind. The state finances are in a bad condition, but not worse than they were previous to the 24 Feb. 1848. Her standing army is too heavy a burthen for her to carry & prevents the equalising of the receipts & expenditures. Belgium however when compared with other states of Europe is rather in a better condition, or less badly off. As to the rest of the

Continent, things look bad indeed. The sword & bayonet is once more become the governing principle. Had France thrown her armies on the Rhine & into Italy there would not have been a monarch upon a throne from the Baltic to the Mediteranean. You perceive that the Republic of France has restored the Pope. That Russia is assisting Austria to crush the Hungarians &c. The probability is that the Governments of Europe, from present appearances, will become more despotic than they have ever been. Liberty & monarchy on the continent appear to be incompatible words. Without instruction the people can not retain power after having conquered it & there is nothing done to prepare them for taking Government into their own hands. Emigration from Europe to the United States is becoming greater. Few have ever gone from Belgium, but it is now becoming quite fashionable here. Some of my friends have sold out their property even at a great sacrifice, and are going with their families and all the property they can scrape.

I have been quite interested in a gentleman, who is now here, from Saxony, and who will shortly leave for the United States. He appears to be a very worthy gentleman & possessed of a great deal of knowledge. He speaks English, French & Spanish almost as well as he does his own tongue, is an author of considerable renown, having written a great deal on the subject of Education (consisting of modes of teaching &c), has been at the head of several schools, & professor at Freyberg. He has also written several works on Hydropathey & been at the head of two or three establishments of that character in Germany. He was wounded in the revolution (late) in Saxony & when the Prussians got possession of that state he with others was obliged to leave. He came here with the intention of obtaining a professorship in Belgium, but has concluded upon going to the United States. He brought me a letter of introduction & consulted me upon his going to the United States either to establish a school in which he could be aided by his wife, who is a very zealous & accomplished lady or put himself at the head of an Hydropathic establishment somewhere in the United States. It immediately occured to me, that it might [be] a fine opportunity for John [C. Calhoun, Jr.,] & said to Dr. [Charles] Munde (the name of the Gentleman) that my brother in law, had the intention to create such an establishment near Pendleton So. Carolina. After making some enquiries about the country & He concluded upon desiring to go to Pendleton with a view either to connect himself with John in some such undertaking or taking charge of the seminaries in Pendleton—or he might combine both. I then told him that I would write to you on the subject, and you could consult John about [it]. He will go shortly in a vessel from Antwerp to New York with his family. His means are restricted & [he] will not have much more than enough to carry himself & family to Carolina should he go there. From what I know of him I take him to be a very sincere, honourable man, particularly well acquainted with the modern languages[,] a man of labour, and good sense & who would strive to make himself useful & to merit the confidence of those who might interest themselves for him. The inclosed letter he wrote me, which will give you an idea of the manner he speaks & writes the English. If you should judge that John & he together could make themselves mutually useful the opportunity is a good one & as he Dr. Munde will not reach N. York before you will have received this you will have an opportunity to write him to New York where a letter addressed to Dr. Munde care of Messrs. Schuyler & Gutmann[,] No. 1 Nassau Street[,] New York, will reach him on his arrival. He, if you should think best, will as soon as possible visit Pendleton with a view to converse on the subject[,] examine the country & then commence operations immediately. From the nature of his past life I should not judge that his habits had ever been expensive & I presume that a life in Pendleton either at the head or connected with the male or Female seminary there or in connection with John in a Hydropathic establishment would suit him well. At all events I have no other motive than that of making myself useful to John & Dr. Munde.

By the last steamer I forwarded a power of Attorney to Mr. [Francis W.] Pickens for the sale of my place [in Edgefield District]. Had I remained in the United States I would not have agreed to sell my place & Negroes for thirty thousand dollars including all my stock[,] implements &c. But as I could not live there, & had no one to attend to my interests, it may be fortunate for me to have sold at any price. It is a lesson that has cost me dear. I hope to be done with Southern property—and shall feel greatly relieved, & thankful when what I have, is safely invested in a country where it will yield me an interest, of which I have been deprived for years.

When I passed through London I heard that [Arthur P.] Bagby [former U.S. Minister to Russia] was there on his return from [St.] Petersburg. He was staying at one of the principal hotels in that city, but awful to relate he had been drunk nearly all the time he was there. No one saw him & the Hotel keeper had to stop his supplies to get him out of his house. Your affectionate son, Thos. G. Clemson.

N.B. I have just seen a letter from Mr. [Edward A.] Han[n]egan [U.S. Minister to Prussia] to an American gentleman in this city.

Mr. H[annegan] says that he will immediately leave Berlin, on account of the Pest having made its appearance in that city. The disease is a frightful one killing in an hour. The Hospitals when he wrote, were all closed. The papers in this city say nothing of it—it may not be true. T.G.C.

[Enclosure]

Dr. Charles Munde to [Thomas G. Clemson]

Brussels, 25th of July 1849

Sir, The political events in my unfortunate country having obliged me to leave it in order to seek a new home and the means of subsistence for my family in the United States of America, I take the liberty of requesting Your Excellency to be so kind as to indicate the ways I am to take and to give me a few letters of introduction to some distinguished families of South Carolina.

The knowledge and talents I can dispose of to make myself useful to the society there, are: a long practice in teaching, especially the modern languages and every thing belonging to them, and an experience of many years in hydropathy. The former have enabled me to the directorship of the Commercial School in Dresden, after having occupied during eight years the place of a professor at the Mining Academy at Freiberg; and the latter I have acquired by a long and repeated visit in Graefenberg, my own treatment and the consecutive direction of two hydropathic establishments, as well as an extended practice in families. My philological works have met with great success in Germany, and my books on hydropathy, translated into several languages, have occasioned a correspondence with nearly all parts of Europe; I even venture to say that my name is not entirely unknown in America.

My project in going to the New World, therefore, is, to make the best of those talents for the benefit of the inhabitants there as well as for my own subsistance and family. If the circumstances should favour my views, I would be happy to establish a school and devote myself entirely to education. Mrs. [Bertha von Horneman] Munde, being well instructed, having an indefatigable zeal in those matters, and knowing German, French and English as well as music, could assist me in the task. If, on the contrary, after having taken the necessary informations on the spot, I should find that I could be more useful in practicing hydropathy, I would try to form an establishment like that of Graefenberg and make the country enjoy the benefit of a system which, I think, might be very efficacious in the bilious diseases of the country.

The Saxon government having deprived me of my books, I can

offer only a few samples of my works—being all I have been able to procure here.

It is necessary to say that my means are very limited; I possess no more than what is wanted to pay the passage and live upon the rest for about a year in a country where the most necessary commodities are cheap. However the produce of my books in Saxony offers me a small resource of from 1200 to 2000 franks a year. To form an establishment of any kind in South Carolina, I would, therefore, be obliged to apply to some persons inclined to favour such a project until I could earn enough to repay them.

If Your Excellency will be kind enough to recommend me, you may rely on my zeal to justify your confidence in me, and to gain the benevolence of those to whom you will kindly introduce me. My will is good: I only wish that my health, shaken by former fatigues and the recent misfortunes, may enable me to prove it. I have the honour to be, with the greatest respect, Your Excellency's most devoted and humble servant, Dr. Charles Munde.

ALS with En in ScCleA; PEx's in Boucher and Brooks, eds., *Correspondence,* pp. 520–521. Note: Dr. Charles Munde, a Dresden physician, immigrated to the U.S. with his wife and settled in Florence, Mass., where he established a sanitorium.

From W[ILLIAM] S. LYLES

Buckhead, Fairfield [District, S.C.]
August 1st 1849

Respected Sir, I venture to enclose you a series of articles written by myself during the past spring and early summer. The object for which they were written will be explained on their perusal. Perhaps in advancing the views I have, I have been premature, but insulted and outraged as we have been, I could not forbear to express the honest convictions of my mind in reference to our duty under certain circumstances &c. There is perhaps too much levity for so grave a subject, pervading some of the articles but I could not let the occasion pass by, without repaying some of the scorn and ridicule which has hitherto been our lot to receive at their hands. I for one think the time has past for forbearance—we should meet taunt with taunt, insult with insult and return blow for blow. To the union as it was I should not object, to the union as it is I do most earnestly.

If it cannot be reformed, the sooner it is dissolved the better for us I think.

Excuse me for trespassing upon your valuable time and accept the assurance of the high regard of the humble individual who addresses you. Resp[ec]t[ful]ly & Truly yours, W.S. Lyles.

ALS with En in ScCleA. NOTE: Lyles (1813–1862), a planter, was a member of the S.C. General Assembly 1838–1840 and 1850–1852 and of the secession convention. Enclosed was the Winnsboro, S.C., *Fairfield Herald* of July 21, 1849, with articles exploring the necessity and feasibility of secession should the North violate the Missouri Compromise.

To [HENRY S.] FOOTE, [Senator from Miss.]

FORT HILL, August 3, 1849

My Dear Sir: My engagements must be my apology for not acknowledging sooner your two letters.

I am obliged to you for securing so prompt an admission of my address [of 7/5] into the columns of the [Washington National] Intelligencer. Col. [Thomas H.] Benton has continued to get so many jobs for that paper, that I had my apprehension, in their wish to keep fair with him, that they would either not publish at all, or delay it so long, as to make the publication of no value.

I am glad that you intended to be present at the meeting of your [Miss.] Convention, in October. It is an important occasion, and your presence will be of great service. You ask me for my views touching the ultimate action of the South in certain events. It is the gravest of all subjects, and must soon demand the attention of the whole Union in tones so deep as to rouse the attention of all.

There is one point, on which there can be no diversity of opinion in the South among those, who are true to her, or have made up their mind not to be slaves; that if we should be forced to choose between resistance and submission, we should take resistance, at all hazards. If we are not prepared for that, we are prepared to sink to the most debased and miserable condition ever allotted to a people, and to become the scorn and by-word of the world. That we will be forced to the alternative, I hold to be certain, unless prompt and the most efficient measures should be taken by the South to arrest the present course of events. They were never moving worse or more rapidly. It is not a mere opinion with me, that we should be forced in the end to choose between submission and resistance, unless the South should take the subject into its own hands, and by a united and decisive movement, stay the course of events. Be assured there is no other remedy—none—not the least, through the action of the general government. Things have gone too far to hope for relief from that quarter.

I have not ventured the assertion, that events were never moving worse, or more rapidly, without due reflection and much observation. I have looked on the movements at the North since the adjournment with close attention. They are, in my opinion, as bad as they can be. At no time have both parties courted the free soilers and the abolitionists with more ardour. I make no distinction between free soilers and abolitionists. They are both equally hostile to us and our institutions. Of the two, the former are the worst and most dangerous. I regard the new platform, called *free democracy*, attempted to be erected at the North, to rally and re-unite the free soilers and the old democrats who opposed them at the last election, as but another name for free soilers, more dangerous than their original, because calculated to deceive and betray the South. There, as yet, has been not a rally on it, that I have seen, in which the free soil doctrines, as to the Wilmot proviso and the territories and denunciation of slavery, did not constitute the platform. The aim of the whole movement is political; and is intended to catch the support of the abolitionists without losing that of the South. If they succeed in that, our doom is fixed. I do not doubt, but we have many and sincere friends among the old democracy of the North, and even among those, who are inclined to favor this unnatural coalition. They do it from what they regard to be a necessity, and as the only way, by which the whigs can be put down, and with reluctance. But that cannot alter its fatal tendency. The whigs at the North are at present doing their best to prevent it, but as soon as they see, that it is like to succeed, and that the democracy of the South are prepared to acquiesce in it, they will wheel right round, and take higher and bolder abolition grounds, and thus control the movement, while the Southern whigs will plead our example, as an excuse for their acquiescing in the bolder movements of their Northern friends. The effects of the whole will be, that the North will become more universally abolition than ever, and the South more derided, distracted and debased than ever; and, of course, less capable of resisting. Even as a political movement on the part of the North democracy, it will fail. It is a game, in which their opponents can ever out play them, and which must end in the destruction and absorption of the democracy there by the other parties. There is but one way they can save themselves, and the party, by boldly planting themselves on the ground, on which the Southern wing of the party occupy on this great question. It would probably place them in a small minority for the time, but it would unite the South, and our united strength, would speedily put them in a majority again. Nothing else can save them. But taking the course, which they appear at present, (at least a considerable portion of them,) disposed to do, will separate the South from them. We cannot countenance, or support the new platform; or recognize any man, or any party that may stand on it, as of us. Thus thinking, nothing future, is to my mind, more certain than that as events are now going, the alternative of submission or resistance will be speedily forced on us, unless we should unite and adopt speedy measures to prevent it; and that presents the question— what can we do? In considering it, I assume that the first desire of every true hearted Southern man, is to save if possible, the Union, as well as ourselves; but, if both cannot be, then to save ourselves at all events. Such is my determination, as far as it lies in my power. Fortunately for us, the road which leads to both yet lies in the same direction. We have not reached the fork yet, if we are ever to do it. Without concert of action on the part of the South, neither can be saved; by it, if it be not too long delayed, it is possible both yet may be. Without it, we cannot satisfy the North, that the South is in earnest, and will, if forced, choose resistance; and until she is satisfied, the causes which have brought the question between the two sections to its present dangerous stage from a small beginning, will continue to operate, until it will be too late to save the Union, and nothing will be left us, but to dissolve the connection. To do that, concert of action would be necessary, not to save the Union, for it would be too late, but to save ourselves. Thus, in any view, concert is the one thing needful. But concert cannot be had without a convention of the South, either formal or informal; and to that point every friend of the Union, and well wisher of the South, ought to direct his effort. It cannot be called too soon. The next session of Congress may make it too late. If nothing is done to bear on its action, the alienation between the sections, which may be caused by its proceedings, may become too great to save the Union. The call then, in my opinion, ought to be made before Congress meets, or early in the session, for a convention in the South, to meet at some convenient central point, in the spring or early in the session. It could not fail to have a powerful effect on the action of Congress, and that followed up by a convention, and a solemn appeal to the North, accompanied by a warning, as to what must be the consequences, unless she should desist from aggression, and cease to agitate the subject, may save the Union. Nothing short of it can; and there is no certainty, that it could if delayed beyond the time stated.

The convention, in my opinion, ought to be informal—such as those so often called by both parties at the North, in taking some new political position. A formal one called by the authority of the government of the Southern States, and to meet in their official character, as representatives of States, ought not to be thought of short of the last extremity. I am also of the opinion, that the call ought to be so made as to ensure a full attendance and harmony of views and action. For that purpose, it should be addressed to all of the South, without distinction of party, who desire to save the Union, and to adopt the most effectual measures for that purpose, but who, in the event it should prove impossible, and the alternative of submission and resistance should be forced on the South, stand prepared to choose the latter. Such a call could not fail to secure a full attendance from every Southern State, and harmony of views and action. The call ought to be accompanied by an address, briefly stating the ground for making it. I trust your convention will make the call. It could come from no better quarter. Your State is the centre of the Southern portion of the great valley of the Mississippi; more deeply, if possible, interested than any other, and would be less likely to excite a feeling of jealousy, than if it came from this, or any of the older States. If your convention should take the stand, and recommend at the same time, a general organization of the Southern States, I would agree to underwrite consequences. Among your other advantages, the whig party would more fully unite in the call than in any other State, but this.

Why cannot Mr. [Thomas] Ritchie and Mr. [Edmund] Burke [editors of the Washington *Globe*] be induced to back the call, if it should be made? It is their true course, whether regarded as patriots or party men. If they would agree to do so, it would ensure its success, and keep the movement in the right direction. Yours truly, J.C. CALHOUN.

PC in the Jackson, Miss., *Flag of the Union*, May 23, 1851, p. 3; PC in the New Orleans, La., *Daily Delta*, May 29, 1851, p. 1; PC in the Charleston, S.C., *Mercury*, June 4, 1851, p. 2; PEx in the Washington, D.C., *National Era*, vol. V, no. 24 (June 12, 1851), p. 94; PEx in Louisa McCord, "Separate Secession," *Southern Quarterly Review* (new series), vol. 4, no. 8 (October 1851), p. 314; PEx in Cleo Hearon, "Mississippi and the Compromise of 1850," *Publications of the Mississippi Historical Society*, vol. XIV (1914), p. 62. NOTE: No ms. exists of this letter. It was published by Foote during controversy over the Nashville Convention.

To DUFF GREEN, [New York City?]

Fort Hill, 4th Aug[us]t 1849

My dear Sir, You are right, as to the source, whence [Thomas H.] Benton draws his support. He has bribed the papers at the seat of Government by jobs at the publick expense; and the only way to put down the corruption is the one you indicate. An Independent Press at Washington has long been a desideratum, but it is difficult to establish, or to maintain such an one there, against the joint influence and power of the publick plunderers, who have got possession of the organs of publick opinion and the machinery of parties.

I am glad to learn that your contract promises so well and hope it will equal your most sanguine hopes. Should you succeed as well as you expect it will give you a commanding position.

With kind respects to Mrs. [Lucretia Maria Edwards] Green and your family I remain.

PC (incomplete) in Jameson, ed., *Correspondence*, p. 771.

From SOLON BORLAND, [Senator from Ark.]

Hot Springs, Arkansas, August 5, 1849

Dear Sir, I have just risen from the perusal of your Address to the people of the Southern States, which I received in the Pendleton Messenger, and cannot resist the impulse to say to you that I have never read a paper which afforded me more satisfaction, and that, as a southern man, I thank you, from the bottom of my heart, for a service so valuable and so seasonable to our great cause. To your own defence against the charges of Col. [Thomas H.] Benton, the common sentiment of the country was it was not necessary, and you might well and safely have rested the vindication of your character to that common sentiment of your countrymen. Indeed, I have ever thought that a reputation which required special defence—apart from the impress it has made upon the minds of men, in its passage through life, was hardly worth having, and could never be regarded as of much value to the country. But regarding Col. Benton's assault upon you, in its true light, of an assault upon the South, you have but represented the South in repelling it; for, in explaining your own course, in connection with the matters discussed, you have, indeed, "vindicated the truth of history", and placed the justice and

13

equity of our cause in a light so clear as, certainly, to convict our enemies of, if not convert them from, "the error of their ways."

It may be that, upon some points touched in your address, but they are intirely apart from its main scope and end, I have not fully concurred with you. I allude particularly to the Ashburton Treaty, and the Oregon question—the former as a matter of principle, and the latter as a matter of policy. But even in them, I have ever accorded to you motives of the loftiest and purest patriotism. And what you have now said upon those topics, while it has not changed my opinions of the questions involved (of principle in the one case and policy in the other), is, I do not hesitate to say, a conclusive refutation of Benton's imputations. Lest I might be, otherwise, misunderstood, I would remark that my objection to your policy upon the Oregon question did not apply to your original view, generally known as the plan of "masterly inactivity." In that, I fully and warmly acquiesced, at the time, and have seen no reason, ["since then," *interlined*] to think otherwise. It was, however, after events had progressed beyond the point where that policy ["was" *interlined and* "impracticable" *changed to* "practicable"], that I concurred with the advocates of 54° 40'. It may have been unwise to have assumed the position in which one found the Government, upon that point— I thought, and still think, it was so, to agitate the question up to the excuse ["of" *canceled*] for assuming such a position. But once assumed, I think the soundest rules, and the most cogent incentives, of moral determination, and political action, required the position to be maintained. And I would have maintained it at all hazards. Nor did I believe that the execution of what were regarded as ["the" *canceled*] ultra propositions would have involved us in hostilities with England. Of late years, I think she has grown, at least indifferent—if not even more than that; to her *western* possessions. Witness, for instance, the aspect of the Hudson's Bay Company's affairs— particularly as developed last winter—and of the condition of Canada. And to my mind, there is a reason for this, which, however it may have occurred to others, I have never heard suggested. It is that England has found our neighborhood unfavorable, ["to" *canceled*] alike, to the promotion of her ["interests" *canceled*] pecuniary interests, and the maintenance of her political influence. It seems to me that she has been relaxing her hold upon this continent (it may be since Mr. [James] Monroe's declaration against European interference this side the Atlantic), while she is assiduously extending and strengthening it in the East—where her superiority is acknowledged (as a ray of light amid the darkness and despotism of those benighted regions), and her avarice and ambition find richer and more ["congenial" *canceled and* "available" *interlined*] fields.

Of the other papers which the speech of Col. Benton has called forth, I have read [Henry S.] Foote's letter to [Henry A.] Wise, and [David R.] Atchison's [Senator from Mo.] reply to the public meeting. The former, I think, contains many good things; but it is so bedizzened and interlarded with the peculiarities of the author—vanity, officiousness and pedantry, that I fear it will do but little good. Besides, the unanimity that prevails in Missi[ssippi] required little or no stimulus. From Wise, should he respond—as I learn he will, something may be expected, especially for effect in Virginia—where, I am sorry to say I cannot expect unanimity, without great effort.

With Atchison's letter I am much pleased. It is plain and direct to the point; and from his great personal popularity in Missouri, much may be hoped. I understand, moreover, that three of the Representatives from Mo. [James S.] Green, [Willard P.] Hall, and [John S.] Phelps, have taken ground with Atchison. With Green and Hall I boarded last winter—and altho they did not sign the Address, they agreed with us in Sentiment, and were decidedly opposed to Benton's reelection.

This brings me to a point, upon which I wish to say a word—altho, doubtless, you have thought it all over. It is the motive of Benton's course.

Until last winter, I looked upon him as one who, embittered by disappointment, had given way to the madness of revenge, and was "fatally bent on mischief"—without any particular end or aim personal to himself—save that of injury to others. A more careful study of him and his circumstances, however, has somewhat altered my opinion; and while it has not, in any degree, mitigated my judgment of his malignity, has, at least, induced me to accord some method to his madness. Indeed, I have concluded that he has a very well defined plan of operations, and a very well defined object—or rather the one of two objects—in view. And, in this, while I think even less favorably of his heart, I cannot withhold a greater respect for his egotistical declaration that he is a man "of head and thought."

His course on the Texas question (which most persons attributed to his unwillingness to follow your lead) almost destroyed him even in his own State. In the election following, he ["was ele" *canceled*] succe[e]ded with great difficulty; being elected by only 8 votes, without any regular ["opposition" *canceled*] opponent. Since then, he has lost strength, and finds and feels that his position in Mo. is very precarious, to say the least of it. Indeed, he is in mortal fear of defeat. To one of his temper such a position is maddening. In casting about him for the means of support, he finds nothing so promising as the Pacific Rail Road. He speculates upon the excitement of a people ever alive to enterprise, especially when it promises some peculiar advantage to themselves—such as securing the terminus of the proposed Road for the capital of their State, and above all stimulated as they are, now, by the glitter of gold upon the Pacific coast. Taking advantage of the enthusiasm of the masses, and helping it to overlook the fact that the comm[en]cement, even, and far more the completion, of ["such" *canceled*] the proposed road must be the work of time—and hoodwinking them (intentionally I must think) in the matter of the *route*, he hopes, and is now attempting, to make Missouri believe that this great project is peculiarly *his own*, for *her* peculiar benefit; but that, as other routes have their advocates, actively at work, *his* services are indispensable to the success of the Missouri route. What opened my eyes to his insincerity in this connection, was a little trick (and ["really" *canceled*] it was really *little*) he played off upon me last summer. You may recollect that towards the close of that session, I offered (and succe[e]ded in passing thro the Senate) an amendment, to the Gen[era]l App[ropriatio]n Bill, of $30,000 to enable [John C.] Frémont [Benton's son-in-law] to complete his 3rd and last exploration. This I did at the special request of Mr. Benton. He requested an interview, and handed me the amendment in question—asking my opinion of it. Having failed to get my joint Resolution from the Land Com[mittee] passed—requiring the Sec. of War [William L. Marcy] to have all necessary explorations & surveys made, I readily agreed to this, as a means of doing something to throw light upon that which was dark and unknown (in its details, at least) to us all. Mr. Benton complimented me upon the course I had taken—agreed with me that the country was not sufficiently known to enable any one to designate a route—and said that such an amendment as the one proposed, being the best that could be done at the time, would come properly from me. He (modestly!) excused himself from moving in it, upon the score of his relationship to Frémont &c. Well, I offered the amendment, and by *begging* a vote from my colleague—who intended to vote against it—I got it thro, by a bare majority. As you know, it was lost in the House—only 29 voting for it. Imagine my surprise, then, at the last session, when Mr. Benton introduced his Bill, and made his speech—in which ["he" *interlined*] boldly and unblushingly asserted that the country had been fully and sufficiently explored & surveyed—and proceeded, with a cool impudence never parralleled, to make St. Louis the starting point, and lay down the route all the way to the Pacific! Comment on this is unn[e]cessary, further than to say that it gave me an insight into the man that I never before had, and it was not (tho promptly done) by "jumping at the conclusion", that I determined him to be uncandid—insincere—dishonest. He is playing his trick, now, on a larger scale, upon the people of Missouri.

But his schemes do not end here. Adept as he is in *humbug*, and believer as he is in its potency, he is not secure in his reliance upon it, in this instance. He knows he reposes on a balloon—which even a feeble adversary may prick, and collapse. But even this might not deter him from [*"his"* canceled] confidence in his skill to patch up, and retain gass enough to float thro, if their [*sic*] was no other difficulty in the way. Unfortunately for him, however, the Southern question comes in as an element—and upon that he stands committed too far to retract. He sees the danger of his position in Missouri. Abolitionism he fears will not sustain him there—nay, not bear its own weight—and even the balloon of the Pacific road may not be able to buoy him over the difficulty. He counts on defeat, for the Senate, as a possibility at least, if not a probability; and he prepares to make what has been his bane prove his antidote—by so shaping his course as to fall completely into abolition arms for the presidential candidacy in 1852. God forbid that such should be the issue; but unless some change more propitious to the fortunes of our country than now portends, take place within two years, I have little hope of any other than a division into Northern and Southern parties, instead of those we have heretofore known. Upon this, however, I will not, now, speculate; for I confess to a strong repugnance to think of such an issue, even. But should such an issue come, I think it easy to estimate Mr. Benton's chances of success; for treason has rarely, indeed, secured reward to the traitor.

Having read over what I have written, I hesitate, and feel almost ashamed, to send you such a crude jotting down of my thoughts. Yet, as they are honestly entertained, tho feebly and plainly expressed, I trust to your well known kindness and candor to excuse their deficiencies, and indulge their freedom.

As I told you on parting, last spring, it was my purpose to address you concerning the Memphis Convention. That purpose was superceded by the invitation of the Committee, and your response which has been published. I expect to attend the Convention (Oct. 23) on my way to Washington. And as I shall, also, on the same trip, visit my brother in Southern Louisiana, I shall go to Washington by the Southern route, and thus execute a purpose, I have long entertained, of seeing a portion of your State—especially its capital.

Pardon me the liberty I have taken to inflict upon you so long a letter, and accept an assurance that I am, with the highest respect, faithfully Your friend, Solon Borland.

ALS in ScCleA.

From F[RANKLIN] H. ELMORE

Columbia, 6 Aug. 1849

My Dear Sir, I have just rec[eive]d yours [*not found*] & feel fully the force of all you say in relation to our condition—the crisis now almost on us, & our ability to meet it successfully if we can but forget all other & vastly minor points of difference & unite our whole energies for this great struggle for safety. But how is this union to be obtained? Here in our own State, unless a timely stop is put to the dissensions now in full preparation, we shall be split into two parties, engaged hand to hand in a question that will control the public attention to a degree that may render all our efforts unavailing. Instead of presenting an example & a rallying point, South Carolina, may herself be the premonitory [*sic*] & type of the fate of the whole South—indeed may be the cause of its degradation & ruin—for, if she, who is looked to as one ever leading in defending these rights, fails or falters, they will surrender as hopeless all effort at resistance & thus rest on us the responsibility. You express the hope that the agitation in regard to the Bank will cease, on the report of the Committees. I have no such hope or expectation unless it is controlled by the higher question & by the action & decided stand of those who see the greater danger & the necessity of union & concert & the concentration of all our energies to meet it. It has become an *object* with *many influences* to destroy this Institution & they have been active—are committed to a great degree—& will, if not checked, press their schemes to a consummation if they can. These influences are of several natures—1. Those originally opposed to Banks & especially to one owned by the State. 2. Those of Private Banks who consider it a rival. 3. The money lenders & shavers & usurers & speculators, whose operations are often defeated by the Bank. 4. These are combined & united for attack by men having political & personal ends to accomplish.

There is no possible way in which their measure can be carried out, that will not cause vast embarrassments, if not ruinous sacrifices—derangement of property—anxiety & alarm—a state of things of all others, the best calculated to crush the spirit of the people & to prepare them for submission & dishonor. The finances & resources of the State will be thrown into confusion—a foreign & domestic ["State" *interlined*] debt of upwards of $2,000,000, which, with an annual interest of near $130,000 must be provided for, while the assetts of the Bank, including liabilities & obligations in every District & Parish & neighborhood, ["will" *interlined*] have to be collected to the amount of $3,000,000, & will not present a state of affairs in which a people can ["easily" *interlined*] be brought resolutely to stand up to greater responsibilities—to face dangers & hazards more even for liberty itself.

And even, my Dear Sir, if they are willing to go into the contest, are they not disarmed? Are they not, in a measure chained down by pecuniary embarrassments personally, & by the fact staring them in the face, that the finances of the State are in no better condition? That their Treasury has been sacked—and that if they have recourse to public credit, to aid the State, that it ["will not be available &" *interlined*] cannot aid them? But I have here stated an idea that requires more explanation. When the State borrowed $2,000,000 under the act of June 1838 to rebuild Charleston, to be repaid in 20 & 30 years, they pledged the Bank as a security for its repayment & for the interest. If the State removes ["or" *interlined*] consumes this pledged security, her credit is blighted in Europe, if not at home. If she feels it necessary to resort to loans to maintain her rights ag[ains]t the Gen[era]l Govt., she will feel this, for I think you will agree she has little to expect from her own monied Institutions in such a contest. Money loves power & goes to it too naturally—in 1832 we had them *all* not only not with us, but decidedly against the State. The same instincts remain—& the same results may be looked for again.

In the volume I sent you there are documents to establish all I have said above in regard to the obligations to our creditors. Gov. [David] Johnson at the last session alluded to these in his Message & they are more developed in a report of 1846 made in the Senate & also in that volume of documents.

With Gov. [Whitemarsh B.] Seabrook I have not exchanged views on this subject. His mind is I think open but as he has not as yet opened the subject to me, I have not brought it to his view. He has notified me of an intention to present inquiries in regard to the Bank, but of what nature I am not fully possessed.

Your idea of a Southern convention I agree with intirely. Our Committee will I feel assured second any move anywhere else for one—*but would you advise us to propose it?* I do not so understand you, & I do not see that we could do so without hazarding more than it seems to me prudent to risk in the present state of affairs. We will keep our attention upon it & be ready to seize the first opening.

Your suggestion as to Mississippi has been acted on already. At my instance the Gov. wrote to Gen[era]l [Daniel] Wallace [Representative from S.C.] & he has agreed to attend it. I expect to see Gen[era]l Wallace myself & you might write to him. If he could arrange it so that this Convention sh[oul]d make the call, would it not be advisable he should do so?

I would be most happy to accept your invitation if it is possible to do so. I would like ["it" *canceled and* "to make my visit" *interlined*] while Gov. Seabrook is in your part of the country & will, if I can, come about that time so that we may confer on public matters togather.

Few things my **Dear Sir** have given me more pleasure than to learn of the near completion of your long expected work. All your friends who have heard of it expect its appearance with anxiety—its appearance just now will I feel assured be most opportune.

Your reply to [Thomas H.] Benton is published alone. I will direct that as many copies be sent to you as you wish. If you will send to Mr. [Henry W.] Conner the names & address[es] of 1000 persons, they will be directed to them at once from Charleston. We have ordered a large edition & don[']t know what to do with them all. Any suggestion from you to Conner will be attended to. He has undertaken this part of the business.

What you have said about "Brutus" surprises me. I had some idea it was written by a Mr. [John C.] Vaughan who removed from Camden to Cincinnati—turned traitor—edited Cassius M. Clays paper after it was expelled from Lexington to Cincinnati, & now is the Editor ["& organ" *canceled*] of a paper at Louisville which is the organ of the Emancipation party of Kentucky.

If you can put us in the way we would gladly trace up the author.

I leave for Limestone [Springs] tomorrow I hope. The excessive rains have kept me & I have fears will even yet keep me here longer. Yours truly, F.H. Elmore.

ALS in ScCleA. NOTE: The "volume I sent you" probably refers to *A Compilation of All the Acts, Resolutions, Reports and Other Documents, in Relation to the Bank of the State of South Carolina, According Full Information Concerning that Institution* (Columbia, S.C.: printed by A.S. Johnston and A.G. Summer, 1848).

From A[BRAHAM] W. VENABLE,
[Representative from N.C.]

Brownsville [N.C.,] August 7h 1849

My Dear Sir, I have deferred writing to you until this moment in order that I might give you a true state of the political history of this part of North Carolina. I arrived at home on the 6h of March our Court Day & immediately declared myself a candidate for Congress upon the platform of my speech of the 4h February 1849[,] the necessity of retaliation on the part of the slaveholding States—Resistance prompt and open. As I expected there was immediately an organised opposition on the part of the whigs and some overtures made to certain Democratic individuals to ascertain whether I could not be effectually opposed by one of my own party with the promise of Whig support. There was on the part of some Hunkerish Democrats an attempt to get up a convention to rule me off upon the ground that my reccommended measures would produce immediate disunion. This signally failed and I declared myself an independent candidate upon the great Southern Question. A whig convention nominated a talented young man [Henry K. Nash] as my competitor and the campaign opened. My health gave away about the middle of May and I was compelled to canvass a large district in a state so feeble as almost to render it impossible for me to travel. Had I been within the reach of the specific influences which produce Cholera I must have had an attack of that disease. But although greatly emaciated & reduced I continued an active canvass. The whole whig press of the State denou[nc]ed me as a factionist, disorganiser and disunionist. The whole north press whig and abolitionist flooded my district with assaults upon my political course; singing hallelujas to the Union, publishing extracts of [George] Washingtons farewell address and one of our own senators together with divers others poured[?] amongst us [Thomas H.] Bentons speech at Jefferson city and [Senator from Conn.] Truman Smith's circulars, and libels, upon the Democracy, covered with Mr. [George E.] Badgers [Senator from N.C.] Frank in many instances were brought to bear in aid of the most zealous and untiring efforts of every whig leader in the

District. The issue was made distinctly resistance or non resistance disunion or union in the event of continued aggression. After a most laborious struggle I have carried my district by a majority of 719 against a majority of 153 two years ago. This is a complete triumph of the high principles announced in the Southern address and the still more definite measures of resistance suggested by myself in my last speech in the house. I must acknowledge ["the" *canceled and* "your" *interlined*] kindness in sending me your reply to Benton. I had however effectualy silenced that speech before it reached me a few days before the election. For the ability to do so I am indebted to facts derived from the perusal of the manuscript which you lent me containing the causes of the disorganization of the Democratic party in 1839 and the many conversations all of which I perpetuated in my memoranda book so far as facts & dates were concerned. My vindication of your course ["and th" *canceled*] was considered perfectly triumphant and Bentons miserable falsehoods fully exposed. But your reply came in time to crush and destroy the last remaining vitality of his miserable attempts. As I expected I was taunted as one of your followers of recent conversion and of course burning zeal. But as those who thrw the taunts had mostly been nullifiers I took a malicious pleasure in illustrating their renegade course.

The battle is fought & victory is won [John R.J.] Daniel [Representative from N.C.] is elected over a Hunkerish Democrat [William J. Clarke] by a majority of 2700—Things look better in this State and I trust that there will be a general reaction. May heaven preserve your health to witness the establishment of Southern rights. I hope to meet you in Washington next winter much restored and in good sperits as the general aspect of affairs must give you cheering hopes for the future. My own health is much improved and my son who is with me presents his kind regards to you. Remember me kindly to Mr. [Armistead] & Mrs. [Martha Calhoun] Burt & your own family. Yours with the most sincere regard, A.W. Venable.

ALS in ScCleA; PEx in Boucher and Brooks, eds., *Correspondence*, pp. 521–522. NOTE: This letter was postmarked at Oxford, N.C.

To H[ENRY] W. CONNER, [Charleston]

Fort Hill, 9th Aug[us]t 1849
My dear Sir, Mr. [Franklin H.] Elmore informs me, that my address [to the Southern people] has been published in pamphlet form, &

that you have the distribution under your superintendence.

I will be much obliged to you to send me a dozen of copies; and would suggest the propriety of sending a copy to each member of the late Congress, &, if you can obtain their names, of the present Congress, who are not members of the late, if you can get their names. They will all soon be elected. Yours truly, J.C. Calhoun.

ALS in ScC; photostat of ALS in DLC, Henry Workman Conner Papers.

From ANNA [MARIA] CALHOUN CLEMSON

Brussels, Aug. 12th 1849

My dear father, We are for the moment so constantly occupied in furnishing our house, that I let again slip the day for sending letters last week, but as now we are nearly through ordering & calculating, I will for the future be more punctual. We found hiring furniture so expensive, & comfortless, that, as we must in whatever part of the world always have furniture, & can never get it handsomer or cheaper than here ["we concluded to buy at once" *interlined*]. At the same time we must be prudent, for the pur[se is] short. We have, therefore, concluded to fur[nish] all the rest of the house substantially, but plainly, & when that is done see what we have left to furnish our pa[r]lours & proceed accordingly. All this takes time to regulate & calculate. It is very easy to furnish very cheaply, when cheapness is the only object, or very extravagantly, when one has plenty of money, but to consult at the ["same time" *canceled and* "at once" *interlined*] economy & good taste, & get at the same time furniture that will be worth carrying with us when we leave, is a problem almost as difficult as any in mathematics or politics to solve satisfactorily.

We are all very well, but the cholera still reigns in Brussels, & keeps us a little uneasy. It is not however worth while leaving the city on that account, as the disease is every where, so we are very prudent, & remain quiet.

The children grow wonderfully as usual, & are thin, but well, & full of life. Floride [Elizabeth Clemson] has almost overtaken [John] Calhoun [Clemson] in height. I always read them whatever is said of them in the letters from home, & they are much gratified to be spoken of. "Oh!["] said Calhoun when I read them your letter[,] "if I was only there I would go all over the plantation with Grandpapa"[;] "& I too said Floride, because grandpapa loves me just as much as he does you." They regret very much [leaving] the country & when any one asks them if they are glad to return to Brussels, they always say No they love their own country best.

We have been received here by every one from the King [Leopold I] down with the greatest kindness & it is gratifying to be so. An American in Europe has only, (at the same time that he asserts his perfect independance on all occasions,) to avoid wounding the feelings of those who sincerely differ from him, in order to be respected & well received every where. Unfortunately our country people fall into one of two extremes generally. Either they think it is impossible to be a good republican, without asserting it on all possible, & *impossible* occasions, & exhibiting their contempt for every body or every thing arround them, or they do what is far worse, affect to despise their country, & ape every thing european. The first class had better never leave home & the other had better never return there. The one render themselves infinitely disagreeable, the other perfectly contemptible.

The weather here is cold & rainy. We have on all our flannel, & still often need fires. The difference strikes me more sensibly between our climate & this, since my winter in Carolina, for our winters are really superior to their summers.

Belgium is perfectly tranquil, & united & quite delighted & amazed to find herself so. They are having all sorts of national fetes to celebrate this happy state of things, & the King from being unpopular, in the extreme, is now received with enthusiasm wherever he shows himself. They are right in remaining tranquil & they have reason to feel content with their situation, when they compare it with the rest of Europe, but should order not be restored elsewhere, they are exposed, from their size & situation to wake up some fine morning in the midst of confusion. For the rest of Europe one nation is more wild & crazy than another & everything is "chaos worse confounded." I have lost all interest in their stupid movements, have given up in despair trying to understand what they are all about.

I do hope you all continue well. Do write me often. I wish I were at Fort Hill to help you write your political treatise[;] I might save you some labour.

I am uneasy about Pat[rick Calhoun] & hope he has left N[ew] O[rleans].

All join in love to every one at home. The children send many kisses & Mimi always begs to be remembered.

I will write mother [Floride Colhoun Calhoun] soon. Your devoted daughter, Anna *Calhoun* Clemson.

ALS in ScCleA.

From Ro[bert] Greenhow

Washington, August 12th 1849

My Dear Sir, I have just returned from the Warrenton Springs [Va.], whither I was forced to go, about a fortnight ["since," *interlined*] in order to obtain rest, and relief, from a painful and dangerous affection of my brain and nervous system, under which I had been labouring for some time, unable to read, think or even frequently to stand. I am somewhat better, but still very unwell, and incapable of mental or bodily exertion, except within a very restricted limit.

The legislature of Virginia was in session at Warrenton, engaged in revising the legal code; Your answer to [Thomas H.] Benton, which arrived while I was there, was read as extensively as the 2 or 3 copies of the [Washington] Union, and as many of the [Richmond] Enquirer, containing it, would allow, and appeared to excite universal commendation. The Governor [John B.] Floyd (though a cousin of Mrs. [Elizabeth McDowell] Benton), was most frank and open in his expressions of adhesion to your views, and satisfaction with the tone assumed by you.

I have seen no one here, since my return, and Mrs. [Rose O'Neal] Greenhow is now confined to the house, so that we have nothing more interesting to tell you—except *in entire confidence*, that an expedition for the overthrow of the Spanish authority in Cuba, is now in progress, and will soon begin active operations. Enterprises of that nature, usually fail; this is however, well arranged, and with means sufficient, apparently to attain the end. I will add, that I am acquainted with all the movements, and *am allowed and requested*, to say thus much to you, about it. The object is, annexation to the United States; the parties being well aware, that their labours to effect independance, without receiving the only guarantee for protection, and order, afterwards, would be only to plunge their country, if possible, into greater evils. This is said *in confidence*—any observations or advice from you, would be received with respect by the leaders of the enterprise, and would reach them through me.

I send you enclosed [*not found*] a slip from the N.Y. Journal of

Commerce of the 30th, which I think that you should see. I have abandoned all hopes as to the mission, and the state of my health is such, as to require all my firmness, and that of Mrs. Greenhow, to sustain my spirits. Mrs. G[reenhow] by the advice of Mr. [John M.] Clayton [Secretary of State] called to see the President [Zachary Taylor], and returned from her interview, very unfavourably impressed as to the capacity and character of the head of our govern-[me]nt, whom she found far more *rough* than *ready*. I am afraid that your mention of documents in the Dep[artment] of State proving the true western extension of Texas, may produce a call from the House, next winter which would seriously detract from the value of my book. Probably however, it will be unnoticed amid the more important points, to which you refer. I must end, with my most grateful respects Y[ou]rs, Ro. Greenhow.

ALS in ScCleA. NOTE: In regard to "my book," Greenhow's *The History of Florida, Texas, and California, and of the Adjoining Countries* .... was privately printed in 1856, two years after his death.

Toast at a dinner at Pendleton, 8/17. At a dinner at the Pendleton Hotel in honor of Captain Barnard E. Bee and Midshipman A[lexander] F. Warley, veterans of the Mexican War, Calhoun proposed: *"The Palmetto*: Already honorably distinguished among the flags of the Southern States of the Union, may it never fail to acquire fresh honors when the patriotism and honor of our citizens are brought to the test." From the Pendleton, S.C., *Messenger*, August 24, 1849, p. 2.

From L[EVIN] H. COE

"that Congress shall abstain from all legislation in relation to the subject of slavery; leaving it to the people of the territories themselves to make the necessary provisions for their eventual admission into the Union, and to regulate their internal concerns in their own way."

Memphis, Aug[us]t 20th 1849

Dear Sir, The foregoing is an extract from the Washington Union of the 6th Inst.

If Northern Abolition seconded by Southern traitors had not deterred our people from removing to California with their slaves by raising the cry of free soilism[,] I possibly for one might have schooled myself barely to bear the foregoing. But the running free-soiler whose life was saved by southern valor at Buena Vista—the same who refusing to fight at Cerro Gordo left the victory to be purchased by the blood of the South, even before the treaty of peace raised the insulting cry that we should not have equal rights in the Country it was foreseen Mexico would have to yield[.]   This has worked its effect. The position of the Union is all the North can desire in view of the orders given by [Zachary] Taylors Cabinet to Gen[era]l [Bennet] Riley—Non intervention as effectually excludes us as if the Wilmot proviso had passed at the date of the peace.

I feel a most solemn conviction that the South must arouse from its negative position and assume that of the lion or this necessary outlet to drain off our surplus slave population will be cut off from us & the doom of our children sealed[.]

What is to be done?

The miscalled Missouri Compromise was forced upon us by Northern votes. In an evil moment it was submitted to[.] The North has reaped the advantage of that oppression upon us. Does not the crisis demand of us to say to the North[,] You forced this line upon us. We yielded. You shall respect the spirit of that enforced rule. It shall be slave territory up to 36° 30′ to the Pacific. This we will maintain if necessary at the point of the bayonet.

Let this be our sine qua non to be enforced "at all hazards and to the last extremity" and I feel an abiding faith that the North will yield. But if I am mistaken in this I feel it is the duty of the South to build the wall of seperation.

I know too well the temper of Arkansas[,] Mississippi & West Tennessee to entertain the least fear of their firmness in meeting the issue. The necessary measures might easily be adopted to bring all the slave States to a common cause.

I have written my own notions plainly[.] This is no time for mincing terms—The South is not aroused to the danger—To sleep a few months longer must be fatal. Very Resp[ect]f[ul]ly, L.H. Coe.

ALS in ScCleA; PC (to "L.S. Hoe") in Boucher and Brooks, eds., *Correspondence*, p. 523. NOTE: Coe served in the Tennessee General Assembly, 1837–1841 and was Speaker of the Senate. An AES by Calhoun reads, "You may print if you should think proper the enclosed [*ms. faded and illegible*]. J.C. Calhoun." An AEI reads, "Return it when done with. J.C.C."

From INGOLDSBY & HALSTED

New York [City,] August 20th 1849

D[ea]r Sir, Your favor of 5th Inst. [*not found*] addressed to our Mr. Ingoldsby, accompanied by a letter from your Son at Brattleboro, was received this day.

In compliance with your request, in the absence of Mr. [J. Edward] Boisseau, we immediately forwarded your Son Wm. L[owndes] Calhoun at Brattleboro' Vt. One hundred & fifty Dollars ($150:).

At your convenience, by and bye, when Exchange can be procured you may please Send us a check for the amount.

Mr. Boisseau is somewhere on the Seashore, we know not exactly where; it is about three weeks since he was last here when he only remained in town a day or two: his health at that time was remarkably good. We remain yours respectfully, Ingoldsby & Halstead.

LS in ScU-SC, John C. Calhoun Papers. NOTE: In an AEU Calhoun recorded that on 12/6/1849 he "Remitted $150 by draft no. 2636 drawn by bank of Metropolis on the Bank of Commerce N.Y."

From A[DAM] B. CHAMBERS and Others

St. Louis, Mo., August 22, 1849

The undersigned, on behalf of a Mass Meeting of the citizens of St. Louis, respectfully invite you to attend a National Convention to be held in this City, on Monday, the 16th day of October next, to deliberate upon the expediency and necessity of connecting, at an early day, the Pacific with the Mississippi Valley, by means of a Railroad and Magnetic Telegraph. We are authorized to tender to you the hospitalities of our city, and shall be happy to have your presence and assistance in furthering this great object of the proposed Convention.

The accompanying address to the people of the United States, to which we beg leave to call your attention, will more fully explain the importance and nationality of the proposed work. A.B. Chambers, R[ichard] Phillips, John O'Fallon, Edward Walsh, John F. Darby.

Printed document (addressed and dated by hand) with En in ScCleA. NOTE: The enclosed printed circular, signed by 25 citizens of St. Louis, is headed "The People of St. Louis, to the People of the United States." It calls for the appointing of delegates from every State and Territory to a convention in St. Louis next month to deliberate upon a railroad from the Mississippi Valley to the Pacific. Chambers was editor of the St. Louis *Republican*, 1837–1854. O'Fallon (1791–1865) was a banker and railroad promoter. Darby (1803–1882) had been Mayor of St. Louis and a U.S. Representative.

From SAM[UE]L TREAT, "(Private)"

[St. Louis, *ca.* August 22, 1849]
Dear Sir: At the ["request" *canceled and* "solicitation" *interlined*] of the Committee on Invitation, I send to you the accompanying request to attend the proposed Convention. I am very anxious, in common with the true-hearted Democrats here, that you shall be present. The Convention is controlled by those who will not give Col. [Thomas H.] Benton an opportunity to make a hobby of the enterprise. As far as the Committee to prepare the Address &c. to be submitted to the Convention have interchanged opinions, they agree upon suggesting that the eastern terminus shall be at some frontier point—say Fort Leavenworth—leaving it to the South to connect with it, *via* Memphis or elsewhere—the North to connect *via* Chicago or elsewhere—the Centre, *via* St. Louis. Thus all questions of a doubtful character may be settled. You have been so grossly misrepresented on this and other subjects, and the people here generally are so favorably disposed towards you, that we are the more anxious that you should visit us.

Col. Benton has at length lost the confidence of the Missouri Democracy. We have printed here in pamphlet form 10,000 copies of your letter to the people of the South, and I caused it to be published in the leading Whig journal, also in the leading Benton paper. It will be read by every voter in Missouri. Every day brings us cheering intelligence from the State. Benton outrages public sentiment and all the decencies of life, wherever he goes; and his journey is proving fatal to him. The people are aroused. Our ablest and best men are on the stump against him: [David R.] Atchison, [James S.] Green, [Thomas B.] English, [Erastus] Wells, [John M.] Krum, [James W.] Morrow, [James H.] Birch, [Claiborne F.] Jackson, Harvey, [James H.] McBride, &c. &c. Not more than three or four prominent men have ventured to defend him publicly. The re-action against him is overwhelming. Now the real question at issue here is—not whether Col. Benton shall be returned to the U.S. Senate, for he is defunct politically—but whether a Whig or Democrat shall succeed him. The arrangements for a true Democratic journal here are not completed. We are at a loss for an editor of commanding abilities and tact—one who will do honor to the cause.

Please send your answer to the invitation to the Committee, under cover to me, and I will present it to them. At all times it will be gratifying for me to hear from you, and to know that the true guarantees of our constitution are meeting with cordial support. Yours truly, Saml. Treat.

ALS in ScCleA.

To T[homas] G. Clemson, [Brussels]

Fort Hill, 24th Aug[us]t 1849

My dear Sir, I got, in the due course of the mail, your letter written in London, and was much gratified to learn, that you had all arrived safely, after a long, but smooth voyage. The last mail brought a letter from Anna [Maria Calhoun Clemson] to her sister [Martha Cornelia Calhoun] written after your arrival at Brussels, and we are all happy to hear, that the children [John Calhoun Clemson and Floride Elizabeth Clemson] look well again, & that you are all in good health. I hope, on your arrival, that both you & she received my letters addressed to Brussels.

I regret to state, that we learn by a note from Mrs. [Marion Antoinette Dearing] Pickens to Mrs. [Floride Colhoun] Calhoun ["written" *interlined*] at the request of Col. [Francis W.] Pickens, who was too sick to write, that Mr. [William A.?] Harris declines to take the place. He had agreed to give $31,000 it seems; but it, also, seems, on examining it, he was not satisfied with the price placed on the hands & stock; Mr. Pickens will doubt[l]ess write you and give a full account of the whole affair; and I only write, because his sickness may prevent him from writing for some time. I regret, that the barg[a]in should be broke[n] off, for I think, the sale [of your plantation in Edgefield District] would have been a good one for you. It was a considerable point to sell the whole to one responsible individual. It would ["have" *interlined*] saved you from a great deal of trouble, & prevent breaking up the gang of negroes, which is always desirable in such cases.

We have had until the last ten days the wet[t]est and coolest summer I ever knew. Dust never rose on the place from the middle of April to the middle of August. It was too wet for any discription of crop; but mine all has turned out well, except the wheat. My corn is very fine. Good judges think it will go beyond 40 [bushels] to the acre. My cotton is equally good. The stand, with little exception, good, & the plant large. It avarages through the whole crop breast high, & promises to be heavily bolled, if the dry weather should not continue so long, as to [*one word or partial word canceled*] destroy, or cut short, the upper bolls. The goodness of the ["cotton" *interlined*] crop is very much the result of the system of manuring, which I have adopted, in the last two years. I find I can make as much manure as I can haul out, and that cow pen leaf manure is nearly equal to the stable. I feel confident that I can raise the product of my cotton to 1,000 pounds per acre on an avarage; & that without lime, or plaster of Paris. When the railroad is finished, this will become a good farming & planting country. It is expected it will be in two years.

Politically I have nothing good to write. The appearance is, that [Zachary] Taylor's administration will prove a failure. I fear he is in the hands of the Northern Whigs, exclusively. In the meane time, the alienation between North & South is daily progressing. [Thomas H.] Benton & [Henry] Clay are both playing for the North. I enclose in pamphlet form my notice of his assault on me. I would have sent it earlier, but only received it in that form, a few days since. It is, as far as I have heard regarded as triumphant. It is said, that he will not be able to sustain himself in Missouri. His colleague, Gen[era]l [David R.] Atchison [Senator from Mo.], says he has no chance to be reelected.

We are all anxious about the fate of Hungary, and the future condition of Europe. Write me in your next fully, what is your impression & [that of] the intelligent portion of Europe in reference to both. If Hungary should be able to maintain herself, the condition of Russia will become critical. What is to become of Germany & France?

I hope, still, Mr. Harris may ["still" *canceled*] agree to take your place. If he should not, you will have to determine what you will do without delay. I am at a loss what to [do]. I do not think, that there is any danger, that the price of negroes will decline, as the prospect of cotton is better than it has been for years.

All join in love to you, Anna & the children. Kiss them for Grandfather. Your affectionate father, J.C. Calhoun.

ALS in ScCleA; PEx in Jameson, ed., *Correspondence*, pp. 771–772.

From J[OHN] L. O'SULLIVAN, "(Confidential)"

Atlanta Ga., Aug. 24, 1849

My dear Sir, Within a period now counting by days & no longer by months or weeks, the flag of Cuban Independence will be raised.

The people of the Island are ripe & ready in point of opinion & feeling; but, timid & overborne by the military despotism under which they have been so long accustomed to cower, they will of course need a respectable *point d'appui*, to induce them to dare to come out. With such a *point d'appui*, moreover, there is little doubt that a large part if not the whole of the Spanish troops would fraternize with the Revolution. Probably ["less than" *interlined*] 1000 will land under Gen. [Narciso] Lopez.

You are aware of the standing threat of the Spanish Govt., to make a San Domingo of Cuba if necessary to keep it.

The South ought (according to an expression which Gen. Lopez has quoted to me from you) to flock down there "in open boats," the moment they hear the tocsin. They will hear it very soon. Will they fulfil this expectation? The answer is of supreme importance. They ought not only to go, but *to go at once.* I write to you (being myself deeply interested in the movement, & now on my way to New Orleans on business connected with) in the hope that you will appreciate at once the thousand & powerful reasons which seem to me to apply to your position, to cause you to strain every nerve at this moment for the promotion of the object. At every considerable point in the South volunteers ought to come forward, & go forward in their own modes. It can easily be done legally. They can go as emigrants, California adventurers *via* Cuba; passengers going to Cuba to see for themselves, and determine there to what side to offer their aid, or to be prepared to act as a ["neutral" *interlined*] police force against servile insurrection in case of danger from the convulsed state of the Island between the two contending parties. Probably the friends of the Revolution can afford them transportation from New Orleans, Charleston, ["Norfolk" *interlined*] or other points—but on this point there can be no practical difficulty. Now, my dear Sir, can not you write to fifty points & fifty proper persons to act and act with the requisite energy, promptitude, head & heart, in this matter? Your aid thus extended would be a tower of strength. All going may rely on generous compensation from opulent Cuba, once liberated. But independent of such motives there are considerations enough of a different character which I should think ought to rouse all the youth & manhood of the Southern States in particular, to rush down to help the Cuban Revolution.

I shall be for a few weeks at New Orleans, where I hope to have the pleasure of hearing from you. This letter is hastily scrawled in the short interval afforded by detention of the [railroad] cars. Very Respectfully & Truly, My dear Sir, Your friend & servant, J.L. O'Sullivan.

[P.S.] If I, a "New York Free-Soiler," am so deeply interested in behalf of this movement, what ought not to be the enthusiasm of Southern Gentlemen?

ALS in ScCleA; PC in Jameson, ed., *Correspondence*, pp. 1202–1203.

From W[ILLIAM] D. CHAPMAN

Aberdeen, Miss., Aug[us]t 25th 1849
Sir: A political controversy of some importance has recently sprung up in this (2nd) Congressional District. Your opinions have been much relied on, but as the controversy has narrowed down to a mere verbal criticism, I feel authorized from having taken an active part, in appealing to you for such information in regard to the subject matter as you may deem proper to impart. I briefly state the points upon which information is desired. To wit

1st Has Congress the power to *legislate* for the Territories? If so, to what extent can it legitimately go? 2nd If Congress can *legislate* to protect citizens in the undisturbed tenure of their property— that is, slave property—can it not also *legislate* for all and any purpose not inconsistent with the Constitution? 3rd If congress exercises the power of legislating in the one, is it not bound to exercise it in the other case? 4th If Congress possesses and exercises this power does it not preclude the necessity for a Territorial legislature or council? 5th If Congress legislates for the Territories is not this *legislation* without *representation*? 6th Are the legislative powers of Congress susceptible of division—i.e., can it confer upon a territorial legislature power to legislate for one kind while it retains the power to legislate for another kind of property—both being recognized by the Constitution as property?

I have affirmed you have nowhere taken the ground that Congress should actively exert its ["legislative" *interlined*] authority to protect slaveholders in the undisturbed tenure of their property in the territories. On the 12th June 1848, you said: [*Pasted-in newspaper clipping*: The United States possess not simply the right of ownership over them, but that of exclusive dominion and sovereignty; and hence it was not necessary to exclude the power of the States to legislate over them, by delegating the exercise of exclusive legislation to Congress. *It would have been an act of supererogation.*] In reply to Col. [Thomas H.] Benton you say [*pasted-in newspaper clipping: All the power it has in that respect, is to recognise as property there*, whatever is recognised as such by the authority of any one of the States, its own being but the united authority of each and all of the States, *and to adopt such laws for its regulation and protection as the state of the case may require.*]

These extracts I think very clearly indicate that you recognize the right in Congress to legislate for the territories, but I lose my way when I attempt to define the limit, or rather I do not see when or at what point legislation ceases. If admitted that Congress *can* exercise this power, it seems clear that a territorial legislature is useless. It is useless for the reason that Congress *can* do all that a territorial legislature could do.

I affirmed you held no opinions so undefinable, and, as I believed, so wholly useless. If our reliance is alone on Congress for protection in the territories, I consider the case as judged—the South as irrevocably excluded. From the large free-soil majority in both houses of Congress the South has nothing to hope. From men who hold that "property in man" ceases to exist in territory belonging to the States of this Union what have we to hope? surely no laws to protect "undisturbed such property tenure." Men who decline to carry into effect a plain provision of the Constitution are little likely to protect by law the existence of an institution they declare cannot exist without direct legislation, and for which there is no constitutional warrant either direct or implied. Several of the States have special statutes rendering the arrest of fugitives from service almost impossible. Knowing this I believed you relied but little on any action by Congress to protect the slaveholder in the territories.

If I have been able to convey my meaning clearly, and you deem the queries worthy of a re[ply?] I beg Sir, that I may be permi[tted] to use it publicly. Directing a public pres[s] adverse to the present administration, I am anxious to defeat a whig aspiring to Congress on grounds degrading, as I contend, to Southern Rights. The result of his doctrines are decidedly free soil. I am Sir Very very high respect Your Ob[edien]t Ser[van]t, W.D. Chapman.

ALS in ScCleA. Note: Chapman edited the Aberdeen, Miss., *Monroe Democrat* in 1849–1850.

From H[erschel] V. Johnson,
[former Senator from Ga.]

Milledgeville Ga., Aug. 25th 1849

Dear Sir, In your reply to Col. [Thomas H.] Benton's Jefferson City speech, you do not deny categorically, his allegation, that whilst a member of Mr. [James] Monroe's Cabinet, you yielded the Constitutional power to Congress to restrict slavery in the territories of the United States. The absence of such a denial is construed, by those who desire to destroy your influence at the South, into an admission of its truth. The discussions of the press, in this State, upon this point, have been characterised by much zeal and some acrimony, and have so directed public attention to it, as to invest it with an importance which it would not otherwise possess. Personally, I regard it as a matter of very little consequence, whether you did or did not yield the power at that time. It is sufficient to know that you do not yield it now, and that the argument against it, which you have given to the public, is unanswerable. But according to my construction of that portion of your reply, touching this charge, it amounts to what is more than equivalent to a denial of it. Your whole argument upon Mr. Monroe's letter to Gen. [Andrew] Jackson and the entry in Mr. [John Quincy] Adam's [*sic*] diary is, not only pregnant with a denial, but shows, that under the circumstances, it is impossible that it can be true. Hence, it is not for my own satisfaction, nor for the gratification of an idle curiosity, that I venture to ask you distinctly, whether I rightly construe your reply, and whether you did, as charged by a portion of the press in Georgia, while in Mr. Monroe's Cabinet, yield the Constitutional power to Congress to prohibit slavery in the territories? A nega[ti]ve reply to this question, which I feel quite confident you will give, will gratify friends, silence enemies and augment the confidence cherished by the people of the South, in your fidelity[?] to her peculiar institutions. Respectfully y[ou]r ob[edien]t S[er]v[an]t, H.V. Johnson.

FC in NcD, Herschel V. Johnson Papers, Letterpress Book, pp. 57–58; PC in Percy Scott Flippin, ed., "Herschel V. Johnson Correspondence," *North Carolina Historical Review*, vol. IV, no. 2 (April, 1927), pp. 195–196.

From H[erschel] V. Johnson

Milledgeville [Ga.,] Aug. 25th 1849

My Dear Sir, Accompanying this, you will receive a letter propounding to you an interrogatory touching your approval of the Constitutional power of Congress to restrict slavery in the territories of the U.S. while in Mr. [James] Monroe's Cabinet. There is no living being who knows that [I] have written or intend to write such a letter; and therefore, you will fully appreciate my good faith, when I assure you, that it is designed to afford you an opportunity to silence captious ["foes" *interlined*], if answered negatively, or for it not to prejudice you in the opinion of any one, if not answered at all. Whether it is judicious for you to reply to it you must judge. But permit me to assure you, that a negative reply will strengthen your friends in Georgia; and I believe will do much good throughout the South. I hope you will pardon the great liberty I have taken, in consideration of the motive which prompts me.

I agree with you very fully in your views as to the admission of California. The movements of the Sec. of War amount to usurpation. What right had he to confer on Gen. [Bennet] Riley the powers of civil Governor? I fear the mission of Mr. [Thomas B.] King of Ga., to California will do infinite mischief to the South. It encourages the people there to revolutionary action and what is worse, commits the administration to its sanction. Then, will not the Southern Whigs sustain their President? If so, united with Northern support, California will be admitted over our heads. The truth is my dear Sir, I despair of the South's vindicating her rights or honor. I fear degradation & submission are certain. A few more months will decide. But for party, we should now all be united as one man. That of itself would save[?] us.

I doubt very much the practicability of procuring a Convention of the Southern States. The Whigs will unite with the hunker democrats and kill the very idea under the cry of "disunion"—Southern "Confederacy" &c. All sensible men can see that there is no harm in a Southern Convention. It is the best & perhaps the only mode of securing harmony and concert of action among the Southern States which have common interests & rights to defend. But O demagogueism! how it can poison and debauch the public mind and defeat every noble and laudable object. It will bring all its miserable pliances to bear against this suggestion. Time however must decide the course best to be pursued. Very soon those who love the Union & love more the rights of the South will have to determine upon their course. That you may long be spared to serve your Country in this her hour of peril is my most ardent desire.

Mrs. [Ann Polk Walker] Johnson tenders sincere regard to you. Truely yours &c, H.V. Johnson.

FC in NcD, Herschel V. Johnson Papers, Letterpress Book, pp. 59–62; variant PC in Percy Scott Flippin, ed., "Herschel V. Johnson Correspondence," *North Carolina Historical Review*, vol. IV, no. 2 (April, 1927), pp. 196–197; PEx's in Flippin, *Herschel V. Johnson of Georgia*[,] *State Rights Unionist*, p. 26.

From WILSON LUMPKIN,
[former Senator from Ga.]

Athens [Ga.,] August 27th 1849

My dear Sir, My long silence must be charged, to the want of something more cheering to dwell upon. To me the political horizon is still overspread with gloom & darkness.

I have to a great extent lost confidence in the virtue & intelligence of our Southern people. I fear they are not capable of *wise self government*. I fear they will, for the sake of a few loaves & fishes, shrink from maintaining their rights & liberty. Many of the political leaders of the present day, are selfish corrupt men; the press to a very great extent is subservient to these men. Thus the people are often mislead, because the truth never reaches them. Since I last wrote to you, I have closely observed passing events. The Southern address, your reply to [Thomas H.] Benton, & every thing else which I have seen in regard to your course, has my undivided approbation. But Sir, upon the slave question, So. Car. is the only State in the Union prepared to do her whole duty. All the other States falter in part. With a single exception in Geo., the Whig press shrink from speaking out in a manly tone. And the Democratic press in this State, is not entirely free from the influence of former associations with [Martin] Van Buren & Benton.

We have an office seeking faction in Georgia, who look to nothing but self agrandizement, & the spoils of office. They have ["been" *interlined*] bred in the New York school of politics, & of course feel but little of the true spirit of Southern Patriotism.

These men with [Thomas] Ri[t]chie at their heard [*sic*], are still ready to fraternize with the Free soilers of New York, upon all questions but that of slavery, & call themselves, the Old Republican party of the Union, & claim Mr. [Thomas] Jefferson as their founder.

The slave question is obviously a vital one to the South. And if we do not stand aloof, from all parties & individuals, who trample upon our constitutional rights touching this subject, we may give up the ship. I plainly see efforts making, & steps taken by many of the leaders of both parties, to prepare the public mind ["of the people" *canceled*] of the South, for that degradation, which fanaticism & designing aspiration, have decreed shall be the fate of our beloved Southern portion of the Union.

The new administration, is obviously using every exertion to avoid responsibility, by urging upon the mixed multitude now found in Calafornia, the speedy formation, of what they call, a State government; & thus exclude the South from all her rights in the Territory. Had Gen[era]l [Lewis] Cass been Elected to the Presidency, the very same course would have been pursued. And I fear, & beleive, a majority of our people, in the slave holding States, will favor submission to this base & vile project of selfish political partizans. [Zachary] Taylors utter want of qualifications for the high office which he holds, leaves us without hope from that quarter. He must be a perfect Automaton in the hands of others.

Corruption has gotten too deep a hold upon ["upon" *canceled*] the politicians & press of our Country, for us to indulge the hope, that we can unite the South in self defence, even upon this vital slave question. And nothing short of union upon this subject, can save us from degradation & horrors, which the strongest language, can but faintly depict. You & myself, may struggle through our few remaining days. But in the last hour, I fear we shall not be consoled with the prospects, which await posterity in this section of our Union. And yet the Almighty has in his goodness lavished upon us, all the blessings of soil, climate, &C. &C. If our political institutions could be preserved, in full force, according to the letter & spirit of the Constitution—I ask no more. And for less than that, I will willingly compromise.

After a manly resistance, I may submit to *Brute* force. But with my dying breath, I will still protest, against the Demon spirit which has thus reduced me. If I was not a beleiver in providence, I should be very unhappy. But I trust in God, & ["hence" *with the "c" interlined*] have I hope.

It seems to me, that a great struggle awaits the Southern States, similar to that which is now going on in Kentucky & Misouri. Men like [Henry] Clay & Benton are to be found in all the Southern States. Men of tallents, determined to rule or ruin. And it appears to me more than probable, that such men, by the progress of things at present going on, will be encouraged at no distant day, to hoist the anti-slavery Banner ["at no distant day" *canceled*], in most of the slave holding States: should this be the case, it will ["soon" *with the last "o" interlined*] be recorded—The slave holding States, [*one word canceled*] *were.*

We still have in Georgia, very many strong & Patriotic men. And we have honest able & Patriotic men, conducting many of our presses. Our Governor [George W. Towns] is sound to the core on the slave question. But there is a *leaven* in both parties working mischief. The *leaven* of love of power & office. Your answer to the Memphis convention Com. was the proper one. If you can say any thing to encourage me, do let me hear from you soon. My family enjoy health. My own health is exceedingly good. My family join me in true regard & high respect for you, Mrs. [Floride Colhoun] Calhoun & family. Truly Y[ou]rs, Wilson Lumpkin.

ALS in ScCleA; PEx in Boucher and Brooks, eds., *Correspondence*, pp. 524–525.

From ROSE [O'NEAL] GREENHOW

Washington, August 29th 1849
My dear Sir, Your last letter to me was received a few days before my departure from Washington upon a brief visit to Pennsylvania— Not however before I had endeavoured to arrouse ["in" *interlined*] Mr. [Thomas] Ritchie a cord responsive to the call of patriotism and Country at this crisis. He says that he agrees with your views upon the cardinal points at issue between the north & South but depricats agitation at this moment as he conceives that the public mind if allowed to rest will be more apt to resume a healthful state. The truth is upon the mere truckling politician there can be little or no reliance, their own interests is the beacon which guides them and the supremacy of party takes precidence of all more sacred obligations.

From the information which I have had of late opened to me I think that the [Washington] "Union" cannot stand much longer with its present Editors [Ritchie and Edmund Burke], universal dissatisfaction exists in regard to it. I think that you will be pleased to learn how compleatly the free soil party has been eradicated in Pennsylvania. It was brought into being by Mr. [James K.] Polks appointments and the Baltimore Convention. Mr. [James] Buchanan has stood by the South most effectively and has done what no other man but him could have done and put down that dangerous agitation. He says that the fate of this Union depends upon the firm and unwavering front which the South may present next winter. That they should ["first" *canceled*] insist upon three things, that the Wilmot Proviso should be droped or rejected, that Congress should pass laws to enable Southern slave holders to reclaim their property wherever found, which is neither more or less than insisting that the Constitution shall be observed and finally that the agitation in regard to abolition of Slavery in the District of Columbia shall cease. He says thus far he will go with you heart and soul, and that Pennsylvania will will [*sic*] stand by you in the assertion of your just rights, and in resisting the encroachments of the north. He says that he thinks all new elements of excitement ought to be droped at this moment as inexpedient—such as the insisting upon the establishment of Slavery in the new territories as it ["can" *interlined*] never be other than the abstract question of right without practical utility and would certainly embarrass the questions at issue. He says moreover, that he thinks the South should concede the establishment of the laws of Maryland over the District [of Columbia], so as to prevent its being a slave market, and the existance of these pens for slaves should be abolished—but not at this crisis would he recommend that they should yield this point even—but simply to drop the question of slavery in the new territories, neither allowing prohibatory laws, or laws in its favor—as the law of nature which ["is" *interlined*] paramount, will settle how far that institution can exist. Mr. Buchanan regrets that the Missouri Compromise line was not adopted as the Cuba question ["would" *altered to* "could"] never be raised, had that been the case. These are his views which had been boldly pressed in correspondance which I have seen when recently written to in regard to the establishment of a free soil paper at Washington, in more than a dozen instances, to my knowledge, for I had seen both sides, ending with most urgent remonstrances against the encroachments of the North, upon Southern rights.

Your letter to Mr. [Robert] Greenhow was received yesterday. Now I must tell you the progress of the Cuba affair. The main spring or mover in the matter [Gen. Narciso Lopez] has just left me, having taken a parting breakfast, before starting on the perilous undertaking. The expedition will sail on Saturday, that is to say a steamer with a thousand men from New York or some point north with one part of the forces—and a steamer of a thousand ton with 12 or 15 hundred more from New Orleans, simultaneously—well armed and equiped composed of picked men, and officers, ready for the perils the ["proffits" *altered to* "profits"] and honours of the venture. We think that all the elements of success are with them, as every chance has been calculated and every thing which prudence and fore-thought could suggest done to ensure full success. The Government here are in the *secret* and have done no more in the matter of the *Proclamation* than *regard for appearances demanded.* The first fifteen days is the time of trial, and they invoke the moral aid, of all true hearts, who desire the incorporation of that ocean gem, in our sisterhood of States—and of all who sympathize with a people groan-ing under the yoke of tyrany, determined to achieve freedom or die in the struggle. I send ["the" *altered to* "an"] extract from the Span-ish paper published in New York under the supervision of [Angel Calderon de la Barca] the Spanish Minister here[;] it speaks for it-self and I think ought to be published in every paper throughout this Union.

Mr. Greenhow has been so unwell all this summer that I have felt and still am under great apprehensions in regard to him. He is at this moment labouring under great depression of the nervous sys-tem—so soon as he is able to travel he will go to the north for a little while as I think that he will not otherwise recover his strength. Mr. Greenhow and myself are both very glad to hear of the progress of your work—it was due to your own future reputation Sir that you should leave what we know must be a great work—apart from the importance to the country that works of such a nature should be left for future guidance and information by one who has stamped his impress upon its history as you have done. I cannot say what my husbands prospects are—yet I do not despair as yet, though I think nothing will be done before the next Congress. Mr. Greenhow['s] paper on the Proclamation has attracted much attention—he is much occupied at this time. I have much to do hence this hurried scrawl. My kindest love to Mrs. Calhoun & family. With affectionate re-gard & respect, Rose Greenhow.

[Appended]

He leido la Cronica de ayer 25 en la cual se reitera al amenazer de los negroes Ese[?] asi "*Cuba belongs to the Spaniards and shall belong to them as long as she be held by a civilized race.*"

The Cronica also said on the 7th of April "The day when Spain should witness her dominions of the Antilles threatened by a *foreign force,* she would oppose it, if not with an equal number of cannons, with that firmness which has been in all ages been the most remark-able trait of her sons. If in consequence of a war signs should be manifested indicating that the *existing hostile elements* now con-

41

trolled by the interests of a common race, were to be set loose, Spain would arm *her* Africans and would guide them as auxiliaries while able to do so and would grant them freedom as a reward for their aid when convinced that such means would be insufficient to resist.

Those Antilles must for many years belong to Spain, or *they shall disappear from* the list of civilized countries."

Returning to the Cronica of Saturday there is the following very curious paragraph, ["]Lastly we beleive that the Spanish authority in Cuba have now imperious and sacred reasons arising from the *right of self preservation,* to exercise the most *unrelenting severity* with the conspirators and to make a *terrible example* with them.

The Government of Cuba *cannot doubt* that the *inhuman* conspiracy now being contrived in this Country and which has occasioned the Presidents Proclamation, *counts upon some traitors in the Spanish territory. These traitors must fall.* The safety of the land, of life and property and of honest commerce (slave trade) so require it. If it should become expedient to soften the measures of severity on which perhaps depends *Cuba's existance* as a member of civilized society, we would implore the interference of the Government of the United States to whom from institutions and Character such a generous and humane service appertains more than to any one else."

ALS in ScCleA; PEx in Jameson, ed., *Correspondence,* pp. 1203–1204; PEx in Boucher and Brooks, eds., *Correspondence,* pp. 525–527.

To ABRAHAM W. VENABLE, [Representative from N.C., Granville County, N.C.]

Fort Hill, August 1849

My dear Sir, I have read your letter [of 8/7] with much interest, and congratulate you and the great cause on your triumphant success. Under all circumstances, it is a great victory for both; and shows what can be done by honesty and boldness in a good cause. Had the other republican members from the State acted with you, the party would have achieved a decided victory in the State in the election. Even as it is, much has been done to restore it to power. Your position is now a commanding one. You are placed by your course and victory at the head of the party in the State. North Carolina has long stood in need of an able, bold and honest man to take the lead in bring[ing] the State into her true position. You can do it.

I am glad to learn your health is good. Mine is as good as I could expect, and I trust sufficiently so to take me through the next session. It will be an eventful one. We must force the issue on the North, so as to know where we are to stand. The sooner it is done, the better for all concerned. I wish to board on Capitol Hill and near the capitol, and would be glad to have you of the Mess, and hope your arrangements will be made accordingly. I am busily engaged on my work, and hope to have it ready for the press before the commencement of the session; so that I can take it with me to Washington.

I hear from Missouri, that [Thomas H.] Benton's days are numbered. Atcheson [*sic*; David R. Atchison] and [James S.] Green say, that he has as good a chance to be made Pope, as to be elected Senator.

My kind regards to your Son [Thomas B. or Samuel F. Venable].

PC in Jameson, ed., *Correspondence*, p. 770.

From BENJ[AMI]N GARDNER

Eufaula [Ala.], Sept. 5, 1849

Dear Sir, I take the liberty of addressing you this letter for the purpose of obtaining your views upon the propriety and practicability of a subject which I desire to bring before the Legislature of this State, (Alabama,) and through that body, before the people of the South, if after mature reflection, it should be deemed advisable. I allude to the subject of our rights in the new territories.

Much has been said and written upon the question of the restriction by Congress of slavery in California and New Mexico; of the injustice and unconstitutionality of the Wilmot Proviso—of the great and unyielding necessity of maintaining our rights and our honor *at all hazards*, and under all circumstances; but I have looked in vain for any proposition by which our rights may be secured, our honor maintained or our equality preserved. I consider the Wilmot Proviso, so far as any *practical* results are concerned entirely harmless, as slavery, in the present aspect of affairs, can never obtain a foothold in the territories, even should that obnoxious and unconstitutional measure never be engrafted upon the statute books, and consequently, we are as effectually excluded, as if ["we we that obnoxious and unconstitutional measure" *canceled*] it were adopted a thousand times over. Now, it is highly important to the South in a political as well as a domestic point of view, that she should have her

43

full share in our late acquisitions. It is unnecessary for me, in addressing *you*, to give the reasons which have led me to this conclusion—they have doubtless suggested them selves to your own mind long since, and I am apprised that you comprehend fully their force and truthfulness. The question then, very naturally arises—what should the South do, in this great emergency, to maintain her equality in the Union and secure her rights in the new territories? I have thought much upon the subject, and have come to the conclusion that there is but one course which she can adopt, which promises any good *practical* results, or which can, in any wise, place her upon an equal footing with the North in our late acquisitions. That plan is this: that each Southern State shall arm and equip a regiment of volunteer emigrants and send them to California, under its own auspices, with positive instructions to conform to all the laws[,] usages and customs of the people there, which do not conflict with the rights of the South, and to protect those who may emigrate with them from among us, in the full enjoyment of their property of whatever description, should any effort be made, either by savages, Mexicans, or others to wrest it from them.

Having been elected a member of the Alabama Legislature from this (Barbour) county, and feeling the great importance of the subject to which I have called your attention, as well as the necessity of union and concert of action on the part of the Southern States in this crisis, I desire to inform myself fully upon this question, that as a Representative, I may act advisedly, deliberately and for the good of the whole country—therefore, having confidence in your judgement and ability as a statesman, I solicit, most respectfully your views upon this important subject. Should your opinions be adverse to the proposition I have suggested, I would be gratified to receive any other from you, which in your judgement, would be productive of more beneficial results.

It may not be amiss for me to add, in conclusion, that I am a *Whig*—an ardent supporter of the present [Zachary Taylor] Administration, and a Southern man by birth, education and in principle. Respectfully Yours, Benjn. Gardner.

ALS in ScCleA; PC in Boucher and Brooks, eds., *Correspondence*, pp. 527–528. Note: An AEU by Calhoun reads, "Ben: Gardner."

From J[OHN] T. TREZEVANT

Memphis, Sept. 6/49

D[ea]r Sir, Some weeks since, I received your last communication; & soon after, your address, in the Pendleton Messenger. You have had the gratification of seeing, ere this, that it has received the approbation of nearly all the Southern prints, and a large portion of the liberal papers of the Northern States. It came in good time, for our State election, and was almost generally published. That it had a decided effect upon the vote of the State, no reading man can doubt; and that the vote of this State has ["had" *interlined*] great influence already in the adjoining States, no one denies. So soon as Miss. saw the vote of Tenn. many of the Candidates withdrew, having found they had assumed ground which they could not sustain before the *people.*

The vote of Indiana, too, has added to the strength of the Southern question, and more, by throwing cold water on [Thomas H.] Benton, than in any thing else.

It is generally conceded here, that he is daily losing ground; especially since Kentucky has so nobly lectured[?] Mr. [Henry] Clay's emancipation project. That State being just east of Benton's, he feels deeply the blow it has given free soilism. His position has brought out opposition that he thought dared not attack him; and that opposition has ["just" *interlined*] discovered that he is vulnerable in hundreds of points, for the reason that attention has not before been directed to them. If Benton is defeated, the question is settled for years to come; for your address from the Senate & Gen[era]l [Lewis] Cass' letter from the North are causing men to *reflect* upon a question that their passions & prejudices have hitherto handled. Benton's capitol lies however, in the credit he arrogates to himself, of founding this great Pacific R.R. project, and, I learn, from some of our merchants just returned from the East, the N.Y.[,] Phi[ladelphia?], Boston, are all lending their energies to the St. Louis Convention; each hoping to reap individual benefit from the convention. This leading desire of each will cause a large attendance of delegates to that Convention Oct. 1st; and to secure their object, they may give such countenance to Benton as to ["render"(?) *canceled and* "clothe" *interlined*] him with an importance that may raise him additional popularity.

I trust your State will send an able & numerous delegation out to our Convention; as, independent of the Pacific project, one of more

45

[*"immediate" interlined*] importance is the connection of this point with Charleston.

Such a connection would have a great political influence, in as much as it would give strength to the South generally. If it be there, but to advocate such a connection, I trust ["tog" *altered to* "to"] see your State in force here then. Yours truly, J.T. Trezevant.

ALS in ScCleA.

From L[UTHER] M. KENNETT and Others

St. Louis, Mo., Sept[embe]r 7th 1849

Hon[ore]d Sir, On the 15th October next, a Convention is to assemble here, with the view of devising measures to secure the establishment of a National Road, connecting, by a common highway, the Atlantic with the Pacific Ocean. To ensure success to this enterprise, in which we cannot doubt but that you, and every other patriotic citizen of the country are deeply interested, requires the earnest and zealous co-operation of those, who, from their long experience in the affairs of our government, their distinguished position, patriotic zeal, great ability, and *unquestioned integrity*, are best qualified to render efficient service in the prosecution of this great national work— a work, national as we hold, in its conception, its construction and in its incalculable advantages.

Your position Sir, as Senator of the United States—your familiar acquaintance with the powers and [*one word altered to* "duties"] of our government, your eminent ability and deservedly great personal influence, make it most desirable to us, that you should be present at the proposed Convention; to instruct us by your Counsel, and encourage our efforts by your patriotic example. In pursuance of this object, and being fully impressed with the very great and beneficial influence which your presence would have upon the deliberations of the proposed Convention; we the undersigned, Citizens of St. Louis, address you this, our earnest request, that you will attend the Convention; give us the benefit of your hearty co-operation, and allow us the pleasure of assuring you in person, how very cordially and truly, we are, Your very sincere friends, L.M. Kennett, J[ohn] Loughborough, George Maguire, John M. Krum, G[eorge] W. Goode, H[ampton] L. Boon, Tho[ma]s B. Hudson, John S. Watson, D[avid] H. Armstrong, I[saac] H. Sturgeon, John B. Thompson, R[obert]

Wash, Thomas P. Veazey, I[saac] A. Hedges, K[enneth] MacKenzie, Joseph B. Wells, D[avid] D. Mitchell.

LS in ScCleA. NOTE: This letter was enclosed with John Loughborough's ALS of 9/11 to Calhoun. An AEU by Calhoun reads, "Invitation to attend St. Louis Convention."

From J[OSEPH] A. WOODWARD, [Representative from S.C.]

Winnsboro [S.C.,] Sept. 7, 1849

My Dear Sir: Yours of the 14th April came to Winnsboro several days after I had left for the West; whither, I was compelled to go. Expecting to return in four or five weeks, I did not direct any letters to be forwarded. But my mother-in-law [Nancy Herndon Rice], who took my letters from the P[ost] Office, supposing yours to be on business of importance, determined, after som[e] days reflection, to forward it to Talladega [Ala.], which place, it might reach before I left. It did not, however, reach Talladega before I had set out for Mississippi. I was there detained much longer than I expected, and by the continued prevalence of "cholera" on Yazoo River, was eventually defeated in the object of my visit.

On my return to Alabama I found your letter in the hands of a relation with whom I staid; but the time had elapsed, when an answer would be of any use or interest to you. And as ["I" *interlined*] was hurrying home, I defered writing to you until ["I" *interlined*] got here. Though, an urgent business and official correspondence, has caused several days procrastination.

I should have defered my visit to the West, for the purpose of attending the [Southern rights] meeting in Columbia [on 5/14], to which you refered, if I had not come to the conclusion, that it would be better for me to be absent. I had seen the Delegates from Fairfield [District], and the leading ones from Kershaw and Richland [Districts], and had spared no pains to impress my own views upon their minds. During court week I made an address in the hearing of all the leading members of the Bar from every contiguous District, in which I spoke temperately, but *without the least reserve.* In my correspondence, too, I have spoken plainly. Deeming, therefore, that I had attempted as much control as I could prudently do, and ["charged being charged" *canceled*] a certain party and interest, endeavouring to get up an impression that I was blinded by my

47

prejudices against [James K.] Polk and Gen[era]l [Lewis] Cass, and thereby ["lead" *altered to* "led"] into an exagerated pincture [*sic*], of the prospect before us at Washington and in the North; I concluded, as my business was urgent to go off, and let the meeting at Columbia appear to have acted upon its own unbiassed judgment.

But the proceedings at Columbia and the documents you sent me touching Senator [Thomas H.] Bentons course, have ceased to be of any importance, since your "Address" in reply to that Senators speech at St. Louis. I regard it a most fortunate event, that Mr. Benton should have made you the occasion he did, and that every issue discussed by you, should have been forced upon you. Like a fool he has made the occasion for you to expose his whole course of treachery, *in* ["nere" *canceled and* "mere" *interlined*] *self-defense.* He has compelled you, *nolens, volens,* to convict him of treachery, and a score of unconscionable lies; and so the matter is every where regarded. He stands disgraced and degraded, in the eyes of all who have not a natural sympathy for a scoundrel.

The state of feeling in the States I have visited, is about what you would infer it to be, from reading the Papers: except, that there is an obscure class of people, in humble condition, composed chiefly of emigrants ["of" *canceled and* "from" *interlined*] East and Middle, Tennessee, who do not sympathize with the Southern movement. But such of them as have read the "Southern Address," were struck with that part which spoke of the probable *enfranchisement* of the Blacks; and if it should be demonstrated, as it can be, that the negroes could never be sent out of the country, this very class of persons, would, for the most part, ["would" *canceled*] be the most bitterly opposed to their liberation. A candidate for the Senate in a mountainous County of Alabama, informed me, that he encountered many individuals who avowed themselves in favour of emancipating the Blacks and *sending them away*—but when assured that we could never send them out of the country, they said they would never tolerate their being set free and kept amongst us—and were shocked at the idea of their being made citizens.

In convicting Benton, you have created an impression, that there may be many other traitors in the South. Till latterly, this was thought impossible. The man who insinuated ["it" *interlined*], was set down as a detractor and an agitator. Now, the people are on the look out. In studying Benton's conduct & motives, they are beginning to see, that it is the interest of every aspirant to betray them—indeed, that he *must needs do so.* The career of the late President [Polk], could not be acted over with impunity.

The election of [Henry W.] Hilliard [Representative from Ala.; "indicates" *canceled*] must not be regarded as indicating an unsound public opinion. He took the highest ground for the South: in consideration of which many thought it but policy to overlook his premeditated treachery, and not seem to persecute one, whoom a large portion of the community honestly thought innocent.

The election of [Williamson R.W.] Cobb, in the Huntsville [Congressional] District is much more to be deprecated. I understood that he appealed to the "hard-fisted" Democracy as having no interest in the question of slavery. It was expected that he would suffer a terrible defeat, but his election was triumphant.

I have some idea of attending the Memphis convention, to which I have an invitation; to see what turns up there, and to hear what is said. Would it be imprudent? I should be glad to have your opinion on this subject. Very truly, J.A. Woodward.

ALS in ScCleA.

From J[OHN] LOUGHBOROUGH

St. Louis, 9th Sept[embe]r 1849

Dear Sir, You have no doubt received ere this will reach [you] a copy of our circular with an invitation to attend the Contemplated Convention in October. I have designed writing to you for some weeks, but have been so much indisposed and so incessantly occupied that I could not do so. The Convention is as the Circular states designed to be a *National* one. We wish to see in attendance all the friends of a Pacific Railway whatever may be their peculiar notions respecting the route for it and other details connected with the great work. Now there is some danger that if the friends of the cause especially from the South will not meet us here, that Mr. [Thomas H.] Benton may drum up force enough to induce the convention here to endorse his bill and his plans. Such a result would be deeply injurious to the Country and especially to the South in many respects. I am sure I need not enter upon details on this point in addressing. The Convention will no doubt be a large one and its action will have great influence upon the public opinion of the Country. Benton got up his project as a Lever to raise him from the depth of degradation to which he foresaw his Abolitionism would consign him in the estimation of the South, his own State included; and if he can contrive to obtain an end[orsement] from this Convention it will be of essential service to him in his ulterior [*one word missing.*] With the exception of two individuals there is no difference of opinion among the Committee of 25 in respect to Mr. Benton. So far as our action is concerned we are determined not to endorse him, or to set him up as the prime mover of the work; and moreover we are determined to use every exertion to prevent the Convention from endorsing him. The people of the State beyond all question are determined not to sustain his unprincipled appeal. If we can only succeed in knocking from under him his Rail road Scheme he will be left without a plank of the wreck to save himself upon. At the request of the Committee of 25 I have prepared an elaborate article for the western Journal on this subject which will be out in a few days. The Committee have ordered several thousand extra copies for gratuitous distribution. In this article I have repudiated Benton's Bill. I have also made a proposition for a Compromise upon which I think all the friends of a Railway can unite. I am laboring to induce the friends of [Asa] Whitney's bill and our Memphis friends to come into my plan and I am gratified to say that thus far the prospect of success is very fair. It would give me pleasure to write a very long letter to you if I could only lean over a table long enough to do so at one sitting, but my health is nearly desperate. The Article now spoken of will be laid before the Convention here by the Committee of 25; and if its suggestions are adopted I have strong hope that our Memphis friends will concur at their Convention which assembles only a week later than ours. For God's sake, for the sake of the ["whole" *canceled*] South, and for the sake of the whole Country be with us. You can effect more than any one else living and has there ever been a period when the services of great ability and high toned Patriotism was more needed? With sentiments of sincere respect and faithful friendship Your ob[edien]t Serv[an]t, J. Loughborough.

ALS with Ens in ScCleA. NOTE: Loughborough apparently enclosed copies of the 8/22 letter of A.B. Chambers and others to Calhoun and its En from the committee of 25 to the people of the U.S. Loughborough was a member of that committee. His article, "Pacific Railway," was published in the September 1849 issue of the *Western Journal of Agriculture, Manufactures, Mechanic Arts, Internal Improvement, Commerce, and General Literature* of St. Louis.

From W[ILLIAM] W. HARLLEE

Office Wilmington & Manchester
Rail Road Co.
Marion C[ourt] H[ouse S.C.,] Sept. 11/49

Dear Sir, As our company are about entering into negotiations for the purchase of some 15,000 tons of T. Iron in England, on terms which would be highly favourable in every respect with the present rates of duty, to be delivered during the next year, I have taken the liberty to trouble you with an inquiry relative to the prospect of an increase of duty on that article. I see by the Rail Road & other journals at the north that a combined effort on the part of the Iron mongers of this country will be made during the next session of Congress to get ["an" *altered to* "not"] only an increased duty but *specific* instead of the present ad valorem duties and I am well satisfied from a correspondence with the owners of Iron factories in New York & Pennsylvania that every demonstration amounting even to a suspension of work will be brought to bear upon the counsels of Congress in favour of a ["greater" *interlined*] protection upon this article, With what effect these ["efforts" *canceled and* "appeals" *interlined*] will be brought to bear I am at a loss to conclude. There is a democratic majority in the Senate, it [is] true, but a great deal of it is just that kind of Democracy which on this & other vital questions to us, not to be relied on.

Will you write me your views as to the probability of an increase of the duty on Iron? and also whether if a contract were now made, stipulating for the delivery of the Iron next year such Iron could by any possibility be exempted from the increased duty?

These are questions in which not only our Company but a vast number of others are deeply interested ["in" *canceled*]. I think our prospect is now fair to conclude a negotiation to secure our Iron (freight & duty at present rates included) at from 40 to $43 per Ton, to be paid for by $200,000 of our Stock at par, $200,000 in our 6 pr. ct. Bonds at 10 years and $200,000 in money which we can easily meet by the ["aid of the" *interlined*] State subscription. You will at once see the advantage we should enjoy by Keeping the duty to its present point.

In case we should be cut off from securing the whole of our Iron we shall then contract for cash & short time for Iron to lay down our Road from its junction with the Camden Branch to the Great Pee Dee River & wait till our resources will enable us to complete the rest, which I hope will not be at too remote a period. I have thought that the large amount of Rail Road enterprises now in their inception in this country would check to some extent the advances of these grasping monopilies of the Iron trade. If protection to home industry and the developement of our physical resources be the object of these protectionists the means are much more certain, to foster and promote Rail Road enterprises which instead of bestowing their benefits upon a few Capitalists are speeding in every direction over our wide domain, stimulating our agricultural & commercial interests, and increasing to so great an extent the availability of our agricultural products, ["and" *canceled*] multiplying so many of our resources & means of support, and furnishing so many inducements of remunerating labour to all classes of our people.

I have been in hopes that this subject would be agitated in some way at the approaching Rail Road convention at Memphis, and that such statistics & demonstrations would be brought forward as to have an influence on public opinion, and especially that portion of the Representation in Congress who are not immediately connected with the Iron interest, for I am satisfied it could be shewn that by increasing now the duties on R.R. Iron there would be more enterprises suppressed or burdened by the operation than whole Iron factories ["in the U.S." *interlined*] are worth put together. The time at which the convention is held places it out of my power to attend it in consequence of my professional engagements in our fall courts but I trust that some person out of this State if practicable would press the matter on the consideration of the convention. It is certainly a legitimate consideration in estimating the capacities and means of the country to engage in great Rail Road enterprises, to look to the removal of burdens upon their construction, not the least of which is the high price of Iron caused by protective duties.

I contemplate writing an article for the ["N.C." *canceled*] Raleigh (N.C.) Standard, and if we could edge in the matter from a whig State it might be the means of ensuring a more impartial consideration. However it might have an important influence to have it discussed from any quarter, and I trust if you are there (which we all hope you will be) that you will if you think it expedient urge the matter so as to attract to it public attention.

If you should not agree with me as to the propriety of this move I hope you will not regard the suggestion as presumptuous, as I feel well satisfied every means in our hands will be required to thwart the movement for protection now going forward. I am Very Resp[ectfull]y Your Ob[edien]t Ser[van]t, W.W. Harllee.

ALS with En in ScCleA. NOTE: Harllee enclosed two pages from an 1849 issue of the *American Railroad Journal* containing articles on "The American Iron Interest" and "Meeting of Pennsylvania Iron Masters." These articles described the depressed state of the U.S. iron industry and blamed the situation on the low tariff duties on English iron.

From J[OHN] LOUGHBOROUGH

St. Louis, Sept[embe]r 11th 1849

Dear Sir, Permit me as an old admirer and friend, and as one true to the rights and the honor of the South to solicit your especial attention to the accompanying letter [of 9/7]. It does not come from ignorant, low bred and unscrupulous partizans, but from a number of ["per" *canceled*] those most estimated among us for every trait which gives dignity and respectability to character.

Mr. [Luther M.] Kennet[t] the first signer is a gentleman extensively known in the West and perhaps to yourself as one of intelligence, and purity of heart. Mr. [George] Maguire was formerly the Mayor of our City and is in every respect an unexceptionable gentleman. Mr. [John M.] Krum was formerly the judge of our highest City court and acquired high character in that station. Messrs. [George W.] Goode[,] Veasey [*sic*; Thomas P. Veazey] and [John B.] Thompson are members of our Bar of high Standing. Mr. Boone [*sic*; Hampton L. Boon] is the Editor of the Metropolitan at Jefferson City[,] the ablest Anti [Thomas H.] Benton paper in the State and besides a first rate gentleman. In short all the signers are "men of mark" and character. If time had sufficed hundreds more of same cast would have become signers.

It is impossible for me within the limits of a letter to state to you how many reasons there are why you should accept this invitation; and I am not sure that I possess sufficient political information and ability to do so. At all events I am very certain that your own reflection will suggest to you better reasons than I can urge. I believe you are under a promise to be at Memphis. Our Convention is only a week before that, and it will be but a loss of the time to visit us. I feel great confidence that the view we have taken of the question will meet the approbation of every true friend of the measure, as it is national and just to all concerned. With Sincere respect Yours, J. Loughborough.

ALS with En in ScCleA.

To A[RMISTEAD] BURT,
[Abbeville District, S.C.]

Fort Hill, 13th Sep[tembe]r 1849

My dear Sir, George [McDuffie Calhoun?] informs me, that you had a good crop when he left home. I hope it continues so. Cotton I think must rise still higher. My information from the west is, that the crop will be very short. Andrew [Pickens Calhoun] writes on 26th of Aug[us]t, that the boll worm was committing great ravages. I fear ours will be cut off more than half. George walked over my crop here, & will tell you what he thinks of it. The weather continues very dry, and I am of the impression the late bolls will yield but little. We have had no rain to wet the ground for about 5 weeks.

The time for leaving for Washington begins to be near at hand. The session cannot but be an important one. Your House [of Representatives] will be so nearly balanced, that, I think, it will be important, that you & our other members should be on the ground some days before hand. The choice of a speaker will be important & difficult to make. I trust our delegation & the sound portion of the South, will be agreed on two points; not to go into caucus to nominate a speaker with any tainted with freesoilism & in no event to vote for [Howell] Cobb of Georgia, as speaker. He will, I doubt not, be a candidate. His course & that of his paper has been infamous. It has been shaped to get the sym[p]athy & support of the worst portion of the Northern democrats.

If I can get off, I wish to be at Washington a day or two before the meeting of Congress. I have made up my mind to board on the Hill, as I wish to be, as little exposed to the weather as possible. I would be glad to have you & Martha [Calhoun Burt] with me, if the Hill would suit you. But if you should prefer any other location, I hope you will not make the sacrafice of selecting it on my account.

My family are all absent but Mrs. [Floride Colhoun] Calhoun & [Martha] Cornelia [Calhoun]. They join their love to you & Martha, & kind regards to Mr. [George] McDuffie & Miss Mary [Singleton McDuffie]. Yours truly, J.C. Calhoun.

ALS owned by Dr. John A. Calhoun.

To [ADAM B. CHAMBERS and Others, St. Louis]

Fort Hill, Sept. 16, 1849

Gentlemen: I regret that I cannot accept your invitation [of 8/22] to attend the Convention to be held at St. Louis, on the 16th of next month, to deliberate upon the expediency of connecting the Valley of the Mississippi with the Pacific. My engagements are of a nature that would not permit me to be present.

No one more highly appreciates the subject of your meeting than I do. I have made up no opinion as to its eastern or western terminus, or the route that should be adopted; nor shall I until I am better informed. My wish is that the best route, all things considered, should be selected, including both termini. The work should look to the whole Union, and the general commerce of both the Atlantic and Pacific oceans. Such will be the views that will govern me, whenever I may be called on to act on the subject. I regard the work to be one of too great magnitude and importance to be influenced by local or private considerations. With great respect, I am, &c., J.C. Calhoun.

PC in the Washington, D.C., *Daily National Intelligencer*, October 31, 1849, p. 3; PC in the Charleston, S.C., *Courier*, November 3, 1849, p. 2; PC in the Spartanburg, S.C., *Spartan*, November 8, 1849, p. 2; PC in the Lynchburg, Va., *Lynchburg Virginian*, November 8, 1849, p. 2; PC in the Edgefield, S.C., *Advertiser*, November 14, 1849, p. 1; PC in the Pickens, S.C., *Keowee Courier*, November 17, 1849, p. 1; PEx in the Georgetown, S.C., *Winyah Observer*, November 14, 1849, p. 2. NOTE: The committee addressed was made up of Chambers, Richard Phillips, Edward Walsh, John O'Fallon, and John F. Darby. Some 137 South Carolinians, including Calhoun, were appointed by Governor Whitemarsh B. Seabrook to attend the convention. (Charleston, S.C., *Mercury*, September 25, 1849, p. 2.)

To SAM[UE]L TREAT, [St. Louis]

[Fort Hill, *ca.* September 16, 1849]

My dear Sir, Agreeably to your request I enclose my answer to the Committee to you. I have left it open for your perusal. After you have read it, wet the seal with your tongue & press it down with your thumb.

I have made my answer short & comprehensive. I thought under circumstances it would be better. If St. Louis should on full deliberation be thought to be preferable as the Eastern terminus I would heart[il]y give it my support; but I think the course you suggest the best, at least for the present, to fix the terminus for the present at Indepen[den]ce or some other place on the Western limits of the State. It will do much to conciliate all the different interests.

I am glad to learn that [Thomas H.] Benton has fixed his doom. It is a wonder that he has been able so long to impose on the country. His fall will be one step to a better state of things. It is vastly important that you should have, at this time, a true & able paper. Yours truly, J.C. Calhoun.

ALS in MoSHi, Judge Samuel Treat Papers.

From F[ITZ]W[ILLIAM] BYRDSALL

New York [City,] Sept[embe]r 17th 1849

Dear Sir, I enclose with this, some newspaper extracts [*not found*], not because they present any new features in the great contest now going on, which involves the existence of the United States Confederacy, but simply because they may be useful in your hands. When we recollect the division of the Methodists, Baptists, &c. into Northern and Southern religious parties upon the subject of ["Negro" *canceled*] Slavery; the breaking up and reorganization of political parties upon the same subject, the long cherished desire which the monarchies and aristocracies of the old world still retain for the dissolution of our Republican Confederacy ["and the sectarian influences they can use to promote that consumation," *interlined*] what American patriot who can foresee future events from existing causes, but will come to the conclusion that "the country, politically is indeed in a bad way. Things cannot go on much farther in the direction they been going for many years?"

The two factions of the Democratic party of this State have united by State Conventions in support of the same State ticket, drawn together by the cohesive motive of the "spoils," each declaring as the basis of Union, hostility to the "extension of slavery" and are proclaiming the constitutional authority of Congress to legislate upon the subject of slavery in the territories and district of Columbia. To me, a union upon such declarations, if sincerely meant, is a union to effect a dissolution of the Union, for what alternative is left for the Southern States but submission or resistance to the North? I confess to you that I see ["an" *altered to* "the"] accumulation gathering against us becoming every year more formidable. The large majority of the people of the New England States are more than ever opposed to the South upon this and other questions. The sentiments of the people of the middle States are tending to the same point; add to these the vast accessions to our voting population from Europe, who come amongst us with as strong, if not stronger prejudices against the slavery of Blacks, as they ["can" *canceled and* "could" *interlined*] feel against the slavery of Whites, and it must be self evident that the longer the denouement of the drama is postponed, the ["worse will it" *canceled and* "harder will the struggle" *interlined*] be for the South. It is absolutely vital to us ["all" *interlined*] that the rights of the people of the Southern States should be admitted and established beyond question, to the same extent as the rights of the Northern people—or that the slave States should separate (and that soon) from the free States. One or the other section of States must give way, but which is the question. I can only say that if we give way, all that we hold dear is lost. Our Southern States would become worse than any other country in ruins, we should forfeit our own self respect and should not deserve neither the respect nor commiseration of mankind. ["Such are my sentiments. A long residence at the north has not changed me—my feelings and my interests politically (for I have still an interest in some slaves) are decidedly Southern." *canceled.*] There is no doubt in my mind if such a calamity as separation should be forced upon us, but that a Southern Confederacy of States could maintain itself against the world. The controll of the whole U.S. coast on the gulf of Mexico would then be ours. The Western States would be dependant on us for an outlet to their exports, capital would grow up amongst us from our own great products. In short give such a confederacy peace and no people ever did, nor could any other people on earth attain such a prosperity as they would reach. But notwithstanding all these and other considerations, I love the Union—its glorious historical associations, its splendid and mighty future in prospect, so much so, that admitting all the blessings which might result to the South in the event alluded to, I should still regard the dissolution or separation of the Confederacy as the worst of misfortunes to the human race— the direst of fatalities to Republican Government. Yet I prefer separation to degradation & wrong.

Were it not for Southern traitors and the best of them deserve no other designation, the difficulty could and would have been settled beyond the reach of agitation two years ago. If I mistake not in my recollections, every slave State except So. Ca. furnishes one or more of those traitors, while to old Virginia must be accorded the high honor of not re-electing one of them for Congress.

There is a growing anti Catholic feeling in this community especially against Bishop [John J.] Hughes and a paper alleged to be under his controll—the Freemans Journal—for denouncing the Roman Republicans and asserting the doctrines of absolutism. The suppression of the Roman Republic in Italy and the collection of Peter's pence in the United States, does not sit well upon the popular mind here. Even one of the chief men, if not the head of the Jesuits here, has come out against the Pope's [Pius IX's] temporal power. After all it may be probable that the Order of Jesuits may have been in former times too republican in sentiment for the pope and the Catholic Kings in Europe who combined to suppress the order. There is an Irish Editor [Thomas D. McGee] of a paper here called the Nation who charges the failure of the late Irish rebellion upon the Roman Catholic priesthood of that country, and recently he accuses the Bishop and the Catholic clergy here of a secret conspiracy to put down his paper.

I hope you are renovating in health. That this and other blessings may be yours is the heartfelt wish of Dear Sir—Your ob[edien]t Servant, F.W. Byrdsall.

ALS in ScCleA.

To A[NDREW] P[ICKENS] CALHOUN, [Marengo County, Ala.]

Fort Hill, 22d Sep[tembe]r 1849

My dear Andrew, I have been waiting anxiously since I received your very discouraging letter of the 26th August, to learn with some certainty, what would be the fate of our crop, especially as you stated you would write again in a few days. I had hoped, the very dry spell of weather we have had since, would improve its prospect, both by deminishing the ravages of the worm and the rapidity with which it ["had" *interlined*] matured the cotton. We have had a drought now of about 7 weeks. The ground has not been wet half an inch in the whole time. Our cotton will soon be all open, except in low places. The leaves are all fall colored to the top. I expect to have out 35,000 [pounds] by the end of the month from 113 acres. It has, I think, been much shortened by the drought, but still I will make a full average. But not so the State generally. From all accounts, the crop of the State will be short at least a third. If you have had the same season, I would suppose it would greatly improve our crop; but I fear, that such has not been the case, as the intelligence from the West still continues to be most unfavourable. If you have not written, write me, as soon as you receive this, & let me know. I shall be very anxious to hear.

I will be glad to meet you in Charleston, as you propose, and hope you will bring a full state of our affairs from the last settlement, as I will bring on my side; so that, among other things, we may adjust our accounts. You had better bring [*one word canceled*] a statement showing that our la[n]ded estate is free from all mortgages & incumberance from the proper office. I think, as good a negotiation, may be made in Charleston, as N. York [City].

Mr. [John R.] Mathew[e]s has written me, that Mrs. [Ann Matthewes] Ioor wishes the bond to her to be discharged this winter. I trust, that I shall be able to take it up from what Dr. [Ozey R.] Broyles' will advance. He speaks with confidence, that he will be in funds.

I gave Mr. [Joseph A.] Scoville, who is travelling in the South as the correspondent of the [New York] Herald, a letter of introduction to you at his request. You will of course treat him civilly; but, I hope, you will not go farther, and make ["him" *interlined*] acquainted in the neighbourhood for I hear, since he left here, that he has taken to his old habit of drinking, and that he boasts of his intimacy with me. He is a kind hearted & obliging man, with good feelings for the South, and, I believe, really & sincerely attached to me; but his intemperance & want of prudence makes him unsafe.

We are all well & all join their love to you & family. Your affectionate father, J.C. Calhoun.

ALS in NcD, John C. Calhoun Papers.

To D[avid] J. McCord, [Columbia, S.C.?]

Fort Hill, 22d Sep[tembe]r 1849
My dear Sir, I regret very much to hear what you say of Mr. [Joseph A.] Scoville, although I cannot say I am surprised. I knew his weakness, and had no great confidence in his reformation of habit. While here, he abstained from touching wine, or sperits and appeared re-

solved to presist in avoiding his former habits, in consequence of which I had cast him off. I know nothing agai[n]st him but that, and a disposition to magnafy his importance. He is a very kind hearted obliging man, of strong attachment and good feeting [*sic;* feeling] for our section, and no small aptitude and industry.

He brought a letter from Mr. [James G.] Bennett of the [New York] Herald to me, from which I learned, he was in his employ, & which gave me some hope he had reformed. I treated him, accordingly, civilly; permitted him to copy my address as I prepared it, for the Herald, & got him to copy the part of the work I have on hand, which was ["then" *interlined*] in the course of execution. As to his boast of any agency he had in the work beyond, it is not worth noting.

I am obliged to you for affording me an opportunity of saying what I have to you, & thereby correcting any erroneous impression, which either his conduct, or expressions may make in reference to myself. I wish him well, & regret that he is so great an enemy to himself. Of his good feelings, in reference to myself, I have no doubt; but his want of prudence, & intemperance at intervals, make him unsafe. With great respect yours truly, J.C. Calhoun.

ALS in ScU-SC, John C. Calhoun Papers; photocopy of ALS in ViU, David J. McCord Papers.

From THO[MA]S G. CLEMSON

Brussels, 7he [September] 24th 1849

My dear Sir, We received by the last steamer your letter dated Fort Hill August 24 together with your reply to [Thomas H.] Benton [*one word changed to* "in"] pamphlet form. I had read it some time since in the News papers. It appears to be triumphant & very severe which he merited. Could you have made it shorter it would have been more generally read, but I do not see how you could have curtailed it.

As to the state of Europe the change that has taken place in the last two months is very great, but neither surprising or unexpected. The people have spent their blood, their enthusiasm & their money, without having gained near as much as they might have done, had their efforts been well matured or well directed. In France, the Republic (such as it is) is fixed upon them in spite of themselves. They would do well under the present form of Government, if the leaders were pure, moral or religious, but as it is, the people are uneducated & have become the pliant tools of those who live by their wits. The longer the present form of Government lasts the stronger will become the conservative party. As to the liberty of the press, it does not exist, but the universal suffrage will be more difficult to take away. Where it will carry them time alone can tell. In France as well as Germany but more particularly the latter property is in the hands of the few. They are adverse to all changes & particularly where the changes are against them. Hungary as you have learned by the papers could resist no longer. The sword & bayonet rule east of the Rhine & monarchy with its accompanying standing armies have nothing to fear at present. Some pretend that other revulsions may be anticipated before a very long time, but I do not think it probable. The people are exhausted & it is impossible for them to compete with power & the well organized armies that have become more wary since the late upheavings. Republicanism here is synonmous with socialism, & the example of France is not calculated to make prosylites. The funds[?] are rising every where & there is as much order & tranquility throughout Europe as ever existed. There is no denying one fact & that is that all the powers of Europe are deeply & I think hopelessly in debt, how they are to escape bankruptcy remains to be seen. What is also true is that the existence of the actual Governments depends on their standing armies, which absorb all their resources. To disarm would be the end of monarchy, & with the present forces ruin stares them in the face. Even in this quiet little country if the army was disbanded, Leopold would not remain two weeks on the throne, & of this monarchs are perfectly aware.

From the fact of my not having heard from Col. [Francis W.] Pickens I was fearful that something had occured when your letter informed me that Col. P[ickens] was sick, & Mr. [William A.?] Harris had declined purchasing my property—& in case it should be true you say I will have to determine without delay what I will do. You also [*one word or partial word canceled*] say that you are at a loss what to say. If you being on the spot & with your experience of southern values can not form an opinion, I am sure I can not. If there ever was a person that should be sick of a country I am the person that should be sick of the South, & if it pleases the Almighty to grant me a safe deliverance I promise never again to place my foot on its soil. I have no confidence in the climate either for myself or family, to live there would be sickness & speedy death, without ["out" *canceled*] one single compensation. Even grant health, to live on my place, would be a seperation from civilisation, & continued privation of the necessities of life, for I have had five years experience in which time the place has not given $1000—it has quit cost & that is all. I have foreseen the possibility of my being forced (notwithstanding my desire to get rid of it) to retain the property nolens volens, & in order to make the best of it I have been desirous to accumulate something that would enable me to live elsewhere a part of the year & repair there during the winter months & scrape along, but that would appear almost hopeless. I have been striving all my life for honourable competency. I have family whose wants are daily increasing, & if I were to resign this place, I could not command $500 from all my property amounting as it should to some where about $50,000. If the property will not sell, I must hold on to it until such time comes (if it ever does) when it will sell. To put it up at public sale would require my presence, & I could not give that without resigning my present position which is at least a support. If I could do any thing with my negroes, the place & the other property might be sold at public sale—& the negroes at leisure. Could any thing be gained by advertising? The difficulty may be, that it is not known to be for sale. I can do nothing & must await until I hear from Mr. Pickens. My affairs have given me so much tribulation that I at times am almost tempted to resign & go & try to put them in a better shape, at all hazards—but I should be relinquishing an existence & the education of my children [John Calhoun Clemson and Floride Elizabeth Clemson]. I have stated to you that this place has not entirely sufficed what I have expended & it has required close shaving. Donnelson [*sic*; Andrew J. Donelson] has had two outfits of $9,000 each with a salary of $9,000 per annum. [U.S. Minister to Prussia Edward A.] Hannegan is going to the United States this winter[;] in the mean time he is amusing himself in England. It is said that now that the Empire is dead, that Mr. Donnelson desires to return to Berlin. If he obtains that position he will have had three out fits in as many years besides his salary. It would be a great lift to me if I could obtain that position, it would put $9,000 into my pocket at once.

When you were in Washington you told me that you anticipated receiving money from Dr. Broryley [*sic*; Ozey R. Broyles], (I think) and that you would apply a portion of it to taking up the bond which will fall due in January. As I have heard nothing from you on the subject, nor from Mr. [John Ewing] Bonneau I judge that you have paid nothing as yet. As the time is fast approaching, when the principal & interest are due, and as you will shortly leave home for the long session I am anxious to know what arrangements you have made. I wish to write to Mr. Bonneau & merely await your answer. I wrote you previous to leaving Europe that I wished my money, but stated at the same time that I should regret distressing you, and should have been satisfied with a portion had it been paid, which however was not the case. I have had two settlements with you, & I now repeat what I said to you in Washington, that I have reason to be dissatisfied with your mode of doing business. Previous to each settlement you failed to pay the interest & the loss occasioned by yourself & son [Andrew Pickens Calhoun], by that delinquency was made to fall on me, because you pleased to call it compound interest. I hope that the time has been ample for you to have made arrangements for the payment of the entire sum, because independent of my want of confidence in the securities of Alabama I have none in the business capacity of your son—besides which I desire to have no pecuniary transactions with any relation or connection, they have in my case proved disastrous. I stated to you before I left Europe & when in the United States that I desired security in Carolina for that portion of the money which you could not pay. This you would not consent to give, lest it might create alarm amongst your other creditors. I wished to avoid the appearance even of my being the cause of distress & therefore consented to another years delay. You will permit me to remark as I am interested, that I think the sum you owe jointly to be large, and a portion of it a very large part of my property & by far too large not to be secured. I have expressed to you verbally & otherwise, years ago, the desire to be paid, & I had hoped that in March the matter would have been closed. It is folly to attempt to raise money in the North on property in the South. The effort should have been made in Alabama & Carolina. When speaking to you of your own affairs in connection with this subject, you told me that Andrew Calhoun stated to you that he would have no difficulty in raising money in Alabama, to purchase your portion of the property in Alabama. If that be the case I should suppose he could have no difficulty in raising the amount of my debt. No one can expect to borrow money, purchase property & disregard his obligations besides. There would be an end to all business if such practices were tolerated. In all the business communities I know of in this world, these questions do not admit of the least doubt. If there be members of your family to whom you feel attached & whose interests you wish to defend, it will not surprise you if I state that I also have affections for my children & that I wish to take care of their interests & so long as I not only ask nothing wrong, but merely what is usual & right it should not be withheld. If after what has occurred difficulty should arise, the responsibility lies else where & not with me. Justice is the highest humanity.

I hope that you have received the portraits which I understood were to have been sent on some time since. Mrs. [Elizabeth Clemson] Barton wrote me some time since that they had or were shortly to go from Phila[delphia]. The main difficulty will be in getting them up from Hamburg.

We are all well. The cholera has almost disappeared from Brussels whilst it lingers in other parts of the Kingdom with considerable violence.

I have not heard from Mr. [Reuben H.] Reynolds in a long time & feel very anxious to know how they are getting along. If as you pass down the goats should not be doing well or have not increased they had better be removed. I was desirous that they should increase & that you & Mr. Pickens should have the benefit of their first offspring. If they appear not to be in good health or you would prefer I will send you a couple direct from Antwerp by the first vessel that leaves for Charleston.

An idea strikes me about my plantation & negroes. Would it be possible to rent [Andrew F.] Lewis's place joining you, so that your overseer Fredericks could attend to both having some one to aid him. We might afford to give him higher wages, if it would pay. My negroes [*one word changed to* "&"] what stock would be necessary might be removed from ["Abbeville" *canceled*] Edgefield & the place & every thing not required in Pendleton might be sold. The waggons could haul up all the farming utensils &c so that they could go right to work on their arrival. I write this suggestion that you may turn it over in your mind, so that if Harris objects to a part[?] he may have the plantation. I must do something & rack my brains to know what I ought to do. Anna [Maria Calhoun Clemson] will write very shortly. We hope that your health is good & if you return to Washington it will be necessary that you should take the greatest care of yourself otherwise you will not be able to stand the long session. Your affectionate son, Thos. G. Clemson.

ALS in ScCleA; PEx in Boucher and Brooks, eds., *Correspondence*, pp. 528–529.

From CHA[RLE]S CARROLL LEEDS

New York [City,] Sept. 24th 1849
Dear Sir, On behalf of "The New York Literary Society," an institution for the advance of literature among young men, I have the pleasure to tender you the acceptance of an Honorary Membership in that body, to which you were elected on Friday Evening Aug[us]t 31, 1849.

The society feel that their little influence over the community will be much widened by the connection, even in a remote degree, of a gentleman whose literary abilities have rendered his name so conspicuous as your own; and by offering such membership they also wish to show their high regard for the many qualifications which have fallen to your share. I Am Sir Yours Very Respectfully, Chas. Carroll Leeds, Corr[esponding] Secretary, 45 William St., N.Y.

ALS in ScCleA.

From H[ENRY] S. FOOTE

Warrenton [Miss.], September 25th 1849
My dear Sir: I am gratified to have it in my power to inform you that several leading gentlemen, of both the two great political parties in Mississippi, have promised me, at our approaching Convention, to act upon your suggestion relative to the recommendation of a Southern Convention. Very recently I have received information from all parts of Missouri touching Mr. [Thomas H.] Benton's movements there, and assuring me of his certain defeat. Among others, [David R.] Atchison writes that his overthrow is beyond doubt. Judge [James W.] Morrow Mr. [Samuel] Treat, and several prominent men besides, write to the same effect. I am invited, as I suppose you are, to the St. Louis Rail-road Convention, & am specially urged to attend by friends who declare their conviction that Mr. Benton's plan will be negatived, and some other adopted. It is also declared to be the wish of several that I should address the citizens of St. Louis in opposition to Mr. Benton's plans & operations generally. I should ["certainly" *canceled and* "willingly" *interlined*] comply with both invitations, but I am not certain, or even confident of any such good effects as seem to be anticipated. Were I sure of your attending, which I think you could do with great advantage to the common cause, I would contrive to meet you, & encounter all the coarser work of the occasion. It would be a great thing to overthrow him at home, and blow up his Humbug project, in presence of his own constituents.

Certain ["indications" *canceled and* "movements" *interlined*] which you cannot fail to have perceived, seem to indicate that the policy of the Administration is to settle the Wilmot Proviso question by admitting California & N. Mexico both as States, upon their formal application next winter. I confess that my mind inclines favorably to the scheme, so far as California is concerned. It appears to me, though, that N. Mexico will hardly be ready to enter the Union so early, as my information is that there are not more than five hundred Americans there altogether. I am not ["so"(?) *interlined*] inclined to move precipitately in the affair at all; and after all that has occurred, should deem it highly indiscreet to take any important step save in full counsel with yourself & others of the South whom I could name. If California could be brought into the Union under Southern auspices, & provision made for the admission of N. Mexico when a sufficient number of persons of American birth shall be ascertained to have become resident therein; all legislation on the subject of slavery, either by Congress or Territorial legislatures being, in the mean time, precluded, it seems to me that the honor of the South would be saved, & the population of both the territories so effectually conciliated, as might in time lead to most advantageous results. Some such plan as this, matured at once, and announced about the time of the Missouri Convention next month, would blow Bentonism *sky-high*; quiet & save the Republic, & sweep away the demagoguism of the present hour forever. I do not urge these things upon you. I only suggest them. Whatever is done hereafter in the settlement of this question, I am desirous, for various reasons, should be done under your lead; but I am willing to perform any subordinate part of the ground work which may be assigned me. I write in great haste, & under the pressure both of bodily disease, & of mental anguish from the decease of several very dear relatives in the neighborhood which has recently taken place. I remain, most cordially, H.S. Foote.

P.S. I enclose you a Missouri newspaper, & a letter of Judge Morrow accompanying it, which I thought might amuse you. H.S.F.

[Enclosure]

J[ames] W. Morrow to H[enry] S. Foote

Jefferson City [Mo.], Sept. 2 1849

My Dear Sir: Pearls continue to pour from the snout of the swine [Thomas H. Benton] in such profusion, that I very much fear I shall become troublesome to you if I continue to send them to you—but the two letters to the people printed in the paper I send you are decidedly too unique to be lost. Do not fail to read his letter of the 30th Aug. 1849. He gives you a very vivid picture of the state of our public morals. The publication of these addresses has produced one general burst of laughter and ridicule. It is plainly to be seen that their author feels the gripe of the monster at his throat. We have the old rebel in our toils, and intend, like the spider, to weave the webb about him until he is powerless. This County (Cole) held a county meeting yesterday and raised the "Wolf howl" of obey or resign. All the leading Democrats (and many of the leading Whigs, who took no part,) of the County were present, and our erudite Governor [Austin A. King] and his promising ["Lieut" *canceled*] adjunct, the Lieut: Gov. [Thomas L. Price], ["saw" *canceled*] who, have both quailed before the old rebels frowns and oaths, saw the ["hand the" *canceled*] hand writing on the wall. Yours very truly, J.W. Morrow.

P.S. He makes a speech tomorrow at Booneville where I hold a Circuit Court, and something rich will grow out of that. J.W.M.

ALS with En in ScCleA; PEx in Jameson, ed., *Correspondence*, pp. 1204–1205.

To J[OHN] A[LFRED] CALHOUN, [Abbeville District, S.C.?]

Fort Hill, 26th Sep[tembe]r 1849

My dear John, I regret to learn that you have had so severe an attack, but am gratified to learn, that you are better & the family all well.

I think you do well, in the present state of your health, to decline going to the Memphis convention, although I would be glad for you to be present.

The news from the West is very bad in reference to the cotton crop. Andrew [Pickens Calhoun] writes, it will not exceed a third of a crop in that section, and that some will not make more than a fourth. Ours will hardly be a third.

My crop is opening fast.

I shall have out nearly 35,000 lb. by the end of the month. It is a good deal shortened by the drought.

All are well & all join in love to you, Sarah [Morning Norwood Calhoun] & your family. Your affectionate Uncle, J.C. Calhoun.

ALS in ScCleA. NOTE: John Alfred Calhoun moved back from Alabama to Abbeville District about this time.

From JAMES AUCHINCLOSS

New York [City], Sept[embe]r 30: 1849

Dear Sir, I assure myself that you will not be displeased at my sending you a copy of the [New York] "Mercury", containing a copy of a letter which I felt it my duty to address to the Rev[eren]d Dr.

[Robert S.] Candlish, of Edin[burg]h, relative to the question of American Slavery, as they call it in Scotland. My motives were honest in writing the letter, and I trust you and others will approve it. With profound respect, I am your ob[edien]t s[ervan]t, James Auchincloss.

ALS in ScCleA.

From HARPER & BROTHERS

No. 82 Cliff Street
New York [City], Oct. 1st 1849

Dear Sir, Your favor of the 22d ult. [*not found*] is at hand. In reply we beg to say, that we should be happy to be the publishers of your proposed work, and to offer you our best terms for the privilege.

Hoping for the pleasure of hearing farther from you on the subject, when your ms. is prepared for the press, we remain, with thanks and respects, Y[ou]r Ob[e]d[ien]t Servants, Harper & Brothers.

LS in ScU-SC, John C. Calhoun Papers.

From MARY L. GARDINER

Sag Harbor, L[ong] I[sland, N.Y.]
Oct. 2nd 1849

My Dear Sir, Having for years been familiar with your name through the public prints, and by your correspondence with my dear Husband, whom you honored with your friendship, and who ever esteemed and valued your early acquaintance and revered your memory, who spoke of you to me, and to our children as One quite above the ordinary mass of men; I take a mournful pleasure in sending you a paper, containing an Obituary of his death. John D. Gardiner slumbers in the grave. No more will his eye search for your name so dear, nor read with nervous impulse the doings and sayings of the Statesman he loved.

The name of John C. Calhoun will ever be a household treasure, and children who now live, and those who are to live will delight in hearing the increasing popularity of one, who subscribed himself the friend and [Yale College] classmate of their sainted Father. With the best wishes for your future happiness, and a prayer for your reunion in a brighter and a better world, I remain Your Friend, Mary L. Gardiner.

ALS in ScCleA. NOTE: An AEU by Calhoun reads, "Mrs. Gardiner."

REPORT AND RESOLUTIONS OF THE MISSISSIPPI CONVENTION

[Jackson, October 3, 1849]

We the delegates to a convention, called by the people of the State of Mississippi, to deliberate on the means to prevent the unfounded pretension, that Congress has power to legislate on the subject of domestic slavery, and to prohibit its introduction and existence in the territories of the United States, have duly considered the important subject committed to our charge, and make the following report, as expressive of the voice of Mississippi.

It is boldly asserted, that Congress possesses an unlimited power of legislation over all the territories belonging in common to the people of these United States—that it, consequently, has power to prohibit slavery in these territories—that the exercise of such power is expedient and necessary, inasmuch as slavery is an evil which must be eradicated from the land. With a few patriotic and honored exceptions, the people of the Northern States seem determined to adopt the Wilmot Proviso, or the principle it contains. Every succeeding year brings forth new expedients for the accomplishment of this object. The press, the pulpit, and the ballot box have all become tributary to this fanatical hostility to the South. It is vain to hope for an abandonment of this settled design. Submission to our wrongs, provokes perseverance on the parts of the aggressors; and it is wise in States, as it is in individuals, to resist encroachment. Unfortunately, we have been but too passive under former encroachments. Our opponents exult in the passage of the Oregon Bill, as a full acknowledgement of the principle, and build their hopes of further success on that. In this unfortunate controversy there are but two alternatives—the one is submission, the other is resistance. To the one we cannot—we will not consent; the other, we are reluctant to adopt.

In the name of our constituents, we solemnly deny the existence of the power claimed, and protest against its exercise. We assert that it will violate the Constitution and will lead to a dissolution of the Union.

We have not met to discuss the question of power or expediency. They have been argued and re-argued; in and out of Congress, by our statesmen and by our people. We have reasoned and remonstrated in terms of conciliation with our Northern brethren, until forbearance has ceased to be a virtue. We have warned them of the consequences of perseverance. They have disregarded our remonstrances, and our warnings; they have disregarded the most solemn compromises, in which we yielded too much. They have refused to submit to judicial determination, preferring to decide by the force of numbers. There is no common arbiter; and we, too, must decide for ourselves. That decision is made. We take our stand on the plain principles of the Constitution, and intend to maintain it, or sink in the effort.

We assert that Congress has no power over the subject of slavery, within the States, or in the territories. That these States by the revolution; by the declaration of independence, and by the treaty of peace, became seperate and independent sovereignties, with all the political power of separate and distinct nations; that they are still so, except so far as they may have expressly delegated part of their power to the general government; that they have not delegated their sovereignty. The Federal Government is not a sovereignty, but a limited federative system, possessing only such powers as have been expressly granted to it by the constitution, with such implied powers as may be indispensably necessary as incidents to the express grant. It follows that it can legislate only on the subjects confined to it, and, on them, only in strict subordination to every principle of the constitution. As power is constantly tending to the legislative department, it is inexpedient that Congress should encroach on the liberties of the people and sovereignty of the States by exercising doubtful powers.

We maintain that the system of slavery was recognized by the constitution—slaves were recognized as property, the full enjoyment of which was guarded and protected; guaranteed by that compact; that Congress has no power over such property; the right of property preceded the constitution—it is co-eval with the history of man; it exists by a paramount law of nature; it is the subject of control by State sovereignty only. This Union never would have been formed, without the full and entire recognition of slavery, and property in slaves, and the guaranty to the owner which is contained in the constitution.

We assert that the territories acquired by the late war with Mexico, are the common property of the U. States; that the people of the States have a right to move to it, and enjoy it; to take with them their property, their religion and their liberty. Congress did not create property in slaves, nor can it say they shall cease to be property. To abolish slavery in the territories, is to diminish their value, and limit their usefulness in the States. It is appropriating the whole of the territory to the use of one portion of the people of the United States, to the exclusion of another. The power of Congress to legislate for the territories is a power to protect the citizen and his property, not to declare what is property: Therefore

1st. Resolved, That we continue to entertain a devoted and cherished attachment to the Union, but we desire to have it as it was formed, and not as an engine of oppression.

2. That the institution of slavery in the Southern States is left, by the constitution, exclusively under the control of the States in which it exists, as a part of their domestic policy, which they, and they only, have the right to regulate, abolish or perpetuate, as they may severally judge expedient; and that all attempts, on the part of Congress, or others, to interfere with this subject, either directly or indirectly, are in violation of the Constitution, dangerous to the rights and safety of the South, and ought to be promptly resisted.

3. That Congress has no power to pass any law abolishing slavery in the District of Columbia, or to prohibit the slave trade between the several States, or to prohibit the introduction of slavery into the territories of the United States; and that the passage by Congress of any such law, would not only be a dangerous violation of the constitution, but would afford evidence of a fixed and deliberate design, on the part of that body, to interfere with the institution of slavery in the States.

4. That we would regard the passage by Congress, of the "Wilmot Proviso," (which would, in effect, deprive the citizens of the slave-holding States of an equal participation in the territories acquired equally by their blood and treasure,) as an unjust and insulting discrimination—to which these States cannot, without political degradation, submit; and to which this Convention, representing the feelings and opinions of the people of Mississippi, solemnly declare they will not submit.

5. That the passage of the Wilmot Proviso, or of any law abolishing slavery in the District of Columbia, by the Congress of the United States, would, of itself, be such a breach of the federal compact as, in that event, will make it the duty, as it is the right of the slave-

holding States, to take care of their own safety, and to treat the non-slaveholding States as enemies to the slave-holding States and their domestic institutions.

6. That the legislature is hereby requested to pass such laws as may, in their opinion, be best calculated to encourage the emigration of citizens of the slave-holding States, with slaves, to the new territories of the U. States.

7. That, in view of the frequent and increasing evidence of the determination of the people of the non-slaveholding States, to disregard the guaranties of the constitution, and to agitate the subject of slavery, both in and out of Congress, avowedly for the purpose of effecting its abolition in the States; and also in view of the facts set forth in the late "Address of the Southern Members of Congress," this Convention proclaims the deliberate conviction that the time has arrived when the Southern States should take counsel together for their common safety; and that a convention of the slaveholding States should be held at Nashville, Tenn., on the 1st MONDAY IN JUNE next, to devise and adopt some mode of resistance to these aggressions; and that this Convention do appoint twelve delegates and twelve alternates—being double the number of our Senators and Representatives in Congress—to attend such convention, and that the other slaveholding States be invited to appoint delegates agreeably to the same ratio of representation.

8. That in the language of an eminent northern writer and patriot—"The rights of the South in African service, exist not only *under* but *over* the Constitution. They existed before the government was formed. The Constitution was rather sanctioned by them than they by the Constitution. Had not that instrument admitted the sovereignty of those rights, it never would have been itself admitted by the South. It bowed in deference to rights older in their date, stronger in their claims and holier in their nature, than any other which the Constitution can boast. Those rights may not be changed—even by a change of the Constitution. They are out of the reach of the nation, as a nation. The confederacy may dissolve and the Constitution pass away; but those rights will remain unshaken—will exist while the South exists—and when they fall, the South will perish with them."

9. That to procure unity and promptness of action in this State, this Convention recommends that a Central or State association be formed at the Capitol, and affiliated county associations within the several counties of the State.

10. That we recommend to the Legislature of this State, that at its next session, a law be enacted, making it the duty of the Gov-

ernor of the State, by proclamation, to call a general Convention of the State, and to issue writs of election based upon the ratio of representation in the State Legislature, upon the passage by Congress, of the "Wilmot Proviso," or any law abolishing slavery in the District of Columbia, or prohibiting the slave trade between the States, to take into consideration the act of aggression, and the mode and measure of redress.

11. That a committee of six be chosen by the Convention to prepare an address to the people of the slave-holding States.

The delegates appointed under the seventh resolution for the State at large, were:

W[illiam] L. Sharkey, A[lexander] M. Clayton, H.T. Ellett and G.T. Sturges. *Alternates*—John I. Guion, A[nderson] Hutchinson, W.R. Cannon and J.T. Harrison.

First Congressional District—Jos. W. Matthews and J.T. [*sic*; T.J.] Word. *Alternates*—H[ugh] R. Miller and J.D. Branford.

Second District—T[homas] N. Waul and J[oseph] B. Cobb. *Alternates*—Reuben Davis and Charles B. Shepperd.

Third District—H[enry] C. Chambers and E[dward] C. Wilkinson. *Alternates*—W[illiam] R. Hill and Patrick Sharkey.

Fourth District—Geo. Winchester and D[ouglas H.] Cooper. *Alternates*—David Hurst and Henry Mouger.

The committee appointed under the last resolution, to prepare an address, is composed of.

W.L. Starkey, A. Hutchinson, Geo. Winchester, C[aswell] R. Clifton, W.R. Hill, Jno I. Guion and E.C. Wilkinson.

PC in the Richmond, Va., *Enquirer*, October 16, 1849, p. 2; PEx in the Washington, D.C., *Daily Union*, October 17, 1849, p. 3. NOTE: The above proceedings are referred to extensively in subsequent Calhoun correspondence, and may have been enclosed in the letter from Anderson Hutchinson on 10/5.

From F[ITZ]W[ILLIAM] BYRDSALL

New York [City,] Oct[obe]r 5th 1849
Dear Sir, The following announcement is going the rounds of the Newspapers: [*Newspaper clipping*: "The Philadelphia North American States that they have positive information that the Hon. John C. Calhoun is about to resign his seat in the United States Senate."]

I confess that I read it with a depression of spirit that was almost crushing. For three days it has lain heavy upon my heart as a death

73

knell. Where is the man upon God's earth can be found ["a man" *canceled*] to supply such a vacancy as will then be made? Who is fit to be our exponent in that body—our cloud by day & our pillar of fire by night? Who, at this juncture when a crisis is at hand so fearful to contemplate? God knows we need every true man we can muster in his proper place, and not one can be spared out of his place and least of all him who is unquestionably the greatest! I can conceive of no greater political misfortune now.

I grieve—but I think [*"not" interlined*] one single thought of censure, because I feel assured that it is not in your nature to retire from a contest of principle unless there ["be" *interlined*] good and ample reasons for your retirement. But it is this firm conviction that strikes the deeper gloom, because of its firmness. There is but one cause or event on which I would like to see you leave the Senate, *that* which I have wished for many years and which I still hope as fondly and with as clear a prospect in my view, as there ever was.

Though I fear you have ample reasons for leaving the Senate, yet I dread it for the sake of our great and good cause. It may be that amid such materials as partly compose that body you may feel you can do no further good there. But the future my dear Sir is in the hands of God and there I am always trustful ["and" *canceled and* "for" *interlined*] my own experience has confirmed my trustfulness in that direction. Parties, principles, politicks are all in a state of chaos, but order will grow out of the present disorder, and surely there can be no order but that which will be based upon the principles, and a strict construction of them, of the Constitution. We have stood upon that platform all the ["way" *canceled and* "time" *interlined*] up to the present moment and there we are still standing for the sake of rights and institutions which make a country dear and sacred and deprived of which we have no Country. No my dear Sir we cannot spare you. We have no right to expect you to toil or expose your health as you have done, nor is it even necessary, but as *the man* who has vision to see, sagacity to direct and public virtue which has never deceived, betrayed, nor demagogued the people, you cannot be spared.

I shall hope that the announcement is not true. Yours truly and with deepest veneration, F.W. Byrdsall.

ALS in ScCleA.

From A[nderson] Hutchinson

Jackson [Miss.,] Oct. 5, 1849

Two of your letters to Gen. [Henry S.] Foote [Senator from Miss.] were enclosed to me, to be used according to my discretion on the question of the crisis. That suggesting a Southern Convention was shown by me to our mutual friends Ch[ief] Justice [William L.] Sharkey & Judge [Caswell R.] Clifton, who, altho Whigs are full up to Southern rights. We adopted the idea with ardor, but all concurred in opinion, that if we should proceed on a course recommended from S. Carolina, we should fail. The idea of a Southern Convention had previously occurred here—but you may well appreciate how much your opinion strengthened[,] confirmed & animated us. I dropped a note to Gen. Foote stating that it had occurred *in Mississippi* that a Southern Convention was the important action required. You will understand this.

In the [Jackson] Mississippian of this date, on its second page, you will find the action of one of the Southern States in Convention, recommending a Convention of the Fifteen Southern States, appointing 12 delegates, with alternates, on the ratio that we have two Senators & four representatives in Congress, being six & that both of the two great political parties should be equally represented. Sharkey & myself thought Washington was the best place of its assemblage; but the majority preferred Nashville as more *central!* All agreed that February or March was the time, but here the majority believed that it would require until the 1st of June to enable the Southern States to act.

There were four or five resolutions concerning the exclusion of California, until organized according to the Constitution; but this, not on principle, but as to detail (fact & law) became a theme of prolonged debate; and the Convention, (impatient to adjourn after three days session,) laid them all aside & appointed a committee to prepare an address to the South, in which it has been agreed that this subject will be submitted to the Southern People & their Conventions.

If the Southern States shall gather around Mississippi & support her the Constitution & the Union will be rescued from the hands of madmen & traitors.

This is the utmost joint action we could obtain. Virginia (my State) I hope will first act—then Alabama—then Louisiana, then Tennessee & Kentucky—then Arkansas—then N. Carolina—*then South Carolina*—& then the *martyred* State of Georgia & the rest. This however is only my wish, the reasons for which I could explain.* [*Foot-*

75

note: "* The second Washington (Zachary Taylor?) at his own table, after his election & before he was conducted to the Capitol as the most renowned specimen of a nation's humiliation, said to his guests, in reference to the extension of the area of slavery, to which he was opposed, that 'if Mr. C(alhoun) sneezed S.C. would sneeze.' A Southern Bishop present told him that (')Va. would sneeze first,' &c."] I trust that our effort will be duly hailed by your nullifying State! Our movement is attempted to be maligned as one of nullification! I am now encouraged to hope that the coalition of the North will soon be compelled to recede & disband. Their politics have too long turned on our affairs: too long has denunciation & actual war upon our agricultural institution been their theme & agitation. I am with the highest esteem, A. Hutchinson.

ALS in ScCleA; variant PC in Jameson, ed., *Correspondence*, pp. 1206–1207. NOTE: Anderson Hutchinson (1798–1853) was a native of Va., a former judge in the Texas Republic, and codifier of the laws of Miss.

From J[OHN] RAVEN MATHEWES

[Clarkesville, Ga.,] 7th Oct[obe]r 1849

My Dear Sir, I rec[eive]d your note & have communicated its contents to my Sister [Ann Mathewes Ioor] & the Doctor [William Ioor] which in their reply is satisfactory. The Elections in this State are over & as much indifference by both parties I have never seen. I freely convers'd with men of distinction on both sides & they ["both" *canceled*] expected the same apathy would be the result. The fact is the Whig & Demo[cra]t extreme wings unconsciously found themselves exposed to be approaching the outstretched arms of the abolitionists & a ["general" *canceled*] murmur of disapprobation was universally made. The Aug[ust]a Sentinel & Chro[nic]l[e] said to be in the Interest of [Robert] To[o]mbs & [Alexander H.] Steph[en]s—the Athens ["Banner" *interlined*] also in [Howell] Cobb & [John H.] Lumpkin. There certainly is a great pause in the activity of all parties in this State & fortunately no election will occur before the Bone[,] muscle & sinew will have time to reflect & see the fatal Gulph yawning at their feet. These two papers used your name as the Pis aller for diverting the Public Gaze & attention from the true reasons why the non conformists to your & Judge [John M.] Berriens papers did not sign but I think they have rather opened the door of investigation through their own Columns. The question which they started was whether J.C. Calhoun or Tommy the Traitor [Thomas H. Benton] stood erect—by universal consent the latter has been plac'd where like Lucifer "never to hope again." The remaining question affords the people to enquire & read what has the former done & been doing all his life. The answer of both parties is that Tommy ["never" *canceled and* "has" *interlined*] betray[e]d the South & that John C. Calhoun has sacrafic'd his own national Rights of Promotion to stand by Southern Constitutional Rights.

Every portion of Georgia has been interchanging Ideas this summer. We here have had Crowds from the Mountains to the Seaboard—and depend upon it that our Rail R[oa]ds & ["northern" *interlined*] cholera have done more for the South in Political enlightenment than Ten thousand Speeches in Congress—and that these will yet be the means of striking more Terror to the Soul of the Northern Tyrant than all that has been done by Congressional Resolutions, Speeches & feuding & provising Editorial squibs. My idea is now to seriously & calmly, but carefully arrange for forming a third or Southern party—making no charges against who *was* wrong or ["rights" *altered to* "right"] in past excitements at Home or at Washington—otherwise we shall have each one that is obnoxious becoming a Sangrado—better the whole village die than his published theories be recanted. Reconciliation should be the watch word—To all save Tommy. The Presidential question by which all our rights have been whitled down will then be in place of our ["growing" *interlined*] weakness ["be" *canceled*] made our pillar of strength. We can tender that office to the party who will most rigidly adhere to the Constitution & protect thereby the Peace & property of the South. This third party may become then the Ballance of power party— whereas we are now like unto the ["2" *interlined*] Litigious cats, the monkey, & the cheese. The Northern Whig & Demo[cra]t Parties— ["agitation of" *interlined*] the Presidential question—& Southern Rights held for ever in the Ballance & at every canvass a piece of cheese is bit off or yielded to ballance the Scale either in favour of the Black or white Cat. I have already fatigued you unintentionally, enclosed is a carricature of my meaning.

Mrs. [Ann Polk Walker?] Johnson wrote last week that you were indisposed with a cough. If it is Chronic permit me to ["advise" *canceled*] suggest the use of Dr. [William J.?] Beachs Pulmonic powders, pills & Drops to be had at Heads[,] Charleston. It is a remedy that has never failed with me—very simple & agreeable.

With our best Respects to Mrs. Calhoun & the family I remain my Dear Sir with esteem Your Wellwisher, J. Raven Mathewes.

ALS in ScCleA; PEx in Boucher and Brooks, eds., *Correspondence*, pp. 529–531.

From JOHN H. HOWARD

Columbus [Ga.,] Oct[obe]r 8th [18]49

At this critical period in the government I should have been pleased to have been in the councils of the State, but have failed more on account of the whig elections for Judges than any other cause. From the returns already in, I think we shall have a democratic majority in both branches of the legislature and if wisely directed much good will result from our success. I enclose you my address. The latter part please read and say whether it is a proper platform for the South to stand on. Had I been elected I should ["have" *interlined*] passed resolutions [*one or two words changed to* "pointing"(?)] to some *definite* action (if I could) and appointed a committee composed of part members and part leading & talented citizens, to bear these resolutions, to each slave holding State. I would if I could have succeeded, had an able committee to present the resolutions for each Southern State so as to have had our views laid before all the States at the same time. These were my views; be kind enough to give them some thought & write me. It is also my opinion that the best move the Southern members of congress can make, is to boldly take the ini[ti]ative and bring in a bill ordering a line to be ["run & " *interlined*] *marked out* upon 36.30. Let the territories on both sides be organized, *neither* though with the Wilmot Proviso. This will leave the South privileged to go beyond 36,30 if they choose subject to be overruled by the opponents of slavery, if they should be in the majority at the time it is proper to be admitted as States. While the marking the line on 36,30 will ["secure them" *canceled*] point to them a place where they will in all probability be secure against such majority. The whigs I presume will desire to get clear of the whole question by admitting the whole country as a State or States. Whether *with* or *without* the proviso it is *too soon*. It is a *fraud* upon the South & should not be submitted to. If California & New Mexico were both now admitted as a State or States without the proviso they would with their present population exclude slave holders the first session after their admission. Will you be kind enough in *confidence* to give me your opinions in regard to the course, South-

78

ern members of congress should pursue at the next session; also what preventive remedy Southern legislatures should present *before* the meeting of congress. I am Respectfully & truly yours, John H. Howard.

P.S. You may rely on the prudent use of your letter or the strictest confidence if you should think proper to impose it. I may be able to do something for the South with our legislature.

ALS in ScCleA; PEx in Boucher and Brooks, eds., *Correspondence*, p. 531. NOTE: Howard's "Address to the Voters of Muscogee [County]" appeared in the Columbus, Ga., *Enquirer*, September 18, 1849, p. 3.

To A[NDREW] P[ICKENS] CALHOUN, [Marengo County, Ala.]

Fort Hill, 9th Oct[obe]r 1849

My dear Andrew, I received yours of the 14th of Sep[tembe]r the day I mailed my last to you. I hope you have got mine.

Yours gives a sad account of our Cotton crop. Its sho[r]tness will throw a heavy money pressure on us this year. The great point will be to keep down interest. We must make every effort to meet interest punctually, & keep up our credit.

I fear from the rate of interest in New York [City], as stated by the papers, we can do nothing there in the way of funding our debt, especially with so small a crop to ship. I hope Dr. [Ozey R.] Broyles will be able to make a large advance, before I leave for Washington. It would do much to relieve us.

I fear, with you, that the worm will prove a perman[en]t drawback on the culture of cotton [*one word canceled and* "in low" *interlined*] latitudes. The only remedy would seem to be the early maturity of the plant. Well selected seed & good culture may do much to facilitate early maturing. I planted this year, seed from petty Gulf (2 years) and ["very" *canceled*] common cotton adjoining. The latter matured fully a week earlier, better bolled, equally easily picked and of as good quality. Would it not be well ["to" *interlined*] try some ["its" *canceled and* "my seedling"(?) *interlined*] seeds? I could, if you should think so, send you two ounces by letter. I had a letter [*not found*] a few days since from M[artin] W. Philips, a planter of Mississippi, proposing to send me some of the best seeds from his vicinity. Among others, he mentions the Sugar loaf. From what he states, it would suit you in every respect. He says, it is from

79

20[?] to 15 days earlier; that its limbs are short, & that it does best in very rich land. He says, it ought to have an 1/8 or 1/9 less distance between the rows, & a 1/6 less in the drill.

I have no personal knowledge of Mr. Philips. He states himself to be a Carolinian by birth, & writes like an intelligent gentleman. I know your aversion to experiments; but, I trust, in a case of so much importance to us, you will obtain some of the seed of a variety appar[en]tly so well suit[ed] to our place. His residence is Edwards, Mississippi. I wrote him, that I had my principal cotton interest in Marengo Ala., which would afford you an opportunity of writing to him. If you write, address him as a gentleman, & not one dealing in seeds. I am sure from the friendly tone of his letter, he would take pleasure in forwarding some of his seed to you.

I find man[u]ring does much to mature cotton early, especially stable. For that purpose, a small ["equantity"(?) *canceled and* "quantity" *interlined*] only ought to be used, to give it a vigorous start.

My crop of cotton is a good deal injured by the drought, & still more by the worm; but I shall make a full average. The crop of the State, as far as I can learn, will be short by a third.

We are well & all send their love to you, Margaret [Green Calhoun] & family. Your affectionate father, J.C. Calhoun.

ALS in NcD, John C. Calhoun Papers.

From J[ohn] Raven Mathewes

[Clarkesville, Ga.,] October 11, 1849

My Dear Sir, I wrote you last week by Mail but cannot omit this private conveyance to write you the result of the Election in this State in favour of the Democracy. "All however is not Gold that Glitters." Their majority will be a unit & several that they claim are "Independents." This will clip the wings of Ultra partyism—which in this State was becoming desperate to the interests & rights of a deluded & infatuated I may add deceived people. Your reply to [Thomas H.] Benton has *since* the Election become a rallying point for both parties; previous—they would not have touched your name with a pair of Tongs—but great is God & so is truth. A Member of Congress today (Demo.) [Howell Cobb] openly said that your position had opened his Eyes & that he no[w] denounced "Tommy" [Thomas H. Benton]. Why not have said so before. His paper at

Athens has been denouncing you & upholding this Traitor 'till the Subscribers have convinced their opinions to the contrary. The Whigs are hopeless—having ralied upon no principles but taking the example of [Zachary] Taylor—they have signally failed & are precipitated in the Chasm without a twig to hold to & have left themselves no rallying point but Northern Whigery which I think at the South is dead & buried. [George W.] Towns' is [*sic*] open & manly letter can be hereafter rallied on. I cut out the ["subjoined" *canceled*] enclosed [*not found*] from one of my last papers. Is it so? I hope that your self & family are in the enjoyment of health & every other blessing. Remaining as ever most truly & respectfully y[ou]rs, J. Raven Mathewes.

ALS in ScCleA. NOTE: An AEU by Mathewes on the envelope of this letter reads, "Fav[oure]d by Grange Simons Esq[ui]r[e] of Charleston So. Ca."

To A[NNA MARIA] C[ALHOUN] CLEMSON, [Brussels]

Fort Hill, 14th Oct[obe]r 1849

My dear Anna, You & Mr. [Thomas G.] Clemson must regard me as a very negligent correspondent this season, but you must attribute it, not to indifference, nor indolence, but to being overtaxed in the way of writing. My correspondence is necessarily heavy. It occupies one day & some times two a week; but what mainly occupies me, is the work I have on hand. I have written between three & four hundred pages of fools cap in the execution of that, since my return from Washington; and have, I think, to write about 40 or 50 more before I conclude the work. I will then have to review, to correct & finish off, which will require some time; but I hope to be able to have it all ready for the press by mid-summer.

It will consist of three parts; a discourse on the elementary principles of govern[me]nt; a discourse on the Constitution & Govern-[me]nt of the United States, and a collection of my speeches & other productions on constitutional subjects. It will make two moderate size Octavo volumes. I think the work is called for by the times, & that it will make an impression. I have stated my opinions on all points, just as I entertain them, without enquiring, or regarding, whether they will be popular ["or" *interlined*] not. Truth is my object, & to that I closely adhere.

As [Martha] Cornelia [Calhoun] and the other members of the

family have kept you well informed in the news line, I will pass over every thing of that kind, and give you some information of ["my" *interlined*] farming operations.

While I have been engaged on my work, I have not been inatentive to my plantation. My crop is a fine one, & the place in good order. I have ["have" *canceled*] just finished hawling in one feild [*sic*] of corn of about 77 acres. It has yielded upwards of 3000 bushels, which for land, that has been cultivated for more than 50 years every year, & three fourth the time in corn and the whole time unmanured, is not bad. I have another feild of about 35 acres to bring in, which will yield nearly as well. In the midest of it, there was something less than 2 acres of land, too low & wet for corn. I planted it in rice. It yielded 130 bushels, thrashed & put up; so your mother [Floride Colhoun Calhoun] will have an ample supply. It yielded about 6 tons of excellent straw, not much inferior to hay. The rice is worth a dollar a bushel, & estimating the straw at $30 the whole will give a profit far beyond any other grain.

My cotton crop is, for the year, very good. It will be more than a full average, although a good deal injured by the boll worm, & the long drought of nearly 2 months in August & September. I expect to make upwards of 60 bales from 113 acres, each bale 400 pounds. I attribute my success to manuring & good cultivation.

The ["cotton" *interlined*] crop is a very short one. There is scarcely any part of the cotton region, where it is not short, and in a greater part of the West, disasterously so; from late frosts, cold spring & summer, excessive rain and [*sic*] one time and drought another, & the ravages of worm. We have suffered with others in the west. Our crop there will not exceed a third, but I hope, the increased price will do a good deal to make up the deficiency.

Say to Mr. Clemson, that I received his letter of the 1st August, enclosing Dr. [Charles] Munde's letter to him. I addressed the Dr. according to his direction at N. York, but have not heard from him. I could not give encouragement of suitable pursuits to one of his talents & acquirements in this quarter, & advised him to try his fortune in the city of N. York, where he would be in the midest of his countrymen, & where there were so many opportunities for employment for one of his high qualifications.

I wrote Mr. Clemson a short time before I got his letter just referred to. I hope he got mine. I have not written him since, as I had been much employed, & had nothing particular to say. Col. [Francis W.] Pickens, I suppose, is in correspondence with him in reference to his Edgefield concerns. I have heard nothing from there lately.

My general health is as good as I could expect, though I am a good deal troubled with my cough.

Your mother & Cornelia, the only part of the family at home, join in love to you all.

Kiss the dear children [John Calhoun Clemson and Floride Elizabeth Clemson] for their grandfather. Your affectionate father, J.C. Calhoun.

ALS in ScCleA; PEx in Jameson, ed., *Correspondence*, p. 772.

From J[OHN] T. TREZEVANT

Memphis, Tenn., Oct. 15/49

D[ea]r Sir, Just as the people of the Southern States are, at the ballot box, sustaining your course upon the great question of Southern rights, rumours reach us that you intend, at an early day, to resign your seat in the Senate of the United States. Your many & warm friends & admirers here at least, must regard this announcement, or this intention on your part as peculiarly unfortunate at this juncture; for the ["late" *canceled*] verdict in every State that has lately voted in the South must be a matter of gratulation to you, & may well susstain you [in] any legislative movement you may feel called upon to make, at the ensuing session of Congress.

That it will be an important session, no one doubts; & that the South will need the aid of all her able & determined sons, none can doubt. To you, more than to any other from the slave region, will the eyes of the South be turned; and for you to resign a position that may—nay *must* be, from recent elections, a commanding one under your lead, would be hazarding all that you have gained, unless you could be sure & the South have confidence, in the ability of your Successor. Another question is of great importance; and requires the boldness & energy of one accustomed to success. It is an investigation into the necessity & legality of that department which will soon be *the* department of the Government. I allude to "the department of the Interior." Under the best hands, it is capable of great evil; but under ambitious, designing men, the prestige it will command is incalculable. It is now used to promote the freesoil fanaticism; and every appointment has some reference to that. This, with the P.O. department in such hands as at present control it, will soon give color to the, or any administration; and power but accumulates power.

To investigate this state of things, & to check what must be regarded by all prudent men, as a rapid tendency towards centreing all power in the Federal head of the Government, & of course taking all from the States, requires the energy & spirit of one familiar with the workings of our Government & ["with" *canceled*] conversant with the distribution, or the originally intended distribution of its powers.

Your friends & political associates look to you as one to whom this duty could be best entrusted, & upon whom it would most appropriately fall.

The South begins to feell that she is not safe, even with a Southern man at the helm, when he is so inefficient & so completely surrounded & controlled by northern influences; and she must be heard, on questions that are rapidly coming to a point. Your long experience, your familiarity with the history of parties & of men now prominent, & your position on this question which rises above all others, in the estimation of Southern men, point you out as one who cannot *now*—not yet, leave a seat, when occupying it may be productive of incalculable good to our common Country. I hope therefore, that the rumour alluded to, is without foundation, and that the ensuing session will find you as vigilant as the criesis may demand. With great respect, J.T. Trezevant.

ALS in ScCleA.

From R[ichard] K. Cralle

Lynchburg [Va.,] Oct. 18th 1849

My dear Sir: On reaching home recently from the mountains, I found your favour of August 24th on my table. I should have replied to it immediately, with the view of soliciting your opinions in detail as to the project contemplated by the Memphis Convention; could I have determined at once to attend it as a Delegate from this Town. I have, however, upon mature reflection declined the appointment for the reason, amongst others, that the movement is premature. We are not certain that the Southern States are to be permitted to participate in the benefits of the acquisition, whilst it is certain that they are to bear their proportion in the costs, should they basely submit to the arrogant pretensions of the non slave holding States, and remain in what is called, *the Union.*

The mail of tonight brings some accounts of the proceedings of the *People of* California and N. Mexico, preparatory to the organization of State Governments. The Mormons, I see, have already completed theirs—settling boundaries, appointing officers, Executive, Legislative and Judicial, and with utmost *sans froid,* proclaiming themselves a sovereign and independent Community! What times are these we live in? Is anarchy *yet to come,* or is it not already at our doors? Unless you can succeed in arousing the spirit of our members of Congress at the next session, I fear all will be irretrievably lost. The infamous *concordat* of [Lewis] Cass & [Martin] Van Buren is by far the most fatal sign of the Times I have yet witnessed. It is an unblushing compact of political scoundrels, uniting for the *avowed* purposes of plunder; and the huckstering character of our Representatives promises nothing, I fear, better than *Protest* and *submission.* Thinking men are looking anxiously to you; and much will depend on your exertions. But the public Papers this evening inform me that your health is so feeble that your friends have advised you to remove to *Charleston.* This seems a strange direction; and I hope the rumour is nothing more than the usual gossip of newsmongers. Should it be otherwise, however, let me advise you to take some relaxation; for I doubt not that, what with the work you have on hand, and your other engagements, you may overtax your physical strength. Could you not anticipate your departure for Washington a few weeks, and take this place on your route? By moderate travelling you could reach here in a week; and stay with me until the commencement of the Session. At this season of the year the roads are generally good, and the temperature propitious. It would give to me, and to all my household, infinite pleasure; and I am sure would be of service to you, should your health be, as is stated, feeble. And even if it should not be so, still, I am confident, the visit would not be without some use, in many respects. The People every where throughout the State need to be conversed with. Roused at a single point the excitement will spread, until a higher tone of feeling shall leaven the masses. We have no man amongst us who has either the ability, or, perhaps, the inclination to move the lethargic mass. There is now no man in Virginia to whom the People look for advice. We are as sheep without a shepherd, and need some controuling intellect to rouse and direct the popular feelings and energies. I am sure if you were to come amongst us, and linger here a few weeks, a flame might be kindled which would spread far and rapidly. This might be done without subjecting you to the pressure of crowds, or unwonted labour or excitement of any kind. My House is large, and will afford ample accommodations for yourself and family. I hope Mrs. [Floride Colhoun] Calhoun will unite with me in urging you to take this plan into consideration. We are all equally anxious to see her and Miss [Martha] Cornelia [Calhoun], who I suppose will go with you to Washington.

Your proposition to meet you during the next Session, I readily accede to, although I may not be able to stay as long as you suggest. I thank you for the flattering opinion implied in the wish that I should look through your M.S.S. before the work goes into the hands of the publisher. I should, indeed, like to do this, not with a view to *criticism* either as to *"style* or *matter"* (for in either the blemishes that might be detected would only be such as the fly might be supposed to discover on the Cupola of St. Paul's) but from a lively curiosity to see how the subject has been treated. I need not say I expect much from it—and such is the general expectation. I see a notice has already appeared that the Harpers of N.Y. would put it to press early in the ensuing Spring.

I have been much engaged since I wrote last, in hunting up old Documents and collecting materials for the Work I propose. I hope during the winter to finish the period extending from 1824 to 1836. The eight previous years I shall have to consult you about, as you were out of Congress, and my information is not as full as I desire it should be. By the bye, a friend from below forwarded to me, by the last mail, a Pamphlet, (consisting of a series of Letters) written by an individual, under the signature of *"Thompson"* in 1823, which contains much interesting matter. He was the advocate of your election at the time—but my friend does not give me his real name. You may probably have, amongst your Papers a good many publications of a similar character which might be of great use to me; and if you could put yourself to the trouble of hunting up and sending them in a box to me, I would take special care of, and return them to you, after I shall have made such extracts as may suit my purpose.

The apprehension you expressed in reference to the course of [Thomas] Ritchie was, as you see, well founded. The Utica Platform takes in, not only [Thomas H.] Benton, but the whole abolition crew. [Zachary] Taylor, I fear, will desert us; and what is more to be apprehended, I much fear the Whigs and Democrats of the South, will after some protestations, submit to act with their respective allies. Should this be the case, the crisis of our fate will be passed, and our destiny sealed. I am engaged, in moments of leisure, on a series of letters addressed to Gen. Taylor, on the subject. The Fifth of the Series will appear next week, in which I shall use the opinions of Messrs. [Charles] Pinckney, [Henry] Baldwin [Representative from Pa.,] and others, on the Missouri Bill in 1820. Was the power of the People of a *Territory* to exclude slavery even so much as mentioned in that Debate? I find nothing that gives colour to such a Doctrine. Baldwin—whose speech I think the ablest, expressly denies the existence of the power, tho' *incidentally*. It is strange the question should have been overlooked—and can be accounted for only on the supposition that the People, or a majority of them were ["known to be" *interlined*] in favour of slavery. Indiana & Illinois had slaves both before and after their admission. How came this to be, if the Ordinance of 1787 was considered binding under the Constitution? Their right to admit slaves seems to have been sanctioned by a vote in Congress of 154 to 36 I think.

I have some letters to write on business to night; and after begging you to excuse this hurried scrawl, and to present my kindest respects to Mrs. Calhoun and Miss Cornelia, subscribe myself very truly and affectionately yours, R.K. Crallé.

P.S. I hope you will have the leisure to notice this at an early day, as I feel anxious about the rumours as to your health.

ALS in ScCleA. NOTE: The pamphlet Crallé mentions was *Presidential Election*, by "Thomson," published in Richmond in 1823.

From R[EUBEN] CHAPMAN, [Governor of Ala.], "Private"

Montgomery Ala., Oct. 19th 1849

Dear Sir; The legislature of this State will meet here in a few weeks (2nd Monday in next mo.) and as my message I believe will be the first since the adjournment of Congress from any executive of a slaveholding State, I am as solicitous as it is certainly important for the interest of the South, that the questions now at issue between the southern and northern portions of the Confederacy shall be presented as strongly as the nature of a message will allow.

I avail myself therefore of my long acquaintance with you, and your own knowledge of my opinions and course on all questions of this sort in Congress to ask your views as briefly as you may think proper upon the following points.

1st. Is not the power of Congress over the territories and public lands within the States identically the same in kind and degree?

2nd. Does the power of erecting territorial Governments result ["from" *interlined*] the terms of the 2nd clause of Sec. 3rd of Article 4th of the Constitution, or is it ["an" *canceled*] incident to the right of acquisition?

3rd. May we not rightfully assume from Gen[era]l [Bennet] Rileys proclamation, that he is acting under instructions from the War Department? and if so, and the ends should be consumated which are in contemplation by that proclamation, would it not be an aggravation of the wrong proposed by the Wilmot proviso?

4th. Under what limitations have the people of a territory a right to erect a State Government?

5th. Are the Mexicans and other foreigners resident in California at the ratification of the treaty citizens of the United States within the meaning of the treaty? and if so, has the treaty making power the right to alter in any particular the general naturalization law of the U.S.?

I have thought of recommending that provision be made for convening the legislature immediately upon the passage of the proviso or any similar measure, or the admission of California as a State through the agency above alluded to. Would it be politic to make any other or different recommendation at present? A State or Southern Convention having neither of them been agitated in this State, I have some fears ["that" *interlined*] the suggestion of either might have a bad effect. The people are however sound on the subject.

I would not trouble you sir, knowing the multiplicity of your engagements but for the vital importance of this subject to our country. As my message must be in readiness some days before the legislature meets, I must ask your reply as early as possibly convenient. With high respect your friend &c, R. Chapman.

ALS in ScCleA; PC in the Tuskegee, Ala., Macon Republican, *November 22, 1849; PC in Jameson, ed.,* Correspondence, *pp. 1207–1208.*

To [DAVID LEVY] YULEE, [Senator from Fla., St. Augustine?]

Fort Hill, 19th Oc[tobe]r 1849

My dear Sir, You will find in the enclosed paper [*not found*] the proceedings of the Mississippi convention, as far as they relate to the report & resolutions.

They embrace the united opinion of both parties. The President of the Convention [William L. Sharkey], who is a very able man, is a whig.

The whole appears to me to be excellent. I see nothing to object to them; and I do sincerely hope, that every Southern State will adopt them, and that both parties will Unite in doing it. It would give unity & concert of action to the South, on the most vital of all questions.

I hope you will concur in these views and use your best efforts to induce both parties to unite & adopt the report & resolutions, & appoint delegates to the Nashville Convention. It may be done, when your legislature meets, by the members acting in their individual character. If the whigs should decline to act, which I hope will not be the case, I trust the democrats will act without them. But it is exceedingly important, that all party divisions should be merged in this vital question.

The course adopted by Mississippi ["holds out," *canceled and* "is" *interlined*], in my opinion, the only one that affords any prospect of saving the Union; or, if that should fail, of certainly saving ourselves. Should the Southern States all adopt it, my hope for the future would be strong; but, if the movement should fail, it would be faint indeed. Concert thereafter, I fear, would be impossible; but without it, nothing can be done. This State will certainly adopt the course of Mississippi with unanimity. Yours truly & sincerely, J.C. Calhoun.

[P.S.] I would be glad to hear from you.

ALS in FU, P.K. Yonge Library, David Levy Yulee Papers.

To ANDREW PICKENS CALHOUN [in Ala.]

Fort Hill, 22d Oct[obe]r 1849

My dear Andrew, ... I have been making good progress in the work I have on hand. I shall finish it, I expect, except revising, correcting and copying before I leave home. John [C. Calhoun, Jr.] who has just returned from the North says it is looked to with great interest there. His health is much improved, and so I understand William's [William Lowndes Calhoun] is, for he went directly to Columbia without returning home, so that I have not seen him.

Mississippi has acted well on the slave question, and I hope Alabama and every other Southern State will back her and send delegates to Nashville. It is all important that they should. Bad would be our condition, if the Convention should fail for want of backing; but bright our prospect should there be a full meeting. . . .

PEx in Jameson, ed., *Correspondence*, pp. 772–773.

From ANNA [MARIA] C[ALHOUN] CLEMSON

Brussels, Oct. 26th 1849

My dear father, I hear from you in all the letters from home, & am delighted to find that your health continues good, but from yourself I have no news. I have only received one letter from you since I left Washington. I know your time is much occupied, but indeed you must spare enough to write me, if only a short letter, from time to time.

We are once more installed at Brussels, & more comfortably than before, (tho' the house in [*sic*] not furnished yet,) because what furniture we have is our own. We made a great mistake in not buying furniture when we first came here. Nothing is so miserable & comfortless as hired furniture, & at the end of a few years you pay nearly the price of the furniture, & have nothing. For instance what we paid for hiring our furniture the four years we spent here, would pay for all we have now in the house. Add to this that we must have furniture wherever we are, & that no where can we get it better & cheaper than here. Our house is smaller than the one we had before, but has a garden, which is very pleasant for the children, & permits them to be more constantly in the open air than formerly. They are always regretting America, & particularly the plantation, where they ran wild. Their journey was of great advantage to them, & developed both mind & body. [John] Calhoun [Clemson] looks very hearty & Floride [Elizabeth Clemson] is almost fat. The[y] grow more rapidly than anything I ever saw, & were they not so well, I should really be uneasy lest they outgrew [*sic*] their strength. They take lessons in Gymnastics & Dancing, which I think very necessary for their health & carriage. Floride has occasionally her attacks of sick stomach, but they grow lighter. The learning goes on slowly, but steadily. We do something every day, & make progress. Tho' they are a little backwards as far as mere books are concerned, I think their mental education, if I may use the term, is more advanced than that of children of their age. They both send many kisses to grandfather & say I must tell him they love him very much.

I hardly know what to say to you of the state of things in Europe. I am, for my part, so disgusted not only with the corruption, (I expected *that*,) but with the childish[ness] & ignorance displayed in the policy of all parties, that I have no patience to read any more politics. The fate of the poor Hungarians, & the conduct of Austria towards that unfortunate people, is a disgrace to the 19th century.

This country is quiet, or rather lethargic, at present. They are so proud of their tranquility, that they are constantly giving festivals in honour of it, but their treasury is in a bad state, & pauperism is far from diminishing. I think myself, that with the example of the rest of Europe before them, they are right to remain quiet, & have reason to be proud of their comparitively happy state.

It is almost time for you to be returning to Washington. You must take care of yourself there, & not work too hard, nor let yourself be too much intruded on by company. Do as I said, & have two days in the week certain hours to receive every one, & the rest of the time receive only your particular friends, or persons on business. Even your friends, especially *Mr.* [Abraham W.] *Venable*, trespass very heavily on you, & you ought to use your privilege of age & position, to get rid of them some times. If I were with you I would soon arrange all that without offending anyone.

Our miserable, wet, dark, & dismal winter is coming on rapidly. I dread it much, after the fine warm winter we passed last ["winter" *canceled and* "year" *interlined*] at the plantation. The children are necessarily confined to the house at [*sic*] great deal by wet weather, which does not suit them at all, & even for me, tho' I go out but little, yet as we keep no carriage, I am often obliged to go shopping about in a manner far from agreeable.

I wish you could see your portrait [by Eugenius Frans DeBlock]. I think you would be pleased with it. You are in the same position as in [Mathew B.] Brady's Daguerretype & look as if you had just finished a speech in the Senate. We have had a magnificent frame made for it, & it is not only a fine portrait but a work of art. How do you like our portraits? I suppose from what mother [Floride Colhoun Calhoun] says they have arrived before this.

Our love to all. I will write mother shortly. I wrote sister [Martha Cornelia Calhoun] last week. Your devoted daughter, Anna C. Clemson.

ALS in ScCleA.

From ROBERT C. ANDREWS

University, Oxford, Mississippi, Oct. 27th 1849
Dear Sir, The members of the Hermean Debating Society of the University of Mississippi, anxious to testify their great admiration of your genius, and their respect for your character have with one voice elected you as an Honorary member. It is a slight but a sincere token of their regard—the disinterested tribute of youth to genius and in permitting us, Sir, to adorn our list of Honorary members with a name consecrated by unshaken public principle and the most un-doubted and various talents you will confer upon us an honor which we will feel very sensibly. With every sentiment of respect, Your humblest admirer, Robert C. Andrews. Cor[responding] Sec[re]-t[ary] Hermean Society.
Hermean Hall, Oct. 27.

ALS in ScCleA. NOTE: An AEU by Calhoun reads, "Honorary membership."

To JA[ME]S ED[WARD] CALHOUN, JR., [Columbia, S.C.]

Fort Hill, 27th Oct[obe]r 1849
My dear James, I intended to write to you to day, and among other things to enquire, when your examination [in South Carolina College] would commence, as I have been appointed a member of the Board of Visitors. But, I received a note from the Sec[re]t[ar]y of the Faculty by the mail of yesterday, which informed me, that it would commence the 12th of next month, which makes the enquiry of you useless.

I regret, that it meets too soon for me to leave to attend, and have accordingly declined accepting the appointment; and notified the Govorner [sic; Whitemarsh B. Seabrook] of the fact, in order that he may fill the place. I wish you to state to the President of the Faculty, that I have declined accepting the appointment, and my reasons. I had hoped it would meet so late, as to enable me to take Columbia on my way to Washington. Ten days or two weeks later would have suited me. My engagements would not permit me to leave in time to be in Columbia by the 12th.

I am glad to learn, that your health & William's is so good, and hope that you will go through your examination well, and that he will make good use of the year. You both will soon be on the stage of life, &, I trust, well prepared to act ["well" *canceled*] your parts. You will both enter on it, at a most eventful period. I fear, it will not be in my power to pass through Columbia on my way to Washington, so that I may not have an opportunity to see either of you before my return home next summer. As it is most probable, that I shall not pass through, I wish you to furnish me with your out standing accounts, before I leave home.

I received a note from Prof[esso]r [Francis] Lieber, informing me, that he had not received my answer to his last note; and in which he says, that he mentions it only to avoid being considered inattentive to my letter should there be any thing in it to require an answer. I wish you to say to him, that I have no distinct recollection of its contents, but am of the impression, it did not require an answer.

We have nothing new in the neighborhood. I have got in all my corn crop. It has yielded well. I find that the boll worm has done my cotton much more injury than I expected; but I will still make a full average.

We are all well & all join love to you & William & kind regards to James Rion. Your affectionate father, J.C. Calhoun.

[P.S.] I enclose a manly & able letter from Jef[ferso]n Davis, Senator from Mississippi. I would be glad to see it noticed in some one of the Columbia papers. Miss[issipp]i & her publick men of both parties have taken the true course, & in the right manner, and ought to receive the approbation & thanks of the whole South. I trust, this & every other Southern State will back her movements. J.C.C.

ALS in ScU-SC, John C. Calhoun Papers. NOTE: Jefferson Davis's letter of 8/18/1849 to Malcolm D. Haynes was made public. In it, he praised the "Address" as a correct statement of the situation and as establishing the necessity for Southern unity.

From H[ENRY] S. FOOTE

Washington, October 28th, 1849

My dear Sir: Your most welcome letter of the 19th instant has just this moment been received, & I hasten to respond to it. The [Washington] Union, as you will have observed, has already published our resolutions & Judge [William L.] Sharkey's opening address; & the Richmond Enquirer has fully and cordially endorsed them. This is all that I have been able to accomplish for the present. I fear that Virginia & the other Southern States will hardly declare their sanction of our Mississippi proceedings, unless some very decided prompting statements[?] should come from S. Carolina. Be not at all uneasy as to our harmonizing hereafter upon every branch of the slavery question. I shall not fail to show, on all occasions, a suitable & just deference for your judgment upon the whole subject, & recognizing you, as the ["wh" *canceled*] people of the South do almost unanimously, as our *Leader* in the grand contest of principle now in progress; I shall evince all becoming respect for you as such. I shall make no ["important" *interlined*] movement without consulting you; & shall express no sentiment willingly that may be calculated to give you offence. I see nothing in your letter to excite the least apprehension that we shall not be of one mind upon the California question; whatever inference you may have deduced from my former letter. If you will do me the honor to read the short introductory note published by me in the Union as prefatory to Judge Sharkey's address, you will not fail to understand my true attitude. With sentiments of profound respect & cordial friendship, I have the honor to be, H.S. Foote.

ALS in ScCleA.

From ELLWOOD FISHER

New York [City,] 10 mo[nth] 29, 1849

Dear Friend, I have received from our friend [Joseph A.] Scoville the lock of hair thee was so kind as to send. As a token of thy recollection and regard it shall be preserved and prized among the most valued testimonials of favour I can receive from man or men. I regret to learn that thy health has not been so good as usual—but I attribute it to the deleterious influences that have pervaded the country this season, affecting the strength of almost every body everywhere, and so very fatal in many places. I have experienced unusual debility myself, but have recovered with the returning health which has come with cooler weather. I trust thee has already experienced its benefit—particularly since the completion of thy book on Government, which I long so much to see, and which Fame will so much delight to receive.

I ought to have made my acknowledgements before for the response to [Thomas H.] Benton. It was anxiously desired by all thy friends with whom I conversed—it was hailed by them with vivid satisfaction, and it has utterly extinguished every symptom of exultation among thy enemies, that was visible after his attacks. It has even abashed his impudence—for his subsequent speeches betray the consciousness of humiliation. For my own part I never doubted thy power to make a triumphant reply—but was apprehensive from our conversations at Washington thee would despise him too much to make it. And this I continued to think as then[?] in the case of [Samuel] Houston would be impolitic—for such men from their very vices have a large circle of abettors and sympathizers—and they also make an impression on the rising generation who are not studious of the past.

I saw a letter not long since from Senator [David R.] Atchison [of Mo.] who speaks confidently—positively—of Bentons defeat in Missouri: an event which after the result in Kentucky would seem to be highly probable. I think it also very probable that [Henry] Clay and his colleague [Joseph R. Underwood] will be instructed by the Kentucky legislature to vote against the Proviso or resign. In this part of the country Abolitionism does not appear to be so strong as it has been. This I think results from the unexpected firmness and unanimity of the South. But it is also owing to the current expectation that California will have population enough to entitle her to admission as a State and that her constitution will exclude slavery. I have suggested to many that even if there are enough people there for a State, they reside on or near the Sacramento and north of 36°30′—and may be admitted with limits proper for a State—leaving all the territory south open to Southern emigration—and that the South will never consent that the few ["the" *canceled*] now in that vast territory shall controul it all, but may agree to their admission with proper limits on the express condition that the South shall have south of that line. Even such an agreement as that however would be rather hazardous for the South, as it would let in a State that might unite with the other northern States to violate such a compact.

The recent union here of the Hunkers and Barnburners does not fully satisfy either party as it is regarded by many of each as a surrender of principle. And in fact it is a mutual surrender of principle to obtain a division of spoils. If the Whig party were not apathetic and discontented it could carry the State—as it is the result is doubtful.

In Virginia where I spent two of the summer months at the springs the tone of sentiment among all parties in reference to the rights of the South, is sounder than it has perhaps ever been. The position assumed by her legislature last winter has been completely sustained by the people—and I understood that of the thirteen dissentients there only three perhaps have been returned. Robert E. Scott the ablest of the Whigs in that body and their leader was defeated in Fauquier County where his influence before had always been overwhelming.

I think therefore thee may rely on more powerful and effective support at the next session of Congress than at any former period.

The lecture I delivered at Cincinnati last winter has I find been republished and diffused over the Southern States to an extraordinary extent. From what I can learn some two hundred thousand copies have been printed. In Kentucky it was ["particularly" *canceled*] received with peculiar favour and with great opposition. The emancipation party there was at first powerful in numbers and remarkably strong in talent and influence, comprehending [Henry] Clay, [George?] Nicholas, the Breckenridges [John and Robert J.?] and a large portion of the Presbyterian clergy. After many attacks that did not satisfy themselves they seem to have finally fixed on President [John Clarke] Young of Danville University, a brother-in-law of the Breckenridges who reviewed it in the Louisville Journal elaborately. I met his first number in Baltimore and replied to that and the succeeding ones from there and from Washington. I am sorry that I have not the numbers but I send [*not found*] as specimens his and my last. Amongst the topics in these is the profit of commerce, as to which the Southern Quarterly in its complimentary notice of the lecture differed from me. That article I am told was written by Governor [James H.] Hammond. May I ask the favour of thee to send him these two papers after reading them—with my respects. I also send [*not found*] a corrected copy of a speech I delivered at Fredericksburg. In the latter I have refered to the extraordinary superiority of the Southern whites in natural increase over the north. That subject I had occasion to examine more particularly in a reply to the [Washington] National Era whose strictures were made soon after the lecture appeared. The reply was in an appendix to another edition of the lecture published in Cincinnati after I left[,] a copy of which I [*partial word canceled*] directed to be sent to thee but it may have been neglected. I think I have there shown conclusively that the natural increase of southern whites over northern in 1830–40 was at least twenty five per cent. And as the wealth of States is held by their adult males, ["it will" *canceled*] and in the lecture it was averaged among the whole white population, it results that the average wealth of the white adult males in the South compared with those of the north ["is much more" *interlined*] than that of the whole white population of the one compared with the other—notwithstanding the burthen of rearing so many more children.

In that appendix and in the controversy with "Justice" every position ["was revie" *canceled*] taken in the lecture was reviewed with care and found ["I think" *interlined*] to be either exactly correct, or far within the limits to which it might have been carried.

I expect to be in Washington in a few days and hope to hear from thee soon. Present my regards most cordially to thy wife [Floride Colhoun Calhoun] and family. Thy friend, Ellwood Fisher.

ALS in ScCleA; PEx in Boucher and Brooks, eds., *Correspondence*, p. 532. NOTE: Fisher's lecture at Fredericksburg, Va., is briefly reported in the Richmond, Va., *Enquirer*, October 5, 1849, p. 4. His Cincinnati lecture was published as *Lecture on the North and the South . . .* (Charleston: A.J. Burke, 1849).

To [HERSCHEL V.] JOHNSON, [Milledgeville, Ga.]

Fort Hill, 1st Nov[embe]r 1849

My dear Sir, The enclosed [*not found*] is a speech of Mr. [Richard K.] Meade [Representative from Va.] to his constituents on the slavery question.

It is able & bold, and I send it as evidence of the increasing sperit of the old dominion on that vital question. Coming from the quarter it does it may contribute something to merge party feelings with you & rouse the sperit of your Legislature.

I do trust, your State will back the Mississippi movement. If she should and the other Southern States should follow, I feel assured it would ["do" *interlined*] more than any thing else to bring the question to a speedy issue. It cannot be made too soon for us.

But, I have written you so fully on the subject, that to add more would be little else than to repeat what I have already written.

With best regards to Mrs. [Ann Polk Walker] J[ohnson], Yours truly, J.C. Calhoun.

ALS in DLC, John C. Calhoun Papers; transcript in DLC, Carnegie Institution of Washington Transcript Collection; PC in Jameson, ed., *Correspondence*, p. 773.

To A[RMISTEAD] BURT, [Representative from S.C., Abbeville, S.C.]

Fort Hill, 5th Nov[embe]r 1849

My dear Sir, I am very desireous, on every account, to be in the same mess with Martha [Calhoun Burt] & yourself. I would prefer the Hill on three accounts; in consequence of a regard to my health; its contiguity to the Capitol; the bleakness of the walk up Capitol Hill in windy weather, & the liability of getting heated in walking up it with the heavy clothing necessary to guard against a Washington winter, & cooling off two [*sic*] suddenly, on throwing off the over coat, or cloak on reaching the Senate Chamber. In all other respects I would greatly prefer the location you suggest. I think, taking it altogether, it is the most protected & best in Washington.

If a satisfactory arrangement could be made on the Hill, & it should not put Martha to too much inconvenience, I would prefer it, but if not, I will join you in the location you suggest, or any other contiguous, rather than seperate from you & Martha.

My arrangement is to be in Charleston on the 25 or 26th & to take the Baltimore boat, which I understand will sail on the 28th, and hope to meet you there & go together. When we arrive at Washington, we can finally decide on our arrangement.

I concur in your suggestion, as to the caucus, with a modification; not to go into it with the free soilers; meaning all, who will vote for the Wilmot proviso; that is, the whole, or nearly the whole of the Northern democrats. To take the ground you suggest, not to go in with those who refused to sign the address, would, I fear tend too strongly to divide the South, and throw from us the Kentucky, Missouri & Tennessee delegations with two or three exceptions.

All join their love to you & Martha. Yours truly, J.C. Calhoun.

ALS in NcD, John C. Calhoun Papers; PC in Jameson, ed., *Correspondence*, pp. 773–774.

From H[ENRY] W. CONNER

Savannah, Nov. 8, 1849

My Dear Sir, I am here on my way to Montgommery Ala. & have just been in conversation with Mess. [John H.] Howard & Gen[era]l [David J.] Bailey of Columbus (two old Nullifiers) & Mr. [Matthew H.] McAllister of this city—the three forming the most influential leaders of the democratic & Southern party of [Georg]ia. They say Geo. is sound & [*mutilation*] spot upon the great questions [*mutilation*] South—that is their party [*mutilation*] harmonize & cooperate [*mutilation*] in common with all the [*mutilation*; S]tates, but the impression [*mutilation*] currency here, & it was [*mutilation*] Charleston that Governor [Whitemarsh B. Seabrook woul]d recommend some seperate [*mutilation*] on the part of So. Ca. [*mutilation*]ing of the Legislature [*mutilation*] character of the movement [*mutilation*] to it as a Carolina & not a Southern movement. They say if he does so it will be fatal to the democratic party of this State & also they think of Alabama & are exceedingly desirous that Governor Seabrook should be induced to modify his views in conformity with what Governor [George W.] Towns has said (which of course is the sentiment of the party) & what the Gov[erno]r of Alabama [Reuben Chapman] will say in his message next week.

I now write to you because [*mutilation*] myself that Gov[erno]r Seabrook is [determined?] upon precipitate & indepen[dent; *mutilation*; action?] on the part of the State & [*mutilation*] know if any body can c[hange his?] views that you can but [*mutilation*] because I believe that [*mutilation*]dation of an ultra [*mutilation*] would do much to [*mutilation*] & concert amongst the Slave [holding?] States that is so rapidly [*mutilation*] & that is so essential to [*mutilation*] interest of the South in either aspect of the case. The gentlemen I have named to you are ready to go the farthest with the farthest & desire the issue to be made at once & finally but they wish it as the act of the South & not of one State, because failure & defeat is the necessary consequence of the one & success & the most happy results the consequence of the other.

[Being?] accustomed to look to you in [all ma]tters of this kind, I take [the liberty?] of invoking your influence [with Governor] Seabrook to prevent a [*mutilation*] move. Authority to [*mutilation*]ntion in case of the Wilmot [*mutilation*] her kindred measure they [*mutilation*] that is now necessary unless [*mutilation*] for delegates to the [convention?] called by Mississippi.

[*Mutilation*] really want to act with us [*mutilation*; *one word illegible*] us to disregard[,] would it not be essential that you visit Columbia so as to be there before the message of the Governor is delivered to the Legislature. I will write you from Montgommery. Very [*illegible*] H.W. Conner.

ALS in ScCleA. Note: Portions of the ms. are missing and words have in some places been supplied conjecturally in brackets.

From W[illia]m B. Johnston

South Carolinian Office
Columbia, Nov[embe]r 8, 1849

Dear Sir, I take the liberty of addressing you for several reasons. Your rumored retirement, you will have noticed probably, we have contradicted in the Carolinian, and we trust we may have been correct in so doing, indeed we cannot think otherwise.

From various indications, I feel assured the proposition emanating from the Mississippi Convention to hold a Southern Convention will eventually be adopted, and though late may yet be effective in doing good. When conducting a neighbouring journal I earnestly and repeatedly urged the necessity of such a measure through its columns; and had the pleasure of knowing that you were convinced that it was *the* action for the South to adopt. Would that the proposition had then received the attention it claimed and deserved! It may not be "too late" now, and there is no doubt but party affiliations have become much weaker since and that there is ["now" *canceled*] a better chance for a complete union of men of all parties at the present time.

Intimately associated with this movement, will be the connection of your name with the Presidency, as an independent or constitutional nominee, irrespective of the nominations of the usual *party* conventions. Now ought not the Democratic presses at the South, take early and decided ground against these conventions—not only the democratic press of the South, but Whig also. But more particularly the democratic press, as the late "Coalitions" at the North are sad evidences of the fact that we have, or can have but few friends there. This can be done without the abandonment of any set of political principles and the mere party associations, are not worth a thought, at such a time as this. It could not involve ["the" *canceled*] any greater sacrafice—none half so great, as the yielding of constitutional rights.

Occupying the position we do, conducting a leading journal, with an extensive and rapidly increasing circulation throughout the State and adjacent States, it is of great importance to us to have benefit of such suggestions as you could give us, and thus be enabled to to [*sic*] aid as far as possible in bringing about a union of the South.

I would consider it a great favor if you had leisure to write me briefly upon these subjects, and any suggestions which you might deem of service to me in my present position would be gratefully received and acted on—premising that any communication you may seem proper to make, being considered strictly confidential. With great respect Yours truly, Wm. B. Johnston.

P.S. I see by the Charleston Courier this evening that they say they have understood you approved of the proposition to hold a Southern Convention. I will probably briefly state in the Carolinian—without saying so authoritatively—that any measure tending to promote union of action will be certain of receiving your sanction.

ALS in ScCleA; PC in Jameson, ed., *Correspondence*, pp. 1208–1210.

From JAMES J. DONEGAN and Others

Huntsville, Alabama, Nov[embe]r 9th 1849

Sir, By a reference to the proceedings of an adjourned meeting of the late Holly Springs Rail Road Convention held at the City of Memphis, you will see that on the 27th Ult[im]o a resolution was adopted, to adjourn to meet at this place on the 26th Inst., with a view to perfect an organization upon the subject of a connection between the South Atlantic and the Mississippi Valley.

Our citizens feeling a deep interest in the contemplated improvement, have most readily adopted the suggestion, and instructed the undersigned to tender you the hospitalities of our town, and invite you to be present on the occasion.

The readiness with which you have embraced opportunities to lend to such enterprizes the influence of your great name, encourages the belief, that if your public engagements should render it impracticable for you to visit us, that we may at least be able to derive in some substantial form, your countenance and encouragement.

Uniting with a high degree of pleasure, our personal Solicitations, to the invitation hereby tendered We remain, with high consideration Y[ou]r mo[st] Ob[edien]t Serv[an]ts, James J. Donegan, George P. Beirne, A[rchibald] E. Mills, Samuel Cruse, J. W[ithers] Clay, Robert Fearn.

LS in ScCleA.

To J**A**[ME]**S** E**D**[WARD] C**ALHOUN**, J**UN**[IO]**R**, Columbia, S.C.

Fort Hill, 11 Nov[embe]r 1849

My dear James, I received yours of the 27th of last month a few days after after [*sic*] I had answered yours of a preceding date. I hope you have got mine [of 10/27].

Nothing of interest has occured since its date. The weather has been fine a greater portion of the time, and I have been busy in writing & attending to the place & my private concerns. My crop is yielding well. I shall make about 13,000 pounds more of seed cotton this year, than the last, off the same ground, although the crop of last year was a fair average.

It will not be in my power to take Columbia in my route to Washington. I expect to leave about the 22d & shall have to be very busy in arranging every thing before I leave.

I had a letter from your brother ["Andrew" *interlined*; Pickens Calhoun] not long since. He writes that his crop [in Ala.] will turn out about what he expected—that is hardly a third of an average crop. It is very unfortunate just at this time, when prices are so good to have so short a crop.

I will send you by Thomas Pickens $150 or 200. You must let me know how much more you will need to square your accounts & return home, & I will remit it from Washington. Take care to take receipts for all you pay.

I hope you will have passed a good examination.

To close your collegiate ["course" *interlined*] is quite a stage in your progress through life. The next step will take you into the most important of all, & for which all the preceeding is but preperation; the business of life, in which, I trust you will act well your part. I hope you will commence the study of law, in good earnest, after you return home. Begin with Blackstone & give him a thorough reading.

We are all well & all join their love to you & William [Lowndes Calhoun] & kind regards to James Rion. Your affectionate father, J.C. Calhoun.

ALS in ScU-SC, John C. Calhoun Papers.

From F[itz]w[illiam] Byrdsall

New York [City,] Nov. 12th 1849

Dear Sir, The Election has taken place in the great State of New York and the result may be thus summed up—the coalition of Hunkers & Barn burners have carried one half of the ticket for State Officers and a sufficient majority in the house of Assembly to give them a majority on joint Ballot. On the other side, the coalition of Whigs and negro voters have carried the other half of the State ticket and a majority of the Senate. Besides, the latter have carried the whole of our city Government which is no small affaire with its patronage and expenditure of some three millions of dollars annually. There are, it is stated, about from 1200 to 1500 negro voters in this county who were recently induced by politicians to hold meetings at Putnam Hall where they resolved to support the Whig party, and to these same negro votes are the Whigs indebted for all or nearly so that they have gained in this election. This is a beautiful state of things proving how capable the whites are of self government when they leave it to negroes to decide who shall rule. Thus each of the political parties in this State are self abased and self degraded.

The paragraphs attached express the opinions of the Barnburner's faction on the result. The Evening Post is at present edited by a Mr. [John] Bigelow who while holding the opinions of W[illiam] C. Bryant, has none of his regard for truth or decency.

[Attached newspaper clipping:]

Anti-Slavery among the Democracy. The *Evening Post* says that the recent election proves that the mass of the two factions of the democracy are now agreed in their opposition to the extension of slavery, and will try to prevent its introduction into New Mexico and California. John Van Buren says ditto. This position breaks up the old party, North and South. The whigs may have the field to themselves.

[Second attached newspaper clipping:]

John Van Buren in Boston.
His opinion of the New York election.

The free-soilers of Boston held a meeting at Faneuil Hall, on Thursday night, at which John Van Buren was present. As soon as he made his appearance he was loudly called for, but there being others on the programme before him, he declined saying anything until his turn arrived, when he was introduced to the meeting, and on stepping upon the platform, was received with immense cheering. He then went on in a strain of remarks which lasted for over an hour, occasionally interrupted by thunders of applause. We intended to give a *verbatim* report of Mr. Van Buren's remarks, but were unable to get it in type for our paper of to-day. It was full of strong points, rich humor, and eloquent appeal, and was received throughout with storms of applause. It was a full commitment of himself and his friends to the Wilmot proviso, and to opposition to slavery at every point, and on every occasion.

In the course of his remarks, he reviewed the policy of the barn-burners in New York in 1848, who, he contended, were more anxious to defeat [Lewis] Cass than [Zachary] Taylor, because Cass was pledged to veto the Wilmot proviso. Besides, he had once been for the proviso; but when the South required him to repudiate his principles before it would consent to put him in nomination for the Presidency, he basely did so. And another thing—Cass belonged to the democratic party—a party which, when it got into power, generally stayed there; while Gen. Taylor was the nominee of a party which came into power only to die. He subsequently alluded to the accusation made against him, of having said the national democratic party was dead. And was it not dead? What is a national party? Is a party which advocates one thing, in South Carolina, and another thing in Vermont, a national party? Unquestionably, the democratic party in Vermont is thoroughly anti-slavery in its sentiments, while the democracy of South Carolina is pro-slavery to the bone; and if a democrat from Vermont should go to South Carolina, and there undertake to advocate what he believes to be democracy, he would be shut up in the Penitentiary. After adverting to and denying the charge of an abandonment of principle brought against the barnburners of New York, he solemnly assured the audience and the country that he and his party still believed slavery to be an unmixed evil, and that he and they would never vote for any man who was not sound on the Wilmot proviso, and pledged to oppose the perpetuation and extension of slavery, wherever the question could be met. Mr. Van Buren was exceedingly humorous and effective in his allusions to the "incomprehensible" Horace Greeley, of New York, and he drew a vivid picture of the versatility of that gentleman's political principles. William H. Seward, too, came in for a scorching rebuke, for his conduct last winter at Washington, with regard to the Wilmot proviso. After some other remarks, Mr. Van Buren alluded to a matter somewhat personal to himself. At the first Barnburners' Convention in New York, a resolution was passed, complimenting, in eulogistic terms, General Zachary Taylor. The paternity of that resolution had been put upon him. He had nothing to do with it. He was not a member of the committee which reported it, and he did not vote for it in convention. The resolution passed in that meeting, it is true, for there were some democrats there who had been made to believe that Gen. Taylor was in favor of the Wilmot proviso; and, in consideration of that fact, they were willing to forego all minor considerations, to sink all former differences, and to go for him on that ground alone. How they were deceived, and how the country was deceived on that point, it was not necessary for him to state.

After alluding to the abolishing of the test question in the Union Convention in New York, and giving a very satisfactory view of that matter, and avowing his determination never to go into a National Convention with slaveholders, Mr. Van Buren closed his remarks.

I am pleased at the defeat of the coalition of Barnburners and hunkers in this county and did my utmost in that direction for I would rather see the Democratic banner trailing in the dirt than conjoined with Van Burenism, free soilism abolitionism &c. A portion of the Republican Committee at Tammany hall with Emanuel B. Hart at their head resisted the barn burners long enough to make their caving in at the eleventh hour the more unprincipled, in consequence of which, the following address was published in most of the city papers on the morning before the election.

[Attached newspaper clipping:]
The Democratic Republican Electors of the City of New York. Fellow Democrats! The brief period which has intervened since the last Democratic Convention met at Syracuse, is marked by events that demand your serious consideration, in view of the Election to-morrow. Already it is apparent that the union from which so much advancement was promised to the Democratic cause, is, in truth, to be employed only as a means of engrafting upon our time-honored principles, a set of Abolition doctrines hostile to the peace and welfare of the Republic, and repugnant to the sympathies and intelligence of the Democratic party. The union upon a State Ticket, agreed to by the Syracuse and Utica Conventions, was based upon a solemn pledge of the good faith of each, that at this Election, and hereafter, no test should be imposed upon any candidate in reference to his opinions upon the powers of the action of Congress on the subject of negro slavery. How has that Union been carried out? How has that pledge of good faith been maintained? By the Democratic party proper, the constituents of the Syracuse Convention, the Union was upheld, and cordially and generously promoted, by the most liberal concessions to the Van Buren faction. In this county we conceded to them a large and undeserved share of the nominations. Throughout the State a similar magnanimity was practised, and especially in the selection of candidates for the Senate, of whom three-fourths consist of members of the late Free Soil party. How has this honorable course on our part been reciprocated? We find that now, in advance of the election, the only Democratic representative of the State of New York in Congress is marked for proscription. War, war to the knife, is declared against Senator [Daniel S.] Dickinson, for the avowed reason that his opinions on the Negro question do not suit the Free Soil Abolition party.

This crusade, begun during the last month by obscure country newspapers, is now daily reinforced by assaults from the leading Van Buren organs in the principal cities of the State. Will the spirit which invokes such hostility be appeased by the sacrifice of Mr. Dickinson? Will one victim satisfy so many executioners? as well might it have been predicted that the Reign of Terror would end so soon as one head had fallen in the streets of Paris. No! it is clear that the same policy which prompts the advocacy now, of only such candidates for the Senate as will proscribe an able and faithful Senator because he is not an Abolitionist, will also pursue every candidate now and hereafter, who professes the opinions of the National Democracy, and refuses to join the fanatical crew enlisted under the black flag carried by Martin Van Buren. If proof is demanded of this, we point to the letter addressed by the Lockport Committee to all the candidates on the State Ticket on the subject of Slavery. The answers of five of these candidates have been published, all of whom agree to swallow the test thus imposed, in violation of all honor and decency, after all controversies had been buried in the Utica and Syracuse Conventions. Messrs. [Henry S.] Randall, [Darius] Clark, [Benjamin] Welch, [Alexander] Campbell and [Levi S.] Chatfield, by recognizing the course persued towards them, by allowing themselves to be chatechised on a subject which has no more legitimate relation to the present election, than the wrongs and sufferings of the white men in the republic of Liberia, who are deprived the right of suffrage, have stigmatized with attempted censure and impugned by a presumptuous effort at rebuke, the conventions from which their nominations were received and a vast majority of the electors to whom they appealed for support. Why have not the answers of the other candidates been also published? Is it because Mr. [John A.] Lott, the candidate for Comptroller, and Mr. [Frederick] Follett, the candidate for canal commissioner, returned such replies as would, by their publication, defeat the malicious intent of the inquisitors? The omission is strange and significant; but its meaning cannot be misunderstood, for the imposition of this test is expressly devised to realize the threatening prediction ventured by John Van Buren, in the Utica Convention, where he declared that "if the candidates did not rightly respond to queries on the slavery subject, they would be defeated by one hundred thousand majority." This threat was deemed, at the time, nothing more than the expiring malediction of a baffled conspirator; no man supposed, that with all his conceded authority over the passions and purposes of his party, it was ever intended by that party to make the denunciation pronounced by their leader, the great end and object of their exertions in the election. This confidence on the part of the democratic masses was created by the subsequent passage in the Utica Convention of a resolution accepting the offer of union made by the Syracuse Convention, on the sole condition—avowed and accepted as clearly and unequivocally as the English language could express it—that no pro-slavery or anti-slavery test should be propounded or enforced against the candidates nominated. What was then a generous and honorable belief in the good faith of the free soil party would be now, if any of us could by possibility entertain it, a false, foolish, and fatal credulity. No democrat can now be so blind as not to see that it is the settled purpose of the Free Soil party to vote to-morrow only for such candidates as have "rightly responded to queries on the slavery subject?" Else, why impose the test? If such be not the design, why did the interrogatories of the Lockport Convention so quickly follow Mr. Van Buren's avowal of the conse-quences of an unsatisfactory answer? Information as to their opin-ions is sought from candidates for no other purpose than to influ-ence the determination of those who are asked to vote for them, and the inference cannot be resisted, that the Free Soil party, as a body, intend to defeat every candidate who, by disdaining the test, places himself upon the platform of the Syracuse and Utica Union.

What, then, shall we do? Fortunately, fellow democrats, the path of duty at this crisis is free from doubt and unobstructed from difficulties. The Syracuse Convention was not invested with any authority to allow one half of our State Ticket to be nominated either by the Free Soil or Whig party. That Convention was not authorized to form either a union or a coalition with any hostile organization. It had no power to commit the constituency it repre-sented to any change or surrender of principle, or to pledge their support for candidates it did not nominate. The union, therefore, which it assumed the responsibility of proposing and which was accepted by the Free Soilers, rested solely for a basis upon the vol-untary adhesion of the Democratic party to its terms; it was a union which could only exist so long as both parties remained faithful to the terms and spirit of the compact; never reposing upon the action of an authorised body, a violation of all the usages of the demo-cratic party, and only tolerated by a spirit of self-sacrifice too often indulged by those we now address, this so-called union having been treacherously violated in its entire scope and meaning of the Free Soil party, no longer deserves even a passive recognition from you. Nay, even more—it is the duty of every Democrat now to denounce it, to repudiate it, to defeat the pernicious objects it is intended to subserve from the action of the adherents to the Utica Convention. The question then again recurs, What shall the Democracy do? Will you vote for candidates whom you did not nominate, for candidates who have insulted the Syracuse Convention by accepting a test which that convention denounced? Can it be expected that you will stand by with your arms folded, and witness the proscrip-tion and degradation of your candidates on the State ticket? see them defeated on an anti-slavery test, and do no act on your part to protect yourselves and save the honor of your party? We think not. The Democracy of this city and State are yet too mindful of their duty to the National Democratic party, to permit a sectional and fanatical brand to be placed on their forehead. The union of the States, with its unnumbered blessings, is more dear to us than a coalition with traitors. Let us, therefore, at the polls, to-morrow, vote only for such candidates on the State ticket as have remained faithful to the cause they represent, and the compact from which their positions emanated. If you and your friends are to be proscribed, then must you proscribe also. Let this be done, and hereafter men will learn that a chivalrous fidelity to the terms and spirit of a treaty can never be disregarded with impunity, by those who seek the advantages of an alliance.

Daniel E. Sickles,	Thomas P. Kettell,
James Lee,	Alexander F. Vache,
James T. Brady,	Geo. J. Gallagher,
Augustus Schell,	Mike Walsh,
Joseph T. Sweet,	John M. Bloodgood,
Alex'r Stewart,	Alex'r M. Alling,

Democratic Republican Executive Committee.

This publication did not aid the incongruous coalition and it accounts in some degree for the almost total defeat of the Democratic party in this county notwithstanding a counter despatch from E.B. Hart & John Van Buren forwarded to Albany on the afternoon of the same day the above appeared in print.

[*Attached newspaper clipping:*]
The Telegraph Monopoly.

The following communication from Mr. Van Buren, which we find in the Albany Atlas, is another instance of the unprincipled management of the Telegraph system in some parts of this State. We give the letter, with the comments of the *Atlas,* and shall avail ourselves of an early opportunity of passing the whole management in review. One of the first duties of the Legislature, upon its assembling, will be to appoint a committee to investigate the whole subject, that the people may know to what a corrupt system of favoritism they are victims:

Editors of the Atlas: Gentlemen—The telegraphic despatch from this city, published by you on Monday, signed "E.B. Hart, Chairman, &c.," was drawn up and forwarded at my instance, and was signed by me as well as by Mr. Hart. The same communication was directed to a prominent democrat at nearly every telegraphic station in the State. Its obvious design was to prevent either of the former sections of the democratic party from retaliating upon the other by scratching a portion of the ticket, and especially to prevent such action on the part of the Barnburners, who might be justly irritated by the card of Messrs. Sickles & Co. The Argus and Atlas both publish it, omitting my name. I have inquired at the office here and am informed that the despatch was forwarded to Albany as written, and strongly suspect that my name was dishonestly suppressed by the operator at Albany, for the purpose of aiding the Taylor and Calhoun men.

Respectfully yours, John Van Buren.
New York [City], November 7, 1849.

P.S. The Argus is requested to copy the above. J.V.B.

"The despatch alluded to," says the Atlas, "was read off by one of the assistants in the office here, when received, and transcribed by one of our clerks. The responsibility for the suppression of Mr. Van Buren's name can hardly attach to Mr. Johnson, who has charge of the office. We think it rests elsewhere than at Albany. We trust that the matter will be investigated, and that responsibility for the violation of a confidential trust may be traced to the parties to whom it belongs.

In regard to the partizan bias manifested by telegraphic correspondents, not only before and after this contest, but in most preceding ones, we can only say that their whig patrons have had, in the end, to pay most dearly, in mortification and money, for the self-sufficiency and ignorance of their dependents."

This Election the first most important one under the new constitution involved more offices of emolument and patronage than any election that ever occurred in this State. It is pretty evident that these considerations super induced the coalition of the factions, and their defeat under those motives and circumstances and by such means as negro votes, is in my view divinely providential if not retributive. And there, as to the two great parties as they will stand in the State legislature, we shall see a droll denouement. The Democratic house can do nothing without the concurrence of the Whig Senate and vice versa. This will be all the better for Senator Dickinson. If the House & Senate unite to instruct him upon Wilmot provisoism, in all probability this proceedure will divide the Democratic party again. If the two houses act upon the basis of party antagonism one of them will oppose necessarily the action of Congress on Wilmot provisoism. The two parties will be in a pretty fix and may heaven in its goodness to the better portion of the Union, encrease their perplexity!

It seems that [James Watson] Webb of the Courier is inclined already to go in favor of Wm. H. Seward for the next presidential term. I cut the following squib from the Herald of yesterday.

[Attached newspaper clipping:]
Too Late.—Col. Webb, in yesterday's *Courier*, makes a deliberate move on the political chessboard, in favor of W.H. Seward for the Presidency. All very well; but he happens to be too late. Downing and the "colored gunmen" have a prior claim upon the little ex-Governor. Their ticket is:

Wm. H. Seward, (free white man) of New York,
For President.
Frederick Douglass, (free black man) of Ohio,
For Vice President.

Unless, therefore, our Wall street neighbor is disposed to join in the movement of the aristocracy of color, he must abandon his man. Seward and Douglass is the ticket—the whole or none.

I am gratified to learn the restoration of your health and that you will be in the Senate the ensuing session. I cannot say to you how much and how earnestly I wish you to be guardian of your own health this winter at Washington in the use of the tepid or warm bath, the flesh brush and such material whether it be silk or woolen under-shirts as will best keep up uniformly the functions of the skin. I take it for granted that you have read Dr. Andrew Combes work "the physiology of health as regards the functions of the skin," or I would if I thought otherwise venture some suggestions to you. But there is one point upon which there are are [*sic*] words in my breast press-ing for utterance and you must excuse them. I urge you to avoid long sessions as much as you can in the day time and especially in the night. I mean do not sit them out from beginning to end.

Reserve yourself for important questions only, and do not impose so much mental labor on yourself as you have done. I mean to say very gently that it is into the latter danger you are most apt to fall, thereby taxing at your time of life, your physique too much. I offer these hints in advance of an important session wherein you will prob-ably need physical energy because the day of reasoning is gone by and the time for action is at hand. Not a single inch—not a whit of compromise should be conceded to the non extension of negro slavery party. The slave States will never be more able for the contest of their rights than now. Within the last few months I have learned from the proceedings of legislatures, conventions, meetings &c in those States, enough to convince me that whatever determined course their Representatives in Congress may adopt in opposition to the proviso partizans, they will be sustained by the people they repre-sent, and God knows—however much I would deplore the necessity of such a step, yet if the members of the Southern States should one and all—withdraw from Congress on the passage of any bill of the Wilmot proviso description, my heart and soul would go with them out and out. I hold that before God & man they would be justified therein because the people of the north—in their publications—in their religious gatherings—in their political meetings have—instead of standing by the South as a part of their common country and common race, held the Southern people up to the odium of the world—ca-lumniated them—got up a persecution against them unrelenting and unjust—unpatriotic and unconstitutional so that no public man, and scarcely any one in private life, dare avow himself in this part of the

Union, wholly with the Southern States on the questions of negro slavery, Wilmot provisoism &c. And finally to cap the climax of wicked injustice the power and right is openly claimed of subjecting the Southern people to spoilation of their rights—their honor and their character as a christian or civilized people.

I think however that with union and firmness on the part of the Representatives from the slave States the tables will be completely turned and that he whom I wish will be our next president as a consequence. Yours with heartfelt respect, F.W. Byrdsall.

ALS in ScCleA.

From H[ERSCHEL] V. JOHNSON

Milledgeville Ga., Nov. 13th[?] [18]49

My Dear Sir, I have rec[eive]d your favours, the one, enclosing the Miss. Resolutions and the other the speech of Mr. [Richard K.] Meade of Va., for which, please accept my thanks. The Miss. Resolutions I fully approve; Mr. Meade's speech I have not yet found time to read except by peace meal.

Our Legislature has been in session nearly two weeks, but nothing has been done except to select Judges & other officers. I have been busy in endeavouring to arrive at what is public sentiment among the members in relation to the vital question of slavery. The Gov. [George W. Towns] in his Message, took strong ground on this subject & recommended that he be authorised by the Legislature, & call a State convention, to determine the course to be adopted in the event of the passage of the Proviso, on abolition in the States. I am persuaded that there is very[?] prudent disposition among the members to carry into effect his recommendations.

The plan you suggested of getting the of getting the [sic] members in their individual character to take action, does not meet with favour, for the reason that there is so much party jealousy, on the part of the Whigs, that they will not co-operate with the Democrats, until stern necessity forces them into it, as the last and only means of saving themselves from annihilation. Hence, I am doing all I can to obtain from the Committee on the State of the Republic, such action as will place the State on the true platform.

Seeing there is little or no hope of having delegates appointed to a Southern Convention, either by the Legislature or the members in their individidual [sic] character, I am pressing the necessity of a

State Convention. The plan I am urging is simply this. To authorise the Governor to call a State Convention, at the earliest possible day, who shall consider the question in all its bearings and decide upon the proper course to be pursued. This Convention to be composed of an equal number of Whigs and Democrats. If we can get such a State Convention I have but little fear that Georgia will promptly take her stand by the side of Miss.

I deem it injudicious, to attempt a direct endorsement of the Miss. Resolutions. They look to a southern Convention, which is an awful scare crow to some of our timid politicians. It however may possibly be done, towards the close of the session, under the indignation which the anticipated movements of Cong. will excite.

The non-signers of the "S[outhern] Address" are alarmed & sick of their position. I am confident they will generally Co-operate in energetic action. [Howell] Cobb however goes to Washington panting for the Speakership. His election will do the South no good & I trust a better man can be chosen. I shall be pleased to hear from you at all times. Yours truely &c, H.V. Johnson.

FC in NcD, Herschel V. Johnson Papers, Letterpress Book, pp. 63–65; PEx in Percy Scott Flippin, ed., "Herschel V. Johnson Correspondence," *North Carolina Historical Review*, vol. IV, no. 2 (April, 1927), pp. 197–198.

From EDWARD HARLESTON

Charleston, 15th Nov. 1849

My Dear Sir, A faction in the Custom House is endeavouring to traduce and undermine the character of our recently appointed Surveyor Mr. W[illiam] Y. Leitch, who I unhesitatingly aver is as good an officer as the Govt. could have appointed, and whose deportment has been uniformly that of the Gentleman. The effort is to prevent his confirmation by the Senate, to subserve the views of men any thing but good, and I beg not to be thought presumptious in proffering my humble testimony to Mr. Leitchs worth and the unworthy motives of his opponents. I am Dear Sir with the highest Esteem & respect yours, Edward Harleston.

ALS in ScU-SC, John C. Calhoun Papers. NOTE: Calhoun's AEU reads: "Mr. Harleston. Relates to the app[ointmen]t of Leitch Surveyor of the Port of Charleston."

To [WILLIAM B. JOHNSTON, Editor of the Columbia *South-Carolinian*]

Fort Hill, Nov. 16, 1849

You are right in supposing that I approve the call of a convention of the Southern States by Mississippi. I regard it as the first great step towards meeting the aggressions of the North, and sincerely hope our State, and every other Southern State, will respond to the call by appointing delegates. Without union and concert of action there can be no effective resistance, and without a convention there can be no union and concert. Such is and has been my opinion in every stage of the abolition agitation.

I concur with you that the Southern press ought to take ground against a convention to nominate candidates for the Presidency and Vice Presidency. To persist in them would be fatal to the South. They, indeed, have been among the means by which the country has been placed in its present dangerous condition; but I do not think the subject of nominating a candidate should be connected with the proceedings of the convention. It would, I fear, lead to distraction and division, and give the meeting the appearance of a political caucus. *The great objects of the convention, in my opinion, should be to make a solemn statement of our wrongs, and an* APPEAL TO THE NORTH *to desist, and to unite on some course of action to repel her aggressions, if she should not.*

Nor do I think that my name should be associated with the Presidency. I feel grateful for the favorable notice in that connection which appeared in your paper and the Charleston Courier. But I do not wish to have the office, and *would not accept it if tendered,* except some imperious consideration of duty should require it. I have no ambition or pride to gratify. MY HIGHEST AMBITION IS TO AID IN CARRYING THE COUNTRY THROUGH ITS PRESENT DIFFICULTIES AND DANGERS. The disease, in my opinion, is now too deeply seated to be remedied through the Presidency, and I fear it is too late even for the power and influence of that high office to control it. I hope you and other friends will take the same view, and omit associating my name with it. If, in the progress of events, THE COUNTRY should think that I could best serve it in that high office, I could not decline it, but it would have to be spontaneous to induce me to accept. Or if the South should think hereafter the use of my name necessary to unite her, I could not object to its use; but I have no anticipation that either will be the case, and as far as I am individually concerned, I have no solicitude that it should be. *I am content to do my duty, without looking farther.* With great respect, I am yours, &c., J.C. CALHOUN.

PC in the Columbia, S.C., *Tri-Weekly South Carolinian,* May 25, 1850, p. 2; PC in the Edgefield, S.C., *Advertiser,* May 29, 1850, p. 3; PC in the Spartanburg, S.C., *Spartan,* June 13, 1850, p. 1.

From JOSIAH S. BROWN

Charleston, 17th Nov. 1849

My dear Sir—On the 1st July last Mr. J[ohn] E[wing] Bonneau kindly associated myself with him in the Factorage & Commission Business under the firm of J.E. Bonneau & Co. You were not informed of it at the time, as Mr. Bonneau was quite unwell & I hoped ere this that his health would have sufficiently improved to enable him to announce it to you himself. I suppose however you must have noticed it through the public prints. His health continuing feeble to the middle of August, he was induced by his physician to travel through the upper parts of our own State & through Georgia for its benefit. He returned about one month since much worse than when he left us and continued declining until Monday last, at which time, it becomes my painful ["duty" *interlined*] to announce to you the unfortunate & melancholy event of his death. He had been a *dreadful* sufferer for some weeks previous. The Business will be continued as heretofore under the firm of J.E. Bonneau & Co. probably until the 1st July next, to enable the parties concerned to close the Business of the present season. At that time I shall commence the Factorage & Commission Business in my own name & on my individual Account. Returning my acknowledgments for the past favours bestowed upon the late Mr. J.E. Bonneau & hoping it may meet your views to continue the same to myself, I Remain D[ea]r Sir with great Respect Yours truly, Josiah S. Brown, surviving copartner in the firm J.E. Bonneau & Co.

ALS in ScU-SC, John C. Calhoun Papers.

To JAMES J. DONEGAN and Others

Fort Hill, Nov. 18th, 1849

Gentlemen: If circumstances had admitted, it would have afforded me a great deal of pleasure to attend your meeting on the 26th inst.;

but the near approach of the session of Congress puts it out of my power.

You are right in thinking, I take a deep interest in connecting the Southern Atlantic ports with the Valley of the Mississippi. Nature points out the way, and I have been one of the earliest and most steady advocates of the connection. When completed, it will be of incalculable advantage both to your great Valley and the Southern Atlantic States. To your section of the Valley, it will be especially so. In its natural state, few portions of it labours under greater disadvantages; but when the connection by Railroads is completed, you may vie with the most favoured section. Instead of being excluded, it will become the very centre of a vast commerce and intercourse, bringing with them great improvement, and increase of wealth and population. With great respect, I am, &c., J.C. Calhoun.

PC in the Huntsville, Ala., *Southern Advocate*, December 14, 1849, p. 2. NOTE: Other addressees were George P. Beirne, A[rchibald] E. Mills, Samuel Cruse, Rob[er]t Fearn, and J. W[ithers] Clay. The Huntsville Railroad Convention met 11/26–28 to accomplish the merger of the Tennessee, Mississippi, and Alabama Railroad and the Tennessee Valley Railroad and to recommend a route for the newly-created company.

From M[ARTIN] W. PHILIPS

Log Hall, [Hinds County, Miss.,] Nov. 19, 1849

Honoured & Dear Sir, Yours of Oct. 9 [*not found*], I rec[eive]d long ago, and but for a crowd of pressing engagements, I would have replied long since.

About the time of receiving yours, I found it fit, proper, & convenient to put into execution a long cherished determination, & I became a Baptist. Altho' I had thought maturely & deliberated calmly, yet when the time arrived to be buried with my redeemer in Baptism, & thus imitating his death, burial & resurrection, it was hard to give up the world. My resolution prevailed & I have had a new round of duties that have so completely absorbed my attention that I have done not much else. About that time, we had an association, then protracted meetings in the Presbyterian & Methodist churches near me, which I could not refuse to attend, even had my *young* feelings not harmonized—then our State Convention of the Baptist church—in which, though so young a member, my brethren confided in me their Treasury department, to square up which required some days of thought & labour. But with all this, I remembered, as I dearly loved, my Countrys friend, benefactor & servant—yourself. For I wrote off hastily a few notes, & sent to the Laurensville [S.C.] Herald, begging the Editor to send a coppy to you. I have written some months for that paper, over the signature of *"Colo."*—and the editor desiring more matter, I thought I could serve you, & thus do more good than by any other writing, for writing to you would draw attention, the name of J.C.C., being so near & dear to every true hearted Carolinian.

I will now endeavour cursorily to give some views, not intending to go over the same ground. But first as to seed & of my little self.

As soon as I can be ready I will send to you "Sugar loaf" seed—these I have selected from the field for 3 yrs.; no one else has done so; therefore I deem them the purest. Upon rich, ["or" *interlined*] fresh ["good" *interlined*] land, these seed yield more than any I have tried in field culture, and all my neighbors on similar lands pronounce the same opinion. I plant them in rows 4½ feet distant & about 20 inches in drill, upon the same land that I plant Pettit Gulph 5 by 30.

"100 seed," I regard nearly as good upon rich land & better upon good to ordinary land. They are only Selected Mexican or Pettit Gulph. Col. H[enry] W. Vick of Vicksburg is the originator, & he was personally selecting for some 5 to 10 yrs. before he sold a seed. They are the vest best Mexican in the S.W.

Prout, is the 3rd & last variety I send you. I am waiting to receive them, as my own is not pure. I bought mine last year, & have selected from them for next crop. Mr. Hogan who planted them in this section, sold the 1st year at 1,000$ per bushel—I *know it*; last year or rather last Dec[embe]r, I paid him 10$ per bushel. They were last year the greatest production I ever saw even in this favoured region. This year not so good, the price selling all seed. Plant these upon *poor land*; I would use a little manure, not much, for over production will break down stalks and lessen crop.

Now Sir—of self. I was a member of S.C. College, 3 yrs., was a member of the University of Penn. near 2 yrs., where I graduated in medicine. I moved here—to this place—in Jan[uar]y 1830 & have as closely followed my calling as any overseer. This country was new, I could not doctor to make money, I had but 4 negroes & in debt 1,400$, could not afford an overseer. I had a beautiful wife & our child, a daughter, my only child now married for near 4 yrs. I began to study my new profession & I *worked* by day. Thus I served my time as an apprentice & have been passed & raised to a masters station by the voice of my peers, who think far more of my abilities than I do. I have predicated my opinions on those of others who were generally my elders, but I have I think invariably proven by experiment, or in other words I have originated no thing, but have weighed in the scales of practice the opinions, precept & practice of others. I take the good of each & discard the bad as far as I am competent.

In the making of any crop, I rely greatly upon the due preparation of the land before planting, in other words upon thorough tilth.

I run off my rows, after the land has been deeply & *thoroughly* plowed, with a short plow & bed to that. I like a full ridge, though not very high nor a steep one. The water furrow well opened, this is done to drain the ridges, that the crop may take an early start. I put in seed *sparingly* having very carefully sunned all my seed after being ginned, so as to have a regular stand—1 bushel per acre is ample. My reason is, I have seen solitary stalks stand a frost that killed corn, where those raised in a hot bed, in bunches were killed. Cotton is healthier & hardier when scattering. I do not plant as early as my neighbors, therefore am but little troubled with lice & sore shin. I never plant even in the mildest weather before the last week in March, & then my freshest land, as it requires longer growing. [On] old land, I prefer to plant about 15th of April. I scrape down ridges, clean the plants perfectly & thin out earlier than my neighbors generally. I only w[ai]t to see a stand in sight. I earth the young plant with a bull tongue plow (scooter plow) as early as the earth is in good order even if the same day. This plan I adopt because the narrow plow makes a water furrow near [*one word or part of a word mutilated*] plants, serves to drain off the superabundant moisture, leaves the narrow [row] dry & warmer, & a little earth is sifted around plants & a covering of [*one word mutilated*] earth is spread over the scraping, making the bed still warmer [so] grass will not vegetate on it so soon.

Pretty generally I scrape [the] 2nd time & sometimes the 3rd [*one word mutilated*] I can throw all earth needed with plows. Upon up land I scrape down all the time pretty much, with the view of having land nearly level[?] by the time I lay by my crop & do not use plows after June on upland, preferring sweeps or cultivators. Low ground needs ridges all year. Cotton requires dry weather, & upland is dry enough without ridges.

I have either selected seed yearly or bought from another site, seed every year since /33. I believe seed from the Miss. River does better [*two words mutilated*] from the hills. I cannot attribute [my] success so much to my [cul]ture, as to my seed, though the culture I proposed some 4 or 5 yrs. ago in [the] American Agriculturist has gained more converts, than my principle of selecting seed.

I cannot regard any one thing, as the thing needful, as planters, we must progress, or we will retrograde. I endeavour to plow deep & to plow up *all* my land & not cover unbroken ridges. I endeavour to cultivate well, frequently stir the earth, though a right clean crop is not lucrative planting—more of this anon. I select the best seed of corn, peas, potatoes, & oats as well as Cotton.

In addition I buy the best plows, having tried full 20 kinds. And I keep a powerful team. Many here call me extravagant, but the proof!—I own 10 hands, worked this year not 11 full hands. I had 9 choice mules, worth 100$ each, 3 geldings & one blooded mare. My objectors of this, say it costs too much to feed, but if so—I *sell corn*. This year I have broken up with a horse team every acre I planted in corn, oats, potatoes & Cotton. I have now ginned 55 bales of cotton[,] can sell 40 head of hogs, now in my pindar & potatoe patches, leaving 40 head of 200 lb. hogs for home use & 130 for next year at least. I can spare 400 bushels of potatoes, corn & fodder. I am sure of 6 bales per hand & may make 7.

The question now is, could I put my land in fine[?] tilth with say 6 mules? for I can cultivate the crop with them. Could I make as much without such tilth? Would my team last as long? And could I make the same articles to spare? Besides all this, I am enabled yearly to save time enough, that I may & do make full 100$[?] worth of shingles per year.

In view of all these matters, I must claim that there should be on every plantation at least 2 *good* work animals for every 3 hands. I believe more food in proportion can be made.

Another change I have been the humble means of spreading far & wide. The change in a great degree of the mode of working negroes, I have pursued for 10 yrs. I cook all food for my hands, having a cook for the purpose. I have all their clothes made. Never allow my foreman to call up hands before day. And when the weather becomes hot say by middle of May, all hands come to the shade, and then lie about, sleep or laugh & talk for 3 *hours*, if a very hot day 4 hours. I never permit my negroes to leave tasks over, or do any work, but feed, after night. I never suffer them to get wet, if to be avoided. And I do more work thereby. I have vegetables the year round, seldom without potatoes from year to year & generally cabbage.

Now my dear & esteemed sir. If these rambling lines can cast a glimmer upon your operations that will lead to good, I will have effected ["a thing of" *interlined*] a great joy to me. If I have been enchained by your writings I can only hope to give you something to think on. Any moment I will add more at your command. Sincerely Y[ou]rs, M.W. Philips.

ALS in ScU-SC, John C. Calhoun Papers. NOTE: Martin Wilson Philips (1806–1889) attained considerable note as a prolific writer on agriculture, educator, and Baptist lay leader.

To JOHN A[LFRED] CALHOUN,
[Abbeville District, S.C.]

Fort Hill, 20th Nov[embe]r 1849

My dear Nephew, I expect to leave for Washington in the morning, and now write principally to remind you of your promise in reference to the oats ["you promised me" *canceled*]. I have come to the conclusion, that our grain crop ought to be, at least in this region, ["principally" *interlined*] corn and oats & that it is of great importance to have a good variety of the latter. The specimen I ["say" *canceled*] saw of yours struck me as being very superior.

If you could leave what you can spare me at Abbeville Court House with directions to send it to Mr. John [S.] Lorton at Pendleton, who will pay the freight I could get it very conveniently. Or if that should be inconvenient, and you could leave it conveniently with Ja[me]s Ed[ward] Colhoun to send it ["by boat" *interlined*] to Anderson Ville to the care of Mr. [James] Harrison, I could get it by sending for it there.

My corn & cotton crop have turned out well. The former has averaged about 40 bushels to the acre round, and my cotton will something more than 70 pounds round. I have now picked 75,500 & several ["tho" *canceled*] thousands weight yet to pick, say from 110 or 112 acres.

I hope your crop has yielded well.

We are all well & all join their love to you & family. Your affectionate Uncle, J.C. Calhoun.

ALS in ScCleA.

From "Colo." [MARTIN W. PHILIPS]

[Edwards, Miss., published November 23, 1849]
HONORED SIR—Will you permit me, through the columns of the [Laurensville, S.C.,] Herald, to reply to your very acceptable letter?

I ask the privilege for this reason, I am determined to give you all the information in my power, on the subjects you have enquired about, and as I am so strongly urged by Maj. [S.A.] Godman to write for his paper, I cannot well refuse; yet I cannot do both, unless I do as now—answer you through the Herald. To me, it is passing strange, that Carolina's favored son, one whom Carolina, and every true Carolinian loves to honor above all men, should ask of one so obscure as "Colo." is, for information. Indeed, it gives joy to my heart that I can contribute to thy weal or pleasure, and this very matter would arouse every dormant energy of my soul—if there were any such—and compel me to resolve to continue laboring in the good cause as long as my energies will permit.

Before I begin the subject of the culture of cotton, allow me to allude to a subject of as prime import, in my humble opinion. And, by the by, I would much prefer to give only general rules, and leave each planter to fill up the minute working parts—yet I assure you, that to answer your wish as expressed in your letter, I deem it a duty, devolving on me, so far your inferior in age and parts.

The subject I desire to press home upon every planter—and beg your especial attention to, because if you will *only assent* to the principle, it will do more than the humble "Colo" could do in years, by persuasion and argument—is, the improvement of seed by a close and rigid selection from the field, as also the duty of drying before put into bulk, so as to prevent the heating of seed.

Every planter should do it to some extent, and in addition thereto, procure an occasional fresh article from the favored region of the cotton plant.

I commence my cotton planting operations by breaking down with clubs the cotton stalk of the past year; if they be large, the limbs are threshed down first, so as to break up, then the stalk broken off as near the earth as possible. Of course this is done when cotton succeeds cotton. I then run off my rows, at such distances as the fertility and age of land as well as the variety of seed demand. The fresher the land, and richer it is, the greater distance; Mexican seed requiring more distance than the cotton I have seen which is called in a part of Mississippi the Hogan seed—a few I have received as a present—and these still more than the Sugar Loaf, another variety from Mississippi, which in some localities in the Gulf States has proved very productive. I have not had occasion to give a greater distance than five 1-2 feet, and am inclined to think, though you claim to be at the Northern extremity of the cotton region, that upon rich and fresh land the cotton stalk may be as large, or larger than some 80 or 90 miles South, on similar lands.

I make it a point to plow out all land as deep as I can, and without any ridge being left under the plowed land. My rows are all laid out by stakes, with a shovel plow, and then two furrows turned to it, one from each side, with an efficient turn plow; this is performed as early in March as I can, endeavoring to postpone my spring plowing until after the heavy rains. Understand I have a clay subsoil, with silicious matter so fine, that no grit is perceived by rubbing with the fingers.

Using due diligence in my early plowing, and planting of corn, I am enabled to have all cotton land with three furrows thrown up, before time to plant cotton. When the time has arrived—which time should not be before the seed will vegetate, and plant grow off—I do not like to plant as early as many do—I then press forward my plowing and planting, thus—enough plows go ahead to ridge up entirely the balance of unbroken earth; harrows follow, openers, droppers, and last coverers. I never wish to sow more than one bushel of seed, and prefer to cover with a board or block, so as to cover shallow, to leave ridge smooth, and to compress earth to seed. Upon level land I require a set of hands to plant 10 acres per day, length of rows averaging 440 yards—a set of hands is, one harrower, one opener, one to sow seed, and one to cover. Now, esteemed sir, we have planted say one half the crop.

If all land had not been plowed with three furrows prior to this, I then turn about and prepare the residue of land, and if corn can be pressed forward, I work all or a part—with the view of having ten days between first and last planting. Then return to planting the residue of cotton. We have now planted the crop, and will talk in our next, why we have done so, for if we have done well, we ought to be able to say why. Yours, &c., Colo.

[*Second published letter:*]
"Colo." to John C. Calhoun

[published November 23, 1849]
ESTEEMED SIR: In the close of my former article, I remarked we had planted our crop, and that we would proceed to show why we did so.

PLOWING AND PLANTING.—I am very particular in requiring rows to be laid off straight, bedded up so, and furrows opened for dropping, equally so, because the plowman in all succeeding labor is able to plow nearer to the plant, and thus lightening hoe labor. An expert plowman, with a sharp turning plow can by letting the share run *level with the ridge,* handles inclined, of course, can scrape so near the plant that a hoe hand can scrape and thin out nearly twice as much.

Many in breaking up land for cotton, leave unbroken earth, some call it—"cut and cover," that is, cover unbroken earth with a furrow— & they insist that the plant bears better, that when the land is all broken up, the plant grows too luxuri[a]ntly. This may possibly be the case upon the rich lands where your plantation in Alabama is, but certainly not in *our State,* and where you live. It is a slovenly culture, to say the least. But how can the tencer spingioles of the root pass through stiff land in dry weather, and how can the plant be sustained when only half the land is cultivated.

The deeper land be plowed when the subsoil is not sandy, or gravelly, if properly drained, the more room for roots to search for their food, and the greater deposite of dew therein, the longer to get hot, and the readier to cool, as well as holding more moisture, less liability to wash from an ordinary rain, and sooner the drying of the surface.

I place two furrows on the one laid off early, that the earth may consolidate—cotton seed vegetating more certain, and grows off more rapidly. I put off breaking out the residue as long as I can; so that the surface may be clean when planted, and thus grass and cotton have an equal start. I use the harrow to remove all trash, clods, &c., as also to level ridge.

I prefer a ridge, with the view of having dry warm soil for the seed, as cotton grows off earlier, and is sooner out of the way of drouths [*sic*], as also that I can scrape down with plow, and cover young grass thinly in the middle.

Early planting gives "sore shin and lice," or rather the plant has so little vitality that its natural enemies soon "take away even that which it hath."

I always strive to keep seed perfectly sound, thereby adding to the vitality of the plant. I have noticed some years the stand to be worse than other years, and some men always to have had the luck of bad stands—this was owing, *I think,* to damp weather, or wet spells, injuring the cotton so as to injure the vital powers of the seed.

I plant seed sparsely, because the plant becomes hardy at once, and then stands almost, if not quite as much cold as does corn.

I regard a crop when planted in first rate order as nearly half made, so much regard I place upon thorough tilth and thorough preparation.

With profound respect, I am, honored sir, Yours, Colo.

PC in the Charleston, S.C., *Richards' Weekly Gazette*, January 5, 1850, p. 4; PC in the Greensborough, Ala., *Alabama Beacon*, January 19, 1850, p. 1; PC in the Laurensville, S.C., *Herald*, November 23, 1849, p. 4; PC in Joseph Addison Turner, *The Cotton Planter's Manual: Being a Compilation of Facts from the Best Authorities on the Culture of Cotton . . .* (New York: C.M. Saxton and Co., 1857), pp. 28–32. NOTE: The extant issue of the Laurensville *Herald* containing this letter is so mutilated that transcription from that source is impossible.

From H[ENRY] W. CONNER

[Charleston] Monday, Nov. 25 1849

Dear Sir, The Bank will renew the existing note as it is for 12 months and will discount [William W.] Allens (late Allen & Hadens) ["note" *canceled*] acceptance of Andrew [Pickens Calhoun] aft[er] endorsed by you ["for" *canceled*] at 12 months at the rate of [*illegible*] off & 2 per cent Exchange making it equal to the Alabama rate of interest. H.W. Conner.

Copy of Mr. Conners note to J.C. Calhoun.

Ms. copy in ScU-SC, John C. Calhoun Papers.

From OGDEN EDWARDS

New York [City,] 30th November 1849

Dear Sir, I have reason for believing that the nomination of Mr. [Hugh] Maxwell for Collector of this port will be insidiously opposed by Governor [William H.] Seward. I have been in habits of friendly intercourse with Mr. Maxwell for a long series of years. His political course has ever been honourable. From the first appearance of Demagogueism in this State under the auspices of Governour Seward he set his face sternly against him; & although he was president of the convention which nominated him when he was elected Governour, he then opposed his nomination. All the factions which have arisen in this State, & upon which Governour Seward has rode into power, from Anti-Masonry, & Anti-Rentism down to Abolitionism, have met with his decided opposition. When Seward was named as a candidate for the U.S. Senate he was met with Mr. Maxwell's indignant and active opposition. All this has produced its natural effect and as Seward can not make him his tool; he will endeavour to make him his victim.

This opposition however will not be avowed. A consummate Jesuit, his tactics will be in conformity to his character. Under the guise of friendship he will resort to the most insidous means. The attainment of the object the great patronage of the office, he will deem sufficient to recompence richly the most strenous efforts & resort to the foulest means. If he suceeds & can place one of his tools in the Collectorship, he will then ["have" *interlined*] means at command to lure a mass of corrupt supporters to his standard.

His candidate originally was James Bowen[?] & his utmost efforts were made to procure his nomination. Mr. Maxwell was not an applicant for this office, but after the resignation of Mr. [Cornelius Van Wyck] Lawrence at the request of the executive, accepted the office & his appointment gave general satisfaction.

I am induced to write not only out of regard to Mr. Maxwell but mainly from a desire to expose the foulest faction that ever reared its crest in this State. Very respectfully Yours, Ogden Edwards.

LS in ScU-SC, John C. Calhoun Papers.

From "Colo." [MARTIN W. PHILIPS]

[Edwards, Miss., published Nov. 30, 1849]
Honored Sir: Having now planted the entire crop of cotton as well as it can be done, in my humble opinion, it falls upon me to continue, in obedience to your kind request, to give the culture thereof.

So soon as I find I have enough cotton out of the ground to give a full stand, I start plows and hoes to scraping and chopping out. Many wait for the third leaf, but I only wait for vegetation unless a cold spell of weather. I run around the plants with a plow, or a cotton scraper, and remove as thin a scraping of earth as can be—when rows are four feet or three and a half, the middles will be covered, so as to keep down grass. The hoes follow, clean the plants perfectly of all the grass or weeds that are up, and to be certain of it, I require the entire bed to show fresh earth, each hand takes his own row, chops through, cutting out the width of hoe of all plants, leave three or four plants, chop through again and so on. I object to any hoe over 10 inches wide, get them of steel, costing $9.75 per dozen, a nine inch hoe is wide enough for any, and eight inches for average hands, sharpen them every day, and if much grass, even twice, with a flat file.

The cotton rows now stand in bunches about 10 inches a part.

After scraping a day or two, start enough bull tongue plows behind hoes, to mould the cotton lightly, so that the plows will be able to earth the plant in a day or two after being scraped. The object is, to have a water furrow near to plants, to serve as a drain, thus make the narrow ridge unbroken dry and warm, the little earth thrown to the plants will serve to add to the warmth, and to prevent choaking growth of plant—at which time the lice by depradating upon the plant, will acquire too great power over it. The healthy plant, will grow off, lice or no lice, and the sore shin is not apt to be seen—but guard closely your hands, that they touch not the stem with the hoe so as to abrade the thin bark, or skin.

My next working is done with a six inch shovel plow, or a small turn plow, or the sweep, or a cultivator—any thing to throw a little earth to it.

My practice is to throw earth with a plow, and draw away with a hoe, my hoe work all year, is of the scraping order. Cotton kept to a ridge, will fruit better and mature earlier, I think. Though, one must know his own locality, and yet should not be bound to "the road his father travelled to mill."

I am not an advocate for garden culture of the cotton plant, yet neat planting demands it. The neat planter will not make the same crops, though he will have at least a greater "pleasure therein."

I forgot to say, that when my land is rich enough to bear five and a half feet rows, I leave the stand of cotton at second hoeing at about 30 inches, sometimes three feet; upon ordinary land I leave plants 18 to 24 inches. I have certainly made more cotton at the last named distance, then when I gave the distance sometimes recommended.

[*Mutilation*] place my first planting of cotton to a [*mutilation*] and working, and last planting, I often do at my first[?] working. The principle is to put to single stalks as early as the season will admit of—there is no question in my mind but what the early thinning and early earthing are important.

By all means clean your crop by the middle of June and keep it clean, the grass that annoys before June does not the harm that June and July grass does.

I have the best piece of cotton in my vicinity, it was not clean before June, and many a laugh was at the expense of my grassy cotton—though the laugh is now over the other shoulder.

We have six months before planting time—should these crude thoughts not be ample, I would be delighted in the employment of a winter's night for a week in replying at greater length. Oblige me, by asking any further of my labor, and thus give your humble fellow citizen even more cause to be thankful to his Maker for giving him the tact, that he may be useful.

With profound Respect, and a heartfelt prayer for our gallant States' success forever, I am your fellow, COLO.

PC in the Laurensville, S.C., *Herald*, November 30, 1849, p. 4.

To AND[RE]W PICKENS CALHOUN, [Marengo County, Ala.]

Washington, 2d Dec[embe]r 1849
My dear And[re]w, I had a very pleasant and safe journey on. The weather was fine throughout; but is now very bad. It snowed during the night, and is now sleeting, with a North Easter; so that I was lucky in taking time by the forelock. I am now quartered at Hills on Capital Hill for the Session.

There is much confusion in the ranks of both parties and it is thought it will be difficult to elect a Speaker. [Robert C.] Winthrop [of Mass.] and [Howell] Cobb [of Ga.] have been nominated by their respective parties; and [David] Wilmot [of Pa.] by the free soilers. There is a Scism in the ranks both of the democrats and the Whigs, as to the Speaker, which will be difficult to heal. The session will be one of great excitement and confusion. . . .

PEx in Jameson, ed., *Correspondence*, pp. 774–775. NOTE: Calhoun was lodged at the boarding house of Mrs. Henry V. Hill on Capitol Hill.

DECEMBER 3, 1849–
FEBRUARY 28, 1850

◫

Calhoun was in his seat in the Senate when the session opened, though he did not choose to speak until December 20. He wrote his son-in-law Clemson on December 8: "There is every indication, that we shall have a stormy session. There is no telling what will be the end. The South is more united, than I ever knew it to be, and more bold & decided. The North must give away, or there will be a rupture."

He added his opinion that the new administration of General Taylor was proving "itself feeble every way." And in the same letter to his kin across the seas he continued with a word about his health: "We have had, thus far, a very mild season. My health is as good as usual. I have resolved to take good care of myself; neither to expose myself or to be overworked." In the same connection, a reporter remarked early in the session that "Mr. Calhoun appears to enjoy better health than he did last summer. He is at his post early and late, and ready for the crisis which is rapidly approaching." (Greenville, S.C., Mountaineer, January 18, 1850.)

Another reporter saw him "on a cold day in December, as, with his closely buttoned surtout, (for he wore no cloak,) he rapidly walked to the capital. His step was firm—his form erect—his eye bright as a star in a moonless sky. Glorious Calhoun! we differ from thee in some things; and yet we admire and venerate thee. Here, now, is a purely intellectual man." (Philadelphia, Pa., Pennsylvanian, March 9, 1850.)

His family was concerned about his health, though not gravely so. Anna Maria wrote on December 22: "Do, my dearest father, . . . do take care of yourself. Dont work too hard—only speak when necessary—Dont go out at night—Dont see too much company—Live generously & drink wine & warm toddy at night . . . ." Probably before Anna's letter had crossed the ocean, Calhoun penned one to her on the last day of the year, describing a matter close to his heart—his works on government and the Constitution to which he was devoting as much as possible of his remaining time and strength.

Optimism about the health of the man who would be sixty-eight years of age in March was mistaken. On January 19, a reporter wrote from Washington: "At this hour of writing, the life of Mr. Calhoun is in imminent peril, from the effects of a severe attack of pneumonia. His indisposition commenced early in the week, and continued to increase until yesterday, when he was compelled to resort to his bed; and . . . it is doubtful whether he will ever recover." (Philadelphia, Pa., Pennsylvania Freeman, *January 24, 1850.)*

Calhoun's condition was from now on daily national news. Thanks to the new telegraph, news could be sent almost instantly from Washington to the Mississippi, the Gulf, and the Great Lakes. Whatever one thought of the Carolina statesman, he was one of the few remaining living links to the early days of the Union. And he was nearly universally respected, except for the Van Buren-Benton wing of the Democratic party who feared his influence.

Attended by his longtime Washington friend Dr. James C. Hall and the North Carolina congressman Abraham W. Venable, who was a physician, Calhoun improved to the point that the Charleston Courier *could report on January 31 that the Senator was "quite convalescent." It was, however, doubtful whether he would be able to continue active in public life. The press widely reported what he was said to have told visiting friends: he would make one last effort to address the crisis. "He remarked," also, "that he was now satisfied that the people of the South were ahead of their leaders in movements on this subject," according to the Charleston* Courier, *February 14, 1850, a report widely repeated.*

On February 18 Calhoun was able to return to the Senate, but only for a short time before he was confined to quarters again. There were many old friends in this Senate. Clay and Webster were back. But there were new faces, too: a militant new breed of Northerners like Hannibal Hamlin, Salmon P. Chase, and William H. Seward. Seward's fellow New Yorker James K. Paulding, who like Calhoun remembered earlier and better days of the Union, wrote on March 19 concerning Seward: "He is one of the most dangerous insects that ever crawled about in the political atmosphere. . . ."

◫

From J A [M E] S T. B R A D Y

New York [City,] Dec[embe]r 4th 1849
D[ea]r Sir, I address you in reference to the office of Collector of the
port of New York, and the action of the Senate on the nomination
of Hugh Maxwell Esq. for that office. What course the Senate should
adopt in regard to the appointments made by General [Zachary]
Taylor is a question which you have no doubt satisfactorily resolved
in your own mind, and I know that your personal action will be
regulated by an honest desire to discharge your public duty with
fidelity. But it can not be improper for me to suggest that if (as I
have every reason to believe) the faction, or *clique* which favours
the political pretensions of William H. Seward, are willing to have
Mr. Maxwell defeated for reasons ["other than" *canceled and* "different from" *interlined*] those which would controul other nominations, they should not be aided in the scheme by any of the Democratic Senators, but the honour, or shame of the Sacrifice should belong to themselves alone. I know that you have a proper appreci-
ation of the Seward faction—of the unworthy means by which it is
sought to give Seward a prominence for which he is neither intellectually nor morally fit. I feel convinced that Some of his admirers
would not be unwilling to have Mr. Maxwell put aside, because although he is, and has been for many years a zealous Whig, he has
not lent himself to the dissemination, or support of the local, Sectional, or fanatical doctrines which now threaten disturbance to our
National Compact. Mr. Maxwell was a friend to my father [Thomas
J. Brady], and cheered me in my first efforts at the bar. I have always
respected and admired him, and should be very sorry if by any
machinations, any of his enemies should obtain an unfair advantage
over him. You also are, I believe, well acquainted with Mr. Maxwell,
and will no doubt concur in my estimate of his character. I hope
that if an occasion should arise in which without impairing any obligation which you owe to principles, it might be in your power to
influence the disposal of nominations, you may feel willing to do
["what" *canceled*] Mr. Maxwell a favour. He was appointed after
the resignation of Mr. [Cornelius Van Wyck] Lawrence, and not as
the mere hungry aspirant to an office held by another. He naturally
feels that to have him excepted, by any contrivance, from the rule
applied to other Nominees of the President, would be a secret Satisfaction to men whom he does not much admire, and with whom he
can never fully sympathize. You will at a glance comprehend his
position, and determine whether any and what interference in this

matter would, on your part, be appropriate. Leaving that question to your decision, and begging you fully to appreciate the friendly motives with which I make this appeal in Mr. Maxwell's behalf, I avail myself of this opportunity to assure you of the continued friendship I entertain for you personally, and of the constancy with which I adhere to the political doctrines essential [*suffix* "ly" *canceled*] to the preservation of State Sovereignty in its full constitutional vigour, as the most reliable, if not the only mode of perpetuating our National Government. Yours very truly, Jas. T. Brady.

ALS in ScU-SC, John C. Calhoun Papers. NOTE: Calhoun's AEU reads: "Mr. Brady[,] relates to Mr. Maxwell." James Topham Brady (1815–1869) was a very successful Irish-American lawyer who turned down many invitations to be a Democratic party candidate for high offices.

To [JOSEPH] N. WHITNER, [Anderson, S.C.]

Washington, 4th Dec[embe]r 1849

My dear Sir, This will be handed to you by my son, Ja[me]s Ed[ward] Calhoun[,] Jun[io]r, who is about to graduate [from South Carolina College].

He wishes to study law with you, and before setting in, to converse with you as to the course he ought to pursue. It is his & my wish that he should remain at home this winter & the greater part of the next summer, & to devote himself to the reading elementary books, connected with ["his profession" *interlined,*] making visits occasionally to Anderson, to converse with you about his studies, & receiving your instructions. Yours truly, J.C. Calhoun.

ALS in NcD, John C. Calhoun Papers.

From ARTH[UR] R. CROZIER and J[AMES] G. M. RAMSEY

Knoxville T[enn.,] Dec[embe]r 6th '49

D[ea]r Sir, It seems to be the opinion of some of our people that the Hon. Jno. Bell will make an effort to reject the nomination of Mr. D[aniel] McCallum the [U.S.] Marshal for the District of East Ten. Mr. McCallum is a whig and a very worthy gentleman, and though differing from us in politics we would esteem it a personal favor if you would give your aid in sustaining the nomination should there be an effort to reject it before the Senate.

Hon. [Hopkins L.] Turney [Senator from Tenn.] has been written to on this subject. Please confer with him. Yours truly, Arth. R. Crozier, J.G.M. Ramsey.

[P.S.] Mr. McCallum was appointed to fill the vacancy occasioned by the resignation of A.R. Crozier.

LS in ScU-SC, John C. Calhoun Papers. NOTE: An AEU by Calhoun reads, "Nomination of McCallum."

To J[OHN] R[AVEN] MATHEW[E]S,
Charleston

Washington, 6th Dec[embe]r 1849

My dear Sir, I was in hope, when I passed through Charleston on my way here, I would meet you there, but was disappointed. We have made arrangement to take up the bond for the negroes purchased of your sister [Ann Mathewes Ioor], on or before the 1st of March, whether our cotton crop should be sold then or not; and I wish you to inform me where the bond is & to whom the money is to be paid.

You will have seen by the papers, that there is great difficulty in electing a Speaker. The result is very uncertain. It depends on the seceeding whigs & the barnburners.

The support of [Howell] Cobb is a bitter dose to the Southern members. They have no confidence in him, & our delegation, with great difficulty, were brought to vote for him. Nothing but the entreaty of our Virginia & other friends and a regard for the cause, could induce our delegation to vote for him. You may wonder why he should be selected as the candidate. It is the work of a caucus and what are called northern democrats, ["and" *canceled and* "who" *interlined*] who [*sic*] with only one or two exceptions ["are" *interlined*] nothing but free soilers. They united on him to a man, because he was the most acceptable to them & least acceptable to us. They, with a few from the South, nominated him & placed the Southern ["the" *canceled*] members in their present awarkward condition.

There has been a scism in the whig ranks, headed by [Robert] Toombs. The seceders will not vote for [Robert C.] Winthrop. It is difficult to say, what they will finally do.

131

The prospect is that there will be a stormy session. Yours truly, J.C. Calhoun.

ALS in ScU-SC, John C. Calhoun Papers. NOTE: The letter bears an AEU by Mathewes: "Answered Dec. 9, 1849. The arrangement concerning the Bond, I will tomorrow write my sister about your desires & when you will give me timely notice of the day I will meet your appointment at this place with all of the necessary papers."

To J[AMES] H. HAMMOND, [Barnwell District, S.C.]

Washington, 7th Dec[embe]r 1849

My dear Sir, I would regard the failure of the Convention, called by Mississippi, to meet from the want of endorsement by the other Southern States to be a great, if not fatal misfortune. It would be difficult to make another effort to rally, and the North would consider it as conclusive evidence of our devisions or indifference to our fate. The moment is critical. Events may now be controlled; but, it will be difficult, if not impossible to control their course hereafter. This is destined to be no ordinary session. We shall need the backing of our constituents; and the most effectual, we can have, would be the endorsement by the other Southern States ["of" *interlined*] the Mississippi call.

I do not think that our State should hold back, and wait for the movement of the other States. If we act at all, it must be through the members ["con" *canceled*] of the Legislature, during the session, and, of course, the movement must be made the next few weeks. If we do not move, other States will be backward to move. As jealous as they may be of us, they still look to us to give the signal. Nor do I think, that we should make the meeting depend on the concurring of 8, or any other number of States. It would, I fear, throw the indifferent against the convention, & tend to defeat it. If the meeting should not be full, it would be a good reason for taking no decisive action & for calling another convention, accompanied by an Address to the other States.

I feel deep solicitude in reference to the subject. With the endorsement by the other States of the call, I see my way; but without it, I do not. If South Carolina backs it, the convention will meet, but without it, it will almost certainly fail. I do hope you will concur in these views, and add your influence to induce the members of our Legislature to appoint delegates.

No one regretted more than I did the course of the [Columbia South-]Carolinian, in reference to the subject to which you allude. I took immediate measures to counteract its ill effect. The disease has got beyond the control of presidential influence. As to the office, I not only do not desire it, but would not accept it, if tendered to me, under existing circumstances. Yours truly, J.C. Calhoun.

ALS in DLC, James Henry Hammond Papers; PC in Jameson, ed., *Correspondence*, pp. 775–776.

To T[homas] G. Clemson, [Brussels]

Washington, 8th Dec[embe]r 1849

My dear Sir, The pressure of my engagements and the expectation of taking your place in my way here, when I might give you some information about your affairs, have delayed until this time my acknowledgement of your last. I was, however, unavoidably prevented from fulfilling my intention of going by your place, which I regret; but I hope Col. [Francis W.] Pickens has kept you informed about your affairs there [in Edgefield District].

I do not know what has been your final decision, in reference to your place, but conclude, that it has been to continue to hold on to it and the negroes and other property ["on" *canceled and* "attached" *interlined*; to] it, for the present. If so, I think, you have decided wisely. Property is on the rise in the South, both lands & negroes, with the prospect of better price for cotton hereafter. Negro men, I understand, will, if likely, command $800 and other discriptions in proportion. Land in our vicinity sell[s] readily at a very considerable increase of price. The crop of cotton is short. It will not, in my opinion, exceed 2,000,000 of bales; and there is a fair prospect, that the demand will keep its price to 8 or 10 cents if not higher for years to come. If so, prices will increase both of lands & negroes, especially the latter. The South has now a fairer prospect ["of prosperity," *canceled*] than it has had at any time for the last 10 years, and already gives signs of returning prosperity.

As short as our Alabama crop is cut short by bad seasons & the worm, I had hoped to make some impression on our debt to you; but all our disposable means will have to be applied to the discharge of the [Ann Mathewes] Ioor debt. In consequence of the age & infirmity of Mr. & Mrs. Ioor, they have determined to give up farming & settle in GreenVille, & desire to have their funds in our hand to vest in that place. Their bond will be taken up the 1st ["of" *interlined*] March, when the year expires. Dr. [Ozey R.] Broyles was not certain, whether he would be in funds, but should he be, whatever may be received from him, will be applied to your bond, and whether he should, or should not be, the interest will be paid punctually at the end of the year. I trust, that we shall be able out of another crop to square with you. You cannot be more anxious to have what is due to you, than we to pay it.

In the meane time, I wish you to inform me to whom the interest & other payments should be made, if we should have funds to make others, as Mr. [John Ewing] Bonneau recently died. His daughter & Henry W. DeSaussure are, I understand, the Executrix & Executor of his estate. The estate is large & the Executor, who will have the management, highly responsible, so that you have nothing to apprehend, as to your bond. He ["(Mr. B.)" *interlined*] had associated with him not long before his death, one of his clerks, Josiah S. Brown, who will continue the factorage business, but whether on the foundation of the old firm, or on his own account, had not be[en] settled, but would be by the first of Jan[uar]y. I shall probably continue ["him" *interlined*] to do my business in Charleston, as he seems to be a worthy & punctual man. You will of course have to determine whether you will select him or some other, as your factor. I think the fact, that Mr. Bonneau had sufficient confidence in him to associate him with him, a strong endorsement in his favour. When you have decided what you will do, & to whom the interest & payments on your bond are to be made let me know.

Congress has been in session now for four days without being able to elect a Speaker. It is uncertain when one can be elected. The free soil party holds the balance between the two parties, and appear resolved not to give away.

There is every indication, that we shall have a stormy session. There is no telling what will be the end. The South is more united, than I ever knew it to be, and more bold & decided. The North must give away or there will be a rupture.

I regard the [Zachary Taylor] administration, as prostrated. It has proved itself feeble every way.

We have had, thus far, a very mild season. My health is as good as usual. I have resolved to take good care of myself; neither to expose myself or to be overworked.

I left all well, when I left home.

Say to Anna [Maria Calhoun Clemson] that I received her last letter after I arrived here. It had gone to Pendleton & was returned here. I will answer it in a short time. My love to her & the children [John Calhoun Clemson and Floride Elizabeth Clemson]. Your affectionate father, J.C. Calhoun.

ALS in ScCleA; PEx in Jameson, ed., *Correspondence*, p. 776. NOTE: Two days after the above letter, James Edward Boisseau, the Calhouns' kin and factor in New York City, wrote Clemson: "The South is all prosperity . . . now is the time to dispose of your Southern property." ALS in ScCleA.

From P[LACIDIA MAYRANT] ADAMS

Pendleton, 1849 [*ca.* 13] Dec[embe]r

Dear Sir, I regret that I am obliged to ask you if it is now convenient to let me have the small ballance that is still due me on the bond. I would not trouble you but if cannot raise some money my property will be levied on, you know [*ms. faded; illegible word*]t sued me last spr[*ms. faded; two or three words illegible.*] In our last settlement you paid[?] me[?] nine[?] hundred & eighty seven dollars including Louisas wages corn & wheat got from Mr. Fred[e]ricks. With respect &, P. Adams.

ALS in ScU-SC, John C. Calhoun Papers. NOTE: An AEI by Calhoun reads: "Mrs. P. Adams, 13th Dec[embe]r 1849. Remitted a check for $47, the amount of the error made in calculating the amount of the bond of my son Andrew & myself to her including the final payment on the bond. It closes all accounts between us. The check drawn by[?] the[?] bank of Metropolis on the Commerce bank of New York in my favour. No. 2771[?]. J.C.C."

From JOHN A[LFRED] CALHOUN

Cedar Grove Abbeville District, [S.C.,] Dec[embe]r 14th 1849

Dear Uncle, I informed you in my last of my intention to visit Columbia. Having just returned from thence, I will give you some account of matters there.

I found quite a strong feeling on the Southern question; but a marked deficiency in concert, and a decided want of intelligence in devising the means of meeting it. The plan finally fixed on (the final action had not been taken) I think will do *tolerably well*. This no doubt you have seen before this letter shall have reached you. The great difficulty of the Legislature's meeting this question properly; arrises in part from a want of general intelligence—but mainly from the influence of faction. I was fourcebly struck with the change of things, since the time of my being a member of that body—ten years ago. Then our Legislature was characterised by a high degree of intelligence, and a marked freedom from the influence of faction. Now the quantity of young men, without experience, and with but little wisdom; added to the fact that there are a set of men now rising into influence in the State, who are premeditatedly infusing into that body an intense spirit of faction—has had a decided tendency to lower the political standard of the State; and, unless checked, will soon prostrate, the heretofore high character, which we have enjoyed. Every question now raised in the Legislature is made to bend somewhat to these factions. Even this great Southern question is not entirely above it.

The next question before the Legislature of most importance (and the first in excitement) is the winding up the State Bank. And here all the virulence of these factions are manifested. I believe a large number of those on either side of this question are honestly contending for what they think is right. But the politicians treat the matter in quite a different light. Whilst one faction look to the Bank as a means of strengthening their ["Bank" *canceled*] influence—The other factions regard it as an obstacle to their aspirations. The center of the two main factions are to be found in *Charleston* and *Barnwell*. And although there are *minor* factions on both sides playing around these leading factions—yet here are the two great centers. The contest I can assure ["you," *interlined*] is most disgusting to every one who is able to rise above these factions. They have not hesitated to mix your name with it, and in my opinion neither have any love for you, but on the contrary a decided dislike. Indeed, this game in connection with your name, was carried to such an extent as to induce me to denounce their conduct in no measured terms. It is evident to my mind, that the leaders of both these factions, as well as some of the subordinates look upon you and your *position* as constituting the chief obstacle to their ambitious schemes. It was my policy to mix freely with all the factions, and in doing so have collected many facts which I think it would be well for you to know: and if you desire, it shall be given. But if it is not your desire to know these this matter can rest between us. I conver[s]ed freely with Governor [Whitemarsh B.] Seabrook on these matters and received some information from him; and he authorises me to say that he concurs in the main with my views. I regard Mr. [Franklin H.] Elmore as your friend. But the *deep interest* he feels in the Bank question has I think made him somewhat indiscrete in the use of your name. The report was that he was using your letter to him to aid the Bank cause. Knowing your desire to keep out of these State issues, I can hardly think this is done with your assent. I have no sympathy for the war now waging against the Bank, and especially the way in which it is conducted. But I think it would be your best policy to keep out of it.

Write me soon and freely on this subject.

We are all well. Your nephew most affectionately, John A. Calhoun.

ALS in ScCleA; variant PC in Boucher and Brooks, eds., *Correspondence*, pp. 532–533.

REMARKS ON ADMITTING THE REV. THEOBALD MATHEW TO THE PRIVILEGES OF THE SENATE FLOOR

[In the Senate, December 20, 1849]

[*It was moved that Mathew (an Irish priest noted for leadership of the temperance movement) be allowed "to sit within the bar of the Senate during the period of his sojourn in Washington." This unusual privilege provoked a lengthy discussion in which many Senators took part pro and con and in which parliamentary questions were raised. Mathew was also considered by some to have indirectly countenanced a call for "warfare against the institutions of the South."*]

Mr. Calhoun. Not supposing that the yeas and nays would be called for, I have abstained from making any remarks upon the question. If the Senate will indulge me in a few remarks—

The Vice President [Millard Fillmore]. With the unanimous consent of the Senate, the gentleman may proceed.

Mr. Calhoun. Mr. President, I intend to limit my remarks simply to the question of laying upon the table. It is now ascertained that there is no precedent whatever to justify the resolution. We are therefore to make a precedent of this case; for let our vote be either affirmative or negative, it is a precedent. Now, sir, setting all other considerations out of view, I am not willing to make a precedent. It

137

appears to me that the Senate itself ought to come to the conclusion, from this very debate, of the impropriety of making this a precedent. It has now occupied us for hours, bringing up a discussion which, so far as the gentleman is concerned who is the subject-matter of it, must wound his feelings much more than the compliment would heal them. The Senate now sees that Mr. Mathew cannot possibly receive the united invitation of this body. It must be a divided vote. The compliment, if it be passed, will be weakened; and I submit it to every Senator, whether it will not be more acceptable to his feelings to lay it upon the table, upon the ground that we do not choose to make a precedent, than to vote for it dividedly.

The Senator from Louisiana behind me, (Mr. [Solomon W.] Downs,) urges the reason for making this a precedent, that it is extraordinary; that the occasion is peculiar, and can scarcely hereafter be repeated. Sir, the very fact that it is extraordinary, is a motive for not making it a precedent. If you vote it down in a strong case, it will establish the rule so that it cannot be broken over hereafter. And if you vote affirmatively upon it, it will draw after it a train that it will be impossible to resist. You may refuse this on the ground that there is no precedent; but if you make a precedent, then, when you come to object hereafter to a resolution of this kind, it becomes a question of merit. Now, sir, gentlemen know, upon a question of merit, how difficult it is to decide.

Sir, I must say that, in many respects, we do not respect ourselves as much as we ought. There is not a parliamentary body in the world that extends compliments of this kind. In the British Parliament it is a high honor to be introduced by a distinguished member of either House privately. No foreigner or other man ought to expect such a compliment from the United States. We owe more to ourselves than to give it; and especially as this goes far beyond any other—admitting him within the bar of the Senate. Sir, I do hope the Senate will pause before they give an affirmative vote. I hope they will consider it, and settle it, that compliments of this kind are not to be expected from us.

[*After further extended discussion, the motion to admit Mathew to the privileges of the Senate floor was adopted by a largely sectional vote of 33 to 18.*]

From *Congressional Globe*, 31st Cong., 1st Sess., p. 58. Also printed in the Washington, D.C., *Daily Union*, December 21, 1849, p. 2; the Washington, D.C., *Daily National Intelligencer*, December 22, 1849, p. 2. Variant in the Alexandria, Va., *Gazette and Virginia Advertiser*, December 22, 1849, p. 2.

From Anna [Maria] C[alhoun] Clemson

Brussels, Dec. 22d 1849

Let me first wish you, my dear father, not "A Merry Christmas," according to the old formula, (for I would hardly wish you to be *merry* & I not there,) but all the blessings you deserve, & which your devoted children desire for you.

I see by the papers that you have arrived in Washington, & I hope in good health, & strength, for the winter campaign. Do, my dearest father, for all of our sakes, & especially for my sake, who love you, I believe, after all, the best of all your children, *for I know you the best*, do take care of yourself. Dont work too hard—only speak *when necessary*—Dont go out at night—Dont see too much company—Live generously & drink wine & *warm toddy at night* & dont let Mr. [Abraham W.] Venable [Representative from N.C.] talk you to death. If you follow these rules & keep your feet & chest warm I think you will go through the winter comfortably & be ready to profit by the fine weather when spring comes.

I suppose the session will be stormy & decisive with regard to the future position of the south. I hope our people will understand, & protect their rights, with firmness. If we fail now, our future is ruined without hope, & we might as well give up everything.

The weather here is very cold & disagreeable, but it has been so dreadfully sloppy & muddy, for a week or two past, that we are all ["able" *canceled*] willing to support the cold, in order to have it dry under foot. Notwithstanding the dampness, we have all fortunately escaped colds, & are all well. Floride [Elizabeth Clemson] & [John] Calhoun [Clemson] have fattened considerably since you saw them, & are much improved in appearance. Calhoun grows very manly, & begins to take some interest in his studies. They both learn well when they choose. In order to excite emulation, I have adopted the old system of medals, which works well so far. They talk a great deal of America & grandpappa[,] grandmamma [Floride Colhoun Calhoun] &c &c. I told them just now I was writing to you, & they gave me a mass of messages, which it would take all my paper to write you, but the principal was that they loved you, & sent you many kisses, & would write you as soon as I would let them. I hold out the permission to write to you & grandmother, as a reward for exertion, & good behaviour. They are amiable & intelligent children, & give me no trouble.

Of politics ["in" *interlined*] Europe I dont know what to say. There seems, (I cannot say a calm but) a *pause*, in the current of events. This may be the pause before the tempest, or the indifference which succeeds over exertion, or hopelessness. Time alone can show what its true nature is. For myself I have not the slightest conception where all this is tending, but I fear it is the begining of an epoch, more or less long of debasement for the people, & tyrany of the leaders. You know I always said there could be no true liberty without a *people* & I saw no people, properly so called, in Europe, except in England, where other causes render the abuses of government as radical, & deeply fixed, as in any country under the sun. In short I fear so far revolution & agitation have rather injured than aided the cause of rational liberty.

If our country fails under the present trying circumstances the future will be gloomy indeed to those who wish well to humanity. Our failure will be the more painful as we shall fall at the beginning of an era of prosperity which su[r]passes the wildest dreams that any other nation ever indulged in & if we are but wise we shall have the world in our hands & an empire more widely extended over it than Rome ever possessed.

Dont laugh at me. I only write so to you & as I grow older gain at least the wisdom to keep my opinions to myself.

All send love. Ever your affectionate daughter, Anna C. Clemson.

ALS in ScCleA.

From Jos[eph] Johnson and Others

Charleston, S.C., 22d December, 1849

Sir: The undersigned, Citizens of South-Carolina, are the Heirs or Legal Representatives of Merchants and Underwriters of Charleston, who were sufferers by the French Spoliations prior to the year 1801.

The very first petition ever presented to Congress on the subject, was from the Merchants of Charleston, so early as the year 1802; and in the same year, Mr. Robert Marion, then a Representative in Congress from South-Carolina, was the Chairman of a Committee which made a favorable report on the subject.

We beseech you, as Guardians of the Interests of your Constituents, to use your utmost endeavors to effect the speedy and full settlement of these our Claims on the General Government.

Craving reference to the enclosed Documents [*not found*], We remain, most respectfully, Your obedient servants, Jos. Johnson for

John Fabre and Fabre & Price, A.M.H. Cox for Tunoro[?] & Cox p. Jos. Johnson, Robert L. Stewart for the Heirs of Tho. Stewart, William B. Heriot for the Representatives of B. & J. Booth, Saml. Alexander, for Estate of John Everingham, Jas. E. Smith for Est. Josiah Smith, H.D. Alexander for Est. David Alexander, Geo. H. Ingraham for self & others, Jane Muir Administratrix of William Muir, Thos. Morris for Self & other heirs of Thos. Morris, R.C. Geyer for self & other heirs of John Geyer, O.L. Dobson one of the Heirs of Daniel OHara & Son and Charles OHara, Jno. Glen for the heirs of Chs. Crowly one of the firm of Cross & Crowly, Ann H. Marsh Daughter of Captain Charles Bishop, Chs. Edmondston Exor. of James Gordon, E.J. Walker for self and heirs of John Teasdall, C.A. Groning for self & heirs of Lewis Groning, Wm. Booth, Chief Mate of the Ship Rainbow of Charleston when captured in 1797, John Woddrop Exor. of John Woddrop dec[ease]d.

PDS in ScU-SC, John C. Calhoun Papers. NOTE: On 1/8/1850, Calhoun presented to the Senate "a memorial of the heirs of James Cox, deceased, asking indemnity for French spoliations prior to 1800; which was ordered to lie on the table." (*Congressional Globe*, 31st Cong., 1st Sess., p. 119.)

To DUFF GREEN, [Dalton, Ga.?]

Washington, 29th Dec[embe]r 1849
Dear Sir, I received your note & your article on the abolition movement. The latter discloses some important facts.

I am glad to see that the Committee made so favourable a report in reference to your rail road. I do hope you may succeed with it to the utmost extent of your hope.

We have done as yet little. The [Presidential] Message is regard[ed] as affording conclusive evidence that the administration [of Zachary Taylor] has taken sides with the North, on all questions, against the South.

The session will be ardeous & stormy. The South is more united & firm on the great issue between it & the North, than I have ever known it to be. The prevailing impression is that the time for action has come, & that nothing but concert & Union among the Southern States can save *the* Union if it is to be saved, or themselves, if it is not to be saved.

Say to Andrew [Pickens Calhoun] that I have not heard from him since we parted in Charleston, & that I wrote him shortly after my arrival here. Say also, that from all I can hear cotton will rise probably to 15 cents, & that he must hold on. With kind regards to Mrs. [Lucretia Maria Edwards] Green and such portions of your family as may be with you I remain yours truly, J.C. Calhoun.

ALS in NcU, Duff Green Papers (published microfilm, roll 9, frames 828–831).

To [ANNA MARIA CALHOUN] CLEMSON, [Brussels]

Washington, 31st Dec[embe]r, 1849

My dear Daughter: Not long after my arrival here I wrote to Mr. [Thomas G.] Clemson and, among other things, requested him to say I would write to you shortly. I hope he received my letter.

If I have not written to you as frequently as formerly, be assured that it has not been caused by any abatement of affection towards you. It is to be attributed simply to the fact that I have been overburthened with writing—a species of labor, which you know, I have ever been especially averse to. I wrote during the recess between 400 and 500 pages of foolscap, besides carrying on an extensive correspondence, which I could not avoid. Under so heavy a pressure I left the correspondence with you almost exclusively to your Mother [Floride Colhoun Calhoun], [Martha] Cornelia [Calhoun] and your brothers. The two former, I know, have been very punctual and full in their communications.

Since my arrival here I have allotted most of my spare time to preparing my manuscript for the press. The discourse, or disquisition, (for I have not yet named it) on Government is finished, and is now copying. It is preliminary to the discourse on the Constitution and Government of the United States. That is much more voluminous. The rough draft is finished. I propose to devote my spare time during the session to preparing it, also, for the press, and hope to have it done and copied before Congress adjourns. I do not know whether I shall put it to press as soon as finished, or not; but I wish to have it off my hands and ready for publication whenever I shall judge it advisable to publish. I trust when published they will do me no discredit, and that they will do much to explode errors and cast light on the subjects of which they treat.

I am truly happy to learn that you are all well, and that the children are growing so finely. They must be a source of great happiness to you. I know not any employment more useful and honorable than that of a wife and a mother superintending her household and the education of her children. By education I mean something far beyond what is to be derived from books. I feel assured that you are discharging faithfully these duties and trust you will find your reward in the character and conduct of your two very promising children when they come to act their part in life.

Your Mother and sister have, I suppose, informed you that the portraits to which you referred in your letter to me were long since received and that they are greatly admired. I think them excellent— good likenesses and well painted. Many think Calhoun's [John Calhoun Clemson] is the best likeness; but I find it difficult to decide which is the best.

I am glad to learn that the same hand that painted yours and the children's has succeeded so well in executing the likeness of myself. I understood from Mr. Henry Gourdin that he had made arrangements to get a portrait of me painted by the Artist [Eugenius Frans DeBlock?] who painted you, and that it would be in Washington this winter. I had supposed it was the likeness to which you referred, but conclude that it is another taken by the same artist.

The question between North and South is daily becoming more and more menacing. It is difficult to say where it is to end. The South is more roused and united than I ever knew it to be; and I trust that we shall persist in our resistance until the restoration of all our rights, or disunion, one or the other, is the consequence. We have borne the wrongs and the insults of the North long enough. It is time they should cease.

My health continues as good as I could expect at my time of life. All were well when I last heard from home.

Give my love to Mr. Clemson and the children.

PC in Jameson, ed., *Correspondence*, pp. 776–778.

From F[RANCIS] BURT

Pendleton [S.C.,] Ja[nuar]y 3d 1850
My Dear Sir, The question of re-chartering the Bank of the State is destined to create much excitement throughout the State at the ensuing election. I should like to have your opinion on the subject not to make public but for my own satisfaction. What is the difference

between the connection with our Bank and the connection of the Federal Government with United States Bank is a question which I would particularly like to have your opinion upon. We have no news here and are going on in our usual quiet way. With esteem & regard, your friend, F. Burt.

P.S. Please send me the Congressional Globe for the last Congress.

ALS in ScU-SC, John C. Calhoun Papers. NOTE: Burt was editor of the Pendleton *Messenger*.

From PERCY WALKER

Mobile, January 3, 1850

D[ea]r Sir, Some months since, Gen[era]l [Zachary] Taylor appointed my brother John J. Walker to the Collectorship of this Port. This appointment has to be submitted to the Senate for confirmation, and I take the liberty of soliciting your support for my brother. Although a Whig, his appointment has been fully acceptable to all parties here and I have reason to know that he will be backed by the Senators from this State [William R. King and Jeremiah Clemens]. Considering their political relations toward him, I can scarcely conceive that his appointment would meet with opposition from other Senators from mere political reasons, but in order to guard against any such contingency, I have determined to appeal to you and to ask you to vote for his confirmation. When I assure you of his entire fitness for the office, you must not attribute it to fraternal affection, for ["such" *canceled*] no one here questions his qualifications.

I have received so many assurances of ["for" *canceled*] your kindly feelings toward myself that I have felt fully warranted in making this demand upon you. Your's very Respectfully, Percy Walker.

ALS in ScU-SC, John C. Calhoun Papers. NOTE: An AEU by Calhoun reads: "P. Walker. See Mr. Clemens [and] Mr. King."

To J[AMES] H. HAMMOND,
[Barnwell District, S.C.]

Washington, 4th Jan[uar]y 1850

My dear Sir, I have delayed answering your last letter until I could ["write" *interlined*] more certainly in reference to the subject to which it relates.

As far as I can judge from indications, I cannot doubt, but that the Convention at Nashville will ["be" *interlined*] well attended. The members from Virginia speak with confidence, that delegates will be ["appointed by" *interlined*] their State. The subject is now before a committee & publick sentiment, in the State & legislature, is said to be strongly in its favour. The legislature of N. Carolina does not meet this winter; but the best informed of her members speaks with confidence, that the State is roused, & that, at least, there will be a partial representation from the State. You can better judge what Georgia will do, than I can. The Alabama members say with confidence their State will appoint and the Florida that theirs will. So say the Arkansas delegation; and Mr. [Hopkins L.] Turney, Senator from Tennessee, who has just left me, feels confident, that Tennessee will. I have but little information as to what Missouri, Kentucky & Louisiana will do; but if the other[s] should act, it is not improbable they will. Even Maryland begins to wake up. Her Governor [Philip F. Thomas] has come out on the Southern side & I have little doubt the State will, from what I hear. Everything that can be done will be done here to ensure a full attendance. There is already much excitement here & it will go on increasing. The debate on the question at issue between the South & North will commence early & be warm. It is becoming a common opinion, that there is little chance ["of" *canceled*] for saving the Union. The subject is freely talked about & discussed in private circles. It is also becoming a prevalent opinion, that the South ought ["not" *interlined*] to remain in the Union, without a complete restoration of all our rights, a full recognition of our equality [in] every respect, & ample security for the future. The contest will not be limited to the territorial aspect of the question between us and them. Every question will be put in issue, & the question of the Union ["be" *interlined*] freely discussed.

It is contemplated, at the proper time, if it should be thought to be necessary, to call on the South to appoint delegates, so as to be fully represented. Georgia is an important State. You can do much

145

there, &, I hope, you will exert yourself, if it should ["be" *interlined*] necessary, to induce her to be represented at Nashville.

As to myself, I lose no opportunity, where I can act with propriety to give the great cause an impulse. I want no reward, no prominence, or even distinction. If the thing is done, I am satisfied, let it be done by whom it may. I have made it a point to throw off no one. Let us be one, is my advise [*sic*] to all parties at the South. You must not think of retiring. The time for action has come. If the South is to be saved now is the time.

The great, pressing, practical question ["of the session" *interlined*] will be on the admission of California. I regard it as worse than the Wilmot Proviso. What the latter proposes to do openly the former is intended to do covertly & fraudulently. It adds insult to injury. The debate on it will be violent and denuncia[to]ry. We may be voted down, but it will not be done without adding fuel to the flame. With great respect yours truly, J.C. Calhoun.

ALS in DLC, James Henry Hammond Papers, 17:21836–21837; PC in Jameson, ed., *Correspondence*, pp. 778–780.

From R[obert] A. Maxwell

Pendleton [S.C.,] Jan[uar]y 4th 1850
Dear Sir, Your's of the 23d Dec[embe]r is just received. I had written to you only by last mail to know whether the statement I forwarded to you a month ago had been received.

I take great pleasure in ratafying the engagement you have made in employing Judge [George M.] Bibb to attend to our case. I concur with you in the necessity and also in the selection. I have no doubt our case will be safe in his hands. We hope to hear soon of its disposal. If we gain a new trial, I shall go immediately to Mobile to prosecute the claim. I shall have strong hopes of gaining the case if we can have it tried on its merits.

I hope Judge Bibb in his argument will not spare the defendant. He will see from the facts which are admitted in the plea of Demurrer, and which may be relied on and can be most incontestibly proven, that the conduct of the defendant in the Judgement was of the most aggravated and blackest character. I cannot believe that a case so marked by crime and villainy and fraud can be sustained in the highest court of our country. I do hope they will give a just rebuke to the Circuit court at Mobile by reversing the decision. I do think the statement of the facts uncontroverted as they are, must carry conviction to the minds of the court and if Judge Bibb can get over the legal difficulties, we are sure of success. I will thank you to let me know as soon as the case is decided.

I will make arrangements in any way you may direct, to meet ["the" *interlined*] engagement with Judge Bibb either by forwarding the money or a draft. Most Respectfully Yours &c, R.A. Maxwell.

ALS in ScU-SC, John C. Calhoun Papers.

To Gov[erno]r [PHILIP F.] THOMAS, Annapolis, Md.

Washington, 5th Jan[uar]y 1850

My dear Sir, I am much obliged to you for a copy of your Message in pamphlet form. I have read it with much pleasure, especially the part in reference to the issue pending between the North & South. I rejoice, that you have put Maryland where she ought to stand. Her old connections, her affinity & her interest are all on the side of the South, & she must share the common fate, whether good or bad, ["with" *canceled and* "of" *interlined*] her sister States of that section.

The time has come, when we must meet the issue. It is forced on us, and cannot be avoided. The sperit of the States south of Maryland is up. We wish to save the Union, if it can be done consistently with our safety & honor, but if we shall find that impossible, we are resolved to save ourselves.

I do solemnly believe the most effectual way to effect both is for the South to meet in convention and tell the North pla[i]nly & directly what we intend to insist on, as our unquestionable rights, and to warn them solemnly of the consequences, if they should continue to violate them. We owe it to them & ourselves to give such warning. If it should be heeded, the Union will be saved, but if not we must take care of ourselves.

Cannot Maryland be induced to send delegates to the NashVille Convention? Her presence there would have a great effect & do much to bring the North to her senses. Truly, J.C. Calhoun.

ALS in ScU-SC, John C. Calhoun Papers.

To Capt. P[ATRICK] CALHOUN, New Orleans

Washington, 8th Jan[uar]y 1850

My dear Patrick, I am ["happy" *interlined*] to learn by your last letter and one just received from your brother Andrew [Pickens Calhoun], written since his return home from his visit to you, that your health is better. He thinks your disease is checked, & that you will recover with time and care, & that your recovery would be expedited by leav[in]g N. Orleans, and being with those who will feel an interest in you & take care of you, & where you can take exercise. He thinks the fresh air of the country would benefit you, and says that you promised him to go to the Cane brake [in Ala.] in January.

I hope, my dear son, that you will fulfill your promise. I am sure, it will be of great service to you, & I will not be [*sic*] cease to be uneasy about you, until I hear you are with him or the family at home. Your brother speaks in the kindest terms of you, & he & his family would nurse you with the greatest care. It is a better climate for you, than Pendleton during the winter. In the spring, when the weather grows warm, you can join the family at Fort Hill, where all will be happy to see, & take care of you. In the meane time, if there should be any particular service in the army, which you would prefer to your position in your regiment, let me know, & I will endeavour to obtain it for you, through my friends here. In making a selection regard ought to be had to a complete restoration of your health. For that purpose, should you be sufficiently restored to be bear [*sic*] the fatigue next summer, it seems to me to be detailed and detached from your regiment on some one of the recognizances or surveys, which will ["be" *canceled*] probably be ordered to be made of the several projected rail road routes to the Pacifick, would be of great service towards a complete restoration of your health & strength. Among them a survey will probably be ordered from Red River, some where just below the raft to the Passo del Norte. If so, I should think to be detailed for that service would suit you well. The route would pass through a high & dry country & fine climate. Let me know your wishes early as you can make up your mind. If it would be desirable, on the restoration of your health, I doubt not, I can get you detailed for the service, should the survey be made.

I had a letter from home a few days ago. All were well. Your mother [Floride Colhoun Calhoun] made anxious enquiry about you & said she had just written to you.

My health continues quite good. The session will be a warm &

148

stormy one. It will probably be protracted until late in the summer. Your affectionate father, J.C. Calhoun.

ALS in ScU-SC, John C. Calhoun Papers.

From Tho[ma]s G. Clemson

Brussels, January 8th 1850

My dear Sir, Your favour dated Dec. 8th came duly to hand and would have been answered immediately, would it have availed, but as the steamers ceased running weekly a letter would not have reached you sooner than this had it been written two weeks earlier.

We were delighted to hear that your health was so good and of the resolve to take care of yourself & not be overworked; however robust you may be at your age, you can not expect to draw upon your recuperative energies as formerly. However sad it may be such is life and we must submit or suffer.

The actual political position of the United States is certainly a very anomalous one. Had the South been true to itself, long since, the present crisis would not have occured. My only fear is that she will give way & suffer the breach to be filled with mud, or make some momentary compromise, that will be set aside at the convenience of the North when they shall have greater strength or the moment lies more opportune for them to carry their views. To postpone the difficulty now will in my mind be a virtual surrender of equality.

The South has in reality been in a tributary state to the North for years, for which they may thank their want of unity. If they give way on this occasion they deserve their fate—what that will be admits of no doubt.

As far as I am able to judge, the present prosperous state of the South is entirely & solely dependent upon the momentary elevation in the price of Cotton, & this has been caused by the short crop coming in upon an exhausted stock, which was the more completely used up, than it would have been, had it not been for the great political revolutions of the last two years. My impression is that cotton will rise still higher before July next & it would not surprise me to see it reach 14 or 15 cents. If the next crop should be a fair one prices will decline again.

Here in Europe there is as much tranquility as I ever saw. Property & securities of every kind are rising rapidly and necessity has compelled every one to go to work to make up for lost time. Revolutions would appear to be at an end for some time to come & even in France the people are becoming accustomed to their new form of Government as imperfect as it may be and in spite of the intrigues & desires of those that led & lived by & under the monarchy of Louis Phillippe. The longer it last[s], the greater will be the difficulty to overthrow it.

Mr. [Francis W.] Pickens wrote me last month & made me an offer of thirty-two thousand dollars for my negroes, land[,] cotton on hand[,] stock &c as it stands. He offered me bonds or sealed notes but for reasons declined giving security or mortgage. I refused the price & terms. His price was 32,000 dols. with interest to be paid in 1854 & 1856. Tho he may be richer than it would require to make payment & of this I have no doubt, I can not in justice to myself & family place so large a part of my property in simple notes or bonds. In case of death or other eventualities there might be infinite difficulty. I answered him to the effect that in any case I must have security, & then made him several propositions. One was that I would take 34,000 dols. for the property[,] negroes[,] land[,] stock &c—or I would take $31,000 for negroes & land, & he to give me the valuation price of the other property on the place. Or I would take $31,000 for land & negroes, he to sell for me the cotton on hand & he to advertise & sell the other property at public vendue & attend to the collection of the debts for me.

Had I known what you write me of the price of negroes I would not have offered the property on those terms. However if he accepts I shall abide by the bargain. My object is to get my property into permanent investment well secured & yielding a regular interest as a means of support. When I have accomplished that I will then turn my attention to getting some employment that will yield me profit & perhaps a living. Neither the climate, the occupation or the mode of doing business in the South suit my temperament or habits. When I purchased the plantation & the negroes, I made the calculation that I should be able to stock it completely at certain prices & this I could have done, it was only about half stocked & on that account has been of no profit & if I save myself it will be from the increase of the negroes & the low prices at which they were purchased. I have had nothing but tribulation since I owned it & wish to get rid of it—which I hope the present rise will enable me to do.

Previous to the offer made me by Mr. Pickens, he wrote me that he would send Mr. [James] Vaughan there as an overseer this year & that he would (Mr. P[ickens]) attend to the selling of my crop in

Hamburg with his own & also purchase my supplies for the plantation, all of which would be an immense saving to me & I hoped that matters would progress better than they have heretofore done, at least my mind was set at ease by the offer, which I consider very kind on the part of Mr. Pickens. So that whether he purchases or not I am partially relieved from anxiety.

This arrangement with Mr. Pickens makes it unnecessary for me to employ a factor in Charleston. Mr. Pickens wrote me of the decease of Mr. [John Ewing] Bonneau & I begged him to procure a statement of my accounts with Mr. B[onneau]'s estate. Also to take charge of the bond from yourself & Andrew [Pickens] Calhoun & keep it for me. There is a small balance due me in the hands or the executors of Mr. Bonneau but not much.

The promise which you now make of paying the interest due me on the bond amounting to $1120 is a great relief to me and will put me at my ease in many respects. I will write to James Ed[ward] Boisseau of New York & give him directions what to do with it. I wish him to invest it for me, so that I can realise the amount immediately to fall back on it in case of emergency. You will oblige me to communicate with Mr. Boisseau & place the money to his credit, for me, when he can draw on Charleston for the sum. I shall write him on the subject by this mail and tell him that I have requested you to place the sum of $1120 to his credit for me. This will be the most simple mode of arranging the matter that occurs to me at this time.

I have never been able to ascertain any thing from Messrs. [J.B.] Crocket[t] & [D.C.] Briggs of St. Louis in reference to the suit with [Lewis F.] Linn & Co. in the affair of the mine La Motte estate. Would you have the goodness to request your colleague of the Senate Mr. [David R.] Atchison to write to some of his friends in St. Louis & request them to call in person on Crockett & ascertain the result, so that I may learn something on the subject. This will be a mode of getting at the truth. I fear there has been foul play there.

[Edward A.] Hannegan [U.S. Minister to Prussia] will shortly leave for the United States. His baggage was sent to Antwerp the other day & he expects to follow. He never should have come to Europe. He has done himself no credit and is another instance of the futility of sending such men to Europe in public capacity. Judging from what I saw of him here he has been drunk ever since he left the U.S. and is about as unfit for the place as a bear. He speaks of you in very kind terms & is one of your political friends.

We are in the midst of a very severe winter for this climate. I never saw so much snow or it continue so long upon the ground.

Notwithstanding the severity of the winter there is much less apparent misery than I have heretofore witnessed. It is explained by the ravages of the Cholera. Last year all the poor & infirm from low living were victims to that pestilence.

Anna [Maria Calhoun Clemson] & the children [John Calhoun Clemson and Floride Elizabeth Clemson] are all well. The latter are improving very sensibly & all join me in love. From your affectionate son, Thos. G. Clemson.

ALS in ScCleA.

REMARKS ON VERMONT ANTISLAVERY RESOLUTIONS

[In the Senate, January 8, 1850]
[*William Upham of Vt. introduced and asked for the printing of resolutions from the legislature of that State opposing the "extension" of slavery and asking that slavery be "excluded" from the District of Columbia. A motion to table the printing motion provoked a long procedural debate and a negative vote of 11 to 46.*]

Mr. Calhoun. I rise simply to explain my [pro] vote upon the motion to lay upon the table the motion to print these resolutions. I did it solely in courtesy to the Senator [Henry Clay] who has the floor upon the question [of suspending diplomatic relations with Austria] left unfinished yesterday. It has been usual, when the hour of adjournment arrives, for the Senator who may have obtained the floor, to yield to the motion to adjourn, upon the assurance that he shall have the floor upon the following day; and I know that it is always unpleasant for a Senator who has thus obtained the floor, and expects to address the Senate, to have the debate procrastinated. I shall therefore oppose further debate upon this, until that other matter has been disposed of.

Mr. President, I intended to say not a word upon this subject; but as I am up, I feel it due to myself and to the occasion to express my simple sentiment upon this matter. I have long labored faithfully—faithfully—to repress the encroachment of the North. At the commencement I saw where it would end and must end; and I despair of ever seeing it arrested in Congress. It will go to its end; for gentlemen have already yielded to the curent of the North, which they admit here that they cannot resist. Sir, what the South will do is not for me to say. They will meet it, in my opinion, as it ought to be met. [*After further discussion, the Senate passed on to other matters without a decision.*]

From *Congressional Globe,* 31st Cong., 1st Sess., p. 123. Also printed in the Washington, D.C., *Daily Union,* January 9, 1850, p. 1; the Charleston, S.C., *Mercury,* January 12, 1850, p. 2. Variants in the Washington, D.C., *Daily National Intelligencer,* January 9, 1850, p. 1; the Alexandria, Va., *Gazette and Virginia Advertiser,* January 9, 1850, p. 3; the Baltimore, Md., *Sun,* January 9, 1850, p. 4; the Philadelphia, Pa., *Pennsylvania Freeman,* January 10, 1850, p. 3.

REMARKS ON FRENCH SPOLIATIONS

[In the Senate, January 9, 1850]
[*Truman Smith of Conn. presented two memorials asking indemnity for French spoliations prior to 1800. William R. King of Ala. supported a motion to refer the documents to a select committee.*]

Mr. Calhoun. Mr. President, I think the very reasons assigned by the chairman of the Committee on Foreign Relations [King] for the course he recommends, are the very reasons why this subject should not go to a select committee. It has been often examined, often reported upon, and elaborately reported upon. No subject is better understood. No further inquiry is to be made upon it, as there are no new facts to be presented for investigation. I think the rule is a very bad one to make exceptions to the regular practice; and all subjects should be referred to standing committees, unless very strong and urgent reasons are assigned for the opposite course.

From the Washington, D.C., *Daily Union,* January 10, 1850, p. 1. Variant in the Washington, D.C., *Daily National Intelligencer,* January 10, 1850, p. 2; the Alexandria, Va., *Gazette and Virginia Advertiser,* January 11, 1850, p. 2; *Congressional Globe,* 31st Cong., 1st Sess., p. 127. NOTE: After further discussion the Senate agreed to the reference to a select committee.

REMARKS ON THE VICE-PRESIDENT'S CASTING VOTE

[In the Senate, January 9, 1850]
[*The question was whether the Vice-President was entitled to break a tie in the election of the Senate Chaplain, or whether his casting vote was limited to legislation.*]

Mr. Calhoun was under the impression that the Vice President has the right to vote in this case.

[*In further discussion, Henry Clay supported Calhoun's position.*]

Mr. Calhoun. As far as the practice of the Senate is concerned, the senator behind me [William R. King] is certainly mistaken, in regard to the power of the Vice President to give a casting vote upon executive appointments. When I presided over this body, I deem it my duty to say, I voted on several occasions upon nominations, and one a celebrated case, the nomination of Mr. [Martin] Van Buren, and on two or three other occasions.

From the Washington, D.C., *Daily Union*, January 10, 1850, p. 2. Variant in the Washington, D.C., *Daily National Intelligencer*, January 10, 1850, p. 2; the Alexandria, Va., *Gazette and Virginia Advertiser*, January 11, 1850, p. 2; the Richmond, Va., *Richmond Whig and Public Advertiser*, January 15, 1850, p. 4; *Congressional Globe*, 31st Cong., 1st Sess., p. 128. NOTE: After further discussion, Calhoun's position was sustained.

To J[OHN] R[AVEN] MATHEW[E]S, Charleston

Washington, 10th Jan[uar]y 1850

My dear Sir, The interest on the [Ann Mathewes] Ioor bond is due on the 1st of March, at which time we shall pay the principal & interest. We have not yet sold our cotton crop & as ours (with others in the west), is cut very short, we are holding back for a higher price in the spring. My son [Andrew Pickens Calhoun] is of the opinion the crop will not exceed 2,000,000 & that it may fall 100,000 or 200,000 below. If such should be the case there must be a considerable advance on the present price.

But whether we shall sell or not between now & March, we will at all events be prepared to take up the bond by the 1st March.

It would [be] more convenient for us to pay what is due in Charleston & I hope arrangements will be made to have the bond there & a person authorised to receive what is due & to deliver up the bond on payment.

Let me know in your next what arrangement will be made, so that I may inform my son in time.

The questions connected with the issue between North & South are the all absorbing topicks here, although the party news papers make little allusion to them. Indeed their editors care for nothing but to live on the government. Disunion is freely talked of in every circle, & many avow themselves to be disunionists, & a still greater number say that they can see no other alternative. The discussion will be warm in both Houses. Yours truly, J.C. Calhoun.

ALS in ScU-SC, John C. Calhoun Papers.

From Jos[eph] J. Singleton

Dahlonega [Ga.,] 10 Jan[uar]y 1850

My Dear Sir, In defiance of all my efforts, I find that I will have to sell about thirty negroes to meet my unfortunate gold mine purchases, and believing that it may be in your power to render me some service in such sale, I take the liberty of asking that favour of you. I would greatly prefer selling all together as they are in families, and would thereby become more suddenly relieved of the usual mortification in such cases. Enclosed you will find a list [*not found*] of ages both male & female, in seperate collums. If you should not want them yourself, you will have an opportunity, (if it ["is" *interlined*] not too much trouble to you) of making enquiry of members from the different Southern States, both as regards their inclination to purchase, as well as the probable value of such property in their respective States. Should it be in your power sir, to render me any assistance in such a sale, it will be most thankfully received, and I hope, ever duly appreciated.

There has been no return from your mine since my last letter to you; in fact the winter has been so excessively wet, that there has been nothing done in any kind of business in this part of the country, much more that of gold digging.

If I only could be so fortunate (which I do not expect) as to blunder upon one of those fat offices in Caliafornia as recommended by Gen[era]l [Zachary] Taylor in his Message, it would in all probability superceed the disagreeable necessity of selling my negroes.

I most *sincerely* hope sir, that the eyes of the American people are now so widely opened, that they will be enabled to place that kind of estimate upon the value of your long and continued councils, which will amount to something, more than an ordinary winding up of a useful life, ever devoted to the practice, and valuable theory of a republican form of Government, the best of all legacies. I am happy to believe that Georgia will do her part.

Do let me hear from you, consistant with your convenience. I have the honor [of] being sincerely yours &C, Jos. J. Singleton.

ALS in ScU-SC, John C. Calhoun Papers.

To James Ed[ward] Calhoun, Jun[io]r, [Fort Hill]

Washington, 11th Jan[uar]y 1850

My dear James, I received your letter with its enclosures a few days since, and promptly addressed a note to the secretary of war [George W. Crawford] in reference to the application of prof[esso]r [Matthew J.] Williams [of South Carolina College]. I hope he may succeed.

I am gratified, that you have received my admonitions, as you have, relative to your expenditures. If you should profit by them, I shall not regret the cause, which occasioned them, as great as has been the embarrassment to which ["the" *canceled*] it has subject[ed] me. Economy is one of the virtues. It is necessary to independence; and without that a man is little better than a slave. Never expend without seeing the means of meeting it, ought to be the maxim of every man, who desires to maintain his dignity & independence.

As there is now a fair prospect, that the price of cotton will continue up, for some time, I trust I shall be able with economy on your part & the rest of the family to free my estate of its incumberance, which would leave ample income to meet liberally all the wants of the family. The pinch with me will be to meet this years expense & the out standing claims of the last, which are heavy.

I trust you will pursue your studies with vigour. Devote the year to reading elevating books. You can occasionally make a visit to Anderson to see & converse with Gen[era]l [Joseph N.] Whitner. I have no doubt, but Mr. [Francis] Burt, who has a good understanding, will take pleasure, should you apply to him, to explain any point you may not fully understand, or to council you, as to the books, you ought to read. If you will write me on any point you desire instruction, I shall always find leisure to give it. When I come home, I shall take the superintendence of your studies myself.

We have little new beyond what you will see in the papers. I enclose the [Washington] Union of this morning in a seperate paper, which contains the speech of Mr. [Jeremiah] Clemens of Alabama, a new member [of the Senate] of great promise. It gave him much reputation.

When you next write give me an account of what you have read & how you are pleased with [William] Bla[c]kston[e].

Give my love to all the family, & let me know how things are go-[ing] on, on the plantation. Your affectionate father, J.C. Calhoun.

ALS in NcD, John C. Calhoun Papers.

To R[ICHARD] F. SIMPSON, [Pendleton, S.C.]

Washington, 11th Jan. 1850

My Dear Sir: I deeply regret to learn, that there is danger that the Bank [of the State of South Carolina] question will cause division and distraction in our District, in consequence of a division of opinion among its delegates [in the General Assembly]. Should such be the case, it would be unfortunate, indeed, at this time, when the united energy of all the South is required to save us from the greatest of calamities. The time has come, when, if we are ever to assert our rights as members of the Union, it must now be done; and then, if we should fail to cause the North to respect and regard them, we must take their protection in our own hands and keeping. To draw off the attention of our State at this time, by subordinate local questions, is to jeopardize our safety and that of the whole South. It must not be forgotten, that we are in the van of the great controversy with the North, and that whatever is calculated to distract and weaken us, will weaken the entire effort of the South. The abolitionists know this, and hence their efforts to do it by circulating documents so freely and at such great expense, among us, to produce that effect.

Entertaining these views, I do hope that the candidates will come to some understanding to leave all questions in reference to the Bank out of the approaching election.

As to the question of the expediency of the Bank, or whether it should be rechartered, I do not feel called on to give an opinion. Although opposed on principle to all Banks of issues, I have, as one of the Representatives of the people of Carolina in their federal character, at all times, abstained from interfering with the local Banks of the State. I have ever left all questions in relation to them to be determined by those, who for the time, are charged with the government of the State; not doubting but that time and experience would prove the correctness of the views I took on the subject of banking.

But while I am on principle opposed to Banks of issue, I have always been aware of the great difficulty and the extreme caution that is necessary to wind up Banks, where they have long existed. With the view to overcome this difficulty, and to avoid the embarrassment and distress incident to winding up, I proposed when the charter of the late Bank of the United States was about to expire, to re-charter it for twelve years, with such provisions as would compel it to unwind itself to a great extent. It is now admitted by the well informed, that if what I then proposed had been adopted, the great catastrophe of 1837 would have been averted. Thinking as I do, I am decidedly of the opinion, that the Bank of the State, if not re-chartered, should be allowed ample time and means to wind up gradually and cautiously. I, in addition, doubt the propriety of deciding the question whether it should be re-chartered or not, at this time. Should the South be bound, as I think it probable she will be, to take her defence into her own hands, we may need all the aid and credit which the banking system of the State will be able to afford, in the undisturbed possession of their means, and the unabated confidence of the public in them. How the question can best be kept out of the canvass, you and other friends in the District can best determine. The press could do much towards it, by showing how adverse the agitation would be to the great and vital question now agitating the State and the whole South, and by making an appeal to the patriotic to interfere to prevent it. The candidates might come to an understanding to leave it out of the issue, and public meetings might pass resolutions condemnatory of all agitation on the subject for the present.

I had a letter from Mr. [Francis] Burt on the same subject as yours, and, as you are on intimate terms with him, and as I am much engaged, I must request you to consider this letter addressed to him as well as you. I have no objection to its being shown to any friend you or he may desire, or using its contents freely, but without publishing.

I continue to enjoy good health, fully as much so as when I left home.

The South is more firm and better united than ever. The session will be stormy. Disunion is a common topic of discussion in all circles. Truly, J.C. Calhoun.

PC in the Pendleton, S.C., *Messenger*, May 17, 1850, p. 2. Also printed in the Sumter, S.C., *Banner*, May 22, 1850, p. 2; the Charleston, S.C., *Mercury*, May 23, 1850, p. 2; the Camden, S.C., *Journal*, May 28, 1850, p. 2; the Edgefield, S.C., *Advertiser*, May 29, 1850, p. 2; the Spartanburg, S.C., *Spartan*, May 30, 1850, p. 2; the Pickens, S.C., *Keowee Courier*, May 31, 1850, p. 1. NOTE: As a preamble to this letter, Francis Burt, editor of the *Messenger*, printed "A Word with the Pendleton Messenger," an article from the Columbia *Palmetto State Banner* alluding to the existence of Calhoun's letter and calling upon the recipients to make it public because "its appearance *now* might do infinite good in preventing a hot and angry contest, which our relations with the Federal Government and the fanatics render it highly desirable to avoid." In response Burt described the circumstances of his and Simpson's writing and Calhoun's response. "With that propriety which always marked his conduct, and which at all times made him studiously avoid thrusting his opinions before the people, upon questions not in the line of his duty, he requested that this letter should not be published; but as he has gone from us, and no charge of dictation or improper interference can now be made, we think the reason for withholding it from the public has passed away, and accordingly comply with the request of the 'Banner.'"

To ANDREW PICKENS CALHOUN, [Marengo County, Ala.]

Washington, 12th Jan[uar]y 1850
My dear Andrew, . . . The issue between the South and the North is the all absorbing subject here, although one would not think so who would judge from the party Organs here. They keep silent in the hope of giving such prominence to mere party issues, as to divert the publick mind from the higher questions and issues. They see in the latter a power sufficient to brake up the old party organization, and with it, the spoils system. The Southern members are more determined and bold than I ever saw them. Many avow themselves to be disunionists, and a still greater number admit, that there is little hope of any remedy short of it. In the mean time the North show no disposition to desist from aggression. They now begin to claim the right to abolish slavery in all the old States, that is those who were original members, when the Constitution was adopted. The Session will be stormy, but I hope, before it ends, a final and decisive issue will be made up with the North. There is no time to loose [*sic*].

Give my love to Margeret [*sic*; Margaret Green Calhoun] and all the children. Kiss them for their grandfather.

PEx in Jameson, ed., *Correspondence*, p. 780.

From GEO[RGE] W. CRAWFORD

War Department, Washington, Jan[uar]y 12th 1850
Dear Sir, Yours of yesterday, requesting the appointment of Professor [Matthew J.] Williams of the College of South Carolina, a "Visiter" to West Point, is received, and at the proper time will be submitted to the President [Zachary Taylor] for his consideration. When the decision is made, I will take pleasure in letting you know the result. I have the honor to be, Very respectfully, Your Ob[edien]t Serv[ant], Geo. W. Crawford, Secretary of War.

FC in DNA, RG 107 (Secretary of War), Letters Sent Relating to Military Affairs, 1800–1889, 30:14 (M-6:30).

REMARKS ON THE EXPENSE OF COLLECTING THE REVENUE

[In the Senate, January 14, 1850]
Mr. Calhoun. One of the members of the Committee on Finance has furnished me with a statement of the revenue from imports, and the cost of collection for the years 1821 and 1849, which I hold in my hand, and which I will state. The revenue of the former year amounted in round numbers to $15,115,000, and the expense of collection to $693,000; that of the latter to $31,500,000, and the expense of collection to $2,700,000.

This statement, of itself, is sufficient to prove that there is something wrong. The expense has increased more than 200 per cent. during the interval between the two periods. I admit that a portion of this increase may be attributed to the increased number of ports of collection, and some other causes; but whatever increase may be attributed to them in increasing the rate percentum of collection is more than made up by the increased amount collected in 1849, compared to 1821. It is more than double; and all know a large revenue, all other circumstances being equal, can be collected for a less rate per centum than a small. Taking every circumstance into consideration, the rate per centum ought, instead of being greater, to be less, in consequence of the increased amount collected. It ought not to exceed $1,500,000, and might be reduced to $1,200,000 with good management and proper economy.

I ought to know something of the revenue and its collection in 1821. I was then a member of Mr. Monroe's administration. There was then as little fraud on the revenue from smuggling or other causes, as cheap and simple as were the laws and mode of collection, as at present.

Something certainly ought to be done to reduce the present enormous expense of collecting the revenue; but I can tell the Senators, from the experience I have had in reference to the reduction of expense, that nothing can be done without the hearty coöperation of the head of the Treasury Department. Little can be done by law. The proposed remedy by specific appropriations will prove a nullity. The head of the department must point out the remedy, and make the application, and call on Congress for any aid he may require. It is only thus it can ever be accomplished. I speak from experience. I trust it will not be regarded as egotism on my part, when I say that I thoroughly reformed the War Department and its abuses when I had the charge of it. I found the expense of the army to be $4,000,000 annually, and I reduced it in three years to about $2,700,000, simply by administration, and that without curtailing its usual supplies.

But, Mr. President, I have no hope of reform or diminution of expenditures. Of all tasks, the reform of old abuses in the expense of the Government is the most difficult. The vast increase of the expense of collecting the revenue has created a large and powerful interest to uphold it. That interest will be opposed to all reduction. But that is not the worst. There is a still larger and more powerful interest, forming in part a majority of the whole country, who are interested in keeping up the present duties on imports. The higher the duties the better for them. They never will enlist in aid of reducing the expense of this Government or correcting its abuses, because that would lead to the reduction of the duties. I have long seen and struggled against the evil, but have utterly failed to remedy it. It will continue and go on, and become worse and worse until it will corrupt and ruin the Government.

From *Congressional Globe*, 31st Cong., 1st Sess., pp. 154–155. Also printed in the Washington, D.C., *Daily National Intelligencer*, January 15, 1850, p. 3; the Washington, D.C., *Daily Union*, January 15, 1850, p. 2.

From J[AMES] L[AWRENCE] CALHOUN

House of Representatives, Jackson [Miss.]
January the 15th 1850

My Dear Uncle, The legislature has bin in session now some ten days[.] nothing of importance has taken place as yet[.] a special message was received from the Governor [John A. Quitman] transmitting sundry resolutions of both houses of the South Carolina legislature ["of" *canceled*] in relation to the action of the State Southern Convention of Mississippi all of which wer[e] refer[r]ed to the Committee on State and federal relations[.] 500 ["coppys"(?) *canceled*] copies of the proceedings of the State Convention had at Jackson last October wer[e] orderdered [*sic*] to be printed & sent to the Governors of the different States to be by them distributed to the members of their respective Legislatures[.] I sent by the mail the inaugural of his Ex[cel]lency Governor Quitman which I hope you will rece[i]ve[.] I would pleased to hear from you at your convienance[.] any docu[ments] you ma[y] think proper to send will be thankful[l]y rece[ived.] I am dear Sir your devoted Relation &, J.L. Calhoun.

P.S. There is no do[u]bt I think of the election of Col. [Jefferson] Davis again to the Senate Though he has strong opposition from the north[.] J[acob] Thompson will be a candidate from that Section[?]—I will write again as soon as the Election is over[.] J.L.C.

ALS in ScCleA. NOTE: Quitman's inaugural address was dated 1/10/1850 and is printed in J.F.H. Claiborne, *Life and Correspondence of John A. Quitman* (New York: Harper & Brothers, 1860), 2:21–25.

From BOLLING HALL

Montgomery [Ala.,] Jan. 15th 1850

Dear sir, I trust that you will pardon the trouble I may give in troubling you with this letter, on account of the importance of the subject and permit me to say that though personally unknown I trust to a hereditary kindness for securing your favorable attention.

I am one of the Committee on Federal Relations on the part of the House of Representatives of this State & have had the Subject of Slavery earnestly under consideration. I am disposed to take the strongest possible Southern ground, but find much difficulty in disposing of the Questions arising out of the peculiar position of California and it is for the purpose of availing myself of your wisdom that I now ask of you what action the State of Alabama can take on this subject that will produce practical results in protecting our rights and equality.

I would likewise ask of you *generally*, what action ["(State)" *interlined*] ought to be had on that subject? What are our present prospects and what will be the result of the anti slavery movements? and how long before a decisive issue is made?

The Committee will certainly report resolutions requiring the Governor to call a convention of the State in case the Wilmot Proviso ["or any kindred measure" *interlined*] should be passed or Slavery abolished in the District of Columbia or any interference with the internal Slave trade. And I believe that I may say that we are prepared for a dissolution of the Union in the last resort. Y[ou]rs with great Respect, Bolling Hall.

ALS in ScU-SC, John C. Calhoun Papers. NOTE: The writer's "trust to a hereditary kindness" rested on the fact that he was the son of Bolling Hall, Representative from Ga. 1811–1817, a friend of Calhoun's in the House of Representatives. The younger Hall was born in 1813 and died in 1866 of wounds received in Confederate service.

From H[ERSCHEL] V. JOHNSON

Milledgeville Ga., Jan[uar]y 19th 1850

My Dear Sir: I have learned to day, from the Chairman, that our joint Com[mit]t[ee] on the state of the Republic have unanimously agreed to report resolutions for the action of our Legislature, endorsing those of Miss. & providing for Georgia to be represented in the Nashville Convention. I believe, beyond doubt, they will be passed. This will place Georgia where she ought to stand, side by side with Miss. & S. Carolina & the Old Dominion.

But I cannot dispel from my mind the most gloomy forebodings for the future. I believe now, as I have always believed, that California will be admitted, at the present session of Congress, And that too by the aid of Southern votes. It is well understood here, that Messrs. [Robert] Toombs and [Alexander H.] Stephens advocate that policy; and I presume that Mr. Speaker [Howell] Cobb, is, as he was at the last session, favourable to it. This of course will utterly emasculate the moral power of the State, either in or out of a Southern Convention; and if other members from other Southern States should vote for admission, it will render such a *Convention* utterly impotent. If California were a small State and its admission with the slavery restriction would settle the question *for ever*, I would, for the sake of the Union, cheerfully yield. But such is not the case. It is large enough for six, as large of [*sic*; as] Georgia; and in the course of time will be divided & subdivided[,] all claiming admittance. The same is true of Oregon. Who then, is so blind as not to see, that at no distant day the free States of the Confederacy will obtain the requisite majority in Congress to change the Constitution to suit their purposes. But will the admission silence the fanatics as to the District [of Columbia]? Will it lead to a repeal of State laws obstructing the reception of fugitives? No, no man pretends that it will. Then, is it not amazing, that any Southern man will vote for admission! I ver[il]y believe if this take[s] place, by the aid of Southern votes, that we may give up the contest and submit to our doom of degradation. If sustained by Southern votes in Cong. it will divide us at home, *& division is submission.* Do drop me a line & tell me what you think is the prospect of admission—this is the great issue. Y[ou]rs truly &c, H.V. Johnson.

FC in NcD, Herschel V. Johnson Papers, Letterpress Book, p. 66; PC in Percy Scott Flippin, ed., "Herschel V. Johnson Correspondence," *North Carolina Historical Review*, vol. IV, no. 2 (April, 1927), pp. 200–201; PEx in Flippin, *Herschel V. Johnson of Georgia*[,] *State Rights Unionist*, p. 28.

From ANNA [MARIA] C[ALHOUN] CLEMSON

Brussels, Jan: 22d 1850

My dear father, I wrote you not to write too much, but I did not tell you *not to write to me*, & yet not one word have we heard from you since you arrived in Washington. Did I not see your name in the papers, I should be uneasy, but Thank God! I see by them, that you are at your post, & doing well. Do neglect, once in two weeks at least, some other correspondent for me. I am so far away from you, & your letters give me so much pleasure, that you might do that much for me I think.

I have been very uneasy about Patrick [Calhoun], since mother's [Floride Colhoun Calhoun's] last letter, & am looking with impatience for farther news from him. He should go home, live quietly, & recruit. I hope the strength of his excellent constitution, may at length triumph over his singular disease.

At this season of the year the mail arrives but once in two week[s], so we are without any very late letters but hope to hear in a day or two.

The long struggle for Speaker [of the U.S. House of Representatives] excited much interest in Europe, & some of those who delight in the failure of republics, began already to triumph, & were sadly disappointed, I believe, when Mr. [Howell] Cobb was elected. Was not his election, by the way, a victory on the part of the South? I considered it as very encouraging, for it seemed to me as tho' each party had determined to make the election of Speaker a test of strength, & that they all felt, that the party who triumphed in that struggle, had the greatest ultimate chance of success. That the South was then victorious seemed to me an excellent sign. I may be mistaken, for at this distance, & with the little confidence one can put in any newspaper statement, it is very difficult to judge correctly, & I am waiting with impatience, a letter from you, *to tell me what to think.*

To show you how much America is rising in position & influence, in the eyes of Europe, it would suffice to see the avidity with which news from that quarter is seized on, & published by the smallest papers. When we first came to Europe, the arrival of the steamers from America was barely mentioned in the larger journals, now *all* contain ample extracts & commentaries on the news. The King [Leopold I] has requested Mr. [Thomas G.] Clemson to send him the American papers, after he had read them, which he does, & from his conversations, the King evidently reads ["them" *interlined*] carefully. If you had been in Europe as long as I have, & knew Kings in general, & this one in particular, as well as I do, this simple circumstance would prove to you how much America has risen in the scale of nations, in the last few years.

The weather is colder, & the cold has continued longer than I have ever known it since my arrival in Europe. The ground is covered with snow, & has been for two weeks, & I see now [*sic*] reason from present appearances why it should ever melt.

With the exception of slight colds, we are all very well, & walk every day, in spite of the cold weather, but notwithstanding, I shall be delighted when the thaw, however disagreeable, commences.

The children [John Calhoun Clemson and Floride Elizabeth Clemson] are very flourishing, & as full of life & spirits as possible. They are so wild that it [is] hard to keep them at their books. They begin however to make some little progress.

It is so cold that tho' I am writing on my knee, at a few inches from the fire, my hands suffer. I do hope you have a milder winter than we have, & are enjoying good health. I do hope you take care of yourself, as I told you to. Where are you staying? Who compose your mess? If cousin Martha [Calhoun Burt] & Mr. [Armistead] Burt are with you, remember us to them, & tell cousin M[artha] I wish she would write & give me the Washington news. I shall be very glad to hear from her. If you could read french, I should perhaps have the vanity to send you a very complimentary notice of Mr. C[lemson] & myself, in one of the papers, in the description of an immense ball which was given the other day by the artists of the country, because I know you love me enough to be pleased at our praises.

I must stop & go to hear the children [recite] their lessons. They send many kisses to grandpapa.

Mr. C[lemson] joins me in love. Ever your devoted daughter, Anna C. Clemson.

ALS in ScCleA.

Memorandum [by JOHN RANDOLPH TUCKER]

[Washington, *ca.* February 1850]

Within a few weeks of the death of Mr. [John C.] Calhoun, and when he was unable to be in the Senate, Mrs. [Maria Dallas] Campbell of Philadelphia, a sister of the late Vice President George M. Dallas, and a woman of remarkable talent and deeply interested in political affairs, met me, then a young man, in the Gallery of the Senate Chamber, and asked me if I would not accompany her on a visit to Mr. Calhoun. I readily assented, for I was a great admirer of the illustrious ["Calhoun" *canceled and* "Carolinian" *interlined*] and knew him quite well considering the difference in our age and position.

Mrs. Campbell was the daughter of Hon. Alex[ander] J. Dallas, Secretary of the Treasury under Mr. [James] Madison, and during the war of 1812, Mr. Calhoun had become well acquainted in Mr. Dallas' family, and an intimacy had grown up between him and Mrs. Campbell which had lasted for nearly forty years. Her admiration for Mr. Calhoun was very great; and she had never faltered in his support during the trying period of nullification. Of all this I was well aware not only from Mrs. Campbell, but from my parents [Anne Evelina Hunter Tucker and Henry St. George Tucker], who were her intimate friends.

Mr. Calhoun was living at the time of our visit in the Old Capitol, and his room was that which is now one of the parlors of Mr. Justice [Stephen J.] Field's residence. In that room he died.

When the servant answered the bell, Mrs. Campbell sent in her name and mine to Mr. Calhoun. I heard his well known voice tell the servant to ask us in; and as we approached his open door, the tall but wasted form of Mr. Calhoun came through the door into the Hall to welcome his visitors. He met Mrs. Campbell as a loving brother would have greeted his sister, and kissed her. It was so simple and genuine a mark of warm regard, as to impress me strongly.

We entered the room. He sat in a large arm chair, and his head frequently rested upon the back of it, from weakness and exhaustion. His iron-grey hair was long, and combed back from his forehead and face, falling upon his shoulders in massive folds. His face was emaciated and pale; his features more marked than usual from the waste of disease; but there remained of his former self, those fiery, restless, and brilliant eyes, through which flashed the undying and undaunted and heroic soul of the great statesman.

In answer to the kind inquiries of his friend, Mr. Calhoun spoke cheerfully, and pleasantly. His face relaxed into smiles of gratification at seeing her; and she with affectionate solicitude laid her hand upon his arm, which was resting on his chair, in earnest inquiries about his health. It was a picture to be remembered of a pure and exalted friendship between noble minds and hearts.

She said, "Mr. Calhoun, I fear you allow yourself to become too much excited by public affairs," referring to the Compromise measures of 1850, involving the Slavery issue.

He replied, "Oh, no, not excited, only intense."

She then asked, "Can nothing be done to save the Union?"

At once all the cheerfulness of expression faded from his face, and a solemnity, which was like the gloom of doom everspread [*sic*] his countenance. His features which had relaxed during the previous conversation, became rigid and fixed. His eyes assumed that expression, so often observed in him of looking "with the mind's eye" at far-distant events, not visible to ordinary men. They had their prophetic gaze, and their solemn and awful expression reflected the convictions of his wiser Soul, and its despondency at results, which his prescience summoned before his view.

He replied, that she would remember, he had always told her, that nothing was or could be stronger than the sentiment for the Union, than the necessity the South felt for self-preservation from the menace to her social institutions.

She then interposed with this question (which and the answer to it are almost accurate, almost in the very words used—),

"But, Mr. Calhoun, can't the Missouri Compromise save the Union?"

He replied with emphasis and decision: "With my constitutional objections, I could not vote for it—but I would *acquiesce* in it to *save this Union!*"

The dying Statesman thus left his sincere testimony to his love for the Union, when ambition, and self-love had ceased to furnish motives for his opinions or his action. This incident ["reflects" *altered to* "refutes"] the oft-repeated charge that Mr. Calhoun was working for a dissolution of the Union, as a means of promoting his personal ambition. In all my intercourse with him, as in this last interview, I never heard him utter any sentiment which did not evince a devotion to the Union, and a desire for its perpetuity.

Typescript in NcU, Tucker Family Papers. NOTE: A letter of 9/8/1915 from C. Braxton Bryan enclosed this typescript to a cousin and stated that it was apparently written by [John] Ran[dolph] Tucker [at an unknown date]. In a letter of 4/14/1898, John C. Calhoun, III enclosed to R. Means Davis an account, heard from Tucker, of a conversation between Tucker and [George] Bancroft in which Bancroft accused Calhoun of being "the original secessionist" and indirectly responsible for the Civil War. Tucker gave a slightly different account of the above interview with Calhoun, upon which Bancroft supposedly replied, "I will never repeat again the charge I made against Mr. Calhoun here to-night." LS with En in ScU-SC, R. Means Davis Papers. John Randolph Tucker (1823–1897), son of Henry St. George Tucker, became a legal scholar of note, held a number of public offices including Representative from Va., 1875–1887, and was president of the American Bar Association.

To [ANDREW P.] BUTLER, "of the Senate"

Wednesday [February 6, 1850]

My dear Sir, I suppose the debate on Mr. [Henry] Clays resolutions will go on at least this week before a vote is taken on them. But should it not, as I am desireous of being heard in the course of the debate, I must request a favour of you to have them postpone[d] to some early day next week, say tuesday [February 12] by which time my strength, I think, will be sufficiently restored to enable me to speak. Truly, J.C. Calhoun.

ALS in CtY, Sterling Library, Betts Collection.

To Tho[mas] G. Clemson, [Brussels]

Washington, 6th Feb. 1850

My dear Sir, I received yours of the 8th Jan[uar]y a short time before the commencement of ["my" *interlined*] recent illness, of which I suppose the papers have informed ["you" *interlined*]. The disease was a modified case of the Pneumonia. I have been for the last week entirely free from disease; and have so far recovered my strength, as to ["be" *interlined*] enable[d] to ride out. I hope to be completely restored by the begin[ni]ng of next ["week" *interlined*] to my usual strength. The disease, I think, will leave no permanent ill effect behind. I took little medicine & lost no blood.

I would gladly make the arrangement you propose of placing the interest on our bond in Charleston to the credit of Mr. [James Edward] Boisseau for you, & to be drawn on by him. But there is a difficulty in the way, which I do not see how it is to be overcome; and that is how are we to receive credit on the bond for the interest, when it is in the hands of Col. [Francis W.] Pickens?

It it [*sic*] seems to me, that the most simple form would be, to pay the amount of interest due to Col. Pickens, as your agent, and he to remit it to Mr. Boisseau or Mr. Boisseau to draw on him for it, as you may direct. He, [that is, Pickens,] as the holder of the bond & your agent in reference to it, would be authorise[d] to credit it with the interest.

Acting under this impression, I have requested my son [Andrew Pickens Calhoun] to remit the interest to Col. Pickens, as your agent with the request to credit the bond with it, as there will not be time to hear from you, before it will be due, and to make other arrangements. I will write to him, to wait your instructions, if he has not already received them.

As soon as I resume my seat, I will speak to Mr. [David R.] Atchison [Senator from Mo.] about [J.B.] Crockett and [D.C.] Briggs, though, I regard it perfectly useless. They have been so often written to, without returning an answer, that I have lost all confidence in them.

The slavery question has at length absorbed the entire attention of Congress & the country. The excitement is on the increase. [Henry] Clay has offered, what he calls a compromise, but will get little support. I do not see how the question can be settled.

Tell Anna [Maria Calhoun Clemson], I received her letter & that I hope she has got mine written a short time before I was attacked by my late illness.

My love to her and the children [John Calhoun Clemson and Floride Elizabeth Clemson]. I often thought of them in my illness. Your affectionate father, J.C. Calhoun.

ALS in ScCleA; PEx's in Jameson, ed., *Correspondence*, pp. 780–781.

Remarks on 2/10. "This morning, some of Mr. Calhoun's friends called upon him, for the purpose of saying that the Senate would cheerfully assign to him any time that he would designate for the purpose of speaking. Mr. Calhoun replied that he felt able to speak now, but he thought it better to defer it for a few days. He did not wish, he said, to reply to any one. He desired to express his own views. He remarked that he was now satisfied that the people of the South were ahead of their leaders in movements on this subject." PC in the Charleston, S.C., *Courier*, February 14, 1850, p. 2; PC in the Camden, S.C., *Journal*, February 15, 1850, p. 3; PC in the Greenville, S.C., *Mountaineer*, February 22, 1850, p. 1.

From F[ITZ]W[ILLIAM] BYRDSALL

New [*mutilation*; York City,] Feb[ruar]y 11th 1850
Dear Sir; I have felt considerable anxiety ever since the announcement of your indisposition. Day after day I looked in all the public prints I could reach for their Telegraphic news and Washington Correspondence, in order to learn the state of your health; and when the news came that the crisis of your attack had passed over favorably, I postponed offering my congratulations untill your re-appearance in the Senate, as I did not wish to intrude upon you before the recovery of your health. But I take it for granted from the silence of the newspapers, that your recovery is no longer doubtful and therefore I take the liberty of writing to you now, because I cannot refrain from doing so, assuring you too that nothing but the apprehension of incommoding you in some way or other restrained me hitherto.

And yet I feel far more disposed to be thankful to divine Providence for your recovery than to offer you my congratulations. For the sake of great principles to which the continuation of your life is so necessary, I feel an humble sense of Gratitude to God too serious to be expressed in the forms of congratulations. No man has nobler motives to regard you above other men than I have. For years your mind has enlightened mine, and I cannot recollect a political or moral sentiment of yours that is not as a household god venerated by m[*ms. mutilated*]standing. Have I not reason to feel more personal [rega]rd than conventional proprieties would allow me to express? I have derived knowledge and instruction from you which I never found in books and I have read as much as any man of my age; and besides add to this, a voluntary act of disinterested friendship, towards one you never saw, and I repeat, have I not reason to feel more personal regard than conventional proprieties would allow me to express?

I have now to inform you that the union among Southern men is working a re-action here. The business men—the owners of real estate are alarmed and so are the holders of the various Stocks, at the prospect of dissolution of the Union. The decrease of trade—the fall of house rents and depreciation of public as well as incorporated Stocks are not pleasant contemplations to those interested therein. They begin to find out that the Southern people are in *earnest*[,] the allegations of the Abolition and Free Soil press to the contrary notwithstanding. How I do hope that the just censure of mankind will fall on the head of that political miscreant [Martin] Van Buren. And yet he is no worse (except perhaps in malicious selfishness) than [Thomas H.] Benton, [Samuel] Houston, [Henry] Clay & Co. These men are recreants from the cause of the South in order to demagogue the North. "He that is not with us is against us," that is the true rule. They do mischief with their projects of [*one or two words mutilated*]. The best way of killing them and their projects [*one or two words mutilated*; is the?] "masterly inactivity" of letting them drop down without discussion.

The South is bound by every motive sacred and dear to the heart of man to maintain intact her own social organization, for it is far preferable to that of Europe and the free States. The latter is calculated for nothing so much as the uttermost development of all the selfish properties of human nature. Every man is in competition with his fellow men, to build himself up on the ruin of others, his hand against every man and every mans hand against him, upon the dog eat dog principle. Such is the modern social system which in the cantology of the day "has fulfilled its mission," and must give way to Socialism or Revolution. The free State legislature[s] have been paving the way for the system of Association for many years, they have engrafted the principle in their institutions and when a people carry a principle into their social organization, they cannot escape carrying it out to its ultimate, except by revolution. For instance, our Rail Road companies, Banking, Insurance, manufacturing companies are all on the principle of association and what is Socialism but an extension of that principle? Now I do hold that our Southern social system is the best that ever existed whether morally or politically considered and that it rests upon moral[,] religious and political principles of the best kind. I for one as a member of a christian church will never consent to change it for the heartless, selfish, vice, misery and crime producing social system of the north. Besides, such is the intense dislike of the proletaires towards the non-producers in the free States in consequence of the wealth and luxury which they create but cannot partake or enjoy, that discontent and hatred exists to an extent scarcely imaginable. More than one man in five is a pauper either in his youth or his old age, in our northern Cities.

Yes my dear Sir, the reaction is going on pretty extensively and we have only to stand firm side by side in order to realize our Constitutional rights. Party considerations are as dust in the balance in this contest of one system of social organization trying to destroy another not necessarily antagonistic but only different. No people ever had so much at stake in any contest as we have in this against northern usurpation. It has not yet come quite home to the northern sense of feeling yet. Their interests are not yet touched. Let the wheels of Government be stopped awhile—Officials unpaid &c &c &c—No appropriations. I have been telling people here for years ["past" *interlined*] that without the South the Exports of the country would not be much, that it is to Slave labor they are indebted for all their national prosperity, rise of property[,] Cities, manufactures, &c—and now I add that dissolution of the Union will ruin their manufactures[,] lay up their ships, lessen their rents & profits & pull down their incomes and they begin to see it. I never hesitate declaring my honest conviction that secession of the Southern States would work for those ["States" *interlined*] a degree of prosperity beyond any other people that ever lived.

I hope my dear Sir that you have kind hearts and gentle hands near you. That your health may be soon renewed with greater vigor and that you may live many years to enlighten mankind in that science, which though the most important has been the least studied, namely the science of political Government, is the devotional prayer of your obliged and ob[edien]t Servant, F.W. Byrdsall.

ALS in ScU-SC, John C. Calhoun Papers. NOTE: After Calhoun's death, Byrdsall wrote to Duff Green: "It is a gratifying recollection to me that Mr. Calhoun the moment he saw it announced in the papers that Mr. [Hugh] Maxwell was appointed Collector [of Customs at New York City], wrote him a recommendatory letter in my favor as strong as could be written for any one, and that too his own voluntary self-prompted act. His letter was dated 9th June [1849] & Mr. Maxwell did not come into office until the first of July." ALS in NcU, Duff Green Papers (published microfilm, roll 10, frames 380–382).

To "Col." ANDREW P[ICKENS] CALHOUN, [Marengo County, Ala.]

Washington, Feb. [*ca.* 15,] 1850

My dear Andrew, I am happy to inform you, that I am so far recovered from my attack, that I hope to be able to resume my seat in the Senate by the end of the week.

It was a modified attack of the Pneumonia. It left me very weak, but I have so far recovered my strength as to be able to ride out when the weather is good.

Mr. [John R.] Mathew[e]s wrote me, that he would take steps to have the Joor [*sic*; Ann Mathewes Ioor] bond in Charleston by the 1st March, ready to be taken up, as soon as the amount is paid. You will of course know how to make arrangement through Mr. [Henry W.] Conner for the purpose of making payment & taking up the bond.

It is proper to state that Mr. John [S.] Lorton wrote to me on the 11th Jan[uar]y that Dr. [Ozey R.] Broyles had advanced $1900, and that he had written to Mrs. Joor that the amount would be paid on the bond according to my instructions (given before I left home) as soon as she would authorise any one to rereceive [*sic*] it. His letter was received about the time I was attacked, and I have not been able to attend to it 'till today. He has not informed me whether it has been paid & credited on the bond, but I presume from his silence it has. I wrote him today to inform me immediately, as it is possible that the bond may have been sent to Charleston under Mr. Mathew[e]'s arrangement. You had better state the facts to Mr. Mr. [*sic*] Conner, and inform him that the payment of the amount has probable [*sic*] been made, but if not to pay the whole amount of the [*sic*] & take it up. If I should hear from Mr. Lorton in time, I will write him ["(Mr. C.)" *interlined*] about it according to the state of the facts.

Mr. Lorton informs me also, that Dr. Broyles requested him to say that he expected in all March to make a farther advance of $4000, or 5000. To which of our debts should [it] be advanced, would it be advisable to apply it? To the debt due to the bank of Charleston or that to the State. It is desirable I should have your opinion in time in order to give instructions to Mr. Lorton, before the money is advanced.

173

I had a letter from Mr. [Thomas G.] Clemson about the time I was taken sick, in answer to one I wrote him after my arrival here & in which I informed him that the interest would be paid on our bond as soon as it became due, which, I think, is the 9th March. He states the amount of interest that will be due at the end of the year ["at" *canceled*] to be $1120; and appears very well satisfied with the arrangement. He writes me that the bond will be placed in the Hands of Col. [Francis W.] Pickens, who it seems has made an offer for his place & negroes. I will write to him if it is in his custody & inform you in time. If it is, the ["check amount of the in" *canceled*] check for the interest will have to be remitted to him.

Mr. Leroy Wiley whom, I believe you know, spent an hour ["to" *canceled*] with me ["yesterday" *interlined*] on his way from the West to New York. He is a large cotton planter & a Savannah[?] merchant, and has attended much to the subject of cotton. He estimates the crop at 1,9000 [*sic*], and is confident the price will rise to 16 cents by the 1st May. I do not think his calculation is extravagant.

Where is Patrick [Calhoun]? I have not heard from him since you left him at New Orleans. I hope he is with you.

I hope you all continue to enjoy good health.

My love to all. Your affectionate father, J.C. Calhoun.

ALS owned by Mrs. Lorton Lewis. NOTE: Calhoun's handwriting in this letter is not quite normal, due doubtless to his illness or from writing in bed.

To J[AMES] H. HAMMOND, [Barnwell District, S.C.]

Washington, 16th Feb: 1850

My dear Sir, It affords me much pleasure to state, that my health is entirely restored and my strength in a great measure. I intend to resume my seat in the Senate tomorrow, & hope to take part in the debate on the great question of the day now pending in the Senate by the end of the week. The discussion before it closes will ["g" *canceled*] cover the whole issue between North & South; and, I trust, it will be of a character to satisfy the South, that it cannot with safety remain in the Union as things now stand, & that ["that" *canceled and* "there" *interlined*] is little or no prospect ["that" *canceled*] of ["there will" *canceled*] any change for the better. The tone of the Southern Senators, with the exception of [Henry] Clay, [Thomas H.] Benton, [Samuel] Houston, and a few others is high. There is an increasing disposition to resist all compromises & concessions and to agree to nothing, that will not settle the entire issue between the two sections on the grounds for which we contend. There is, I think, little prospect, that the North will come to our terms, or that any settlement of the questions at issue will be agreed on. That ["is my own impress" *canceled*] I think is the general impression. The impression is now very general, & is on the increase, that disunion is the only alternative, that is left us.

I regret greatly to learn, that you cannot take Washington on your way to NashVille. I regard it of great importance you should, ["if" *canceled*] even if your stay should be short. A few days would put you in full possession of the state of things here, which I regard as very desirable. Without flatery, I know no one better informed, than you are, on the great subject that now agitates the country, or more capable of deciding what should be done, with the knowledge you would acquire of the state of things here, or of preparing whatever papers the Convention may think proper to put out. It is, indeed, highly desirable, that at least two members from each of the de[le]gations, should visit Washington on their way to NashVille, in order to consult freely with the members from the South who are true ["to the South to it" *canceled*] to her.

I trust you may be induced to reconsider your conclusion. The reasons you assigned for it, are, indeed, strong; but they cannot be stronger than those in favour of the opposite conclusion. Never before has the South been placed in so trying a situation, ["and" *canceled*] nor can it ever be placed in one more so. Her all is at stake. Yours truly, J.C. Calhoun.

ALS in DLC, James Henry Hammond Papers; PC in Jameson, ed., *Correspondence*, pp. 781–782.

From ANNA [MARIA] C[ALHOUN] CLEMSON

Brussels, 18th Feb. 1850

My dearest father, You cannot conceive how miserable I am, at seeing by the last papers that you are ill. Mr. [Joseph A.] Scoville, who wrote to Mr. [Thomas G.] C[lemson] the 16th, says nothing of your illness, yet the letters, & papers, of the 21st, say you have been ill for *ten days.* I do not know how to reconcile this, but I know that you are ill, & suffering, & I am not near you, & am forced to wait till next week before I can have tidings of you. You do not know how I suffer from all this. Do, if you are not able to write yourself, get Mr. [Armistead] Burt, cousin Martha [Calhoun Burt], Mr. Scoville, or some one, to write us fully. Mr. Clemson feels almost as much as I do. No one can feel *quite* as much as I do, where *you* are concerned, but he is really deeply attached to you.

You must quit Washington, my dear father, & resign. It is now certain that the climate, & the life you lead there, are not favourable to your health. You have spent a long life in the service of your country, & it is now time to take care of yourself for our sakes. You can even be as much service to your country, by influencing the movements of your friends from Fort Hill, as you can at Washington. Go home then, my dearest father, live quietly, & generously, & be a good deal in the open air, without fatiguing yourself. Oh! if I could only be near to nurse you, read to you, write for you, & anticipate every wish. But we have all our trials in this world, & mine is my separation from you. When you are all well, I content myself in hearing from, & writing to you, but when any one is ill, I then remember the ocean that rolls between us. God grant that the mail of next Wednesday may bring tidings of your entire restoration, & *return to Carolina*. Even should you feel well & strong again, you should not remain at W[ashington]. There is danger that the same causes, may again produce the same results, & at your time of life these repeated attacks will in the end rack the constitution, & are therefore to be avoided. I do hope some of the family came on immediately to nurse you. If so, say they must write me fully about you. If mother [Floride Colhoun Calhoun] is with you, say I have written her to Fort Hill.

Again I repeat, return home as soon as you can bear the journey. The spring is coming on, & the weather will be delightful, & the plantation will give you agreeable occupation. I long to hear you are at Fort Hill.

[John] Calhoun [Clemson] has had a bad cold for a week past, but has gone out to day & as the weather is fine, I hope he will soon be entirely well. He is one of the healthiest boys I know of, but a cough always last[s] a long time with him & goes very hard so I am always uneasy when he has one. Floride [Elizabeth Clemson] is uncommonly well. Both are shedding their teeth, which disfigures them somewhat. Dancing & gymnastics are causing their bodies to develope finely, & keeping them straight. Calhoun's mind is also developing well, & he bids fair to be a man of talent. In addition to that, his character is very noble, & his heart good. For Floride, she is one of the very smartest, & most practical little bodies, you ever saw. No danger of her. She will always be able to take care of herself I assure you. They were both much distressed to hear of your illness, & send "a thousand kisses to grandfather."

Adieu, my dear father; do make some one write me immediately, & regularly about you.

Mr. Clemson joins me in love to you. Your ever devoted daughter, Anna C. Clemson.

ALS in ScCleA.

From [NATHANIEL HEYWARD]

[Charleston?] 18th Feb[ruar]y 1850

My dear Sir, Since my being (when a Youth) in Camp during the Revolutionary War where my Brother [Thomas Heyward, Jr.] (the signer of the Declaration of Independance) Commanded, the three numerous generations of my own descendants ["however strong may have been their desires on several occasions yet they" *interlined*] have never in ["any" *interlined*] one instance entered the throng of solicitants for Government military appointment and now for the first time towards the close of my long life at the age of 85 It would gratify me ["much" *canceled*] & my numerous family much, if you could procure for us the appointment of my Grandson Gabriel E. Manigault as Cadet in the Military Academy of West Point.

He is a fine tall healthy & highly educated youth of sixteen—of unexceptionable deportment & morality—just entering Junior at the Charleston College—well grounded in Mathematics & ["all" *canceled*] other studies requisite to an admission as Cadet & speaking French just as well as he does English having been partly educated in France—under the supervision of his parents who went with him ["there" *interlined*] for that purpose. I remain &c.

Ms. copy in ScU-SC, Manigault Family Papers. NOTE: An AEU on this ms. reads, "Copy of a Letter to be written to Hon. J.C. Calhoun by Nat[hanie]l Heyward." Gabriel Edward Manigault (1833–1899) did not receive the West Point appointment, but he later became a notable Charleston physician.

From Curtis Field, Jr.

Richmond Ky., Feb[ruar]y 22d 1850

Dear Sir: Allow me to request of you the favour to send me for preservation in the Madison [County] Library any speeches which you have recently delivered in Congress or elsewhere, a copy of which you can conveniently spare. You have in the Library two volumes of your speeches published several years ago, in which is embraced a great deal of the wealth of our country. We shall also be gratified to receive any public document worthy of preservation *from you*, which you may think proper to send us. In sending either speech or public document you will place us under additional obligations to you by sending your autograph upon it.

The Madison Library was chartered by the Legislature of Ky. in 1833 and now contains upwards of 2000 volumes of valuable works. With Respect Y[ou]rs, Curtis Field Jr., Librarian M.L.

ALS in ScU-SC, John C. Calhoun Papers.

To J[ohn] S. Lorton, [Pendleton, S.C.]

Washington, 22 Feb: 1850

My dear Sir, It will not do to hazard so large a sum by mail. I see no alternative but to wait for a good opportunity to send it by a safe private conveyance, ["excepting" *changed to* "except"] paying the money to Mrs. [Ann Mathewes] Ioor, to whom the amount due on the bond belongs, taking her receipt, that it is a payment in part of ["a bond" *interlined*] given by A[ndrew] P[ickens] Calhoun, Th[omas] G. Clemson & J.C. Calhoun to John [R.] Mathew[e]s as her trustee for the purchase of a gang of negroes. The receipt could be taken in duplicate, one to be held by you & the other transmitted to us[,] Mr. Mathew[e]s to be credited on the bond. You could prepare the receipts, one marked duplicate; and employ Mr. Miller, if ["you" *interlined*] could spare him, or some perfectly trust worthy person, if you cannot, & charge the expense to me. You can explain by note to Mrs. Ioor your reason for taking the course & may, if you think proper enclose this note to her, but to be returned to you.

I would, however, if there is any prospect of any safe opportunity to Charleston in a reasonable short time prefer sending it direct to Mr. Mathew[e]s.

I have not yet sold my cotton & desire to hold back to May. If however Mr. [Ozey R.] Broyles should make another payment in the meane time, you may retain & credit the note you refer to with the am[oun]t. Truly, J.C. Calhoun.

[P.S.] Let me hear, as possible what course you have adopted.

ALS in ScU-SC, John C. Calhoun Papers.

To J[OHN] R[AVEN] MATHEW[E]S, Charleston

Washington, 23d Feb. 1850

My dear Sir, The mail of yesterday brought me your letter of the 20th Inst. I received the day before yesterday, a letter from Mr. [John S.] Lorton on the same subject; and was both mortified & disappointed the ["sum" *canceled and* "money" *interlined*] in his hand had not long since been paid on the bond. I left instructions with him to pay it to Mrs. [Ann Mathewes] Ioor to be credited on the bond. He informed me, as soon as he received it, of the fact; and, also, that he had written to Mrs. Ioor, informing her of the fact, that he had $1900 on hand, which he [said] would be paid, as soon as a person duly authorised to receive it should apply to him. I infer that the bond had ["been" *interlined*] previously sent to Charleston to you & that, that was the cause the payment was not made.

I have written to him, and in answer to the question what he should do with the money, as it was unsafe to send so large a package of bank notes by mail, have requested him to send a trusty person with it to GreenVille, & to pay the money to Mrs. Ioor, & take her receipt for the amount, to be credited on the bond & to transmit it to you by mail, unless there should be an early opportunity of sending it by some trusty individual going to Charleston. In that case, to address the package to you & if you should not be in town ["to re(?) & to guard" *canceled*] to leave it with the President, or cashier of the bank of Charleston to be delivered when you came to town. I hope by ["one or" *canceled*] the ["other" *canceled*] arrangement the money will ["be" *canceled*] either be received, or the receipt of its payment by the 1st of March, or a short time afterwards.

I informed my son, that a payment of $1,900 would be made on the bond, so that it is probable he will remit no more than will be necessary ["than"(?) *canceled*] to pay the balance.

My restoration to full health & strength has been retarded by a

179

severe cold, which is now epidemick here. I am gradually recovering from it & hope to be well enough to attend to my publick duties in a short time. I am very desireous of expressing my views on the on[e] great question now under discussion in the Senate. Truly, J.C. Calhoun.

ALS in ScU-SC, John C. Calhoun Papers. NOTE: An AEU by Mathewes dated at Charleston on 3/2 reads: "Answered & mailed Mr. Calhoun my disappointment again quoting his positive promises & that to avoid all censure & delay will leave the Bond & Mortgage with Mr. [Oliver L.] Dobson for settling &c & urging his immediate paym[en]t here to Dobson."

To J[AMES] ED[WARD] CALHOUN, JR., [Fort Hill]

Washington, 24th Feb. 1850

My dear James, I am so much pressed by my correspondence at this time, that you must excuse the brevity of my answer to your long & well written letter.

My recovery has been interupted the last week by a bad cold, which I attribute to the state of the atmosphere, rather than any imprudence or exposure on my part. ["Colds" *canceled*.] Coldes have, indeed been so common for a week or ten days, as to be almost considered as ["an" *interlined*] influenza. I am now much better. My cough is loose, & I expectorate freely. My general health, aside from the cold, is good.

I am happy to hear, that every thing is going on well on the plantation; and hope Mr. Fred[e]ricks may succeed in making a good crop.

I cannot give my assent to your going to California at this time. It will not do to go, before you have acquired a profession. You would utterly fail, should you go before. I had a full talk with Dr. [William M.] Gwin, who you know they elected as Senator, before I got your letter, or knew of your desire to go. He says, that none but labourers, including merchants, capatilists & lawyers can succeed. That young men without capatal & not acustomed to labour, must decided [sic] to ["be" *interlined*] waiters in Hotels, or ["to" *interlined*] some subordinate station, or become work[er]s in the mines, and that a vast number, who ["are" *interlined*] forced to do so, die. That bowel complaints are the most common ["complaints" *canceled*] at the mines, & the principal cause of death, to which disease you know you are very liable. He represents the practise ["of" *canceled*] of law to be very profitable and ["that it" *interlined*] is likely to continue so, as the field for litigation is great. Under such circumstances your course is clear. Turn in and persue the study of your profession with vigour, &, if you should then continue your desire to go, ["I will n" *canceled*] after you have completed your studies, I will not oppose your wishes.

Before then, I cannot give my assent. If ["the" *interlined*] country is as rich in gold, as it is said to be, no time will be lost. In the meane time the facility of getting there will be increased & the expense of living there greatly reduced.

My love to your Mother [Floride Colhoun Calhoun] & [Martha] Cornelia [Calhoun]. Say to the latter I forwarded her letter to Mrs. [Elizabeth Clemson] Barton & will forward hers to her sister Anna [Maria Calhoun Clemson] by the next steamer. Your affectionate father, J.C. Calhoun.

[Marginal P.S.] Dr. Gwin says ["Phys" *canceled*] Doctors were not doing well. That diseases were generally of the same kind & most persons kept medicine & applied it themselves.

ALS in ScU-SC, John C. Calhoun Papers.

To A[nna Maria] C[alhoun] Clemson, [Brussels]

Washington, 24th Feb. 1850

My dear Anna, I would have answered your last by the steamer which brought it, had it not been received too late to do so. The next is daily expected, by which this & one from [Martha] Cornelia [Calhoun], and one from myself to you of an old date, but just returned to me as a dead letter with one from Mr. [Thomas G.] Clemson of the same date, or rather a short note to him.

I fear from your complaint of the want of punctuality on my part as a correspondent, that one or two others have failed to reach you. I must have written you as many as four or five since we parted last spring. If I have not written to you more frequently, my dear daughter, you must attribute it to ["the" *interlined*] extent of my correspondence and the great amount of writing I had to do in addition, and also to the fact, that you have had in your mother [Floride Colhoun Calhoun] & Cornelia two very punctual correspondents in the family. Besides my correspondence, which, with Mr. Clemson ["comprehends" *canceled and* "extends" *interlined*] when from home ["to" *interlined*] nine ["persons" *interlined*] in my own family, & when at home usually five or six, I have written between 350 & 400 pages of fools cap in execution of the work I have on hand, since we parted, & have reviewed, corrected & ["have" *canceled*] had copied the elementary disquisition on govern[men]t (["now" *interlined*] ready for the press) containing 125 pages of fools cap. When I add, that I have done all this in the midest of a round of company, & and [*sic*] my many other engagements, I think you will see, that I have a very good excuse, if I have not written you as frequently as formerly.

I answered Mr. Clemson's last, shortly after I received it. I hope he has got my answer. I gave him an account of my illness, & the state of my health at the time. My strength gradually continued to return, but slowly, until I had so far recovered, that I was enabled to take my seat in the Senate last Monday[?] and hoped to be able to address the Senate on the great question, which now absorbs all others, in a few days. The next day, the weather was very bad, and I did not go out. The day after I found myself in the incipient state of a cold, which increased the next, accompanied by a slight fever. I have the last three days been free of any febrish symptoms, & my cold is now broke. I cough still a good deal but the phlem is loose, & I expectorate freely. It has thrown me back a week, but there has been nothing serious about it. I do not think it is to be attributed to any exposure, or imprudence on my part, but to the state of the atmosphere. Indeed colds are so common as to be almost epidemick.

I am affraid Patrick's [Patrick Calhoun's] health is seriously impaired. He is now staying with his brother Andrew [Pickens Calhoun], & is much better. I hope when the weather gets warm & settled he will go to Fort Hill, & remain there until he gets fully able to join his Regiment. A frontier life, away from the pleasures of a city, may fully restore him.

The excitement, in reference to the slave question continues on the increase. I see no prospect of any satisfactory adjustment of it. You were deceived, if you supposed the South gained any thing, by the election of [Howell] Cobb [as Speaker of the House of Representatives]. He was forced on us by the Northern democrats, as they call themselves, but free soilers, as they should be called. They could not be induced to rally on any other Southern man; and the only reason they rallied on him was, that he was the least true of all ["the" *interlined*] Southern members, of the South, to the South. Indeed, such is the state of things in which we are placed, that it is indispensable to the elevation of any Southerner, that he should be false to his section.

I am exceedingly anxious to be heard in the debate now going on in the Senate; and as my ["health" *canceled and* "strength" *interlined*] may not be sufficiently restored in time, I have resolved to write out what I intended to say, & have it read, should it not be.

I am happy to hear you are all well, & the children [John Calhoun Clemson and Floride Elizabeth Clemson] doing so well. My love to Mr. Clemson & them, with a kiss from grandfather.

May God bless you all. Your affectionate father, J.C. Calhoun.

[P.S.] This is my second letter to one of the family today & I have another to write.

ALS in ScCleA; PEx in Jameson, ed., *Correspondence*, pp. 782–783.

To F[RANCIS] W. PICKENS,
[Edgefield District, S.C.]

Washington, 24th Feb: 1850

Dear Sir, Mr. [Thomas G.] Clemson informed me in his last letter, that he had made arrangements to place the bond of my self & Andrew [Pickens Calhoun] in your hands. I now write to ascertain, whether he has done so; and if he has, whether you would feel yourself authorised to receive the interest that would be due on it at at [*sic*] the end of the year, & credit ["it" *interlined*] on the bond? If he has not placed it in your hand, I will thank you to ["let" *canceled and* "inform" *interlined*] me, if you know, in whose hands it is.

I would be obliged to you, if you would write me at your early conven[ien]ce. With respect I am & &, J.C. Calhoun.

ALS in CtY, Sterling Library, Miscellaneous Manuscripts. NOTE: On 4/10/-1850, Pickens wrote A.P. Calhoun that Clemson had wished him to take the bonds "but I refused to do so, & have never had or seen them. I answered one from your father on the same subject, just before the sad & melancholy event which has filled the country with gloom." (ALS in ScU-SC, Francis Wilkinson Pickens Papers.) Given Pickens's frequently recorded claim that he had been mistreated by Calhoun, a letter [of *ca.* 5/1850] from Patrick Calhoun to Anna Maria Calhoun Clemson is apposite: Patrick asks that Thomas Clemson not appoint Pickens as his agent in this country. "I would beg for myself and all my brothers that he not be selected as, it would be exceedingly disagreeable to all of us, to have any personal intercourse with him." (ALS in ScCleA.)

To [JAMES G.] BENNETT, "National Hotel"

Sunday Morning [February 26, 1850]

Mr. Calhoun's respects to Mr. Bennett, and would thank him, if Mr. [Joseph A.] Scoville has returned from Richmond and he should meet with him, to say to him that Mr. C[alhoun] would be glad to see him. Mr. Calhoun would not trouble Mr. Bennett, but he is not certain where Mr. S[coville] is to be found.

PC in the New York, N.Y., *Herald*, May 3, 1850, p. 4.

MARCH 1–31, 1850

⚏

Calhoun's health continued to be what would later be called a running news story, Unionwide. There was also continued speculation as to whether he would be able to address the Senate for the crisis, whether that effort would finish him, and what it would contain. Unusually, his speech was printed up in advance, and was read in the Senate by James M. Mason of Virginia on March 4.

On that day, Calhoun entered the already packed chamber a little after noon and "was greeted and welcomed, in the most enthusiastic manner, by the Senators, who immediately surrounded him. . . . Mr. Calhoun almost immediately took his seat, being, apparently, very feeble and emaciated; but his eye was as bright, his smile as cheerful, and his heart as firm as ever." (Charleston, S.C., Courier, *March 9, 1850.)*

Another reporter's description: ". . . it seemed generally understood that Mr. Calhoun will never again be seen, certainly not heard, in that Chamber. His appearance is a guarantee for the truth of that impression; for, physically, he seemed barely alive. Yet, his nervous, restless and brilliant eye glared and loomed around him more remarkably than ever before, it seemed to me. The pallor of death seemed to be upon him." All present knew that the speech contained the sentiments of "a patriot—conscious that he was speaking his last words to his country. . . ." There was a rush for printed copies that were already available in Washington at two cents. (Philadelphia, Pa., Pennsylvanian, *March 6, 1850.)*

The last important words were thus given to history. The message was clear. The Union could not be saved by eulogies on the Union. It could only be saved by sincere efforts at harmony. This meant that an increasingly self-serving Northern majority would have to make the strenuous moral effort to deal justly with the minority region and its differing interests. That evening he wrote Henry W. Conner in Charleston last words for the South: "If we flinch we are gone; but, if we stand fast . . . we shall triumph, either by compelling the North to yield to our terms, or declaring our Indepen-[den]ce of them."

A few days after the speech, Daniel Webster, who was working

185

on his own response to the crisis and would see almost no one, spent two hours alone with the Carolinian.

Calhoun made the effort to speak again on March 5, 7, and 13, trading points with Henry S. Foote, Webster, and Lewis Cass on the compromise proposals. Then he sank into bed-ridden decline while his friends in the city and the country at large maintained the death-watch that was part of the custom of the times.

Son John C. Calhoun, Jr., who was a doctor, arrived around March 11 to keep his father company and oversee his care. Calhoun wrote a few letters and dictated others to John and to Joseph A. Scoville, who had reappeared as his volunteer secretary. As the month wore on, it became clear that Calhoun had no hope of recovery in Washington. Plans were made to take the railroad to Richmond, where Richard K. Crallé would meet Calhoun and his son and convey them by carriage to his home in the piedmont hills of Virginia. For this purpose, a trunk, containing valuable papers, was sent ahead. Calhoun remained alert and ready to see worthwhile visitors.

About 4 a.m. on March 31, Calhoun woke John, Jr. and remarked that he felt he was going. He was, it was said, calm and conscious, though after a while he was unable to speak. Some colleagues who roomed at the same house kept watch, and death came about 7:30 a.m. (Charleston, S.C., Courier, *April 1 and 5, 1850.)*

There was now the telegraph to broadcast news. It was received the same day in the capital city of South Carolina, where the town bell was set to tolling. (Robert W. Gibbes, Columbia, to Dr. James G. Morton, March 31, 1850, ALS in PPL.) The New-York Historical Society received the news that evening while meeting and by resolution expressed the members' profound veneration for Calhoun's "high character, unsurpassed abilities, and pre-eminent public services." (Washington, D.C., Daily National Intelligencer, *April 5, 1850.)*

Ⅱ

Memorandum of a conversation with James M. Mason, [Washington, 3/1850]. In a memo detailing a conversation with John C. Calhoun shortly before his death, Mason wrote, "sitting with him [Calhoun] in his chamber, the conversation turned on the various propositions and the questions before the Senate on the subject of slavery, as arising out of the acquisition of California and New Mexico." Calhoun said, "The Union is doomed to dissolution, there is no mistaking the signs. I am satisfied in my judgment, even were the questions which now agitate Congress settled to the satisfaction and with the concurrence of the Southern States, it would not avert, or materially delay, the catastrophe. I fix its probable occurrence within twelve years or three Presidential terms. You, and others of your age, will probably live to see it; I shall not. The mode by which it shall be done is not so clear; it may be brought about in a manner that none now foresee. But the probability is, it will explode in a Presidential election." From Virginia Mason, *The Public Life and Diplomatic Correspondence of James M. Mason,* pp. 72–73.

To [JOHN T.] TOWERS, [Washington]

Washington D.C., March 3, 1850
D[ea]r Sir, You will please let Mr. [Joseph A.] Scoville have ten thousand copies of my speech [of 3/4/1850] as soon as possible. Yours resp[ectful]ly, (signed) J.C. Calhoun.

Copy in ScU-SC, John C. Calhoun Papers. NOTE: The copy is written on the back of a claim of 5/14/1851 by Towers on Calhoun's estate for $95 for 9,500 copies of his "Speech on the Slavery Question, as per order." Calhoun's speech of 3/4 seems to have been printed before it was delivered, which was certainly a unique circumstance. According to the account given by Joseph A. Scoville in a letter of 4/30/1850 to James G. Bennett, editor of the New York *Herald,* and printed in the *Herald* of May 3, Calhoun had dictated the speech to Scoville, took the sheets Scoville had written and revised them in his own hand, and Scoville had made a fair copy. James M. Mason wanted the speech printed for easier reading in the Senate, and Scoville persuaded Towers and his printers to work Sunday night to have Mason's printed copy ready.

SPEECH ON THE SLAVERY QUESTION

[In the Senate, March 4, 1850]
[*In opening remarks reported in the* Congressional Globe, *Calhoun said: "As much indisposed as I have been, Mr. President and Senators, I have felt it to be my duty to express to you my sentiments upon the great question which has agitated the country and occupied your attention. And I am under peculiar obligations to the Senate for the very courteous manner in which they have afforded me an opportunity of being heard to-day.*

I had hoped that it would have been in my power during the last week to have delivered my views in relation to this all-engrossing subject, but I was prevented from doing so by being attacked by a cold which is at this time so prevalent, and which has retarded the recovery of my strength.

Acting under the advice of my friends, and apprehending that it might not be in my power to deliver my sentiments before the termination of the debate, I have reduced to writing what I intended to say. And, without further remark, I will ask the favor of my friend, the Senator behind me to read it.

Mr. (James M.) Mason (of Va.). It affords me great pleasure to comply with the request of the honorable Senator, and to read his remarks.

The honorable gentleman then read Mr. Calhoun's remarks as follows" (from Congressional Globe, 31st Cong., 1st Sess., p. 451):]

I have, Senators, believed from the first that the agitation of the subject of slavery would, if not prevented by some timely and effective measure, end in disunion. Entertaining this opinion, I have, on all proper occasions, endeavored to call the attention of both of the two great parties which divide the country to adopt some measure to prevent so great a disaster, but without success. The agitation has been permitted to proceed, with almost no attempt to resist it, until it has reached a period when it can no longer be disguised or denied that the Union is in danger. You have thus had forced upon you the greatest and the gravest question that can ever come under your consideration—How can the Union be preserved?

To give a satisfactory answer to this mighty question, it is indispensable to have an accurate and thorough knowledge of the nature and the character of the cause by which the Union is endangered. Without such knowledge it is impossible to pronounce, with any certainty, by what measure it can be saved; just as it would be impossible for a physician to pronounce in the case of some dangerous disease, with any certainty, by what remedy the patient could be saved, without similar knowledge of the nature and character of the cause of the disease. The first question, then, presented for consideration, in the investigation I propose to make, in order to obtain such knowledge, is—What is it that has endangered the Union?

To this question there can be but one answer; that the immediate cause is the almost universal discontent which pervades all the States composing the Southern section of the Union. This widely extended discontent is not of recent origin. It commenced with the agitation of the slavery question, and has been increasing ever since. The next question, going one step further back, is—What has caused this widely diffused and almost universal discontent?

It is a great mistake to suppose, as is by some, that it originated with demagogues, who excited the discontent with the intention of aiding their personal advancement, or with the disappointed ambition of certain politicians, who resorted to it as the means of retrieving their fortunes. On the contrary, all the great political influences of the section were arrayed against excitement, and exerted to the utmost to keep the people quiet. The great mass of the people of the South were divided, as in the other section, into Whigs and Democrats. The leaders and the presses of both parties in the South were very solicitous to prevent excitement and to preserve quiet; because it was seen that the effects of the former would necessarily tend to weaken, if not destroy, the political ties which united them with their respective parties in the other section. Those who know the strength of party ties will readily appreciate the immense force which this cause exerted against agitation and in favor of preserving quiet. But, as great as it was, it was not sufficient to prevent the wide-spread discontent which now pervades the section. No; some cause, far deeper and more powerful than the one supposed, must exist, to account for discontent so wide and deep. The question, then, recurs—What is the cause of this discontent? It will be found in the belief of the people of the Southern States, as prevalent as the discontent itself, that they cannot remain, as things now are, consistently with honor and safety, in the Union. The next question to be considered is, what has caused this belief?

One of the causes is, undoubtedly, to be traced to the long-continued agitation of the slave question on the part of the North, and the many aggressions which they have made on the rights of the South during the time. I will not enumerate them at present, as it will be done hereafter in its proper place.

There is another lying back of it, with which this is intimately connected, that may be regarded as the great and primary cause. That is to be found in the fact that the equilibrium between the two sections in the Government, as it stood when the Constitution was ratified and the Government put in action, has been destroyed. At that time there was nearly a perfect equilibrium between the two, which afforded ample means to each to protect itself against the aggression of the other; but, as it now stands, one section has the exclusive power of controlling the Government, which leaves the other without any adequate means of protecting itself against its encroachment and oppression. To place this subject distinctly before you,

I have, Senators, prepared a brief statistical statement, showing the relative weight of the two sections in the Government under the first census of 1790 and the last census of 1840.

According to the former, the population of the United States, including Vermont, Kentucky, and Tennessee, which then were in their incipient condition of becoming States, but were not actually admitted, amounted to 3,929,827. Of this number the Northern States had 1,977,899, and the Southern 1,952,072—making a difference of only 25,827 in favor of the former States. The number of States, including Vermont, Kentucky, and Tennessee, were sixteen; of which eight, including Vermont, belonged to the Northern section, and eight, including Kentucky and Tennessee, to the Southern, making an equal division of the States between the two sections under the first census. There was a small preponderance in the House of Representatives, and in the electoral college, in favor of the Northern, owing to the fact that, according to the provisions of the Constitution, in estimating federal numbers, five slaves count but three; but it was too small to affect sensibly the perfect equilibrium, which, with that exception, existed at the time. Such was the equality of the two sections when the States composing them agreed to enter into a Federal Union. Since then the equilibrium between them has been greatly disturbed.

According to the last census the aggregate population of the United States amounted to 17,063,357, of which the Northern section contained 9,728,920, and the Southern 7,334,437, making a difference, in round numbers, of 2,400,000. The number of States had increased from sixteen to twenty-six, making an addition of ten States. In the mean time the position of Delaware had become doubtful as to which section she properly belongs. Considering her as neutral, the Northern States will have thirteen and the Southern States twelve, making a difference in the Senate of two Senators in favor of the former. According to the apportionment under the census of 1840, there were 223 members of the House of Representatives, of which the Northern States had 135, and the Southern States (considering Delaware as neutral) 87, making a difference in favor of the former in the House of Representatives of 48. The difference in the Senate of two members added to this, gives to the North in the electoral college, a majority of 50. Since the census of 1840, four States have been added to the Union: Iowa, Wisconsin, Florida, and Texas. They leave the difference in the Senate as it stood when the census was taken; but add two to the side of the North in the House, making the present majority in the House in its favor of 50, and in the electoral college of 52.

The result of the whole is to give the Northern section a predominance in every department of the Government, and thereby concentrate in it the two elements which constitute the Federal Government; majority of States, and a majority of their population, estimated in federal numbers. Whatever section concentrates the two in itself possesses the control of the entire Government.

But we are just at the close of the sixth decade, and the commencement of the seventh. The census is to be taken this year, which must add greatly to the decided preponderance of the North in House of Representatives and in the electoral college. The prospect is, also, that a great increase will be added to its present preponderance in the Senate during the period of the decade by the addition of new States. Two Territories, Oregon and Minesota, are already in progress, and strenuous efforts are making to bring in three additional States from the territory recently conquered from Mexico; which, if successful, will add three other States in a short time to the Northern section, making five States; and increasing the present number of its States from fifteen to twenty, and of its Senators from thirty to forty. On the contrary, there is not a single Territory in progress in the Southern section, and no certainty that any additional State will be added to it during the decade. The prospect then is, that the two sections in the Senate, should the efforts now made to exclude the South from the newly acquired Territories succeed, will stand, before the end of the decade, twenty Northern States to fourteen Southern, (considering Delaware as neutral,) and forty Northern Senators to twenty-eight Southern. This great increase of Senators, added to the great increase of members of the House of Representatives and electoral college on the part of the North, which must take place under the next decade, will effectually and irretrievably destroy the equilibrium which existed when the Government commenced.

Had this destruction been the operation of time, without the interference of Government, the South would have had no reason to complain; but such was not the fact. It was caused by the legislation of this Government, which was appointed, as the common agent of all, and charged with the protection of the interests and security of all. The legislation by which it has been effected may be classed under three heads. The first is, that series of acts by which the South has been excluded from the common territory belonging to all of the

States, as the members of the Federal Union, and which have had the effect of extending vastly the portion allotted to the Northern section, and restricting within narrow limits, the portion left to the South. The next consists in adopting a system of revenue and disbursements, by which an undue proportion of the burden of taxation has been imposed upon the South, and an undue proportion of its proceeds appropriated to the North; and the last is a system of political measures, by which the original character of the Government has been radically changed. I propose to bestow upon each of these, in the order they stand, a few remarks, with the view of showing that it is owing to the action of this Government that the equilibrium between the two sections has been destroyed, and the whole powers of the system centered in a sectional majority.

The first of the series of acts by which the South was deprived of its due share of the Territories, originated with the Confederacy which preceded the existence of this Government. It is to be found in the provision of the ordinance of 1787. Its effect was to exclude the South entirely from that vast and fertile region which lies between the Ohio and the Mississippi rivers, now embracing five States and one Territory. The next of the series is the Missouri compromise, which excluded the South from that large portion of Louisiana which lies north of 36° 30′, excepting what is included in the State of Missouri. The last of the series excluded the South from the whole of the Oregon Territory. All these, in the slang of the day, were what are called slave territories, and not free soil; that is, territories belonging to slaveholding powers and open to the emigration of masters with their slaves. By these several acts, the South was excluded from 1,238,025 square miles, an extent of country considerably exceeding the entire valley of the Mississippi. To the South was left the portion of the Territory of Louisiana lying south of 36° 30′, and the portion north of it included in the State of Missouri. The portion lying south of 36° 30′, including the States of Louisiana and Arkansas, and the territory lying west of the latter and south of 36° 30′, called the Indian country. These, with the Territory of Florida, now the State, makes in the whole, 283,503 square miles. To this must be added the territory acquired with Texas. If the whole should be added to the Southern section, it would make an increase of 325,520, which would make the whole left to the South, 609,023. But a large part of Texas is still in contest between the two sections, which leaves it uncertain what will be the real extent of the portion of territory that may be left to the South.

I have not included the territory recently acquired by the treaty with Mexico. The North is making the most strenuous efforts to appropriate the whole to herself, by excluding the South from every foot of it. If she should succeed, it will add to that from which the South has already been excluded 526,078 square miles, and would increase the whole which the North has appropriated to herself to 1,764,023, not including the portion that she may succeed in excluding us from in Texas. To sum up the whole, the United States since they declared their independence, have acquired 2,373,046 square miles of territory, from which the North will have excluded the South, if she should succeed in monopolizing the newly-acquired territories, about three-fourths of the whole, leaving to the South but about one-fourth.

Such is the first and great cause that has destroyed the equilibrium between the two sections in the Government.

The next is the system of revenue and disbursements which has been adopted by the Government. It is well known that the Government has derived its revenue mainly from duties on imports. I shall not undertake to show that such duties must necessarily fall mainly on the exporting States, and that the South, as the great exporting portion of the Union, has in reality paid vastly more than her due proportion of the revenue; because I deem it unnecessary, as the subject has on so many occasions been fully discussed. Nor shall I, for the same reason, undertake to show that a far greater portion of the revenue has been disbursed at the North, than its due share; and that the joint effect of these causes has been, to transfer a vast amount from South to North, which, under an equal system of revenue and disbursements, would not have been lost to her. If, to this be added, that many of the duties were imposed, not for revenue, but for protection—that is, intended to put money, not in the treasury, but directly into the pocket of the manufacturers, some conception may be formed of the immense amount which, in the long course of sixty years, have been transferred from South to North. There are no data by which it can be estimated with any certainty; but it is safe to say, that it amounts to hundreds of millions of dollars. Under the most moderate estimate, it would be sufficient to add greatly to the wealth of the North, and thus greatly increase her population by attracting emigration from all quarters to that section.

This, combined with the great and primary cause, amply explains why the North has acquired a preponderance over every department of the Government by its disproportionate increase of population and States. The former, as has been shown, has increased in fifty years 2,400,000 over that of the South. This increase of population, during so long a period, is satisfactorily accounted for, by the number of emigrants, and the increase of their descendants, which have been attracted to the Northern section from Europe and the South, in consequence of the advantages derived from the causes assigned. If they had not existed—if the South had retained all the capital which has been extracted from her by the fiscal action of the Government; and, if it had not been excluded by the ordinance of '87 and the Missouri compromise, from the region lying between the Ohio and the Mississippi rivers, and between the Mississippi and the Rocky mountains north of 36° 30'—it scarcely admits of a doubt, that it would have divided the emigration with the North, and by retaining her own people, would have at least equalled the North in population under the census of 1840, and probably under that about to be taken. She would also, if she had retained her equal rights in those territories, have maintained an equality in the number of States with the North, and have preserved the equilibrium between the two sections that existed at the commencement of the Government. The loss then of the equilibrium is to be attributed to the action of this Government.

But while these measures were destroying the equilibrium between the two sections, the action of the Government was leading to a radical change in its character, by concentrating all the power of the system in itself. The occasion will not permit me to trace the measures by which this great change has been consummated. If it did, it would not be difficult to show that the process commenced at an early period of the Government; that it proceeded, almost without interruption, step by step, until it absorbed virtually its entire powers; but without going through the whole process to establish the fact, it may be done satisfactorily by a very short statement.

That the Government claims, and practically maintains, the right to decide in the last resort, as to the extent of its powers, will scarcely be denied by any one conversant with the political history of the country. That it also claims the right to resort to force to maintain whatever power she claims, against all opposition, is equally certain. Indeed it is apparent, from what we daily hear, that this has become the prevailing and fixed opinion of a great majority of the community. Now, I ask, what limitation can possibly be placed upon the powers of a government claiming and exercising such rights? And, if none can be, how can the separate governments of the States maintain and protect the powers reserved to them by the Constitution, or the people of the several States maintain those, which are reserved to them, and among others, the sovereign powers by which they ordained and established, not only their separate State Constitutions and Governments, but also the Constitution and Government of the United States? But, if they have no constitutional means of maintaining them against the right claimed by this Government, it necessarily follows, that they hold them at its pleasure and discretion, and that all the powers of the system are in reality concentrated in it. It also follows, that the character of the Government has been changed in consequence, from a federal Republic, as it originally came from the hands of its framers, into a great national consolidated Democracy. It has indeed, at present, all the characteristics of the latter and not one of the former, although it still retains its outward form.

The result of the whole of these causes combined is, that the North has acquired a decided ascendancy over every department of this Government, and through it a control over all the powers of the system. A single section governed by the will of the numerical majority, has now, in fact, the control of the Government and the entire powers of the system. What was once a constitutional federal Republic, is now converted in, reality, into one as absolute as that of the Autocrat of Russia, and as despotic in its tendency, as any absolute government that ever existed.

As then, the North has the absolute control over the Government, it is manifest, that on all questions between it and the South, where there is a diversity of interests, the interest of the latter will be sacrificed to the former, however oppressive the effects may be, as the South possesses no means by which it can resist, through the action of the Government. But if there was no question of vital importance to the South, in reference to which there was a diversity of views between the two sections, this state of things might be endured, without the hazard of destruction to the South. But such is not the fact. There is a question of vital importance to the Southern section, in reference to which the views and feelings of the two sections are as opposite and hostile as they can possibly be.

I refer to the relation between the two races in the Southern section, which constitutes a vital portion of her social organization. Every portion of the North entertains views and feelings more or less hostile to it. Those most opposed and hostile, regard it as a sin, and consider themselves under the most sacred obligation to use every effort to destroy it. Indeed to the extent that they conceive they have power, they regard themselves as implicated in the sin, and responsible for suppressing it, by the use of all and every means. Those less opposed and hostile, regard it as a crime—an offence against humanity, as they call it; and although not so fanatical, feel themselves bound to use all efforts to effect the same object, while those who are least opposed and hostile, regard it as a blot and a stain on the character, of what they call the Nation, and feel themselves accordingly bound to give it no countenance or support. On the contrary, the Southern section regards the relation as one which cannot be destroyed without subjecting the two races to the greatest calamity, and the section to poverty, desolation, and wretchedness; and accordingly they feel bound, by every consideration of interest and safety, to defend it.

This hostile feeling on the part of the North towards the social organization of the South, long lay dormant, but it only required some cause to act on those who felt most intensely that they were responsible for its continuance, to call it into action. The increasing power of this Government, and of the control of the Northern section over all its departments, furnished the cause. It was this which made an impression on the minds of many, that there was little, or no restraint, to prevent the Government from doing whatever it might choose to do. This was sufficient of itself to put the most fanatical portion of the North in action for the purpose of destroying the existing relation between the two races in the South.

The first organized movement towards it commenced in 1835. Then, for the first time, societies were organized, presses established, lecturers sent forth to excite the people of the North, and incendiary publications scattered over the whole South, through the mail. The South was thoroughly aroused. Meetings were held everywhere, and resolutions adopted, calling upon the North to apply a remedy to arrest the threatened evil, and pledging themselves to adopt measures for their own protection, if it was not arrested. At the meeting of Congress petitions poured in from the North, calling upon Congress to abolish slavery in the District of Columbia, and to prohibit what they called the internal slave trade between the States, announcing at the same time, that their ultimate object was to abolish slavery, not only in the District, but in the States and throughout the Union. At this period, the number engaged in the agitation was small, and possessed little or no personal influence.

Neither party in Congress had, at that time, any sympathy with them, or their cause. The members of each party presented their petitions with great reluctance. Nevertheless, as small and contemptible as the party then was, both of the great parties of the North dreaded them. They felt, that though small, they were organized in reference to a subject which had a great and a commanding influence over the Northern mind. Each party, on that account, feared to oppose their petitions, lest the opposite party should take advantage of the one who might do so, by favoring their petitions. The effect was that both united in insisting that the petitions should be received, and that Congress should take jurisdiction of the subject for which they prayed. To justify their course, they took the extraordinary ground, that Congress was bound to receive petitions on every subject, however objectionable it might be, and whether they had or had not jurisdiction over the subject. These views prevailed in the House of Representatives, and partially in the Senate, and thus the party succeeded in their first movements in gaining what they proposed—a position in Congress, from which agitation could be extended over the whole Union. This was the commencement of the agitation, which has ever since continued, and which, as is now acknowledged, has endangered the Union itself.

As for myself, I believed at that early period, if the party who got up the petitions should succeed in getting Congress to take jurisdiction, that agitation would follow, and that it would in the end, if not arrested, destroy the Union. I then so expressed myself in debate, and called upon both parties to take grounds against assuming jurisdiction, but in vain. Had my voice been heeded, and had Congress refused to take jurisdiction, by the united votes of all parties, the agitation which followed would have been prevented, and the fanatical zeal that gives impulse to the agitation, and which has brought us to our present perilous condition, would have become extinguished from the want of fuel to feed the flame. *That* was the time for the North to show her devotion to the Union; but unfortunately both of the great parties of that section were so intent on obtaining or retaining party ascendency, that all other considerations were overlooked or forgotten.

What has since followed are but the natural consequences. With the success of their first movement, this small fanatical party began to acquire strength; and with that, to become an object of courtship to both the great parties. The necessary consequence was, a further increase of power, and a gradual tainting of the opinions of both of the other parties with their doctrines, until the infection has extended over both; and the great mass of the population of the North, who, whatever may be their opinion of the original abolition party, which still preserves its distinctive organization, hardly ever fail, when it comes to acting, to co-operate in carrying out their measures. With the increase of their influence, they extended the sphere of their action. In a short time after the commencement of their first movement, they had acquired sufficient influence to induce the Legislatures of most of the Northern States to pass acts, which in effect abrogated the provision of the Constitution that provides for the delivery up of fugitive slaves. Not long after, petitions followed to abolish slavery in forts, magazines, and dockyards, and all other places where Congress had exclusive power of legislation. This was followed by petitions and resolutions of Legislatures of the Northern States and popular meetings, to exclude the Southern States from all Territories acquired, or to be acquired, and to prevent the admission of any State hereafter into the Union, which, by its Constitution, does not prohibit slavery. And Congress is invoked to do all this expressly with the view of the final abolition of slavery in the States. That has been avowed to be the ultimate object from the beginning of the agitation until the present time; and yet the great body of both parties of the North, with the full knowledge of the fact, although disavowing the abolitionists, have co-operated with them in almost all their measures.

Such is a brief history of the agitation, as far as it has yet advanced. Now I ask, Senators, what is there to prevent its further progress, until it fulfils the ultimate end proposed, unless some decisive measure should be adopted to prevent it? Has any one of the causes, which has added to its increase from its original small and contemptible beginning until it has attained its present magnitude, diminished in force? Is the original cause of the movement, that slavery is a sin, and ought to be suppressed, weaker now than at the commencement? Or is the Abolition party less numerous or influential, or have they less influence over, or control over the two great parties of the North in elections? Or has the South greater means of influencing or controlling the movements of this Government now, than it had when the agitation commenced? To all these questions but one answer can be given: no, no, no. The very reverse is true. Instead of being weaker, all the elements in favor of agitation are stronger now than they were in 1835, when it first commenced, while all the elements of influence on the part of the South are weaker. Unless something decisive is done, I again ask, what is to stop this agitation, before the great and final object at which it aims—the abolition of slavery in the States—is consummated? Is it, then, not certain that if something decisive is not now done to arrest it, the South will be forced to choose between abolition and secession? Indeed, as events are now moving, it will not require the South to secede to dissolve the Union. Agitation will of itself effect it, of which its past history furnishes abundant proof, as I shall next proceed to show.

It is a great mistake to suppose that disunion can be effected by a single blow. The cords which bound these States together in one common Union are far too numerous and powerful for that. Disunion must be the work of time. It is only through a long process, and successively, that the cords can be snapped, until the whole fabric falls asunder. Already the agitation of the slavery question has snapped some of the most important, and has greatly weakened all the others, as I shall proceed to show.

The cords that bind the States together are not only many, but various in character. Some are spiritual or ecclesiastical; some political; others social. Some appertain to the benefit conferred by the Union, and others to the feeling of duty and obligation.

The strongest of those of a spiritual and ecclesiastical nature consisted in the unity of the great religious denominations, all of which originally embraced the whole Union. All these denominations, with the exception, perhaps, of the Catholics, were organized very much upon the principle of our political institutions; beginning with smaller meetings corresponding with the political divisions of the country, their organization terminated in one great central assemblage, corresponding very much with the character of Congress. At these meetings the principal clergymen and lay members of the respective denominations from all parts of the Union met to transact business relating to their common concerns. It was not confined to what appertained to the doctrines and discipline of the respective denominations, but extended to plans for disseminating the Bible, establishing missionaries, distributing tracts, and of establishing presses for the publication of tracts, newspapers, and periodicals, with a view of diffusing religious information, and for the support of the doctrines and creeds of the denomination. All this combined contributed greatly to strengthen the bonds of the Union. The strong ties which held each denomination together formed a strong chord to hold the whole Union together; but, as powerful as they were, they have not been able to resist the explosive effect of slavery agitation.

The first of these cords which snapped, under its explosive force, was that of the powerful Methodist Episcopal Church. The numerous and strong ties which held it together are all broke, and its unity gone. They now form separate churches; and, instead of that feeling of attachment and devotion to the interests of the whole church which was formerly felt, they are now arrayed into two hostile bodies, engaged in litigation about what was formerly their common property.

The next cord that snapped was that of the Baptists, one of the largest and most respectable of the denominations. That of the Presbyterian is not entirely snapped, but some of its strands have given away. That of the Episcopal Church is the only one of the four great Protestant denominations which remains unbroken and entire.

The strongest cord, of a political character, consists of the many and strong ties that have held together the two great parties which have, with some modifications, existed from the beginning of the Government. They both extended to every portion of the Union, and strongly contributed to hold all its parts together. But this powerful cord has fared no better than the spiritual. It resisted for a long time the explosive tendency of the agitation, but has finally snapped under its force—if not entirely, in a great measure. Nor is there one of the remaining cords which has not been greatly weakened. To this extent the Union has already been destroyed by agitation, in the only way it can be, by snapping asunder and weakening the cords which bind it together.

If the agitation goes on, the same force, acting with increased intensity, as has been shown, will finally snap every cord, when nothing will be left to hold the States together except force. But, surely, that can, with no propriety of language, be called a Union when the only means by which the weaker is held connected with the stronger portion is *force*. It may, indeed, keep them connected; but the connexion will partake much more of the character of subjugation, on the part of the weaker to the stronger, than the union of free, independent, and sovereign States, in one confederation, as they stood in the early stages of the Government, and which only is worthy of the sacred name of Union.

Having now, Senators, explained what it is that endangers the Union, and traced it to its cause, and explained its nature and character, the question again recurs—How can the Union be saved? To this I answer, there is but one way by which it can be, and that is by adopting such measures as will satisfy the States belonging to the Southern section that they can remain in the Union consistently with their honor and their safety. There is, again, only one way by which that can be effected, and that is by removing the causes by which this belief has been produced. Do *that*, and discontent will cease, harmony and kind feelings between the sections be restored, and every apprehension of danger to the Union removed. The question, then, is—By what can this be done? But, before I undertake to answer this question, I propose to show by what the Union cannot be saved.

It cannot, then, be saved by eulogies on the Union, however splendid or numerous. The cry of "Union, Union—the glorious Union!" can no more prevent disunion than the cry of "Health, health—glorious health!" on the part of the physician, can save a patient lying dangerously ill. So long as the Union, instead of being regarded as a protector, is regarded in the opposite character, by not much less than a majority of the States, it will be in vain to attempt to conciliate them by pronouncing eulogies on it.

Besides, this cry of Union comes commonly from those who we cannot believe to be sincere. It usually comes from our assailants. But we cannot believe them to be sincere; for, if they loved the Union, they would necessarily be devoted to the Constitution. It made the Union, and to destroy the Constitution would be to destroy the Union. But the only reliable and certain evidence of devotion to the Constitution is, to abstain, on the one hand, from violating it, and to repel, on the other, all attempts to violate it. It is only by faithfully performing these high duties that the Constitution can be preserved, and with it the Union.

But how stands the profession of devotion to the Union by our assailants, when brought to this test? Have they abstained from violating the Constitution? Let the many acts passed by the Northern States to set aside and annul the clause of the Constitution providing for the delivery up of fugitive slaves answer. I cite this, not that it is the only instance, (for there are many others,) but because the violation in this particular is too notorious and palpable to be denied. Again: have they stood forth faithfully to repel violations of the Constitution? Let their course in reference to the agitation of the slavery question, which was commenced and has been carried on for fifteen years, avowedly for the purpose of abolishing slavery in the States—an object all acknowledged to be unconstitutional—answer. Let them show a single instance, during this long period, in which they have denounced the agitators or their attempts to effect what is admitted to be unconstitutional, or a single measure which they have brought forward for that purpose. How can we, with all these facts before us, believe that they are sincere in their profession of devotion to the Union, or avoid believing their profession is but intended to increase the vigor of their assaults and to weaken the force of our resistance?

Nor can we regard the profession of devotion to the Union, on the part of those who are not our assailants, as sincere, when they pronounce eulogies upon the Union, evidently with the intent of charging us with disunion, without uttering one word of denunciation

201

against our assailants. If friends of the Union, their course should be to unite with us in repelling these assaults, and denouncing the authors as enemies of the Union. Why they avoid this, and pursue the course they do, it is for them to explain.

Nor can the Union be saved by invoking the name of the illustrious Southerner whose mortal remains repose on the western bank of the Potomac. He was one of us—a slaveholder and a planter. We have studied his history, and find nothing in it to justify submission to wrong. On the contrary, his great fame rests on the solid foundation, that, while he was careful to avoid doing wrong to others, he was prompt and decided in repelling wrong. I trust that, in this respect, we profited by his example.

Nor can we find any thing in his history to deter us from seceding from the Union, should it fail to fulfil the objects for which it was instituted, by being permanently and hopelessly converted into the means of oppressing instead of protecting us. On the contrary, we find much in his example to encourage us, should we be forced to the extremity of deciding between submission and disunion.

There existed then, as well as now, a union—that between parent country and her then colonies. It was a union that had much to endear it to the people of the colonies. Under its protecting and superintending care, the colonies were planted and grew up and prospered, through a long course of years, until they became populous and wealthy. Its benefits were not limited to them. Their extensive agricultural and other productions, gave birth to a flourishing commerce, which richly rewarded the parent country for the trouble and expense of establishing and protecting them. Washington was born and grew up to manhood under that union. He acquired his early distinction in its service, and there is every reason to believe that he was devotedly attached to it. But his devotion was a rational one. He was attached to it, not as an end, but as a means to an end. When it failed to fulfil its end, and, instead of affording protection, was converted into the means of oppressing the colonies, he did not hesitate to draw his sword, and head the great movement by which that union was forever severed, and the independence of these States established. This was the great and crowning glory of his life, which has spread his fame over the whole globe, and will transmit it to the latest posterity.

Nor can the plan proposed by [Henry Clay] the distinguished Senator from Kentucky, nor that of the [Zachary Taylor] Administration, save the Union. I shall pass by, without remark, the plan proposed by the Senator, and proceed directly to the consideration of that of the Administration. I however assure the distinguished and able Senator, that in taking this course, no disrespect whatever is intended to him or his plan. I have adopted it, because so many Senators of distinguished abilities, who were present when he delivered his speech, and explained his plan, and who were fully capable to do justice to the side they support, have replied to him.

The plan of the Administration cannot save the Union, because it can have no effect whatever towards satisfying the States composing the Southern section of the Union, that they can, consistently with safety and honor, remain in the Union. It is in fact but a modification of the Wilmot proviso. It proposes to effect the same object, to exclude the South from all territory acquired by the Mexican treaty. It is well known that the South is united against the Wilmot proviso, and has committed itself by solemn resolutions, to resist, should it be adopted. Its opposition *is not to the name*, but that which it *proposes to effect*. That the Southern States hold to be unconstitutional, unjust, inconsistent with their equality as members of the common Union, and calculated to destroy irretrievably, the equilibrium between the two sections. These objections equally apply to what, for brevity, I will call the Executive proviso. There is no difference between it and the Wilmot, except in the mode of effecting the object, and in that respect I must say, that the latter is much the least objectionable. It goes to its object, openly, boldly, and distinctly. It claims for Congress unlimited power over the Territories, and proposes to assert it over the Territories acquired from Mexico, by a positive prohibition of slavery. Not so the Executive proviso. It takes an indirect course, and in order to elude the Wilmot proviso, and thereby avoid encountering the united and determined resistance of the South, it denies, by implication, the authority of Congress to legislate for the Territories, and claims the right as belonging exclusively to the inhabitants of the Territories. But to effect the object of excluding the South, it takes care, in the mean time, to let in emigrants freely from the Northern States and all other quarters, except from the South, which it takes special care to exclude by holding up to them the danger of having their slaves liberated under the Mexican laws. The necessary consequence is to exclude the South from the Territory, just as effectually as would the Wilmot proviso. The only difference in this respect is, that what one proposes to effect directly and openly, the other proposes to effect indirectly and covertly.

But the Executive proviso is more objectionable than the Wilmot, in another and more important particular. The latter, to effect its object, inflicts a dangerous wound upon the Constitution, by depriving the Southern States, as joint partners and owners of the Territories, of their rights in them; but it inflicts no greater wound than is absolutely necessary to effect its object. The former, on the contrary, while it inflicts the same wound, inflicts others equally great, and, if possible, greater, as I shall next proceed to explain.

In claiming the right for the inhabitants, instead of Congress, to legislate for the Territories, the Executive proviso, assumes that the sovereignty over the Territories is vested in the former; or to express it in the language used in a resolution offered by one of the Senators from Texas, (General [Samuel] Houston, now absent,) they have "the same inherent right of self-government as the people in the States." The assumption is utterly unfounded, unconstitutional, without example, and contrary to the entire practice of the Government, from its commencement to the present time, as I shall proceed to show.

The recent movement of individuals in California to form a constitution and a State government, and to appoint Senators and Representatives is the first fruit of this monstrous assumption. If the individuals, who made this movement, had gone into California as adventurers, and if, as such, they had conquered the Territory and established their independence, the sovereignty of the country would have been vested in them, as a separate and independent community. In that case, they would have had the right to form a constitution, and to establish a government for themselves; and, if afterwards, they thought proper to apply to Congress for admission into the Union as a sovereign and independent State, all this would have been regular, and according to established principles. But such is not the case. It was the United States who conquered California, and finally acquired it by treaty. The sovereignty, of course, is invested in them, and not in the individuals who have attempted to form a constitution and a State, without their consent. All this is clear, beyond controversy, unless it can be shown that they have since lost or been divested of their sovereignty.

Nor is it less clear, that the power of legislating over the acquired territory is vested in Congress, and not, as is assumed, in the inhabitants of the Territories. None can deny that the Government of the United States have the power to acquire Territories, either by war or treaty; but if the power to acquire exists, it belongs to Congress to carry it into execution. On this point there can be no doubt, for the Constitution expressly provides, that Congress shall have power "to make all laws which shall be necessary and proper to carry into execution the foregoing powers," (those vested in Congress,) "and all other powers vested by this Constitution in *the Government* of the United States, or in *any department* or *office* thereof." It matters not, then, where the power is vested; for, if vested at all in the Government of the United States, or any of its departments, or officers, the power of carrying it into execution is clearly vested in Congress. But this important provision, while it gives to Congress the power of legislating over Territories, imposes important restrictions on its exercise, by restricting Congress to passing laws necessary and proper for carrying the power into execution. The prohibition extends, not only to all laws not suitable or appropriate to the object of the power, but also to all that are unjust, unequal, or unfair, for all such laws would be unnecessary and improper, and, therefore, unconstitutional.

Having now established, beyond controversy, that the sovereignty over the Territories is vested in the United States—that is in the several States composing the Union—and that the power of legislating over them is expressly vested in Congress, it follows, that the individuals in California who have undertaken to form a constitution and a State, and to exercise the power of legislating without the consent of Congress, have usurped the sovereignty of the State and the authority of Congress, and have acted in open defiance of both. In other words, what they have done is revolutionary and rebellious in its character, anarchical in its tendency, and calculated to lead to the most dangerous consequences. Had they acted from premeditation and design, it would have been, in fact, actual rebellion; but such is not the case. The blame lies much less upon them than upon those who have induced them to take a course so unconstitutional and dangerous. They have been led into it by language held here, and the course pursued by the Executive branch of the Government.

I have not seen the answer of the Executive to the calls made by the two Houses of Congress for information as to the course which it took, or the part which it acted, in reference to what was done in California. I understand the answers have not yet been printed. But there is enough known to justify the assertion, that those who profess to represent and act under the authority of the Executive, have advised, aided, and encouraged the movement, which terminated in forming what they call a Constitution and a State. General [Bennet] Riley, who professed to act as civil Governor, called the Convention, determined on the number and distribution of the delegates, appointed the time and place of its meeting, was present during the session, and gave its proceedings his approbation and sanction. If he acted without authority, he ought to have been tried, or at least reprimanded and disavowed. Neither having been done, the presumption is, that his course has been approved. This of itself is sufficient to identify the Executive with his acts, and to make it responsible for them. I touch not the question, whether General Riley was appointed or received the instructions under which he professed to act from the present Executive, or its predecessor [James K. Polk]. If from the former, it would implicate the preceding as well as well as [sic] the present Administration. If not, the responsibility rests exclusively on the present.

It is manifest from this statement, that the Executive Department has undertaken to perform acts preparatory to the meeting of the individuals to form their so-called Constitution and Government, which appertain exclusively to Congress. Indeed, they are identical in many respects, with the provisions adopted by Congress, when it gives permission to a Territory to form a constitution and government, in order to be admitted as a State into the Union.

Having now shown that the assumption upon which the Executive and the individuals in California acted throughout this whole affair, is unfounded, unconstitutional, and dangerous, it remains to make a few remarks, in order to show that what has been done is contrary to the entire practice of the Government from its commencement to the present time.

From its commencement until the time that Michigan was admitted, the practice was uniform. Territorial Governments were first organized by Congress. The Government of the United States appointed the Governors, Judges, Secretaries, Marshals, and other officers, and the inhabitants of the Territory were represented by legislative bodies, whose acts were subject to the revisions of Congress. This state of things continued until the government of a Territory applied to Congress to permit its inhabitants to form a constitution and government, preparatory to admission into the Union. The preliminary act to giving permission was, to ascertain whether the inhabitants were sufficiently numerous to authorize them to be formed into a State. This was done by taking a census. That being done, and the number proving sufficient, permission was granted. The act granting it fixed all the preliminaries—the time and place of holding the convention; the qualification of the voters; establishment of its boundaries, and all other measures necessary to be settled previous to admission. The act giving permission necessarily withdraws the sovereignty of the United States, and leaves the inhabitants of the incipient State as free to form their constitution and government, as were the original States of the Union after they had declared their independence. At this stage, the inhabitants of the Territory became for the first time a people, in legal and constitutional language. Prior to this, they were, by the old acts of Congress, called inhabitants, and not people. All this is perfectly consistent with the sovereignty of the United States, with the powers of Congress, and with the right of a people to self government.

Michigan was the first case in which there was any departure from the uniform rule of acting. Hers was a very slight departure from established usage. The ordinance of '87 secured to her the right of becoming a State, when she should have 60,000 inhabitants. Owing to some neglect, Congress delayed taking the census. In the mean time her population increased, until it clearly exceeded more than twice the number which entitled her to admission. At this stage she formed a constitution and government without the census being taken by the United States, and Congress waived the omission, as there was no doubt she had more than a sufficient number to entitle her to admission. She was not admitted at the first session she applied, owing to some difficulty respecting the boundary between her and Ohio. The great irregularity, as to her admission, took place at the next session, but on a point which can have no possible connexion with the case of California.

The irregularities in all other cases that have since occurred are of a similar nature. In all, there existed territorial governments established by Congress, with officers appointed by the United States. In all, the territorial government took the lead in calling conventions, and fixing the preliminaries preparatory to the formation of a constitution and admission into the Union. They all recognized the sovereignty of the United States, and the authority of Congress over the Territories; and wherever there was any departure from established usage, it was done on the presumed consent of Congress, and not in defiance of its authority, or the sovereignty of the United States over the Territories. In this respect California stands alone, without usage, or a single example to cover her case.

It belongs now, Senators, for you to decide what part you will act in reference to this unprecedented transaction. The Executive has laid the paper purporting to be the Constitution of California before you, and asks you to admit her into the Union as a State; and the question is, will you or will you not admit her? It is a grave question, and there rests upon you a heavy responsibility. Much, very much, will depend upon your decision. If you admit her, you endorse and give your sanction to all that has been done. Are you prepared to do so? Are you prepared to surrender your power of legislation for the Territories—a power expressly vested in Congress by the Constitution, as has been fully established? Can you, consistently with your oath to support the Constitution, surrender the power? Are you prepared to admit that the inhabitants of the Territories possess the sovereignty over them, and that any number, more or less, may claim any extent of Territory they please; may form a Constitution and Government, and erect it into a State, without asking your permission? Are you prepared to surrender the sovereignty of the United States over whatever territory may be hereafter acquired to the first adventurers who may rush into it? Are you prepared to surrender virtually to the Executive Department, all the powers which you have heretofore exercised over the Territories? If not, how can you consistently with your duty and your oaths to support the Constitution, give your assent to the admission of California as a State, under a pretended constitution and government? Again, can you believe that the project of a constitution which they have adopted, has the least validity? Can you believe that there is such a State in reality as the State of California? No; there is no such State. It has no legal or constitutional existence. It has no validity, and can have none, without your sanction. How, then, can you admit it as *a State,* when according to the provision of the Constitution, your power is limited to admitting new *States.* To be admitted, it must be a State, an existing State, independent of your sanction, before you can admit it. When you give your permission to the inhabitants of a Territory to form a constitution and a State, the constitution and State they form, derive their authority from the people, and not from you. The State before admitted is actually a State, and does not become so by the *act of admission,* as would be the case with California, should you admit her contrary to constitutional provisions and established usage heretofore.

The Senators on the other side of the Chamber [the Whigs] must permit me to make a few remarks in this connection particularly applicable to them, with the exception of a few Senators from the South, sitting on that side of the Chamber, when the Oregon question was before this body, not two years since. You took (if I mistake not) universally the ground, that Congress had the sole and absolute power of legislating for the Territories. How then, can you now, after the short interval which has elapsed, abandon the ground which you took, and thereby virtually admit that the power of legislating, instead of being in Congress, is in the inhabitants of the Territories? How can you justify and sanction by your votes, the acts of the Executive, which are in direct derogation of what you then contended for? But to approach still nearer to the present time, how can you, after condemning, little more than a year since, the grounds taken by the party which you defeated at the last election, wheel round and support by your votes the grounds which, as explained recently on this floor by [Lewis Cass] the candidate of the party in the last election, are identical with those on which the Executive has acted in reference to California? What are we to understand by all this? Must we conclude that there is no sincerity, no faith in the acts and declarations of public men, and that all is mere acting or hollow profession? Or are we to conclude that the exclusion of the South from the territory acquired from Mexico is an object of so paramount a character in your estimation, that Right, Justice, Constitution, and Consistency, must all yield, when they stand in the way of our exclusion?

But, it may be asked, what is to be done with California, should she not be admitted? I answer, remand her back to the territorial condition, as was done in the case of Tennessee, in the early stage of the Government. Congress, in her case, had established a territorial government in the usual form, with a Governor, Judges, and other officers, appointed by the United States. She was entitled, under the deed of cession, to be admitted into the Union as a State as soon as she had sixty thousand inhabitants. The Territorial Government, believing it had that number, took a census, by which it appeared it exceeded it. She then formed a Constitution, and applied for admission. Congress refused to admit her, on the ground that the census should be taken by the United States, and that Congress had not determined whether the territory should be formed into one or two States, as it was authorized to do under the cession. She returned quietly to her territorial condition. An act was passed to take a census by the United States, containing a provision that the Territory should form one State. All afterwards was regularly conducted, and the Territory admitted as a State in due form. The irregularities in the case of California are immeasurably greater, and offer much stronger reasons for pursuing the same course. But, it may be said, California may not submit. That is not probable; but if she should not, when she refuses, it will then be time for us to decide what is to be done.

Having now shown what cannot save the Union, I return to the question with which I commenced, How can the Union be saved? There is but one way by which it can with any certainty, and that is, by a full and final settlement, on the principle of justice, of all the questions at issue between the two sections. The South asks for

209

justice, simple justice, and less she ought not to take. She has no compromise to offer, but the Constitution; and no concession or surrender to make. She has already surrendered so much that she has little left to surrender. Such a settlement would go to the root of the evil, and remove all cause of discontent, by satisfying the South, she could remain honorably and safely in the Union, and thereby restore the harmony and fraternal feelings between the sections, which existed anterior to the Missouri agitation. Nothing else can, with any certainty, finally and forever settle the questions at issue, terminate agitation, and save the Union.

But can this be done. Yes, easily; not by the weaker party, for it can of itself do nothing—not even protect itself—but by the stronger. The North has only to will it to accomplish it—to do justice by conceding to the South an equal right in the acquired Territory, and to do her duty by causing the stipulations relative to fugitive slaves to be faithfully fulfilled—to cease the agitation of the slave question, and to provide for the insertion of a provision in the Constitution, by an amendment, which will restore to the South in substance the power she possessed of protecting herself, before the equilibrium between the sections was destroyed by the action of this Government. There will be no difficulty in devising such a provision—one that will protect the South, and which, at the same time, will improve and strengthen the Government, instead of impairing and weakening it.

But will the North agree to do this? It is for her to answer this question. But, I will say, she cannot refuse, if she has half the love of the Union which she professes to have, or without justly exposing herself to the charge that her love of power and aggrandizement is far greater than her love of the Union. At all events, the responsibility of saving the Union rests on the North, and not the South. The South cannot save it by any act of hers, and the North may save it without any sacrifice whatever, unless to do justice, and to perform her duties under the Constitution, should be regarded by her as a sacrifice.

It is time, Senators, that there should be an open and manly avowal on all sides, as to what is intended to be done. If the question is not now settled, it is uncertain whether it ever can hereafter be; and we, as the representatives of the States of this Union, regarded as Governments, should come to a distinct understanding as to our respective views, in order to ascertain whether the great questions at issue can be settled or not. If you, who represent the stronger portion, cannot agree to settle them on the broad principle of justice and duty, say so; and let the States we both represent agree to separate and part in peace. If you are unwilling we should part in peace, tell us so, and we shall know what to do, when you reduce the question to submission or resistance. If you remain silent, you will compel us to infer by your acts what you intend. In that case, California will become the test question. If you admit her, under all the difficulties that oppose her admission, you compel us to infer that you intend to exclude us from the whole of the acquired Territories, with the intention of destroying irretrievably the equilibrium between the two sections. We would be blind not to perceive in that case, that your real objects are power and aggrandizement, and infatuated not to act accordingly.

I have now, Senators, done my duty in expressing my opinions fully, freely, and candidly, on this solemn occasion. In doing so, I have been governed by the motives which have governed me in all the stages of the agitation of the slavery question since its commencement. I have exerted myself, during the whole period, to arrest it, with the intention of saving the Union, if it could be done; and if it could not, to save the section where it has pleased Providence to cast my lot, and which I sincerely believe has justice and the Constitution on its side. Having faithfully done my duty to the best of my ability, both to the Union and my section, throughout this agitation, I shall have the consolation, let what will come, that I am free from all responsibility.

From *Speech of Mr. Calhoun, of South Carolina, on the Slavery Question. Delivered in the Senate of the United States, March 4, 1850* ([Washington: John T.] Towers, printer, [1850]); rough draft (in the hand of Joseph A. Scoville) in DLC, John C. Calhoun Papers. Also printed in *Congressional Globe*, 31st Cong., 1st Sess., pp. 451–455; the Washington, D.C., *Daily Union*, March 5, 1850, pp. 1–2; the Washington, D.C., *Daily National Intelligencer*, March 5, 1850, pp. 1–2; the Baltimore, Md., *Sun*, March 5, 1850, p. 1; the New York, N.Y., *Herald*, March 5, 1850, p. 1; the Alexandria, Va., *Gazette and Virginia Advertiser*, March 6, 1850, p. 3, and March 7, 1850, p. 2; the Charleston, S.C., *Mercury*, March 7, 1850, p. 2; the Charleston, S.C., *Evening News*, March 7, 1850, pp. 2–3; the *National Era*, vol. IV, no. 10 (March 7, 1850), p. 39, and no. 11 (March 14, 1850), p. 41; the Washington, D.C., *National Era*, March 7, 1850, pp. 3–4, and March 14, 1850, p. 1; the Charleston, S.C., *Courier*, March 8, 1850, p. 2; the Richmond, Va., *Enquirer*, March 8, 1850, p. 1; the Columbia, S.C., *Tri-Weekly South Carolinian*, March 9, 1850, pp. 1, 4; the Richmond, Va., *Whig and Public Advertiser*, March 12, 1850, p. 4; the Camden, S.C., *Journal*, March 12, 1850, pp. 1–2; the Georgetown, S.C., *Winyah Observer*, March 13, 1850, pp. 1–2, and March 16, 1850, pp. 1–2; the St. Louis, Mo., *Missouri Republican*, March 13, 1850, p. 2; the New York, N.Y., *National Anti-Slavery Standard*, March 14, 1850, pp. 1–2; the Spartanburg, S.C., *Spartan*, March 14, 1850, p. 2, and March 21, 1850, pp. 1–2; the Greenville, S.C., *Mountaineer*, March 15, 1850, pp. 1–2; the Pickens, S.C., *Keowee Courier*, March 16, 1850, pp. 1–3; the Sumter, S.C., *Ban-*

ner, March 20, 1850, and subsequent issues; the Vicksburg, Miss., *Sentinel*, March 23, 1850, and subsequent issues; *Speech of Mr. Calhoun, of South Carolina, on the Slavery Question. Delivered in the Senate of the United States, March 4, 1850* ([Washington:] Buell & Blanchard, [1850?]); *Speeches of Hon. John C. Calhoun, and Hon. Daniel Webster, on the Subject of Slavery. Delivered in the Senate of the United States, March, 1850* (New York: Stringer & Townsend, 1850), pp. 1–12, under the half-title *Address of the Hon. John C. Calhoun, in the Senate of the United States, on the Subject of Slavery*; Crallé, ed., *Works*, 4:542–573; Benton, ed., *Abridgment of Debates*, 16:403–414; Jenkins, *Life of John Caldwell Calhoun*, pp. 415–439; Briggs, ed., *Noted Speeches*, pp. 139–172; Anderson, ed., *Calhoun—Basic Documents*, pp. 298–324; Lence, ed., *Union and Liberty*, pp. 573–601. Partly printed in [Musson,] *Lettré a Napoleon III*, pp. 155–160; [Musson,] *Letter to Napoleon III*, pp. 123–128; Bradley, ed., *Orations and Arguments by British and American Statesmen*, pp. 271–297; Johnston, ed., *American Orations*, 2:123–160; *Library of Southern Literature*, 2:703–710; McClure, ed., *Famous American Statesmen and Orators*, 3:327–356; Warner, ed., *Library of the World's Best Literature*, 6:3098–3100; Cook, *John C. Calhoun— The Man*, pp. 97–115; Wilson, ed., *The Essential Calhoun*, pp. 390–393. NOTE: For a partial history of the text of this speech, see above Calhoun's note of 3/3 to John T. Towers and its footnote. The extant draft cited above is too rough to have been the fair copy used for typesetting. In a letter to James G. Bennett on 4/30/1850 (New York, N.Y., *Herald*, May 3, 1850, p. 7), Joseph A. Scoville stated that the fair copy was "in my possession now, and intended for his daughter, Mrs. Clemson. . . ." That ms. has not been found and Richard K. Crallé does not mention having any such ms. (*Works*, 2:v–vi). The Charleston, S.C., *Courier*, May 14, 1850, under the heading "Mr. Calhoun's Last Speech," reported the availability of this speech "printed on white Satin in a form suitable for framing," at $5 per copy printed in gold and $2 in ink. Also an edition printed on vellum, $2 per copy in gold and $1 in ink.

To [HENRY W. CONNER, Charleston]

[Washington, March 4, 1850]

My speech, of which a copy will be enclosed to you by the mail, which takes this, was read today in the Senate. My friends think it among my most successful efforts, & that it made a profound impression. I, trust, that our friends in Charleston will give it a wide circulation. You will see, that I have made up the issue between North & South. If we flinch we are gone; but, if we stand fast on it, we shall triumph, either ["of" *canceled*] by compelling the North to yield to our terms, or declaring our Indepen[den]ce of them. Truly, J.C.C.

ALI (incomplete) in ScC; photostat of ALI in DLC, Henry W. Conner Papers. NOTE: This letter has been dated from its content.

Remarks in Reply to Henry S. Foote

[In the Senate, March 5, 1850]
[*Foote made critical remarks in regard to Calhoun's speech of yesterday. Andrew P. Butler of South Carolina rose to reply and while he was speaking Calhoun entered the chamber.*]

Mr. Calhoun, (in his seat.) What is the question before the Senate? Is there any, sir?

The Vice-President [Millard Fillmore]. There is no question pending.

Mr. Calhoun. I must really express my great regret that a member of this body, in my absence this morning before the hour for the consideration of this question, should have engaged in commenting on my remarks in reference to the important question that is under discussion. I had not the advantage of hearing the remarks of the Senator from Mississippi? Did he accuse me of disunion? Did he mean to insinuate that?

[*Foote apologized. He had spoken in Calhoun's absence only because he expected him to be absent a long time, and avowed that he "had not the slightest intention to impute to him designs hostile to the Union." He feared that Calhoun would find his remarks in bad taste when he read them in the newspapers.*]

Mr. Calhoun. My friend from Mississippi might have been saved from the necessity of making these solemn protests that he has never followed a leader, for I have never pretended to be the leader of any man. When I speak, I speak for myself—upon my individual responsibility—and not for the Senator from Mississippi, nor any other Senator. Sir, I desire that my words shall go out and be received by the public as they stand, and not as they may be attempted to be explained here by any gentleman.

Mr. President, the Senator from Mississippi has unfortunately overlooked the character of my remarks. What was the great object I had in view? It was to ascertain the cause of the disquiet which prevails: and could I overlook the cause which is so obviously to be traced to the utter inability of the southern States to defend themselves through Congress, upon this or any other subject, upon which the northern States choose to act? Could that be overlooked? It is the great and manifest cause. If we had the same power now that we had formerly, we could defend ourselves here; but that power is gone. And it is the sense of weakness that the South feels—it is the conviction that they cannot defend themselves here, that is the cause of the deep excitement which prevails in that section of the Union.

Could I overlook that? And what was my summing up? It was that, unless this question is finally and forever settled now, it is not probable that it will be settled at any future time, and that it never can be satisfactorily settled, unless the cause which has led to that disquiet, be removed. I said nothing about *sine qua non*; I did not allude to any *sine qua non*—that is an inference of the Senator from Mississippi, not to be deduced from any language that I used.

But I will say, and I say it boldly—for I am not afraid to say the truth on any question—that, as things now stand, the southern States cannot with safety remain in the Union. When this question may be settled, when we shall come to a constitutional understanding, is a question of time; but, as things now stand, I appeal to the Senator from Mississippi, if he thinks that the South can remain in the Union upon terms of equality?

Mr. Foote. We cannot, unless the pending questions are settled; but in my opinion, these questions may be settled, and honorably settled, within ten days' time.

Mr. Calhoun. Does the Senator think the South can remain in the Union upon terms of equality without a specific guarantee that she shall enjoy her rights unmolested?

Mr. Foote. I think she may, without any previous amendment of the Constitution. There we disagree.

Mr. Calhoun. Yes, there we disagree entirely; and there, I think, he disagrees with our ancestors. I agree with them. They thought liberty required guarantees; they thought that it required protection; and so believe I. Mr. President, I will not dwell upon this topic, which has been brought up in this irregular manner.

The Senator from Mississippi accuses me of another thing: that I condemned the whole North in the gross, as being hostile to the South. What did I say? I stated that there were three divisions of sentiment in the North on the subject. The first, and it constitutes but a small portion, believe the institution of slavery to be immoral; a larger portion believe it to be criminal; and all believe it to be a blot upon our national escutcheon. What more did I say? I said that whenever it came to a question, all parties would join in fighting against the South.

Mr. Foote. This passage in the Senator's speech struck me as being too severe. I am very glad to hear it explained.

Mr. Calhoun. Every portion of the North entertains feelings more or less hostile to the South.

Mr. Foote. I cannot think so.

Mr. Calhoun. More or less hostile. What I mean is, that they declare that the institution is a blot upon our national escutcheon. Is that not being more or less hostile? And is there a northern man who will rise up and make a declaration to the contrary? Sir, I must express my deep regret that the Senator from Mississippi should think proper to call on me in this irregular way, and at this early stage, for an explanation. If he differed from me there would be a suitable occasion, in the course of the debate, to express his sentiments. No, Mr. President, we cannot disguise the fact that this feeling in the North exists; and unless there be a provision in the Constitution [to protect us] against that feeling, the two sections of this Union will never live in harmony.

Now, sir, as to the question of disunion. I talk very little about whether I am a Union man or not; because I put no confidence in professions. I leave it to my acts to determine whether I am a Union man or not. Sir, I challenge comparison with any man here—I challenge a comparison by the Senator from Mississippi—I appeal to him if there is any man who has ever abstained more carefully from what he believed to be a violation of the Constitution, or who has ever been more forward to arrest all infractions of the Constitution. It is in vain for a man to say he loves the Union if he does not protect the Constitution; for that is the bond that made the Union. If I am judged by my acts, I trust I shall be found to be as firm a friend of the Union as any man within it. Sir, I do not know that there are any points I have left unexplained; if my friend from Mississippi— for I will still call him my friend—wishes for explanation upon any other point I shall be glad to accommodate him.

[*Foote avowed that he had been misunderstood and had not accused Calhoun of disunion. He prized Calhoun's friendship.*]

Mr. Calhoun. The Senator exhibits, I think, a little anxiety to misconstrue; at all events, he does not construe my remarks liberally. He calls my attention to a meeting in New York, at which, he says, sentiments were expressed that were favorable to the South. It is true there were many sentiments expressed there that I approve of, but I am not to be deceived by them; that meeting was for depriving us of all our rights in California. I like to attend to things, and not to the names by which they are called. Sir, I should be most happy to think that we should have the votes of the Senators from New York, and of other Senators of the North, in favor of preserving our rights in California. But there are two modes of treating the subject: one is by speaking, and the other by acting—of the two, the latter is the most effective. I had hoped that this discussion would go on regularly, and I hope it will hereafter; and if any Senator, in the course of his remarks, chooses to comment upon what I have said, I trust I shall have health enough to defend my own position.

From *Congressional Globe*, 31st Cong., 1st Sess., pp. 463–464. Also printed in the Washington, D.C., *Daily National Intelligencer*, March 6, 1850, p. 3; the Alexandria, Va., *Gazette and Virginia Advertiser*, March 8, 1850, p. 2; the Columbia, S.C., *Tri-Weekly South Carolinian*, March 9, 1850, p. 2; the Charleston, S.C., *Courier*, March 9, 1850, p. 2; the Richmond, Va., *Whig and Public Advertiser*, March 12, 1850, p. 2; the Spartanburg, S.C., *Spartan*, March 21, 1850, pp. 2–3. Variant in the Washington, D.C., *Daily Union*, March 6, 1850, p. 1; the Richmond Va., *Enquirer*, March 12, 1850, p. 4. Other variants in the Baltimore, Md., *Sun*, March 6, 1850, p. 4; the Charleston, S.C., *Evening News*, March 8, 1850, p. 2; Crallé, ed., *Works*, 4:574–578.

From J[AMES] H. HAMMOND

Silver Bluff, 6 March 1850

My Dear Sir, I am greatly rejoiced to hear of your improved health, & by the telegraph that you were in the Senate day before yesterday. I trust that as warm weather advances you will recover entirely & feel well enough to retain your seat through this crisis. If I may judge of your particular views by the three or four sentences which the telegraph devotes to an abstract of your speech on Monday, I should regard your retirement at this moment as a peculiar calamity to the South. Under any circumstances your loss would be irreparable, but your ideas as to the precise course necessary at this exigency, as I understand ["them" *interlined*], are so clearly, in my judgment the only safe & sound ones, that to be deprived of your powerful aid in developing & enforcing them, would almost make me doubt that Providence was on our side. I have no sort of faith in any Constitutional Compacts with the North. She never has regarded them & never will. On mere Legislative Compromises I look with horror. They are the apples of Hippomenes cast behind him in the race. Our only safety is in *equality of power*. We must divide the territories so as forever to retain that equality in the Senate at least, & in doing so we should count Delaware with the North. She is no Southern or Slave State. I would infinitely prefer disunion to any thing the least short of this—& I would rather have it I believe *any how* for fear of future [Henry] Clays, [Thomas H.] Bentons, [Samuel] Houstons & [John] Bells. If the North will not consent to this I think we should not have another word to say, but kick them out of the Capitol & set it on fire. We must act *now*, & decisively. We will be in ["a" *inter-*

lined] clear minority when California comes in & in twenty or thirty years, there will be ten more free States west of the Mississippi & ten more north of the St. Lawrence & the Lakes. England would gladly surrender Canada to us now, if she had a decent pretext that would save her pride. Long before the North gets this vast accession of strength she will ride over us rough shod—proclaim freedom or something equivalent to it to our slaves & reduce us to the condition of Hayti. She would not even do as England did to Jamaica. She would do what the Constituent Assembly did to Hayti. If we do not act now—we deliberately consign our children—not our posterity, but *our children* to the flames. What a holocaust for us to place upon the altar of that Union, for which the South & West have ["(had)" *interlined*] such a bigoted & superstitious veneration.

It seems to me that Congress will leave nothing for the Nashville Convention to do. If you make a truce—however fatal—we cannot violate it. If you make an impassable breach, the powers of the Convention under the Virginia instructions will be inadequate to any useful purpose. The only thing to be done will be to call a General Congress of the South. The Nashville Convention might recommend that—but I presume an equally potent impulse would come from Congress. Should things remain—contrary to every appearance— pretty much as they are, I think that will be the proper course for the Nashville Convention to take. I am decidedly opposed to any Address either defiant or remonstrant, or conciliatory to the North, & nothing need be said to the South after the Southern Address. A very short Preamble & a couple of resolutions would answer every purpose & these I could draw in five minutes. In fact I have had them by me for some time. The substance of them is in this letter. I am not ambitious myself to "Bell the Cat" & will not push to make the move, but would rather second it. But would make it. I would send you a copy of this paper, but fear to involve you unnecessarily in its consequences. You must preserve yourself for the Convention to frame the New Constitution. You must be there with your full powers. In the mean time I am extremely anxious to see your Book on Government. I trust you have taken the ground that the fundamental object of Government is to *secure* the fruits of labour & skill— that is to say *property*, & that its forms must be moulded ["after" *canceled and* "upon" *interlined*] the social organization. Life & liberty will then be secured, for these are naturally under the guardianship of ["civilization" *canceled*] society & that civilization which is the fruit of its progress. "Free *Government*" & all that sort of thing has been I think a fatal delusion & humbug from the time of Moses.

Freedom does not spring from Government but from the same soil which produces Government itself: & all we want from that is a guarantee for property fairly acquired.

I fear it will be impossible for me to go to Washington. I must endeavour to put my affairs in a proper train, to be neglected hereafter if circumstances require it, as every man must do his duty when the tug comes. In the last eight crops I have sunk four & two of these in the last three, & just now a heavy pecuniary responsibility has devolved on me, because two years ago—after paying $18,000 for [James] Hamilton [Jr.], I again in a critical moment, lent him a hand, on a solemn pledge of his *honor, in writing,* to meet the engagement, which he has wholly failed to do. It is melancholy to think of what he once was & what he is now. I *would* not believe it until too late. Altho' I have the strongest hopes that I have my lands now in a condition to repay me rapidly all I have sunk in their improvement—I must at this time act with exceeding caution & dare not leave them to any management but my own until I see my crop fairly on the way. Do write me as fully as you can. I think the Atlantic & Gulf States are by an immense majority ready for any thing, & less patient than their leaders. Six months has produced an immense change & it is going on rapidly. If the leaders will only *lead,* neither they nor we have any thing to fear. Yours sincerely, J.H. Hammond.

P.S. I sent you some Addresses I delivered lately. When you find time to read them I hope you will concur in my views of Southern manufacturing.

ALS in DLC, James Henry Hammond Papers; PEx (misdated 3/5) in Jameson, ed., *Correspondence,* pp. 1210–1212. NOTE: An AEU by Hammond reads: "Returned to me by Jos[eph] A. Scoville after Mr. C's death." Hammond had lately published *An Address Delivered Before the South-Carolina Institute, at Its First Annual Fair, on the 28th November, 1849* (Charleston: Walker & James, 1849), and, perhaps, *An Oration, Delivered Before the Two Societies of the South Carolina College, on the Fourth of December, 1849* (Charleston: Walker & James, 1850).

To J[OHN] R[AVEN] MATHEW[E]S, Charleston

Washington, 6th March 1850

My dear Sir, You cannot regret more sincerely than I do, that there should have been any disappointment in reference to making final payment of the bond of my son Andrew [Pickens Calhoun] & myself on the day appointed. I hoped [*sic*] the whole has been paid ere this and the transaction closed. The difficulty, I suppose, resulted from the change of the President of the bank [of Charleston?]. We made our arrangement with Mr. [Henry W.] Conner, and I have every reason to believe, if he was not in funds on the 1st of March, he was shortly afterwards. But to avoid all delay, I wrote to him, as soon as I received your letter last evening, that you had left the Bond & mortgage with Mr. [Oliver L.] Dobson with powers to act for you, and requested his early attention to the subject, if he had not already Paid the bond.

It may be, that there may be some delay as to the $1,900 in the hands of Mr. [John S.] Lorton. I wrote to my son long since, that the money was in his hands & that I had instructed him to pay it to Mrs. [Ann Mathewes] Ioor & have it credited on the bond, supposing it was in her hands, as I had previously payed the interest several times to her, without any question being made as to her authority to receive it, but I at the same time, to avoid accidents, wrote him to remit ample to cover the whole, which I hope he has done. I authorized Mr. Lorton [at Pendleton] should there be any difficulty made to receiving the money and giving a receipt, to transmit ["it to you by the to(?)" *canceled and* "the money by the first safe opportunity" *interlined*] in a package addressed to you, & to be delivered to you, should you be in town, and if not to leave it at the bank of Charleston, to be delivered to you. If you should receive it, or if it should be left at the bank, & the bond be discharged, I wish you to deliver it to Mr. Conner, who has my instructions what to do with it, but if it should not be fully discharged to ["apply it to" *canceled*] credit ["it" *interlined*] on the bond.

Should Mrs. Ioor receive the money & receipt for it, I trust there will not be any difficulty in crediting the amount on the bond, if not already paid, and if it is, to pay over the amount to Mr. Conner for me. If one or the other is not done it will place the affair in a very awarked [*sic*; awkward] condition. All the embarrassment about it has been owing to my absence from home.

I ["enclose herewith" *canceled and* "transmit by the mail that takes this" *interlined*] a copy of my speech. It has been well received here. My health is improving. Truly, J.C. Calhoun.

ALS in ScU-SC, John C. Calhoun Papers. NOTE: In the John Raven Mathewes Papers in ScU-SC is a letter from William Ioor, in Greenville, S.C., to Mathewes in Charleston, April 1, 1850, reading: "We are all truly sorry you have had so much trouble with the Calhoun business, are rejoiced you have got so well over it, and happy you have determined to take charge of the money yourself, being well aware we shall have no difficulty about the Interest money hereafter. Above is the receipt you wished." The receipt appears on the same manuscript, signed by Ann [Mathewes] Ioor, dated 3/1/1849 [*sic*], and reads: "Received of Mr. John C. Calhoun Four hundred and twenty Dollars ($420.00) being the balance due for Interest on his Bond to John R. Mathewes as Trustee for myself and Children, up to the above date."

Remarks during Daniel Webster's Speech on the Compromise Resolutions

[In the Senate, March 7, 1850]

[*In the course of his oration, Webster stated that Calhoun, as Secretary of State, had forwarded the annexation of Texas "to strengthen the slave interest of this country."*]

Mr. Calhoun. Will the honorable Senator permit me to interrupt him for a moment?

Mr. Webster. Certainly.

Mr. Calhoun. I am very reluctant to interrupt the honorable gentleman; but, upon a point of so much importance, I deem it right to put myself *rectus*. I did not put it upon the ground assumed by the Senator. I put it upon this ground: that Great Britain had announced to this country, in so many words, that her object was to abolish slavery in Texas, and through Texas, to accomplish the abolishment of slavery in the United States and the world. The ground I put it on was, that it would make an exposed frontier, and, if Great Britain succeeded in her object, it would be impossible that that frontier could be secured against the aggression of the Abolitionists; and that this Government was bound, under the guaranties of the Constitution, to protect us against such a state of things.

Mr. Webster. That comes, I suppose, sir, to exactly the same thing. It was, that Texas must be obtained for the security of the slave interest of the South.

Mr. Calhoun. Another view is very distinctly given.

[*Webster resumed his remarks as to the annexation of Texas being in the interest of the slave States, remarking that Calhoun "did avow it boldly and manfully; he did not disguise his conduct."*]

Mr. Calhoun. Never, never.

Mr. Webster. What he means he is very apt to say.

Mr. Calhoun. Always, always.

[*Webster continued his speech for some time, after which:*]

Mr. Calhoun. I rise to correct what I conceive to be an error of the distinguished Senator from Massachusetts, as to the motives which induced the acquisition of Florida, Louisiana, and Texas. He attributed it to the great growth of cotton, and the desire of the southern people to get an extension of territory, with the view of cultivating it with more profit than they could in a compact and crowded settlement. Now, Mr. President, the history of these acquisitions I think was not correctly given. It is well known that the acquisition of Florida was the result of an Indian war. The Seminole Indians residing along the line attacked one of our fortresses; troops were ordered out; they were driven back; and, under the command of General [Andrew] Jackson, Pensacola and St. Marks were seized. It was these acts, and not the desire for the extended cultivation of cotton, which led to the acquisition of Florida. I admit that there had been for a long time a desire on the part of the South, and of the [James Monroe] Administration I believe, to acquire Florida; but it was very different from the reason assigned by the honorable Senator. There were collected together four tribes of Indians—the Creeks, the Choctaws, the Chickasaws, and the Cherokees—about thirty thousand warriors—who held connection, almost the whole of them, with the Spanish authorities in Florida, and carried on a trade perpetually with them. It was well known that a most pernicious influence was thus exercised over them; and it was the desire of preventing conflict between the Indians and ourselves in the South, as I believe, which induced the acquisition of Florida. I come now to Louisiana. We well know that the immediate cause for the acquisition of Louisiana, was the suspension of our right of deposit at New Orleans. Under a treaty with Spain we had a right to the navigation of the river as far as New Orleans, and a right to make deposits in the port of New Orleans. The Spanish authorities interrupted that right, and that interruption produced a great agitation at the West, and I may say throughout the whole United States. The gentlemen then in opposition, a highly respectable party—the old Federal party, which I have never said a word of disrespect in regard to—if I mistake not, took the lead in a desire to resort to arms to acquire that territory. Mr. [Thomas] Jefferson, more prudent, desired to procure it by purchase. A purchase was made, in order to remove the difficulty, and to give an outlet to the west to the ocean. That was the immediate cause of the acquisition of Louisiana. Now, sir, we come to Texas. Perhaps no gentleman had more to do with the acquisition of Texas than myself; and I aver, Mr. President, that I would have been among the very last individuals in the United States, to have made any movement at that time for the acquisition of Texas; and I go farther: if I know myself, I was incapable of acquiring any territory simply on the ground that it was to be an enlargement of slave territory. I would just as freely have acquired it if it had been on the northern as on the southern side. No, sir; very different motives actuated me. I knew at a very early period—I will not go into the history of it—the British Government had given encouragement to the Abolitionists of the United States, who were represented at the World's Convention. The question of the abolition of slavery was agitated in that convention. One gentleman stated that Mr. [John Quincy] Adams informed him, that if the British Government wished to abolish slavery in the United States, they must begin with Texas. A commission was sent from this World's Convention to the British Secretary of State, Lord Aberdeen; and it so happened, that a gentleman was present when the interview took place between Lord Aberdeen and the committee, who gave me a full account of it shortly after it occurred. Lord Aberdeen fell into the project, and gave full encouragement to the Abolitionists. Well, sir, it is well known that Lord Aberdeen was a very direct, and, in my opinion, a very honest and worthy man; and when Mr. [Richard] Pakenham was sent here to negotiate with regard to Oregon, and incidentally with respect to Texas, he was ordered to read a declaration to this Government, stating that the British Government was anxious to put an end to slavery all over the world, commencing at Texas. It is well known, farther, that at that very time a negotiation was going on between France and England to accomplish that object, and our Government was thrown, by stratagem, out of the negotiation; and that object was—first, to induce Mexico to acknowledge the independence of Texas upon the ground that she would abolish it. All these are matters of history; and where is the man so blind—I am sure the Senator from Massachusetts is not so blind—as not to see, that if the project of Great Britain had been successful, the whole frontier of the States of Louisiana and Arkansas, and the adjacent States, would have been exposed to the inroads of British emissaries. Sir, so far as I was concerned, I put it exclusively upon that ground. I never would run into the folly of re-annexation, which I always held to be absurd. Nor, sir, would I put it upon the ground—upon which I might well have put it—of commercial and manufacturing considerations, because those were not my motive-principles, and I chose to assign what were. So far as commerce and manufactures were concerned, I would not have moved in the matter at that early period.

The Senator objects that many northern gentlemen voted for annexation. Why, sir, it was natural that they should be desirous of fulfilling the obligations of the Constitution; and, besides, what man at that time doubted that the Missouri compromise line would be adopted, and that the territory would fall entirely to the South? All that northern men asked for, at that time, was the extension of that line. Their course, in my opinion, was eminently correct and patriotic.

Now, Mr. President, having made these corrections, I must go back a little farther, and correct a statement which I think the Senator has left very defective, relative to the ordinance of 1787. He states very correctly that it commenced under the old Confederation; that it was afterward confirmed by Congress; that Congress was sitting in New York at the time, while the [Constitutional] Convention sat in Philadelphia; and that there was concert of action. I have not looked into the ordinance very recently, but my memory will serve me thus far, that Mr. Jefferson introduced his first proposition to exclude slavery in 1784. There was a vote taken upon it, and I think on that vote every southern Senator voted against it; but I am not certain of it. One thing I am certain of, that it was three years before the ordinance could pass. It was sturdily resisted, down to 1787; and when it was passed, as I had good reason to believe, it was upon a principle of compromise—first, that the ordinance should contain a provision similar to the one put in the Constitution, with respect to fugitive slaves; and next, that it should be inserted in the Constitution; and this was the compromise upon which the prohibition was inserted in the ordinance of 1787. We thought we had an indemnity in that, but we made a great mistake. Of what possible advantage has it been to us? Violated faith has met us on every side, and the advantage has been altogether in their favor. On the other side, it has been thrown open to a northern population to the entire exclusion of the southern. This was the leading measure which destroyed the compromise of the Constitution, and then followed the Missouri compromise, which was carried mainly by northern votes, although now disavowed and not respected by them. That was the next step; and between these two causes, the equilibrium has been broken.

Having made these remarks, let me say, that I took great pleasure in listening to the declarations of the honorable Senator from Massachusetts upon several points. He puts himself upon the fulfillment of the contract of Congress, in the resolutions of Texas annexation, for the admission of the four new States provided for by those resolutions, to be formed out of the territory of Texas—all that was manly, statesmanlike, and calculated to do good, because just. He went farther: he condemned, and rightfully condemned—and in that he has shown great firmness—the course of the North relative to the stipulations of the Constitution for the restoration of fugitive slaves; but permit me to say, for I desire to be candid upon all subjects, that if the Senator, together with many friends on this [Democratic] side of the chamber, puts his confidence in the bill which has been reported here, farther to extend the laws of Congress upon this subject, it will prove fallacious. It is impossible to execute any law of Congress, until the people of the States shall coöperate.

I heard the gentleman with great pleasure say, that he would not vote for the Wilmot proviso, for he regarded such an act as unnecessary, considering that nature had already excluded slavery. As far as the new acquisitions are concerned, I am disposed to leave them to be disposed of as the hand of nature shall determine. It is what I always have insisted upon. Leave that portion of the country more natural to a non-slaveholding population, to be filled by that description of population; and leave that portion into which slavery would naturally go, to be filled by a slaveholding population—destroying artificial lines, though perhaps they may be better than none. Mr. Jefferson spoke like a prophet, of the effect of the Missouri compromise line. I am willing to leave it for nature to settle; and to organize governments for the territories, giving all free scope to enter and prepare themselves to participate in their privileges. We want, sir, nothing but justice. When the gentleman says that he is willing to leave it to nature, I understand he is willing to remove all impediments, whether real or imaginary. It is consummate folly, to assert, that the Mexican law prohibiting slavery in California and New Mexico, is in force; and I have always so regarded it.

No man would feel more happy than myself, to believe that this Union, formed by our ancestors, should live forever. Looking back to the long course of *forty* years' service here, I have the consolation to believe, that I have never done one act which would weaken it—that I have done full justice to all sections. And if I have ever been exposed to the imputation of a contrary motive, it is because I have been willing to defend my section from unconstitutional encroachments. But I cannot agree with the Senator from Massachusetts, that this Union can not be dissolved. Am I to understand him, that no degree of oppression, no outrage, no broken faith, can produce the destruction of this Union? Why, sir, if that becomes a fixed fact, it will itself become the great instrument of producing oppression, outrage, and broken faith. No, sir! the Union can be broken. Great moral causes will break it, if they go on; and it can only be preserved by justice, good faith, and a rigid adherence to the Constitution.

Mr. Webster. Mr. President, a single word in reply to the honorable member from South Carolina. My distance from the honorable member, and the crowded state of the room, prevented me from hearing the whole of his remarks. I have only one or two observations to make; and, to begin, I first notice the honorable member's last remark. He asks me, if I hold the breaking up of the Union, by any such thing as the voluntary secession of States, as an impossibility? I know, sir, this Union can be broken up; every Government can be; and I admit that there may be such a degree of oppression, as will warrant resistance, and a forcible severance. That is revolution—that is revolution! Of that ultimate right of revolution, I have not been speaking. I know that that law of necessity does exist. I forbear from going farther, because I do not wish to run into a discussion of the nature of this Government. The honorable member and myself have broken lances sufficiently often before on that subject.

Mr. Calhoun. I have no desire to do it now.

[*Webster made a few more remarks.*]

Mr. Calhoun. One word, and I have done; and that word is, that notwithstanding the acquisition of the vast territory of Texas, represented by the Senator from Massachusetts, it is the fact that all that addition to our territory, made it by no means equal to what the northern States had excluded us from before that acquisition. The territory lying west, between the Mississippi and the Rocky Mountains, is three fourths of the whole of Louisiana; and that which lies between the Mississippi and the Ohio, added to that, makes a much greater extent of territory than Florida, and Texas, and that portion of Louisiana that has fallen to our share.

[*Adjournment was then moved and agreed to.*]

From *Congressional Globe*, 31st Cong., 1st Sess., pp. 479–484. Also printed or partly printed in Washington, D.C., *Daily National Intelligencer*, March 8, 1850, pp. 2–3; the Alexandria, Va., *Gazette and Virginia Advertiser*, March 11, 1850, p. 3, and March 12, 1850, p. 2; the Charleston, S.C., *Mercury*, March 11, 1850, p. 2; the Charleston, S.C., *Evening News*, March 11, 1850, p. 2; the Richmond, Va., *Whig and Public Advertiser*, March 12, 1850, pp. 5–6; the Sumter, S.C., *Banner*, March 20, 1850, p. 2; the Greenville, S.C., *Mountaineer*, March 22, 1850, p. 1; the Pickens, S.C., *Keowee Courier*, March 22, 1850, p. 2; the Spartanburg, S.C., *Spartan*, March 28, 1850, pp. 1–2; *Congressional Globe*, 31st Cong., 1st Sess., Appendix, p. 273; Benton, *Abridgment of Debates*, 16:423–434; *Writings and Speeches of Daniel Webster* (1903), 10:76–77. Variants in the Washington, D.C., *Daily Union*, March 8, 1850, pp. 1–2; *Speech of the Hon. Daniel Webster, in the Senate of the United States, on the Subject of Slavery* (no publisher, no date), pp. 30–32.

To Ed[mund W.] Hubard,
[Buckingham County, Va.]

Washington, 9th March 1850
My dear Sir, I have read your kind and approving letter, with all ["with" *canceled*] the emotions it was so well calculated to excite. Your approval of my course, I value far more highly, than all the shouts, which the popularity of the day could raise.

I ["enclose" *canceled and* "send herewith" *interlined*], in pamphlet form, my recent speech, read by Mr. [James M.] Mason of your State. The views it takes, I hope will meet with your approval. It has met with the hearty approbation of all the Southern representation here, except open traitors to the cause of the South, and a few, who are still anxious to retain party connection, when all the ties, which, ["who" *canceled*] held the respective parties together are dissolved except the desire for the "Spoils of the government["]. Both have weaken[ed] the the [*sic*] cause of the South much, by offering propositions for compromise. Our true course was to place before the country in their full strength our just complaints, and leave it to our aggressors to offer terms of settlement. But most unfortunately, both classes of the individuals refered to have taken the opposite course, and, instead of waiting, have eagerly come forward & offered terms to our opponents, when they have not deigned to make a single offer. Mr. [Daniel] Webster ["yesterday" *canceled*], in his speech yesterday, without making an offer, indicated the grounds, on which he was disposed to act, and, although far short of our just demands, I must say, that they are better than [Henry] Clay's Bills, or any yet offered by Southern men. It is yet uncertain, what will be done, but there is no prospect, I can see, of making a final settlement of the questions between the two sections—one that will ["finally &" *canceled*] forever settle them. None has yet been offered which will terminate the agitation, about slavery & while that continues, the South cannot ["be" *canceled*] safely & hon[our]ably continue in the Union.

Present my kindest regards to Mrs. [Sarah Eppes] Hubard. I hope yours & hers fondest anticipation as to your son & daughter may be realized. Very truly & sincerely, J.C. Calhoun.

ALS in DLC, Personal Papers—Miscellaneous.

To Tho[mas] G. Clemson, [Brussels]

Washington, 10th March 1850
My dear Sir, I answered Anna's [Anna Maria Calhoun Clemson's] last letter by the last steamer; ["which" *canceled*] I hope she has received my letter.

Since then, my health continues to improve & my strength is so far returned, that I am able to take my seat in the senate & a part in the discussions of the body.

I send you a copy of my speech on the great question of the day. My friends insisted, that I should not undertake to deliver it, as it might over tax my strength. In conformity to their wishes, I wrote it out, and had it read by a friend [James M. Mason], I being present. It has made a decided impression. Since, then, Mr. [Daniel] Webster delivered his views. He took grounds more favourable to the South, than Mr. [Henry] Clay, but still far short of a permanent settlement of ["the question" *interlined*]. His speech, however, shows a yielding on the part of the North, and will do much to discredit Mr. Clay & other Southern Senators, who have offered less favourable terms of settlement. If he should be sustained by his constituents & N. England generally, it is not improbable, that he will take still stronger grounds; & that the question may be adjusted, or patched up for the present, to brake out again in a few years. Nothing short of the terms, I propose, can settle it finally & permanently. Indeed, it is difficult to see how two people so different & hostile can exist together in one common Union.

I wrote some time ago to Col. [Francis W.] Pickens and asked him to inform me, whether the arrangement, which you stated in your last letter to place our bond in ["your" *canceled and* "his" *interlined*] hand, had be[en] carried out, & whether, if the bond was in his hand, he would feel himself authorised to receive the interest & credit it on the bond; and, if the bond was not placed in his hands, to let me know, if he knew, ["wh" *canceled*] in whose hands it was. I have not yet heard from him.

I am happy to say that, I think, ["my" *canceled*] neither my late attack, nor ["that of a" *canceled and* "the" *interlined*] prevailing influenza, which, I took, in my convalescent state, & which so much retarded the restoration of my health, have left any permanent derangement of my system. The weather is now becoming mild, which will permit me to take exercise in the open air, & which only is required to a full restoration of my strength.

My love to Anna & the children [John Calhoun Clemson and

Floride Elizabeth Clemson]. Kiss the ["children" *interlined*] for their Grandfather. Your affectionate father, J.C. Calhoun.

ALS in ScCleA; PC in Jameson, ed., *Correspondence*, pp. 783–784.

To [GEORGE W.] CRAWFORD, [Secretary of War]

Washington, 10th March 1850

Dear Sir, Professor Leiber [*sic*; Francis Lieber] of our [South Carolina] College, has a son (Hamilton Leiber) whose name is on file in your Department, & he is very desireous to know what prospect he has of receiving a midshipman's warrant. He is well recommended, I learn, for the place & I would be gratified to hear of his success. Truly, J.C. Calhoun.

ALS in DLC, Gideon Welles Papers, 36:25790. NOTE: Calhoun addressed this letter in error to "Mr. Crawford," the Secretary of War. It was answered on 3/19 by William Ballard Preston, the Secretary of the Navy.

Richard Rush, Sydenham, [near Philadelphia,] to J[ames] M. Mason, [Senator from Va.], 3/12. Rush thanks Mason for a copy of Calhoun's speech, which he thinks was "powerful" and "patriotic." Rush asks that his friendly respects be given to Calhoun and regrets that Rush was able to see Calhoun only once when Rush was in Washington recently. He would be glad to hear Calhoun discuss European affairs, because he found himself agreeing with all that Calhoun had to say during their last visit. ALS in Vi, Robert Mercer Taliaferro Hunter Papers; PC in Ambler, ed., *Correspondence of Robert M.T. Hunter*, p. 106.

FINAL REMARKS ON THE COMPROMISE

[In the Senate, March 13, 1850]

[Lewis Cass of Michigan spoke against the views of William H. Seward of New York, placing himself on the Constitution and fearing danger to the Union.]

Mr. Calhoun. I have a few words to say in reply to the observations of the Senator from Michigan, and, as it is in reference to a point of some importance, I desire that what I say shall go out with his remarks. I regret very much that the state of my health does not permit me to enter fully into the argument, and that I shall be under the necessity of economizing my words, as well as my strength.

Mr. President, the Senator could not have heard me with more regret, make the declaration to which he has alluded, than I have heard him this morning make the declaration which he has made. Sir, the Senator and myself have two distinct and different conceptions as to the mode of saving this Union. His whole course has been a course of palliatives. And, sir, of all courses, that is far the worst. Why, sir, you might as well treat a cancer, that is about striking into a vital part, with palliatives, as to treat this question with palliatives. No, sir! my idea has been from the first, that it was a disease that would be fatal if not finally arrested; and I have acted upon that impression. If I am wrong, it is because the impression is wrong; and in order to arrest it, it is necessary at every stage of it, to understand the real causes and progress of the disease, and the causes by which it endangers the Union. In my late speech, which the Senator has heard with such profound regret—and I am amazed that my meaning should be so utterly misunderstood by the honorable Senator from Michigan—I stated simply, and in as few words as I could, what would certainly, according to my judgment, save the Union, promote conciliation, and restore harmony and good feeling throughout all sections of the Union. That was the amount of what I said. Now, I ask, can the Senator believe that the South is safe, while one portion of the community hold entire possession of the power of the Government, to wield it for their own benefit, in any manner they please, and while they see fit to interfere between the two sections of the Union? Can any man believe that the South is safe while this state of things exists? No man can say that he believes it. I do not, at least; and, therefore, all the wonder of the honorable Senator upon that point may cease. But the Senator says, it is impossible to comply with the requisition of giving us a new constitutional guaranty. Well, that very declaration goes to show—

Mr. Cass. The honorable Senator entirely mistakes. I certainly did not say anything of the kind.

Mr. Calhoun. I said, in my remarks the other day, that such amendment in the Constitution must be made as would give to the South—

[*Cass requested Calhoun to permit him to return to his remarks prior to a discussion of a constitutional amendment.*]

Mr. Calhoun. I understood the argument of the Senator as leading to that.

Mr. Cass. I hope the honorable Senator will defer his remarks until to-morrow morning.

Mr. Calhoun. I do not know that an opportunity will then be afforded me of saying what I desire to say upon this point. The Senator says that new guaranties cannot be given by amendments to be made in the Constitution. Sir, I insist that that is the legal and constitutional mode—it is the mode pointed out by the Constitution itself. Why, who ever before heard of such a suggestion as, that to amend the Constitution would be treason? It shows a state of feeling existing in the mind of the Senator which, in my opinion, is inconsistent with judicious action.

I intended to branch off here, and to show, that the distinguished Senator, if this Union is ever to be dissolved, will have contributed his full share to its dissolution; that the very entanglement we are now in, originated in the last Presidential election, and, as I think I have demonstrated, originated in a violation of the Constitution, and in a violation and disregard of the sovereignty of the States. Whenever the Senator chooses to go into a discussion upon this point, I am ready to meet him.

Mr. President, I must necessarily abbreviate what I have to say. The distinguished Senator heard me with painful feelings designate Washington as the illustrious Southerner. Why, the Senator ought to remember, that every effort has been made to take Washington out of our hands; but it seems that the morality of the present time is, that the assailant is perfectly innocent, and the assailed the only guilty party. Yes, sir! it was endeavored to take him out of our hands; and we are to be stigmatized as disunionists, and his message—his farewell address—to be quoted against us, while I venture to assert, that the greater part of that message bears directly upon the assailants, and not the assailed. It was to meet this, that I reminded the Senate and the world—and rightly reminded them—that Washington was an illustrious Southerner; he was not the less an illustrious American; but I must say, that the whole proceeding here, for the last fifteen years, has been such that, if carried out and consummated, as it will be, unless some definite understanding is arrived at, the end of the whole will be the holding up of Washington as a miserable slaveholder. I do not insinuate that Washington should be regarded exclusively as a southern man; I only say, we have a right to claim him as an illustrious Southerner, for he was a southern man—a southern planter—and we do not intend that he shall be taken out of our hands.

Mr. President, with these remarks, I will content myself for the present, without detaining the Senate further.

[*Cass replied that he had no intention to condemn Calhoun's proposal to amend the Constitution. He assured the Senate "that was not the difficulty at all."*]

Mr. Calhoun. What was it, then?

[*Cass replied that the problem was in Calhoun's assertion that failure to amend would be fatal to the Union.*]

Mr. Calhoun. Certainly; it would, in the end, be fatal.

[*Cass said that it was Calhoun's remark that the amendment must be made "immediately" that caused his dissent.*]

Mr. Calhoun. No, sir; that is not the language I used.

[*Cass quoted Calhoun's speech: "If the question is not now settled it is uncertain whether it can ever be settled hereafter."*]

Mr. Calhoun. Certainly.

[*Cass understood Calhoun's remarks to suggest that the Constitution must be amended and that the admission of California be made a test of the North's willingness to compromise.*]

Mr. Calhoun. Certainly.

Mr. Cass. That if California were admitted, it would be followed by a dissolution of the Union.

Mr. Calhoun. No, sir. I wish the Senator would read the remarks I made in reference to that point.

[*Cass read parts of Calhoun's speech of 3/4 relating to the need for compromise and his suggestion that the admission of California would "test" the North's willingness to compromise.*]

Mr. Calhoun. Read on—read the whole.

[*Cass read another paragraph. He stated that he thought California should not be a test and reiterated his opposition to a Constitutional amendment.*]

Mr. Calhoun. I must say there has been a strong disposition manifested on the part of the honorable Senator, to misconstrue my expressions—and plain expressions they are. The Senator says I asserted, that a dissolution of the Union would follow the admission of California. I did not assert that. I stated that it ought to be considered a test question; but I leave it to my constituents to determine what course they will take. Let the gentleman give the words I used, and I am willing to stand by them; but he must not expect me to be responsible for his interpretation of them. Well, in regard to the word "now," I did not intend to be understood as asserting that the amendment must be made instanter, but that an indication should be given now, that such amendment would be agreed to, and let it then be carried through the ordinary process.

[*Henry S. Foote of Miss., while declaring that no Senator was more devoted to the South than himself, suggested that Calhoun had put a wrong interpretation on his own words.*]

Mr. Calhoun. The Senator from Mississippi, in his ardor, much mistakes. He has just declared, solemnly, that I was engaged—as if he knew the fact—in preparing a compromise, and was also opposed to this committee.

Mr. Foote. Has the honorable Senator not told me that he was opposed to this committee? Did he not say to others that he was opposed to it? This is a fact which he cannot deny.

Mr. Calhoun. I am opposed to raising a committee at the present time; but I have invariably said, that if any gentleman desired to have a committee at the close of the debate, I would not oppose it.

I appeal to my colleague—to my friends around me—if that has not been my position. Now, sir, I trust this controversy will not be carried further.

[*Foote avowed that his controversy with Calhoun was painful for him and had been forced upon him by "circumstances."*]

Mr. Calhoun. The Senator complains that I did not consult him upon my speech. Well, sir, I never did consult any man upon any speech I ever made. I make my speeches for myself. When my friends called upon me in my room, I would propose some interrogatories to them; but I did not suppose that I could not come up here to express my individual feelings without the consent of the Senator from Mississippi.

[*Foote thought that Calhoun "was bound to consult us, who have an equal interest with him in this matter, before he made a new issue." He then mentioned a mass meeting in St. Louis which had sustained Thomas H. Benton against Calhoun.*]

Mr. Calhoun. Was it not a telegraphic report?

Mr. Foote. I believe it was.

Mr. Calhoun. I distrust all telegraphic reports. Mr. President, it is a common trick to send out telegraphic reports, and letters with them, and as soon as possible—perhaps in advance of the speeches and movements made—before the truth can be known. Well, sir, I think the Senator from Mississippi is the last man to complain of not being consulted.

Mr. Foote, (in his seat.) Never, sir—never.

Mr. Calhoun. He makes movements in which he does not ask the assistance of all his friends. He says he knows the opinions of all the Senators upon this floor, except two or three. But I say to him that I know, on the contrary, five or six who differ from him.

[*Foote replied.*]

Mr. Calhoun. He is far more familiar in his social intercourse with the Senators, in his habit of consulting them, than I am.

Mr. Foote, (in his seat.) I am on good terms with everybody.

Mr. Calhoun. I am not—I will not be on good terms with those who wish to cut my throat. The honorable Senator from New York [Seward] justifies the North in treachery. I am not the man to hold social intercourse with such as these.

Mr. Foote, (in his seat.) I think he (Mr. Seward) will have to be given up.

Mr. Calhoun. I recognize them as Senators—say good morning, and shake hands with them—but that is the extent of my intercourse with those who I think are endangering the Union.

From *Congressional Globe*, 31st Cong., 1st Sess., pp. 518–520. Also printed in the Washington, D.C., *Daily Union*, March 14, 1850, pp. 2–3. Partly printed in the Alexandria, Va., *Gazette and Virginia Advertiser*, March 16, 1850, p. 2; the Charleston, S.C., *Mercury*, March 18, 1850, p. 2; Benton, *Abridgment of Debates*, 16:439–443. Variants in the Washington, D.C., *Daily National Intelligencer*, March 14, 1850, pp. 2–3; the Alexandria, Va., *Gazette and Virginia Advertiser*, March 14, 1850, p. 3; the Baltimore, Md., *Sun*, March 14, 1850, p. 4; the Charleston, S.C., *Evening News*, March 16, 1850, p. 2; the Columbia, S.C., *Tri-Weekly South Carolinian*, March 19, 1850, p. 4; the New York, N.Y., *Herald*, April 1, 1850, p. 1.

J[OSEPH] A. SCOVILLE to [Thomas G. Clemson]

Washington, March 13, 1850

My dear Sir, I have to acknowledge receipt of your esteemed letter of the 18th Feb[ruar]y. John [C. Calhoun, Jr.] arrived day before yesterday and has just handed me the enclosed [*not found*]. I did not say any thing of Mr. Calhoun's illness when I last wrote for I did not think it would be very serious, and when he was worst I did not write for I did not want to worry you. He began to get better about the 14th of last month, and on the 20th commenced dictating his speech to me. I never expected to see him go out of his room again, but on the morning that he had arranged for [James M.] Mason to read it in the Senate, he made me get a carriage—and go with him to the Senate chamber. He coughed less than he had done for some days. After the delivery I hurried him as much as I dared to get him away from the excitement of the congratulation &c. To my surprize he was better that evening—and the next day insisted upon going again, and I went with him. He was better and spoke in reply to [Henry S.] Foot[e]. Wednesday the 6th it rained and he staid at home and gave me names to send his speech to. On Thursday he went over to the Senate & replied to [Daniel] Webster. He spoke very firm—was not near as weak as he has been, and his cough is visibly improved. I that day made up my mind that he would get well again. Still he raise and coughs a great deal and the excitement which is constantly kept up by people calling (He *will* see them) is very bad. He wont listen to any ["idea" *canceled*] suggestion of retiring. On the contrary I am certain that he will remain at what he calls his post as long as the breath of life is in him. His mind is made up. Things look very gloomy. There will be no compromise. The North are determined, and the South—are not. There is a jealousy on the part of would be great men such as [Henry S.] Foot[e] & others. If the South remain firm and stand by Mr. Calhoun—the north might grant Something—they may compromise—but I doubt it. It will be a mere piece of patch work. All is dark. No man can forsee what will take place. The South would be better of if a separation was to take place, but it would cause bloodshed. There will be no peaceable separation. I am at hand when any thing can be done to aid Mr. Calhoun & shall not leave him while he is here. He is accustomed to me, and I understand him.

I am the "Patrick Henry" the "Rabelaise" & the "Alexander" of the New York Herald.

The "Davis" of the Charleston Mercury.

The "Bascombe" of the "Columbia S.C. Telegraph"

The "Sentinel" of the "Georgia Telegraph" at Macon"

The "Paul" of the North Carolina Standard at Raleigh

So you see I am very busy.

Mr. Calhoun told me to write you and to put the letter in [Francis] Markoes hands which I will do at once in order to save the mail by the next steamer.

Present my kind regards to Mrs. C[lemson] and the little people, & Believe me, Yours Truly &c., J.A. Scoville.

ALS in ScCleA.

To H[ENRY] W. CONNER, [Charleston]

Washington City, March 18th, 1850
My dear Sir: I return the Bill herewith, endorsed as you requested. When the whole credits are entered, I should be glad to have a statement, showing the exact state of ["my account, as well as that of" *canceled and* "mine and" *interlined*] my son's [Andrew P. Calhoun; "account" *interlined*] with the Bank [of Charleston].

Mr. [Daniel] Webster's Speech [of 3/7] may have produced, in the first instance, the impression you deprecate; but there is no apprehension it will be permanent. It is universally understood here that he could not sustain himself at the North with either Party; and that, to protect himself from their assaults, he has taken shelter under the [Zachary Taylor] Administration. Can anything more clearly evince the utter hopelessness of looking to the North for support, when their strongest man finds himself incapable of maintaining himself on the smallest amount possible of concession to the South; and on points too clear to admit of Constitutional doubts? Very truly, J.C. Calhoun.

P.S. Mr. [John S.] Lorton informs me he has already made the deposit of nineteen hundred Dollars in the Bank.

LS in ScC; photostat (of LS) in DLC, Henry Workman Conner Papers; PEx in Wilson, ed., *The Essential Calhoun*, p. 363. NOTE: This letter is in the hand of Joseph A. Scoville and signed by Calhoun.

From J[AMES] K. PAULDING

Hyde Park, Dutchess [*sic*] County [N.Y.], March 19, 1850
My Dear Sir: I have received and read your speech with the deepest interest and attention. It traces the present crisis to its source, and points out the means of avoiding its consequences with perfect clearness, without declaration and without passion[.] It appeals to our reason and asks only justice. It will not perhaps be so much praised as some others; but hereafter when its predictions will be fulfilled, as I presume they will be ere long, unless the spirit of fanaticism is effectually checked in its career, you will be quoted as one who foretold the danger and pointed out the only means by which it could be avoided. It gives me pleasure to see that you take the same ground, with one exception, which I assumed in a pamphlet I had prepared on the same subject, but for which I could find no pub-

lisher. I was also desirous of publishing a second edition of a work of mine on slavery, now out of print, but was met by the same obstacle. The literary as well as the political press is enthralled in the North, and *audi alterem partem* becomes an obsolete maxim.

If you will permit me, I will suggest to you a doubt of the policy as well as efficacy of the guarantees you propose for the future safety of the South, which will be equally denounced with the Constitution as "violations of the law of God and the rights of nature" by the fanatics. They will be but burnt flax in their fiery furnace. I mention this, because it would seem that several of the representatives of the South are not prepared to go with you to that extent; and, as I have formerly stated, I think unanimity of the last consequence to the South[.] It astonishes me to see the distinction of parties still kept up in that quarter, and that when such momentous interests are at stake, instead of embarking to a man in one bottom, each one seizes his own plank and paddles away in different directions.

I cannot express the contempt and disgust with which I have read the speech of our [N.Y.] Senator, [William H.] Seward, though it is just what I expected from him. He is one of the most dangerous insects that ever crawled about in the political atmosphere, for he is held in such utter contempt by all honest men that no notice is taken of him till his sting is felt. He is only qualified to play the most despicable parts in the political drama, and the only possible way he can acquire distinction is by becoming the tool of greater scoundrels than himself. Some years ago, after disgracing the State of New York as Chief Magistrate, he found his level in the lowest depths of insignificance and oblivion, and was dropped by his own party. But the mud has been lately stirred at the very bottom of the pool, and he who went down a mutilated tadpole has come up a full-grown bull-frog, more noisy and impudent than ever. This is very often the case among us here, where nothing is more common than to see a swindling rogue, after his crimes have been a little rusted by time, suddenly become an object of popular favor or executive patronage. The position taken and the principles asserted by this pettifogging rogue in his speech would disgrace any man—but himself.

I fear it will not be long before we of the North become the tools of the descendants of the old Puritans, who had not the most remote idea of the principles of civil liberty, and no conception of religious toleration, but the most unrelenting intolerance. The despotism of parsons is taking the place of that of kings; and the gown and the petticoat have conspired to usurp the breeches. Our freedom is in great danger of being sacrificed to texts of Scripture, and fanatical dogmas; the Twelve Tables are becoming our law, and we shall be obliged to study the Pandects of Leviticus.

I fear, too, you will be tempted to trespass too much on your strength in defending yourself from your foes and friends. Let me beg of you to bear in mind that at your age and mine, nature is not often strong enough to make more than one rally, and that every successive effort is productive not of vigor, but exhaustion. Remember that, in all probability, the future will require your exertions as well as the present. I rejoice to hear the favorable opinion of your physicians. Don't trouble yourself to reply. I am, my dear sir, Yours, very truly, J.K. Paulding.

PC (from the Mobile, Ala., *Register*) in the Richmond, Va., *Daily Dispatch,* April 2, 1862, p. 1; PC in Jay B. Hubbell, ed., "James Kirke Paulding's Last Letter to John C. Calhoun," *North Carolina Historical Review,* vol. XXXII, no. 3 (July, 1955), pp. 412–414; PC in Aderman, ed., *The Letters of James Kirke Paulding,* pp. 514–516. NOTE: Paulding's *Slavery in the United States* was published first by Harper & Brothers in 1836.

From W[ILLIA]M BALLARD PRESTON, [Secretary of the Navy]

Navy Department, March 19th 1850
Sir, I have the honor to acknowledge the receipt of your letter of the 10th instant in relation to the appointment of young Leiber [*sic*; A. Hamilton Lieber] as a Midshipman in the Navy.

There were two Midshipmen to be appointed from South Carolina. The Department selected [William L. Butler] the Son of the late Colo[nel] P[ierce] M. Butler for one, and young Mr. [Thomas W.] Heywood for the other.

There is now no vacancy in that grade of officers from South Carolina. When one shall occur, the claims of Mr. Leiber will be most respectfully considered. I have the honor to be Very respectfully Your ob[edien]t Serv[an]t, Wm. Ballard Preston.

FC in DNA, RG 45 (Naval Records), Miscellaneous Letters Sent by the Secretary of the Navy, 1798–1886, 43:176 (M-209:16).

To ———

Washington, March 20th '50

My dear sir, I find from experience, that there is no hope of recovering my health, as long as I remain in the city. For that purpose I retire into the country, and a perfect exemption from the cares and exertions of public life are indispensible. I have accordingly determined to leave here in a few days and spend a few weeks with my friend Mr. R[ichard] K. Cralle. His residence is near Lynchburg Virginia, to which place during the period of my absence I wish my letters & papers to be sent.

I will thank you to prepare a notice to the above effect to be published in the [Washington Daily National] Intelligencer & [Washington Daily] Union. The publication may be delayed until the day of my departure. With great respect yours truly, J.C. Calhoun.

LS in ScU-SC, John C. Calhoun Papers. NOTE: This letter was written and signed by John C. Calhoun, Jr., for his father. The addressee was perhaps Robert Beale, Sergeant-at-Arms of the Senate.

From FRANKLIN SMITH

Canton Missi[ssippi], March 22, 1850

Sir, In common with most of my countrymen I have been denouncing Mr. [Daniel] Webster for 20 years. But he has come so much nearer right than was expected that it gives me pleasure to testify that he is now hailed in this region as a great man, and the sentiment is prevalent that if you and he were to take counsel together and adopt a plan—any plan that John C. Calhoun and Daniel Webster would now *both* approve—that such plan would bring larger armies of freemen into the field from all parts of the country to make it good, than could be mustered by all the Presidents, Secretaries and generals on earth.

Before the honors now within his grasp and yours, the Presidency, the Popedom and the Autocracy of Russia dwindle into helpless, infantine and utter insignificance and contempt. Such honors are already yours. Mr. Webster has now the opportunity to make them his, which if neglected can never occur again.

So far as I have heard an expression of opinion on the part of Democrats or States' rights men here, there is no sympathy felt in Gen[era]l [Henry S.] Foote's quasi attack upon you. As evincing a division in our ranks his remarks are regretted. So far as interpreted into a design to weaken your influence or break the force of the positions taken in your speech, his course is repudiated and condemned. God bless you and surround you with his heavenly guards! Very respectfully Your ob[edien]t S[ervan]t, Franklin Smith.

ALS in ScU-SC, John C. Calhoun Papers. NOTE: This letter possibly was never read by Calhoun.

From ANNA [MARIA] C[ALHOUN] CLEMSON

Brussels, Marc[h 2]4th 1850

My dear father, I see by the papers that you are recovering, which is a great comfort to me, but not a line have I received from any one about you. I think some one at Washington might have written, if it were only two lines, to Mr. [Thomas G.] C[lemson] or myself, for they might have known how we should feel, to see by the papers that you were ill, & have no intelligence. Do, my dearest father, go home, & take care of yourself, & come no more to that miserable Washington. The climate & the life you lead there, are both injurious to you, & I long to hear you are in Carolina once more.

I had letters from mother [Floride Colhoun Calhoun] & sister [Martha Cornelia Calhoun], the other day, but both were written before they had heard of your illness.

They all seem very fond of Anzie [Adams Calhoun], & I do hope John [C. Calhoun, Jr.] has a wife who will make him happy, & aid him on through life. From all I hear she has intelligence, energy, & good temper, & these are three sterling qualities in a woman. They all say they think she resembles me in appearance. I dont know, from my remembrance of her, how that can well be, but I am sure if it is so, you do not love her the less for that. By the way, talking of resemblance, a Belgian gentleman told me last evening, that he had recognised an engraving of *you*, which he had met with in a book, from its resemblance to me. "That must be Mrs. Clemson's father," he said immediately, & as the children say, "sure enough it was." This pleased me much, for I thought my full moon face had lost all the original likeness to you. The painter [Eugenius Frans DeBlock] who made your portrait told me that in painting it he was forceably struck with the resemblance also. This thing of likeness is very singular. [John] Calhoun [Clemson] is also thought strikingly like you yet he certainly does not resemble me in the least. Floride

239

[Elizabeth Clemson] on the contrary is said to be my image yet no one thinks her like you. If my son only resembles you in every thing, dearest father, I shall have nothing to wish for him. I fear he will want your calm & *fixity* of character. He is full of talent, of I think a high order in some respects, & the warmest & most generous impulses, but the most nervous & susceptible temperament, & the greatest imaginative powers I ever saw. I try to control these points of his character, or rather to teach him to control them, by making his education practical, & by cultivating as much as possible his reason, & also by taking the greatest possible care of his physical & moral faculties. Both of them are out in the open air as much as possible, & follow a regular course of gymnastics, which has had the most remarkable effect in developing their bodies, & I have a small garden, where when the weather is warmer, they may be in the open air all day, & dig & work as much as they please. I think I deserve to succeed with [my] children for I devote myself [to] them, & [tr]y to study their characters, & direct my efforts accordingly, but I often feel very anxious, least I should judge falsely, & not be acting right. For my daughter I fear but little. The sphere of a woman is more limited, & certain qualities are equally suited to whatever station she me [*sic*; may] be placed in, but in a man it is different, & I am more in the dark. However if I conscientiously do my best I dont think I can go far wrong.

To give you an idea of how well Calhoun's mind responds to a high idea I will mention a little conversation we had the other day. We were speaking of the mottoes on the arms of different families here & I said I thought grandfather's motto "The duties of life are greater of [*sic*] life itself" better than any. He thought for a moment or two & then said "Mama will you write that down for me & put that it is my grandfather's motto & when I am a man I will take it for mine & be a great man too." Well said Floride "I can take it for mine mama too, cant I, tho' I am not a *man*." I write these little things because I think they will please you.

We are all well tho' the changeable weather has given every one bad colds.

Mr. C[lemson] joins in love & the children send many kisses. Your devoted daughter, Anna C. Clemson.

[P.S.] Do get some one to write me if you do not feel well enough to write yourself.

ALS in ScCleA. NOTE: Because of a slight mutilation the exact day of this letter is not certain but it seems fairly certain that Calhoun could not have received it before his death.

CIRCULAR in Behalf of John C. Calhoun

Charleston, 25th March, 1850

The continued and alarming illness of Mr. [John C.] Calhoun fills the public mind with painful anxiety and profound regret. All feel his great importance to the country at this eventful period; all are sensible that his health has been sacrificed to his public duties; and all are deeply impressed with gratitude for his devoted and long tried public service.

Under convictions so solemn, a sense of public justice and of private affection prompt us to make such a manifestation of our feelings, as will testify our gratitude to one who has never faltered in the path of duty, and whose commanding talents have been surpassed only by his own exalted virtues and his devotion to his country's good. We would be instruments, in the hands of a Gracious Providence, *if it be His Will,* for restoring him, in renewed health and vigour, to the councils of the nation.

To discharge this solemn and grateful duty, and that we may with more propriety *urge* his temporary retirement from present labor, and the use of means necessary for the restoration of his health, we claim the privilege of raising, by subscription, an amount of money sufficient to enable Mr. Calhoun, should it be expedient, to visit Cuba and the Continent of Europe. Or, should this excursion not be deemed advisable, then we propose that the amount so raised be applied in such manner as may be considered best calculated to promote his health, his peace, and his happiness. And we trust that this movement will be regarded as a tribute and an offering to the true interests of this whole Republic.

We, the undersigned, therefore, do hereby agree to pay to Hon. Daniel E. Huger, H[enry] W. Connor [*sic*], or H[enry] Gourdin, Esqs., the sums opposite our respective names: and we do also hereby appoint these gentlemen our representatives to carry into prompt effect, and in such manner as they may deem most advisable, the intentions of this subscription.

Printed document in NcD, Sallie Donelson Hubert Papers. NOTE: This copy of the circular was addressed to Nathaniel Heyward at Collin's Cross Roads, S.C. Nathaniel Heyward, James B. Heyward, and William Henry Heyward signed this copy as subscribing for $1,000, $200, and $200, respectively. In the Charleston, S.C., *News and Courier,* February 3, 1893, p. 5, Robert N. Gourdin described Calhoun's refusal of the proposed subscription. The plan was revived after Calhoun's death and successfully paid off debts for the benefit of his family.

From E. W. GOODRICH, J. M. DUNN, and J. F. GREEN

Chestnut Grove Polemic Hall
Chestnut Grove [Va.?], Mch. 25th 1850
Dear Sir, At our meeting on Saturday the 23d Inst. the unde[r]signed were appointed a committee to notify you of your election as an honorary member of our institution. In discharging that duty we cannot repress the expression of our admiration for your eminent talents as a statesman orator and patriot nor can we forego the pleasure of returning to you our eternal gratification for the distinguished services which you have exercised in promoting the prosperity honor and glory of our common Country. We have the honor to be yours, Most Respectfull, E.W. Goodrich, J.M. Dunn, J.F. Green.

LS in ScU-SC, John C. Calhoun Papers.

E[LIZA GREEN REID] to Mrs. Andrew P. [Margaret Green] Calhoun, [Marengo County, Ala.]

Carrol Place [Washington,] 25th March 1850
My Dear Sister, Mamma [Lucretia Edwards Green] has just returned from Mr. Calhouns & glad am I to tell you that he is better, he sat up to day 1½ hours and walked across the room with the assistance of his nurse. He told mamma yesterday when she called to see him, (for you must know that she goes ["& visits" *canceled and* "to see him" *interlined*] *every day*), that he thought he would be well enough to come up here in a day or two. This evening he told her he would not venture out whilst the weather was so cold & as he expected Mrs. [Floride Colhoun] Calhoun the last of this week he would not make any change until she arrived. I need not tell you how glad we would be to have him with us and that we would do every thing in our power for his comfort & I may add that we are better able to have him here & can give him more comforts than we could this time last year, thanks to the hard labour of our dear Papa [Duff Green], & I know it would give him more happiness than I can express to have Mr. C[alhoun] stay with us until he recovers and as long afterwards as he could find it pleasant, he said as soon as he got home "I wanted Mr. C[alhoun] to stay here in my house all winter." I am so glad

Mrs. C[alhoun] is coming on for he requires some one to watch him all the time & who can do it as well as she. He does not appear to have any idea of how ill he is & has been. Dr. [James C.] Hall says the least imprudence now would be fatal[;] he could not live through annother attack. With care we have every thing to hope for.

I have not time to write more to night as I wish this to go in the mornings mail & if I do not send it to night it will not be in time. I write since tea so as to send you the latest news of him who is so dear to us all. You have never known how dearly I love him[;] it is a feeling which has grown with my gro[w]th and strengthened with my strength but I am not one to make professions.

The dream you speak of in your letter I had never heard of, in truth I have thought of nothing but Mr. C[alhoun] & the state of his health since we reached home. I have inquired however & learn that most persons think he never had such a dream as the one in the papers[;] he had a dream but I cannot get the correct account of it. I have heard several, all different, as soon as he is well enough I will see him and get his own version of it. You speak of the danger we are in here you would be surprised to see[?] how quiet every thing is since Mr. [Daniel] Websters speach every one, or most persons seem [to] think the question settled and very little is said about dissolution.

I will write [to] you again soon. Ever your aff[ectionate] Sister, E[liza Green Reid].

[P.S.] Love to Brother A[ndrew Pickens Calhoun] & all from [*one word changed to* "both"] ma & myself.

ALS in ScU-SC, John C. Calhoun Papers.

"RESOLUTIONS Dictated to Joseph A. Scoville by John C. Calhoun a Few Days Before His Death"

[Washington, March *ca.* 25, 1850]

Resolved That ["to deprive" *canceled*] the States composing the Southern portion of the Union ["the right belonging to them as members of it to emigrate with" *canceled and* "cannot be deprived" *interlined*] of their full and equal rights in the territory acquired from Mexico, or any other belonging to the ["States of this Union, United States" *canceled*] to the Union without violating the Constitution, pe[r]petrating an act of gross injustice, destroying their equality as members of the Union, and by retarding their growth and accelerating that of the States composing the northern portion of the Union, destroying the equilibrium of Government.

Resolved that the assertion that the inhabitants of the territories have [*blank space*] is utterly destitute of foundation, is in derogation of the sovereignty of the States composing the Union to which the territories are declared by the Constitution to belong and in whom the sovereignty over them resides is revolutionary & anarchical in its character, treasonable in its tendency and wholly unsustained by the practice of the Government.

[*The following canceled:*] Resolved that to make a constitution & to form a State involves the highest powers of sovereignty and ["beyond the competency of the inhabitants residing in the territories of the United" *canceled*] and that they cannot of course be rightfully performed by ["the" *canceled*] inhabitants residing in the territories ["belonging to the United States" *canceled*] without the per [*blank.*]

Resolved that to make a constitution and form a State involves the highest powers of sovereignty and that it cannot of course be rightfully performed by inhabitants residing in the territories without the permission of Congress as the representative of the United States to whom the territories belong or in whom the sovereignty over them resides.

Resolved that the attempt of the inhabitants of California to make a constitution and form a State without the permission of Congress is an offence against the joint sovereignty of the States of the Union and that the instrument purporting to be the Constitution of California is utterly void and of no binding force on the inhabitants thereof, nor on this government, or the States it represents & and [*sic*] the so called State but a name without any reality whatever.

Resolved that all acts on the part of any department of this Government or of the citizens of the U.S. intended to encourage, or aid the inhabitants of California to make a constitution and form a State (["if" *interlined*] without the permission of Congress there has been such acts) are utterly unauthorized by the Constitution and inconsistent with the allegiance ["to" *canceled*] due to the joint sovereignty of the States of the Union.

Resolved that it is not within the Constitutional competency of Congress to give validity to the instrument purporting to be the Constitution of California (or) and to admit the inhabitants of California into the Union as a State under it, because according to the fundamental principles of our system of Govt., constitutions derive their validity from the people by whom and for whom it was made, and because it would [be] inconsistent with and subversive of this principle to act on the assumption that Congress could [give] validity to the instrument and make it a consti[tu]tion by the act of admitting of its inhabitants into the Union.

Resolved that the States of the Southern portion of the [Union] are not opposed to the proviso, which usually bears the name of its author [David Wilmot], because it ["bears it" canceled] bears it but because its aim is to ["defraud" canceled and "deprive" interlined] the States (South) of their due share in the territories of the Union, by a palpable violation of the Consti[tu]tion by a total disregard of every principle of justice and equality, to be followed if adopted by a subvertion of their equality as members of the Union.

Resolved that any attempt to admit the inhabitants of California with the intention to evade the opposition to the proviso ought to excite a still more stern and indignant opposition because it would accomplish the same thing in a manner more objectionable and involve other Constitutional objections peculiar to itself and of a deeper and graver character if possible [than] what have been set forth in the preceding resolution.

Resolved that they are more objectionable because it would effect indirectly and surreptitiously what the proviso proposes to effect openly and directly because it would exclude the said States more effectually from said territory by being inserted in the instrument purporting to be a consti[tu]tion and what would be claimed to be a ["Constitution" canceled and one word or abbreviation illegible] if Congress should endorse than it would be if inserted in the provisions of a territorial Govt. while it would be equally unjust and unfair ["as if excluded by an ins(ti)tution(?) of the Proviso(?) by act of Congress" interlined] in as much as the citizens of said States have been precluded from emigrating to said territory by the action of this Govt. and thereby of being a voice in the formation of said instrument.

Resolved that the time has arrived when the said States owe it to themselves and the other States composing the Union to settle fully & forever all the questions at issue between ["the" changed to "them"; "two sections of this Union" canceled].

DU in DLC, James Henry Hammond Papers, vol. 18:22106–22109; PC in Jameson, ed., Correspondence, pp. 785–787. NOTE: Joseph A. Scoville wrote to James H. Hammond on April 18, 1850: "Mr. Calhoun commenced dictating some resolutions a few days before he died—he did not finish them, whether he intended them for the Senate or for Nashville [convention] I never knew. I will send them to you when I have time to make a copy. They are about 2 Sheets of paper in my hand writing." (ALS in DLC, Hammond Papers, vol. 17:21919–21921.)

J[ohn] C. Calhoun, Jr., to R[ichard] K. Crallé, [Lynchburg, Va.]

Washington, March 26th 1850
6 o'clock P.M.

Dear Sir, Father's health has continued to improve since you left, and for the last four days, his pulse has not indicated the slightest febrile action.

The weather has been so unfavourable, that the Doctor has advised him to keep his bed, so that, he is yet quite weak. I have no doubt, but that a few days of good weather, will complete his restoration to health, and that he will soon be strong enough to travel, with perfect safety.

Write by the return mail, and let us know what Hotel in Richmond, you will meet us at. Father thinks, that if it should not put you to too much inconvenience to come down in your own carriage it will probably be the most agreeable mode of travelling, to go up in your carriage. He leaves it to you to determine the arrangements, as you can so much better judge.

As soon as we fix upon the time for leaving, I will inform you, the time we will reach Richmond I will designate. I remain yours respectfully, J.C. Calhoun, Jr.

ALS in ScCleA.

William O. Goode, [former Representative from Va.], Boydton [Va.], to R[obert] M.T. Hunter, [Senator from Va.], 3/29. Goode discusses politics at length. He asks Hunter to offer to Calhoun assurances of Goode's highest respects and thanks for a copy of Calhoun's speech. A friend of Goode, who for years teased Goode as being "a Nullifier[,] Disunionist and Worshiper of John C. Calhoun," has recently said: "I acknowledge Mr. Calhoun is the greatest man now living. He has made it all plain as day; why did we not see it before?" ALS in Vi, Robert Mercer Taliaferro Hunter Papers; PC in Ambler, ed., *Correspondence of Robert M.T. Hunter*, pp. 109–110.

From R[ichard] K. Crallé

Lynchburg [Va.], March 30th 1850

My dear Sir, I have just received Dr. [John C.] Calhoun's favour of the 26th inst. and am much gratified to hear of your continued improvement. The inclement spell through which we have passed is, I hope, the last of the season; and as a milder and more regular temperature may be expected, I doubt not your health will be soon restored. With such aids, combined with a more quiet and peaceful retreat, I see no reason why you may not again enjoy your usual strength and elasticity.

I wrote to you the day after I reached home; but omitted, I think, to mention the Hotel in Richmond where I would advise you to go. *"The American"* is perhaps, the best; but I would rather reserve the selection until I got to Richmond myself; and to this end John must give me timely notice of the day when you will leave Washington— noting the time required for a letter to reach me, and the two days travel from this to Richmond. A letter written from Washington on Sunday, Tuesday and Thursday *morning*, before the mail leaves, will reach me on the suc[c]eeding Tuesday, Thursday & Saturday nights— and I could leave ["in" *interlined*] the *mornings* after, and reach Richmond in 36 hours.

I mention these particulars in order more surely to anticipate your arrival in Richmond. The arrangements after will depend on contingencies. If the Packet-boats be crowded—as they may be, we will take the cars to Charlottsville; and thence to a point on the canal from whence you can reach Lynchburg without sleeping on the Boat. I would prefer this as you might be too sensible to the dampness. I could readily meet you with a carriage, but in the present state of our roads, I fear the travel of 120 miles would too much tax your strength. We can easily reach here by 25 or 30 miles of land travel in a private conveyance should we think it advisable to shun the canal at night. There will be no difficulty in determining on the proper course when we meet.

Mr. [Thomas?] Bolling of Richmond desires that you should stay at his House on your arrival. He expects it—tho' I informed him it would be better to get as near the Canal as possible, should we take that route. He has been very kind in making all necessary arrangements for the journey on the Boat; but if it be crowded, I should prefer the Rail Road to Charlottsville, which will leave us only *day travel* by the Boat, after reaching the Canal from that point. This would, perhaps, save fatigue and exposure. But I will arrange all these matters in the way most conducive to your comfort. Let me urge you to leave the City as soon as you safely can. I trust the weather will now oppose no barrier; and that your strength will allow you to travel some time during the next week.

Mrs. [Elizabeth Morris] Crallé desires her kindest regards to you and to Mrs. [Floride Colhoun] Calhoun, should she be with you. She looks forward with great pleasure to the day when she shall see you both again. In haste, ever truly yours, R.K. Crallé.

ALS in ScU-SC, John C. Calhoun Papers.

Diary entry by Joseph Henry, Secretary of the Smithsonian Institution, [3/31]. "John C. Calhoun died this morning at 7 o'clock. Was sensible until the last—I called upon him about a month ago. Was to have seen him again—he promised to give me a sketch of his views relative to government—I have found no man in congress so interesting in conversation as Mr. C. no one ["so" *interlined*] quick to catch an idea and to give it back to you enlarged and improved. He was not friendly to the Smithsonian Inst[itution] but was very friendly to me personally. He thought the money should not have been accepted [from a foreigner]. I made several appointments to discuss with him the subject of the institution but we always got on some other subject." Entry in DSI, Joseph Henry Collection, Desk Diary. (Henry's diary for January 20, 1850 indicates an earlier visit to Calhoun. To that entry Henry added a note in 1862: "This visit was to Mr. Calhoun while he was on his death bed but a short time before his death. His servant said he was too ill to receive company but Mr. Calhoun hearing my voice asked that I would come in. I remained with him for some time and talked on the subject of Government[,] promised to read his book.")

"The Last Moments of Mr. Calhoun's Life," by J[OSEPH] A. S[COVILLE]

Washington, D.C., March 31—P.M.

This morning, at the age of sixty-eight, John C. Calhoun expired. Long as his death has been apprehended, it comes upon us as an unlooked-for bereavement.

The star of the western hemisphere has been stricken from the firmament. It belongs now to another universe. All unite in feeling that our republic has lost its most brilliant ornament, and a large section its almost idolized champion. During nearly half a century of public life, in which Mr. Calhoun has gone through all the various stages of political advancement, save one—from the local to the general Legislature—from the cabinet to the Vice Presidency, and from the Vice Presidency back again to the Senate—he has been regarded as the great statesman and patriot of the age. He now slumbers in death.

His last hours were in unison with his whole career.

Yesterday it became very apparent that he could survive but a very short period. He was restless, and evidently weaker but notwithstanding, he sat up for two hours, in the early part of the day. He conversed very little until evening. Some letters were read to him, upon which he commented. He spoke of the feeling of the South on the present agitating subject, and expressed his confidence that there would soon be but one sentiment—that the Southern people would unite as one man against Northern aggression. His confidence in the Southern people was unwavering to the last.

At half-past twelve he commenced breathing very heavily, which occasioned some alarm to his son, Dr. [John C.] Calhoun, the only member of his family who was present during his last illness. He remarked that he felt unusually wakeful, and requested his son to lie down, who objected. Then he asked his son if he felt uneasy? His son replied, "I do; had you not better take some wine, father?" He replied, "No; I don't require any more stimulus." His son felt his pulse, remarking that it was very low. Mr. Calhoun said, "I feel that I am sinking, but you had better lie down, John." His son did as was requested but felt very uneasy, as the difficulty of breathing still continued.

At two o'clock this morning, he called in a very feeble voice, "John, come to me." He did so, when Mr. C[alhoun] put out his arm, and asked him to feel his pulse, remarking, "I have no pulsation at the wrist. Take my watch on the table and put it in your trunk" which was done. He then pointed to a bureau of drawers, and said, "Take my papers and put them also in your trunk." (These papers are the manuscript works on government and the constitution.) He then remarked "The medicine has had a delightful effect. I am in a pleasant perspiration." At about 5 o'clock his son took a seat by the fire, desiring his father to take some rest, who said he had not rested at all. His son asked if he had any pain? He replied, "No,

I have not felt the slightest pain throughout this whole attack." His son asked, "Are you comfortable now?" He replied, "I am perfectly comfortable." These were the last words of Mr. Calhoun.

At about a quarter before six, he made a sign with his hand for his son to approach the bed. Holding out his hand, he took that of his son's, grasped it very closely, looking very intensely into his face, moving his lips, as if he desired to speak. His son, perceiving that he was speechless, at once called the Hon. Mr. [Abraham W.] Venable, of North Carolina. When the latter went to his bedside, Mr. C[alhoun] took hold of his hand, pressed it, and presented his wrist, apparently to indicate his approaching dissolution. He looked Mr. V[enable] in the face very intently while he was feeling his pulse. Mr. V[enable] remarked, "You are pulseless, sir, and must take some wine," and called for Madeira. Mr. C[alhoun] pointed to the wardrobe. Mr. V[enable] got the wine from thence, and poured out half a tumbler full. Mr. C[alhoun] took it in his hand, raised his head, and drank it. Mr. V[enable] then left the room, to summon some friends, and was gone about five minutes.

Soon after, the Hon. Mr. [James L.] Orr, and also the Hon. Mr. [Daniel] Wallace, both of South Carolina entered the room. When the door opened, his eyes were directed towards it, and were fixed upon Mr. O[rr], as he walked towards him, until he reached the bed. Mr. O[rr] leaned over to feel his pulse. Seeing his purpose, Mr. C[alhoun] extended his arm. He was asked if he would have the physician, Dr. [James C.] Hall, sent for. He shook his head. He then presented his wrist to Mr. Venable, who remarked, "The wine has produced no effect—there is no return of pulsation." He adjusted his head on the pillow, looked Mr. V[enable] in the face, with an expression which seemed to say, "I am perfectly conscious that it's all over." A few moments after, when breathing with some difficulty, he put one hand to the top of his head, then passed it through his hair, and brought it down again upon his breast. He then breathed quietly, except a slight rattle in his throat, his eyes retaining their brightness, and his countenance its natural expression, until the last breath, (which was drawn with a deep inspiration,) when his eyes suddenly became dim. They were immediately closed by Mr. Venable. His countenance was that of one who had fallen quietly asleep. He was conscious to the last moment.

At about eight o'clock on the evening previous to his death, Mr. Calhoun remarked that his mind was never clearer; that he had great facility in arranging his thoughts; and in reply to a remark of his son, that he was fearful that he was occupying himself too much with thinking, he said: "I cannot avoid thinking of the political affairs of the country. If I could have but one hour to speak in the Senate, I could do more good than on any previous occasion of my life."

The funeral will take place on Tuesday. To-morrow, Mr. [Isaac E.] Holmes will announce the death of Mr. Calhoun in the House of Representatives, he being the oldest member of the South Carolina delegation. In the Senate, Mr. Butler will make the announcement.

Yours truly, J.A.S.

PC in the New York, N.Y., *Herald*, April 2, 1850, p. 4; PEx in the Charleston, S.C., *Mercury*, April 5, 1850, p. 2; PEx in the Spartanburg, S.C., *Spartan*, April 11, 1850, p. 2; PEx in the New Orleans, La., *Daily Picayune*, April 14, 1850, p. 7; PEx in *Littell's Living Age* (November 11, 1854), pp. 265–266. NOTE: Scoville wrote a long letter to James Gordon Bennett, editor of the New York *Herald*, which was published in the *Herald* of May 3, 1850, p. 7, in which he gave a further detailed account of Calhoun's last days, including those who visited him and attended him regularly. And on April 18, 1850, he wrote a long letter to James H. Hammond (ALS in DLC, James Henry Hammond Papers) which gives further details and circumstances of the last few weeks of Calhoun's life. The PEx versions of this report omit only the short paragraph preceding the close.

D[aniel] W[ebster, Senator from Mass.], to [Fletcher Webster], "Sunday two oclock," 3/31. "Mr. Calhoun died this morning at 7 oclock. It is remarkable, that his body servant, who has waited upon him for thirty years, died also last night. Mr. Calhoun was just about my own age, born in the same year. I found him a prominent member of the House of Representatives, when I first took my seat in that body, in May 1813, the year of your birth. The Secretary of the Senate [Asbury Dickins] has come to signify Mr. [Andrew P.] Butler's [Senator from S.C.] wish, that I should say something in the Senate tomorrow, which I shall try to do." ALI in NhHi.

POSTSCRIPT
APRIL–AUGUST, 1850

〔

On April 1, in New Orleans, the courts were closed and a militia artillery battalion fired minute guns from dawn to dusk in observance of Calhoun's passing. (New Orleans, La., Courrier de la Louisiane, April 2, 1850.) *Public meetings were held the next day in Raleigh and many other places.*

On April 2, funeral services were conducted by the Senate chaplain in the Capitol. The text was from Psalm 82: "I have said ye are gods; and all of you are children of the Most High. But ye shall die like men, and fall like one of the princes." Memorial orations were made by members of Congress, Daniel Webster's being particularly generous and eloquent. Then Calhoun's remains were placed in the Congressional cemetery temporarily. (All reported abundantly in the press.)

The London Times *reported the news of Calhoun's death on April 10. The Oregon City* Oregon Spectator *announced the news on June 13, having received it by sea from San Francisco to Portland.*

On April 19, it was reported to Calhoun's son-in-law, the U.S. Chargé in Belgium, that at the port of Antwerp the flags of the consulate and of the American ships in harbor had been flown at half mast in recognition of the Union's loss. (William H. Vesey to Thomas G. Clemson, April 19, 1850. ALS in ScCleA.)

One of the strangest reactions to Calhoun's passing was that of the inveterate naysayer James H. Hammond, who recorded in his diary: ". . . he certainly sacraficed his last chance by going to Washington. I feel his death even more sensibly than I expected. Our intercourse for the last twenty [years] all recurs to me. . . . I grieve for the loss of the man more perhaps than I do for the Statesman. Pre-eminent as he was[,] intellectually above all the men of this age as I beleive—he was so wanting in judgement in the managing of men . . . that he never could consolidate sufficient power to accomplish anything great, of himself & in due season." The South had no one to replace him, and moreover the passing of Calhoun and other national men of his cohort would break "the last links of the chain of the Union." (Entry of 4/7/[1850] in ScU-SC, James Henry Hammond Diary.)

On April 22, Calhoun's earthly remains, in charge of Robert Beale, Sergeant-at-Arms of the Senate, and accompanied by an official delegation of Senate and House members and Calhoun's sons Andrew, Patrick, and John, went by rail to Richmond, where they rested overnight in the capitol. Then on by rail to Petersburg, Raleigh, and Wilmington, with public observances along the way, and by boat to Charleston.

It was assumed by the family that Calhoun would be buried at Fort Hill (on his own plantation ground, like Washington, and Jefferson, and Jackson). The town of Aiken had already made arrangements to observe the passage of the remains on their way upcountry and the citizens of Pendleton had organized to greet the last return of their distinguished neighbor. At Charleston, however, the sons were persuaded to let Calhoun rest there, in St. Philip's churchyard, pending the State's erection of a suitable memorial at Columbia. (The temporary resting place was to become a permanent one except for a slight interruption to avoid federal vandalism during the War for Southern Independence.)

For the interment services on April 26, government and business closed. The funeral procession accompanying what was described as "the lofty hearse" took two hours to pass and was thought to be the largest gathering ever seen in Charleston.

Calhoun's demise, not surprisingly, inspired artists. Clark Mills took a death mask from which he produced a bust. Numerous busts and paintings were commissioned. Likenesses were for sale in all the bookshops of Charleston and elsewhere. During the course of 1850 a lifesize wax image, a huge painting with accompanying musical composition, a "panorama," and a "diorama" featuring Calhoun were exhibited.[1]

The most curious event in this connection involved Hiram Powers's long-awaited statue, which had been commissioned by a group of Charlestonians. On July 19, 1850, the brig Elizabeth, *bringing the statue from Italy, was wrecked off Fire Island, New York, and sank in two fathoms, taking to the bottom the statue and*

---

[1] The Charleston *Mercury* and *Courier* are full of notices from April through December, 1850. A large file of information about Calhoun iconography from all periods will be available with the permanent Calhoun Papers collection at the University of South Carolina, South Caroliniana Library. See also Clyde N. Wilson, *John C. Calhoun: A Bibliography*, pp. 162–164.

drowning eight people including Margaret Fuller Ossoli. The operations of retrieving the statue were a running newspaper story until success was achieved in late October. (Contemporary newspapers.)

Calhoun's religious and theological views erupted into a minor controversy a few months after his passing and have presented for some observers a puzzle that perhaps can never be satisfactorily solved. Though he seems to have talked over these matters, as he did all significant questions of knowledge, with friends, including clergymen, he made no public declarations. Indeed, as a republican statesman he was correct not to encourage either the popularity-seeking such declarations might imply or the sectarian disputes that might ensue from competing efforts to gather his prestige for particular churches (as they did after his death).

He has at various times been characterized as a Calvinist, a Unitarian, and even a Swedenborgian.[2] *His supposed lack of trinitarian orthodoxy has called forth pervervid attacks from Calvinists well into the late twentieth century—not a major question but one seriously contested to those who are interested in Calvinism. It should be remembered, in connection with his supposed Unitarianism, that Calhoun had little to do with the organized New England-centered church of that name. If he was a "unitarian" it was in a Southern tradition following upon Jefferson that was quite different.*[3] *Calhoun was said to have remarked that no one could doubt the truth of Christianity,*[4] *which would put him a step or two further than Jefferson toward orthodoxy. His views and conduct were well within the easy folds of his wife's Episcopal Church, which he attended.*

Perhaps the most balanced and informative answer to the question was given by Anna Maria Calhoun Clemson when she was asked by Charles Edward Leverett, an Episcopal clergyman, to comment upon Calhoun's faith: "I approach with some little delicacy the subject of my fathers religious belief, because he himself was always reserved as to the particular tenets of his belief. This was from no carelessness or indifference on the subject, which occupied much of his thoughts. Should their be any doubt on this subject, his answer

[2] The charge of Swedenborgianism must have originated in the fact that his intimate, Richard K. Crallé, was interested in that philosophy. Crallé's denial appeared in *De Bow's Review*, vol. XXVI, no. 4 (April, 1859), p. 482.

[3] See John A. Macaulay, "Truth Over Fanaticism: The Independence of Southern Unitarianism, 1790–1860" (Ph.D. dissertation, University of South Carolina, 1998).

[4] Daniel Ravenel to Henry Gourdin, April 30, 1850, ALS in ScU-SC, John C. Calhoun Papers. This letter contains a judicious discussion of Calhoun's beliefs.

when the Rev. Mr. Butler of Washington, called & sent up word (during his last illness) he wished to converse with him, on religion would be sufficient. He said, "tell Mr. Butler I am too ill to see him, but I have not put off to my death bed, the consideration of a subject so important." He read, & studied the Bible constantly, & earnestly & conversed often, & beautifully about it, & his life was regulated, & governed, by an earnest & simple faith. His family was Presbyterian, but he always attended the Episcopalian Church, which was that of my mother, & grandmother, & all remarked, as you did, his reverential air during the services, but he never spoke of any particular form of worship, with preference, so far as I know, nor do I believe he ever did, to any one, tho I know there has been an effort made to prove he was this, that, or the other. I enjoyed, I am proud to say his confidence, & to me he never broached the subject, tho we often conversed on religion." [5]

⫴

From S. Newel Dada, Fulton, N.Y., 4/1. He writes to obtain a copy of Calhoun's recent speech on the admission of California and to secure Calhoun's autograph. Dada hopes that his wishes may be granted and that "your life, already past its meridian may be spared yet many years for our Countrys good." ALS in ScU-SC, John C. Calhoun Papers.

JOSEPH A. SCOVILLE to Tho[ma]s G. Clemson, [Brussels]

Washington D.C., April 1st 1850

My Dear Sir, I am writing this within a few feet of the venerated corpse of Mr. Calhoun. I sat up with him the last night. I hardly know where or how to commence my letter. After the last debate in which Mr. Calhoun took part in the senate, he returned to his room at ["the" *canceled*] Hills and never has left it since. His lungs were affected and so was his heart. I was with him night and day until John [C. Calhoun, Jr.] came, and when he arrived I relieved him a

[5] Anna Calhoun Clemson to Leverett, April 22, 1867, in *The Leverett Letters: Correspondence of a South Carolina Family, 1851–1868*, ed. J. Tracy Power et al. (Columbia: University of South Carolina Press, 1998), pp. 426–427.

part of every night. He would be better one day, and worse the next. He intended to have gone to Virginia. No *immediate* danger was apprehended until Saturday. On that evening he frequently remarked that he was sinking, and requested John to place his watch and papers in his trunk, soon after his pulse was completely gone. He spoke the last words about 6 AM yesterday morning[,] "I am very comfortable." His eyes continued bright, and his count[en]ance as expressive as ever for an hour afterwards, and he was conscious to the last moment. At 10 minutes past 7 he raised his right hand to his head, passed it through his hair, and then dropped it on his breast. His eyes became fixed, and he gave a long breath, something like a whistle, and all was still. His face even now is completely and exactly as it was in life. He died with a smile on his countenance, that same smile he always had. He told me ["not" *canceled*] to write you or Mrs. [Anna Maria Calhoun] Clemson, but to write nothing about being very ill. I did not write at all, for I felt that he was on his death bed. John says he cant write to day. Mrs. [Floride Colhoun] Calhoun is not here, and she had not even reached Charleston yesterday. Andrew [Pickens Calhoun] will come on at once. I telegraphed him to do so yesterday. James [Edward Calhoun] is at Pendleton, Willie [William Lowndes Calhoun] at Columbia. Not a female hand was nigh him except that of the Nurse. Mrs. [Martha Calhoun] Burt is in So. Ca. & Mr. [Armistead] Burt is ill. I begged, prayed and tried to persuade both Burt & John to send for Mrs. Calhoun in time. I could not assume the responsibility, for he had expressly told me not to write. I did write Mrs. M. Calhoun [Martha Maria Davis Colhoun?] & told her his exact situation.

I have but one moment to write you to be in time for the mail which leaves here in an hour. Let me refer you to the [N.Y.] Herald files. Yesterday I sent on a Telegraphic Despatch with nearly all the particulars, and last night I sent a more full letter, at the request of the So. Ca. delegation who read & endorsed it before it went. You will there find many of the ["events of the" *interlined*] last hours. John is the only one of the family here. The Body will be placed in a metallic Coffin and deposited in ["the" *canceled*] a vault in the Congressional Burying Ground, until ["you" *changed to* "Mrs."] Calhoun is heard from.

I sent you two letters this morning from home via the Department of State.

This will be a sad blow to Mrs. Clemson, and I am sorry to be the communicator of such an affliction, but I have tried to do my duty, and I have the future consolation in store to know that he approved and appreciated my devotion to him. He is dead, and the tie that bound me to this place is gone. I have done now with politics. I will never serve under a lesser man, and his equal will never be found. With respect I am in haste, Joseph A. Scoville.

ALS in ScCleA.

P[atrick] Calhoun, "Charleston Hotel," to Florid[e Colhoun] Calhoun, [Fort Hill], 4/3. He commiserates with her on the death of John C. Calhoun and hopes she will bear the affliction with becoming fortitude. "At the request of Governor [Whitemarsh B.] Seabrook I had an interview with him this morning, in which after expressing the deepest sympathy for yourself and the family[,] he requested to know whether it would meet the views of the family that Fathers remains should be intered in this City or Columbia. I answered that if Father had left no particular request on the subject I felt confident that no opposition to this request would be made by the family but that I could give no definite answer before communicating with you. I wish therefore that you would write me by return mail giving your consent. It is a reasonable request and one that we should willingly agree to as a tribute of great respect. I shall remain until I hear from you and then hasten to Fort Hill with all speed." ALS in ScCleA.

F[loride Colhoun] Calhoun, Fort Hill, to A[nna Maria] C[alhoun] Clemson, [Brussels], 4/4. Mrs. Calhoun informs Anna of John C. Calhoun's death in Washington and explains why she was not present there. She expects Calhoun's body to be sent from Charleston shortly. "Begin from this hour, to give your children, religious instruction. Tell them how calmly, and resigned, their Grandfather, died. He called John [C. Calhoun, Jr.], to him, and asked him, ["if" *interlined*] he thought he was worse, he said he did, then he calmly, told him, he was sinking fast, and that he must put his watch, in his trunk, and his papers, and lock them up, then, called him the second time, and reached out his arm to let him see he was dying, took him by the hand, and held it firmly between his, and gave up the Ghost. As to religion, he thought more deeply, on the subject, than many who, were public professors. In all his last letters to me, [he] concluded with God, bless you all, which was never before done by him. I never for a moment thought, thought [*sic*] your father, would be taken from us before he reached 70, but feared he would not live over that period, he failed so rapidly the last two years. God, has taken him to himself, and he could not have departed, at a better time, for his country, as it is supposed his death, will add much to settling this important question, which if it does, will be another call for us to give him up cheerfully. Every arrangement, is making to receive his body here, to be deposited on forthill, the highest rise on the top of the hill, which I mention that you may know precisely where he is laid, and think of the spot. We will inclose an acre at least, and have it walled in, with either stone, or brick. It is to be hereafter, a resting place for us all." ALS in ScCleA.

J[ohn] C. Calhoun [Jr.], Richmond, to R[ichard] K. Crallé, Lynchburg, 4/4. Calhoun writes concerning John C. Calhoun's trunk, now in Crallé's possession, which he wishes to take to Fort Hill when he returns. "If you have not sent it [in response to a request by Joseph A. Scoville], I would be glad, if you would keep it, until you hear from me again. Do be careful of the papers in it, and not let any one else, even borrow them from you. Father was sanguine to the last, that he would be able to visit you soon, and spoke of it, with anticipations of great pleasure." ALS in ScCleA.

[Bvt. Maj. Gen.] N[athan] Towson, [Paymaster General], Washington, to James L. Orr, [Representative from S.C.], 4/11. In reply to a letter of 4/8 in which Orr asks "what agency Mr. [John C.] Calhoun had whilst *Secretary of War* in establishing the exercise in Flying artillery tactics," Towson gives a short history of light artillery before Calhoun's service as Secretary of War. He then says, "The act to reduce and fix the military peace establishment approved March 2nd 1821 was prepared by Mr. Calhoun and bears the impress of his master mind. He conferred freely with the officers of the army, ascertained to a great extent the causes of failure and the defects in the army pending the war of 1812 and provided a remedy for them in future wars, as far as was practicable with the small force retained, and to that bill in a great degree the country is indebted to our success in the late Mexican War. That act provides that there shall be four regiments of artillery of nine companies each, one of which was to be designated and equipped as light artillery. This furnished a due proportion of this arm for an army the size of the one retained, and being distributed among the different regiments removed the inconvenience felt in the war of 1812 of having more of the arm than was required to serve at any one point to furnish commands for field officers. It was Mr. Calhoun's intention that these four companies should be constantly mounted and drilled as light artillery but Congress made no appropriation to meet the expense of purchasing and keeping the horses while Mr. Calhoun remained Secretary of War, and it was not until the year 1838, when Mr. [Joel R.] Poinsett was Secretary of War, that the companies were mounted and drilled as light artillery. . . . Mr. Calhoun did much for the improvement of all arms and all branches of the service, by the appointment of boards composed of intelligent and experienced officers to examine into and report on different subjects and to suggest alterations where they deemed them necessary." Ms. copy in ScCleA. (In a letter of 4/12 to James H. Rion, Orr enclosed this letter for Rion's use in preparing a eulogy on Calhoun. Ms. copy in ScCleA.)

[Martha] Cornelia [Calhoun], Fort Hill, to [Anna Maria Calhoun Clemson, Brussels], 4/12. "It has been decided that his [John C. Calhoun's] remains are to be intered here, as almost all the great men of the country are buried on their own places. The people of Charleston, & Columbia, are very anxious, that he should repose at either of those places. I suppose his remains will soon be here, brother Patrick has gone to Washington for them." Various members of the family are soon expected to reach Fort Hill. ALS in ScCleA. (Expecting Calhoun's remains to pass through on the way upcountry, the town of Aiken was already making preparations for the reception. Samuel Brooks to Charles G. Wagner, Intendant of Aiken, April 8, 1850; ALS owned by Elizabeth C. Teague.)

J[OHN] C. CALHOUN [JR.] to Governor W[hitemarsh] B. Seabrook

Charleston, April 19, 1850

DEAR SIR—I have to acknowledge the receipt of your Excellency's letters of the 17th and 18th insts. Since my brother Major [Patrick] CALHOUN and I had the honor of an interview with you, further reflection had induced us not to interpose our wishes to the temporary interment of our Father's remains in Charleston, keeping in view their removal to Columbia, or elsewhere, at a future day.

Indeed, considerations with which it is unnecessary now to occupy your Excellency's attention, seem to us to point out the expediency and propriety of their reposing here for the present. These were our views, when I addressed your Excellency on the 16th inst., but still we did not feel ourselves authorized to act in behalf of the family on this very delicate subject. Our brothers, Mr. ANDREW P. CALHOUN and Mr. J[ames] E[dward] CALHOUN, have since arrived in Charleston, and confirm our opinions as stated above. With the concurrence of so many members of our family as to the course proper to be pursued, and, under all the circumstances, should our fellow citizens of Charleston still be ready to receive the remains of our lamented Father, and afford to them a temporary resting place in their city, with your Excellency's concurrence, we cheerfully resign them into their custody, leaving the question, as to the place of their final repose, open to future consideration. With the highest respect and esteem, I remain yours, sincerely, J.C. Calhoun [Jr.].

PC in the Charleston, S.C., *Courier*, April 24, 1850, p. 2; PC in the Charleston, S.C., *News and Courier*, March 25, 1880.

AND[RE]W P. CALHOUN to R[ichard] K. Crallé, [Lynchburg]

Charleston, April 26th/50

My dear Sir, On opening my Fathers papers today we find none of the manuscript of his treatise upon the Constitution. We are aware that a part was placed in your hands a few days before his death, and are in hopes you have the entire work. If such is the fact we wish you to retain it untill you complete the revisal, for we are satisfied there is no one more capable to perform the task, or who had his confidence to a greater degree, or understood his views better.

As the original will be prized by the family may I ask you to preserve it carefully for us. His first work we perceive is entirely completed, and I trust the work in your hands was finished—he wrote me last winter it only wanted a few pages of being complete.

As he reposed so much of his fame upon these works, you may imagine with what solicitude his family feel for their security—and being brought properly before the publick. You stand prominent in our affection as his friend, and will be consulted as an advisor as to the best course to be taken with respect to them.

If you have completed the work retain it untill you hear from me. My post office is *Union town, Perry co., Alabama.* Very sincerely your friend, Andw. P. Calhoun.

ALS in ScCleA.

ANDREW P. CALHOUN to Gov[ernor Whitemarsh B.] Seabrook

Charleston, April 26, 1850

Dear Sir: On my arrival in Charleston, last week, from my residence in the West, after consultation with my brothers, P[atrick] and J[ohn] B. [*sic*] CALHOUN, we determined to accede to your Excellency's request that the remains of our father "should be temporarily deposited in the Metropolis, there to await the final action of the Legislature," provided it met the approbation of our surviving parent [Floride Colhoun Calhoun]. With this view, we addressed our mother, and she entirely concurs in our decision, and has placed the matter entirely in my hands, as the eldest of the family, to say to your Excellency, and through you to the people of the State, that we now place the remains of our father in their charge, to make such disposition as their feelings and wishes may dictate. I am, sir, with great respect, Your obedient servant, Andrew P. Calhoun.

PC in the Charleston, S.C., *Courier*, April 27, 1850, p. 2; PC in the Charleston, S.C., *News and Courier*, March 25, 1880.

AND[RE]W P. CALHOUN to R[ichard] K. Crallé, [Lynchburg]

Fort Hill, May 4th 1850

My dear Sir, I wrote you from Charleston respecting the manuscript of my fathers that he left in your hands. He expressed to me about a year ago his intention to place such papers in your hands as would aid you in writing his biography. I find in looking over his papers a vast mass of material that doubtless will be useful to you, and would be very happy if you could make it convenient to visit Fort Hill this summer for the double purpose of aiding us to prepare his works for the press—and to obtain such papers as you may desire. My mother urges me to insist upon your bringing your family and spending the months of July & August with us. I will leave for Alabama day after tomorrow, and expect to return here about the first of July. My fathers study shall be at your disposal[;] the dwelling is a large one, and independent of the particular object that now induces me to urge you to come, there is no one who our family would greet with more heartfelt pleasure than yourself. The country is entirely healthy about here, and by taking the mountain route, or even by rail road to Augusta Geo., would be perfectly healthy. The family join me in kind regards to yourself and family.

Direct to Union Town—Perry co., Ala. Very truly yours, Andw. P. Calhoun.

ALS in ScCleA.

J[OHN] C. CALHOUN [JR.] to R[ichard] K. Crallé, [Lynchburg]

Fort Hill, May 19th 1850

My dear Sir, I received your kind and interresting letter a few days ago, enclosing one from Gen: [James] Hamilton [Jr.] to yourself.

I remained two or three weeks in Charleston, after my return from Washington, to see what disposition would be made of father's remains. On reaching home I found your letter and perceived from the date, that it had been written several weeks previous.

You cannot imagine how much pleasure if afforded me, to hear from you, my father's long tried and faithful friend. I have long been cognizant with the intimate relationship, which has existed between yourself and father, and have often heard him speak in the highest terms of your tallents and character. The day after you left Washington, he remarked to me, that he missed you very much, and that "your manners were so quiet, and you seemed to feel so much for his situation." He often alluded to his contemplated visit to your residence, and said, he knew that your good lady and self, would do everything possible to add to his comfort and happiness. He told me, that it was his wish for you to prepare his work for the press, and that you intended writing his biography. I feel confident, that there is no man living, who from his intimate acquaintance with father, could better be assigned the task than yourself.

You have requested me to give you a sketch, of the last moments of my dear father, which I will endeavour to comply with, as well as my limited space will admit of. Father's last moments were in many respects in conformaty with his past career. He met death with calm dignity; silent because he had no past regrets to recount, and thoughtful and dignified because he was a Philosopher, who had no fear of the king of terrors. About a week previous to his death, he had what appeared to me a change for the worse, he lost his appetite, and for the first time in my life, I heard him speak despondently about himself. In reply to the enquiries of his friends concerning his health, he would observe, that he "did not seem to improve, but on the contrary was evidently becoming daily weaker" and he once remarked to me, that "if a change did not soon take place for the better, he could not long weather the ravages of diseased action." At this juncture of the disease, he requested me to have an interview with Dr: [James C.] Hall, which we had, in his room, in his presence. We came to the conclusion, that from the insidious nature of the disease, it was uncertain, as to its prognosis, he might linger for months, or sink in the course of a few days, from an acute turn of the inflamation, which evidently existed, in the air cells and substance of the lungs. He was generally apathetic, but I could sometimes cheer him, by reading the reviews and under the general head of the newspapers. I abstained, as much as possible, from referring to politics, and would request him to try and drive it from his thoughts, which to some extent, he succeeded in doing. He never suffered the slightest pain, throughout the whole course of the disease. On Saturday (the day preceeding his death) he appeared in better spirits, and said he felt stronger. He sat up most of the day and eat [*sic*] quite heartily, he insisted upon my taking some exercise (as I had not left the house for a week) remarking, that he felt a great deal better, but that he could not spare me for more than one hour. I left at one and returned at two o'clock, and found Dr: Hall on the eve of leaving[;] he told me, that father was a great deal better, but as the fever had just subsided, I had better give him a little wine occasionally.

About 7 o'clock PM, he seemed a little exhausted from the continuance of the expectoration which had then increased to an alarming extent. Soon (about 9 o'clock) a difficulty of breathing supervened, which arose from his inabilaty to raise the mucous from the lungs. Every succeeding hour seemed to increase his weakness, which caused me great uneasiness, and prevented me from lying down. At 4 o'clock he called me, and offered his arm, remarking that there was no pulsation at the wrist. His whole body was suffused with perspiration, which at once convinced me, that he was dying, he noticed my agitation, and asked me, "if I was uneasy about him," which I answered in the affirmative, he then said, "I feel that I am sinking," and directed me to put away in my trunk his important papers.

After I had arranged everything, as he had requested, I returned to him, and endeavoured to give him some relief, by turning him on his side, but he soon asked me, to place him again on his back, and when I asked him if he felt easier, he remarked, "I am now perfectly comfortable"—these were his last words. His loss of speech arose from the want of sufficient air in the lungs, to give articulation, even his last words were uttered so feebly, as to require me to place my ear very near, to hear what he said. He was speechless for an hour before his demise, but even then, his consciousness remained so clear, as to enable him to make intelligent signs to those around him. About five minutes before he expired, he beconed me to approach nearer, he then squeezed my hand, gazing intently into my eyes, moved his lips as if to speak, and breathed his last, without a pang or strougle.

My brother Andrew [P. Calhoun] & mother [Floride Colhoun Calhoun] have written urgently for you to pay us a visit this summer. Allow me to join them in the sincere hopes, that you will come. It would afford us unspeakable pleasure to have you & your family with us, and no pains will be spared to make your time pass off as agreeably as possible. I remain dear sir, your sincere friend, J.C. Calhoun [Jr.].

ALS in ScCleA.

ARMISTEAD BURT, [Representative from S.C.], to Thomas G. Clemson, [Brussels]

Washington City, 20 May 1850

My dear Sir, Information from the United States, will have informed you, that Mr. [John C.] Calhoun's death occurred before your letter could have reached me. I did not receive it until ["the" *changed to* "a"] fortnight after that sad event. I have been very indisposed ever since, and too much overcome by it to trust myself, with an attempt to write you, about the illness and last moments of one, whose loss is so heavy a bereavement to his whole country and such an affliction to his friends and relations.

On our way to this City, before the meeting of Congress, we met Mr. Calhoun in Charleston, as I thought, in his usual health. I thought it quite as good, as I could have expected, and better than when I last saw him. His complexion was good, and he seemed to have his customary strength. We came together, and he appeared to have borne the fatigue of the travel well. We were at the Hotel together, and talked of our arrangements for the winter. I submitted that matter to him, and Martha [Calhoun Burt]. Mr. C[alhoun] finally determined to go on Capitol Hill, and took lodgings at Hills boarding house. He believed it would be best for him, as it would save the ascent from the avenue to the Capitol, which he believed had injured ["the" *canceled and* "him" *interlined*] last winter. I earnestly advised against it, but without avail. Martha was so much opposed to going on the Hill, that we remained on the avenue all winter. For the first time, we were, thus unfortunately separated. His health remained quite good, until he took a cold, which affected him very much. Of this he became much relieved, but was quite feeble, when he determined to attend the sittings of the Senate. I observed, he coughed more than usual, and his expectorations were more frequent, and copious, than formerly. A visit to the Senate when he was quite too feeble to leave his lodgings, and the excitement of debate, threw him back, and produced slight fever. I did not regard it as serious, and did not doubt, he would recover. He thought, he would soon recover, and I had always found him so calm and accurate an observer of his situation, that my opinion was, in a degree, influenced by his own. Dr. [James C.] Hall, his Physician, believed he would recover, but advised that he should leave Washington, as soon as he had strength enough to travel. He was opposed to it, but finally yielded to my entreaties, and consented to go to Mr. [Richard K.] Crallé's his old friend, at Lynchburg, in Virginia. He sent on one of his trunks. I saw he did not, improve as fast as I expected, and consulted him, about the propriety of writing for Mrs. [Floride Colhoun] Calhoun. He insisted he was gaining every day, slowly, and strenuously opposed ["to"(?) *altered to* "my"] writing. About two weeks before his death I determined to write to Mrs. C[alhoun] without letting him know it, and did so, asking her to come without delay. But even then I had no fear of his death. But I observed him closely, seeing him from twice to three times in the day and night, and could not see that he was gaining strength, as he thought he was. Three days before his death, I was violently attacked with fever, and saw him no more. Dr. Hall, reported to me that he was slowly improving, and I ["neither" *interlined*] knew nor heard, to the contrary, until half [an] hour before he expired. Martha had gone home on a hasty visit and was absent also. Everything that skill or kindness could effect was done. I had procured an excellent & faithful female nurse. Indeed, nothing was omitted. His death came upon him unexpected, and from all I heard, he was not aware of its approach until about an hour before he ceased to live. But he died, as quietly as an infant sleeps. The sensation which his death produced, can scarce be imagined, in Congress and throughout the country. No American, whatever his station, had higher honors paid to his memory. The whole nation not only mourned, but wept, his loss. I send a few of the many tributes to his virtues and his character which were called forth. I have thought Mrs. [Anna Maria Calhoun] Clemson and yourself would value them. I can hardly realise that he is no more, and Martha's health has been seriously affected by her grief. Martha sends her love to yourself, Mrs. Clemson, and the children, with mine. Martha begs that I shall add a word more to Mrs. Clemson. She says she did not forget the miniature of Mr. Calhoun, which Mrs. C[lemson] asked her to have painted, this winter. But that Mr. Calhoun, said he could not have it done well here, and that Mrs. Clemson, must have it painted from the one she has in Brussels. She hopes Mrs. C[lemson] will believe that the miniature, was not neglected by her, and that Mrs. C[lemson] will not be disappointed on account of it. Sincerely and truly yours, Armistead Burt.

ALS in ScCleA.

AND[RE]W P. CALHOUN to Rich[ar]d K. Crallé, [Lynchburg]

Marengo co. [Ala.], May 20th 1850

My Dear Sir, Yours of the 4th inst., was rec[eive]d yesterday—and it was so full, and consoling, upon every point that I wished information upon, that it has set my mind at rest upon points that much perplexed me. My brother John [C. Calhoun, Jr.] thought you only had a few pages of the manuscript on the Constitution, and could give no account of the rest of the work. I knew how much time—thought—wear of body, and health, that work had cost father, for years he has condensed the ample volume of thought untill now nothing but the essence of ideas are left. I knew furthermore that he reposed much of his future *fame* upon these elementary works, and it was a great object in life to complete them while in the full possession of his faculties[.] Last november he wrote me to meet him in Charleston as he went to Washington. I did so, and spent a week with him. Being his eldest son, by two years, he has always, for the last 18 years, made me a confidential friend. He told me at our last interview on this earth, all his designs respecting his works. His intention was to bring out one of them immediately in view of the alarming conjuncture of the country. I objected to his doing so on the ground that it might divert the great issue, and give his enemies an opportunity to turn public attention to points in his book that might be in advance of the rec[eive]d notions of the times. He said he would consider about it. His intention was to consult with you in preparing the works. He had the profoundest reliance upon your friendship and intelligence. So much so my dear sir, that I feel in writing to you—altho personally unacquainted—as if addressing an old personal friend, and I must beg the honor of being so considered, for your name, I do, and shall ever connect with my fathers. To return to the works. It was his opinion in publishing, that his speeches illustrative of different points should be incorporated in the body of the book. My impression was different. I thought they should form an entirely seperate work, and to this end your suggestions become very interesting. My father told me the Harpers wished to issue another edition of his speeches & as the first edition was exhausted, and remarked that he had retained a copy of each document he wished preserved at Fort Hill among his papers. We had not time the other day to inspect any thing, and as I expected to return there in July I postponed all examination untill then. If it would not impose too much upon you, and it met your approbation I would prefer yourself to arrange and compile these papers exclusively for yourself. I shall write the Harpers that the compilation will be made and to make no publication without the sanction of the family. I have so much to say that I must condense. You rec[eive]d I trust, my letter from Fort Hill asking the favor of your presence there this summer. I designated July as I could not leave my planting interest here before, but I regretted doing so afterwards as the month of June would be the most pleasant to come south. My mother [Floride Colhoun Calhoun] was very anxious for you to bring Mrs. C[rallé] & family, and wrote to you before I left. Now I wish to say to you that the family will be delighted to see you as early as possible. I will come on as early in July as possible, and as administrator of the estate look over all his papers, and place such as you may require in writing his biography at your disposal. You he preferred, and you in the opinion of his family are the most competent. Very truly your friend, Andw. P. Calhoun.

ALS in ScCleA.

J[OHN] C. CALHOUN [JR.] to Mrs. A[nna Maria] C[alhoun] Clemson, [Brussels]

Fort Hill, June 20th 1850

My dear sister, I must begin my letter by craving your pardon for my long silence, not that this is the first time that I have been at fault, for you know, at best, that I am a poor correspondent, but I think, at this particular juncture of our lives, it is a duty we owe one another, to draw still closer together those ties of relationship, which is now our sweetest consolation, since our sad bereavement.

Before leaving Washington I wrote briefly to you, announcing fathers' death, and inclosed a lock of his hair, but as you make no alusion to it, I fear that it was lost. I have made some ineffectual attempts to write to you, but was prevented by the developement of a large boil on the end of my right thumb, which for sometime threatened to become a whitlow. Fortunately it has disappeared, without any serious consequences, but has left the finger so tender, that even now I can with difficulty hold my pen.

You have expressed a desire, for me to give you an account of fathers' death, which I will endeavour to do, but I feel, that, I can add very little, to the accounts which you have seen in the New York Herald and other papers. Being the only member of the family present, perhaps I may be able to add something of interest, connected with that sad event.

I reached Washington on the 28th of February, and found father much better than I expected to see him, although so weak as scarcely to be able to walk to the Capitol without assistance, altho' his spirits were as good as usual. He continued perceptably to improve, until he was provoked by Senators [Lewis] Cass and [Henry S.] Foote, to enter into an exciting debate, which was entirely too great a shock, for the weak state of his physical system. I accompanied him after the debate to his room which he reached in an exhausted state. After undressing and putting him to bed, he remarked to me, he had never before felt so much the need of physical vigour. For the first time in my life, I heard him speak despondingly about himself. His affection of the throat took an acute form, and a continued fever supervened, which lasted eight days. The second day after his relapse he remarked to me, that it was the severest attack which he had ever suffered from, and how providential it was, that I was with him. I did all in my power to cheer him up, by conversing and reading the reviews, & under the general head of the newspapers. Sometimes he would arouse himself, but generally he preferred to remain perfectly quiet. In reply to the enquiries of his friends concerning his health, he would shake his head despondingly and say, that "he did not seem to be getting better, but on the contrary seemed daily to be growing weaker." He once remarked to me, that "if a change did not soon take place for the better, he could not long weather the progress of diseased action." For the first week, he would allow no one but myself to attend him, but finding the confinement beginning to effect my health, I prevailed upon him to let me engage a nurse. When the fever left him, he seemed a great deal better, so much so, that his appetite returned, and he sat up most of the day. Even the day preceeding his death, (Saturday) he sat up and ate with considerable apetite, and seemed in decidedly better spirits, than he had for sometime previous. About eleven o'clock Saturday night a change for the worst took place. He breathed with difficulty, owing to the inability to raise the mucous from his lungs. As he grew weaker the difficulty of raising the mucus increased, until finally the lungs became so full, as to exclude the inhalation of air, which was the immediate cause of death. At 4 o'clock he called me, and told me he was rapidly sinking, and asked my opinion about the case, I confirmed what he had said, he then gave directions about his papers, and told me to take his watch. He then requested to remain silent, (about 5 o'clock AM) but at the end of half an hour, feeling uneasy I approached the bed, and asked him a question, he only moved his lips as if to speak—he was speachless. I called in Mr: [Abraham W.] Venable, who asked for some wine, which father pointed out to him, he drank it eagerly, but soon shook his head, as if to say, it is all over the wine has no effect, at the same time placing his hand upon his pulse. I held his hand, until overcome with sorrow, I sank into an arm chair near the bed; missing me, he looked at each of the gentlemen and shook his head. Mr: Venable told me that father wanted to see me. When I approached he smiled, took my hand in his and squeezed it, at the sametime gazing intently into my face. About one minute before he died, he shook my hand in token of farewell, relaxed his, raised it to his head, brought it down on his chest and breathed his last, with a sweet smile on his countenance.

You cannot imagine my feelings at that solemn moment, my dear sister, when the sad reality flashed upon me, I wept like an infant. The past and preasant crowded upon my memory. I thought of father, as the most affectionate of parents, and how utterly impossible it was, for any one to fill his place in our memory. We have truly lost the most affectionate of parents, and our country her most illustrious and patriotic citizen.

Father often spoke to me, in the most affectionate terms of you and all the rest of the family. He once said to me, "I am afraid, that Anna feels very uneasy about me"; and that he hoped soon to be able to write to you himself, saying that he was entirely convalescent. I enclose a sprig of box, which Judge [Andrew P.] Butler took off fathers' coffin, and beged me to send to you with his best respects and kindest sympathy. I have a lock of hair, which I preserved for you, in case the other was lost.

We are uncertain as to our future plans, as our share will be very small, I have determined to visit the west this fall, with a view of locating myself in the practice of my profession, indeed, father advised me before his death to pursue that course, if I found that there was no opening in this State. It is probable that Jimmy [James Edward Calhoun] or Willie [William Lowndes Calhoun] (especially the latter) if they do not acquire professions, will have no other alternative but to live at Fort Hill. As a married man, I am not contented to live on the small amount that I now have, but some of these days if I meet with success, I will return to our old and honored South Carolina, to spend the declining years of my life.

All are well on the place but old Tom, who has had a very severe attack of Pneumonia, which together with his old age, has left him in prostrated and dying state, in fact, I doubt if he lives twenty four hours longer; he has been a faithful negro, and it really makes me sad, to see him placed beyond my power of doing him any good.

Willie is still at Uncle James [Edward Colhoun]; they & Jimmy were quite well when last heard from, and will be up sometime in July.

Anzie [Adams Calhoun] joins me in much love to all, and believe me, your ever affectionate brother, J.C. Calhoun [Jr.].

ALS in ScCleA.

ANNA [MARIA] C[ALHOUN] CLEMSON to [Patrick Calhoun]

Brussels, June 24th 1850

I cannot tell you, my dearest brother, the pleasure your letter gave me, & with what a painful interest I read the details with regard to father. While I think of it, let me reply to one part of your letter. I infer that you think that I accused the family of neglect, in not going on to Washington, to be near father. I never had such an idea, in the smallest degree. I know too well how much all loved him, to suppose that for an instant, & I know also how we were kept hopeful to the last moment. It was not till the week before we heard of his death, that Mr. C. & myself had our eyes opened to his danger. He wrote me a cheerful, long, & firmly written letter, not a week before his death, saying that he thought his constitution had not received a permanent shock, & that he hoped to be soon in his usual health. With all this it was impossible to suppose we should lose him so soon, but Mr. C., who has, you know, some medical knowledge, began, from certain things he saw in the papers, to dread the event, & immediately wrote to Mr. [Armistead] Burt, desiring him to consult with father's physician, & if there was any immediate danger, to get leave of absence for us to return to the U.S., from Mr. [John M.] Clayton. Before Mr. Burt received his letter, our dearest father was no more. I could not then think that any of the family supposed him in danger, but I thought him very ill, & I knew so well how light he always made of sickness, & I feared that others who did not know all this, might accuse us of neglect. It was for this reason I urged that some one should go to him & no other. I merely mention this lest you should think me unjust. All these retrospections can be of no avail. Our noble father can never be restored to us. We shall never look upon his like again. In all history I find no man who combined so much talent, heart, philosophy, & simplicity. Truly do you say that his death is one of the noblest on record. An enemy to all parade, he made no exhibition of firmness, but calmly & quietly fell asleep, like an infant. And surely if any one could leave this life without dread, it was he, who never in the course of his long & useful life, failed in the performance of every duty. Knowing how he prized his well earned reputation, I feel at times, that had I the power to recall him, I should hesitate to use it, certain that it could be only to satisfy my selfish affection, so glorious is the spectacle of such a man, in the full splendour of his intellect, & at so critical a period, sinking into the grave, like the setting sun in unclouded splendour, amidst the tears of a nation. His life & death are bright & encouraging examples to every one, for they prove that a firm adherence to truth & principle, will in the end be appreciated as they deserve. I have not the sad pleasure, that you have, of mourning him at Fort Hill, where every object recalls his presence, but in imagination I often repass the years that are gone, when we were all so happy there together, & so vividly sometimes to [*sic*] I see my father, that I feel as tho' he must speak to me. Can we ever forget his sweet smile, &

his ready sympathy in all our pleasures & pains? He was our friend our guide our head & he is gone.

I regret deeply that he left no will. We should then have known that we were fulfilling his wishes exactly. Mr. Clemson, having no one in America to attend to his affairs, had already written to Mr. Burt, requesting him to act for him, when called upon by the family, for the arrangement, with regard to the debt, owed him jointly by father & Andrew [Pickens Calhoun]. He has written, since I received your letter, again to Mr. Burt, mentioning what you say, about the partition, & requesting him to represent us in that also. I do not suppose he will refuse, more especially as Mr. C. of course told him he expected to pay all expenses. If there were need I suppose then he might be written to, by some of you, & told when you will all meet. It will be a sad occasion of meeting, & in some sort like the breaking up of the family. The thought that the old place, in which he took so much pride, must now be divided, & perhaps some of the negroes, to whom he was so kind a master, sold, or at least separated, is very painful to me.

We are all quite well, & in the midst of dust, which renders Brussels a very disagreeable summer residence, but we are too poor to move. It takes the strictest economy to get along on the pay, & buy our furniture, which we do as more profitable than hiring. We cannot even keep a carriage, which would enable us to go from time to time into the country, & breathe the fresh air. The children grow as fast as ever, & so far from forgetting you, often speak of "uncle Paddy," particularly Floride [Elizabeth Clemson], with whom you contrived to render yourself a special favourite. She is shedding her teeth at present, which disfigures her. I wish you could come here, & I think with a little effort you might contrive it. See what you can do. We should be so happy to have you & I want to see some one of the family so badly. Mr. C. joins me in much love & the children also. Do write me often, fully, & freely. Truly your affectionate sister, Anna C. Clemson.

ALS in ScU-SC, John C. Calhoun Papers.

Tho[ma]s G. Clemson to Maj. Patrick Calhoun

Brussels, August 6th 1850

My dear Patrick, Your favour of July 6th has just come to hand. I lose no time in answering it, as tomorrow I send off my despatches. I wrote you some time since informing you that I had in accordance with your request nominated someone (that person was Mr. [Armistead] Burt) to represent Anna's interest at the family meeting, which will take place this month at Fort Hill, for the settlement of your fathers estate. Mr. Burt wrote me in answer that his public duties would prevent him from acting, expressing at the same time a regret that such was the case. I then sat down & wrote to Mr. [Joseph N.] Whitner of Anderson C[ourt] H[ouse] & wrote you a few lines on the subject. We are anxious that our absence should not be the cause of delay in any arrangements which may be necessary. So that I have done all that I can do & hope that what has been done by us may meet the approval of all the family. Fearing that my presence might still be required, I wrote a letter to Mr. [John M.] Clayton requesting him to give me leave of abscence to visit the United States to be used if I thought necessary. But owing to the death (I suppose) of the President [Zachary Taylor] & the change of the Cabinet I have received no answer, nor do I now expect it & shall have to remain quiet until I hear from the new Secretary of State informing me of his appointment. Then I shall write him & request permission to visit the United States should my affairs require it, some time during this fall. You speak of leaving Fort Hill in October. I hope that you will not leave until you hear from me, whether I shall be allowed to go home or not. I presume that next week will bring me the official announcement of Mr. [Daniel] Websters appointment. I shall then immediately write him on this subject. Should he give me leave & I decide to go, I will start at once for the United States & in that case shall hope to be with you in October or in the month of November. My journey will necessarily be rapid so that I shall be forced to leave my family here. There is another reason which renders it almost indispensable that I should return home viz: to endeavour by some means or other to dispose of my estate, negroes, plantation & all in Edgefield. That property has been a weight upon my back & given me a great deal of trouble without any profit. Besides which I have had no one to give it any attention & have been obliged to trouble Mr. [Francis W.] Pickens when I could have wished to avoid it. Had I imagined when I purchased it, that it would have caused so much difficulty I would most certainly have had nothing to do with it. But soon after I made the purchase I found that it would be almost impossible to struggle against all the obstacles in the way of success. I then came here & it has yielded me no profit & been the cause of great unhappiness. No wonder to quote an expression in your mothers last letter that I should be at times "irritable."

I pass from that to another subject upon which you ask my opinion viz., The destination which ought to be given to the manuscripts written by your father. I look upon those works as invaluable to the world & of great intrinsic value to the family. Your fathers great life was passed in serving the state of South Carolina & the whole South. Had his exertions been used in augmenting his fortune it may reasonably be supposed that you would all have had a large inheritance. As it is you have no reason to regret the almost unprecedented legacy he has bequeathed to you all in his name. No man ever died leaving so many sincere mourners. He defended the people of the South as his children during a long life. It is proper & right that the state he loved should possess his last legacy to his country & the family should not hesitate to give them up to her. I do not know what directions your father left with Mr. [Richard K.] Crallé but it is impossible they could interfere with this design. Naturally he could not foresee nor calculate in what he said to Mr. Crallé on this desire of the state, but I am sure it is an honour to his memory which he would have highly appreciated, & as his wish was to be useful to his countrymen even after his death he would feel the additional weight given, even his ideas, by their being thus so to speak, solemnly adopted by his beloved state. Anna entirely concurs with me in this view. I therefore think Governor [Whitemarsh B.] Seabrook should be informed that the family hold these valuable papers at the disposition of the state. The price paid by her for the work will doubtless be handsome & it is money that the family should be proud to receive & the state proud to give. Anna to whom her father often wrote & spoke on the subject says you are mistaken in saying there are "two works." The Disquisition on Government in general, is intended as an introduction to that on the constitution of the U.S. & they should be published together, one being necessary to the perfect understanding of the other.

I have thus fully given my views as to what I think should be done, whether the reputation of your father or the family interests are considered. I loved & venerated Mr. Calhoun as tho he had been my own parent & I am interested in all that concerns his memory or the well being of his family. [Matha] Cornelia [Calhoun] mentions that

James [Edward Calhoun] has written that Mr. [Henry] Gourdin is to go to Pendleton to see your mother [Floride Colhoun Calhoun] about paying the debts of the estate by subscription. This should be accepted. No false delicacy should stand in the way of this tribute offered by his friends. He spent his life & neglected his private interests to protect & defend his state. It is her proud duty to care for that family he loved so well. The estate once unincumbered will permit also the preservation of Fort Hill so hallowed to us all by his presence. I should think that the sale of the Alabama property *which I consider in all events* a necessity would permit a division to be made which would enable your mother[,] Cornelia[,] James & Willie [William Lowndes Calhoun] to preserve entire Fort Hill as a place of solemn pilgrimage to us all where we may go from time to time to honour our mother & recall more freshly to our minds the great & good man we have lost.

I wrote you and requested your advice as to what I should do with regard to the disposal of my property in Edgefield. How can it be done without risk? & who ought I to employ to do it for me? Since my abscence from the United States Mr. [John Ewing] Bonneau has died & I have no agent in Charleston to attend to any business that I may have. Can you name to me any one there in whom I can place implicit confidence, to attend to my business. In thinking over such person I shall consider it as a sine qua non that, the person I may select, should be at his ease in money affairs.

I have fifty or more negroes on my property. What are they worth? & what would they bring if sold?, & how am I to sell them & my land, Horses stock &c without running any risk in getting the money.

We are delighted to know that your health is improving so rapidly & hope that you will take care of yourself. Give my respects to Mr. Gourdin when you see him and say to him that I hope the portrait of your father gave him pleasure. Mr. [William W.] Corcoran of Washington wrote to me that he had received it & that it was very much admired and it was his intention to expose it in the Capitol for a few days.

We are all of us well with the exception of [John] Calhoun [Clemson] who is weakly and has a kind of cough but I hope he will get rid of it for we are doing all that we can to invigorate his constitution. Floride [Elizabeth Clemson] used to suffer from frequent sick head aches giving rise to fits of vomiting, which gave us great uneasiness, but I have, by great attention mainly to her diet and manner of eat-ing, managed to get her well or rid of them so that she is now taking on flesh & grows rapidly so much so that I fear she will be taller than her brother who as yet is the tallest by an inch or more.

Anna & the children join me in sending much love to yourself & the family. Your affectionate brother, Thos. G. Clemson.

ALS in ScU-SC, John C. Calhoun Papers.

[By ANNA MARIA CALHOUN CLEMSON]

Brussels Belgium, August 15th 1850

Sacred to the memory of the best of Fathers.

This imperfect collection, made in a distant land & under many disadvantages, is intended for my dear son, John Calhoun Clemson, with the hope that its perusal may induce him to follow the noble example of his Grandfather.

Imitate, my son, his unostentatious virtues, & cheerful philosophy. Be ever guided by the sentiment which regulated his every action, & was often on his lips—*"The duties of life are greater than life itself."*

ADU in ScCleA.

SUPPLEMENT, 1804–1848

▯

Documents that were not published in chronological order because not discovered or identified soon enough, or for other reasons.

▯

SUPPLEMENT, 1804–1817

◫

[Yale College diploma, 9/1804]. William Pinkney Starke saw and quoted from this document about 1886: "Senatus Academicus, Collegii Yalensis, in Civitate Novo-Portu, Reipublicae Connecticut-tensis," signed by "Timotheus Dwight, Preases." Abs in ScCleA, Starke's ms. life of Calhoun, typescript, p. 66.

Record of law studies, Charleston, 12/24/1804. An entry made in the records of the DeSaussure & Ford law firm indicates that Calhoun entered their office on this date as a student for a fee of "100 Guineas." Entry in ScHi, DeSaussure & Ford Cashbooks, vol. 3, no. 26.

HENRY W[ILLIA]M DeSAUSSURE to
Robert Goodloe Harper, Baltimore

Charleston, May 13th 1805
Dear Sir, Permit me to introduce to your acquaintance, Mr. [John C.] Calhoun, son of old Mr. Patrick Calhoun, & a near relation of our late respected friend Mr. J[ohn] E[wing] Colhoun.

This young Gentleman has been educated at New Haven, and has acquired more knowledge than is usual at his age—and there are indications of a superior mind.

He accompanies Mrs. [Floride Bonneau] Colhoun, the widow of Mr. J.E. Colhoun, who is going to the northward, where she has placed some of her Children for education.

Should ["you" *canceled*] they remain in Baltimore your attentions, to them will oblige me.

When shall we have the pleasure of seeing you here? It would give me & many of your old friends much pleasure, if you would pass a winter here.

I congratulate you on the acquittal of *Judge* [Samuel] *Chase*, a Dignified Senate, of considerable permanency, & high responsibility is an Important check on the wild measures of democracy. If there is any hope that our republic shall escape the fate of almost all other republics, destruction by the arts of demagogues, it is in the stability of our Senate. God grant it may escape. With great respect & Esteem I am Dear Sir yours very truly, Henry Wm. DeSaussure.

ALS in ScU-SC, Henry William DeSaussure Papers.

[Speeches and writings in behalf of Selleck Osborn, Litchfield, Conn., late 1806.] An anonymous 1823 biography of John C. Calhoun states, in regard to his stalwart republicanism, his activities on behalf of Osborn, a Republican editor of the Litchfield *Witness*, prosecuted for libel against the State: "The law-student JCC warmly interested himself in behalf of Osborne [*sic*], and by his writings, speeches, and other exertions, was in no little danger of sharing the fate of the persecuted editor." PC in the Richmond, Va., *Enquirer*, November 21, 1823, p. 1.

[Certificate from Litchfield Law School, 7/29/1806.] William Pinkney Starke saw and quoted from this document, which certified that "John C. Calhoun has read law as a regular student under the tuition of the Hon. Tappan Reeves [*sic*] and James Gould from the 22 July, 1805, to the date hereof, and that during that period he has applied himself to no other regular business, and has attended diligently and faithfully to the study of law." Abs in ScCleA, Starke's ms. life of Calhoun, typescript, p. 76.

Theodore Dehon to FLORIDE COLHOUN

Newport, Rhode Island, 17th March 1807
[*Inscription in a copy of* The Book of Common Prayer:]
Presented to Miss Floride Calhoun [*sic*] by the Rector, Wardens, & Vestry of Trinity Church, in Newport, as a small token of their sense of her skill & kindness, in performing upon the Organ of the Church, while the Church is unavoidably destitute of an Organist. By order of the Vestry, Theodore Dehon, Rector.

ADS in Prayer Book, Fort Hill. NOTE: In this volume are Colhoun and Calhoun family births, marriages, and deaths from 1764 to 1956.

By M[oses] Waddel, Abbeville District, S.C., 2/6/1808. Waddel renounces his claim to any part of the estate of the late Patrick Calhoun in behalf of William, Patrick, James, Jr., and John C. Calhoun "in consideration of the natural love and affection which I bear unto" them. ADS in NcD, John C. Calhoun Papers.

Remarks to the Republican caucus of the S.C. General Assembly, *ca.* 11/1808. PC in *Life of John C. Calhoun* (New York: Harper & Brothers, 1843), p. 7: see *The Papers of John C. Calhoun*, 17:10–11.

REPORT as Chairman of the Committee on Claims

[S.C. House of Representatives, December 12, 1808] The Committee on claims report

On the petition of Dr. George Carter for services rendered during the late war, that the prayer of the petition be not granted, as on examination they find that he has already been fully compensated.

On the petition of Alex[ander] Kincaid; that on examination they find the facts stated in the ["petion" *canceled*] petition to be true (viz.) that the petitioner purchased a tract of land sold under a mortgage to the loan office; and that an action was afterwards brought for the recovery of said land by Louisa Rose and others; ["for"(?) *changed to* "that"] the State was duely vouched; and that the plaintiffs in said action recovered nearly one half of the land purchased by the petitioner; so as wholly to destroy the object of his purchase. They, therefore, recommend that provision be made to reimburse the petitioner the sum of one hundred and thirty dollars (the sum paid for said land) with interest from the 15th April 1808[,] the time of eviction; also the sum of one hundred and twenty five dollars twenty two cents, the costs and charges incurred in defending said action; on the said Alexander's reconveying to the ["treasury" *canceled and* "State" *interlined*] the above tract of land.

On the petition of Absolem Shurley and others, Heirs of Champanions Shurley, praying payment of an indent to the said Champanions not drawen [*sic*]; sufficient vouchers not being exhibited ["exhibit as" *canceled*] to them they recommend that the said petition be refered to the Comp[trolle]r General to report on ["the" *canceled and* "its" *interlined*] merits at the next session of the Legislature.

On the petition of Jno. and Wm. Graham p[r]aying to recover a lost indent; they recommend that the petition be refered to the

Comp[trolle]r to report on its merits at the next session of the legislature.

On the petition of Stephen Fuller praying compensation for a horse placed in the publick service in the late war. The truth of the statement in said petition not appearing they recommend that ["its" *altered to* "it" *and* "prayer" *canceled*] be rejected.

On the petition of Isaiah C. Fitten praying payment for a horse and Clothing furnished in the ten months service; it not appearing what clothing was furnished; or what the value of the horse was they recommend that ["the prayer of" *canceled*] the petition be rejected.

On petition of Jacob Lazerus [*sic*; Lazarus] praying to be paid $100 on account of a ["counterfit" *canceled*] bank note which he received from the treasurer and which has turned out a counterfit; that as it appears, that the said note was received in exchange from the treasurer ["fr"(?) *imperfectly erased*] acting in his individual character, that ["the prayer of" *canceled*] the petition be rejected.

On the petition of Wm. Pledger Praying compensation for services; that, as it does not appear what services were rendered, ["tha"(?) *canceled*] the petition be rejected.

On the petition of Benj[amin] Reynolds praying to be indemnified for a tract of land sold by the commissioners of Confiscated estate to him and which has been recovered by an older grant; that the petition be rejected for want of vouchers to substanstiate the truth of its statement.

["On the petition of ("Richard Winn and others" *canceled*; "of" *imperfectly erased*) H. Milling praying a compensation for a negroe. That on investigation it appears that the said negroe was apprehended for wounding a Mrs. Kenedy, and that before trial he committed suicide; the committee are of a opinion that the petition ought to be rejected." *This entire section was canceled and the word* "rejected" *written in the margin opposite it.*]

On the petition of ["George" *canceled and* "Joseph" *interlined*] Palmer ["praying" *interlined*] for a grant of pine land out of the secretary's office that the prayer of the petition be rejected.

On the petition of Martha Anderson praying to be enabled to draw the annuity of John Calhoun; that, as it appears that the said Calhoun is not absent, as represented in said petition, that it be rejected. J.C. Calhoun[,] Ch[air]m[an].

ADS in Sc-Ar, Records of the Comptroller General, Accounts Audited of Claims Growing out of the Revolution, 1778–1867, 1105-E. NOTE: An AES of 12/17 by R[ichard] Gantt, Clerk of the House, indicates that the House agreed to the report and that it was ordered to be sent to the Senate.

Lattimer and others vs. Robert Elgin and wife, and Lewis Gannt, Ninety-Six District Court of Chancery, 2/1809. Calhoun represented the defendants in this suit over an estate. Printed report in DeSaussure, *Reports of Cases Argued and Determined in the Court of Chancery of the State of South-Carolina, and in the Court of Appeals in Equity,* 4:26–33.

Benjamin Houston vs. John Gilbert, "Notice of Motion for a new trial, Laurens Dist[rict Court of Common Pleas]," 11/1809. Calhoun represented Houston and the trial jury found in his favor in a suit to recover the cost of a slave who was "a most intollerable rogue and runaway . . . to the knowledge of the Defendant." [Abraham] Nott represented Houston in the appeal. ADS (by attorney Samuel Farrow) in ScU-SC, Thomas Waties Papers.

RESOLUTION on Court Expenses

[S.C. House of Representatives, December 2, 1809]
Resolved that it ["is" *interlined*] expedient to remedy by some means the exorbitant expe[n]ce in small cases above magistrate jurisdiction and that some effectual means be taken ["to" *canceled*] this session to remedy the same.

ADU in Sc-Ar, Records of the General Assembly, Resolutions, 1779–1847. NOTE: Below the text of this resolution and written by someone other than Calhoun, are the words, "On motion—referred to." An AES on the reverse side reads: "referred to a Committee, see the names attached within—considered & agreed to. John S. Richardson, Chairman."

REPORT for the Committee on Claims

[S.C. House of Representatives, December 5, 1809]
The committee on Claims Report,
On the petition of Leonard Dozier praying for compensation for a negro executed; that the same be granted; and the petitioner be allowed one hundred and twenty two dollars forty four cents for the same.
On petition of John Rose praying compensation for a negro exe-

cuted, that the same be granted; and the petitioner be allowed $122.44.

On the petition of John Moncrief ["that"(?) *canceled*] praying to be allowed a ballance of a claim against this State that on examination of the same, they find that this committee at the last session reported in favour of the petitioner to the amount of $1813 but by some mistake provision was only made to the amount of $1500; they thererefore [*sic*] recommend that the prayer of the petition be granted; and he be allowed $313. J.C. Calhoun.

ADS in Sc-Ar, Records of the General Assembly, Committee Reports, 1776–1862, 1809, no. 126. NOTE: An AES of 12/6 by R[ichard] Gantt, Clerk of the House, indicates that the House agreed to the report and sent it to the Senate for its concurrence. A final endorsement reads: "Lay on Table."

REPORT as Chairman of the Committee on Claims

[S.C. House of Representatives, December 6, 1809]
The Committee on Claims Report;

On the petition of Richard Gains praying compensation for a negro executed for rape, that the prayer of the petition be granted; and that the petitioner be allowed the compensation allowed by law in such cases viz. ["$122.50" *altered to* "$122.44"].

On the petition of Thomas Duckett for the same as the above, the committee Report as in the above case.

On the petition of Francis Lafilly praying compensation for a negro executed for Arson that the prayer of the petition be granted; and the petitioner be allowed one hundred and twenty two dollars ["fifty" *canceled and* "forty four" *interlined*] cents. John C. Calhoun, Ch[airma]n.

ADS in Sc-Ar, Records of the General Assembly, Committee Reports, 1776–1862, 1809, no. 131. NOTE: An AES by R[ichard] Gantt, Clerk of the House, shows that the House approved the report on 12/6 and that it was sent to the Senate for its concurrence. A final note reads: "Lay on Table."

REPORT for the Committee on the Abbeville Court House

[S.C. House of Representatives, December 6, 1809]
The Committee to whom were refered the presentment of the grand Jury as to the condition of Abbeville Court, report; that they have taken the same into consideration; and are of opinion that the court house is extremely inadequate to the use of so large; and populous a district. That the court house is small, inconveniently constructed, old and leaky. Your committee farther state, that the papers belonging to the former district of Ninety-Six are deposited in the court house of Abbeville; and that from the leaky condition of the same are daily destroying, to the great detriment of the State generally; your committee therefore recommend that an appropriation be made not exceeding the sum of $5000 for the purpose of erecting a new Court house; and that five commissioners be appointed to carry the same ["to" *imperfectly erased*] into effect. John C. Calhoun.

ADS in Sc-Ar, Records of the General Assembly, Committee Reports, 1776–1862, 1809, no. 23.

REPORT as Chairman of the Committee on Claims

[S.C. House of Representatives, December 7, 1809]
The committee on Claims Report; that they have taken into consideration, the report of the commissioners appointed at the last session of the legislature to enquire into the account of the Justices of the County court of Fairfield, and to investigate the claim of John Buchan, Richard Winn and others ["as" *interlined*] presented by their petition ["at" *interlined*] the last session; that after mature deliberation they find, the return of the said Commissioners to be correct; that the said petitioners have expended out of their owen [*sic*] purse the sum of $327.99 including interest to the first day of January next; and also that there is a judgement against them in the district court of Fairfield on a bond given to the builder of said Court house to the amount of $953.14 including costs of said suit, principal and interest to the first of January next. Your committee, farther state, that there appears to be due of good debts to the treasurer of the county court of Fairfield £152.13.10. They, therefore, recommend that provision be made in the appropriation bill to the amount of the principal, interest and costs due on the bond aforesaid (viz.) $953.14; and that the

solicitor of the midle circuit be directed to take immediate steps to recover the ["goods"(?) *canceled*] debts due to the said Treasurer of the county court of Fairfield; and when recovered the sum of ["thre" (?) *canceled*] $329.99 ["be paid" *interlined*] to the said petitioners, or their order; and the ballance to the treasurer to this State. John C. Calhoun.

ADS in Sc-Ar, Records of the General Assembly, Committee Reports, 1776–1862, 1809, no. 12. NOTE: An AEU of 12/14 by R[ichard] Gantt, Clerk of the House, indicates that the House concurred in this report and directed that it be sent to the Senate. An AEU of 12/16 by B[enjamin] H. Saxon, Clerk of the Senate, shows that the Senate concurred in the report.

REPORT as Chairman of the Committee on Claims

[S.C. House of Representatives, December 8, 1809]
The Committee on Claims Report,

On the petition of Charles C. Ash praying compensation for a negro executed that the petition be granted; and he be allowed one hundred and twenty two dollars forty four cents.

On the petition of John B. Earle praying compensation for a negro executed that the petition be granted and the petitioner be allowed $122.44.

On the petition of William Thompson praying that a double Tax, which he has paid, be returned; that, the double tax, without the ["costs" *altered to* "cost"] of suit, in collecting the same (viz.) $52.35, be refunded.

On the petition of Peter Oliver praying to be allowed the amount of interest that may be found due him ["him" *canceled*] as administrator of Joseph Short ["&" *canceled*], Jacob Schene and others late mariners on borard [*sic*] the ship South Carolina, that the prayer of the petition be granted and that the petition be refered to the Comptroller to ascertain the amount of the interest; and that the petitioner be allowed one half thereof. John C. Calhoun.

ADS in Sc-Ar, Records of the General Assembly, Committee Reports, 1776–1862, 1809, no. 46. NOTE: Appended is an AES of 12/14 by R[ichard] Gantt, Clerk of the House, affirming the concurrence of the House in the report and stating that it was sent to the Senate for its concurrence.

REPORT of the Committee on Gabriel Benson's Petition

[S.C. House of Representatives, December *ca.* 10, 1809] The Committee to whom were refered the petition of Gabriel Benson praying for the establishment of a turnpike road; Report that they have taken the same into consideration; and are of the opinion that the establishment of the turnpike requested will considerably facilitate the intercourse between this State and the western country, to the mutual advantage of each; your committee find on investigation, that the contemplated turnpike will shorten the distance to the state of Tennessee from the western part of this State [*one or two words canceled*] near fifty miles; and will furnish a road nearly as good a[s] the one now in use. Your committee are farther of opinion that it will be extremely difficult to keep ["the" *interlined*] said road in a passible condition, unless on the principle of vesting an interest in some individual for that purpose; your committee therefore recommend that power be vested in the petitioner to open and keep in repair a turnpike from Saluda river throug[h] douthett's gap to pegion river in the State of Tenessee; and that the petitioner be vested with power to take a moderate toll, to be established by law [*partial word canceled*] in himself and his heirs and assigns for the turm of 21 years; on condition that he ["p"(?) *canceled*] keep ["the" *interlined*] said road in a good and passable condition; and also on condition that he ["closes" *canceled*] leaves open all roads and paths way now in use. J.C. Calhoun.

ADS in Sc-Ar, Records of the General Assembly, Committee Reports, 1776–1862, no date, no. 664. NOTE: Benson's petition was referred on 11/29 to a committee headed by Calhoun. The S.C. House of Representatives adjourned on 12/19.

REPORT as Chairman of the Committee on Claims

[S.C. House of Representatives, December 11, 1809] The Committee on Claims Report,

On the petition of James and Elizabeth Ken[n]edy praying compensation for a negro executed that the prayer of the petition be granted and they be allowed $122.44.

On the petition of Timothy Barton praying compensation for a negro executed that the prayer of the petition be granted and he be allowed $122.44.

On the petition of Joseph Wood praying to be rembursed money expended by him in repa[ir]ing the court house that the prayer of the petition be granted; and he be allowed $41.87.

On the petition of John Bird in right of himself and as administrator to his brother for services rendered during the last war; your committee have taken the above Claim into serious and mature deliberation, and are of the opinion that the prayer of the petitioner ought to be granted. It appeared by the most undoubted evidence to your committee that the petitioner and his brother were faithful soldiers [*one word or partial word canceled*] in the cause of our country during ["the whole" *canceled*] nearly the whole of the revolution; and that the petitioner was taken a prisoner at the capture of Charleston and continued a prisoner till the summer of 1781. That the petitioner has made application to the general government for a compensation for his services but his application owing to his not having heard of the provision made ["for such services" *interlined*], from his remote situation, was not [made] till after the final liquidation of the Claims of the several States against the [*partial word canceled*] United States. Your Committee therefore recommend that petitioner be allowed the sum of $331.87 being the principal sum due the petitioner and his brother after ascertaining the difference betwen the depreciated currency in which the petitioner was paid; and the sum of ["three"(?) *canceled*] $333.13 [*one word or partial word canceled*] being one half of the interest on said sum; being in the whole $665. John C. Calhoun.

ADS in Sc-Ar, Records of the General Assembly, Committee Reports, 1776–1862, 1809, no. 47. Note: An AES of 12/14 by R[ichard] Gantt, Clerk of the House, reads: "Resolved that this Ho[use] do agree to the within report, Or-d[ere]d that the same be sent to Senate for their Concurrence."

REPORT as Chairman of the Committee on Claims

[S.C. House of Representatives, December 13?, 1809]
The Committee on Claims Report

On the petition of William Knox praying for a pension; and payment for a mare killed in the publick service; that the prayer of the petition be rejected as to the pension; and as to the payment for his mare, your committee report that they have the most satisfactory vouchers that the said mare was killed in a very meritorious and dangerous atempt on the Cong[a]ree fort; and that the petitioner has never received payment for the same[;] your committee therefore recommend, that ["p" *canceled*] the petitioner be allowed the sum of eighty dollars the value of the said mare without interest for the same. John C. Calhoun.

ADS in Sc-Ar, Records of the Comptroller General, Accounts Audited of Claims Growing out of the Revolution, 1778–1867, 4373. NOTE: The manuscript S.C. House of Representatives Journal for 1809, p. 92, indicates that this report was made to the House on 12/14/1809; that it was agreed to by the House and sent to the Senate for its concurrence.

To [BENJAMIN TALLMADGE, Representative from Conn., Litchfield, Conn.]

Abbeville [S.C.], 10th Feb[ruar]y 1810

D[ea]r Sir, Give me leave to introduce to your acquaintance Mr. William D. Martin a young gentleman of my acquaintance; who expects to spend some time at Litchfield in the law school. Mr. Martin is a young gentleman of reputable connections; and is much esteemed among his acquaintances for his many good qualities. Whatever attention your politeness may prompt you to extend to him ["will" *interlined*] be thankfully acknowledged by ["your" *canceled*] me. I am with sentiment of esteem your's &c, John C. Calhou[n].

ALS in ScU-SC, John C. Calhoun Papers.

To BENJ[AMIN] TALLMADGE, [Representative from Conn.], Litchfield, Conn.

Laurens So. Ca., 18th April 1810

D[ea]r Sir, I take the liberty of introducing to your acquaintance my friend Mr. Robert Cunningham. He intends to spend a year, or more at Litchfield in taking a course of law Lectures. From a very intimate acquaintance with him, I can say with certainty you will find him a young gentleman deserving your attention. He is of an excellent character, and of very respectable connections; and I have no doubt, from his close attention to his studies, his acquirements already and his abilities, that he will rank high among the members of the law school in Litchfield. I leave all farther recommendation to your farther acquaintance with him; and will be always ready to acknowledge any attention you may be pleased to show. I am with much esteem your's &c, John C. Calhoun.

ALS in ScU-SC, John C. Calhoun Papers.

Richard Quarles et al. vs. the administrators of the estate of Hugh Middleton, Ninety-Six District Court of Chancery, 6/1810. Calhoun and George Bowie successfully represented Quarles et al. in a case concerning dower rights and a S.C. law abolishing primogeniture. Printed report in DeSaussure, *Reports of Cases Argued and Determined in the Court of Chancery of the State of South-Carolina, and in the Court of Appeals in Equity*, 4:145–148.

HICK[SON] BARKSDALE vs. John Nelson Newby

In the [Court of] Common Pleas
West[ern] Circuit, At Abbeville Octo[be]r Term 1810
Tried before his Honour Judge [Elihu H.] Bay. ["Verdict for Pl(ainti)ff" *canceled.*]
On the trial of this case it came out in evidence that the plaintiff Hickoson [*sic*] Barksdale and the Defendant Jno. N. Newbey [*sic*] had traded horses and that the note on which the action was [f]ounded was given in boot between the horses by the defendant. The Defendant set up a defence of unsound property. To substantiate this defence Williams was sworn who proved that the same horse was owned by his father before he came into the possession of the Plaintiff and that he had at that time the string halt; that the horse could stand a ride for a few miles without discovering the defect; but after he became heated it in a great measure prevented his traveling; that he did not think the horse worth thirty dollars; and that he thought it impossible for the horse to be any length of time in the possession of one without discovering the defect. John Scudy, ["James Beckley" *interlined*] and Williamson Norwood ["both" *canceled*] proved that the horse is still disordered with the string halt; that the defendant had gave full value if the horse had been sound[;] that the horse gave in exchange was worth eighty five dollars; and that the string halt horse is not worth more than thirty dollars[;] ["They are both we" *canceled*] and that they were ["both" *canceled*]

well acquainted with the horse. They also proved the tender of the horse back to Plaintiff. Norwood farther proved that the defendant had bought the horse for a special purpose (viz) to go on a journey to Raleigh Nor. Carolina and that, the horse gave out on the journey by which defendant was compeled to purchase another and was put to great inconvenience; also that he [Norwood] was about to trade for the horse ["once" *canceled and* "with the plaintiff" *interlined*] but ["that" *canceled*] brother of the plaintiff gave him to un[der]-stand that the horse was disordered by which he was prevented.

Joseph Lee was called in on behalf of the ["defendant" *canceled and* "Plaintiff" *interlined*] who swore that he had seen the horse strained in a race while in the possession of the Plaintiff and that he did not perceive any thing the matter of him; and that the plaintiff was offered one ["hundred" *interlined*] thirty dollars ["for him" *interlined*] which he refused to take. The Judge charged favourably to the plaintiff and the jury brought in a verdict for twenty five dollars. The Defendant will move for a new trial on the following [gr]ounds[:]

1st. That from all the circumstances of the case it is presumable that ["there was" *canceled*] Plaintiff had knowledge of the defect; and of course practised a fraud on Defendant by concealing it.

2dly. That the object for which the horse was purchased failed and of course destroyed the contract.

3dly. That the horse got by Plaintiff in exchange was worth much more than the string halt one and the Plaintiff ["not" *canceled*] on that account ["not" *interlined*] entitled to recover.

4th. Verdict contrary to law and evidence.

ADU (in Calhoun's handwriting) in ScU-SC, Thomas Waties Papers. NOTE: Calhoun represented the defendant and George Bowie represented the plaintiff. An AEU by Judge Thomas Waties, the appellate judge in this case, reads: "Let this Verdict sleep—Sanctioned by both Judge & Jury." Another copy of this brief, partly in Calhoun's handwriting but mainly in George Bowie's, is found in the Waties Papers. Appended to this second copy is Judge Elihu H. Bay's report on the case, which reads in part: "Observing that it was almost every day[']s Practice for men who had been disappointed in their Bargains ["of this kind" *interlined*] to come into a Court of Justice to get them Rescinded—and to endeavour by a multiplicity of Witnesses, to endeavour to bias a Jury in their Favor—but unless there was some very evident Fraud or imposition practiced it was better to uphold Contracts than to set them continually afloat."

Edmond Foreman vs. James and Jesse Lawson, "Motion for non-suit or new trial," Abbeville [District Court of] Common Pleas, 10/-1810. Calhoun represented the Lawsons in a suit over the sale of a slave whose title proved to be uncertain. Judge Elihu H. Bay directed the jury to find in favor of Foreman. Calhoun filed this motion for consideration by the "next constitutional court" (circuit judges sitting as an appellate court) at Columbia. An AEU by Judge Thomas Waties of the Constitutional Court indicates that the motion was discharged. ADU (in Benjamin C. Yancey's handwriting) in ScU-SC, Thomas Waties Papers.

BENJAMIN LOVE vs. Abraham Hadden

Western Circuit, Abbeville District
[Court of Common Pleas] October term 1810
Motion to set aside Nonsuit. Tried before Judge [Elihu H.] Bay.

This was an action of trespass to try title &c. The Plaintiff claimed the land in question as Heir at Law to his Mother Jane Love. To substantiate his claim he gave in evidence under the usual restrictions, a Copy Grant, for the lands in dispute, to one Sarah Fee, who was cousin to Pl[ain]t[i]ff. He then called as a Witness John Love, his son, to prove his Pedigree. John Love, said, that his Grand Mother, had two brothers, Hugh Fee, who was the elder, and John Fee. That Hugh Fee was born in Ireland, & removed to this Country previous to the American revolution, & settled in Charleston; The other brother, John, went into the British Armey previous to the American Revolution & has never been heard of since. That Benjamin Love, the Plaintiff in this action is an only son of John Love, & that Sarah Fee was the Daughter of Hugh Fee the Brother of Plaintiff's Mother. A Mr. Hawthorne, a very old man, was then called, who said that he was well acquainted with Sarah Fee the Grantee, and she was dead; That he also was acquainted with her Father Hugh Fee, who was also dead, & died about the year 1760 leaving a son, John Fee, who took as heir at law to his sister Sarah. That he saw John Fee, son of Hugh, during the American revolution; he was then residing in Charleston, a cripple. That since the death of Sarah Fee, and Hugh Fee, Witnesses Mother had made considerable enquiry after John Fee, son of Hugh, and has never been heard of since Witness last saw him, which was during the American Revolution. The identity of the land was then established, & the trespass being proved, Plaintiff rested his case.

The Defendant then called for a Non Suit which the Judge granted, on the following grounds only.

That at the death of Sarah Fee the Grantee, who died since the American revolution, the land descended to her brother John Fee, an American citizen having resided in Charleston at the time of the decleration of Independence; & that Plaintiff being an Irishman (born in Ireland previous to the Revolution) was an Alien, and incapable of taking a descent cast since our Revolution.

1st. [*sic*] The Plaintiff[']s Attorney, moves, to have this Non Suit, set aside, on the following grounds.

1st. That the Plaintiff being an *Anti Nati*, still retains all the privilages of Birth, which he had previous, to the ["American"(?) *canceled; sic*] of this Country from Great Britain. That during the Colonial Situation of this Country, he was by birth capable of inheriting lands, in this Country, of which his Ancestors were seized. Therefore he is and was, capable of taking & holding these lands at the death of John Fee.

2nd. That admitting the incapacity insisted on, the British Treaty, commonly called Jays treaty, provided for his case.

ADU (in an unknown handwriting) in ScU-SC, Thomas Waties Papers. NOTE: Calhoun and George Bowie represented the defendant and Benjamin C. Yancey represented the plaintiff. An AEU by Judge Thomas Waties, the judge in the appeal of the case, reads "Submitted. To be considered."

JOHN NELSON "NEWBEY" ads. "Hickoson" Barksdale

[Abbeville District Court of Common Pleas
October Term 1810]

Take notice that at the next constitutional court at Columbia the defendant will move for a new trial on the following grounds:

1st. The contract between the parties was void ["as" *canceled and* "because" *interlined*] there was sufficient evidence to presume a knowledge of the disorder of the horse in the plaintiff of course he must have practiced a deceit on the defendant.

2dly. Because the object for which the purchase was made wholly failed.

3dly. If the contract was not void the plaintiff was not entitled to recover as he had received a horse (together with the notes sued on) in exchange of greater value than the horse, purchased of Plaintiff.

4th. Because verdict contrary to law and evidence. Calhoun, atty.

ADS in ScU-SC, Thomas Waties Papers. NOTE: AEU's by Calhoun read "Motion for new trial" and "Notice for his Honor Judge [Elihu H.] Bay." An AEU by Bay described the case and explained his actions in trying the case.

W[illia]m Smith vs. Robert Young, "Motion to set aside" a judgment, Abbeville District Court of Common Pleas, 10/1810. In a suit over a $9 debt, Calhoun was attorney for the plaintiff whose plea was dismissed. This motion seeks to set aside that action. ADU (in Benjamin C. Yancey's handwriting) in ScU-SC, Thomas Waties Papers.

A[LEXANDER] SPENCE vs. John Spence

In the [Abbeville District Court of] Common Pleas
Western Circuit [October 1810]

Tried before his Honor Judge [Elihu H.] Bay. Verdict for Pl[ainti]ff.
This was an action of trespass to try titles brought by the plaintiff Alexander Spence against the Defendant John Spence. The Plaintiff gave in evidence a copy of the original Grant to Mark the father in law of Plaintiff, a mesne conveyance from Mark to himself. The locus in quo was admited and trespass proved. The defendant on his part proved declerations made by Mark in the presence of Plaintiff that he had sold the land many years ago [*two words canceled*] to ["a" *interlined*] certain Williamson living in Charleston and that he had made conveyance of it to the said Williamson and had been paid for the same. Isreal Davis proved that he once offered to purchase the land from Mark and that he informed him that he had sold it ["to" *interlined*] Williamson; upon which the witness offered to give him six dollars for a conveyance of it; which Mark seemed disposed to take; but took time to consult Robert Smyth. He Smyth proved that when consulted he gave it as his advice that it would be a dishonest act as he had once sold it and had been paid; on this Mark refused to sell. This took place in the presence of Plaintiff and before he purchased of Mark. The defendant also proved that Williamson had not been heard of for many years; and offered to prove farther declerations of Mark that he had sold and conveyed the land and that Plaintiff had knowledge of ["them" *canceled and* "it" *interlined*] before ["the" *canceled*] his purchase when defendant['s] counsel were stopt and a point made to the court by the plaintiff's that evidence of that kind was inadmissable; and that the defendant

293

ought first to account for the loss of the deed of conveyance; and then prove the contents by a copy, or some one who had seen the original; and could prove its contents. The court sustained the objection made by Plaintiff's counsel; and verdict was given for plaintiff.

The Defendant will move for a new trial on the ground that the evidence given and offered to be given by him is in its nature legal and admissiable to prove that Mark had conveyed the land to Williamson and that the plaintiff had notice thereof; and ought to have been admited by the court to go to the jury.

ADU (in Calhoun's handwriting) in ScU-SC, Thomas Waties Papers. NOTE: Calhoun represented the defendant, John Spence, and Benjamin C. Yancey represented the plaintiff. AEU's by Judge Thomas Waties, appellate judge in the case, summarized the case and legal points made in the appeal. Another copy of this brief, in Benjamin C. Yancey's handwriting, and Judge Elihu H. Bay's autograph report on the case and his original decision, are also found in the Waties Papers. The brief in Yancey's handwriting bears an AEU by Waties which reads "discharged."

Marriage license of John C. Calhoun and Floride Colhoun, 12/-27/1810. An entry indicates that on this date a license was issued to John Caldwell Calhoun of Abbeville, "Esquire," and Floride Colhoun of Charleston, "Spinster," to be married by Theodore Dehon. Entry in Sc-Ar, Charleston County Court of Ordinary Minute Book, 1808–1812.

From GEO[RGE] WARREN CROSS

[Charleston, S.C.] 25 Feb[ruar]y 1812

D[ea]r Sir, I have taken the liberty to enclose you certain certificates which were thought necessary to obtain the release of an American Citizen, from the prison at Halifax. Mr. [Richard] Hancock shipped on board the Adele, a brig which was taken off our Bar in June last by Emulous Sloop of War. I understand that he has a large family, and a distressed family that he shipped on board of this vessel, on account of the high wages, but that this as you will see by the Consul's Certificate, was not a cruiser. If you think proper, will you make use of his Certificate and I have assured the Brother of Mr. Hancock, that every exertion consistent with propriety will be made ["by" *interlined*] you in behalf of an american Citizen confined in the prison of a foreign Country. Y[ou]rs very respectfully, Geo: Warren Cross.

ALS in DNA, RG 59 (State Department), Miscellaneous Correspondence regarding Impressed Seamen, box 5, Richard Hancock. NOTE: An EU reads, "Hancock Richd., a Prisoner of War at Halifax. Rec[eive]d from Mr. Calhoun, of the Senate [*sic*]."

Minutes of a meeting of the House Committee on Foreign Relations, 3/[12]/1812. Calhoun was among nine members present. [John] Randolph stated that he knew a person who could, if summoned, "give important information on the subject matter of" [James Madison's] message of 3/9. Randolph declined giving the name of the person "untill the committee should have determined whether it would or would not be proper to send for him. On motion of Mr. Calhoun, the committee agreed [5 to 3] to postpone untill tomorrow the further consideration of the said communication of Mr. Randolph." Incomplete DU in NBuHi, Peter B. Porter Papers, document A-7 (published microfilm, roll 2, frames 31–32).

Peter B. Porter, John Smilie, and J. C. Calhoun to JAMES MONROE, Secretary of State

Committee Room, March 24, 1812

Sir, We have been appointed by the [House] Committee of Foreign Relations to confer with the Executive [James Madison] on the various important measures which it may appertain to them to prepare, & recommend to the House of Representatives: and, more especially at this time, to ascertain the views of the Executive on the following points (viz.)

Are the forces already provided for, by law, adequate to the objects in contemplation of the Executive? And, if not, what addition or alteration is desired?

At what time may we prudently calculate that the military preparations now going on, under the direction of the Executive, will be in a state to justify the commencement of ["open" *changed to* "active"] hostilities against G. Britain?

Would it be adviseable that a declaration of war should be preceded by an Embargo? and, if so, at what time should the Embargo be laid?

We will thank you to appoint a time when we may have the honor to wait on you or the President, for the information desired. We have the honor to be, with great respect, your very hum[b]le servants, Peter B. Porter, John Smilie, J.C. Calhoun [Representatives from N.Y., Pa., and S.C., respectively].

LS in NN, James Monroe Papers; unsigned draft in NBuHi, Peter B. Porter Papers, document A-9 (published microfilm, roll 2, frames 35–36). NOTE: The fourth paragraph of the draft, stricken by order of Smilie and Calhoun, read: "Will a declaration of war against G. Britain be advisable, in the opinion of the Executive? and, if so, when?"

To JOSIAH BARTLETT, [Representative from N.H.], Stratham, N.H.

Washington City, April 15, 1812
Dear Sir, Under the injunction of the most inviolable Secrecy, we make the following request; that you forthwith repair to your Station in Congress—the time is important—this is no idle intimation. Read and come on quickly. Your friends, Felix Grundy [Representative from Tenn.], John A. Harper [Representative from N.H.], J.C. Calhoun.

LS in NhHi, Bartlett Papers.

To HENRY W. DESAUSSURE, Columbia, S.C.

Washington, 8th Dec[embe]r 1812
Dear Sir, The gentleman who will deliver this to you is Mr. Ellis of Richmon[d]. He proposes to visit our State; and will probably make some stay in Columbia. Should he do so, I am confident, it will afford you pleasure, to extend to him, that polite attention, which you have been in the habit ["to" *canceled and* "of" *interlined*] exercising towards respectable strangers. I am with much esteem, J.C. Calhoun.

ALS in NjMoN, Lloyd W. Smith Collection (Morristown National Historical Park published microfilm, Reel 8).

Calhoun and W[illia]m W. Bibb, [Representative from Ga.], to William Jones, Secretary of the Navy, 3/1/1813. They recommend the appointment of William Butler of S.C. as Surgeon's Mate in the Navy. LS (in Calhoun's handwriting) advertised as item 221 in Catalog 19 (1917) of Dawson's Book Shop, Los Angeles.

From Thomas Lehre, Charleston, 5/5/1813. He anticipates that the office of U.S. Marshal in that District may become vacant. He provides evidence that he has served long and faithfully as Sheriff, and he hopes that he will be considered for the position of Marshal. ALS in DNA, RG 59 (State Department), Letters of Application and Recommendation during the Administration of James Madison, 1809–1817 (M-438:5, frames 180–183).

J[ohn] C. Calhoun and Others to
[JAMES MONROE, Secretary of State]

[Washington, May 28?, 1813]

We the Subscribers, understanding that the Office of Marshal for the District of South Carolina is vacant, do hereby recommend, for that important Station, Col. Thomas Lehre, as a gentleman every way qualified to perform the duties attached to it. Col. Lehre is a gentleman of high respectability—has filled the office of Sheriff of Charleston district with great credit to himself and essential service to the community; is in the confidence of his fellow citizens and represents them in the Legislature of South Carolina, and is, in our opinion, ["in" *interlined*] every ["way" *canceled*] respect intitled to the confidence of the government. Sam[ue]l Farrow, Elias Earle, D[avid] R. Evans, J.C. Calhoun, John Gaillard.

LS in DNA, RG 59 (State Department), Letters of Application and Recommendation during the Administration of James Madison, 1809–1817 (M-438:5, frames 189–190). NOTE: An ALS of 5/28/1813 from Earle to James Monroe states, "Herewith you will receive the ["papers" *interlined*] Recommending Col[one]l Thomas Lehre as the proper person to fill the office of marshall of ["Charleston" *canceled and* "S. Carolina" *interlined*] Distr[ict]."

J[ohn] C. Calhoun and R[ichar]d Skinner to
W[ILLIA]M JONES, [Secretary of the Navy]

Washington City, June 8th 1813

Sir, We take the liberty of soliciting your attention to the application of George B. Webster of Litchfield in the State of Connecticut for an appointment in the Navy. We are personally acquainted with the Gentlemen who have recommended this young Man to you and know them to be Citizens of irreproachable character. We are Sir Respectfully your obed[ien]t Serv[an]ts, J.C. Calhoun, Rd. Skinner.

LS in CLU, Miscellaneous Papers. NOTE: Skinner was Representative from Vt., 1813–1815, and a graduate of the Litchfield Law School. He was later Governor of Vt.

J[ohn] C. Calhoun and Langdon Cheves to Gen. [JOHN] MASON

[Washington] 23d July 1813

Mr. Huger is a gentleman of respectability; and his statement in relation to the case of Mr. [G.] Simpson may be implicitly relied on. J.C. Calhoun, Langdon Cheves.

LS (in Calhoun's handwriting) in DNA, RG 45 (Naval Records), Subject File, Prisoners and Prisons (including Prison Ships): Aliens, Civilian, in U.S. (RN), Correspondence Relating to Aliens, Enemy and Neutral.

[JOHN MASON] to [John C.] Calhoun and [Langdon] Cheves

Office Comm[issar]y Gen[era]l of Prisoners
July 24, 1813

J. Mason presents his Respects to Mr. Calhoun and Mr. Cheves & regrets that he happened to be absent from the office when they did him the honor to call yesterday.

He begs leave to inform them that the policy of the Government has been for some time past to refuse passports to british Subjects to leave the country—six months after the declaration of War having been ["given" *canceled*] given to all who chose to do so within that Period.

Under these ["circumstances" *interlined*] desireable as it might be, and he has no doubt is—on account of the merits of the individual to yield to his wishes on this occasion, under the ["powers" *canceled and* "authority" *interlined*] vested in him J. Mason has not the power to interfere in the case of Mr. [G.] Simpson—he thinks it however proper to apprise Mr. Calhoun and Mr. Cheves that ["the" *canceled and* "an" *interlined*] application ["of" *canceled*] from Colo. [Thomas]

Barclay the british Agent Gen[era]l for Prisoners of War was made some time last month for passports for Mr. Simpson, on the ground ["of" *canceled and* "that" *interlined*] his ["connection" *canceled*] case differed from that of aliens generally because of his agency for Prisoners, to whom, it was replied from this office, that no decision on that ground could be made here—and it was recommended that the application be made to the Department of State.

It is believed that the Secretary of State [James Monroe]—has had the case before him, but his descision ["if made" *interlined*] is not known.

J. Mason has the honor to return herewith the letter [*not found*] of Mr. Huger.

Draft in DNA, RG 45 (Naval Records), Subject File, Prisons and Prisoners (including Prison Ships): Aliens, Civilian, in U.S. (RN), Correspondence Relating to Aliens, Enemy and Neutral.

Power of attorney from John C. Calhoun and Eliza[beth Barksdale] Pickens, Pendleton District, S.C., 9/13/1813. They authorize George Bowie to be their agent in settlement of the estate of Ezekiel Pickens, of which they are executors. DS owned by Mr. Augustus D. Graydon.

To GEORGE BOWIE, Pendleton

Willington [S.C.,] 26th Oct[obe]r 1812 [*sic*; 1813] D[ea]r Sir, By Mrs. Calhoun I transmit a bundle of papers relating to the estate of Mr. [Ezekiel] Pickens; which may be of use to you in the management of the estate. If any of the debts can be collected I would wish immediate steps to be taken to that effect. I have examined the papers relating to the estate of J[ohn] E[wing] C[olhoun] and find that the $100 to[?] which you gave me a memorandum has been paid to Mr. Pickens.

I have heard with regret of the death of Mr. [Samuel B.] Jones. Another agent must be named immediately. I wish I could be at Pendleton but it is quite out of my power. I am yours &c, J.C. Calhoun.

[P.S.] I wish the lands in Laurens could be sold immediately. I have it in my power to make some arrangements that would make it convenient. However let no sacrafice be made.

ALS in ScU-SC, John C. Calhoun Papers.

Langdon Cheves and J[ohn] C. Calhoun to Gen. [JOHN] MASON, Commissary General of Prisoners, Georgetown, D.C.

Washington, 19 Decem[be]r 1813

Sir, We have been requested to apply to the proper authority for permission for George Birnie ["who is a subject of Great Britain" *interlined*] to reside in Charleston, So. Carolina, the place of his permanent residence for some ["time" *canceled and* "years" *interlined*] past. We know the Gentlemen who have signed the enclosed Certificate to be persons of character & much respectability & nearly all of them natives of the U:S: & from the information & knowledge we have of Mr. Birnie & his friends we believe that "neither the interest welfare or tranquillity of this Government will be in the slightest degree affected" by his residence in the City of Charleston. It will be observed that were he a professed artist, instead of a student, he would be permitted to remain there under the standing regulations of the Government & yet probably his case is one equally entitled to the favour of the Government. Of this view of the ["subject & the" *interlined*] accompan[y]ing certificate we respectfully ask as early a consideration as may be convenient to you & your determination thereon. We are Sir, with great respect, Y[ou]r ob[edien]t S[ervan]ts, Langdon Cheves, J.C. Calhoun.

LS (in Cheves's handwriting) in DNA, RG 45 (Naval Records), Subject File, Prisoners and Prisons (including Prison Ships): Aliens, Civilians, in U.S. (RN), Correspondence Relating to Aliens, Enemy and Neutral.

To [WILLIAM] JONES, [Acting] Secretary of the Navy

1st Feb. [1813 or 1814]

D[ea]r Sir, Should ["the" *interlined*] place mentioned in the enclosed letter [*not found*] be vacant, I am satisfied, that Mr. Robertson will make an excellent officer. He is a man of property, stead[i]ness [of] character, and business. I am with respect yours &c, J.C. Calhoun.

ALS in DNA, RG 45 (Naval Records), Subject File—Rejected Applications. NOTE: An EU reads, "Hon. J.C. Calhoun—favor of Mr. Robertson of Charleston should the Navy Agent be changed."

From [JOHN MASON]

[Georgetown, D.C.] Jan[uar]y 10, 1814
Sir, I have received [*not found*] your letter of the ["10" *canceled*]
1st Inst: and that enclosed from Mr. Joshua Brown. I have the
honour to inform you, that it has been decided at the Treasury Department that the Bounty ["of 25$ per th(?)" *canceled*] payable on
each Prisoner ["of War" *interlined*] brought into port ["und" *canceled*] captured by private armed vessells ["under the Law of the 2d
Aug(us)t last" *interlined*]—should be paid at the Treasury in Washington, on Evidence furnished from this office of the requisite facts
in each case; and to this end, that the different collectors and marshalls in the United States have been instructed as by the circulars
herewith transmitted to furnish ["returns" *canceled*] such receipts
and returns for Prisoners ["so delivered" *interlined*] as will enable
us to ["certify" *canceled*; "furnish" *interlined and then canceled*;
"return" *interlined*] to Treasury Department the necessary proofs.

In the cases mentioned by Mr. Brown the only ["pa" *canceled*]
Information received here on the Subject—was from the Marshall of
So. Carolina in a letter dated 28 Oct[obe]r—in the following passage
"The owner of the privateer Decatur has made application to me for
the head money due to him for the Prisoners of War. The Clerk of
the Court having certified the number of those engaged on board
the Dominican I herewith forward his certificate to you and will be
glad to have your Instructions on the Subject. I ["will" *canceled*]
enclose you ["Sir" *interlined*] a copy of the Clerk's certificate for
your Information from which it will be readily seen—that this being
only an indirect Evidence of the Persons on board the prow the action ["commenced"(?) *interlined*] and no proof of the number of
Prisoners actually brought in and delivered—it was not applicable to
the case.

Soon after the reception of the Marshalls letter quoted above, the
["Inst" *canceled*] printed Instructions herewith were sent under
which it was presumed, he would be at no loss to determine what
Proofs would be requisite as to the prisoners of whom he had spoken.
As however ["by" *canceled*] at the close of Mr. Browns letter they
do not seem to have acted on it—I have this day addressed a special
letter to the Marshall on his case.

Draft in DNA, RG 45 (Naval Records), Subject File, Prisoners and Prisons (including Prison Ships): Miscellaneous (Impressed Seamen, RV), Correspondence
Relating to Payment of a Bounty for British Prisoners of War . . . , 1813–1814.

To the Rev. [MOSES WADDEL]

Washington, 12 Feb[ruar]y 1814

I think you are almost too anxious for peace. I know it much to be desired; yet secure and permanent peace can only be the result of fortitude and spirit. It is like fame—scarcely to be acquired by those who desire it vehemently. This I think has ever been the fault of our policy; and till changed must be [sic] inevitably result in the very opposite of what it desires. The spirit of a Nation ought not to be inferior to its sense of justice. It is the junction of the two which forms a great People. Whether the negociation will result in peace I will remain in my former opinion. We have had our late arrivals which tend to confirm the hope that it will be favourable. Our last comes down to the 25th of December. It contains Bonapartes speech to his Senate in which he states that the Allies had offered and that he had accepted preliminaries to a general peace. Lord Castlereigh [sic] had gone to the continent it is supposed in consequence. This looks well. I believe the world needs repose. So many years of violent struggle must have exhausted Europe. But we must not give way to these pleasing prospects. In all things immediate ease and pleasure is to be suspected. As a public Trustee I can only regard the interest[,] the honor and the duty of our country.

Ms. copy in ScCleA, Richard W. Simpson Papers, A-5613. NOTE: According to an AEU by Richard F. Simpson, Representative from S.C. 1843–1849, he copied the document transcribed above from one in the possession of Levi [that is, David Levy Yulee] about 1843–1845. Yulee had made his copy from an original in the possession of Moses Waddel's son William W. Waddel.

To "JOHN MAYSON [sic; Mason], C[ommissary] G[eneral] of Prisoners"

5th March 1814

D[ea]r Sir, Mr. Joshua Brown the owner of the privateer Decatur has sent me on a power of attorney to receive the money due to him for prisoners delivered to the proper agent at Charleston. I have applied to the Treasury office for the money; but am informed that the prisoners must be audited at your office. I will thank you to have it done immediately as there is a safe conveyance to Charleston, which will leave this in a few days. J.C. Calhoun.

ALS in DNA, RG 45 (Naval Records), Subject File, Prisoners and Prisons (including Prison Ships): Miscellaneous (Impressed Seamen, RV), Correspondence Relating to Payment of Bounty for British Prisoners of War Captured by American Privateers. NOTE: An EU reads, "ans[were]d 7 March."

To [JAMES MONROE, Secretary of State]

Willington [S.C.,] 15th June 1814

D[ea]r Sir, A friend of mine residing in the Mississippi Territory has written to me that the place of the district attorney in that territory is now vacant and that he wishes to obtain the appointment. My friend, whose name is Abner J. Lipscomb is a gentleman of undoubted talents and integrity. If you can obtain the appointment for him, I will take it as a singular favour.

We have had great changes since the adjournment. It will, I think be difficult to appreciate their effects on our relation with England. Should the worse happen, from the good sense and virtue evinced by the country, nothing disasterous is to be feared. My best respects to Mrs. [Eliza Kortright] Monroe. With much esteem your's &cc, J.C. Calhoun.

ALS in PHi, Dreer Collection.

From Barkley M. Blocker, James Bonham, and 11 other citizens, Edgefield District, S.C., 11/1/1814. They recommend James G. Butler, Jr., "a Sobre & moralised young man," for appointment as an Ensign in the Army. (An AES by Calhoun indicates that he is not acquainted with the applicant but that he does "know most of the Subscribers. They are very respectable.") LS in DNA, RG 94 (Adjutant General), Letters Received, 1805–1821, 4801 (M-566:38, frames 802–804).

From William Devlin, Abbeville [S.C.], 11/4/1814. He requests Calhoun's assistance in securing a commission in the Army, preferably in the 18th [Infantry] Regiment, in which Devlin has served successfully as a recruiting Sgt. He encloses testimonials. (Calhoun wrote in an AEU that he believed Devlin to be "a worthy young man.") ALS with Ens in DNA, RG 94 (Adjutant General), Letters Received, 1805–1821, 5198 (M-566:41, frames 1052–1060).

From Harriet Duvall, Abbeville District [S.C.], 11/8/1814. Having no doubt of Calhoun's "friendly exertions respecting the promotion of my son Thomas P. Brown," but thinking the situation somewhat propitious since [John] Armstrong is no longer Secretary of War, Mrs. Duvall requests that Calhoun exert himself in Brown's favor. (An AES by Calhoun states: "I am not acquainted with the applicant.") ALS in DNA, RG 94 (Adjutant General), Letters Received, 1805–1821, 4737 (M-556:38, frames 381–384).

From [JOHN JACOB ASTOR]

New York [City,] 23 Nov[embe]r 1814

Dear Sir, I had to regret the necessity of leaving Washington without having had the pleasure of again seeing you. I have read with much Interest the amendment which you made to the 2d section of the Bank Bill on ideas which occured to me but which is certainly calculated to place the whole community on a more equal footing as to the advantages arising from the Institution than the original Bill. Whether this plan will produce the same good effect on public credit is yet to be ascertained; from what we have seen the effect has been the revers[e] as Stocks have already fallen 2 to 3 p. ct. Although I see in your plan a proposition to relieve the heavy pressure of the Stocks yet I think it doubtful if or whether the purchase of the 15 millions of Stock as proposed will be so effectual on the price and credit of public Stocks as the other mode would have been. Whether the Bank will fill [its stock subscription list] is also a matter of doubt and cannot well be judged untill the details of the Bill are finished & agreed on. The public opinion here is against it and if the government should have no connection with the Bank and the notes are not to be received in all payments of taxes and pay[men]ts to gover[nmen]t generally I should doubt much whether the Bank will have *any Subscribers* for I do not see whence the advantages of this Bank are over that of any other whose stock is plenty in this city at 20 p. ct. below par and the U.S. Stocks at 24–25 p. ct. under par and declining. I am sorry to observe in the minds of the community of this city a depression which since the declaration of the War has not been so visible before[.] The fear of a commotion appears to increase and which I think arises from the appearent want of Union among the ruling powers[.] Since these few Days Exchange on London has advanced considerably from the circumstances of wealthy men transferring a part of their property to England where they think it more secure. I do not well see how Govern[men]t is to get money to supply these present demands if some measure is not quickly taken to revive public credit which is at present very low and declining. We have here a report which I hope is without foundation viz: that Mr. [Alexander J.] Dallas is about to retire from office [as the new Secretary of the Treasury]. This, I think, would be a misfortune to our country. Should you wish any information from this quarter such as I can give to you I shall be at all times happy to communicate. I am with great respect, Dear Sir Your Ob[edien]t Serv[an]t [John Jacob Astor].

FC in MH, John Jacob Astor Papers, Letterbook for 1813–1815, pp. 368–369.

To Samuel H. Smith, [U.S. Commissioner of Revenue], 12/23/-1814. "I will comply with your request on the subject of naming of a suitable person for the place of assessor for the 4th collection district of S. Carolina as soon as I can get an answer to a letter which I have written in relation to it." ALS advertised in Catalogue 77 [1972] of Kenneth W. Rendell, Inc., Somerville, Mass., p. 10.

John Babcock, New Haven, to [David] Daggett, [Representative from Conn.], 2/15/1815. Babcock requests that Daggett give Calhoun an appended receipt. The receipt indicates that in 12/-1805 Calhoun had purchased for three dollars a copy of "Currans Speeches," [that is, *The Speeches of John Philpot Curran, Esq.* . . . (Dublin: Stockdale, 1805)] from John Cooke and Co., of London. In 2/1815 Calhoun paid the bill, which, with "8 $\frac{8}{12}$ Years interest," totaled $4.50 to John Babcock, Cooke's agent in New Haven. ALS in CtY, Sterling Library, David Daggett Papers.

From Richard M. White, New York [City], 2/21/1815. White informs Calhoun that he has talked with Capt. [Alden] Partridge about the possibility of appointment to the Military Academy. Partridge feels that White should be given an appointment if he is qualified. White appreciates everything that Calhoun has done to help him obtain this appointment, but he can wait only 20 more days for a definite answer. If no such answer is obtained by then, White will have to return to Charleston. ALS in DNA, RG 94 (Adjutant General), Application Papers of Cadets, 1805–1866, 1815, 23 (M-688:4, frames 100–102).

J[ohn] C. Calhoun and Others to [JAMES] MONROE, Secretary of State

Washington, 25 feb[ruar]y 1815

Sir, We have the honour to enclose a letter from [Isaac Harby] the Editor of the "Southern Patriot," a Gazette published in Charleston, So. Carolina, which is of the same tenour as one addressed to each of us, which will, better than anything we can state, express his views and wishes. He is a native of the country & we believe him to be a man of good talents, good moral character, devoted to the Republican institutions of the country & friendly to those who now administer the ["country" *canceled*] Government.

We think him worthy of the patronage of the Government as far as may be compatible with the public interest & so far we take the liberty to present his application for your consideration. We have the honour to be, Sir, with great respect, y[ou]r Ob[edien]t S[ervan]t, J.C. Calhoun, Wm. Lowndes, Theo. Gourdin, Langdon Cheves.

LS in ScU-SC, John C. Calhoun Papers.

John C. Calhoun and Others to the President [JAMES MADISON]

House of Representatives, 3 March 1815

Sir, Should it become necessary to appoint commissioners to ascertain and survey the boundary lines fixed by the treaty with the Creek Nation of Indians concluded on the 9th day of August 1814 we take the liberty to recommend Mr. John Kershaw and William Barnett late members of Congress as persons in whom the government may place the most implicit confidence and quallified to perform the duty. We are Sir very respectfully Your ob[edien]t Serv[an]ts, A[lfred] Cuthbert, Bolling Hall, Jno. Forsyth, Wm. Lowndes, John C. Calhoun, Langdon Cheves, Geo. M. Troup, Theo. Gourdin [Representatives from Ga. and S.C.].

LS in DNA, RG 59 (State Department), Letters of Application and Recommendation during the Administration of James Madison, 1809–1817 (M-438:4, frames 1045–1046); PC in Carter, ed., *Territorial Papers*, 6:512. NOTE: Kershaw and Barnett were retiring Representatives fom S.C. and Ga., respectively.

A[ndrew] Pickens, Jr., St. Thomas, to Dr. John Noble, Charleston, 3/19/1815. This letter concerns various small matters of personal business that Pickens requests Noble to perform for him in the city and is endorsed: "Attention of Mr. Calhoun." Transcript in TxU, Patrick Noble Papers, p. 4.

W[illia]m Tennent, Abbeville, S.C., to William H. Crawford, Secretary of War, 3/21/1815. Tennent's son Charles wishes to attend the Military Academy. Calhoun and other S.C. citizens add their endorsements to the application. ALS in DNA, RG 94 (Adjutant General), Application Papers of Cadets, 1805–1866, 1814, 107 (M-688:3, frames 525–526).

To [JAMES MONROE, Secretary of State]

Bath [Abbeville District, S.C.,] 2d April 1815
Dear Sir, A friend of mine Nathaniel A. Ware of the Mississippi Territory has requested me to apply for the place of the secretary of that territory made vacant by the death of Mr. [Henry] Da[i]ngerfield. If the place is not already filled, I can recommend my friend as well worthy of the attention of the government. He is a [*one word canceled*] man of excellent information and correct principles; and I believe every way well qualified for the office which he wishes to obtain. Mr. Da[i]ngerfield was also register of the land office which place Mr. Ware would desire if he should be appointed to continue annexed to the secretary's.

I hope you find yourself quite recovered from the effect of your incessant labour the last winter. The peace here is universally approbated, not from ["*the*" *canceled*] being weary with war or disgusted with its policy, but from a conviction that it is every way honorable, and that it has substantially effected all of the great objects which it had in view at its commencement. I look forward with anxiety to see what effect it will have on the next Massachusett's election. I see the factionists in that quarter have been incessant in their old trade of suppressing and misrepresenting the truth. My respects to Mrs. [Eliza Kortright] Monroe. I am with esteem your's &c, J.C. Calhoun.

ALS in DNA, RG 59 (State Department), Letters of Application and Recommendation during the Administration of James Madison, 1809–1817 (M-438:8, frames 549–550).

To [JAMES MONROE?, Secretary of State]

Willington [Abbeville District, S.C.,] 17th June 1815
D[ea]r Sir, The enclosed letter [of 5/22] from [Isaac Harby] the
Editor of the [Charleston] Southern Patriot will best speak for itself.
I have nothing in addition, to the recommendation alude to in the
letter, to say, but that I believe it to be edited with more ability and
as firmly attached to the interest of the country and the administra-
tion as any paper in the State. I am with much respect yours &c, J.C.
Calhoun.

ALS in Ia-HA. NOTE: For Harby's letter of 5/22 to Calhoun, see *The Papers of*
John C. Calhoun, 1:284–285.

Toast by John C. Calhoun at Abbeville, S.C., 7/4/1815. At a
Fourth of July dinner Calhoun made the following toast: "The People—the only source of legitimate power—may France, acting on that
principle, prove invincible; and may its truth and energy disperse
the combination of crowned heads." From the Charleston, S.C.,
City Gazette and Commercial Daily Advertiser, July 27, 1815, p. 3;
also printed in Theodore D. Jervey, *Robert Y. Hayne and his Times*,
p. 65.

By John C. Calhoun, John E[wing] Colhoun [Jr.] (for himself
and in behalf of Andrew Norris, James E[dward] Colhoun's guardian), and Floride [Bonneau] Colhoun, 11/14/1815. They state that
that have examined and found to be satisfactory the accounts of
Henry W. DeSaussure as executor of the estate of John Ewing Colhoun [Sr.]. They acknowledge the receipt of all accounts and papers
pertaining to the estate in DeSaussure's possession at this time. John
Reid witnessed this document; it was recorded on 12/21/1815. Recorded copy in Sc-Ar, Records of the Secretary of State, Recorded
Instruments, Miscellaneous Records (Main Series), 1671–1973,
C:221.

To [ALEXANDER J.] DALLAS, [Secretary of the Treasury]

[Washington] 21st Dec[embe]r 1815
D[ea]r Sir, The committee [on the currency] has had a meeting this
morning and have unanimously determined that a national bank is

the best means of restoring specie payment. They directed me to call on the treasury department for its ideas on the subject in detail. ["It will" *canceled.*] The questions directed to be put will comprehend 1st the amount; 2d the detail other than mere form in the organization; 3d those measures best calculated to support the bank in its effort to restore specie payment to the country. As far as the committee has developed its views, on the part of each member it has been such as we could desire; and I hope the difficulty will not be so great as, I, at first, expected, in its passage. I will call for a few moments this evening to have a little farther conversation on the subject. J.C. Calhoun.

ALS in ScU-SC, John C. Calhoun Papers.

From R[eturn] J. Meigs [Jr., Postmaster General], 12/23/1815. "I have the honour to observe that we have balanced Mr. Waddle's [*sic*; Moses Waddel's] account as postmaster at Willington for the quarter ending 31 March 1815—he having transported the mail between Willington & Vienna for the neat [*sic*; net] proceeds of the Willington Post Office. This circumstance was overlooked or that gentleman would not have been written to on the subject." FC in DNA, RG 28 (Post Office Department), Letters Sent by the Postmaster General, 1789–1836, J:351 (M-601:19, frame 207).

By "A.C.M.," [1815]. Among the Calhoun pamphlets at Dartmouth is a copy of A.C.M.'s pseudonymous *The Second Crisis of America, or A Cursory View of the Peace Lately Concluded between Great Britain and the United States, ... By a Citizen of Philadelphia* (New York: John H. Sherman, 1815). The author inscribed the work "With the High Respect of his Ob[edien]t Ser[vant,] The A[uthor]." Printed pamphlet in NhD, John C. Calhoun Pamphlet Collection.

To CHARLES J. INGERSOLL, Philadelphia

Washington, 10th Ap[r]il 1816
Dear Sir, I received your letter by yesterday's mail; and cannot refrain from making an early acknowledgement for the personal consideration which you have been pleased to express. The good opinion of the discerning and virtuous has ever been precious to me. It is the appropriate and best reward for efforts in our country's service.

This session has done much; and what is of still greater importance[,] on principles so solid and wise, that if future Congresses continue to act on the same, we cannot fail to realise the fond wishes of the founders of this republick. Two great subjects yet remain to be acted on; the navy and internal improvements. The first will doubtless this session receive due attention; the latter so important every way, will be postponed, I fear, to the next.

You expressed a curiosity to see my observations on the state of the nation; you will find it in the enclosed Intelligencer; and, I hope, it may in some measure meet your expectation. You are too well acquainted with me to expect any of the beauties of eloquence, for in fact, I have never aspired beyond the humble sphere, of perspicuity of argument. The speech is not written by me; but from [Joseph] Gales notes, with verbal corrections only on my part; but it in main fairly expresses my views.

On the subject of prohibiting the exportation of specie, I can only say that I think the merchants are mistaken in thinking it necessary. The demand for specie on account of our measures ["will be so great" *interlined*] as to induce an importation, to a considerable extent. I do not fear any injurious exportation. With much esteem yours &c, J.C. Calhoun.

ALS in PHi, Ingersoll Papers.

To ANDERSON CRENSHAW, Newberry (C[ourt] H[ouse]), S.C.

Washington, 11th April 1816

D[ea]r Sir, I received your letter this morning and take a pleasure in complying with your request. The bank has passed; and in my opinion, tho the dividends to be made by it will not probably be greater than the state banks; yet the stock will have a greater rise. If I were situated as you are, I would [in]vest in the national bank. The subscription is to be opened 1st July; and subscription may be made in Charleston. The shares are $100 each; of which at the time of subscribing $5 dollars ["in" *altered to* "on"] each share is to be paid at the time of subscribing; $10 six months thereafter in gold or silver coin and $10 six month thereafter in like manner, making in the whole $25 in specie on each share. Of the remain[in]g $75 it is to be paid in three instalments also at the same time with the payment of the specie part but with this difference that it may be in specie or United States stock. Information will be published for the benefit of the community. I am with respect yours &c, J.C. Calhoun.

ALS owned by T.H. Crenshaw, Jr., Paris, France; copy of ALS in A-Ar, Crenshaw Family Papers; copy of ALS in AU, T.H. Crenshaw, Jr., Papers. NOTE: This letter bears a postmark of "Apr[il] 8."

REPORT OF THE COMMITTEE ON CURRENCY

[In the House of Representatives, April 13, 1816] The Committee appointed upon so much of the Presidents [James Madison's] message as relates to an uniform National Currency who were required by a reso. of this House of yesterday to enquire into the expediency of prohibiting by law the exportat[ion] of bullion & specie from the United States for a limited period have had the same under consideration, & submit thereon the following reso. (See other side).

Resolved that it is inexpedient to prohibit the exportation of bullion or specie at the pre[se]nt time.

DU in DNA, RG 233 (U.S. House of Representatives), 14A-C17.5; variant PC in *Annals of Congress*, 14th Cong., 1st Sess., col. 1365; variant PC in *House Journal*, 14th Cong., 1st Sess., p. 643. NOTE: The words "prohibiting by law the exportat" and the resolution are in Calhoun's handwriting. This report is endorsed, "Report of the Committee on Currency on prohibition of exportation of Specie. April 13, 1816. Ordered to lie." Another endorsement reads simply, "Recorded."

From R[OBERT] B[RENT, Paymaster General, U.S. Army]

Wash[in]g[ton], 17 April 1816
Sir, The case of William Willson is prepared for payment to you and I would have sent the check with the account under cover hereof could I know on what Bank you would wish the money.

The case of William Pettigrew is defective on which the amount can not be safely paid, because it is certified that the claimant is a brother of the deceased—*one of his heirs*—a payment on a power of Att[orne]y of that Kind would not secure me a credit in the accounting offices for such payment. I enclose you both claims. If you will have the goodness to sign the receipts in the case of Wilson [*sic*], and signify the Bank on which you wish the draft, when you return the voucher, I will endeavour to accommodate you.

The case of Pettigrew, you can if you think proper, take with you to the south, and get it settled by a payment in that quarter—the man claiming (to settle all difficulty) can take out letters of administration in the case, and on shewing this letter to the Paymaster on whom he may call, with the evidence of administration, all difficulties will be removed.

I regret Sir, that any circumstance should intervene in a case presented by you, to prevent the pleasure I should have in paying the claim due to the representative of a deceased soldier. R.B.

FC in DNA, RG 99 (Paymaster General), Letters Sent, 9:67. NOTE: On 4/26 Brent forwarded Calhoun a check on the Bank of Columbia for $51.09 paying the claim of William Pettigrew, deceased. (FC in *ibid.*, 9:84).

To Dr. WILLIAM W. BIBB, Mallory, Ga.

Washington, 4th Dec[embe]r 1816

Dear friend, I can scarcely inform you how much, I and the rest of your friends here miss you both in a social and political point of view. The old mess is reconstituted with the addition of [Daniel M.] Forney and [William C.] Love [Representatives from N.C.], at the old place; and almost every incident tends strongly to bring you to our remembrance.

The result of the election in your state legislature has on all sides excited but one sentiment, that of strong reprobation. So soon to forget your services and devotion to the publick interest argues but little in favour of their intelligence or virtue. From your perfect self control the feelings excited is doub[t]less less sensibly felt by your self than your friends.

Your absence has weakned the [James Madison] administration much in the Senate. In fact, I know not how they will supply your place. The talents of the Senate is great on the side of the opposition. On our side it must be acknowledged, that there are many who are very respectable for intelect; but, I do not know one, who combines the requisite talents, address, industry and firmness. Who will aspire to lead there, I cannot even conjecture. If the times were difficult, it would be almost impossible for our side to hold its own in the Senate.

The repeal of the compensation law is already agitated in both bodies. [Joseph B.] Varnum [of Mass.] in the Senate and [Thomas M.] Nelson [of Va.] in our house commenced the work of popularity. They both were eager to be first. I hope they may meet the deserved reward. There is not a man in Congress who would be more mortified at the reduction of their pay than Varnum, yet it is he, who wishes to appear to the people as the disinterested patriot. Col. [Richard M.] Johnson [Representative from Ky.] moved on the subject yesterday. His speech was the strangest jumble, I ever heard. I do not pretend to divine his object by his speech. Both [Henry] Clay and Johnson deny that they are committed; but I expect they will be in favour of a repeal. My best respects to Mrs. [Mary Freeman] Bibb. Your friend, J.C. Calhoun.

ALS in MH. NOTE: Bibb was Representative from Ga. 1807–1813 and Senator 1813–1816. In 1817 he became governor of Ala. Territory.

From G eo[rge] Graham, Acting Secretary of War

Dept. of War, 8 D[ecembe]r 1816

Sir, I have examined the papers which you put into my hands relative to Gen[era]l [Wade] Hampton['s], claim, and am very doubtfull whether any of the principles heretofore acted upon in this Dept. can be applied, so as to admit this claim. The measures pursued by Gen[era]l Hampton in relation to Mr. McConnell [*sic*; James McConnel] was so directly in opposition to the principle recognized in the 2d section of the act for establishing rules & articles for the government of the Armies of the U. States passed the 10th April 1816, as to involve his claim with questions of great delicacy, and on which this Dept. must act with much precaution. I will however submit the papers to the President [James Madison] and if he cannot find himself justified in admitting the claim, they will at least relieve his mind from any unfavorable impressions in relation to Gen[era]l Hamptons conduct in this affair, if it has imbibed any such. I have the honor to be & &, Signed, Geo. Graham, Act[in]g S[ecretary] of War.

FC in DNA, RG 107 (Secretary of War), Letters Sent Relating to Military Affairs, 1800–1889, 9:209 (M-6:9). NOTE: In 1813 Hampton had McConnel ar-

rested for espionage and furnishing false information about the enemy. Mc-
Connel was acquitted and released; he sued Hampton in New York for false im-
prisonment, obtaining a $6,000 judgment. Hampton asked that the U.S. as-
sume the judgment and other expenses he may incur in this matter.

To [WILLIAM JONES?]

Washington, 13th Dec[embe]r 1816

Dear Sir, Mr. Buckner Thruston, one of the Judges in this district [of
Columbia], is desireous, in case a branch of the United States bank
should be established here, to be appointed one of the directors. I
have known Mr. Thruston for many years; and have always considered him ["as" *interlined*] a gentleman of excellent talents and great
integrity; and have no doubt, that should he be appointed he would
discharge the duties of a director faithfully. With esteem your's &c,
J.C. Calhoun.

ALS in PHi, Gratz Collection.

J[ohn] C. Calhoun and Others to "the President [WILLIAM JONES] & Directors of the Bank of the United States, Philadelphia"

Washington City, 23d Dec[embe]r 1816

Gent[leme]n, The undersigned have been requested to recommend
to you for the appointment of Cashier of the Branch Bank of the
United States to be established at Savannah two gentlemen either of
whom they believe qualified for and deserving of the trust. James S.
Walker Esq[ui]r[e] of Augusta Georgia late a Commissioner for receiving subscriptions to the U.S. Bank there, and Col: Edward Har-
den of Savannah late a Commissioner likewise, are the applicants.
They are both gentlemen of the first respectability, both active and
intelligent and competent to fill with ability any employment of this
Nature to which their attention should be directed. Justice requires
us to state that Mr. Walker has been regularly bred to mercantile
business and if experience in that way is an advantage he possesses it.
In point of character and talents it would be invidious if it were even
possible to make a distinction. We are anxious only that the office
should be well filled and either will be well deserving of it.

We have therefore submitted their pretensions to your consideration with a full belief that they will be fairly regarded[?]. John Forsyth, Bolling Hall, Wilson Lumpkin, R[ichard] H. Wilde [Representatives from Ga.].

[Autograph endorsement:] I am personally acquainted with Mr. Walker and believe him in every respect well qualified for the place for which he applies. J.C. Calhoun.

LS with AES in PPL.

From Sam[uel] R. Marshall, Washington, 1/6/1817. He discusses at length a petition before Congress concerning the rank and pay of medical officers in the Navy. Whatever the fate of the petition, "it will ever be a source of satisfaction to me, that it was favored with your approbation and honored by the support of your talents." ALS in DNA, RG 46 (U.S. Senate), 16A-D9.

To [WILLIAM G. POINDEXTER]

Washington, 30th Jan. 1817

Dear Sir, Inclosed you will find the writing which [William] Hix gave me at the time of sale and the affidavit, which you require, as to the materiality of certain witnesses named. William Calhoun Jun[io]r who signed the receipt was present at the time of the sale, and will prove that [Jacob B.] Fowler was present at the time. He resides at Willington So. Carolina and acts as my agent. To him you will please to direct whatever papers you may transmit. Benton Walton of Lincoln County Georgia, will prove that Hix and Fowler resided for some time preceeding the sale at his house with the negroes and that they acted as if there was a joint owner ship in the property. If material, proof can be furnished that Fowler in some instances sold in his own name from the same gang. I am not certain but Walton can prove it. If he cannot Robert Ware of the same county, if am correctly informed can. This testimony will I presume be sufficient to establish the collusion. As to the identity Meredith McGehee will positively prove it as to Tomkins. He happened to be in Virginia at the time Tomkins was condemned & will prove him to be the same. As to Anthony the proof will not be so direct. You can of course ["of" *canceled*] obtain the proof of a sale of a negro of his name at the Penitentiary to Fowler, with the discription of his person; and either of the witnesses named except Ware can give the

315

discription of the fellow which I bought of Hix. A man of the name of Clement Townson, who lives 12 miles of Linchburgh in your State, was present when Fowler bought the negroes at the Penitentiary. His testimony may perhaps be important. You can best judge. On the point of damage Mr. Calhoun & McGehee can testify. My actual loss in money is between $500 & $600. Mr. McGehee lives ["at" *canceled and "in" interlined*] the same neighbourhood with Mr. Calhoun. You do not mention whether the action is brought against both Hix & Fowler; and I have made the affidavit in the alternative. I suppose it will do. The testimony of the two Witnesses resident in So. Carolina may be taken at Willington; and if it be necessary to direct the commission to persons by name, that of Dr. Moses Waddel, Ezekiel Noble & Peter Rodgers may be inserted. That of the two resident in Georgia may be taken at the Residence of Mr. Walton, and the commission filled with the names of John H. Walton, William Stokes & Samuel Duboise. As to the time, you had I suppose better fix that. From Richmond to Willington the mail is usually 8 days. To prevent accidents from delay you had better allow as much time as the sitting of the court will permit. If the papers are directed to William Calhoun he will be punctual in his attention to the business. If I have omited any thing let me know what is necessary as soon as possible. I am anxious to have the trial as soon as possible. I hope there is no doubt of obtain[in]g the money in case I get a judgement. Yours &, J.C. Calhoun.

[Enclosure]

Affidavit of John C. Calhoun

District of Columbia S[uperior?] C[our]t

This day John C. Calhoun of the State of South Carolina member of Congress made oath before me one of the Judges of the circuit court of the United States for the said district that Benton Walton and Robert Ware of Lincoln County & State of Georgia and William Calhoun jun[io]r & Meredith McG[e]hee of Abbeville District South Carolina, are material witnesses for him, in the suit depending in the superior court of Law for the County of Goochland State of Virginia, between himself Plaintiff and William Hix and Jacob B. Fowler or one of them are defendants; and that he cannot safely go to trial, without the benefit of their testimony given under my hand at Washington in the said District this 29th January 1817.

B[uckner] Thruston.

John C. Calhoun.

[Enclosure]

Receipt of William Hix

[Abbeville District, S.C.] 25th June 1816
Received of John C. Calhoun forteen hundred dollars in full of two negro ["boys" *canceled and* "fellows" *interlined*] Tompkins and Anthony, whom I warrant to be of sound constitution and, as far as I know, of good and honest character. I also warrant the tittle of said negroes.

William Hix

W[illia]m Calhoun Jr.

ALS with Ens in Vi, Goochland County Judgments, 1820, April, Calhoun vs. Fowler and Hix. NOTE: EU's on the affidavit read, "Calhoun vs. Hicks & Fowler, Affidavit," and "Filed 9th Dec. 1817 & 2 Coms. iss[ue]d." The bill of sale is in John C. Calhoun's handwriting and has his endorsement reading, "Mr. Hix's bill of sale and receipt for Tompkins and Anthony." Anthony and Tompkins were slaves purchased by John C. Calhoun in Abbeville District, S.C., from Hix and Fowler who bought them at the Virginia Penitentiary when their sentence to be hanged was commuted to transportation outside the U.S. After Calhoun purchased them, they ran away but were found and returned for a $52 reward. Calhoun then sold them for $1,000 and sued Hix and Fowler for fraud in the Goochland County Circuit Superior Court. On April 19, 1820 Hix confessed Judgment with $15 damages and court costs. The case against Fowler was discontinued. William Calhoun was an older brother of John C. Calhoun.

From R[obert] B[rent], 2/25/1817. He transmits a draft on the Bank of Columbia for $400 due to "the widow Noble" on her half-pay pension. FC in DNA, RG 99 (Paymaster General), Letters Sent, 10:62.

J[ohn] C. Calhoun and Others to [JAMES MONROE?]

Congress Hall, Feb. 28th 1817
Sir, We beg leave to recommend to your consideration Colonel *Alney McLean* of Kentucky for the office of Govenor of the new territory intended to be formed out of the Territory of Mississippi. Colonel McLean is a gentleman of talents and integrity; and his servises during the late war and particularly at New Orleans has endeared him to all his countrymen. We have the Honour to be your Humb[le] Serv[an]ts, Solomon P. Sharp, Stepn. Ormsby, T[homas] Fletcher, Tho: Newton, Wm. McCoy, Jonathan Ward, B[artlett] Yancey, Jno. Kerr, Ben Hardin, John Alexander, Wm. Creighton, Jun.

I concur with great pleasure in recommending Col. McClean to office above mentioned. S[amuel] D. Ingham, N[ewton] Cannon, J.C. Calhoun, W[eldon] N. Edwards, J[ohn] G. Jackson, James Pleasants, Jr., Wm. Lowndes.

LS in DNA, RG 59 (State Department), Letters of Application and Recommendation during the Administration of James Madison, 1809–1817, Alney McLean (M-438:5, frames 534–535). Note: All the signers of this letter served in the House of Representatives at this time. Sharp, Ormsby, Fletcher, and Hardin were Representatives from Ky.; Newton, McCoy, Kerr, Jackson, and Pleasants from Va.; Alexander and Creighton from Ohio, Ingham from Pa., Cannon from Tenn., Calhoun and Lowndes from S.C., Yancey and Edwards from N.C., and Ward from N.Y. McLean also served as a Representative from Ky. until March 1817.

From R[obert] B[rent], 3/1/1817. He transmits by messenger a check for $400 for Gen. M. Coale and requests Calhoun to send to the office the proper power of attorney or receipt. FC in DNA, RG 99 (Paymaster General), Letters Sent, 10:67.

Deed executed by Eliza Pickens, Andrew Pickens, Jr., and John C. Calhoun, executors of Ezekiel Pickens, Charleston District, 3/15/-1817. For $4,100 they sell to Isaac Ball that plantation called Brick Yard, containing approximately 2,470 acres of land in St. Thomas's Parish. Recorded copy in Sc-Ar, Charleston County Deeds, V-8:210–211 (microfilm).

From Sam[ue]l Wragg, "Wedgefield," [Georgetown District, S.C.], 5/20/1817. He is requesting "gentlemen of my acquaintance in Congress," including Calhoun, to aid in the appointment of his son Samuel Wragg to the Military Academy. ALS in DNA, RG 94 (Adjutant General), Application Papers of Cadets, 1805–1866, 1818, 61 (M-688:8, frame 12).

From Jacob Bond I'On, Charleston, 5/28/1817. He asks Calhoun's help in securing a Cadet appointment for his nephew, Samuel Wragg, Jr. ALS in DNA, RG 94 (Adjutant General), Application Papers of Cadets, 1805–1866, 1818, 61 (M-688:8, frames 10–11).

Land grant signed by A[ndrew] Pickens, Jr., Governor of S.C., Columbia, 6/2/1817. In accordance with a S.C. law of 2/19/1791, John C. Calhoun is hereby granted 840 acres of land in Abbeville District, situated on "branches of Savannah river" and bounded by the lands of James Collier, Maj. George Robertson, John C. Calhoun, and an unknown person. This tract was surveyed for Calhoun on 5/15, and a plat of 5/30 [recorded copy in Sc-Ar, Records of the Secretary of State, Office of the Surveyor General, State Plats, 44:404] certified by Josiah Kilgore, Surveyor General, shows the shape and bounds of the grant. Retained copy in Sc-Ar, Records of the Secretary of State, Recorded Instruments, Land Grants, Columbia Series, 61:197.

Power of attorney executed by J[ohn] C. Calhoun, A[ndrew] Pickens, Jr., and Eliza Pickens, Pendleton District, 6/11/1817. As executors to the will of Ezekiel Pickens, they appoint Henry W. De-Saussure their agent to sell the tract of land containing about 6,500 acres called Robert's Barony on the Little [Salkehatchie] River. G[eorge] Bowie, M[oses] Waddel, and John E[wing] Colhoun [Jr.] witnessed this document; it was recorded on 6/2/1818. Copy in Sc-Ar, Records of the Secretary of State, Recorded Instruments, Miscellaneous Records (Main Series), 0-4:396–397.

Commission as Interim Secretary of War, Washington, 10/8/-1817. President James Monroe appoints Calhoun Secretary of War "during the pleasure of the President of the United States for the time being, and until the end of the next session of the Senate of the United States and no longer." This document is signed by James Monroe and Secretary of State John Quincy Adams. DS in ScCleA.

From Brig. Gen. J[oseph] G. Swift

New York [City], 18 October 1817
Sir, Having been informed that Major [Christopher] Van de Venter, a Native of New York, is desirous of obtaining the principal Clerkship of the War Department, in case that station should be vacant— I take the liberty of stating to you, that I am intimately acquainted with this Gentleman; he is an accomplished Officer & a man of business; his education was finished at the Military Academy, he has been ten years in the Army & possesses the respect of every Officer of my acquaintance, who has had an opportunity of knowing him. From Major Van de Venter's general acquaintance with military subjects, from his habits of Official business & from my acquaintance with the routine of the War Office (having transacted business there for many years) I can recommend Major Van de Venter to your notice as pos-

sessing qualities eminently fitting him for the Station which he is desirous of obtaining. I have the honor to be your most respectful humble Servant, J.G. Swift, B. Gen[era]l, Chief Engineer.

LS in MiU-C, Christopher Vandeventer Papers.

To [ANDREW PICKENS, JR.]

Abbeville, 12th Nov[embe]r 1817

Dear Sir, Since my arrival at this place, I have been informed of the division of your brother's [Ezekiel Pickens] estate; and the principle on which that division was made. I regret, that I have not a copy of the will, so that I might again review my opinion, as it differs considerably from yours; but I think my memory, both of its general provisions, and of that part on which, I understand, the mode of dividing particularly rest, is sufficiently accurate, to enable me to venture my opinion. I have stated my view of it in detail to Mr. [Patrick?] Noble and have requested him, as the most satisfactory mode, to state them to you; and will therefore only present an outline. I conceive the great and leading object of your brother, which pervades every part of his will, was to produce an entire equality, as far as it was in his power, between his children; particularly those of the first and last marriages, and that if any particular part ["of his will" *interlined*] is doub[t]ful, yet this general object so clearly expressed must prevail. Nor can I admit, that the portion of it, which was supposed to justify the present division, is in the least opposed to the general spirit of the will, as I have stated; but on the contrary it appears to ["be" *canceled*] me, to discover great solicitude to preserve an equality among the children. I will state my opinion a little more fully on this point, as it is one of importance. The object of your brother it appears to me was two fold. In the first place to make an equal division among his children in the first instance; and to preserve it ["in" *interlined*] case any of them died before they were of age, by dividing their share among the others so as still to keep them equal. ["The necessity of this last" *canceled*] To effect this last point, was the object of the clause, on which the present division was made. The necessity of the clause, will be appearant, if we reflect, that by law, in case of the death of a child of the last marriage its share would go wholly to its full brother or sister, in exclusion to the half, and vice versa, in case of the death of one of the first marriage. Without persuing the argument farther, it appears to me the result of the construction given will be to set the will wholly aside, except as to the specifick legacies; and; probably the effect, which it might have on the event of the death of one of the children under age. If the testator had died without a will, or if the will had been set aside before the ordinary, precisely the same division would take place by law ["which" *canceled*] with that which has been made; or[?] if the children of the last marriage ["had n" *canceled*] were not entitled to a cent under their grand father's will the division would be the same. This appears to me not to be giving an effect to the wishes of the testator as clearly expressed. If on review of the subject yourself & Mrs. [Elizabeth Barksdale] Pickens agree with me in opinion, the proceeding can easily be corrected; but if not, I do think the Ex[ecuto]rs right to make application to the court of equity; and divide under their direction. With esteem yours &c, J.C. Calhoun.

ALS in ScU-SC, John C. Calhoun Papers.

From H[arry] Toulmin, Fort Stoddert [Ala. Territory], 11/12/-1817. He encloses a petition signed by about 500 residents of Ala. urging Congress to reject the rumored applications "about to be made . . . by the new state of the Mississippi for an extension of the boundaries of the said state so as to include at least the whole of the settlements on the western side of the Mobile & Tombigby rivers." He asks Calhoun to present and support this petition because the Territory has no Delegate yet in the House. ALS with En in DNA, RG 233 (U.S. House of Representatives), Territorial Papers, Alabama Territory; PC with En in Carter, ed., *Territorial Papers*, 18: 190–201.

From HENRY WHEATON

New York [City], 17 Nov. 1817
My dear Sir, Permit me to introduce to the honor of your acquaintance my friend Major [Christopher] Van De Venter of the army.

Maj. Van De Venter visits the seat of Government fortified with strong recommendations, as a candidate for the situation of First Clerk in the War Department, a post that in my opinion he is eminently qualified to fill as to talents, acquirements, & merits. His sufferings alone during the late war give him a very strong claim on the gratitude of the Country & the government. It would I am sure give ["you" *interlined*] great pleasure to promote his views in any mode that may be compatible with your feelings of propriety & your relations with the administration. Any attention that you may find it convenient to shew him will be gratefully requited by me, & will be bestowed on an enlightened & honest man, who is altogether worthy of your friendship & confidence, but who is too modest to be the herald of his own pretensions. I am with great respect & esteem your most obedient humble servant & faithful friend, Henry Wheaton.

Ms. copy in MiU-C, Christopher Vandeventer Papers. NOTE: In the lower left of the manuscript, under Wheaton's name, this letter was addressed to "The hon. John Calhoun, N.C. [*sic*]."

From [Col.] H[ENRY] ATKINSON

New York [City], Nov. 19, 1817
Sir, I have the honor to address you by Major [Christopher] VanDe-Venter, who goes to Washington with a hope of procuring a situation in the Department of War. A long acquaintance with Maj[o]r V[andeventer] justifies me in recommending him to your notice. His talents, integrity & merit cannot be doubted, & may be received as sure pledges of his fitness & capacity to discharge any duties, that you may have occasion to employ him in. With great respect Sir I have the honor to be Your mo[s]t ob[edient] Ser[van]t, H. Atkinson.

Ms. copy in MiU-C, Christopher Vandeventer Papers.

From Brig. Gen. M[OSES] PORTER

Head Quarters 4th Mil[itar]y Dept.
Phil[adelphia,] Nov. 21, 1817
Sir, Understanding that Major [Christopher] VanDeVenter of the Quarter Masters department is an applicant for the Situation of First Clerk in the Department of War, I take the liberty of recommending him to your notice as particularly competent to the discharge of the duties of that office, having served two years in the Army in a variety of Military Situations of high responsibility & trust; the duties of which he has ever discharged with honor to himself & Country. I

have the honor to be Sir Very respectfully Y[ou]r Mo[st] Ob[edien]t Serv[an]t, M. Porter, Brig[a]d[ier] General.

Ms. copy in MiU-C, Christopher Vandeventer Papers.

[DE WITT CLINTON, Governor of N.Y.], to the Secretary of War

New York [City,] 24 Nov[embe]r 1817

Sir, This letter will be delivered to you by Longbolen[?] and Nicholas Cuzuk[?], two Tuscarora Indians residing in this State. Their journey to the South is to receive the benefits of some lands belonging to the[?] Tribe in North Carolina And as they are men of good character I am persuaded that you may rely on the fidelity of their representations and I take the liberty of recommending them & the interests of their Nation to your protection.

Draft in NNC, De Witt Clinton Papers, Letterbooks, 4:20.

From STEVENSON ARCHER, [former Representative from Md.]

Belle Air Md., Dec[embe]r 1817

My dear Sir, As the Spring circuits in the Alabama Territory are rapidly approaching & I have been unable to dispose of my property here, I have been under the necessity of resigning my appointment [to be a Judge in Miss. Territory]. I shall ever feel grateful to you for the assistance which you rendered me in procuring the appointment & have to request that you will add to the obligations under which I lie to you. My friend Henry H.B. Hays a citizen of the Territory & a practicing attorney therein is desirious of being my successor. I wish if possible to aid his views by obtaining your influence in his behalf. I assure you he is in every way qualified to discharge with ability the duties of such a situation, & I am convinced, as he is a citizen of the territory that his appointment would be very agreeable to the people of that section of the country.

With the best wishes for your success in the discharge of your

official duties & for your prosperity in every situation of life I remain y[ou]r friend, Stevenson Archer.

ALS in DNA, RG 59 (State Department), Letters of Application and Recommendation during the Administration of James Monroe, 1817–1825, Hays (M-
439:8, frames 759–760).

From J A C [O B] B R O W N

Head Quarters, Brownville [N.Y.], Dec[e]m[ber] 5th 1817
Sir, I perceive that it is announced by the news papers that the office
of Sec. of War has been assigned to you. I presume therefore to address you as chief of the Dept. of War and to congratulate you on this
occation. The President [James Monroe] can inform you how deep
an interest I felt on this Subject and the pleasure the selection of
yourself must afford me.

By the mail that conveys this Letter the report of the Insp. Gen-
[e]r[a]l of my [Northern] Div[isio]n will be forwarded to Adj. &
Insp. Gen[e]r[a]l [Daniel] Parker to be laid before you. This report and that of Dr. ["Jos." *interlined by someone else*] Lovell ["H.S."
interlined by someone else] forwarded some time since to Mr.
[George] Graham will afford some information on the state of my
command. You will, I am sure, observe with pleasure that the labour
performed by the Troops on military Roads, Fortifications and Barracks has not impaired their discipline and that the Corps most distinguished for the performance of labour are also entitled to the
highest praise for their military Character.

I had the honor to name Croghan, brother of Col[o]n[el]
[George] Croghan to the President as a suitable person to do the
duty of Judge Advocate. Permit me to recommend this Gent. to you
to fill the vacancy occationed by the rejection of the nomination of
Mr. Lybe [*sic*; John L. Leib]. We have but few Gent. in the Army
from Kentucky and I hope that it may be considered proper to
strengthen our interests by good selections from that portion of the
Union. Several names have been presented to me for this office, but
I find among them none equal to that of Croghan. The young Gent.
for whom I solicit this appointment is every way qualified to perform
the duty.

With your permission, I hope to have the pleasure of paying my
personal respects to you, in Washington, by the tenth of January.

With high consideration I have the honor to be y[ou]r humbl[e] Serv[an]t, Jac: Brown.

ALS in DNA, RG 94 (Adjutant General), Letters Received, 1805–1821, 4719 (M-566:38, frames 259–262); CC in DLC, Jacob Brown Papers, Letterbooks, 2:83. NOTE: John L. Leib had been appointed as a Judge Advocate, but his appointment had been negated by the Senate.

From H[ENRY] CLAY, [Speaker of the House of Representatives]

[Washington] 3d Dec. 1817

D[ea]r Sir, I have just heard of your safe arrival, & congratulate both that ["account" *canceled and* "event" *interlined*] & your recent appointment: with regard to the latter however not without some feeling of regret at our loss of you in the H. of Representatives.

You will have to appoint a first Clerk in your department forthwith. It is an appointment in which your personal convenience as well as the public interest, must be much concerned. Maj. [Christopher] Van De Venter (to whom I beg leave to introduce you) is, unless I am greatly deceived, precisely the person you want. Educated at West Point[,] well acquainted with tactics, familiar with the actual condition of the Army, & conversant with all its details, he will be of vast relief to you. Such is the character I have of him by letters, & from Gen[era]l [Joseph G.] Swift, & other officers: & such is the character which I think he deserves from what I know of him. I therefore, unite with his friends in expressing to you a wish for his appointment ["he"(?) *canceled*] to the situation in question. Y[ou]rs cordially & faithfully, H. Clay.

Ms. copy in MiU-C, Christopher Vandeventer Papers.

From W[ILLIA]M H. CRAWFORD, [Secretary of the Treasury]

Washington, 3rd Dec. 1817

Dear Sir, I have this moment heard of your arrival, & seize the occasion of presenting for your consideration the application of Maj[o]r

[Christopher] Van DeVenter, for the office of Chief Clerk which it is understood will be vacated [by George Graham] upon your entering ["of" *canceled*] on the duties of your office.

Major Van DeVenter is an officer of great merit who has been long on the Staff of the Army, & will I am persuaded be more useful to you in the Situation which he seeks, than any person whose services ["it is probable" *interlined*] you will be able to engage.

A desire to serve him & at the same time to place in your possession the information which may be necessary to a judicious selection are the inducements which impel me to this step.

Should you find proper, [to] confer the appointment in question upon Major Van De Venter I shall always consider myself under obligations for the confidence ["wh" *canceled*] with which you may honor him. I remain with Sentiments of the highest respect your most ob[edien]t & very humble Servant, Wm. H. Crawford.

Ms. copy in MiU-C, Christopher Vandeventer Papers.

Oath of office as Secretary of War, 12/8/1817. Calhoun put his signature to an oath promising to uphold the Constitution and faithfully fulfill the duties of the office of Secretary of War. DS in ScCleA.

From R[ic]h[ard] M. Johnson, [Representative from Ky.]

[Washington] 10th Dec. 1817

Sir, My Friend Lt. [Henry S.] Mallory is ordered to Nashville ["$"(?) *canceled*] 750 ["miles" *interlined*]—he is without money or friends at this place. It is usual I believe to advance in such cases money to make the officer easy as to his expences. Will you be so good as to give him a line to the Paymaster stationed in this City to advance him his transportation & 3 months pay & this in case of death & shall bind me to refund the money to govt. Your[s] Sincerely, Rh: M: Johnson.

ALS in NhHi, Salmon P. Chase Papers. NOTE: An AES by D[aniel] Parker reads, "The Paymaster Gen[era]l. The advance required will promote the service."

To Maj. C[HRISTOPHER] VANDEVENTER, Washington

War Department, 10th Dec[embe]r 1817
Sir, I have concluded to offer you the appointment of cheif Clerk in this Department, and would be glad that you could attend to the duties attached to ["it" *interlined*; to]morrow. With great respect &c, J.C. Calhoun.

ALS in MiU-C, Christopher Vandeventer Papers.

From [WILLIAM HENRY HARRISON, Representative from Ind.]

[Washington,] Saturday ["11th" *altered to* "13th"]
Dec[embe]r [1817]
Gen[era]l Harrison presents his compliments to the Sec[retar]y of War & requests to be informed when he can wait upon him with a prospect of finding him at leasure to hear a Statement which the Wyandot & Seneca Indians now in Town are desirous of making & which they wish to do in the presence of Gen[era]l H[arrison.] I[t] would be extremely gratifying to those people if they could be permitted to deliver what they have to say to the President personally.

Gen[era]l Harrison assures Mr. Calhoun that these Chiefs deserve this mark of respect as well from their characters as men as for the services they have rendered the United States.

ALU in InHi, Harrison Miscellaneous Collection.

From OSWALD H. HOUSTON and SAMUEL C. CALHOUN

Southcarolina, Abbeville Dist., Decemb[e]r 15th 1817
Dear sir, I am led to beleive that you will or has Accepted of the office of the secretary of war. My friend Samuel C. Calhoun and my self will trouble you with a few lines concerning the Milatary Academy. We are desireous to be Acquainted with the terms of that place and the duties we would have to undergo. Will you be so accommodating as to write us a few lines as quick as these come to hand. You will

lay us under obligation. Give us a full statement of the place and your advice if you please. We want to know if there is a sertain time of the year that we can enter or not or if we can Enter when we please. If you write and we are as well satisfied with the discription you give it as we are of the Idea we have of it we will undoubtedly go provided we can get Admittance.

After receiving your letter we will immediately answer it, with pleasure whether we like the place or whether we intend going or not. Our dependance will alltogether rest upon you to get admittance.

Sir, you will lay us under further obligation for a compleate discription of the place, And your Advice as we are determ[in]ed to abide by it. This from yo[u]r young friends Oswald H. Houston and Samuel C. Calhoun.

LS (with both signatures in the same hand) in DNA, RG 94 (Adjutant General), Application Papers of Cadets, 1805–1866, 1817, 70–71 (M-688:6, frames 392–394).

Commission as Secretary of War, Washington, 12/16/1817. President James Monroe, "with the advise and Consent of the Senate" appoints Calhoun to be Secretary of War. This document is signed by Monroe and Secretary of State John Quincy Adams. DS in ScCleA.

From [DE WITT CLINTON, Governor of N.Y.]

Albany [N.Y.,] 17 Dec[embe]r 1817

Gov[erno]r Clinton's compliments to Mr. Calhoun & transmits to him the Reports on the northern & western Canals of this State as a token of his respect for Mr. C[alhoun]'s distinguished efforts in favor of internal improvements.

Draft in NNC, De Witt Clinton Papers, Letterbooks, 4:56.

SUPPLEMENT, 1818–1825

〔0〕

To Thomas Dougherty, Clerk, House of Representatives, 1/7.
"Sir. Mr. Jefferson has interested himself to procure the admission
of a claim of Mr. [Joseph Léonard] Poirey an aid-de-Camp and Secretary to major general La Fayette, during the war of the American
revolution. This claim was brought before the American government, at the instance of the Marquis La Fayette, by General Washington. In 1801, Mr. Jefferson assured Mr. Poirey, that his claim
should be presented to Congress. Permit me to enquire of you,
whether anything was done by Congress in relations to this claim.
The destruction of the journals of Congress which belonged to this
department, by fire causes me to trouble you with this application."
Text or partial text of an LS in *Profiles in History*, a catalog of Joseph
M. Maddalena, Beverly Hills, Cal., [1988], Item 76, p. 27.

From W[ILLIA]M FINDLEY, [former
Representative from Pa.]

Youngstown, Westm[orelan]d County [Pa.],
Jan[uar]y 19, 1818
Dear Sir, If health had permitted and it had been my lot, to have been
a Member of the present Congress, I would have regretted the want
of those displays of talents and industry by which my attention was
so frequently and so agreeably entertained during several Congresses
in which you Sir and myself were members, and in which the respectability of your talents and usefullness were acknowledged by all
parties, at ["a" *interlined*] period too when the violence of party conflict disgraced the nation and embarrassed her measures. Your usefullness would have in my opinion been of ["so" *interlined*] great
advantage to the present house, composed of a greater proportion
than heretofore of new members, as abates in some measure the satisfaction I would have otherwise in your being put at the head of the
War department, though in that department I am confident your
usefullness will be great. Be pleased to execuse this introduction by
setting it to account of past friendship.

My object however in calling your attention is to request the admission of a promising young lad of ["15 or" *canceled*] 16 years of age as a Cadet in the Milatary Accedemy at West Point, or to inform me by the bearer how such application should be made. His name is Thomas Johnston, son of Alex[ande]r Johnston, a friend of mine and ["a" *interlined*] respectable citizen. That the young man[']s character is amiable and promising is admitted by them that know him, and is certified in the inclosed letter from J.S. Findlay, a very respectable teacher in Greensburgh our county town, and Brother to the Gov[erno]r of Pennsylv[ani]a [William Findlay].

Notwithwithstanding [*sic*] the oppertunities I have had and the votes I have given to support that institution, yet as none of my friends in this part of the [*partial word canceled*] State were applying for admission, I never made myself acquainted with the mode prescribed for obtaining admission or the quallifications necessary for the applicant, only I know that the institution is under the superin[ten]dance of the War office and subject to such rules as are ["theirby" *canceled and* "thereby" *interlined*] prescribed, and that provision is made for the instruction of the pupils in every necessary branch of learning in the Accedemy.

I will only add what I know will be agreeable to you Sir, that notwithstanding my advanced age, it has pleased God that my health is recovered beyond all probability. I am with sincere esteem yours very respectfully, Wm. Findley.

ALS with En in DNA, RG 94 (Adjutant General), Application Papers of Cadets, 1805–1866, 1818, 67 (M-688:8, frames 76–77 and 68–69). NOTE: The enclosed letter from J.S. Findlay was dated 12/3/1817 and addressed to William Findley. In a letter of 6/2/1818, Thomas Johnston accepted his appointment to the Military Academy; he graduated with the class of 1822.

From JOHN JOHNSTON, [Indian Agent]

Piqua [Ohio,] Jan[uar]y 26, 1818
Sir, I have been lately written to by Governour [Jonathan] Jennings of Indiana, on the subject of purchasing from the Indians what is called the White River Country within the limits of that State. Himself as well as many of the leading men ["in" *canceled;* "that" *altered to* "there" *and* "State" *canceled*] has [*sic*] expressed great solicitude on the subject. It will be perceived on a reference to the map that the Indian lands at this time approaches within forty miles of the

Ohio River. In communicating with Governor Jennings and The Hon[ora]ble Messrs. [Waller] Taylor & [James] Noble of the Senate on this subject, I have ventured to give it as my opinion, that if proper measures are pursued the Country can be purchased the approaching summer. Seeing that public opinion in Indiana and the adjoining parts of Ohio is so much in favour of a Treaty [I] have made out an estimate for the purpose, accompanied by such remarks as appeared necessary. A Duplicate of this estimate was forwarded to Messrs. Taylor & Noble of the Senate from Indiana with a view that if a Treaty was concluded on the appropriations and other arrangements might be made before Congress would rise. The Representation from Indiana will no doubt confer with you on the subject.

I propose that the Treaty be held at Greenville in Ohio, a place celebrated in the history of our intercourse with the natives. Once the Head Quarters of Gen[era]l [Anthony] Waynes Army and where two pacifications took place with the Indians. It will be easy getting forward to this point all the stores and provisions necessary for the Treaty. The expence of holding a Treaty at Greenville will be Ten thousand Dollars less than at any place in the Indian Country.

I recommend that all the annuities for the Miamies, Delawares, Weeas, Eel Rivers, Kickapoos[,] Putawatimies *who receive at Fort Wayne*, Shawanoye & Wyandotts for the present year, take the route of Pittsburgh descend the Ohio to Cincinnati and there be deposited with The House of Jeremiah Neave & Son to remain subject to my orders. My object is to have them transported to Greenville and delivered at the Treaty, thereby saving the trouble and expence of collecting the Indians a second time to receive them. I beg that this circumstance may be particularly attended to.

In the event of a Treaty being ordered I want to receive your commands as early as practicable as much previous management is necessary among the Indians, and as the Tribes who will be parties to it are scattered over a great extent of Country. My opportunities of communicating, at this season of deep snow, with His Excellency Gov[erno]r [Lewis] Cass is seldom and this I hope will be my appology for addressing myself direct to you. I have the Honor to remain with very great respect Sir y[ou]r mo[st] ob[edient] S[ervan]t, Jno. Johnston, Indian Agent.

ALS in InHi, Benjamin Parke Papers.

To JOHN WILLIAMS, "Ch[airman] of the Mil[itar]y Com[mitt]ee of the Senate U.S."

Department of War, 5th February 1818
Sir, I have given to the enclosed resolutions of the Senate all the attention, which their importance demands, and my other engagements would admit. Feeling as I do, the importance of a well organized staff, I regret that want of minute knowledge in relation to it, which would enable me to state my ideas with greater decision, both as to the present system and such amendments as it may be susceptible of.

If the Committee should think that so much of the act of 1816, as creates the office of Hospital surgeon's and Hospital surgeon's mate, and judge advocates, ought to be repealed, I would respectfully suggesting the propriety of creating in lieu of them, the office of Surgeon general and Judge advocate general. I have already offered to you my ideas in relation to them, in conversation, and now will only briefly restate them.

The medical staff at present is without responsibility; and must, I conceive, remain so 'till its duties are brought to a center. To introduce responsibility, it should be the duty of the surgeons of the army to make quarterly returns of the manner in which they have performed their duties. These returns ought, among other particulars, to contain a list of the sick, their disease, the prescriptions and issues of medical stores. It must be apparent, that there ought to be a medical character of eminence, to report to the head of the department, on these returns. It is thus that the character of each surgeon in the army will come to be known, and important checks imposed on the improper consumption and waste of medical stores. It is not to be doubted, that the public sustains great losses for the want of such a system.

The Judge Advocate General would be the adviser of the department in all cases touching martial laws, and would, in important trials, be ordered to act as the Judge advocate. It seems to me, the importance of such an office is apparent, when we reflect that points of the most difficult character, are involved in the decisions of courts martial, and that those decisions may involve the life of a fellow citizen.

The Quarter master's department may, I conceive, be rendered more simple and efficient. I would suggest the propriety of one quarter master general, with one deputy for each division, and as many assistants as the service may require. No branch of the general staff is more important and difficult to manage than the Quarter master's;

none requires more eminently the control of a single and responsible head.

I would also respectfully suggest, that in the dispersed condition of the army, the Chaplains might be dispensed with, without injury to the service, except the one at West point. I know of no farther retrenchments, that would not impair the efficiency of the staff. I am, very respectfully, Sir, your obed[ien]t Servant, J.C. Calhoun.

LS in MB; FC in DNA, RG 107 (Secretary of War), Reports to Congress from the Secretary of War, 1803–1870, 1:435–437 (M-220:1); PC in Jameson, ed., *Correspondence*, pp. 133–134.

From ——, Sta[u]nton [Va.], 2/21. This writer informs Calhoun that Capt. Samuel Miller, "the proprietor of a large Iron Establishment on the waters of the Shenandoah," wishes to sell his iron establishment. If the government wishes to buy this land, the writer wants to be informed of it so that he can make known to Miller the views of the government. (An EU on this letter reads: "Col. [George] Bomford"; another EU reads: "Proposals for making Cannon.") ALI in NcD, John C. Calhoun Papers.

From Th[omas] S. Jesup

Washington City, March 18th 1818

Sir, Having been informed that certain *Majors* of the staff ["of the army" *canceled*] have protested against my appointment as Adjutant General, it is due to myself to say that I never applied for that appointment, but consented, at the request of General [Jacob] Brown, to receive it, should the Government think proper to confer it upon me. But altho' it is a matter of perfect indifference to me whether I receive the appointment or not, I feel it to be a duty which I owe to the field officers of the army, to enter my most solemn protest against the promotion of any *Staff Major*, over the Lieut. Colonels of the army.

Should the protest of the gentlemen alluded to, be placed upon the files of the War Office, I must request that this letter be filed with it: and have the honour to be, Sir, your ob[edien]t serv[an]t, Th: S. Jesup, Lt. Colo. 3rd Inf[an]try & Colo. by brevet.

ALS in U.S. Army Military History Institute, Carlisle Barracks, Pa., Thomas S. Jesup Papers.

To Capt. "JOHN OCONNER [*sic*; John M. O'Connor]," New York [City]

War Dept., 10th April 1818

Sir, Inclosed is the letter which you requested to Mr. [Albert] Gallatin [U.S. Minister to France]. I hope it will procure you the advantages of the course of lectures which you are desireous of attending. With sentiment of esteem I am &c, J.C. Calhoun.

ALS owned by Mr. Dirk F. Bollenback. NOTE: An endorsement on the address page of this letter reads: "J.C. Calhoun, War Department 10th April 1818[,] rec[eive]d 15 [April 1818]." Calhoun's letter of 4/10/1818 to Gallatin is published in *The Papers of John C. Calhoun*, 2:238.

ACT REGULATING THE STAFF OF THE ARMY

[Washington, April 14, 1818]

Be it enacted by the Senate and House of Representatives of the United States of America, in Congress assembled, That so much of the act "fixing the military peace establishment of the United States," passed the third of March, one thousand eight hundred and fifteen, as relates to hospital stewards and wardmasters, and so much of the "Act for organizing the general staff, and making further provision for the army of the United States," passed April twenty-fourth, one thousand eight hundred and sixteen, as relates to hospital surgeons, hospital surgeon's mates, judge advocates, chaplains, and forage, wagon, and barrack masters, and their assistants, be and the same is hereby, repealed.

SEC. 2. *And be it further enacted,* That there shall be one surgeon general, with a salary of two thousand five hundred dollars per annum, one assistant surgeon general, with the emoluments of a hospital surgeon, one judge advocate, with the pay and emoluments of a topographical engineer, to each division, and one chaplain, stationed at the military academy at West Point, who shall also be professor of geography, history, and ethics, with the pay and emoluments allowed the professor of mathematics; and that the number of post surgeons be increased, not to exceed eight to each division.

SEC. 3. *And be it further enacted,* That so much of the act of the twenty-fourth of April, one thousand eight hundred and sixteen, aforesaid, as relates to the quartermaster general of division, shall be repealed; and the quartermaster's department shall consist, in addition to the two deputy quartermasters general, and the four assistant deputy quartermasters general, now authorized, of one quartermaster general, with the rank, pay, and emoluments, of a brigadier general, and as many assistant deputy quartermasters general as the President shall deem proper, not exceeding, in the whole number, twelve.

SEC. 4. *And be it further enacted,* That to each commissioned officer who shall be deranged by virtue of this act, there shall be allowed and paid, in addition to the pay and emoluments to which they will be entitled by law, at the time of their discharge, three months' pay and emoluments; and that the provisions of this act shall be carried into effect on or before the first day of June next.

SEC. 5. *And be it further enacted,* That the pay and emoluments of the inspector generals of divisions be, and is hereby, raised to be equal to the pay and emoluments of the adjutant generals of division.

SEC. 6. *And be it further enacted,* That as soon as the state of existing contracts for the subsistence of the army shall, in the opinion of the President of the United States, permit it, there shall be appointed by the President, by and with the advice and consent of the Senate, one commissary general, with the rank, pay, and emoluments, of colonel of ordnance, who shall, before entering on the duties of his office, give bond and security, in such sum as the President may direct; and as many assistants, to be taken from the subalterns of the line, as the service may require, who shall receive twenty dollars per month in addition to their pay in the line, and who shall, before entering on the duties of their office, give bond and security, in such sums as the President may direct. The commissary general and his assistants shall perform such duties, in purchasing and issuing of rations to the army of the United States, as the President may direct.

SEC. 7. *And be it further enacted,* That supplies for the army, unless, in particular and urgent cases, the Secretary of War should otherwise direct, shall be purchased by contract, to be made by the commissary general on public notice, to be delivered, on inspection, in the bulk, and at such places as shall be stipulated; which contract shall be made under such regulations as the Secretary of War may direct.

SEC. 8. *And be it further enacted,* That the President may make such alterations in the component parts of the ration as a due regard to the health and comfort of the army and economy may require.

SEC. 9. *And be it further enacted,* That the commissary general and his assistants shall not be concerned, directly or indirectly, in the purchase or sale, in trade or commerce, of any article entering into the composition of the ration allowed to the troops in the service of the United States, except on account of the United States, nor shall such officer take and apply to his own use any gain or emolument for negotiating or transacting any business connected with the duties of his office, other than what is or may be allowed by law; and the commissary general and his assistants shall be subject to martial law.

SEC. 10. *And be it further enacted,* That all letters to and from the commissary general, which may relate to his office duties, shall be free from postage: *Provided,* That the sixth, seventh, eighth, ninth, and tenth, sections of this act shall continue and be in force for the term of five years from the passing of the same, and thence until the end of the next session of Congress, and no longer.

APPROVED, April 14, 1818.

PC in Peters, ed., *Statutes at Large,* 3:426–427. NOTE: This bill was based on a draft by Calhoun. See above Calhoun to John Williams, 2/5/1818 and the correspondence between Calhoun and Williams in *The Papers of John C. Calhoun,* 2:132, 147.

From Maj. Gen. ANDREW JACKSON

Head Quarters, Divi[sio]n South
Fort St. Marks [Fla.], 26 March [*sic*; April] 1818

I wrote you from Bowlegs Town on the 20th Inst[a]n[t]. On the night of the same day I received the expected despatch from my aid de camp Lt. [James] Gadsden, communicating the success of his expedition, and on the next day as soon as the sick of my army were dispatched down the Suwaney river to be conveyed in the captured Schooner to St. Marks I took up the line of march for that Fort. I arrived at this place last evening performing a march of 107 miles in less than five days. Lt. Gadsden had reached it a few hours before me. He communicates having found among the papers of [Alexander] A[r]buthnot, Armbrister [*sic*; Robert C. Ambrister] and [Peter B.] Cook letters, memorials &c all pointing out the Instigators of this savage war & in some measure involving the British Government in the agency. These will be forwarded you in a detailed report I purpose communicating to you as early as practicable.

The old woman spoken of in my last communication to you, who had promised to use her influence in having [Peter] McQueen Captured and delivered up has not been heard of. From signs discovered on the opposite shore of the St. Marks river I am induced to believe that that Indian party are still in this neighbourhood. A detatchment will be sent out to reconnoitre the country to receive them as Friends if disposed to surrender, or inflict merited chastisement if still hostile.

I shall leave this in 2 or 3 days for Fort Gadsden, and after making all necessary arrangements for the security of the positions occupied—and detatching a force to secure the country west of the Appalacha-cola, I shall proceed direct for Nashville. My presence in this country can be no longer necessary. The Indian Forces have been divided, and scattered, cut off from all communication with those unprincipled agents of Foreign nations, who have deluded them to their ruin[,] they have not the power, if the will remains, of again annoying our frontier. I remain respec[tfull]y your Ob[edien]t Ser[van]t, Andrew Jackson, Major Genl. Comdg.

LS in MiU-C, Southwest Territory Collection; CC in DNA, RG 84 (Foreign Service Posts), Diplomatic Posts, Spain, 1801–1935, Correspondence, 1818; PC in *Annals of Congress*, 15th Cong., 2nd Sess., Appendix, cols. 2072–2073 and 2189; PC in House Document No. 14, 15th Cong., 2nd Sess., p. 55; PC in House Document No. 65, 15th Cong., 2nd Sess., pp. 181–182; PC in *American State Papers: Military Affairs*, 1:701; PC in *American State Papers: Foreign Relations*, 4:600; PC in Bassett, ed., *Correspondence of Andrew Jackson*, 2:363–364.

From Maj. Gen. ANDREW JACKSON

Fort Gadsden [East Fla.], May 6, 1818
Head Quarters, Div[isio]n South
Sir, I have to acknowledge the receipt of your letter of the 2d March last. The testimony of Col. [David] Brearley shall be taken as directed, with that of [William] McIntosh who seized the Africans, and such other as may be deemed necessary to elucidate & explain the whole transaction. The active operations in which I am engaged will prevent my taking the depositions myself, Col. Brearley is now at Fort Hawkins under arrest, a confidential officer however will be charged with the duty.

I have no doubt that the evidence when collected will convict the agent [David B. Mitchell] of the charges preferred. Your most ob[edient] Serv[ant], Andrew Jackson, major Genl. Comdg.

LS in ScU-SC, John C. Calhoun Papers. NOTE: A Clerk's EU reads, "Fort Gadsden, 6 May 1818. Genl. A. Jackson, Has recd. letter 2d March—A confidential Officer will be appointed to take depositions in the affair of the smuggled Africans."

From MARCUS MORTON, [Representative from Mass.]

Taunton [Mass.], May 6, 1818

Dear Sir, It is with reluctance, that, I at this time intrude myself upon your attention, already fully occupied, by the important business of your office. But a sense of duty to my Country and its Government constrains me to make known to you some of the abuses of the Law for the relief of some of the soldiers of the Revolutionary Army, which are attempted to be practised and which, I trust you have the power to prevent. I learn, since my return to Massachusetts, that the applications for pensions under this law, are numerous beyond the expectations of any one; and that there are among the Applicants a very great number, who do not come within the literal or equitable provisions of the Act.

I have no doubt that the Officers of your department will exercise due vigilence (and no small share will be necessary) in preventing *Militia* and *State troops* from placing themselves upon the "*Continental Establishment.*"

The great abuses to which I wish to call your attention, consist in the applications of men who are not in "need of assistance from their Country for a support." Your directions allowing this fact to be proved by the oath of the applicant while it promotes and encourages perjury and gives the knave an advantage over the honest man, do not in any considerable degree check the abuses of which I complain. A great many in comfortable and easy and some in affluent circumstances, have already taken the oaths preparatory to their applications to your Department. Each one seems to find a justification for his conduct in the examples of many others, whom he considers less needy than himself. The consequence is that a few only of the more worthy and conscientious are to be excluded from the benefit of the law. I do not perceive how these abuses are to be prevented but by a change of the rule which you have prescribed in relation to this subject. It is not now so late that any great inconvenience would result from such a change. I think that in addition to or without the Applicants own oath other evidence of his *need of assistance* ought to be required. No material inconvenience would be experienced by the real object of the Law, because in all cases he could obtain such additional evidence with very little trouble. Still further to prevent imposition, I think this evidence ought to be obtained from persons, who from their situation in Society would be entitled to credit. Probably by requiring affidavits from Selectmen of towns, or Overseers of the Poor, or some Magistrates of the County in which the Applicant resides as to his *need of assistance,* you would effectually prevent abuses of the law, without imposing any hardship upon any class of Applicants. In my opinion, this would remove the present temptation to perjury; would deprive the knave of the advantages he now posses[ses], and would prevent one of the most popular Acts of the present Administration from being converted into a source of discontent. Confident I am that some means ought to be adopted to prevent these abuses of the law or the law ought to be so amended as to include all classes of Revolutionary Soldiers, without reference to their circumstances in life or to be wholly repealed.

Dear Sir, please to excuse the freedom with which I have expressed my sentiments, and to believe me to remain with the highest respect and Regard Y[ou]r Obedient Servant, Marcus Morton.

FC in MHi, Marcus Morton Letterbooks, 1:1–4.

From the Rev. ELIAS CORNELIUS

Washington, July 10, 1818

Sir, Among the duties which, as agent for the American Board of Commissioners for Foreign Missions, I have been instructed to perform, has been that of selecting a few promising Indian youth, of influential & distinguished families, with a view to their regular & more liberal education in the State of Connecticut. The selection has been made: and I ["now" *interlined*] have the honour to state, that I have with me in this city, one such youth from the Choctaw nation, & three from the Cherokee Nation.

The name of the Choctaw youth is *McKee Folsom.* He is a brother of David Folsom, a distinguished half breed chief whose signature is to be found to the last treaty held between the United States & the Choctaw nation. The Lad is 16 years of age—and apparently possessed of a mind susceptible of great improvement.

One of the Cherokee youths is the son of the well known half breed Charles R. Hicks, at present the second chief in office in his nation, though in influence, the first. This chief has been a reputable professor of the Christian religion in the Moravian church, for five years past and is in every respect so far as a stranger can decide, a civilized & enlightened man. I enclose you a copy of a sealed letter of instructions to his son which he put into my hand at the time of our

339

departure, and which I am happy to communicate as furnishing at on[ce] a specimen of Indian intellect & Indian affection. Leonard, his son, has already received in his nation a good common education—he is not 14 years of age and obviously ["possessed" *altered to* "possesses"; "of" *canceled*] a mind, strong & active. Another of the lads, about the same age as Hicks, is a Nephew of Major Ridge, an officer under Gen. [Andrew] Jackson during the former Creek War. He is also nephew to Charles Reece, a halfbreed chief, who distinguished himself so eminently at the Battle of the Horseshoe—being the first of the three Cherokees, who swamp [*sic*; swam] the Tallapoosa & brought away the Canoes of the enemy. For this act of bravery he received an elegant silver mounted rifle from ["the" *canceled*] President [James] Madison. His Nephew is a youth of a good common education, & promises fair, as do the others, of becomeing at a future day conspicuous in his Nation. The remaining Cherokee though not so particularly distinguished by his connexions is an amiable & promising boy: having no mixture of ["the" *canceled and* "foreign" *interlined*] blood ["of the white people, in his veins" *canceled*]. The first is a half breed; the other two are 3/4 Indian blood.

The Parents & friends of these youth, have expressed to me the most earnest desire that their children should be educated, & have testified their sincerity by furnishing them with horses & other necessaries for their long journey and about one hundred dollars in money. From my own knowledge of their circumstances I should judge this bequest a large proportion to their real ability.

Beleiving that the Government can in no way more effectually subserve the cause of humanity & national policy among these people, than by lending their patronage & support to efforts which are made to fit their children for active and useful life, I have thought it would not be an improper subject on which to address the Secretary of War.

I do not ask for such an appropriation, as would ["would" *canceled*] defray the whole expence of their education. Christian Benevolence, happily coinciding in her views, with the best policy of the Government, is not reluctant to sustain her proportion of the burden—while it is expected another item will be defrayed by the friends of the youths in the Indian country. Could the Government make an annual appropriation of one hundred dollars only to each of the youth while obtaining their education, and grant something to assist in defraying the necessary expences of their journey, which have already become considerable, it would enable the American Board, much to extend their benevolent efforts, while by such an appropriation, the policy of the Government would be as effectually subserved as by a larger sum. The sum now asked for the *four* youth if I mistake not, is the same as that which the Government has already annually appropriated for the education of *one* Indian Youth ["in" *canceled and* "late in" *interlined*] Baltimore. An additional argument however, in the present case for seeking a small appropriation, is derived from the expectation that soon several more promising youth from the Indian country will join their companions in Connecticut—["for" *canceled and* "to" *interlined*] whom ["we trust" *canceled and* "it is presumed" *interlined*] the present answer of the Secretary, will be considered as applicable.

As I hope to have the satisfaction of introducing the youth in whose behalf the present communication is made to the personal acquaintance of the Secretary of war I will not prolong my letter. I will only add that while the natives of our forests are fast resigning their ["own" *canceled*] political existence, to strengthen & perpetuate our own—while they are yielding up—their lands—to them *their last*[,] *their only hope* of support, ["and lands" *canceled*], the sale of which ["has" *canceled*] throws millions into our National Treasury, their humble & affecting prayer, for a remuneration so small will not be unavailing. And in the full hope of assurance that it will not—I have the honour to subscribe myself yours humbly & sincerely, Elias Cornelius, Agent for the A[merican] B[oard of] C[ommissioners for] F[oreign] M[issions].

ALS in CtHi.

From JER[EMIA]H EVARTS and ELIAS CORNELIUS

Washington, July 15, 1818

Sir, As agents of the American Board of Commissioners for Foreign Missions we beg leave to offer the following suggestions & inquiries. We need not trouble you with a long introduction, as there are several documents in your department relative to the general subject of this communication.

Permit us to observe, however, that the Society, in whose behalf we speak, entertains the most large & liberal designs; that its members reside in seven States of the union, and the only reason why they are not found in every state is the impracticability of their meeting to transact business, if so widely dispersed; that it has patrons & friends in all the States; that its members are not confined to any religious denomination; that it disowns all narrow, local, or party views, & seeks to do good by aiding in the moral improvement of our fellow men, wherever accessible, who have not yet enjoyed the blessings of civilization & Christianity; that it regards with peculiar interest the wants of the Aborigines within our own borders; that it acknowledges with gratitude the favorable regards & the important aid of government; & that it will not solicit the patronage of government for any object, to which the members of the Society are not ready to contribute of their property, their time, & their labor. Permit us to add, that as the various concerns of the Board are becoming weighty, both on account of the expense & responsibility attached to them, and as prudence, circumspection, & economy, are highly necessary, the Committee, & other agents of the Board, will not make any communications to government without great care & deliberation.

After these remarks we would respectfully inquire,

1. Whether the government may not with propriety give further assurances, that, in case the Indian title to the land, on which our schools are & shall be established, should hereafter be extinguished, the Board shall enjoy the land occupied & improved by them, it being understood that all the avails & profits of such tenements shall be applied solely to the benevolent objects for which the Board was formed? It is proper to state here, that it is a favorite plan of the Committee to exhibit a favorable & thorough specimen of agriculture before the eyes of the Indians, & to cultivate all the grains, grasses, & fruits, which are suited to the various climates of our stations. For these purposes, & to prevent annoyance from near neighbors, probably no man would think a mile square too large a reservation. This inquiry will be deemed proper, when it is considered that great expense has already been incurred in improving the farm among the Cherokees, & similiar expenses are contemplated at other stations.

2. Will not the government supply a greater number of implements of husbandry, & of domestic manufacture, than have as yet been promised? At the school among the Cherokees, there are already more than twenty boys, who can handle the hoe, & the axe, very dexterously.

3. As it is found desirable to give some promising Indian youths a more thorough education, than they can receive in their own tribes, & to give them a fair & full view of the benefits of civilized society, will not government bear a moderate part of the expense of their journey & residence for this purpose? Four youths of this descrip-

tion are now under our care in this city, on their way to an excellent school, designed particularly for their benefit, & the benefit of others in similar circumstances.*

[Note:] *As a particular account has already been given of these youths to this department by one of us, it is not necessary to repeat the account here.

4. Will not the government assist in the erection of a corn-mill near each station, provided it can be done at a moderate expense, with the approbation of the public agent, & with a prospect of success? So important is a mill to the comfort of the [mission-]family & school, that the Board have already expended five hundred dollars in building one among the Cherokees. It was not quite completed on the 1st of June last.

5. Should the Board feel able to comply with the earnest desires of the emigrants to the Arkansas, & send a mission-family & schoolmaster thither as soon as possible, will not the government afford some extraordinary aid? particularly, as the distance is great, the passage circuitous & expensive, & the obtaining of supplies difficult?

Expressing a confident opinion, that the civil & moral improvement of the Indians, will promote the true policy, the interest, and the dignity of the United States, we are, Sir, with sentiments of great respect & consideration, your obedient servants, Jerh. Evarts, Elias Cornelius.

LS (in Evarts's hand) in NbHi, Eli S. Ricker Collection. NOTE: Calhoun's reply is published in *The Papers of John C. Calhoun*, 2:397.

To JAMES MONROE, "President of the U.S.," Albemarle [County], Va.

War Dept., 24th Sep[tembe]r 1818
Dear Sir, I enclose you a copy of my letter to Gen[era]l [Edmund P.] Gaines in reply to his of the 8th Inst.; a copy of which I have also transmitted to Gen[era]l [Andrew] Jackson.

I enclose a letter from Gen[era]l [Samuel] Smith and from Gen[era]l [William Henry] Winder recommending Col. [Nathan] Towson to fill the place lately held by Col. [Franklin] Wharton [Commandant of the Marine Corps]. You know Col. Towson personally; and it will be useless for me to state the high estimation in which he is held in the army. The act of the last session has left him without his

343

brevet pay; and he only draws that of a Captain, on which he has to support himself & family. He finds it so inadequate, that, he states, he will be compelled to leave the service. I do not know how far it would be proper to fill the vaca[nc]y by one out of the Corps; but if it should be so determined, I am sure a more worthy & deserving ["an"(?) *canceled*] officer cannot be found.

Accept the assurance of my respect & esteem. Yours sincerely, J.C. Calhoun.

ALS in ViW, Monroe Papers (James Monroe Papers in Virginia Repositories, published microfilm, roll 13, frames 121–123).

To JAMES E[DWARD] COLHOUN "of the Congress Frigate, Norfolk"

[Washington, *ca.* October 25, 1818]

Dear James, ["Since" *canceled*] Since writting the within I have rece[ive]d a letter [of 10/2] from Mr. [Andrew] Norris with one for you which I enclose. William Norris says that your mother [Floride Bonneau Colhoun] will not be here probably for two weeks. Should you desire it, a draft will be sent you on the Branch bank at Norfolk for the $300. J.C.C.

[Enclosure]

Andrew Norris to James E[dward] Colhoun, "U.S. Frigate Congress," Norfolk

28 Sept[embe]r 1818[,] Walnut Grove Abbeville Dist. S.C. Dear James, Your two letters of Dates 9th July & 4th August ult. came to hand together on the 22nd instant they gave me Pleasure in informing me of your safe Return to your Native Continent. I am indeed happy to hear, that when distant from relatives you found friends to assist you. I hope you have been able to reimburse them out of what you rec[eive]d thro' the medium of our mutual friend Mr. Calhoun at Washington. Should it, or should it not be so—I will by the first Private conveyance transmit you $500 in addition to the $300 to Mr. Calhoun as requested in your letter. The conveyance by mail is so dangerous & almost always uncertain that I do not like to risque any amount in a letter & in the part of the Country I live there is no chance of getting Bills of exchange nor even Post Notes, the Circulating Paper here generally comes from Savannah and Augusta. If any opportunity Should offer earlyer than by Mr. [Eldred] Simkins

our Representative in Congress I will certainly forward you the above. I am sorry to think of your going to the China Sea the length of time you will be absent, will I fear entirely wean your affections from all your relatives and former friends & a matter of still greater importance to yourself on the next 4th July Twenty one years will have passed since you breathed vital air. I then would be glad that you should be Home to take charge of, or give directions about those things that are at present between me and Mr. Speed. I have frequently been applied to—to sell your Pendleton land. I have refused to sell telling the Applicants when they might apply to yourself, provided you would be at that time Home. How the Crop at Midway may turn out this year I cannot tell you—it was well set & worked but suffered with drought. Since writing the above an opportunity offers by W[illia]m C. Norris of sending this under cover to Mr. J.C. Calhoun to whom I inclose the Three Hundred Dollars you mention to have received from him in your's of 4th Ult. The sum herein before promised you, I will send on by your Mother [Floride Bonneau Colhoun] or some other private conveyance to the care of Mr. J.C.C. Your Aunt [Anna Wrainch Norris] joins me in best wishes for your Health and Happiness, believe us my dear James Your's Sincerely, Andrew Norris.

P.S. Please make my Compliments to Mr. & Mrs. Calhoun.

ALI in ScCleA; ALS of En in ScU-SC, James Edward Colhoun Papers. Note: Andrew Norris (1765–1824) was a son of Robert Norris and Jean Ewing Colhoun Norris. He was an Abbeville attorney and a half-brother of John Ewing Colhoun, Sr., father of John Ewing Colhoun, Jr., James Edward Colhoun, and Floride Colhoun Calhoun. Calhoun's letter has been given the date of its postmark.

From [former Governor] ANDREW PICKENS, [JR.]

Hopewell [Pendleton District, S.C.], 29th Oct[obe]r 1818
Sir, Major [Adam] Carruth is going on to Washington for the purpose, as I understand, of extending his contract for the manufacture of arms & wishes me to say what I think of his machinery. A few weeks since, I was at his manufactory, & so far as I was competent to judge, I thought the arms, which he had completed, were excellent & was much pleased with the facility & ingenuity with which every operation appeared to be performed & think, from its situation & command of water, that his machinery is capable of being increased to any reasonable extent. I know no man, in this country, better

calculated to manage & carry on such a manufactory. I have the honor to be &c, Andrew Pickens.

ALS in DNA, RG 156 (Chief of Ordnance), Letters Received, 1812–1894, 1818, P. NOTE: A War Department Clerk's EU reads, "And[re]w Pickens, late Gov[erno]r of So. Carolina in favor of Mr. Carruth's Fact[or]y for Arms. Oct[obe]r 1818."

From J[AMES] B. REYNOLDS, [former Representative from Tenn.]

Clarksville, Ten., 18th Nov[embe]r 1818
Dear Sir, It is probable that at this Session of Congress there will be a new territory erected on the Arkansas or Red-River. Should this happen, you will please present my name to the President [James Monroe] for any office you conceive me capable of filling.

My people here have put me down in consequence of the compensation law, and I feel too much wounded to ask from them a renewal of their favours. I regret the circumstance; for no man ever has, or ever will have their interest at heart more than I had. And it seems now that all the States are endeavouring to forget the measure, and electing the old members, yet in this quarter the subject still lives. It has been an unfortunate one to me, for it has even mingled itself with my professional pursuits, and has curtailed its profits very sensibly. It is too much to bear, and I ought to have torn myself from the country long since. But I remained with lingering hope, that all would be well.

I have no person now to look up to under the President but yourself on subjects of this kind. The present representation from this State have, with a very few exceptions, rode into congress on the unpopularity of the compensation law. I have therefore no favours to ask ["of" *interlined*] them. There are two worthy friends from the adjoining State who I believe would lend their names to promote my interest if called upon, I mean Messrs. [Henry] Clay & [Richard M.] Johnson. I remain very sincerely your much obliged friend, J.B. Reynolds.

ALS in DNA, RG 59 (State Department), Letters of Application and Recommendation during the Administration of James Monroe, 1817–1825, Reynolds (M-439:14, frames 330–333).

To [HENRY CLAY,] Speaker of the House of Representatives

Department of War, 14th January, 1819

Sir, In conformity with the resolutions of the House of Representatives of the 6th and 7th instant, "directing the Secretary of War to report to the House of Representatives, the present strength and distribution of the Army of the United States; and to subjoin to such report, the number and value of the extra day's labour, performed by the several detachments thereof, respectively, in the year, ending on the 30th day of October last, upon roads or other objects of fatigue duty; together with a statement of such objects, if any there are, of a similar nature, to which it is contemplated to direct the labour of the troops in the current year, distinguishing the sums expended on roads: and also to include in the report of the strength of the Army called for by the resolution of the 6th instant, the amount in value, if any, of the extra compensation in subsistence, clothing, or pay allowed the troops for extra labour during the year ending on the 30th of October last, in fatigue duties, distinguishing that which has been bestowed in compensation for labour on roads," I have the honor to state, that the report which I had the honor to lay before the House the 18th November last, in compliance with the resolution of the House of Representatives of the 20th of April, 1818, gives the strength and distribution of the Army of the United States.

The report of the 3d Auditor of the Treasury Department [Peter Hagner], transmitted herewith, furnishes "the number and value of the extra day's labour, performed by the several detachments of the army, in the year ending the 1st day of October, 1818, upon roads and other objects of fatigue duty." In relation to "such objects of a similar nature, to which it is contemplated to direct the labour of the troops in the present year," I have to state, that it is contemplated to employ the soldiers, as far as practicable, upon the road between Plattsburgh and Sackett's harbour, in the State of New York; upon the road from Detroit to Fort Meigs, in the State of Ohio; upon the road from the Muscle Shoal, in Tennessee, to Madisonville &c., and upon fortifications and the repairs of barracks, particularly in constructing the barracks at Baton Rouge. No extra subsistence, except Whiskey, nor extra articles of clothing, are allowed to soldiers while employed on extra labour; when a greater quantity of clothing than what is allowed by fixed regulations is issued, its value is deducted from the pay of the Soldier. I have the honor to be, Your most obed[i-en]t Serv[an]t, J.C. Calhoun.

LS with En in DNA, RG 233 (U.S. House of Representatives), 15th Cong., 2nd Sess., Original Reports, War Department; FC with En in DNA, RG 107 (Secretary of War), Reports to Congress from the Secretary of War, 1803–1870, 2:83–84 (M-220:1); PC with En in *American State Papers: Military Affairs*, 1:822–823; PC in Crallé, ed., *Works*, 5:61–62.

From M[ARTIN] D. HARDIN, [former Senator from Ky.,] "Private"

Frankfort [Ky.], Jan. 24th 1819

D[ea]r Sir, I understand that there is a probability that the Masouri territory will be divided at the ensuing session of Congress, and that some gentlemen from this State will probably be brought before the President [James Monroe] for the government of the [new Ark.] territory. Mr. George Robertson now of the House of Reps. I understand is one. He is a young man of good standing & respectable talents, and I think decidedly ["super"(?) *canceled*] preferable on many accounts to any other from this State that I have heard of.

I learn that Maj[o]r David Trimble also of the H. of Reps. will be willing to accept the office of Secretary. Maj[o]r Trimbles standing is also good & his talents respectable.

I should be gratified if it should meet the views of the President to favour the pretentions of these gentlemen. I have the honour to be very respectfully Your most ob[edien]t, M.D. Hardin.

ALS in DNA, RG 59 (State Department), Letters of Application and Recommendation during the Administration of James Monroe, 1817–1825, Robertson (M-439:14, frames 678–680).

To [MARTIN D. HARDIN?, former Senator from Ky.]

War Dept., 27th Jan[uar]y 1819

Dear Sir, I have received your letters of the 30th December and the 4th of this month [*not found*]; and I can assure you that it afforded me much pleasure to hear from one for whom I have so much respect.

On the same day your letters came to ha[n]d, I received one from our friend [Fidelio C.?] Sharp, in which he expressed a desire to be appointed governor, should a new territory be formed on the Arkansaw [*sic*; River]. I shall give his application my aid with pleasure. I have known him long and intimately. He has few superiors of his age in any part of our country.

With Mr. [George] Robertson [Representative from Ky.] I am not so intimate; but I am very favourably impressed both as to his talents and character.

The proceedings here this winter will, I presume, have considerable bearing on your State politicks. The appearance of combined and systematick attack on the administration is much diminished from your quarter. Col. [Richard M.] Johnson has in particular been open and marked in his support of the measures of the government; and I think it due to candour to say, that I have no doubt of the sincerity of his friendship. I think he cannot be identified with any oposition party which may grow up in your State.

With yourself and many of your political friends in Kentucky I am well acquainted; and nothing can be more unjust and absurd than an attempt to attach the odious name of Federalists to such men.

Accept the assurance of my sincere respect and esteem. J.C. Calhoun.

ALS in MHi, Perry-Clarke Collection, James Freeman Clarke Autograph Collection.

From G[EORGE] ROBERTSON, [Representative from Ky.]

House of Representatives, 24th Feb[ruar]y 1819

Sir, My Friends have brought me before the President [James Monroe], during the present week, for the office of Gov[erno]r of Arkansas [Territory]. The opinions and wishes of many of them have been disclosed to Mr. Monroe, but the Letter [of 1/24/1819 from Martin D. Hardin] which I take the liberty to enclose to *you*, cannot come to his view or knowledge, except through your intermediation. When you are informed that I did not determine to be a Candidate until last Monday, you will readily perceive the reason why this Letter was not sent to you at an earlier period.

It was enclosed to me unsealed—and I am instructed to inform you, that that part of it which speaks of Mr. [David] Trimble is not to be considered. He does not desire the office which it asks for him.

I regret to learn, *much to my surprise,* that I've come into collision with Mr. [Fidelio C.?] Sharp.

I regret it the more, because, my Letters from Kentucky, informed ["me" *interlined*] that he was to be a Candidate, *only* upon the contingency of my declining to ask for the office—in confirmation of which, a Letter recommending *him* was enclosed to me, *to use for him if I should not offer.*

But as Mr. S[harp] is unconditionally before the President, I do not desire, that the communication of *this fact,* should operate ag[ains]t him, or in favor of me. But mentioned it *only* because, I feel bound to give some reason for a competition with Mr. S[harp]. If it should be consistent with your feelings or sense of propriety, to communicate the enclosed Letter to the President, you would by so doing confer a favor on Sir y[ou]r m[os]t ob[edien]t h[umbl]e S[ervan]t, G. Robertson.

ALS with En in DNA, RG 59 (State Department), Letters of Application and Recommendation during the Administration of James Monroe, 1817–1825, Robertson (M-439:14, frames 674–680).

From GEO[RGE] BOWIE

Cahawba [Ala. Territory], March 19th 1819
Dear Sir, I have been here for some weeks making preparations to remove to this Territory but now shall go further. Upon the news of the Cession of the Floridas And[re]w ["&" *interlined*] Joseph Pickens[,] Dr. Casey and myself started for Pensacola from St. Stephens [Ala. Territory]. I returned to attend to the sales here, the others went on with all the funds we could raise. I trust they will be able to make a profitable return. It has long been my wish to settle in Pensacola & I rejoice much that that [*sic*] I will now have it in my power to gratify that wish.

I ought not, in your present situation, to trouble you with my personal interests but as Congress is not now sitting I must for once intrude.

If there is any situation in that Country in which you think I can be servicable I would be glad to accept of it. You know I have never been much of an Office hunter, and you may be assured I shall not be mortified if in this instance I should fail.

Please remember me to Mrs. [Floride Colhoun] Calhoun & believe me yours Sincerely, Geo. Bowie.

P.S. I expect to return to Abbeville in all the month of May.

ALS in DNA, RG 59 (State Department), Letters of Application and Recommendation during the Administration of James Monroe, 1817–1825, Bowie (M-439:2). NOTE: An AEI by Calhoun reads, "I am well acquainted with Mr. Bowie. He is a good lawyer and an excellent man."

To Maj. C[HRISTOPHER] VANDEVENTER, Washington

Savannah, 9th May 1819

Dear Sir, We arrived here last evening and will probably remain three days in this place, and then will proceed to Augusta. The weather has become exceedingly hot, and that by a very sudden transition from a long continuation of cold weather, which renders it proper that we should leave the flat country as soon as possible.

I was very glad to learn by your last letter that you had returned to Washington, and to hear of the improved state of Mrs. [Sally Birckhead] Van De Venter's health. I do since[re]ly hope that a change of air and the return of summer, will restore her to the greatest of all earthly blessings.

Before I received your letter I had directed the advance to be made to Col. [Richard M.] Johnson, which I trust will prevent any interruption in our military movement to the west.

I return the application of Sam[ue]l T. Cooper for a cadets appointment. I had promised an appointment to a lad in Beaufort in So. Carolina, of the name of Rich[ar]d La Boulardrie De Treville and it became necessary to fill up the blank appointment sent on by Mr. [Lewis] Edwards in his name. You will add him to the list of those who have been appointed.

I return also the papers in the case of David Wood. You will as he requests return the papers to him; and inform him his claim cannot be allowed. He cl[e]arly acted as the agent of Mr. [Matthew L.] Davis and to him he must look. Mr. Davis cannot be charged as there was no failure; and if he could he has already been advanced by the Department as far as was thought expedient.

I return you Col. [William] McRee's letter; and I have directed Gen[era]l [Daniel] Parker to inform him of the acceptance of his resignation.

I enclose a statement of Mr. Virgra[?] in relation to his application for a pension; and you will request Mr. [James L.] Edwards to give it an immediate consideration.

You will transmit to Willington a cadet's appointment for my signature for Mr. James Hamilton. You will find the papers in relation to his case among those returned.

I regret very much the delay, which has taken place in the case of young [William] Earnest referred to in the letter of Mr. Coale herewith ["referred to" *canceled and* "returned" *interlined*]; nor can I now decide the case, as I have not the act referred to. You will examine the act, and, if it gives discretionary powers to the Department to expend the pension for his education, you will immediately signify the wish of the Department that he should be sent to the Hartford Asylum for education, and express to ["him" *canceled and* "Mr. Coale" *interlined*] my regret for the delay, which has taken place. I would have decided the case immediately, but was in hopes, I might obtain the act in time. In case he should be sent to the Hartford, you will write to the person ["or persons" *interlined*] at the head of the institution; and state to them the wishes of the Department to have him educated; and that the pension granted by Congress, to the extent which may be necessary, will be applied to that purpose.

Mr. Edwards of the pension office informs me, that Mr. [David] Robinson, the former agent for Vermont, has neglected to pay over the money in his hand to the present agent [Heman A. Allen]. The course proposed by Mr. Edwards appears to be a correct one. The pensioners ought not to suffer by the neglect of the former agent; and, if he has not yet paid over the money, a sufficient sum ["will" *canceled and* "ought to" *interlined*] be transmitted to Mr. Allen, the present agent, to enable him to pay the pensions due; and a suit commenced without delay to recover the money from Mr. Robinson. With esteem Yours &c &c, J.C. Calhoun.

ALS in DNA, RG 107 (Secretary of War), Letters Received (Unregistered Series), 1789–1860, H-1829 (M-222:25, frames 269–273). NOTE: Calhoun addressed this letter to "Maj. C. Van De Venter, Chief Clerk, Washington City," and franked it "War Dept., J.C. Calhoun."

From ELDRED SIMKINS

Edgefield C[ourt] H[ouse, S.C.,] 1 June 1819
Dear Calhoun, I have been requested to write to you in favor of
Angus Patterson Esq[ui]r[e] an excellent lawyer ["and member of
the Legislature" *interlined*] residing at Barnwell in this State, who
wishes an appointment in the civil department of East Florida. He
is so good a lawyer, and so fair a character that I scarcely know any
appointment of judge, solicitor or indeed any other, the duties of
which he would not well fill. I believe he aspires to the office of solicitor or att[orne]y gen[era]l and perhaps if not attainable, would
accept of another. I should like to see him succeed next in order
to Wm. Ellison Esq[ui]r[e] whose high claims I have ventured frequently to interest you in.

Please make the application for Mr. Patterson, not forgetting our
friend Ellison. With great regard, I am dear Sir y[ou]rs truly, Eldred
Simkins.

ALS in DNA, RG 59 (State Department), Letters of Application and Recommendation during the Administration of James Monroe, 1817–1825, Patterson
(M-439:13, frames 237–240).

To Mrs. [LOUISA C.] ADAMS

[War Department,] 28th July 1819
Mr. Calhoun presents his best respects to Mrs. Adams, and assures
her it will afford him much pleasure, to grant the leave of absence
to Mr. [George] Boyd [Indian Agent at Michilimackinac], which she
requests, if in the opinion of Gov[erno]r [Lewis] Cass, the superintendent, it can be done without serious injury to the publick service.
Gov[erno]r Cass will be immediately written to on the subject.

At the request of Mr. [Henry?] Middleton, I send "Waxall's
own Time" to you, with the request that after you have perused the
volumes to return them to me.

ADU in MHi, Adams Papers, Letters Received and Other Loose Papers (published microfilm, roll 447). NOTE: The "volumes" referred to are Sir Nathaniel
Wraxall, *Historical Memoirs of My Own Time* (London: Cadell & Davies, 1815),
2 vols.

From JAMES MONROE

Oak hill, [Loudoun County, Va.] Sep[tembe]r 16th 1819
Dear Sir, I have yours of the 14th. I return the proceedings, in the cases of Lt. [William B.] Davidson & Dr. [Hanson] Catlett, and concur in the view which you have taken of them. Let the sentence in the first be approved, to which I think, that it will be proper to add, a disapprobation of the manner of the defence, it being an abusive attack on the prosecutor, [and] the commander who arrested him, rather than a defence of his own improper conduct. It may also not be improper, to notice ["tht"(?) *canceled*] the irregular manner, in which the order was given to the Lieut[enan]t, it being an order rather to be infered, than distinctly to be understood, especially in the first instance. Orders should be positive & explicit. It is evident however, that it was understood by the Lt., which is sufficient for the confirmation of the sentence. I am aware, that there will be some difficulty, in drawing the order, so as to express this sentiment, without justifying, in a certain degree the conduct of the Lt. If you cannot avoid that consequence, to your satisfaction, omit the idea altogether; and indeed I wish you to do it, if you see the slightest objection to it.

In the case of Dr. Catlett I would also approve the sentence, but restore him, in consequence of the recommendation, & his long service & good conduct. You will judge how far it may be proper to notice his conduct in this whole business; insubordinate conduct while under arrest, breaking his arrest &ca, not to have been expected from an officer so long in the service, & so well acquainted with the necessity of subordination. I think that it will be proper to notice the act of Major [Abram R.] Wool[l]ey, in putting a sentinel over the surgeon it being contrary to law & oppressive. If may be better to take the lead, in expressing that sentiment, than to wait for the occasion being presented, at the instance of another trial. The act will not justify the conduct of the surgeon, great part of his offence, having been committed before it, and the breach of the arrest itself, tho' in a less exceptionable manner, than afterwards.

I cannot be down till the latter end of the approaching week, when, especially if you can make it convenient to stay, till then, I certainly will, of which, inform me by return of the mail. Say nothing of my intention to visit the city, for the reason mentioned in my last. Very sincerely yours, James Monroe.

[P.S.] I send you a communication from Judge [Archibald?]

Stuart of Virg[ini]a respecting some military claims. Examine them & inform me what answer I shall give.

ALS in PHi, Daniel Parker Papers. NOTE: Calhoun's letter of 9/14, mentioned above, is published in *The Papers of John C. Calhoun,* 4:326. An earlier letter from Calhoun, dated 9/8, relating to the courts-martial of Davidson and Catlett is published in *The Papers of John C. Calhoun,* 4:309–310.

From JAMES MONROE

Oak hill, Sep[tembe]r 20th 1819

Dear Sir, By some accident, the proceedings at West point, in the case of the Cadets, were put out of view, untill the receit of your letter [of 9/18] by yesterdays mail. I have examin'd them with attention, and entirely concur with the attorney general, in the opinion, that they are subject to the rules & art[icle]s of war, and approve the course which you propose, for the further prosecution of the business. Let the same court be convened again, & the opinion of the A[ttorney] G[enera]l be read to it, & then, let it decide, for itself, on the point in question. The Professor [Claudius] Crozet, will be tried also by the same court, on charges to be presented by Major [Sylvanus] Thayer, to whom, instructions, to that effect, should be given. I return you all the papers, with a letter, I have just receiv[e]d from Mr. Loring, father of [Nathaniel H. Loring,] one of the young men, who appears to be misinformed, respecting some circumstances attending the trial, particularly the fact, alledged by him, that neither of the accused cadets was permitted to give evidence in the case.

(It is strange that the deposition of Capt[ai]n [Alden] Partridge should have been admitted in evidence, & not less so, ["than" *canceled*] that the Cadets should have interrogated ["him" *interlined*] respecting the veracity of Major Thayer. It is presum[e]d however, that these matters will be duly weighed by the court.)

I suspect that the present temper is to be imputed, to the former proceeding, and originates principally, with the former Superintendant [Partridge], or his friends. Still I think that too much rigor ought not to be exerted with these young men; I mean in the general adm[inistratio]n of the institution. The severity of martial law, can hardly have been intended, to be applied, in all circumstances, to young men at school. Some liberality, & a generous confidence, would succeed better, than severity. This dread of a mutiny, in

355

boys, seems to me to be carried very far. Nothing however can be done, in the present stage, ["best" *canceled and* "but" *interlined*] to proceed in the route tried[?].

If the weather permits I shall be with you to morrow or next day. very sincerely yours, James Monroe.

ALS in ViU, James Monroe Papers (James Monroe Papers in Virginia Repositories, published microfilm, roll 13, frames 153–155); CCEx in PHi, Daniel Parker Papers.

To C[HRISTOPHER] VANDEVENTER, [War Department]

Spartanburgh, So. Caro:, 4th Nov[embe]r 1819
Dear Maj[o]r, I am this far on my way (65 miles) and if the weather should continue good you may expect me about the 19th Inst. I do not wish the estimates [of appropriations requests for 1820] to be made before my return; at least I wish them not to be submitted to the Treasury Department.

I have rec[eive]d your several communications in the due course of the mail and am very glad to learn that nothing has yet occured which renders my presence necessary.

Will you be so good as to inform Mrs. [Elizabeth Pinckney] Lowndes of the time of our expected arrival. Mrs. [Floride Colhoun] Calhoun wrote her from PickensVille, but her letter may miscarry. Yours sincerely, J.C. Calhoun.

ALS in MiU-C, Christopher Vandeventer Papers.

To C[HRISTOPHER] VANDEVENTER

Fredericksburgh [Va.,] 2d Dec[embe]r 1819
Dear Maj[o]r, I arrived here last evening. I am still very weak; but have recovered rapidly. I expect to be in Washington tomorrow evening. I will thank you, to request Mr. [Lewis?] Edwards to have the box of silver, which he deposited in the bank, sent to my house; and to send the enclosed letter immediately to Miss Stillings at Mr. [William] Lownde[s]'s. Yours sincerely, J.C. Calhoun.

ALS in MiU-C, Christopher Vandeventer Papers.

To ——

[1820 or earlier?]
Dear Sir: I do not know Gen[era]l Davies' [*sic*; William R. Davie's] Post Office, but his residence is not far from Cambden [*sic*] So. Carolina. A letter directed to that place with a request to the Post Master to forward it, would I think reach him without much delay. Yours &c, J.C. Calhoun.

ALS in CLU.

To T[HOMAS] WORTHINGTON, [former Senator from Ohio], Chillicothe

Department of War, Washington, 27th Jan[uar]y 1820 Sir, I have received yours of the 27th and 31st December. I regret that I cannot make the additional advance of 20,000$ which you require. In the advertisement of the Commissary General of Subsistence [George Gibson] it was distinctly stated that no more than 1/4 of the amount of a contract would be advanced except on the contracts of St. Louis and Detroit, on the former one half and on the latter one third.

A departure from this rule in any case would subject me to the charge of partiality, and I beg you to believe that could the rule be dispensed with in any case yours would have been the exception; I can assure you however that additional advances will be made immediately subsequent to your deliveries at New Orleans, Natchitoches and Fort Smith, and the amount found due on your Saint Louis contract will be promptly paid. I am Sir respectfully Y[ou]r ob[edient] Ser[van]t, J.C. Calhoun.

LS in OHi, Thomas Worthington Papers (published microfilm, Worthington Papers, roll 12, frames 394–396). NOTE: For Worthington's letters of 12/27 and 12/31, see *The Papers of John C. Calhoun*, 4:509–511 and 534.

To [Nicholas] Van Dyke, [Senator from Del.], 2/16/1820. "Mr. Calhoun requests the favour of Mr. Van Dyke's company at dinner on Tuesday night at 5 OClock. The favour of an answer is requested." (An EU records that Van Dyke had a previous engagement with [Nathan] Sanford, Senator from N.Y.) LU in DeGE, Longwood Manuscripts.

To H[ENRY] CLAY, Speaker of the House of Representatives

Department of War
23rd Feb[rua]ry, 1820

Sir, In compliance with the resolution of the House of Representatives of the 26th of Feb[rua]ry, 1819, "that the Secretary of War be instructed to report to the House, at an early period of the next session of Congress, a copy of such rules and regulations as shall have been adopted for the government of the Military Academy; together with a list of the Cadets which were attached to the Academy, on the 1st of Jan[ua]ry, 1815, and of such as shall have been appointed between the said 1st of Jan[ua]ry and 30th Sep[tembe]r 1819; exhibiting the date of their several appointments, with the States and territories from whence they came; a list of such as shall have resigned or have been dismissed, and at what period; also, a list of such as shall have been commissioned in the Army, with the date of their commissions, and of such as shall have resigned, with the date of their resignations; also, the said Secretary be instructed to report as aforesaid, whether any, and, if any, what legislative provisions are necessary for the more convenient organization and government of the said Academy the better to ensure a strict obedience to all proper orders, and a suitable respect for all rights of those whose duty it may be to yield obedience," I have the honor to transmit a report from the Engineer Department, marked A, which contains the rules and regulations for the government of the Academy, and a list of cadets, as required.

In reply to so much of the resolution as relates to the better organization and government of the Military Academy, I would respectfully submit a copy of a report from the Academick Staff to this Department, marked B, and a copy of a report of the Superintendent of the Military Academy, containing propositions for its' new organization, marked C, with a copy of a report of Gen[era]l [Simon] Bernard & Col[one]l McRee [*sic*; William MacRea], containing remarks on the plan proposed by the Superintendent, marked D. The improvements of which the Military Academy is thought to be susceptible are so fully discussed in these reports, as to render unnecessary many additional observations; and the few, which I propose to make, will be principally confined to the propositions, to separate the Academy from the Corps of Engineers, to increase the number of professors and assistants, and to equalize the compensation of the former.

The Military Academy has acquired a character and importance which seem not to have been contemplated in its' original institution. It originated in the act of the 16th of March, 1802, which created the Corps of Engineers. By that act the President was authorized to establish a corps of Engineers, to consist of one principal Engineer of the rank of Major, with six Assistant Engineers of the rank of Captains and Lieutenants, to which were added ten cadets; and the act directed, that the corps thus organized should be stationed at West Point, and should constitute a Military Academy. The principal Engineer, and, in his absence, the next in rank, was made Superintendent of the Academy, and the Secretary at war was authorized to purchase such books, implements, and apparatus, as should be necessary for the use of the institution. In the next year, by the act of the 3rd Feb[rua]ry, 1803, the President was authorized to attach to the Engineers two teachers, one of the French Language, and the other of drawing. The Institution remained without any change in its character until 1808, when, by the act of the 12th of April of that year, authorizing the raising of an additional military force, two Cadets were attached to each Company of Infantry, riflemen and Artillery, authorized to be raised under it, making in the whole, with the ten cadets originally attached to the Corps of Engineers, one hundred and fifty Cadets. The Institution was farther enlarged, and changed in its' character, by the act of the 29th of April, 1812. Three Professors were then added, one of Natural and Experimental Philosophy, another of Mathematicks, and the other of the Art of Engineering in all of its branches, with an Assistant to each professor; and the Cadets, including those that were authorized to be appointed in 1808, were increased to two hundred and fifty, without being attached to any particular Corps. The act also provides, that the cadets, after passing through the respective classes, should receive regular degrees from the Academick Staff, and should be promoted into any Corps, according to the duties which they may be deemed competent to perform. The Academy was thus increased from ten Cadets to two hundred and fifty; and instead of being constituted wholly of the corps of Engineers, as at its original institution, and being intended to educate officers exclusively for that corps, it now comprehends within its' scheme of education officers of every arm of the Service. Under its' present organization, it is, in fact, as intimately connected with one corps of the Army as another, yet the provisions of the act of the 16th of March, 1802, which places the Superintendence of the Institution under the Charge of the chief of the Corps of Engineers, and, in his absence, the next in command, still continues. It is obvious that the organization would be more simple, and would correspond more perfectly with its' present character, if the Academy were wholly separated from the Engineer Corps, and the President was authorized to select the Superintendant from any Corps of the Army in which the most suitable character might be found. The field of Selection for so important an office, would thus be enlarged, and the Institution be brought more directly under the control of the government. An additional reason will be found for the change proposed in the fact, that the station originally assigned to the Corps of Engineers at West Point, since the enlargement of that corps and the great increase of its duties, is not the most suitable. Experience has proved that, in time of peace, the cheif of the Corps should be stationed at the Seat of government, to superintend, under its immediate controul, the great and important duties assigned to the corps. Most of the officers belonging to it, are, in fact, assigned to important duties at a distance from the Academy. The Original connexion with the Corps, has thus become almost nominal; and the interest of the Institution would, it is beleived, be promoted, as has been stated, by their entire separation.

The number of professors and assistant professors, is believed to be too few for the wants of the Academy; and the two additional professors, one of Chemistry, and the other of ["Astronomy" *canceled and* "Artillery," *interlined*] with the increase of the assistant professors and teachers recommended in the report of Gen[era]l Bernard and Col[one]l McRee, would greatly increase the usefulness and respectability of the Academy. The professor of Chemistry might perform the duties of Post Surgeon, as in our country the medical profession and that of Chemistry are usually united. The number of Assistant Professors is found to be so inadequate, at present, that Cadets are appointed to perform the duties of assistants. The objections against the employment of Cadets for that purpose, contained in the report of the Academick Staff, are deemed satisfactory.

I entirely concur in the opinion of the Superintendent of the Academy, that the pay of the professors ought to be equalized, and that the compensation of the other professors ought to be made equal to that of those of Natural and Experimental philosophy, who receive the pay and emoluments of a Lieutenant Colonel. Neither the difference in the duties of the Professors, nor the difference in the capacity to perform those duties, is so considerable as to justify the present difference in their pay; and less compensation than that proposed, it is beleived, will not always command suitable talents. The compensation proposed in the report of the Superintendent for the teachers and assistant professors, appears to be just and proportionate to that of the professors. The pay of the Superintendent of the Academy depends, at present, on his commission and rank; and as the most suitable officer for the post may hold an inferior rank, and as his duties and expences as Superintendent are the same, let his rank be what it may, it is conceived, that it would be proper to allow the Superintendent the pay and emoluments of a Colonel, provided his rank does not give him a greater compensation. The present Superintendent, who has performed his duties with zeal and ability, receives only the pay and emoluments of a Major of Engineers, and it is known, that his compensation is inadequate to meet the expenses to which he is subjected, as Superintendant, in a place so frequented by Strangers as West Point.

The additional number of Professors and Assistants, and the change in the compensation which has been proposed, will add something to the expenses of the institution, but the great improvement, which it will make, will much more than compensate the publick. The pay of Superintendent and Professors, constitutes but a small portion of the expense of the Academy. The pay and subsistence of the Cadets, the cost of buildings, fuel, stationary, books, &c, constitute the body of the expenses; yet it is manifest, that these, without a suitable number of able and experienced professors, are of little avail. The annual expenses will be but little effected, whether the number and pay of the professors are adequate or inadequate; but the prosperity of the institution must necessarily depend almost wholly on their number and ability. Without a sufficient number of professors, every branch of knowledge necessary to perfect an officer to discharge his duties cannot be taught, and, without a sufficient compensation, adequate talents and experience to teach that well, which may be directed to be taught, cannot be commanded. A just degree of liberality in the compensation of the Superintendent, professors, and teachers, is thus necessarily connected with true economy, by rendering the other, and most heavy expences of the institution in the highest degree effective.

It will not be necessary to appoint an additional Quarter Master, or paymaster, as recommended in the report of the Superintendent, as one of the Assistant Dep[ut]y Quar[te]r Masters has been assigned to West Point; and no great inconvenience is experienced in making payments to the officers and cadets belonging to the institution, under the present law.

The [*"altering" canceled and "change" interlined*] of the age for admission from fourteen to twenty one, the periods now fixed by law, to that proposed in the report of the Superintendent, namely, from sixteen to twenty, would, for the reason assigned, be proper, and the other changes proposed, with the alterations contained in the remarks of Gen[era]l Bernard and Col[one]l McRee, appear judicious; and would, doubtless improve the condition of the Academy. Many of them may, however, be made, perhaps advantageously, the Subject of regulation rather than law.

In addition to the alterations in the organization of the Military Academy proposed in the documents, which accompany this report, I am of opinion, that the rules and articles of war are not suitable to the Institution, and that a system ought to be formed for its' government. Whether the Cadets are, under the existing laws, subject to the rules and articles of war, appears in some degree doubtful. The court-martial in the case of [Thomas] Ragland, [Wilson M.C.] Fairfax, [Charles R.] Holmes, [Charles R.] Vining, & [Nathaniel H.] Loring, determined that they were not, and, although the Attorney General dissented from that opinion, yet the Court, on its' being reassembled to reconsider its' opinion, adhered to its original decision, notwithstanding the opinion of the Attorney General. The interposition of Congress, to settle a point of so much importance, would seem to be necessary. The duties and rights of the Superintendant, professors, and cadets, ought to be rigidly defined, or collisions of the most dangerous character to the Institution, must occur. But should Congress remove the present doubt, by subjecting the professors and cadets expressly to the rules and articles of war, it is beleived, that much uncertainty would still exist as to their respective duties and rights. Many of the provisions contained in the rules and articles of war, appear not to be applicable to the Military Academy; and of those, which of themselves appear to be so, it might be doubtful, under the rigid construction, which an act so highly penal, as that which contains the rules and articles of war, ought to receive, whether, as the professors and cadets are not named in any of the provisions, and as most of them expressly refer to officers or soldiers, they could be so constructed as to comprehend the former. Besides this uncertainty, other objections of a weighty character exist against extending the rules and articles of war to the professors and cadets. Many of the provisions which a system for the government of the Institution ought to contain, are entirely omitted; and the punishments, both as to kind and degree, which are necessary for the government of the Army, are not required for that of the Military Academy. To remove these objections, I would respectfully suggest, that the President be requested to prepare a suitable system for the government of the Military Academy, to be laid before Congress, at their next Session, for their approval.

I cannot refrain from observing, on a subject of so much importance as the education of those who may be charged with the defence of the country, and on whose skill and fidelity our honor and security must so much depend, that, whatever degree of perfection may be given to the Military Academy at West-Point, as an elementary school, yet our military education, in the higher branches of the art of war must remain imperfect, without a school of application and practice. The education at the Military Academy will be full and complete for officers of Infantry, but those who may be promoted into the Artillery and the Corps of Engineers, ought to have the means, in a school of application and practice, to complete their theoretical knowledge in the higher branches of the Science connected with their profession, and to apply the knowledge acquired to practice. It ought never to be forgotten, that the Military Science, in the present condition of the world, cannot be neglected with impunity. It has become so complicated and extensive, as to require for its acquisition extensive means and much time to be exclusively devoted to it. It can only flourish under the patronage of the government, and, without such patronage, it must be almost wholly neglected. A comparatively small sum expended, in time of peace, to foster and extend the knowledge of Military Science, will, in the event of war, be highly beneficial to the country, and may prove the means of its' safety. A school of practice and application, with the exception of the cost of the necessary buildings, would be attended with but a small expense; and, with such an institution, officers would be trained, who would be masters of every branch of knowledge connected with their profession, and who, by their Science, would be, not only highly useful, but an ornament to the country. Without pursuing the subject any farther, I would respectfully refer the House to a report on this interesting subject, made in obedience to its order, on the 15th of January, 1819. I have the honor to be, Your most obed[ien]t Serv[an]t, J.C. Calhoun.

LS with Ens in DNA, RG 233 (U.S. House of Representatives), 16A-F4, Original Reports, War Department; variant FC in DNA, RG 107 (Secretary of War), Reports to Congress from the Secretary of War, 1803–1870, 2:122–126 (M-220:1); CC with Ens in DNA, RG 233, 16C-C3, 211:137–196; PC with Ens in House Document No. 88, 16th Cong., 1st Sess.; PC with Ens in *American State Papers: Military Affairs*, 2:75–98; PC in Crallé, ed., *Works*, 5:72–80. NOTE: An endorsement dated 2/25 reads, "Read, and referred to the Committee on Military Affairs."

From E[THAN] A[LLEN] B[ROWN, Governor of Ohio]

Columbus, Feb[ruar]y 28th 1820
Sir, I take the liberty to send you the inclosed copies of an Act, and of a resolution of the legislature of Ohio, relative to a proposed Canal between Lake Erie and the Ohio River.

As no sacrifice, even temporary, is is [*sic*] asked of the Gen[era]l Govt., I hope, from your liberal and patriotic character, and from the obvious advantage, of such a work, to the War Department, that the application to Congress will meet with your support. I am Sir, very respectfully &c, E.A.B.

FC in OHi, Governors' Letterbook, December 1814–May 1821, p. 254 (published microfilm: William S. Jenkins, ed., Records of the States of the United States, Ohio, reel E.1).

To L[ANGDON] CHEVES, [President, Bank of the United States, Philadelphia]

War Dept., 23d March 1820
D[ea]r Sir, General [Jacob] Brown, for reasons which he will explain to you, is desireous of obtaining of the U. States Bank a loan, on an extended credit, of $10,000, or $15,000 upon an indorsement, which he assures me, will be perfectly satisfactory to the Bank.

I know not whether the interest of the institution, or the rules, which have been adopted for its administration, will permit you to make such loans in *any case*; but if they do I hope and believe, that you will find this one of the cases, in which such accommodation ought to be granted. Independent of the eminent merit and distinguished services of Gen[era]l Brown, you will, I think, perceive in the reason, which he will state to you for the loan, an additional motive to accommodate him, as it goes to show, that the cause why it would now be convenient to him, has arisen from a disposition, which, while it sought reasonable profits from an investment of part of his capital, at the same time was calculated to add to the productive powers of the country. With sincere respect, J.C. Calhoun.

ALS in ScU-SC, John C. Calhoun Papers.

To Mrs. [Louisa C.] Adams

[War Department,] 27th March 1820

Mr. Calhoun's best respects to Mrs. Adams and he is happy to state, that on an examination of the case of Mr. [George] Boyd [Indian Agent at Michilimackinac], he found he could with propriety make the allowance to him, which she desired. The 2d Auditor [William Lee] has been directed to allow his Salary from the 1st Dec[embe]r 1819. Mr. Boyd's letter is herewith returned.

ADU in MHi, Adams Papers, Letters Received and Other Loose Papers (published microfilm, roll 449).

To L[angdon] Cheves, "Confidential"

War Dept., 11th April 1820

Dear Sir, Col. [Richard M.] Johnson informs me, that some difficulty has occured in carr[y]ing into effect the arrangement, which had been made to take up his debt and that of his brothers to the United States bank. I am not informed of the nature of the arrangement, or the difficulty to which [he] refers; but he assures me, that if the former [arrangement] could be fai[r]ly carried into effect, as intended by the Board of the mother bank, it would enable him and his brothers to get through their monied difficulties; but if that cannot be done, and the present difficulty in effecting the arrangement should continue, there [sic] situation is very critical.

It has become my duty to look into the monied concerns of Col. Johnson and his brothers, as his elder brother James Johnson is a contractor to a very considerable ["extent" *interlined*] with the government and the others are his security. There [sic] property is very considerable, but there embarrassment is not less considerable, and will require in my opinion all of *their* energy with indulgence to get through. It may be material to observe, that their means to meet their engagements this year will be much inferior to the last, as the advances of the government on the existing contracts with James Johnson will be comparitively small. I make this communication with the assent of Col. Johnson, in the hopes, that it may prove beneficial to him and not injurious to the bank; and I am sure that whatever assistance you can afford, one of his real worth, labouring under great difficulties, not rising out of speculation, but voluntarily assumed on

365

account of his brothers, you will with pleasure extend to him. With great respect & esteem I am &cc, J.C. Calhoun.

ALS in ScHi, Langdon Cheves I Papers.

To L[ANGDON] CHEVES, [Philadelphia]

War Dept., 18th April 1820

Dear Sir, Permit me to introduce to your acquaintance Mr. [John T.] Mason, the [U.S.] Marshal for Kentucky. Mr. Mason's standing and connections are of the first respectability; and your attention to him will confer a personal obligation on me. With sincere respect & esteem I am &c, J.C. Calhoun.

ALS in ScHi, Langdon Cheves I Papers.

To H[ENR]Y W. DeSAUSSURE, Columbia, S.C.

War Dept., 28th April 1820

Dear Sir, I have received your favour of the 18th Inst. [*not found*]; and if you would permit me to advise you for your son [Louis M. DeSaussure], I would recommend him to return his letter of appointment, and to obtain another for June 1821. Were he to rec[ei]ve an order for admission in Jan[uar]y, as you suggest, he would labour under many disadvantages, from not having ["an" *canceled*] the same advantages as the rest of his classmates, who will commence their course in June next. If, however, you should prefer his admission in Jan[uar]y or Sep[tembe]r an order will be given to that effect.

I have read with surprise and deep mortification, that part of your letter, in which you state the effects, which the discussion of the Missouri question has had on some of our most intelligent and patriotick citizens. That an attempt to emancipate our slaves by our northern brethren should rouse the deepest indignation in the slave holding States, and that we should prefer disunion rather than submit to the consequences of emancipation is natural, and, for the reasons to which you refer, just to ourselves; but that any thing has yet occured, which ought to induce any reasonable and virtuous mind to beleive that "there is no more safety to the Southern States in the Union" is what I cannot in the sleightest degreee assent to. Mr. [N.Y. Senator Rufus] King's speech [of 2/11], which gave the greatest offence, was very exceptionable, but it would be giving a very dangrous importance to it, or that of any other member, if we were to permit ["to" *and an unintelligible word canceled and* "it to" *interlined*] destroy our attachment to the Union. Had he and those with whom he acted avowed their object to be emancipation, still I would suppose the natural effect ["would be" *interlined*] to excite our indignation against the individuals, but not to excite a jealousy, or distrust of the Union. Such, however, I do not beleive to be his object, or that of any respectable politician in the non slave holding States. The fact is, that the Missouri question had no connection with emancipation. Its object was political power and preemmince. That the struggle was so conducted as to excite dangerous feelings on both sides is certain, but the topicks which were resorted to were intended for victory on the point of the contest; and not to endanger our property in our slaves. With this view of the subject, I cannot but think it very dangerous to permit an opinion to be formed which can only be justified when it becomes necessary to resist an actual attempt at emancipating some slave holding States. It is at least not necessary to propagate such an opinion now; for when it becomes necessary, it will exist in suffic[ie]nt force. Against such an attempt the South would be as one man. But to entertain the opinion *now* that there is no safety in the Union for the South, would be to permit ourselves to be governed by an unfounded suspicion as to the object of a great majority of the non slave holding States; and to act on it, could not fail finally to disgrace us, and most justly. With wisdom and moderation the slave holding States will ever have influence not only suffic[ie]nt for their protection, but to secure their just weight in the Union. They have always had it; and they, in my opinion, possess great and permane[n]t political advantages, to maintain their respectability and just influence. But should our fidelity to the union be once fairly called in question, then our weight will and ought to be lost.

In the very free observations which I have made, I can of course have no personal referrance, as I am unacquainted with the sentim[ents] of our distinguished citizens with one or two exceptions, in relation to the point to which I have refered. I am simply actuated by a strong desire, that what I deem a dangrous mode of think[in]g should not take root; and I am satisfied that the respectable individuals to whom you refer, will when they reflect more cooly agree with me in opinion. Very respectfully & since[re]ly, J.C. Calhoun.

ALS in ScHi, DeSaussure Family Papers.

To [JAMES MONROE, "Oak Hill," Loudoun County, Va.]

War Dept., 30th May 1820

Dear Sir, I enclose the proceedings of the court martial at Troy [N.Y.] in the cases of [former] Capt. [and Military Storekeeper Peter] Faulkner and Artificer Whitman. In the former case, the court sentenced the accused to be dismissed the service ["the service" *canceled*] of the U. States; and in the latter to be confined with the ball & chain for six months. I have examined the proceedings with care. The charges against Capt. Faulkner are well sustained and are of such a nature as to merit the sentence of the court. In that of Whitman, under all of the circumstances of the case, the punishment appears severe. In fact, I doubt the propriety of such punishment in the case of a mere artificer. That of dismissing him from the service would be more appropriate, as the pay of the artificer ($16 per month) is such as to enable the government to obtain persons of that discription with ease. I think it would be well to order his punishment to be remitted, and that he be dismissed from service.

I send also some vouchers, which, in the settlement of the account of the late Gen[era]l [Zebulon M.] Pike, require your sanction. They are for secret service, and appear to be such as are proper to be allowed.

I will thank you to return the papers after you have acted on them. The trial of Capt. Faulkner you will find in the first part of the record and Whitman in the latter.

I hope you had a pleasant journey to Loudo[u]n [County] and that the ladies were not fatigued with the ride. Yours sincerely, J.C. Calhoun.

ALS in NjMoN, Lloyd W. Smith Collection (Morristown National Historical Park published microfilm, reel 8).

To L[ANGDON] CHEVES, [Philadelphia]

War Dept., 10th June 1820

Dear Sir, I write to you at the request of Mr. [Stephen C.] Carpenter, whom you formerly knew in Charleston, and who informs me, that he is about to proceed to Philadelphia in order to seek employment; and that he hopes, that it may be in your power to render him some assistance. Mr. Carpenter was employed for some months in the Pension office, but as his qualifications were found not to be such, as the duties assigned to him, which were almost wholly mechanical, required, I was under the necessity of saying to him, that he could not be continued, and that he must look out for some other employment.

He fears that this occurrence may have reached you, and caused unfavourable impressions on your mind against him. Tho' I presume such is not the fact, yet as he desires it, I have been induced to write to you in relation to it. There was no other reason for removing Mr. Carpenter, but his unsuitableness to the duties which were assigned him. As a transcribing clerk, he was reported to me by Mr. [James L.] Edwards, who has charge of the details of the pension office, to be slow, not very accurate, and not sufficiently punctual to office hours. In a situation, which would require some exercise of the mind, and which would not require a fixed routine of duties to be performed at certain hours, I am of opinion he would be very capable and useful. With great respect & esteem I am your ob[edient] Ser-[van]t, J.C. Calhoun.

ALS in ScHi, Langdon Cheves I Papers.

To L[ANGDON] CHEVES, Philadelphia

War Dept. 10th Aug. 1820

My dear Sir, When you were last in Washington, I mentioned to you, that I intended to take an excursion to the north this summer. My publick duties have prevented me from carr[y]ing into effect my intention, as early as I then expected; but I have, at last, determined to set out on tuesday next. As the season is late, I will proceed direct to Niagara, without stopping on this side of Albany. On my return I will move less rapidly, and ["then" *interlined*] propose to spend a few days in Philadelphia where I hope to have the pleasure of seeing you.

Mrs. Calhoun has ["been" *interlined*] deterred from accompanying me from the lateness of the season. She joins her respects to yourself & Mrs. [Mary Dulles] Cheves. With sincere friendship, J.C. Calhoun.

ALS in ScHi, Langdon Cheves I Papers.

Subscription list for building a Unitarian Church in Washington, 9/1820. Calhoun subscribed fifty dollars to the construction of the First Unitarian Church. Other subscribers were John Quincy Adams, William W. Seaton, and William Elliott, Representative from S.C. The organization of the Unitarian Society was to be "strictly *Congregational*, the Pastor & officers chosen by the People, and all Committees of management elected only for limited periods & specific purposes." DS (copy) in All Souls Unitarian Church, Washington, D.C.

To L[ANGDON] CHEVES

War Dept., 23d Oct[obe]r 1820

My dear Sir, I take the liberty of introducing to your acquaintance Mr. Samuel Calhoun a young friend and relative of mine, who goes to Philadelphia with the intention to take a course of Medical lectures.

As he is wholly unacquainted in Philadelphia, and as I have not the pleasure of a personal acquaintance with any of the Lecturers in the Medical school, I must beg the favour of you to give my young friend the necessary introduction. Dr. Casey with whom he has been stud[y]ing medicine speaks in the most favourable terms of his talents and habits. With the most sincere regard, J.C. Calhoun.

ALS in ScHi, Langdon Cheves I Papers. NOTE: Samuel Calhoun was a grandson of Calhoun's uncle William Calhoun.

Proposed Plan for the Reorganization of the Army

[Washington, December 12, 1820]

A. Organization of the Army as proposed under the Resolution of the House of Representatives of 11th May 1820.

General Staff

  2 Major generals
  4 Aids-de-camp
  4 Brigadier generals
  4 Aids-de-camp
  1 Judge advocate
  5 Topographical engineers
  4 Assistant Topographical Ditto
  1 Adjutant and Inspector general
  2 Adjutant generals
  4 Assistant adjutant generals
  2 Inspectors general
  4 Assistant inspector general
 10 Battalion adjutants
  8 Battalion adjutant

Quarter master's Department

  1 Quarter master general
  2 Deputy quarter master generals
 16 Assistant deputy quarter master generals
 10 Regimental quarter masters
  8 Battalion quarter masters

Paymaster Department

  1 Paymaster general
 19 Paymasters

Purchasing Department

  1 Commissary general
  1 Assistant commissary general
  2 Store keepers

Subsistence Department

  1 Commissary general, with as many assistant commissaries as the service may require.

Medical Department

  1 Surgeon general

371

   2 Assistant surgeons general
   1 Apothecary general
   2 Assistant Apothecaries general
 25 Surgeons
 44 Assistant Surgeons

Engineer Corps
   1 Colonel
   1 Assistant Engineer
   1 Lieutenant Colonel
   2 Majors
   6 Captains
   6 Lieutenants
   6 Second Lieutnants

Military Academy
 12 Professors and masters
250 Cadets

Artillery
   1 Colonel commandant
   1 Colonel of ordnance
   1 Lieutenant Colonel of Ordnance
   2 Majors of Ordnance
   5 Lieutenant Colonels of Regiments
   5 Major   ditto
   7 Captains of Ordnance
   5 Do   of light Artillery
 40 Do   of Artillery
 10 Lieutenants of light Artillery
 80 Do   of Artillery
 10 Second lieutenants of light Artillery
 80 Second   do   of Artillery
247 Officers
 15 Sergeants of Light Artillery
120 Do   Artillery
 30 Corporals   Light Artillery
240 Do   Artillery
   5 Do   of the Train
   5 Armorers
   5 Smiths (light Artillery)
   5 Trumpeters (light Artillery)
 40 Drummers

```
   90  Gunners (light Artillery)
  720  Do        Artillery
  180  Matross, light Artillery
1,440  Do        Artillery
   10  Workmen,
   45  Soldiers of the train, light Artillery
2,950  Privates
```

Infantry
```
    9  Colonels
    9  Lieutenant Colonels
    9  Majors
   90  Captains
   90  Lieutenants
   90  First Lieutenants
   90  Second Lieutenants
  297  Officers
  360  Sergeants
  360  Corporals
    9  Armorers
    9  Drum Majors
   90  Drummers
2,520  Privates
   18  Workmen
3,336  Privates
   75  Artificers, workmen of ordnance
6,391  Men, rank and file
```

Staff

The chief reduction which is practicable in the staff, is that of the purchasing department. It is reduced to one commissary general, stationed at Washington; one assistant and two storekeepers, at New York and Philadelphia, where all stores purchased for the army will be concentrated, and from whence they will be distributed to the quarter-masters of every corps. By abolishing the distinction between the battalion and regimental paymasters, several corps may occasionally, when assembled on one point, be paid by the same officers. The difficulty of finding suitable persons willing to accept of the appointment of surgeons mates has likewise been the reason for suppressing that rank, and allowing in their steads a certain number of of [sic] assistant surgeons with the rank and appointment of post surgeons, and abolishing all distinctions of rank and pay between surgeons employed in a post, battalion, or regiment. In small posts the assistant commissaries of subsistence may be charged with the functions of quartermasters.

Artillery

By uniting the three corps of the Ordnance, light artillery, and artillery, in one, appointing one general staff at the head of it, & making its officers pass in relation, through the three services, the organization of the army will be rendered more simple and the instruction of the officers much more complete. The present regiment of light artillery being organized to manoeuver sixty guns, is stronger than our occasions require; being on foot, and performing garrison duty, it cannot practise its peculiar manoeuvres, nor qualify itself for the service which it will be called upon to perform in the field. It is therefore proposed to convert it into an additional regiment of foot artillery, which will only be changing its denomination, and to add a company of light artillery to each of the five regiments of artillery. This arm will thus be distributed on the frontier, and by allowing twenty eight saddle and thirty two train horses to each company, with ten soldiers of the train, to serve them, it will be enabled to manoeuver two pieces, at a time, with their caissons.

Two lieutenants and two second lieutenants in each company are more than the service indispensably requires. A certain number of officers of this rank can, therefore, always be spared from regimental service, and appointed as assistants in the ordnance department. But it is necessary to maintain some supernumerary captains for this purpose, for, if their number did not pass that of the companies of artillery, it would be impossible to spare a captain of artillery from his company. Lest misapprehensions should arise on this subject, it is proper to state, that officers of artillery detailed on the ordnance service, are exclusively under the controul of the ordnance department. The service of the arsenals is to be provided for out of the artillery; and the cannoneers will thus perfect themselves in the composition of fire works. A single company of ordnance artificers will be retained in peace.

As three or four experienced pointers are sufficient for each piece, it is proposed to form them into a peculiar class, as in Europe. All augmentations or reductions of the artillery will then fall on the matrosses, who can be trained in a few weeks. The proposed organization allows three sergeants, commanding two guns, to each company, (of whom the senior may perform the duties of orderly and quarter master Sergeant), six corporals, commanding each one gun, three gunners, and six matrosses (the least number that can manoeuvre it) to each gun. By raising the force of each company to 100 men, in time of war, the whole corps will be able to manoeuvre 90 guns in the field—viz. 30 by the light artillery, and 60 by ten companies of foot, and 900 or even 1800 guns in forts and batteries by allowing six cannoneers, or even three, with the aid of the militia, to serve alternately two guns.

Infantry

The proposed organization in the reduction of each regiment to the minimum force, will leave it adapted to the purposes of military service and instruction, by preserving in each corps all its necessary component parts. To execute the modern manoeuvres of the field, each battalion must divide itself in two half battalions, four divisions, eight platoons, and sixteen sections, and thirty two squads, exclusive of its flank companies. Experience has pointed out that in time of war its front should not pass 200 files, exclusive of flank companies, lest it become weak and wavering. But it cannot in peace be reduced below 128 files, or 64 to a half battalion, 32 to a division, 16 to a platoon, 8 to a section, 4 to a squad, as the various fractions would become too diminutive for any service, if reduced below that number.

The propriety of reducing each regiment to its minimum force, rather than reducing the number of regiments, and making them somewhat stronger, has been chiefly deduced from the following principle: the desire of avoiding to create new regiments, with raw inexperienced officers at their head, in the time of war. Each regiment of the army can be formed into two battalions, equally intermixed with old soldiers at the approach of war, and that by a very simple operation, provided that, some time previously, care may have been taken to augment the number of their officers, and fill up their ranks to a higher complement. Nine regiments which, on the proposed organization, form only 3,663 men in time of peace, may then be raised to near 16,000 in time of war, without creating new corps—by doubling the number of battalions, and raising their front to 250 files, including the flank companies, and forming them in 3 ranks. It is, therefore, evident, that the reduction of each regiment of infantry, when formed on this small scale, whilst it makes a very trifling economy, for the present, deprives us of the power of forming a large and effective force in time of war.

The mode of doubling the battalion is simply to form a battalion of each half battalion, a division of each platoon, a platoon of each section, [*partial word canceled*] and fill up their ranks to the proper number, with a care to place the recruits in the second ranks.

Note. As this estimate is predicated on the smallest numbers that can perform the requisite manoeuvres in the school of company and battalion, and, as experience proves that no organization can be kept full, an increase of one sixth to the rank and file, would render the corps at all times efficient and perfect, and would greatly improve the proposed organization.

FC in DNA, RG 107 (Secretary of War), Reports to Congress from the Secretary of War, 1803–1870, 2:160–164 (M-220:1); variant PC in *American State Papers: Military Affairs*, 2:191–193. NOTE: A copy of Calhoun's proposed reduction and reorganization of the Army was enclosed with his report of 12/12/-1820 to John W. Taylor, Speaker of the House of Representatives (see *The Papers of John C. Calhoun*, 5:480–491).

From T[IMOTHY] PICKERING, [former Representative from Mass.]

Salem [Mass.], Dec[embe]r 26, 1820

Dear Sir, I have just been reading your report of the 12th instant, on the military peace establishment for the United States. You will doubtless recollect, that my opinion has been at all times in favour of its reduction to five, or, at the highest number, to six thousand men. At the close of the late war [of 1812], when the question came before the House of Representatives, Gen[era]l [Joseph] Desha [Representative from Ky.] offered a resolution to reduce it to 6000. With this I readily concurred, as more likely to obtain (from the quarter whence it came) than the number of 5000, which [*several words canceled and* "I intended to propose" *interlined*]. The subject ["(of reduction)" *interlined*] rested until near the close of the last session of the Congress in which I was a member—February 1817. I remember I then in a few words ["gave" *canceled and* "offered you" *interlined*] my ["principal" *interlined*] reason for its reduction—That we did not need a single soldier, on the whole Northern Frontier, eastward of Detroit. ["You then(?)" *canceled.*] You assented to the correctness of my view of the subject, but remarked that it was then too late to ["bring"(?) *interlined and then canceled and* "introduce" *interlined*] the measure ["forward"(?) *canceled*], as there would be little hope ["of accomplishing" *canceled*] of bringing it to a satisfactory conclusion before the termination of the session: and so indeed it was. In the following summer, Mr. [James] Monroe made his Eastern tour. He was accompanied by that intelligent officer, General [Joseph G.] Swift, chief of the corps of Engineers. ["I sought an opportunity to converse with" *canceled and* "To" *interlined*] him ["on" *canceled and* "I mentioned" *interlined*] the subject. He anticipated ["my re(?)" *canceled*] my remarks, by saying promptly—"We do not need a man on our Northern Frontier, eastward of Detroit—except at one point, to facilitate our entrance into Canada, in case of a future war with G. Britain." This point was on or near the northern part of Lake Champlain—I suppose Chazy—where a fortress ["was begun by(?)" *canceled*] has since been partly constructed, but which now, it seems, falls within the British line of Canada. If it does, I frankly avow to you that I consider it fortunate for the United States—as it will save us from a large [*one interlined word canceled*] and useless expenditure of money—not merely in ["completing" *interlined*] its ["own"(?) *canceled*] erection—but in ["maintaining" *canceled and* "supporting" *interlined*] there a perpetual garrison. For what have we to apprehend on the side of Canada? The British will never ["from thence" *interlined*] invade the U. States, because they know a conquest of ["the" *canceled*] territory in that quarter cannot be maintained. And they will never cross the line for the purpose of devastation, ["because(?) they" *canceled and* "know" *changed to* "knowing"] we can amply retaliate. Let the British erect as many forts as they please: it may [*one interlined word canceled*] be expedient for their security against a sudden attack ["& conquest" *interlined*]—as their efficient protectors are on the other side of the Atlantic. But however many points it will be practicable for them to fortify, they cannot ["possibly" *canceled*] close every passage into Canada. Before another war, ["if a war must occur," *interlined*] the country will ["be" *interlined*] opened, ["and" *canceled*] & roads formed, leading to every part of the Canada border; and an army moving with a competent ["number" *interlined*] of batteaux would cross the St. Lawrence ["& other waters" *interlined*] at many places, with little opposition, and particularly without ["first"(?) *interlined*] encountering their fortifications.

Under this view of the subject, I ask, of what use was the Northern army—the increasing or strengthening of the military posts—and the naval establishment preserved on the lakes, eastward of Detroit? I consider the expenditures on these objects a public waste—beneficial only to the inhabitants of New York, for whose ["products" *interlined*] markets were thus provided, & roads constructed, at the "Expense" *and an illegible word canceled and* "expense" *interlined*] of the United States. I am therefore well pleased that the army is likely to be reduced—I hope to the number (6316 ["noncommissioned officers, musicians & privates" *interlined*]) on which your estimates [*one or two interlined words canceled*; "is" *canceled and* "are" *interlined*] formed. The organization you recommend I think perfectly correct; and its principles ["to be" *canceled*] incontrovertible. [*Several words canceled.*] Such a body of commissioned & noncommissioned officers, would, ["as you remark(?)," *interlined*] very soon bring to a good state of discipline all the additional troops required to form an army of twenty thousand men. They could do more— for if a formidable invasion were justly to be apprehended, ["a portion" *canceled*] and it were deemed necessary to embody a portion of the militia, a part of the officers & noncommissioned officers, ["and" *canceled and* "with" *interlined*] a selection of the best & most intelligent privates, might be employed to instruct ["such embodied militia" *canceled and* "them" *interlined*]. And with such instructors, ["the" *canceled*] militia-men would acquire more knowledge in ten days, than ["they" *canceled*] in training, even according to the practice in ["New England" *canceled*] Massachusetts ["(where they regularly turn out four days in a year)" *interlined*] from the age of eighteen to forty five. I pronounce this opinion with confidence, from my experience in the militia, when a young man, and ["from" *interlined*] what I have since observed. In other States, at least those south of New England ["& New York" *interlined*], militia ["exercises" *canceled and* "training" *interlined*] are [*sic*] still more insignificant. I except from this description the select corps & companies in cities & large towns. Such select militia I would have maintained, and sufficiently encouraged to persevere, altho' all the rest of the militia should be ["excused"(?) *canceled and* "wholly exempt" *interlined*] from military musters, ["excepting one"(?) *canceled*] unless it should be deemed advisable to assemble them in companies, or, if in scattered settlements, by sections of companies, for the inspection of their arms. Such a system for the militia I have ["for" *canceled*] long thought to be desirable, & wished to see authorized by Congress. The select corps & companies of militia above mentioned might be required to be formed in the several States, according to their population: ["and" *canceled*] the whole number to be ["at least" *canceled and then interlined*] double ["to" *interlined*] that of the standing army on the peace establishment. This exemption of the great mass of militia from ["mili" *canceled*] mustering four days in every year, ["would produce" *canceled*] (and when they assemble in brigades and divisions, once a year, their whole loss of time would equal five or six days) ["whi"(?) *canceled*] would effect ["so vast" *interlined*] a saving ["from which" *canceled*] as to enable each State to give a ["handsome" *canceled and* "reasonable" *interlined*] indemnity to its quota of select militia for the greater expense of ["time(?) and" *canceled*] money and time in equipping themselves, and performing the requisite exercises. Every *patriot-talking* citizen sounds & sounds the phrase "a well disciplined militia"; as if it existed in the United States, and was ["a" *canceled and* "our" *interlined*] sure defence ["when our whole" *canceled*]. The truth is, a well disciplined militia has been unknown since the early days of the Roman commonwealth—except in *Switzerland,* a country bordering on powerful nations, against whose enterprises it was necessary to be constantly armed & prepared for defence. The whole mass of able bodied men were [*sic*] trained to ["arms;" *interlined*] military exercises ["being performed" *interlined*] every Sunday after public worship, under ["those"(?) *canceled and* "the direction of" *interlined*]; "those experienced fellow citizens" *canceled and* "officers" *interlined*] who had ["served in the Swiss regiments" *canceled*] acquired knowledge and experience in the Swiss regiments engaged in foreign service, & who at certain periods returned home. But for more than a century the Swiss militia system has been [under]going decay, & is now, probably, ["totally" *canceled and* "quite" *interlined*] inefficient. What I have suggested concerning it is derived from Stanyan's Account of Switzerland, written, ["I believe, a" *canceled and* "early in the last" *interlined*] century, ["ago, &" *canceled*] & which I read 40 or 50 years ago. I recollect seeing ["it also" *interlined*] among the books which Mr. [Thomas] Jefferson sold to Congress—a small duodecimo volume. *Constantly Impending danger from superior neighbouring Powers, can alone induce any government to impose, & reconcile the* ["subjects" *canceled and* "body of the people as a militia" *interlined*] *to submit to, the* [*about two words canceled*] *heavy expense of time, & the toil* [*about two words canceled*] *necessary to obtain* ["any" *canceled*] *material knowledge of the military art.* And as the people of the United States are not in this situation, all attempts to *discipline* the ["whole body of" *canceled*] the [*sic*] militia ["at large" *interlined*] must be fruitless: the time and money devoted to it are thrown away. I wish therefore to see the project abandoned. The citizens from 21 to 40 might be ["regimented(?), and the regiments which should compose brigades, & the latter(?) to compose divisions, might be (*about two lines illegible*) formed into" *canceled*] organized ["bodies" *canceled*], as for actual service, but exempted from all military ["duty, except, as before (*about two lines illegible*) and even that may be dispensed with, if every State should become provided (as in a series[?] of years they will be) with adequate magazines of arms & equipments for its militia" *canceled and* "exercises" *interlined*].

I have taken the liberty to make these observations to you, ["as" *canceled*] the ["Directing" *interlined*] Head of the War Department, [*one word canceled*] knowing [*several words canceled*] the readiness with which you can justly estimate, and fully persuaded of your disposition to promote every measure calculated to advance the public welfare. With a friendly & respectful remembrance I am, dear Sir, ["with sincere respect" *canceled*] your obed[ien]t serv[an]t, T. Pickering.

Draft in MHi, Timothy Pickering Papers, 15:237–239A (published microfilm, reel 15).

To C[HRISTOPHER] RANKIN, [Representative from Miss.]

Department of War, December 29th 1820

The Secretary of War's compliments to the Hon[ora]ble C. Rankin, and informs him in reply to his note of this date, that altho he has no doubt upon the subject, yet he feels a delicacy in expressing an opinion to the Committee of ways & means, without a formal call upon him. He would respectfully suggest that Mr. Rankin would effect his object by a motion directing that Committee to enquire into the expediency of changing the appropriation as he proposes. I have &c, J.C.C.

FC in DNA, RG 107 (Secretary of War), Letters Sent Relating to Military Affairs, 1800–1889, 11:134 (M-6:11).

From [JOHN B. C. LUCAS]

[St. Louis, *ca.* 1821]

Sir: Having lately received information that it has been circulated during the last session of Congress that I had written to divers members of Congress from the non slave holding States and informed them that the persons opposed to slavery wer[e] getting in power in Missouri, in order to induce them to hold out against the admission of this State into the union; that in consequence of this Missouri is largely indebted to me for the humiliation to which she has been subjected last winter.

I also understand that such a report has been credited by some members from the slave holding States and other gentlemen. Permit me therefore to assure you that these reports are utterly unfounded; that I never have written anything at Washington or elsewhere to any person directly or indirectly for or against the questions for authorizing the territory of Missouri to become a State or for admitting Missouri into the union. That I believe such report has originated with agents and partners of the Spanish land claimants at Washington whose object is to interrupt the good understanding that may exist between me and numbers of gentlemen from the south as they suspect that I correspond with them on subject of land claims and may again alarm them. Yours respectfully, [John B.C. Lucas].

PC in John B.C. Lucas, ed., *Letters of the Hon. J.B.C. Lucas from 1815 to 1836,* pp. 98–99.

From Tho[ma]s Aspinwall

Consulate of the United States
London, 5 January 1821

Sir, Having met with the enclosed statement of the present distribution of the British Military Forces, I have ventured to transmit it to you, presuming that it might be acceptable, and have the Honor to remain, With great respect, Your Obedient Servant, Thos. Aspinwall.

LS with En in DNA, RG 107 (Secretary of War), Letters Received (Registered Series), 1801–1860, A-59 (M-221:88). NOTE: The En covers the British Isles (including Ireland), the East and West Indies, British America, Gibraltar, and the Mediterranean.

To [Samuel L.] Southard, [Secretary of the Navy]

Friday [February 9, 1821?]

D[ea]r Sir, I did not discover that the enclosed note, by some accident was omitted to be taken by my boy till it was too late last night. With sincerity, J.C.C.

ALI in NjP, Samuel L. Southard Papers.

To OLD BIG BEAR in N.C.

Department of War, February 12th 1821

Sir, I have received your letter of Nov[embe]r last in which you express a fear that you will be turned off your lands reserved to you by treaty. I am exceedingly sorry to hear it & hope it will not be the case as I have no doubt your rights under the treaty will be properly protected in the courts of North Carolina. As you appear ignorant of your rights & the laws which protect them, I advise you to select some one of your neighbors who is prudent & can be wholly confided in by you to be your agent to manage your affairs.

The general government cannot interfere in the question between you & the State further than to recommend your claims to the protection of the governor [Jesse Franklin] to whom I have written on the subject. I have, &c, J.C.C.

FC in DNA, RG 75 (Bureau of Indian Affairs), Letters Sent by the Secretary of War, 1800–1824, E:51 (M-15:5); CC in Nc-Ar, Governors' Letterbooks, vol. 24, p. 27 (misdated 2/13).

ACT TO REDUCE AND FIX THE MILITARY PEACE ESTABLISHMENT OF THE UNITED STATES

[Washington, March 2, 1821]

Be it enacted by the Senate and House of Representatives of the United States of America, in Congress assembled, That, from and after the first day of June next, the military peace establishment of the United States shall be composed of four regiments of artillery, and seven regiments of infantry, with such officers of engineers, of ordnance, and of the staff, as are hereinafter provided for.

SEC. 2. *And be it further enacted,* That each regiment of artillery shall consist of one colonel, one lieutenant colonel, one major, one sergeant major, one quartermaster sergeant, and nine companies, one of which shall be designated and equipped as light artillery; and that there shall be attached to each regiment of artillery one supernumerary captain to perform ordnance duty; and that each company shall consist of one captain, two first lieutenants, two second lieutenants, four sergeants, four corporals, three artificers, two musicians, and forty-two privates, That each regiment of infantry shall consist of one colonel, one lieutenant colonel, one major, one sergeant major, one quartermaster sergeant, two principal musicians, and ten companies; each of which shall consist of one captain, one first lieutenant, one second lieutenant, three sergeants, four corporals, two musicians, and forty-two privates; and that to each regiment of artillery and infantry there shall be one adjutant, who shall be taken from the subalterns of the line.

SEC. 3. *And be it further enacted,* That the corps of engineers, (bombardiers excepted,) and the topographical engineers, and their assistants, shall be retained in service as at present organized.

SEC. 4. *And be it further enacted,* That the ordnance department shall be merged in the artillery; and that the President of the United States be, and he is hereby, authorized to select, from the regiments of artillery, such officers as may be necessary to perform ordnance duties, who, while so detached, shall receive the pay and emoluments now received by ordnance officers, and shall be subject only to the orders of the War Department; and that the number of enlisted men in the ordnance department be reduced to fifty-six.

SEC. 5. *And be it further enacted,* That there shall be one major general, with two aids-de-camp, two brigadier generals, each with one aid-de-camp; and that the aids-de-camp be taken from the subalterns of the line, and, in addition to their other duties, shall perform the duties of assistant adjutant general.

SEC. 6. *And be it further enacted,* That there shall be one adjutant general, and two inspectors general, with the rank, pay, and emoluments, of colonels of cavalry.

SEC. 7. *And be it further enacted,* That there shall be one quartermaster general; that there shall be two quartermasters, with the rank, pay, and emoluments, of majors of cavalry; and ten assistant quartermasters, who shall, in addition to their pay in the line, receive a sum not less than ten dollars, nor more than twenty dollars, per month, to be regulated by the Secretary of War.

SEC. 8. *And be it further enacted,* That there shall be one commissary general of subsistence; and that there shall be as many assistant commissaries as the service may require, not exceeding fifty, who shall be taken from the subalterns of the line, and shall, in addition to their pay in the line, receive a sum not less than ten, nor more than twenty, dollars per month; and that the assistant quartermasters, and assistant commissaries of subsistence, shall be subject to duties in both departments under the orders of the Secretary of War.

SEC. 9. *And be it further enacted,* That there shall be one paymaster general, with the present compensation, and fourteen paymasters, with the pay and emoluments of regimental paymasters; and that there shall be one commissary of purchases, and two military storekeepers, to be attached to the purchasing department.

Sec. 10. *And be it further enacted,* That the medical department shall consist of one surgeon general, eight surgeons, with the compensation of regimental surgeons, and forty-five assistant surgeons, with the compensation of post surgeons.

Sec. 11. *And be it further enacted,* That the officers, non-commissioned officers, artificers, musicians, and privates, retained by this act, except those specially provided for, shall have the same rank, pay, and emoluments, as are provided, in like cases, by existing laws; and that the force authorized and continued in service under this act, shall be subject to the rules and articles of war.

Sec. 12. *And be it further enacted,* That the President of the United States cause to be arranged the officers, non-commissioned officers, artificers, musicians, and privates, of the several corps now in the service of the United States, in such manner as to form and complete, out of the same, the force authorized by this act, and cause the supernumerary officers, non-commissioned officers, artificers, musicians, and privates, to be discharged from the service of the United States.

Sec. 13. *And be it further enacted,* That there shall be allowed and paid to each commissioned officer who shall be discharged from the service of the United States in pursuance of this act, three months' pay, in addition to the pay and emoluments to which he may be entitled by law at the time of his discharge.

Sec. 14. *And be it further enacted,* That the system of "General regulations for the army," compiled by Major General [Winfield] Scott, shall be, and the same is hereby, approved and adopted for the government of the army of the United States, and of the militia, when in the service of the United States. (a)

Approved, March 2, 1821.

PC in Peters, ed., *Statutes at Large,* 3:615–616. Note: The plan which went into this act was drafted by Calhoun, though it underwent some revision in the House of Representatives before final passage. See Calhoun's original recommendations in House Document No. 45, 16th Cong., 2nd Sess. See also letters from David Trimble in *The Papers of John C. Calhoun,* 5:529, 537.

To W[ILLIAM] H. CRAWFORD, Secretary of the Treasury

War Department, March 3d 1821

Sir, I will esteem it as a favor, if, whenever you receive information as to the failure of any Bank, in which the public funds are deposited, you will communicate the same to this Dept. Such information is rendered desirable in consequence of the inconvenience & disapointment which U.S. Pensioners sometimes experience in being obliged to receive sums due them in a depreciated paper currency. The Bank of Vincennes, in Indiana, I understand, has suspended specie payments, and their notes are of but little value. Funds were transmitted to that Bank for the purpose of paying the Pensioners in that State, before I was apprised of these facts. I am &c, J.C. Calhoun.

FC in DNA, RG 15 (Veterans Administration), Letterbooks of the Pension Office: General, 1812–1831, 10:293.

To [JAMES P.] PRESTON, [former] Gov[erno]r [of Va.], Brown's [Hotel, Washington]

[Washington] 20th March [1821]

Mr. Calhoun's respects to Gov[erno]r Preston and would be glad of his company this evening, which besides the personal pleasure, it will afford an opportunity of conversing with him in relation to his duty under the Creek treaty as a commiss[ione]r which place he is happy to learn he has accepted.

ALU in ViHi, Preston Family Papers.

To T[HOMAS] LAW

War Dept., 28th July 1821

Dear Sir, I received your note covering your address; and ["your" *interlined*] reflections on slavery, and as requested, I herewith return them. I thank you for the perusal of them. They breath that ardent philanthropy, which constitutes so distinguished a trait in your character; but, I cannot accord in all of your views. It seems to me, that as to the increase of slaves in proportion to our free popu-lation, ["that" *canceled*] in the U. States, that you must be in an error, notwithstanding, that you quote from so respectable an authority as Mr. [Daniel?] Raymond. I tooked [*sic*] into the subject formerly, and my impression is different from yours; and, if I remember rightly, Mr. [Henry] Clay, in one of his Missouri speeches, stated that in the first census, ["that" *canceled*] the slave population was 22 in the 100, in the next 20 and in the last but 18 or thereabouts. If I am not mis-taken, Dr. [Adam] Seybert estimates the slave population of our country to double in about 25 or 26 years, while that of the ["Whites" *canceled and* "free" *interlined*] does the same in less than 22. The subject is interesting, and I hope before you publish, that you will make sure of the facts. It is possible, that, in the States to which you refer, ["that" *canceled*] the slave population advances more rapidly, than the free; but that, I am satisfied must arive from the fact, that the emigrants, who are numerous from those States, are commonly not the rich, or large slave holder, but those, who are in moderate circumstance, or from the introduction of slaves from other States. Either of these causes, if the true, ["ones"(?) *canceled*], will probable prove temporary.

Very alarming, indeed, would be the fact, if so, that in[?] the entire of our population the race of slaves increased faster than the free. Respectfully, J.C. Calhoun.

ALS in CtY, Beinecke Library, James Weldon Johnson Collection. Note: Thomas Law (1756–1834) wrote numerous pamphlets during the 1820's. His reply to Calhoun is published in *The Papers of John C. Calhoun*, 6:328–330. Daniel Raymond (1786–1849) and Adam Seybert (1773–1825) wrote books on the political economy of the U.S.

From W[illia]m Lowndes,
[Representative from S.C.]

[Charleston, S.C., *ca.* August 15, 1821]
Sir, I have been desired to mention to you that a Youth of this town (Charleston) ["is desirous" *canceled*; John E.] Carew is desirous of being appointed a Cadet & that his Father [Edward Carew] who has ["his"(?) *canceled*] brought him up carefully & well, concurs in his wish. The Youth is said to be about 14 years of age & from what I have heard there is I think a greater probability if he shall be ap-

pointed of his entering, & continuing in, the army than there has been in the greater number of our Carolina appointments.

I know nothing of this Young Man except from the information which has been given me by my friend Mr. [Matthew I.] Keith. He will write to you on the subject & in any recommendation which he may give will consider the interests of the Institution as well as the wishes of the Individual. The simple [reason] which leads to this is not very common but it adds very much to the force of any recommendation which he may give. I am With very great respect &ca Y[ou]r obed[ient] Serv[an]t, Wm. Lowndes.

ALS in PHi, Dreer Collection, American Statesmen.

To P[ETER] HAGNER

[Washington, August 19, 1821]
D[ea]r Sir, I saw Col. Nisbett [*sic*; Wilson Nesbitt?] this evening, and he says that his child is so ill, that it is doubtful whether he will be able to start in the morning. From what he says, I think the chance is against his going, and of course you cannot rely on the arrangement. If, however, contrary to expectation he should start you will fall in with us by the stage, provided you take it on Tuesday [8/21]. Unless your health should be very perfectly restored, I do not think you ought to give up the trip. Even if your health should not immediately require it, it will give such confirmation ["of" *canceled and* "to" *interlined*] it as to afford you much benefit. Yours sincerely, J.C.C.

ALI in NcU, Hagner Family Papers.

To C[HRISTOPHER] VANDEVENTER, [Washington]

Bedford Springs [Pa.], 2d Sep[tembe]r 1821
Dear Sir, I have received your letters of the 27th & 29th Inst. [*sic*] with the letters and papers accompanying them.

I have no doubt but that such a report in relation to the Military Academy as M[a]j[o]r [Sylvanus] Thayer suggests would be serviceable, and that Let. [William Theobald Wolfe] Tone would perform the duty satisfactorily; but I am at present inclined to think, that the duty ought to be performed through ["the C(hief) Eng(i-nee)r as" *interlined*] the inspector, whose duty it will ["be" *interlined*] under the new regulation, to inspect the situation once a year. I will however come to no conclusion till my return to Washington.

I return Col. [Abram] Eustis' letter to Col. [George] Bomford; and it will be proper for Col. Bomford in answer to give him a full explination of the difficulty which prevented the President [James Monroe] from carr[y]ing into effect the promotion of Col. Eustis as was at first intended. I am aware of his merit and have been anxious to see him advanced in proportion to the length of his service and his ["just" *interlined*] claims, and did hope when it was rumoured, that [Bvt.] Col. [George E.?] Mitchel[l] would resign, that an opening would be made ["for" *canceled*] to do justice to him and Maj[o]r [James B.] Many; but on a more detailed view of all of the circumstances, I found it impossible to advance Col. Eustis and restore Maj[o]r Many to the Artil[ler]y without doing manifest injustice to others. By furnishing Col. Eustis with a statement of the effect that would result by filling Col. Mitchel[l]'s vacancy by his promotion and the transfering of Maj[o]r Many back to the Art[iller]y compared to that by filling it in the manner which has been adopted he must, I think, be satisfied with the impossibility consistently with the rights of others, to carry the first intention of the Department into effect.

Will you ["to" *canceled*] say to Mrs. [Floride Colhoun] Calhoun, if in Washington, that we would have written to her but was [*sic*] induced to believe from your letters and Mr. [Peter] Hagner's statement, that we should see her at the Springs.

We are all well; and shall set out on our return at the fartherest on the 9th and it may be as early as the 7th.

Mr. [James L.] Edwards will examine the enclosed [property] schedule and if it is one of those cases in which there is no difficulty he will admit it and deliver the [pension] certificate to judge Parker of Virginia, who will call for it about the 20th Inst. With great respect I am & &, J.C. Calhoun.

ALS in MiU-C, Christopher Vandeventer Papers.

Notice of L.L.D. degree, 9/10/1821. "The Degree of L.L.D. has been conferred on the Hon. John C. Calhoun, of this State, by Hamilton College, [Clinton,] N. York." From the Charleston, S.C., *Courier*, September 10, 1821, p. 2.

From JAMES MONROE

Oak hill [Loudoun County, Va.], Oct[obe]r 5: 1821
Dear Sir, The rise of the streams between this & albemarle [County], in consequence of heavy rains, detained me two days longer on the road than I had expected, & will prevent, in this, the[?] reply, to yours of the 28th ult[im]o, a deficiency however which I hope to supply in some degree at least by Mr. [Samuel L.] Gouverneur who leaves this tomorrow morning for the city, on his way to N. York. Some few matters however I will notice in this. Sometime since I received a private letter from Gen[era]l [Andrew] Jackson, communicating his sentiments on several subjects, particularly, the conduct of the Gov[erno]r [José Maria Callava] who preceded him, of what was said of Mr. [Eligius] Fromentin &ca, and in regard to the military arrangments. I sent this letter in confidence to Mr. [William] Wirt, & I wish you to inform him that it is my desire that he hand [it] to you in like confidence. To this letter I gave a friendly answer, without going into much detail, but with an assurance, that his opinions would be attended to and have weight on all topics to which they applied. Since then the Gov[erno]r has been arrested, Mr. Fromentin has issued a writ of habeas corpus, which was disregarded, & other things have occurred there of an unpleasant nature. The Spanish laws &ca.[?] operating there, in all cases, except what concerns the revenue, & slave trade, & our district district [*sic*] being appointed for the execution of these only, I cannot see on what principle Mr. Fromentin interfer[re]d.

I think with you, that you had better inform Gov[erno]r [John] Clark [of Ga.], that it is not the practice or rule of the dept., to deliver papers, under the circumstances applicable to this case, it being not to vindicate private character, none being attacked, nor promote the public interest. You will of course take your own mode, & under such guards, as the rule of the office admits, & will prevent complaint or reply.

I am glad to hear of your return with Mrs. [Floride Colhoun] Calhoun in good health. Sincerely yours, James Monroe.

ALS in DLC, James Monroe Papers.

From THOMAS HEMPSTEAD, Act[in]g P[artner,] M[issouri] F[ur] Company

St. Louis, Oct. 16, 1821

The Missouri Fur Company have the pleasure of presenting to J.C. Calhoun Esq. Secretary of War one Doz. and a half of Buffaloe Tongues which was taken in the fall of 1820 on the upper Missouri river and which is sh[ip]ped and consigned to Messrs. Hurd & Sewall of the City of New York subject to his order. I am Respectfully Sir Your ob[edien]t Serv[an]t &, Thomas Hempstead, Actg. P.M.F. Company.

FC in CtY, Beinecke Library, Western Americana Collection, Thomas Hempstead Letterbook. NOTE: Hempstead also sent the same gift to President James Monroe and Secretary of the Treasury William H. Crawford.

From OLIV[ER] WOLCOTT, [Governor of Conn.]

Litchfield (Conn[ecticu]t), October 18, 1821

Sir, At the request of Eli Whitney Esq[ui]r[e] of New Haven, I have the honour to represent to you, that a considerable proportion of the muskets ["at present deposited" *interlined*] in the Arsenal of this State, and in the hands of our Militia, ["and" *canceled*] were manufactured by Mr. Whitney and ["as" *canceled and* "that as" *interlined*] far as my knowledge extends, they have been universally approved.

I ["have" *canceled and* "feel" *interlined*] no hesitation in expressing to you my opinion, that in the future ["distristion" *canceled*] distribution of Muskets to this State, those manufa[ctu]red by Mr. Whitney, will be preferred to any other, which are now known. I have the honour to be with perfect respect, Sir, your obed[ient] ser[van]t, Oliv: Wolcott.

ALS (retained copy) in CtHi, Oliver Wolcott, Jr. Papers.

To Hon. J[OHN] B. GIBSON, [Philadelphia]

Washington, 30th Oct[obe]r 1821

Dear Sir, I am very happy to perceive, that your college [Dickinson College] is reorganized; and I do hope, that under the superintendence of one so distinguished, as is Dr. [John M.] Mason for abilities and energy, it will realize the anticipations of its warmest friends. The location [Carlisle, Pa.] appears to me to be in every respect most fortunate.

If I remember correctly, in conversing with you in relation to the College, I mentioned with approbation the Maryland resolutions preposing to vest in the old States, the same proportion of the publick land for the purpose of education, as that, which has been vested in the new States. The resolution appears to me to be founded in strict justice, and that nothing is wanting, but its adoption and a prudent management of the fund, to place the education of the country for ever, on the most solid foundation. Believing, that you might take an interest in the subject, and that through your influence, ["an" *canceled*] some influential member of your Legislature might bring it before that body at the next session, I have taken the liberty of enclosing you a copy of the report & resolution. I am no other way connected with the subject, but as any enlightened citizen must be, with whatever he may suppose to be calculated to advance the intelligence of the community.

Mrs. Calhoun joins her best respects to yourself & Mrs. [Sarah Galbraith] Gibson. With great esteem I have the honor &c, J.C. Calhoun.

ALS and CC in PHi, William W. Porter Papers, John B. Gibson Correspondence. NOTE: Gibson was an Associate Justice and later Chief Justice of the Supreme Court of Pa.

To Stephen "Girrard" [*sic*; Girard], Philadelphia, 11/17/1821. "I introduce to you Major General [Alexander] Macomb, who will hand you this, on visiting Philadelphia." LS in Girard College Library, Philadelphia, Pa., Stephen Girard Collection (microfilm of collection in PPAmP).

From C[HARLES] W. PEALE

Philadelphia, Dec[embe]r 3d 1821
Dear Sir, When I was last at Washington I waited on you respecting the application of my Brother James Peale, who was after that placed on the ["pention" *altered to* "pension"] list, and under the act of 18 March 1818 received one years pension, but never [under] the additional act of 1820 owing to his having formed a wrong conception

of its provisions. My object in now troubling you is to know whether you think he can be continued on the list under the last act. His situation is peculiarly a hard one as he is now past 72 years of age, and has a family consisting of 10 persons; his wife, 5 Daughters[,] one son and two grand children, all of whom live togather—two of his Daughters paint, one does a little by teaching Musick, and his Son is a Clerk, yet knowing that his Children with great difficulty support even themselves, and that he has not for many years been able to support himself, my Brother wishes to be continued under the additional act. His only property (which remains unaltered since the act of 1818) consists of some old furniture amounting to about $150. He owes debts to the amount of about 600$[?] leaving out those he owes his Children.

With every apology for thus intruding on you, I shall be pleased if it does not interfere with your many important duties to receive an answer in a few days. A single line may be sufficient, and you ["will" *interlined*] confer an obligation on Dear Sir, your friend, C.W. Peale.

P.S. My son Rubens meditates the Establishment of a Museum in Washington, but I think it very doubtful whether he will receive sufficient encouragement from Public bodies. If he visits Washington this session its probable that I may accompany him.

ALS (retained copy) in PPAmP, Peale-Sellers Papers (published microfiche of *The Collected Papers of Charles Willson Peale and his Family*, Series II-A/ 66Fl); PC in Miller et al., *The Selected Papers of Charles Willson Peale and his Family*, 4:94–95.

To Joseph Lancaster

Washington, 25th Dec[embe]r 1821

Dear Sir, I rece[i]ved your favour of the 7th Inst. [*not found*] in the due course of the mail, and would have given an earlier reply, had not the pressure of official duties in consequence of the commencement of the session of Congress prevented me.

I regret very much, indeed, to learn that your success in Baltimore has not equalled your expectation. It is mortifying to think, after your great and useful efforts in favour of education, that you should, in any part of our country, fail to receive the most ample patronage. That such should be the fact in Baltimore, I am wholly at a loss for a cause, unless one should be found in the unparalleled commercial difficulties, which she has experienced for some years.

I have duly reflected on the plan which you have suggested for your future operations; and I am bound in candour to say, that I fear that it cannot succeed. The President [James Monroe] very early determined, to apply the small appropriation for the civilization of the Indians, only to schools established *within their country* and supported *in part by individual* resources. It was believed, after much reflection, that it was only by adopting this mode of applying the appropriation, that much good could be effected by so small a sum. What has been so deliberately adopted cannot now be departed from; particularly as its wisdom has been fully tested by experience. The plan, which you prepose, contemplates a very different mode of applying the appropriation, and, consistently with the system adopted, cannot receive the patronage of the [War] Department.

The donation of land can only be made by Congress; and, altho' I do not doubt, but that the members of that body very highly appreciate your distinguished labours in the great cause of education, yet, I very much doubt, whether they would feel themselves justified in making a donation, on the principles, which have heretofore governemed [*sic*] them, in relation to the publick land. With great esteem I am & &c, J.C. Calhoun.

ALS in CtLHi, Ransom Collection, 8:40. NOTE: Lancaster (1778–1838), an Englishman, was creator of the Lancasterian system of education. In 1821 he made a U.S. lecture tour and began a school in Baltimore.

From JED[IDIA]H MORSE, "Private"

Washington, Jan. 4th 1822
Dear Sir, I enclose a letter to the President, wh[ic]h should accompany the Report, for its explanation, when sent to Congress.

Something was said the last winter on the subject of my securing the copy right of my Report. I wish this business may be correctly understood by the Govt. & myself, & that done wh[ic]h shall meet the views of both. There is a *property* in this Report, (probably I overate its value) wh[ic]h it seems would be right, in existing circumstances, in some way, to secure to me. No other way occurs to me, than securing the *Copy right* of the Report, with the understanding, that Congress shall print as many copies of it, as they may want for their own use.

I know not whether any thing of this kind has been done in regard to other reports; or whether it would be deemed honorable in the Govt. to reward their servants in this way, or to [*sic*; for] their servants thus to receive ["claims"(?) *canceled*] compensation for their services. I can only say, that another course, of more certainty as to the issue, & less liable to public remark, would [*illegible word altered to* "be"] much more grateful to my own feelings.

With these remarks I willingly submit the subject to the decision of the President.

It will be necessary that this decision be known to me before the Report goes to the press, that the Certificate may be put on the back of the Title page.

I am not very well this morn[in]g. This indisposition, with the severity of the weather, will confine me to my room to-day.

You will do me a particular favor to bring my business to some speedy issue—as I cannot long sustain the expense of time, of health & of money, to wh[ic]h I am necessarily subjected while I remain— Yours very respectfully, Jedh. Morse.

ALS in Schenking-Diederichs Collection, University of Amsterdam Library; microfilm of collection in DLC. NOTE: Morse's *Report to the Secretary of War of the United States, on Indian Affairs* .... (New Haven: printed by S. Converse, c. 1822) was published in 6/1822.

To PHILIP P. BARBOUR, Speaker, H[ouse] of Rep[resentative]s

Dep[art]m[en]t of War
January 15th 1822

Sir, The Secretary of War, to whom was referred the resolution of the House of Representatives of the 10th inst: "directing that the Secretary of War communicate to that house a Statement (so far as the same may be in his power to make) of the items of all expenditures made, and expenses incurred in the Indian Department during the years 1820 and 1821, together with abstracts of the estimates furnished for said years by the Indian Agents upon which funds have been advanced, or expenses incurred, and also a Statement of the several amounts to which their respective expenditures were limited by the instructions of said Secretary," has the honor to enclose herewith a Statement of the 2nd Auditor [William Lee], marked A. shewing "the ["items of all" *canceled*] expenditures made, and expenses incurred in the Indian Department for the years 1820 and 1821" as far as the actual expenditures can be ascertained from the vouchers received. Statement marked B. containing "abstracts of the estimates furnished for said years by the Indian Agents upon which funds were advanced, or expenses incurred" and documents marked C. containing a circular of the 19th March 1821 to the Superintendents and Agents, by which will be seen "the several amounts to which there [*sic*] respective expenditures were limited" together with an estimate of the arrearages of the Indian Department at the termination of the last year, and the general regulations which have been adopted to control the expenditures of that Department.

The estimates on which advances were made are necessarily imperfect for the year 1820, as the regulation changing the mode of making advances to Agents and Superintendents was adopted on the 19th February of that year. Before that period the Disbursments of the Indian Department were made without estimates, principally on drafts drawn on this Department by the Agents and Superintendents, care being taken in accepting the drafts not to exceed the sum allotted to each, without satisfactory explanation. This mode of covering the disbursments of the Indian Department was, however, found to be defective, as it gave no previous check over the disbursments, and exposed the Government to fraud in disposing of drafts on it, by the Agents without accounting for the premium which they might obtain. It is not however known that any fraud of the kind has been committed, but it was a strong objection to the mode of making disbursments, that it was liable to abuse. Under the system adopted, if rigidly enforced, the possibility of such frauds is excluded.

Believing it to be within the intention of the Resolution, I have annexed to the copy of the circular to the Superintendents and Agents of the 19th March last which contains the Amount to which their respective expenditures were limited, copies of various other circulars which had been at different times adopted in order to introduce economy and accountability, and thereby diminish the expenditure of the Indian Department. In addition to these, Special instructions, applicable to the peculiar state of each agency, have, with the same view, at various times been given to the different agents. On account of its amount, and liability to abuse the expenditure, which particularly claimed the attention of this Department, was that on account of rations issued to Indians. Not long after the commencement of the present Administration of the Department, the circulars in relation to issuing rations, copies of which accompany this report, were issued to the Agents and Superintendents. It is believed that the regulations, which they contain, have had a very happy effect in preventing impositions on the government and diminishing the disbursements of the Indian Department.

By referring to the accompanying documents it will appear, ["it will appear" *canceled*] that the aggregate amount allotted to the Agents and Superintendents under the circular of march last is $79,500, leaving $20,500 to meet such general charges against the appropriation as belonged to no particular Agency, such as the debits which might be brought against it, in the settlement of former accounts of expenditures, for the expenses of rations issued to the Indians through the Commissary of Provisions, of visits of Indians to the seat of Government, general expense under the Indian intercourse act of 1802; transportation of annuities &c. The sum allotted to these various objects have proved insufficient. Even with the addition of the balance of the appropriation of the last year, it has not been sufficient to meet the debits ["the" *canceled*] arising from the Settlement of old accounts. It was believed, when the estimates of the last year were made, that the balance of the appropriation of the preceeding year, with such Credits as might be brought to the Indian appropriation from the Settlement of old accounts would be Sufficient to cover the debits. Such however has not proved to be the fact, as will appear by reference to the Statement of the 2nd Auditor of the Treasury which accompany's this report. It is proper to remark that the debits which have been brought against the Indian Appropriation in the last and preceeding years have risen principally out of the Settlement of the Accounts of Army contractors under contracts made before the establishment of the present System of Supplying the Army with provisions, which commenced on the 1st of June 1819. The amount of rations issued to Indians could not under the old System be ascertained till the contractor rendered his accounts for Settlement, on which the provisions issued to Indians were charged to the proper Appropriation and the appropriation for the Indian Department for the year, was thus liable to be effected by the disbursements of former years. As the accounts of the former Army contractors have been all audited, and as the prompt Settlement of accounts under the present System of supplying the Army with provisions prevents the accumulation of outstanding claims, it is believed that the appropriations for the Indian Department will not hereafter be effected materially by the Settlement of outstanding accounts; but as balances remain due the United States in several cases on account of Subsistence, for the recovery of which suits have been instituted against the Contractors, it may occur that awards may be made in their favor on items chargeable to the Indian Department, which on Settlement by the accounting Officers, have been decided to be inadmissible. In such cases the appropriation for the Indian Department will be charged, and the Subsistence credited with the Amount.

In conclusion it may not be improper to State that altho' $200,000 has been the amount of the annual current appropriations for the Indian Department from the termination of the late war till last year, yet the disbursments considerably exceeded that sum previous to the year 1820, the difference being made up from time to time by appropriations for arrearages. The Acting Secretary of War, Mr. [George] Graham estimated the disbursments of the Indian Department at $250,000 in the year 1817. In his letter to the Chairman of the Committee of Ways & Means of the 4th of January of that year he states "The expenses of the Indian Department have been estimated at Two hundred thousand dollars; it is however recommended that this estimate should be increased, so as to make a permanent annual appropriation for this object of $250,000 at least. The circumscribed limits of most of the Indian Tribes, East of the Mississippi and Illinois Rivers having rendered their dependence upon the chace for Subsistence more precarious, has produced a more frequent intercourse between those Indians and the Agents of the United States and a consequent increase of the issue of rations and of presents to them." In addition to these causes the number and importance of the Treaties which have been held with the Indians since the late war, the great increase of the annuities and extension of the frontier, have tended very much to increase the disbursements of the Indian Department. Believing it, however to be the intention of Congress that the expenditure should not exceed $200,000 per annum, efficient measures were adopted shortly after the commencement of the present administration of this Department to reduce the amount of the expenditure within that Sum.

Acting on the same principle after the reduction of the appropriation of the last Session to $100,000 for the expenses of the Department every effort was made to reduce the Disbursement within the amount appropriated, which could be made without deranging the System established under existing laws. The consequence has been a very considerable reduction in the disbursements; but it has not been practicable to bring the expenditure within the appropriation. Though ["the" *canceled*] measures were taken immediately after the passage of the act making the appropriation, yet at points so remote as those at which most of the agencies are fixed nearly one half of the year had elapsed before any considerable diminution could be effected in the rate of expenditure authorized by previous appropriations, by which time, (the previous expenditure being at the rate of $200,000 per annum) the appropriation was nearly exhausted, and the expenses of the Department have, been accumulating against the Government, without the means of meeting them.

All which is respectfully Submitted. J.C. Calhoun.

LS with Ens in DNA, RG 233 (U.S. House of Representatives), 17A-E4, Original Reports, War Department; FC with Ens in DNA, RG 107 (Secretary of War), Reports to Congress from the Secretary of War, 1803–1870, 2:198–207 (M-220:1); CC with Ens in DNA, RG 233, Record of Reports from the Secretary of War, 17th Cong., 1st Sess., 240:4–14; PC with Ens in House Document No. 24, 17th Cong., 1st Sess.; PC with Ens in *Annals of Congress,* 17th Cong., 1st Sess., pp. 724–728; PC with Ens in *American State Papers: Indian Affairs,* 2:266–271; PC in Crallé, ed., *Works,* 5:94–98. NOTE: An endorsement on the last page of this report reads, "Report 24 of the Secretary of War, relative to disbursements for the Indian Department—made in obedience to a resolution of the House of Representatives of the 10th of January, 1822." A second EU reads, "Read, and committed to that com[mitt]ee of the whole to which is committed the bill making partial appropriations for the military service for the year 1822." A final endorsement reads, "To be printed with all practicable despatch. W[illiam] W. S[eaton]."

To [John Quincy] Adams

[Washington,] 21st March [1822]

Dear Sir, If you have had time to investigate the claim of Mr. [Joel R.?] Poinsett which I left with you a few days since[,] I would be glad to know the result. I am &c, J.C.C.

ALI in MHi, Adams Papers, Letters Received and Other Loose Papers (published microfilm, roll 454). NOTE: This letter is addressed in Calhoun's hand, "Mr. Adams, or if absent Mr. [Daniel] Brent."

From Henry R. Schoolcraft, Washington, 4/2/1822. He submits a geological report of an "expedition sent to explore the upper Mississippi, by the way of the Lakes," begun in May of 1820. Lewis Cass accompanied the expedition. Schoolcraft gives an account of his route, departing Detroit and coasting along the shores of lakes St. Clair, Huron & Superior to the Fond du Lac. The expedition then proceeded up the St. Louis River, portaged across land to the Mississippi, sailed up the Mississippi and then portaged across land to Lake Huron and sailed down to Detroit. Schoolcraft gives an outline of the geology of this region. He seeks "to determine the limits between the primitive & secondary formations, and to test, by actual observation, its conformity or non conformity of structure, with the principles of generalization, set up in other countries." He "consider[s] the changes wrought upon the ["secondary" *canceled and* "whole series of" *interlined*] formations," i.e. surface strata. He also discusses the four kinds of geological action which exerted an influence on the region: oceanic, lake, volcanic and disintegration. He also seeks the actual sources of the Mississippi. 3 drafts in DLC, Henry Rowe Schoolcraft Papers.

To J[OHN] P[ENDLETON] KENNEDY, [Baltimore]

Washington, 12th May 1822

Dear Sir, I duely received your note of the 1st Inst., but have been prevented from answering it, as early as I desired, by the pressure of official duties incident to the termination of a session of Congress. The President, after mature deliberation, determined not to make the appointments of the ministers to South America for the present; and it is not probable that they will be made till we hear from their governments. I received the ["packet" *altered to* "pacquet"] with the letters to which you refer and laid them before the President. They are now filed in the State Department, and will be brought regularly before the President, when he comes to make the appointment to which they refer. I will be happy to give you such information, as you may at any time ["to" *canceled*] request. With great respect I am &c, J.C. Calhoun.

ALS in MdBE, John Pendleton Kennedy Collection (published microfilm of the John Pendleton Kennedy Papers, reel 13). NOTE: A defective transcription of this letter appears in *The Papers of John C. Calhoun,* 7:106–107.

To J[AMES] P. PRESTON

Washington, 22d May 1822

Dear Sir, I have been requested by a friend of mine to bring to the notice of the board, of which you are a member, the application of Mr. [Samuel] Niles a son of [*mutilation*; the] gentleman [Hezekiah

Niles], who edits the [Niles' Weekly] Re[gis]ter in Baltimore. I am [no]t acquainted with the young gentleman, but the letter of my friend [*not found*], which I enclose is entitled to the highest cred·t; as from my personal knowledge of him, I can vouch for the fidelity of his representation in such cases.

You will perceive the qualification which he claims, ["&" *interlined*] which, if you should think sufficient for the place, I will be much gratified with his success. I would have also written to your colleague Mr. [Nathaniel A.] Ware, [but] am ignorant of his ad-dr[ess] at present. You will be so good, in making the solici[ta]tion as to lay the Doctor's letter before him and state to him that I wish [*mutilation;* him] to consider this note addressed as well to him as to yourself. I am with great respect Yours &c, J.C. Calhoun.

ALS in ViHi, Preston Family Papers.

MEMORANDUM Concerning the House Report on the Elijah Mix Contract

[Washington, *ca.* late May 1822]

A. By reference to the marginal mark A in the report of Genl. [Alexander] Macomb ["of the 29th of April" *interlined*], it will be seen that the sentence immediately following that above quoted explains the circumstances under which advertisements were deemed to be indispensable and cites the contracts for the Gulf of Mexico in illustration.

B. This is erroneously stated. The report of Genl. Macomb whence it is pretended to be derived states that the practice of advertising in all cases had existed since the "Complete Organization of the Engr. Dept." And it states that the Engr. Dept. was established in Apr. 1818 but it does not state that it was completely organised as soon as it was established. It was not considered to be so organized until more than a year after its establishment.

C. This statement with respect to Alanson [*sic*; Allason] Crandall is calculated to produce an impression very different from that which the facts in the case will warrant as will distinctly appear on examination of ["his" *canceled and* "Crandall's" *interlined*] statement herewith marked C ["by reference to which adverts to" *canceled and* "by reference to which it will (*"appear" canceled and* "be seen" *interlined*) that" *interlined*] stone ["of an inferior quality &" *interlined*] obtained in the cheapest manner without quarrying would cost $3 per perch no allowance being made for profits—the experiments being professedly made to ascertain the lowest possible rate at which it could be obtained under the most favorable circumstances. He does not offer, as the Committee states, to furnish ["stone" *interlined*] at $3 per perch.

D. The Committee omit to state that [Frederick] Perley by his own confession, even admitting him to be entitled to credit, admits that his proposal, ["altho" *canceled and* "was" *interlined*] put into the post office at Aquia and not handed to Genl. [Joseph G.] Swift and that he was under the belief that Genl. Swift had never recd. them. See ["Colo. (George) Bomfords &" *canceled*] Capt. [John L.] Smiths letter ["of 2d May & Colo. Bomfords of May" *interlined*] to Gen. Swift marked D.

E. Mr. [Edgar] Patterson's statement is obviously not to be relied on. ["as he admits he was not engaged in the quarrying business and is contradicted by Genl. (John) Mason who professes to have had experience" *canceled and* "It is contradicted by that of Genl. Mason who professes to have had experience in the quarrying business in which Mr. Patterson by his own account had no knowledge at the time the contract was formed." *interlined*.] The Committee keep out of sight the statement of Mr. [John W.] Baker accompanying the Rep[or]t of the Engr. Dept. & marked E in which ["it is stated that" *interlined*] the contract was ["stated to be" *canceled*] a disadvantageous one and ["which" *interlined*] refutes wholly the reasoning drawn from his statement ["made" *interlined*] before the Committee.

F. The argument of the Committee as to nonfulfilment of the contract is fully answered by the letter of Colo. [Charles] Gratiot ["the Engr. superintending the work" *interlined*] to Genl. Macomb dated the 26th May ["1822" *canceled*] and marked F ["by which it appears that stone to the full amt. of the sum allotted to the contract was not delivered" *canceled*].

G. This is incorrectly stated as will appear by inspection of Major [Christopher] Vandeventers statement made to the Committee ["at the" *interlined and* "marked" *altered to* "mark"] G.

H. The italicised "yet" here introduced is sufficient to shew the temper with which the investigation has been made—That temper of mind which has induced the Committee to dwell in the minutest manner upon every circumstance however trivial or insignificant which ["was" *canceled and* "appeared to be" *interlined*] calculated in the slightest degree to implicate the contract and to pass over or notice but slightly ["the" *canceled*] statements of the strongest and most decisive character in its favor. Among those wholly passed over are the proposal of Mr. Yeatin [*sic*; W. Yeaton] the certificates of ["Mr. (Joel) Cruttenden Mr. Baker" *canceled*] Mr. [Lloyd] Pumphrey ["Mr. Baker & Mr. Cruttenden" *interlined*] to the Engr. Dept., and Mr. [Josiah] Meigs letter ["as to" *canceled and* "stating" *interlined*] the practice[?] with respect to advertising ["under his administration" *canceled and* "in the Dept. over which he presides. The" *interlined*] statem[en]t of Mr. Mix shewing the actual loss sustained by him on the deliveries made the first year ["which is" *interlined*] founded on the quarriers bill ["to shew the cost of the stone" *interlined*] and the charter parties ["of the vessels employed in its transportation" *interlined*] to shew the cost of freight. The Chief Engr. report ["of the 1st of May" *interlined*] as to the construction given to Mixs contract ["as" *canceled and* "with reference" *interlined*] to the quality of stone to be delivered ["under it" *interlined and* "See his letter dated the 1st of" *canceled*] May. Colo. Bomfords statem[en]t of a conversation between him & Mr. [Robert] Leckie respecting the cost of stone &c—Mr. Stewarts [*sic*; William Steuart's] statement. Not to mention the stight [*sic*; slight; "notice taken of" *canceled*] manner in which they pass over those they do notice particularly Genl. Mason's, Com. [John] Rodgers', Colo. [Walker K.] Armistead's, &c.

DU (in an unknown hand) in MiU-C, Christopher Vandeventer Papers. NOTE: This undated rough draft was in response to a report submitted by a Select Committee of the House of Representatives on 5/7/1822.

To JOHN P[ENDLETON] KENNEDY,
"Confidential"

Washington, 29th June 1822

Dear Sir, It is not in my power to give any precise answers to the ["your" *canceled*] inquiries in your note of the 27th Inst. The President is now deliberating on the appointments to which you refer; but it is not probable, that he will come to any decision till after the arrival of the Minister, who is shortly expected from Mexico. Should he arrive, it is not improbable that appointments will be made, at least to Mexico & Colombia.

I am under obligations to you for the interest which you take in my young friend [George] McDuffie. My solicitude on his account has been very great. His life ought to be considered as publick prop- erty. I fear, however, that Col. [William] Cum[m]ing will revive the contest from what I observe in the publick papers. He appears to be actuated by a spirit not common on such occasions.

I have been deprived of the pleasure of my intended visit to Caro- lina by the lateness of the session of Congress and the accumulation of business which required my attention at the close of the session. I am with great respect yours &c, J.C. Calhoun.

ALS in MdBE, John Pendleton Kennedy Collection (published microfilm of The John Pendleton Kennedy Papers, reel 13). NOTE: A defective and misdated version of this letter is published in *The Papers of John C. Calhoun,* 7:365.

To "Messrs. A[nthony] C. Cazenove," Alexandria, 7/5/1822. "I acknowledge the receipt of your letter of the 2nd [*not found*], and would have availed myself of the opportunity you mention of pro- curing wine from Madeira, had I not already engaged a supply of that article; through Mr. John Herbert of your City." LS in MoSM.

To L[ANGDON] CHEVES, "Private"

Washington, 19th July 1822 Dear Sir, A friend of mine [Christopher Vandeventer] finding it necessary to have an acceptance in Philadelphia for the sum of $2,500 payable 45 days hence, has applied to me to aid him in his difficulty, which I have agreed to do, tho with great reluctance in giving you any trouble, by drawing on you, which I hope you will find it con- venient to accept. My friend is punctual and competent, and you will without doubt be put in funds by the maturity of the bill. I hope I have not taken too great a priviledge.

I regret to see you retire from the [presidency of the U.S.] Bank, tho I do not doubt that you must be quite exhausted with your fatig[u]ing duties. You see the papers are speculating on your future course. I hope you do not intend retirement, for which you formerly expressed so much fondness. Its charms show best at a distance. You are too young, and with too good a constitution to withdraw yet from the active scenes of life. With sincere friendship I am &c, J.C. Calhoun.

ALS in ScHi, Langdon Cheves I Papers. NOTE: An AEI by Cheves reads, "I ac- cepted Mr. Calhoun's draft in favour of Vandeventer for $2,500 this day at 45 days sight—22d July 1822. If I should be obliged to pay this Bill this letter will shew that Mr. Calhoun is liable to repay it to me."

From C[HARLES] W. PEALE

Belfield [Pa.,] Aug[us]t 30, 1822

Dear Sir, My Son Rubens is desirious to know what encouragement might be obtained to establish a Museum in the City of Washington, provided the undertaker was qualified to render it a scientific and well organized Institution for difusing general knowledge, whether a building would be given that would be sufficiently large to make a beginning & capable[?] of being extended with an increasing collection of Nature & arts.

Rubens proposes that it might begin with Mr. Delaplanes [*sic*; Joseph Delaplaine's; "Collections" *altered to* "Collection"] of Portraits and some subjects of natural History, and he wishes to assertain to [*one word missing*] what amount of Income might be expected Pr. Annum in the first beginning of such an undertaking, and if it would qualifie[?] him to an increasing family he would make exertions to accomplish what he conceives would in the Issue be a public benefit.

The parting with Rubens would ["be" *interlined*] a loss to the Philadelphia Museum, but if it [is] for Rubens's interest I cannot withhold my assent, as I have other Children to be provided for and who of course must supply his place. Titian is now in my pay to mount those subjects which he collected in the late tour with Major [Stephen H.] Long. I did hope to have had them all mounted and in public view ["before this time" *interlined*] but the labour of mounting in proper form, a variety of Animals which was collected and hastily[?] skined and hurried from place to place, under many fold disadvantages, require more time to put them in order, than Subjects freshly obtained. Some of the Small birds are mounted, also some of the small Quadrupids—all the Snakes of which there ["is" *interlined*] a pretty variety, ["they" *interlined and then canceled*] are done—but the large birds and Quadrupids are yet on hand, and I expect that I must lend my aid to complete them.

Since my Museum has been incorporated, the Professors have given their aid to the further improvement of it. The Minerals are splendid and importantly arranged to give a facil & perfect knowledge, to those who incline to persue that study.

My son Titian yesterday urged me to make application to get an appointment of him as a Naturalist in a tour of discovery ["with"(?) *canceled and* "that" *interlined*] Commodore Steward [*sic*; Charles Stewart] commands. Mr. Pierce Butler advises me to let Titian go, and he offers to write a letter to the President ["if" *altered to* "to"] obtain his patronage of it. Titian is well qualified to preserve as well as to collect Subjects of natural history generally.

Your occupations allow you very little time to write letters, and therefore unless you can find some occassion on[?] which I can serve you I cannot expect a line from you, unless you can oblige me in giving your opinion on the first subject of this Scrole. I am Dear Sir with much esteem your friend, C.W. Peale.

ALS (retained copy) in PPAmP, Peale-Sellers Papers (published microfiche of The Collected Papers of Charles Willson Peale and his Family, Series II-A/ 67D12–13); PC in Miller et al., *The Selected Papers of Charles Willson Peale and his Family*, 4:77–79.

To L[angdon] Cheves

War Dept., 2d Sep[tembe]r 1822
Dear Sir, Since I received the bank notice to day I saw my friend [Christopher Vandeventer] who informs me, that the amount required by the note will be remitted in time, which I do not in the least doubt. Should any accident, however, occur, I must request you as a particular favour to attend to it for me, and I will transmit the amount to you without delay from my own resources. I make the request ["as an" *canceled and* "from" *interlined*] extreme precaution, not that I expect any disapointment. Yours truly, J.C. Calhoun.

ALS in ScHi, Langdon Cheves I Papers.

From [Charles G. Haines?]

[New York City, *ca.* October 1822]
Sir: You will deem this letter a very singular [one], and think correctly, in doing so.

You will be nominated for the next President of the United States. I shall give you all the support that zeal, industry, and fidelity can produce. I make you this frank tender of my confident [*sic*] and ardor, before I know your strength, before the line is drawn, before I can anticipate the result of things with any degree of certainty.

I do this because I think you would give to this Union, a system of national policy, at once bold, elevated, and enlightened; one that will reveal the resources of a great country, and ["advance" *canceled*] rapidly advance him in the paths of ["national" *canceled*] greatness & renown.

It is also proper for me to say, that in thus speaking, I have no hopes of office. I am ["engaged" *canceled*] young in my profession, have fair prospects, and do not wish to leave it. Any of your friends in New York can inform you, what I claims [*sic*] I have on your confidence, and what services I can render to your cause—the cause of the nation. I would particularly refer you to [former Bvt. Brig.] Gen. [Joseph G.] Swift.

There is no time to be lost, ["now(?) there is no no" *canceled.*] Boldness and victory will go together. ["Sill" *canceled*] Still prudence should be consult[ed]. I would be sory to say [*sic*] any premature public step. Your friends throughout the Union should understand each other. ["You" *canceled*] We must ["rest your hopes on" *canceled and* "keep together" *interlined*] the old democratic party—["& try" *interlined*; to] come forward as the man of the people; ["without regard to state parties & local" *canceled.*]

["I would like to have an an" *canceled.*]

I expect no answer to this. It would [be] improper for me to look for, and equally so for you to ["make the" *canceled*] confide in ["an entire" *canceled and* "a" *interlined*] stranger. You are a young man. I am still younger. In aiding[?] you to stand at the head of the Republic, I even think that ["I" *canceled*] you will feel ofended at my frankness. ["and" *canceled*] I have much mistaken your character, If I judged incorrectly.

Etenim semper magno ingenio
adolescentes repenandi potius a
gloria, quam inatandi fuerunt.

Draft in N, Henry Post Collection; Abs (dated ca. 6/30/1823?) in The Papers of John C. Calhoun, *8:142–143.*

From Eli Whitney, New Haven, Conn., 10/25/1822. He "encloses vouchers for having delivered 500 muskets 'for the use of the U. States, in conformity with my arrangement . . . with the Ordnance Dept. . . . be pleased to direct a remitance of six thousand five hundred dollars . . .'" "It would have been more agreeable to my wishes, to have made a statement, including the incidental expenses of Boxes &c, but the state of my health has been & continues to be such as to put it out of power at present." ALS offered for sale as item 206 in catalog 3 (*ca.* April 1, 1962), pp. 20–21, by Paul C. Richards, Brookline, Mass.

To C[HARLES] G. HAINES, [New York City], "Private"

War Dept., 1st Nov[embe]r 1822

Dear Sir, Entertaining, as I do, a high opinion of your character and talents, I am much gratified with your favourable opinion; a continuance of which, I shall endeavour to merit.

If I have any political standing, it has been acquired by a fearless adherence to principles. I have ever been directed by a decided impulse, which in my political course, has left me but little discretion in calculating personal consequences. I am contented with our political institutions, and as they presuppose the people to be virtuous and intelligent, I have acted on the maxim, that what is wise would be popular. It ought at least to be so, and if it is not generally so, the very basis of our system is erroneous. As a consequence of this maxim, every effort of my political life has been directed to the developement morally and physically [of] the mighty resources of this country. I would not assent to rise on any other principle. I have no ambition simply to administer the government. If I have ambition this is too poor an object for it.

From these principles, my friends will, I hope, be at no loss to infer my course. Whether they will lead to my elevation, or not, time alone can decide. I have seen nothing yet in my political course to distress them, even in that point of view. The period, at which the people will be called on to choose, is yet so remote, and the number of those, whose claims are thought to entitle them to consideration, so great, that we must expect a thorough canvass. Unfounded pretentions will not be able to stand the test; and the bold assertion of popularity, unless ["having" *canceled and* "it should have" *interlined*] a just foundation, will avail nothing. The subject has been, fortunately for the country, early agitated, and he whose claims can best stand a free and full discussion, will, as he ought, ["to" *canceled*] have the best prospect of success. With great esteem & respect I am &c, J.C. Calhoun.

ALS in N, Henry Post Collection.

From [Maj. STEPHEN H. LONG, Topographical Engineers]

Philadelphia, Nov[embe]r 29, 1822

D[ea]r Sir, I beg leave to request your attention to a subject of peculiar interest to me and hope that my views in relation to it may meet your approbation. The subject alluded to is the appointment of Civil Engineer for the State of Virginia, which is to be made in January next by the Board of Publick Works, of that State, and which I am very desirous to obtain, while at the same time, I wish to take no steps in relation to the business, that you may not approve.

My object in soliciting the appointment is twofold. Viz. to ameliorate my condition, and engage in pursuits congenial to my taste and wishes, and for which I think myself better qualified than for any other. I am moreover inclined to believe that in point of national importance, the facilities and advantages for internal improvements in the State of Virginia are second only to those of New York which renders the object in view still more desirable.

But as I have very few personal acquaintances in Virginia, whose friendship and patronage would be likely to serve me in the present case, I am induced to build my hopes of success, principally upon the aid & support I may receive from another quarter, and with the conviction that your influence would be of essential service to me, I beg indulgence in asking your friendly aid.

I beg leave here to enumerate some of the more prominent duties of Civil Engineering, for the performance of which I fancy myself competent, having had experience in most of them.

Topography and Hydrography, comprehending surveys, delineations, descriptions, and the construction of maps.

Location & Construction of Forts, Arsenals, fortified lines &c

Survey, location, and construction of Roads & canals and their several appendages, such as Locks, Bridges, Tunnels &c

The application of waterpower to mechanical operations including the construction of Hydraulic & Hydrostatic machines

The planning & Construction of Steam Engines &c

Geometrical construction of drafts & plans, appropriate in the several operations above mentioned

Although I have had no immediate experience in the construction of Canals, I have taken much pains to acquire a practical knowledge of this branch of duty and feel confident that I should be able to superintend all the opperations appropriate in their Construction.

408

Ex (enclosed in an LS of 12/4/1822 from Calhoun to George Newton) in Vi, Board of Public Works, Administrative Papers, Applications for Position of Chief Engineer, 1816–1823.

To N[ICHOLAS] BIDDLE, [Philadelphia]

Washington, 2d Dec[em]b[e]r 1822

Dear Sir, Feeling as I do deep solicitude in the prosperity of the Bank [of the U.S.], I have been very much gratified with your nomination to the Presidency of that institution and most sincerely hope, that you may be elected.

The prosperity of the government is intimately connected with the good management and prosperity of the Bank; and altho' the latter may not have realized the expectations of the stockholders, it has fully discharged its duty to the government, and is entitled to its support. Without the institution it is difficult to realize the embarrassment under which the government ["must" *canceled and* "would" *interlined*] have laboured.

If at any time, I can render aid to the institution, it will afford me much pleasure, and should you be elected, of which there can be no reasonable doubt, the pleasure would be still farther advanced by cooperating, as with the present President [Langdon Cheves], with one, for whom I have so great an esteem. With great respect & esteem I am &c, J.C. Calhoun.

ALS in the Biddle Family Papers, Andalusia, Pa.; Abs in Reginald C. McGrane, ed., *The Correspondence of Nicholas Biddle Dealing with National Affairs, 1807–1844*, pp. 28–29.

Check payable to John C. Calhoun, 12/2/1822. This check for $150, drawn on the Office of Discount and Deposit of the Washington Branch of the Bank of the United States, is signed by R[ichar]d Smith, Cashier. An endorsement making the check payable to W[illiam] B. Finch of the U.S. Navy was signed by Calhoun. DS in NN, Personal Miscellaneous Papers.

To George Newton, Norfolk, [Va.], 12/4/1822. "Since I addressed you yesterday on the subject of a Civil Engineer, I have received a letter [of 11/29/1822] from Major [Stephen H.] Long of the Topographical Engineers, requesting that I would lay his name before the Board of Publick Works as a Candidate for the vacant office. As Major Long is esteemed well qualified for the situation, I take particular pleasure in recommending him to the consideration of the Board." (George Newton, 1786–1835, was a large-scale merchant and canal promoter.) LS in Vi, Board of Public Works, Administrative Papers, Applications for Position of Chief Engineer, 1816–1823; FC in DNA, RG 107 (Secretary of War), Letters Sent Relating to Military Affairs, 1800–1889, 11:449 (M-6:11).

By "Atticus," [1822]. Among the Calhoun pamphlets at Dartmouth College is a copy of *A Few Considerations, in Relation to the Choice of President, Written with a View to the Approaching Election, and Respectfully offered to the Citizens of the United States* (n.p.; 1822). Calhoun annotated the copy "Not worth reading except to gratify curios[ity]." Printed pamphlet in NhD, John C. Calhoun Pamphlet Collection.

By [Edwin C. Holland, Charleston?, 1822]. Among the Calhoun pamphlets at Dartmouth College is a copy of Holland's *A Refutation of the Calumnies circulated against the Southern & Western States, Respecting the Institution and Existence of Slavery Among Them. To Which is Added, a Minute and Particular Account of the Actual State of and Condition of their Negro Population. Together with Historical Notices of All the Insurrections that have taken place since the Settlement of the Country* (Charleston: A.E. Miller, 1822). Holland inscribed the cover of the pamphlet "The Hon. John C. Calhoun from his Ob[e]d[ien]t Serv[an]t, The Author." Printed pamphlet in NhD, John C. Calhoun Pamphlet Collection.

From H[ENRY] S[T]. G[EORGE] TUCKER, [former Representative from Va.]

Richmond, Jan[uar]y 21, 1823

Dear Sir, I recieved a few days past from Mr. John Cooke of Martinsburg, a letter informing me of his desire to place his brother St. George at the military academy. Supposing that it must on all occasions be more satisfactory to the Departments to recieve their information from one who is personally known to them he has requested my agency in this business which I lend with particular pleasure.

The young gentleman alluded to is I think a very promising

youth, and manifests even at this early period those feelings and that proper pride which afford a presage of his possessing the high and honourable principles which have always distinguished his brother in a very remarkable degree. His brother thinks that he possesses much of the military spirit; and no one can better Judge than he; for during the late war altho he held no commission even in the militia he subjected himself cheerfully to all the fatigues and privations of a soldier in the ranks of a troop of cavalry.

I can say nothing of the acquirements of St. George Cooke tho his intelligence and the attentions of his mother & brother leave no room to suppose his proficiency is not greater than that of youths of his own age. I am Dear Sir with great respect and personal regard yours, H.S.G. Tucker.

LS in DNA, RG 94 (Adjutant General), Application Papers of Cadets, 1805–1866, 1823, 253 (M-688:27, frame 42).

From [JOHN B. C. LUCAS]

St. Louis, Jan[uar]y 31st, 1823
Sir: Presuming that you are not ignorant that a large balance of the Spanish land claims reported upon by the commissioners remain in statu quo, and that the land claimants have made various attempts to procure the passage of an act suitable to their wishes, permit me to suggest to you that far from being discouraged, their eagerness and industry increases with the difficulties, and that the absence of Mr. [William] Lowndes, perhaps of others, will probably give them this session a fresh encouragement to renew their attempts. Unfortunately the interest of many influential men here is at variance with that of the U.S. Nothing is more just though at the same time more objectionable to land claimants that to have their claims referred to a court of justice. Finding that they could not avoid in the bill reported last year the reference to the judiciary, they endeavored to chide its effects by interpolating principles unknown to the Spanish laws [and] trammel the court. Knowing perfectly your devotion to the service of your country, I make no doubt but you will put your friends in Congress upon their guard. Yours, &c., &c., [John B.C. Lucas].

PC in John B.C. Lucas, ed., *Letters of the Hon. J.B.C. Lucas from 1815 to 1836,* pp. 99–100.

[Floride Colhoun Calhoun, Washington], to William D. Lewis, [*ca.* 2/1823]. "Mrs. Calhoun requests the pleasure of Mr. Lewis's company, on Thursday Evening 13th Feb." DU in PHi, Lewis-Neilsen Papers.

To V[IRGIL] MAXCY [in Maryland], "Private"

[February 1823?]

Dear Sir, I had written my letter of the 22d before I received your last favour of the 21st Inst. Mr. [George M.] Dallas writes with a st[r]ong and manly tone of feelings, and I have no doubt, but that one who stands so well with the majority in Pennsylvania, and who is prepared to act so decisively will have great weight in the election. The election will certainly turn on Pennsylvania. She must, if decisive in her cour[se] carry both Virginia & New York. I do not think it would be prudent to attempt the movement at Annapolis which he sugges[ted]. A failure would have the worst ["of" *interlined*] consequences, and consequently no attempt ought to be made, without a certain[ty] of success.

Before I received your last, I had supposed, that you alluded to a number on your resolutions, which I had not received. I now infer, that you transmitted but one number to me. If such be the fact, there has been no miscarriage of the mail. I received the number and sent it immediately to the editors and was under the impression that it had appeared in the [Washington Daily National] Int[elligence]r. I will see the Editors [Joseph Gales, Jr., and William W. Seaton] to day to know if they have received it, & why it has not appeared. Sincerely, J.C. Calhoun.

ALS in DLC, Galloway-Maxcy-Markoe Papers, vol. 37.

From JOHN TAYLOR, [Senator from Va.]

Washington, Feb: 20, 1823

Major Adam Hoops, then of Pensylvania, became an officer in a continental regiment, of which I was a major, very early in the revolutionary war. He was at the time under eighteen years of age, but he soon attracted the particular respect and esteem of his superiours; and was considered as possessing in an eminent degree, the qualities essential to a military character. He was present at the battles of Staten Island, Brandy wine, and German town with this regiment, and conducted himself in such a manner, as to obtain its approbation. Soon afterwards he exchanged into another, and having myself subsequently resigned, I know nothing further of him, nor was apprised of his existence, until I met with him a few weeks past in Washington, when, after a seperation of forty five years, the impression he had made on me, whilst we were in the army together, caused me to recognise him instantly. John Taylor.

ALS in DNA, RG 107 (Secretary of War), Personnel Papers, 1838–1912, Applications for Appointment, 7.

From ELI WHITNEY

New Haven, 20th Mar. 1823

Sir, Accompanying this communication you will receive an improved Model of a Guarde for the Musket. The only difference between this & the Model adopted, or intended to be adopted, as a standard, is in the form of that end of the Bow of the guard, to which the swivel is attached. The plate of the guard is precisely the same. The advantages of this construction are, that it is something stronger, much more easily made & meets the eye, at least, equally well, in its appearance. It is easier made both in the forging & finishing.

Both ends of the Bow of this Guard can be forged in a pair of matched Dies, each having a similar, circular, concave impression. Dies of this description are more easily made & are more induring than any other—they leave the metal in a firm, sound state & the work more free from scales & *without any fire.* Both ends of the Bow, can then be finished by Milling or Turning, with more expedition & accuracy than those of the other form can be filed.

Under an impression that the subject of its adoption might be refered to the Armories, I have furnish[e]d Col. [Roswell] Lee [Superintendant of the Springfield Armory] with a model exactly similar to the one sent herewith—which is put in such a manner that it can be sent to Mr. [James] Stubblefield by mail. With much respect, I am, Sir, Y[ou]r very ob[e]d[ien]t Serv[an]t, Eli Whitney.

ALS in PPL, Penrose Hoopes Collection. NOTE: A Clerk's EU reads "Rec[eive]d 29th[,] ans[were]d May 7th." An Abs of Whitney's contract of 8/15/1822 to produce muskets for the U.S. is in *The Papers of John C. Calhoun*, 7:244.

To E[BENEZER] PETTIGREW "of Lake Phelps," Plymouth, N.C.

Washington, 26th March 1823

Dear Sir, I have delayed answering your letter of the 12th Nov[ember]r till after the rising of Congress, in order that I might give you the general opinion, which was entertained of your wine; and am much gratified to say, that with little exception, it has been found to be excellent. It was, however, generally thought, that it would still be better, if instead of the apple brandy, the French, or some other less dissimilar in its taste from the ["wine" *canceled*] wine, had been used; or if it had been manufactured without brandy at all. These were, however, mere conjectures and probably were erroneous.

Your wine was so much esteem[ed], that I was continually asked, if it could be obtained of the same quality; and I promised to request you to send ["me" *canceled*] a cask to Mr. [James] Lloyd, Senator from Massachusetts, at Bost[on], Another to David B. [*sic*; David A.] Odgen Esq[ui]r[e former Representative] of New York, and Virgil Maxcy Esq[ui]r[e] Near Annapolis, to be sent to Baltimore. I would be much gratified, if you could send each of them a cask, as it would contribute to extend the knowledge and reputation of so fine a domestick ["a" *canceled*] wine, they being all gentlemen of the first standing in society. Very Respectfully, J.C. Calhoun.

ALS in Nc-Ar, Pettigrew Family Papers, vol. 3, p. 61; PC in Lemmon, ed., *The Pettigrew Papers*, vol. 2, p. 37. NOTE: The wine referred to had doubtless been produced by Pettigrew from scuppernong grapes which were famous in his region.

To ——

Washington, March 30, 1823

I am very much obliged to you for the copies of the canal reports, which you were so good as to transmit to me. It is the subject, in which I believe I may with truth say I take the deepest interest, not only as connected with our commercial and monied prosperity, but with the existence of the union itself. The canal through Ohio, and the one uniting the waters of the Chesapeake with the western waters through the route of the Potomac, I consider of prime importance, and hope that we may both live to see them completed.

PEx (from the Chillicothe, Ohio, *Supporter*) in the Washington, D.C., *Republican and Congressional Examiner*, June 21, 1823, p. 2. NOTE: The PEx above was prefaced with the following: "Extract of a letter from the Hon. John C. Calhoun, to a gentleman in this neighborhood."

To P[ETER] B. PORTER

[Washington, April 13, 1823]
... my own ground unconnected and uncommitted, and intend to do so. I look to those principles, and that policy, which I have ever struggled to maintain. I would rather sink with them, than rise with any others. My friends, thinking that they could be thereby better supported, thought proper to bring forward my name, and have seen nothing calculated to change their opinion. On the contrary, they are Zealous and not without confidence in the result; but are disposed to rest their hope more on the appeals to the good sense and virtue of the people, than exagerated calculation of strength.

For your good opinion accept of my kindest acknowledgement. My long acquaintance has taught me to value your judgement and integrity, and I hope ever to merit your esteem, whether we shall be found in the great struggle ["or not" *canceled*] on the same side or not. With sincere esteem I am &, J.C. Calhoun.

ALS (fragment) in NBuHi, Peter B. Porter Papers (published microfilm, reel 10, frames 372–374). NOTE: Calhoun addressed this letter to Porter in Albany, from which it was postmarked on 7/7 and forwarded to Black Rock.

From ELI WHITNEY

New Haven, 18th April 1823
Sir, Herewith inclosed you will receive Vouchers for my having made a further delivery of 500 Muskets, whereupon be pleased to direct a remittance of Six Thousand five Hundred Dollars to be made to Your very respectful & Ob[e]d[ien]t Serv[an]t, Eli Whitney.

ALS in PPL, Penrose Hoopes Collection. NOTE: A Clerk's EU reads, "Bill forwarded to the [2nd] auditor [William Lee] 23 Apl. 1823."

To [Episcopal] Bishop J[ohn] H[enry] Hobart, New York [City], 5/8/1823. "The allowance made for the education of a young Chief of the Onondaga tribe will be remitted to you, or paid in any other way you may be pleased to indicate. An apology is due to you for not earlier answering your inquiry on the subject." LS in Archives and Historical Collections of the Episcopal Church, Austin, Tex., John Henry Hobart Papers.

To B[ushrod] Washington

Washington, 8th May 1823

Dear Sir, I take great pleasure in recommending to your civilities the Rev[eren]d Dr. Baldwin and the gentlemen, who accompany him. They are members of the convention of the Baptist denomination now in session in this city; and are desireous of visiting a spot, for ever endeared to the American as the residence of the father of his country. With great esteem & respect I am & &, J.C. Calhoun.

ALS in ScU-SC, John C. Calhoun Papers. NOTE: Bushrod Washington (1762–1829), a nephew of George Washington, was an Associate Justice of the U.S. Supreme Court from 1789 until his death.

To Brig. Gen. S[imon] Bernard and Lt. Col. J[oseph] G. Totten, Board of Engineers, Philadelphia

Engineer Department, Washington, June 7, 1823

Gentlemen: Your being ordered to Philadelphia, had reference, not only to the aid you might afford in determining the route for the canal to connect the Chesapeake and Delaware, but to such as your professional experience, joined to that of Commodore [William] Bainbridge of the Navy, who will be associated with you for the purpose, would enable you to render towards carrying into effect the objects contemplated by the 6th section of an act of Congress, approved on the 7th of May, 1822, for providing, near Cape Henlopen, the means of securing vessels against the effects of floating ice, a copy of which is herewith enclosed; accordingly, on your arrival at Philadelphia, you will consult with Mr. [William] Meredith and the other directors of the Canal Company, and in concert with Commodore Bainbridge, Mr. Robert Ralston the chairman, and the members of the Chamber of Commerce of Philadelphia, who have volunteered their assistance in the establishment of the Breakwater, and will be governed by the result, as to which of these undertakings your attention shall first be directed.

The Secretary of War desires that you furnish at your leisure, to this Department, a report of your proceedings in relation to the Canal, accompanied with any remarks you may deem to be pertinent to the subject; and, as soon as practicable, a report respecting the Breakwater, to be addressed to the Secretaries of War and Navy Departments, by yourselves and Commodore Bainbridge jointly, to embrace an examination of the utility of the undertaking, and practicability of accomplishing, and these being established, a development of the plan you may recommend, accompanied with the requisite explanatory drawings, and a detailed estimate of the expense. J.C. Calhoun.

PC in William Jones, *Remarks on the Proposed Breakwater at Cape Henlopen, communicated, by request of the Secretary of the Treasury . . . to which are added, the Report of the Board of Engineers, and Captain Bainbridge of the Navy; the Memorial of the Chamber of Commerce of Philadelphia, &c. &c.* (Philadelphia: Printed by order of the Chamber of Commerce of Philadelphia, 1825), pp. 8–9; CC in DNA, RG 45 (Naval Records), Miscellaneous Letters Received by the Secretary of the Navy, 1801–1884, 1823, 4:24 (M-124:96).

To Gen. W[ILLIAM] H. SUMNER, [Adjutant General of Mass.]

Washington, July 4, 1823

Dear Sir: I have been so much pleased and instructed by the perusal of your letter on the militia, that I should be much gratified to see it in the hand of every citizen of our country.

Though my official duties have connected me more immediately with the regular establishment, I have never undervalued the militia; but, on the contrary, have never, for a moment, ceased to consider [it] as the natural and proper bulwark against foreign aggression or domestic usurpation. Every other force is more or less mercenary, and the tendency of all such force is hostile to freedom. Still, in the present condition of the world, and improved state of the military science, a regular force to a certain extent is necessary. You cannot give to the great body of citizens all of the instruction and experience, which the present state of the military art renders necessary. Hence the necessity of a standing force; but, the organization ought to be such, as to give the greatest amount of science with the smallest amount of force; or, in other words, to substitute science for numbers. To this point my attention has been incessantly directed for the last six years; and, I think I may say, with so much success, that though our present establishment does not equal twice the number of that on the reduction in 1802, it contains ten times its science, and is in that proportion better calculated to effect the only legitimate object of a standing force. This great improvement has been effected mainly by attention to military education; by a more perfect organization both of the staff and line; and by a great improvement in the system of regulations and discipline. I think it may be confidently affirmed, that there never was an establishment which, in proportion to numbers, contained so much of the military elements.

In giving this perfection to the regular force, I do hope that a foundation is laid to extend some portion of it to the militia. The regular establishment may be viewed as a small pattern farm, in which a perfect process of cultivation is introduced, and which ultimately will gradually diffuse itself over the whole country.

I tender you my acknowledgments for the copy of your letter, with which you have been pleased to favor me. With sincere regard, I am, &c. &c., J.C. Calhoun.

PC in the Washington, D.C., *Republican and Congressional Examiner*, May 11, 1824, p. 2.

From EDWIN JAMES

Saint Louis, July 11, 1823

Sir, Enclosed, are a few seeds of a species of tobacco, indigenous to the Rocky mountains, about Santa Fe, and to the hilly parts of North California, whence I received them by a gentleman recently from that quarter. Some plants have been reared from seeds of the same parcel, and are now growing in the garden of Gen. William Rector of this place. This species is abundantly distinguished from the common tobacco, also from that cultivated by the Aborigines of the Missouri, by the long and conspicuous foot stalks of the leaves; it is also, as I think, (judging from recollection,) distinct from the *rustico*, the only remaining species heretofore noticed in North America, and which has been met with, principally, if not entirely, in the vicinity of the old French or Indian stations in the interior of New

York. The leaves of this plant possess, as I am informed, in a great degree of concentration, the peculiar properties of the common tobacco, and it is probably much better adapted than that species, to the climate of the more cool and temperate parts of the United States.

I have taken the liberty to transmit the seeds to you, as I am persuaded you will attach so much importance to any attempt to spread the knowledge of our indigenous productions, as to cause them to be planted in the ensuing spring, and in the following summer it is probable a quantity of seed will be produced, sufficient to be distributed to every part of the Union. I have the honour to be, With great respect, Your ob[edien]t serv[an]t, Edwin James.

PC in *The American Farmer*, vol. V, no. 21 (August 15, 1823), p. 167. NOTE: James in 1823 dedicated a book to Calhoun: "To The Honourable J.C. Calhoun, Secretary of War, whose liberal views, enlightened policy, and Judicious Measures, while they have been prosecuted with the utmost circumspection and economy, Have at the same time contributed in an eminent degree to the ADVANCEMENT of the NATIONAL CHARACTER OF THE UNITED STATES Both in Science and Politics; These volumes are most respectfully dedicated by the Authors, as a humble testimonial of their high sense of his talents and patriotism, and as a grateful acknowledgment of his indulgence and patronage." PC in *Account of An Expedition from Pittsburgh to the Rocky Mountains, Performed in the years 1819 and '20, by order of the Hon. J.C. Calhoun, Sec'y of War: under the Command of Major Stephen H. Long. . . . Compiled by Edwin James. . . .* 2 vols. (Philadelphia: H.C. Carey and I. Lea, 1823). A London edition published in three volumes by Longman, Hurst, Rees, Orme, and Brown in 1823 contains a slightly different version of the dedication.

From JAMES MONROE

Oak hill [Loudoun County, Va.] July 11th 1823
Dear Sir, Mr. [William P.] Craighill, the person who applied some weeks since, for the appointment of Storekeeper &ca at Harpers ferry, has returnd to ascertain the result, & will deliver you this. He brings a letter from Col: [James] Stephenson, the member [of the House of Representatives] from that district, & is accompanied by Dr. Creamer[?], who resides near the post, who assures me that his appointment will give general satisfaction in that quarter. He is connected with the family of the late Col: [John P.] McGuire, the revolutionary officer who held it lately, & his appointment, I understand, will be very gratifying to the young man who resigns it. I think therefore if you see no objection to it, that the appointment had better be given to him, without delay.

419

I send you another letter from Mr. [James] Madison, rec[eive]d here, on the subject, of the other two. Be so kind as to procure for me, all the documents requested by him, & send them to me, that I may forward them to him. Return me also his letters.

I have been much engaged since my arrival, in domestic concerns, but shall always be ready to attend to any of a public nature. I shall I presume, return in a week or ten days more. Very sincerely yours, James Monroe.

ALS in Washington's Headquarters, Newburgh, N.Y., Thomas F. Balfe Collection. NOTE: James Madison was seeking information from Monroe on the commission of Andrew Jackson to be a Major General in 1814. The Madison Papers at DLC contain three memoranda dated 8/1/1823 from the Adjutant General's Office concerning the commission (Presidential Papers Microfilm, James Madison Papers, reel 20).

BERNARD FARREL to Floride [Bonneau] Colhoun, [Georgetown, D.C.]

[Charleston] 17 Jully 1823
Hounoured Madam, I aply to your Goodness once more. I am sure you will help me as I know it is in your power. You befrinded me when I Lived at the Blessing plantation for Mr. [Henry] Laurens [Jr.]. You spoake well of me and I am sure you will Doe so still. I have 5 small Children[,] the most of them fit to Goe to school and I have not the means to school them[,] the times is so hard. I am Living in a poor parrish that is Christchurch. My health wont permit me to Live on Rice plantations. A Good word from you Madam to your Hounourabel son would get me in to one of the Light houses to superintend it. I would get Recomendations to satisfie you from a Good many Gentelmen. Nathaniel Hayward [*sic*; Heyward], James S[c]hoolbred & Fred[e]rick Rutledge Esquires would Recomend me[,] and others. I know madam you will help me as I know you are Good to those that stands in need of help if you know them. Your son John E[wing] Colhoun [Jr.; "Esqr." *interlined*] would write to his Brother[-in-law, John C. Calhoun] for me. But I Cant see him as he seldom Comes to town. I sent you two letters Before this. I hope you Rece[ive]d them. I make Bold to Continue writing to you untill I hear you Rece[ive]d my letters and then I will stop. Perhaps the[y] may be mislayed and not Reach you. I am with the

Greatest Respect your most Humbel and obeidient servant, Bernard Farrel.

[P.S.] Hounoured Madam, if you Could spare the time a Line Derec[te]d to me, to be left at the office of Mesrs. Kershaw & Lewis[,] I would soon Get it.

ALS in DNA, RG 26 (U.S. Coast Guard), Early Light House Correspondence, Miscellaneous Letters Received, 1780–1910. Note: This letter was addressed to Floride Bonneau Colhoun "To be Left at the Hounourabel Secetarry of Warr's office, Citty of Washington."

By [John A. Dix, New York City, *ca.* 8/1823]. Among the Calhoun pamphlets at Dartmouth College is a copy of Dix's *On the Mode of Constituting Presidential Electors. Addressed to the People of New-York* (New York: Charles Wiley; Johnstone and Van Norden, Printers, August, 1823), upon which Calhoun wrote "When you have read the enclosed, please to return it. J.C.C." Printed pamphlet in NhD, John C. Calhoun Pamphlet Collection.

From J[OHN] B. C. L[UCAS]

St. Louis, Aug. 8, 1823

Sir: The peace which we have enjoyed in Missouri and particularly at St. Louis, has always been since a great while, precarious and of short duration. It has only lasted so long as [Thomas H.] Benton and his confederates have been able to awe into silence the editors of public papers and their correspondents. The attempts which have been made from time to time to discuss in the papers various subjects of a public nature, no matter how temperate, how fair, and how decorous, have never failed to be attended with scenes of violence and blood if they operated in any shape against Benton or his associates.

The violent death of Joshua Barton is the latest instance we have of the kind at St. Louis. Mr. Barton was attorney of the U.S. for the district of Missouri. Seeing that his brother David Barton was cried down for the vote he had given in the Senate against the nomination of Wm. Rector to fill the office of Surveyor of public lands for the State of Illinois, Missouri and Arkansas, [Joshua Barton] undertook to publish a statement of the public conduct of the surveyor in the Missouri Republican, printed at St. Louis, and justify the vote of his brother. Immediately after these, he received a challenge from one of the brothers of the surveyor. He endeavored to avoid a duel by offering to prove the truth of every part of the statement he had made, but this was of no avail. He must fight. I am well satisfied that it was with the greatest reluctance he accepted the challenge, but from the well known violence of that party on former occasions it is generally believed, and for my part I doubt not that if he had not fought then he would have been assailed at the first opportunity and received a treatment worse than death. It is consolatory to see that these extremities have made the deepest impression upon the public. It has roused it to the highest degree of indignation against the surveyor and his abettors. The paragraph of Mr. B[arton] under the name of Philo which was published in the Missouri Republican of the 25th of June, has been republished in the other papers of the State and the public conduct of the surveyor is closely investigated and loudly censured under every respect. This appears to be the commencement of a reaction from which the most beneficial effects may be anticipated. It may be proper to observe that like Chas. Lucas, Mr. B[arton] was district attorney for the U.S., that he had not less disposition than C. Lucas to be watchful and do scrupupously [sic] his duties, not only with respect to Indian agents, public surveyors, &c., but with respect to Spanish land claimants, in case a law should be passed to direct them to bring their claims before the court of the District of Missouri. This may the better explain why they both have ended in the same way, and have been dispatched by the same set of men. As to myself, the same men have exhausted every means of annoyance against me short of actual violence. They knew perfectly well that I was not a man to tamper or compromise with, hence I met with their constant and strenuous opposition. They have not even blushed to contrive and circulate the report that I was a pardoned rebel in Pennsylvania and that I was elected to Congress by the old stock of rebels. Permit me to repeat to you that no man could have been more popular than me, and amass more wealth provided I had confirmed every claim, not exceeding one league square and reported in favor of the others. I presume to say that my services in Louisiana, since Missouri, have redounded to the public benefit, whilst they have been to me a real source of vexation and persecution. Respectfully, J.B.C.L.

PC in John B.C. Lucas, ed., *Letters of Hon. J.B.C. Lucas from 1815 to 1836*, pp. 57–59. NOTE: Charles Lucas, son of John B.C. Lucas, had been killed in a duel with Thomas H. Benton in 1817.

From [Brig. Gen.] J[oseph] G. Swift

New York [City,] 4 Oct. 1823
My dear Sir, [John Q. MacNeill] The son of Col. A[rchibald] F.
M[a]cNeill of Wilmington N.C. has been passing the summer in my
family. He is an intelligent & well behaved youth of 22 years—Has
been very ill, but has recovered his health & is now unusually hearty.
He wishes, & His Father wishes him, to enter the Navy as a Surgeons
Mate. He has applied & forwarded the certificate, of Dr. [Armand
J.] DeRosset Senr. of Wilmington, of His studying. If you could say
any thing favourable to this matter to Mr. [Samuel L.] Southard, &
inform Him of the respectibility of Dr. DeRosset (upon all which I
have written Mr. Southard) it would in my opinion serve a very
worthy man & be acceptable in many respects.

Should Mr. M[a]cNeill succeed I shall recommend Him to revise
his medical pursuits Here by taking a full course at the Med[ica]l
College. Your most Resp[ectfu]l friend & Servant, J.G. Swift.

ALS in DNA, RG 45 (Naval Records), Subject File, Commissions, Appointments, Applications, Acceptances, Oaths, Resignations, Discharges, and Similar Documents (NN): Surgeons and Surgeon's Mates, Unsuccessful Applications for Appointment.

From J[oseph] G. Swift

[New York City] 28th Oct. [1823]
My dear Sir, The Prospects brighten & I do not know but I may say
as you to to [*sic*] Mr. [Henry] Wheaton y[ou]r "victory is in New
York." However you will judge for yourself by the following *solemn
facts.* On Saturday last there was a meeting, of Republican[s] from
every Ward in the City, in favour of the People & on unanimous
agreement in a Ticket to be proposed as a substitute. Last night the
great Tammany meeting was called at 7. 20 minutes before about
300 got into the Hall & there was a cry for [William?] Paulding &
[John P.] Anthony to the Chair. Anthony having been recommended
by the Nom[inatin]g committee was actually permitted to take the
chair. He then cried citizens wait 'til the time 7—on the mark (when
from 2000 to 3000 were in the Hall) the Preamble to the proceedings
of the nom[inatin]g Committee was commenced & before even that
was half through the mass cried[,] away with that stuff give your
Ticket[,] the Ticket. Upon Anthonys pronouncing the first name

Gen. [Robert] Swartwout spoke audibly enough, with the lungs of Stentor, & in order Mr. Ch[airma]n I hold in my hand a substitution for your Ticket & I call on you to put the question for it in order. Ch[airma]n replied I know its in order but what shall I do. Swartwout put the substitute. Anthony then cried out to Swartwout to come up & help him keep order. I will says S[wartwout] if you will put the substitute, I will says Anthony who then was whispered to by the oppos[itio]n no—no—then says Anthony I will adjourn y[ou]r meeting. Swartwout said the People will not let you adjourn[,] put the substitute. Swartwout looked & acted in the most elegant style of self possession & the People crying that tried old Democrat Swartwout in the Chair says Swartwout my good friends the day is yours the Ticket is yours. It cannot be put down. I pray you be patient & keep order. Then there was a lull when Anthony said again I will adjourn, the People cried in a voice of Thunder No—then says Anthony I will leave the Chair & so turned off. Instanter the People cried Swartwout in the Chair—in He went & the result you see in the [New York] Patriot.

There was not a solitary being who spoke to the Committee Ticket save Major N[athan] Hale (Major [Christopher] Vandeventer knows him). [William A.?] Davis was in his speaking plan, but so dum[b] struck & crest fallen that he did not utter a Word. Yours most Resp[ectfull]y, J.G. Swift.

ALS in DLC, Galloway-Maxcy-Markoe Papers, box 68.

To HUGH NELSON, [U.S. Minister to Spain]

Washington, 1 November 1823

Dear Sir, I take the liberty of making you acquainted with Lieutenant [William T.] Washington of the United States Army who visits Europe for the improvement of his health and the cultivation of Military Science.

Lieutenant Washington is a graduate of West Point where he stood High, and is considered among the most promising officers in our service.

I feel confident that you will cheerfully afford him any facilities which may be in your power & effect the laudable objects which he has in view. With great respect & esteem I am your obedient servant, J.C. Calhoun.

Typescript in NcD, Francis Warrington Dawson Papers. Note: An endorsement on this letter reads: "Now Vice President of the United States."

To "Gen[era]l" R[obert] Swartwout, [New York City?]

Washington, 9th Nov. 1823

My dear Sir, The hatred of the enemy show[s] how conspecious and effective ["a" *interlined*] part you have acted in the great contest, which has just terminated; nor does he alone bare testimony. All of our friends concur in attributing much to your energy, and good conduct. It is a glory of no ordinary kind. The victory was over a foe prepared and powerful, and whose triumph would have prostrated the best interest of the country. Tho' the battle is won, let us not commit the error of many, otherwise able generals, ["neglect" *interlined*] to secure the fruits of our victory. The Radical is fallen, but much remains to ["be" *interlined*] done to give a permanent ascendency to sound principles and enlightened national policy. Our strength is in our principles and policy; in the pure democracy of the one, and the true wisdom of the other.

Move on as you have commenced, and New York will obtain a power and influence in the nation at once satutary [*sic*] to the community and honorable to the State. With great regard I am & &, J.C. Calhoun.

ALS in NN, Robert Swartwout Papers. Note: "The great contest, which has just terminated," refers to elections for members of the N.Y. legislature, in which those who favored giving the vote for Presidential Electors to the people had reportedly triumphed over those who favored the legislature's retaining the selection of Electors.

To O[gden] Edwards, [New York City?]

Washington, 23d Nov. 1823

My dear Sir, The meeting of Congress which is just at hand, renders it necessary, that we should fix definitely on our course in relation to several important points and among others in relation to a Congressional caucus. It is a subject surrounded with difficulties, which I will state, so as to inable you to judge of the course, that ought to be pursued.

As far, as I can judge, and I have been an attentive observer, I think it doubtful whether a caucus nomination will not defeat the election of any of the candidates on whom it may fall. I feel quite confident, that no State, but Virginia[,] Pennsylvania, Delaware and New York is inclined to such nomination, and that it would immediately combine a large majority of the rest of the Union against it. But this is not all. It is quite certain, that the friends of the other candidates will immediately call a convention of delegates to make a nomination ["to" *canceled*] against the caucus. Nor will there be any insurmountable difficulty in the course. Each Congressional district would appoint one, and where the member of Congress had the confidence of his constituents he would be nominated. It is easy to see, that a Caucus nomination would be defeated by the convention nomination. It is certain that it would be defeated in Penn-[sylvani]a, for in that State the nomination by caucus by the members of the legislature has for many years been abandoned, as too unpopular; and that by convention substituted. I should consider its defeat as pretty certain in your State also, in the present state of the publick mind; for besides the superior fairness of a convention nomination, those very arguments in favour of giving the choice of electors to the people, would apply to a convention nomination. Should we be on the side of a caucus nomination, we will be seperated from the people, which must prove fatal. Besides it is ascertained, that the friends of Gen[era]l [Andrew] Jackson, Mr. [John Quincy] Adams and Mr. [Henry] Clay will oppose a caucus; & should our friends in Congress advocate it, we would be thrown into the Ranks of Mr. C——d's [that is, William H. Crawford's] radical friends, which could not fail to weaken us, and impair our standing with the people. In addition to these views, I may add, that it is fully ascertained, that Mr. C——d is stronger, by far with the members of Congress, than with the people and there might be some hazard in Caucus, without ["any" *canceled and then interlined*] advantage to compensate it.

For these reasons, my friends are of the opinion, that we ought to take grounds in Congress against a caucus by the members of Congress; and in order that the people may fully understand our grounds, the subject ought to be brought into discussion in Congress. In fact there is little doubt it will be so brought by the members from Tennessee, who are instructed by the Legislature of the State. By taking our grounds against it in the discussion, we will have the advantage of acting on principles, and being on the popular side; and if a caucus should be attempted to join in the call of a convention of delegates to make a nomination. I have no doubt, but that our Penn[sylvani]a friends would prefer a convention, and if the legislature of that State does any thing, it will be to recommend their members to use their exertions to obtain a call of a convention. Should it be thought advisable to do any thing in your legislature; I would advise the same course. It is more constitutional, more popular, less liable to abuse and will prevail over the caucus system. Unless it should become necessary to act, the better way would be to let things take their course. We stand on truth, and principles, which if events take their own direction must prevail. Should our cause grow as much in the next six ["months" *interlined*] as in the last, the election would not be doubtful. But should it become necessary to act, we ought to take care never to seperate from principles, or the popular side.

Let me hear from you on these important topicks. I value your judgement much, and I hope it will be found in accord with our present opinion.

Our friends are sanguine in North Carolina & Georgia. In the latter State there is another election before the choice of electors, and the small majority of Radicals will only tend to unite our friends so as to secure the victory next fall. Sincerely, J.C. Calhoun.

ALS in MHi, G.L. Paine Papers. NOTE: Edwards (1781–1862), was a native of Conn. He was in N.Y. a judge, state legislator, and unsuccessful Whig nominee for Governor.

By L.H. Clar[ke, New York City, 1823]. Among the Calhoun pamphlets at Dartmouth is a copy of *Report of the Trial of An Action on the Case, Brought by Silvanus Miller . . . Against Mordecai M. Noah . . . for an Alleged Libel* (New York: J.W. Palmer, 1823), upon which is inscribed "Hon[ora]ble J.C. Calho[un] From L.H. Clar[ke]." Clarke was a N.Y. court reporter. Printed pamphlet in NhD, John C. Calhoun Pamphlet Collection.

From Ch[arle]s Fisher, [Raleigh, N.C., 1824]. Fisher sends to Calhoun a pamphlet entitled *Debates on Mr. Fisher's Resolutions Against Caucuses in the House of Commons of North-Carolina. In Dec. 1823* (Raleigh: J. Gales & Son, 1824) and endorses the pamphlet "Ch[arle]s Fisher to Mr. Calhoun." Printed pamphlet in NhD, John C. Calhoun Pamphlet Collection.

Andrew Norris, Walnut Grove, S.C., to "Col." John E[wing] Colhoun [Jr.], Columbia, S.C., 1/31/1824. "I have lately received from your Brother [James Edward Colhoun] a letter in which he mentions to me the want of some pecuniary assistance. Particularly to a transaction between him and J.C. C[alhoun] relative to an exchange of Negroes in April 1822 in which exchange he fell in Debt to J.C. C[alhoun] $1147.47[;] this sum he wishes you to settle for him with the interest that may have accrued thereon since that time with Mr. J.C. C[alhoun] as soon as you Possibly can as he is in much want of it—the unusual expense he is at (as you may expect) far exceeds his income; when you settle this sum for your Brother he ["he" *canceled*] will deduct it from the integral part of the Debt you owe him." Norris mentions other business matters about which John Ewing Colhoun should write to James Edward Colhoun. ALS in ScU-SC, James Edward Colhoun Papers.

From J A M E S L E G A R É F R E E R

Philadelphia, 27th Febr[uar]y 1824
D[ea]r Sir, The slight acquaintance which I had with you, when a youth (at Dr. Waddle's [*sic*; Moses Waddel's school]) would not warrant the liberty I take of addressing you on the present occasion; nor have I any friends or patrons to extol my merits or grant me a recommendation; but, Sir, my situation demands that I should make some desperate effort for its relief. I have neither friends, money, or any occupation whereby I can possibly subsist. From most desperate exertions I have been enabled to attend two courses of medical lectures in this place; but for want of pecuniary means I am debared taking the degree as conferred at this Institution, 'tho' should I be so fortunate, it would require means that I could not possibly command, to establish myself as a practitioner. Thus have I plainly unfolded my real situation and have only to ask you, to endeavour to gain me ["a situ(?)" *canceled*] an appointment, 'tho' its emolument should be but sufficient to afford me a subsistance. Trusting that you will excuse the liberty I have taken and that you will do something for the relief of my unpleasant situation, I subscribe myself Your's respectfully, James Legaré Freer.

N.B. I am thirty year's of age and a native of S.C.

ALS in NNC, Jay Family Papers.

From DAN[IE]L WEBSTER, [Representative from Mass.]

Saturday morning [February 28, 1824]

My Dear Sir, I wish to see you, for a half hour, this morning or Evening, as may best suit your leisure, in regard to this troublesome business of the road over the Public Grounds [of the Watertown Arsenal] at Washington [*sic*; Watertown, Mass.]. Some of my Constituents have sent me a Petition to Congress, on that subject, which I am unwilling to present, or at least to have it acted on, if any other mode of accomplishing the proper end could be thought of. I am very much inclined to think that what is called the "compromise rout" is most expedient to be adopted, in relation as well to the accomodation of the public travel, as to the more particular interest of the U.S. Considering the present posture of the case, it has occurred to me that perhaps this course might properly enough be taken. Let the Petition be presented, & referred to the Military Com[mitt]ee. On your being informed of this, a letter might be written from your Department, to the persons to whom you gave your assent, stating that the subject was before Congress, & intimating that it might be inexpedient for them to act on your permission until the sense of Congress should be expressed. The immediate effect of this course, I am very confident, would be an ["immediate" *canceled*] agreement of the parties among themselves; an event much to be desired. The Gentlemen interested on both sides of this controversy are highly respectable, & I am anxious that the affair should take ["such" *canceled*] a direction the most likely to terminate in an amicable result.

The bearer will wait for a line in answer. Most truly, Y[ou]rs, Danl. Webster.

ALS in MHi, G.F. Hoar Papers (microfilm edition of The Papers of Daniel Webster, roll 4, frame 4020); PC in *The Writings and Speeches of Daniel Webster* (1903), 16:91–92. NOTE: An EU on the ALS reads: "Concerning objections to the passage of a Road over public grounds at ["Washington" *canceled*] Watertown." Another EU provides the date "1824."

From [ANDREW JACKSON]

Washington, March 14th 1824

Gen[era]l Jackson returns his compliments to the Secratary of war, acknowledges the receipt of his note of yesterday, and informs him that by appointment he is to meet the committee of the Senate on military affairs on Monday 10 oclock A.M., before whom there are some very important business. The General, if it meets the convenience of the President of the united States [James Monroe], would prefer to pospone the receipt of the Medal proposed to be delivered; untill Tuesday next 11 oclock. The Gen[era]l requests to be informed whether this alteration will meet the approbation of the President.

ALU in InU, War of 1812 Manuscripts.

To JOHN FLOYD, Chairman of the House Committee on the Occupation of the Columbia River

Department of War, April 19th 1824

Sir, In answer to your letter requesting me to communicate to the "Committee on the occupation of the Columbia, or Oregon River, any facts or views which may be in the possession of the War Department, relative to the proposed occupation of that River in a military point of view, the ease with which troops may be marched to that point, and the importance in checking foreign encroachments, and controuling the Indians within our Territory," I have the honor to state that on an examination of the files of this Department, I have not been able to find any information of the kind referred to by your letter.

For the facility with which troops may be marched to the point contemplated to be occupied, I would refer the Committee to the report of the Quarter Master General which accompanied my letter to the President of the United States [James Monroe] of the 17th of February last. There is no doubt, but that the occupation of the mouth of the Oregon, would give the government more complete controul over the Indians within our Territory, west of the Rocky mountains, and tend to check the encroachments of foreign traders in that quarter; but it is believed that so long as the Traders of the British Fur Company have free access to the region of the Rocky mountains from the various posts, which they hold upon our northern Boundaries, they will in a great measure monopolize the Fur Trade west of the Mississippi, to the almost entire exclusion in a few years of our Trade. J.C.C.

FC in DNA, RG 107 (Secretary of War), Reports to Congress from the Secretary of War, 1803–1870, 2:304 (M-220:1); PC in Jameson, ed., *Correspondence*, pp. 217–218.

From J O H N R O S S, [Cherokee Delegation]

Washington City, April 20th 1824

Sir, When I last had the honor of an interview with you accompanyed by Gen[era]l [Robert] Houston, you will recollect that I laid before you a plat of Lewis Ross' reservation as run out agreeably to its location by the treaty of 1819, and also exhibiting the survey as made by the United States Surveyor agreeably to your order, in consequence of John Spears [*sic*; Speers] setting up a claim for a life ["estate" *interlined*] reservation, and also the surveys made under the authority of the State of Tennessee, by which you will discover the survey as made for John Spears ["under your order," *interlined*] came in contact with a part of Lewis Ross' claim as secured to him by Treaty, and that the reservation laid off for John Spears was sectioned off & sold by the State of Tennessee; in consequence of these circumstances, a part of Lewis Ross' claim is involved by litigation with Spears and the State of Tennessee. In addition to the verbal statements made to you by Gen[era]l Houston on the subject of Spears' claim for a reservation, I beg leave to lay before you ["a copy of" *interlined*] his letter to me on the subject. And I am requested by Lewis Ross to say that When these facts are made known, that you will at once see that he has been unjustly led into ["useless" *interlined*] difficulties and expense by the representations made to the Department in favor of Spears' claim, and as it cannot be the intention of the Government to make the reservations of less value than contemplated by the parties under the provision of the Treaty stipulation, nor to subject them to unnecessary litigation in law, it is confidently expected that you will reinvestigate the subject, in the end that the land reserved to him under the Treaty of 1819 may be secured to him without further Trouble & expence, or otherwise should the Government insist that Spears ought to have a reservation he would be willing to surrender his claim altogether provided the Government would pay him a reasonable price for it; or else pay him the value of the difference of the land as secured to him by Treaty and as laid off for him by your Order in consequence of Spear's claim. These propositions I am directed to state, are made solely with the view and a desire to be freed from an unjust and an unnecessary law suit, produced by the contravening claim allowed to Spears by the Government. I therefore beg your early attention and decision of the subject. I beg leave further to add that on my arrival in this city, I handed you a letter from Ja[me]s Brown in relation to Charles McClung instituting a suit against him for the land granted to him by reservation, you will please to inform me whether the subject of that letter has been acted on, and the result. I have the honor to be Sir, Y[ou]r V[e]ry Ob[edien]t H[um]ble Serv[an]t, Jno. Ross.

ALS in TU, Penelope Johnson Allen Papers. NOTE: A Clerk's endorsement on this letter reads: "Washington Ap[ri]l 20 1824. Cherokee delegation, East of the Mississippi—Relative to the Reservation of Lewis Ross, and the difficulty occasioned by the interference of the reservation selected by Speers with it." A second endorsement reads: "information as to the intruders on the Cherokees has rec[eive]d—the delegation that they are more numerous than ever, since Capt. [Archibald R.] Turk burned their houses &c."

From W[ILLIAM] H[ENRY] HARRISON

Cincinnati, 11th May 1824

Sir, I beg the President to accept my thanks for his referrence to me of the application by Mr. Cassady [*sic*; George Cassedy, Representative from N.J.] for a copy of my official letters to the Secretary of War in relation to the movements of the N[orth] W[estern] Army in the Campaign of 1812.13.

I have not the least objection that copies of *all* my letters should be furnished him. So far from it if by any accident the files of the War office do not contain them all I will immediately upon being informed of it transmit ["the" *altered to* "a"] book to your office containing them—All in the hand writing of my Aid de Camp the Hon[ora]bl[e] Waller Taylor [of Ind.] now of the Senate of the U.S. & from which copies can be taken. I have the Honour to be Very Respectfully Sir y[ou]r Hum[ble] Serv[an]t, W.H. Harrison.

ALS in InHi, Harrison Miscellaneous Collection.

MEMORANDUM by John C. Calhoun

[*Ca.* June, 1824]

The enclosed letters were prepared on the occasion to which they refer[,] to be sent to the [House] Committee [investigating Ninian Edwards], but there being some uncertainty as to the State[men]t to which they refer, the Pres[iden]t [James Monroe; "and" *canceled*] Mr. [William] Wirt [Attorney General] and Judge [Secretary of the Navy, Samuel L.] Southard whom I consulted advised me not to send them. Mr. [John Quincy] Adams [Secretary of State] was doubtful, but inclined to think they ought to be sent. I informed Mr. [Daniel Pope] Cook [Representative from Ill.] at the time I passed the address, that I had not read it. I received ["it" *interlined*] by the morning mail and passed it without delay to him. It was in my possession about half an hour.

ADU in ScCleA. NOTE: Calhoun added an endorsement to this memorandum which read, "Letters proposed to be sent to Mr. [Daniel] Webster and the [House] Com[mit]tee on Gov[erno]r [Ninian] Edwards Memorial." The "enclosed letters" mentioned herein have not been identified.

To LEVI WOODBURY, [Governor of N.H.], Concord

Department of War, June 28, 1824

Sir, In pursuance of a request of the Governor of South Carolina [John L. Wilson], I forward to you herewith, a map of the State of South Carolina, together with a letter; which were transmitted to me for that purpose. I have the honor to be, Sir, very respectfully Y[ou]r Ob[edient] Serv[an]t, J.C. Calhoun.

LS in NhHi, Levi Woodbury Collection.

From JEFFERSON DAVIS

Lexington [Ky.], July 7th 1824
Transylvania Univer[sity]

Sir, The commission of Cadet granted the undersigned March 11th, and remitted to Natchez, on account of my absence was forwarded here. I accept it.

[I] am not able to go on before Sept. for reasons I will explain to the superintendent on my arrival. Yours &c, Jefferson Davis.

ALS in OFH, George W. McCrary Papers; PC in Haskell M. Monroe and James T. McIntosh, eds., *The Papers of Jefferson Davis*, 1:10–11. NOTE: A letter such as the above would normally be found in the War Department Records of the National Archives. George W. McCrary, among whose papers it is preserved, was Secretary of War under Rutherford B. Hayes.

Toast at a dinner for Commodore [John] Rodgers, Washington, 7/22/1824. "The Stars and the Stripes." PC in the Washington, D.C., *Daily National Intelligencer*, July 24, 1824, p. 3.

To President [JAMES MONROE, Oak Hill, Loudoun County, Va.]

Washington, 24th July 1824

Dear Sir, I enclose you a letter from Mr. [John] Norvell in relation to Mr. [John] Conard the Marshall of Pennsylvania.

He was formerly a member of Congress, and stood at that time very fair as a man of sound sense and great independence; and I have no doubt enjoys at this time the confidence of a large portion of the people of Pennsylvania.

I am, of course, not particularly acquainted with the facts, which may have been brought against him, but would ["suggest" *interlined*] the propriety at this particular period, of taking no step on them, unless absolutely necessary, without affording the Marshall an opportunity of explaining, and defending himself.

Mr. [Joel R.] Poinsett [Representative from S.C.] has acknowledged my letter and is disposed to accept; but had come to no conclusion. He, however, informs me, that I shall hear from him definitely in a few days.

I enclose the [Philadelphia] National Gazette, which contains the fullest account of the last news from Mexico. It is interesting. There can be no doubt but that French intrigue is at work there. With great and sincere regard, J.C. Calhoun.

ALS in ScU-SC, John C. Calhoun Papers; photostat of ALS in AzTeS, Information Exchange Database Collection. NOTE: Poinsett had been offered appointment as U.S. Minister to Mexico.

To "The President" [JAMES MONROE]

Washington, 14th Sep[tembe]r 1824

Dear Sir, I enclose for your consideration and decision the proceedings of the Courts Martial in the cases of Brevet Maj[o]r [Morrill] Marston, Capt. [James S.] Gray and L[ieutena]nt [Alfred] Mitchell, all of whom have been sentenced to be cashiered, but the two latter are recommended to be restored. The first is a very clear case; and altho' the court has recommended, that Maj[o]r Marston should be permitted to resign, I am of the opinion, that the sentence ought to be approved and carried into effect, in order to make the example the more stricking, and to avoid the long delay, which would follow, at so distant a post, by giving him the permission to resign.

The recommendation of the court in favour of Capt. Gray and L[ieutena]nt Mitchell, I think correct, for the reasons, which it has assigned. In the case of the latter, I do not think that Col. [Henry] Leavenworth [commander of Fort Atkinson, Council Bluffs], the officer ordering the court is free from blame. The whole affair was trivial and not deserving to be brought before a court martial, and the offer by the Col. not to proceed, if L[ieutena]nt Mitchell would resign, has the appearence of taking advantage of ["him, and" *altered to* "his situation"] which in some degree sanctions the charge brought against him by L[ieutena]nt Mitchell, in his defense, of oppression. With sincere regard and esteem I am & &, J.C. Calhoun.

ALS in MWA, Miscellaneous Manuscripts. NOTE: Marston was dismissed on 9/27 while Gray and Mitchell remained in the army.

To T[HOMAS] WORTHINGTON, [former Senator from Ohio]

Washington, 4th Sep[tembe]r [*sic*; October] 1824

Dear Sir, I received your letter of the 24th Sep[tembe]r by this morning's mail, and can assure you, that a visit to Ohio would have delighted me. I am of the impression, that not one State in this Union possesses greater advantages, and that in a short time, she will rank with the very first in population and wealth, provided the nation performs its duty as to internal improvement. My arrangement was to proceed along the line of the projected Canal to Lake Erie and on my return to take a short circuit through Ohio. The severe indisposition of one of my children [John C. Calhoun, Jr.] prevented me from carr[y]ing the arrangement into effect, and has postponed the pleasure of visiting your noble State to another period.

The time has not yet arrived for opening the bids. I wish you success, as I am never disposed to change those that I know will do well from past experience. With great respect I am & &, J.C. Calhoun.

ALS in OHi, Thomas Worthington Papers (published microfilm, Worthington Papers, roll 13, frames 488–490).

From V[IRGIL] MAXCY

Tulip Hill [Md.,] Nov. 14, 1824

My dear Sir, I enclose you a letter just rec[eive]d from a friend on the Eastern Shore of Maryland in which he desires me to make application for the admission of his only son [Tench Tilghman] into the military Academy. He is a gentleman of the highest respectability and I think, that the associations which the name of his son's grandfather still revives in Maryland, would render his appointment highly acceptable in this State. Permit me to add I should feel highly gratified if his wishes can with propriety be complied with & am With faithful Attachment always yours, V. Maxcy.

[P.S.] I go to Philad[elphi]a day after tomorrow & thence to New York. If you have any commands in either place should be happy to receive[?] them. I shall be there a fortnight.

[Enclosure]

Tench Tilghman to Virgil Maxcy, "Near Annapolis"

Near Easton, Talbot Co. E[astern] S[hore] of Md.
November 6th 1824

You are a father, my dear Sir; it would be superfluous therefore to attempt to describe to you the anxiety of a parent for the improvement and future welfare of his offspring. And yet I believe I may safely state that he, who has the good fortune to have several children to divide and share his affections, cannot appreciate that extreme solicitude, which too often preys upon the parent, who has had tie after tie severed, until he feels but one ligament entwining his heart, often with delight; but too often stretched and strained to agony.

The best course to make my boy a virtuous, well informed, and useful citizen is the chief object, the absorbing motive of my life. And after much reflection I have determined to endeavour to place him at West Point. To make him by obligation and gratitude a child of the Republic as well, as by nativity.

Certain that it would afford you pleasure to serve me on such an occasion, it has been for a year past my wish to desire you to make a communication for me on this subject to your distinguished friend, Mr. Calhoun. So long however as he was before the publick as a competitor for the presidency, tho' my judgement had selected him as the most consistent and fairest character among the candidates, I felt indisposed to make this communication. It has not only been the study of my life to act right; but I would willingly keep my motives above suspicion. This reason for delaying to make this ["communication" *canceled*] request of you has ceased to exist.

I have ever understood the first idea in organizing this school was to educate and train the sons of the soldiers of the Revolution; assuredly one of the most judicious modes, in which our country could testify its gratitude to this band of patriots and heroes. This work has been accomplished; that generation has been sent forth; and the community must be well satisfied with the effect; for the Institution is continued, increasing in strength, usefulness, and popularity.

I know not the rules, which now govern the selections; but this Institution was certainly brought within my consideration from the belief, that my boy had claims exceeded by few, if by any, now in a situation to receive its benefits. These I will succinctly state. His maternal grand father, Colo. Tench Tilghman, was selected by general [George] Washington, and taken into his family as early as 1776. I have in my possession letters, that would bear me out in the assertion, that he became and continued his confidential Aid till the close of the war. I need not state to you, Sir, that he was *the* Aid, selected by the Commander in Chief, as the chosen Messenger to bear to Congress the glorious news of the final victory, the surrender of York. The Congress bore their testimony to his services and worth by a conspicuous vote, and the presentation of a sword and horse. By Maryland he has been placed in a group where Washington and Fayette are the only other personages, and the painting is the conspicuous ornament of the Representatives Chamber of the State.

This gentleman left two daughters; but no male issue, no son to receive the profered boon of his Country's gratitude. My boy is the only remaining child of his eldest daughter, and bears his grand father's names. He was 14 in March last, and is tolerably advanced in his education. He has read Caesar and Lucian, is finishing Virgil and Cicero, and has commenced Xenophon. My wish is to ground him as thoroughly as possible at least in the classics usually read, before I send him to West Point—(understanding that the course there is destitute and defective in this essential of a finished education). I am by no means certain that I can prepare him, as I wish, for the usual time of entering, (June I beleive) in the year 1825. But I have made application thus early to endeavour to render it the more certain, and that I might have more time to give my arrangements for him the proper direction. I have therefore to request, should my application be successful, that the order, commission, or warrant to entitle him to present himself, a candidate for examination and admission, if it can be done, be so made out, as to authorise his application in 1825, or 1826. And if not too indefinite in 1827.

Why is it, that the course in this Institution is not more extended and complete. While we are putting some of our best ore into the furnace, forging it to the firmest texture, and skilfully preparing it with the keenest and most terrible edge, why should we not add the purest refinement, the finest potion, the highest temper. A fool hardy veteran, well practiced in battle, can sink a ship, or butcher an opposing regiment; but a polished scholar and a gentleman—a [William] Bainbridge can give a ten fold effect to victory. His urbane and courtly attack on ["the hearts of" *canceled*] the vanquished was far more powerful and the effects far more extensive, than the irresistable lightning of his cannon on their ship. His skilful gunnery riddled her hull, and the huge mass, and her gaping wounds were both swallowed by the ocean. But the impression, which he elegantly engraved on the hearts of the enemy, is truly ore pereminis.

Does not the highest, the purest concern for the happiness of our country dictate the most thorough and perfect moral and literary training for the youths, who will most probably become not only her future heroes; but be called to fill her highest civil stations. The man, who is surrounded by a halo of military glory will be conspicuous; will be popular in a free country. In a competition for civil station, depending on popularity, on the votes of the whole community—the ripest scholar—the most thorough bread statesman enters the lists with fearful odds against even a miteor [*sic*] hero. But if this hero has been taught only a thorough drill in the arts of destruction—his skill in the tactics of war only inciting and inflaming his ambition; the true happiness of his country will no[t] be in all—nay—in any of his thoughts—He will be seeking the bubble glory in the cannons mouth. He may, like Buonaparte make his country gigantic and terrible; but while the blaze of her glory is throwing a fearful light over surrounding nations, the flame, that feeds it, will be most grievously consuming and destroying her own vitals.

In these modern days, when we boast the sway of the better feelings and a milder philosophy—when Christian information, and we would fondly hope Christian principles too are on a more rapid and widely spread march to universal sway, if a remnant of soldiery be still necessary, is it not our bounden duty to endeavour by every means in their training to fill them also with peaceful knowledge? to liberalize their minds, and humanize—nay Christianize their hearts? Is not the Christian hero McDonnaugh [*sic*; Thomas Macdonough] among the most brilliant, the most precious ornaments of our gallant navy? I am far from wishing to see ["the" *interlined*] athletic and hardy portions of their education diminished; I would indeed extend them too. I would certainly have them trained as first rate cavalry; especially as mounted riflemen. And I would give them thorough training in the bold and useful as well, as healthful exercise of swiming. For this purpose a floating bathing house without much cost, would be safe and convenient; and assist also in inducing the excellent habit of personal cleanliness. But enough.

I will feel obliged to you to make a communication for me as soon, as your convenience will permit; and beg leave to assure you of the sincere respect and esteem, with which I am Y[ou]r Ob[e]d[ient] Ser[vant], Tench Tilghman.

P.S. If you have a spare copy of the laws and rules of the Institution, I would thank you for it.

ALS with En in DNA, RG 94 (Adjutant General), Application Papers of Cadets, 1805–1866, 148 (M-688:30, frames 381–382 and 401–408). NOTE: Tench Tilghman (1810–1874) who was appointed several years later, graduated from the Military Academy in 1832. He served in the Artillery before resigning from the U.S. Army in 1833, when he returned to Maryland, serving in the State militia from 1837 to 1861, when he entered Confederate service. He was Commissioner of Public Works in Md., 1841–1851, Superintendent of the military department of the Md. Academy, 1847–1857, U.S. Consul at Turks Island and at Mayaguez, 1849–1850, and later held several prominent posts.

From W[ILLIAM] H. ROANE, [former Representative from Va.]

Richmond, Nov. 24th 1824

My D[ea]r Sir, A visit to my farm which I had not seen for more than a month, has prevented an earlier acknowledgement of the receipt through our friend Mr. [George] Hay, of your ["esteemed" *canceled*] valued favour of the 10th Inst.

I do indeed consider it as a mark of your confidence & friendship, and ["believe me Sir" *canceled and* "take leave to assure you" *interlined*], that from our earliest acquaintaince, I have ["ever" *canceled*] felt a strong and involuntary desire to reciprocate all & every such manifestation; the cordiality & kindness which has ever marked your conduct to me, the consistency of your public course, the fearless & independent manner in which you have at all times declared your opinions, and the zeal & ability with which you have supported them, have all combined to ["make" *canceled and* "render" *interlined*] me your admirer and personal friend; and be assured there is nothing in my composition which renders such feelings incompatible with any existing, or probable difference of political opinion. Unless we differ much more than your letter to me would indicate we all here in Virginia have certainly done you great injustice: for it has been supposed & I really know not exactly from what cause, that you are particularly hostile to the opinions which Virginia has ever maintained in regard to the constitutional powers of the General Government. I had myself ["supposed" *canceled and* "believed" *interlined*] that you were disposed to [*ms. torn; one word missing*] to the Fed[era]l constitu[tio]n a construction much broader than the one agreed on by the Republican party in 1798. I am indeed happy to ["hear" *canceled and* "find" *interlined*] that in this respect I have been mistaken. No ["man" *canceled and* "republican" *interlined*] can desire a construction of that instrument other than the one adopted during Mr. [Thomas] Jefferson's Administration. You have also been considered in this State as friendly to a tariff, having for its ["exclusive" *interlined*] object the protection of manufactures, regardless of its consequences ["to the other great interest of the nation" *interlined*] to ["a" *canceled*] revenue from imposts. ["Thus supposed to entertain opintertain [*sic*] opinions so oposite to the" *canceled and* "Labouring under the imputation of these opinions it is not surprizin(g) that you are not a favourite in Virg(ini)a" *interlined*]. Whilst your patriotism & talents are acknowledged by all, you have become unpopular in this State in a ratio almost commensurate to your great ability to thwart & destroy those principles which with a great majority of the people here in Virginia have grown up into fixed habits of thinking, if not into prejudice. I have not myself ever believed that you entertained views of the ["theory &" *interlined*] principles of the constitution, whatever you might think of ["its" *canceled and* "their" *interlined*] application to the supposed necessities of the country much variant from those expressed in the letter before me. Nor have I for a moment ["thought" *canceled*] supposed that you would sanction any tariff of duties which ["would prostrate the agriculture & commerce of the country & which" *interlined*] did not closely & certainly combine the great objects of defence & revenue with a gradual and easy protection to our rising manufactures. I think a conversation with you last winter authorized this latter belief.

Being raised in the Virginia school, I early and strongly imbibed the politics which have distinguished her character and course as a member of the union.

I consider the Gen[era]l Gov[ern]m[en]t as one of very limited powers *quo-ad* all matters concerning the internal police or domestic happiness of the people; those being ["carefully" *canceled and* "cautiously" *interlined*] & wisely left by the constitution to the care and protection of the State governments. I consider that every power which ["is not" *canceled*] is not clearly and expressly granted to the Gen[era]l Gov[ern]m[en]t, for some defined or express purpose, is absolutely reserved ["by" *changed to* "to"] the States, either to be by them excercized for the happiness of the people or to prevent its excercize to their injury by the Gen[era]l Government: and that whenever implied or incidental powers of an original ["stamp" *canceled and* "substantive character" *interlined*] are claimed, that the States should be consulted as to their ["excercise" *canceled*; "existence" *interlined and then canceled*; "enforcem(en)t" *interlined*] or at least, that those who are to excercise should not themselves ["assume them" *canceled and* "be the sole judges of their existence & extent" *interlined*]. And I have ever viewed every infraction of these doctrines as, inevitably tending to the destruction of the government either by a dissolution or consolidation of the union.

I am Sir most forcibly struck with your view of the present situation of my beloved State. I have long felt the mortification of the fact that she has lost much of her former influence ["in the union" *interlined*] and without examining minutely into causes, have only consoled myself with a hope, that her position, extent of population and above all integrity of principle would sooner or later restore her to it. This subject is quite new to me & I ["frankly" *interlined*] acknowledge my ["utter" *canceled and* "entire" *interlined*] incapacity to take the correct view of it. ["Whatever remarks I may make are only such as occur at the moment & are offered with all possible diffidence to your superior judgement" *interlined*], but the picture which you draw of the present ["posture" *interlined*; and] condition of Virg[ini]a is too gloomy to receive my assent. It is true that she is at this moment most probably differing in regard to the important election now pending, from a majority of those States with whom she has

441

heretofore cooperated, on occasions not less important. That is a difference from its nature temporary; it must terminate in a short time & ought not nor cannot leave unpleasant recollections with the other States. It does not appear to me that, this fact or any other known to me amounts to a seperation of the interests or feelings of Virginia from the Gen[era]l Govt. or from her sister States. None of the great principles of her original union or of any subsequent alliance with any of the States are as far as I can percieve atall concerned in the pending contest, it being one on which individuals or States may freely & fairly differ. Permit me now to enquire what are some of the facts in regard to Virginia & her old associates and allies in those political struggles to which you refer. In the year 1798 Virginia became alarmed at the monstruous encroachment by the Gen[era]l Govt. on the constitution of the country: she sounded the tocsin to the whole ["union" *canceled and* "nation" *interlined*], summoning country and its relative [*ms. torn; several words missing*]ys of foreign nations have reque[*ms. torn; several words missing*]ement of measures and the excercise of [*ms. torn; one or two words missing*]ch the most fastidious disciple of the school of [17]98 cannot ["object" *canceled*] on principle object. Because an army[,] a navy[,] fortifications &c &c were then opposed it does not follow that they are now wrong; any more than because ["a" *canceled and* "protecting" *interlined*] tariffs[,] Bankrupt Laws &c are now ["opposed" *canceled and* "objected to as premature & partial in their operation" *interlined*] they may not at some future ["day" *canceled and* "time" *interlined*; "be" *changed to* "become"] necessary to the prosperity of the whole nation: The power to do these things has always existed, it is only its excercise which has been contested. Virg[ini]a as far as I know has fully acceeded to all the measure[s] of this class which have been suggested by the altered situation of the country or by the experience of the late eventful war.

I cannot but think you are mistaken as to the feelings of this ["State" *interlined*] towards the present administration. If ["Virg(ini)a" *canceled and* "she" *interlined*] is seperated from or opposed to it, I am ignorant of the fact. Engaged as this adm[inistratio]n has been in perfecting measures already begun & carrying the nation from a state of war to ["one" *canceled and* "that" *interlined*] of peace, its course has been tranquil[,] easy & uneventful compared to any previous time; and if Virg[ini]a has seen in ["its" *canceled and* "that" *interlined*] course nothing to praise & admire, I certainly think shee has manifested no marks of hostility to it. As far as our worthy president [James Monroe] is concerned I am certain there is no [*ms. torn;*

a few words missing] belief. The manifold evidences of the alla[*ms. torn; one or two words missing*]ative State which more than once has "sav[*ms. torn; one or two words missing*] near drowning he swam" are certain sureties that she will never ["*desert*" *canceled and* "abandon" *interlined*] him so long as he ["*proves*" *canceled and* "continues" *interlined*] true to ["*his country*" *canceled and* "the principles which have heretofore endeared him to her" *interlined*]. I do certainly think that Mr. Munroe has lost some ground in Virg[ini]a because of his supposed desire to obliterate the former traces & land marks of the great parties of the country, and to produce an amalgamation of them, which could not be durable & might ultimately divide & settle themselves on principles less desirable than those of their former seperation. ["*For*" *canceled*] there must ever be parties in the country & there can be no doubt, that their differences had better be based on abstract principles of controversy, ["*than on local*" *canceled*] than on measures of mere policy—the former are coextensive with the ["*nation*" *canceled and* "whole union" *interlined*]. The latter only appeal to local prejudices or sectional interests, & always subject the country to danger from designing politicians or ambitious demagogues. But even this cause has not ["*been strong enough to*" *interlined*] withdrawn Mr. Munroe from the affection of the people of ["*Virg(ini)a*" *canceled and* "this State" *interlined*]. We view ["*him*" *interlined*] as one of the last hopes of Virg[ini]a as a patriot and statesman who has rendered distinguished service to the country. For my self I entertain towards him no other than fillial affection.

I do not atall disagree with you as to the present unhappy state of things in the U. States—and not considering that any of the principles of ["*our*" *canceled and* "this" *interlined*] State are summoning them to vindica[*ms. torn; one or two words missing*] charter of their liberty. The summons [*ms. torn; one or two words missing*]regarded, but opposed & ridiculed by [*ms. torn; one or two words missing*]tes, and Virginion was by them charged with disaffection and hostility to the union. The ability[,] zeal & persevereance ["*however*" *interlined*] with which she ["*pressed &*" *interlined*] sustained her doctrines, ["*soon*" *interlined*] enlightened the whole ["*union*" *canceled and* "nation" *interlined*] as to the true principles of the constitution, and most of the States & all her neighbours, formed an alliance with her & succeeded in breaking down a power usurped & wielded against the liberty of the people. The struggle eventuated in a revolution as decisive & complete as was that of 1776. In those times the rights of the States was the watch word of every republican; they then thought that the happiness of the people & the perpetuity of the gov-[ern]m[en]t itself required that the Gen[era]l Gov[ern]m[en]t should not only not excercise any doubtful power, but should excercise those expressly granted, in a cautious[,] circumspect & sparing manner, always awaiting the maturity of events which might require their action. On all these points & many others then the order of the day Virg[ini]a now stands alone and is even much divided in herself. Can it then be ["fairly" *interlined*] said that she has seperated herself ["either" *canceled*] from the Gen[era]l Govt. or ["from her" *canceled*] deserted her quondam friends & allies? May not the present Isolated condition of Virg[i]nia in regard to the other States (if ["indeed" *interlined*] such be her condition), & even her divisions at home, be in part attributed to ["her the" *canceled*] her continued & persevering efforts to maintain the original principles of [*ms. torn; a few words missing*], & to their yielding to the gradual & [*ms. torn; a few words missing*]action of those principles to the State [*ms. torn; a few words missing*]y were ["found" *interlined*] when the struggle of [17]98 commenced? As far as these and all other constitutional principles are concerned in the seperation to which you allude, I do not think it can be fairly said that Virg[ini]a has deserted her allies or as yet (but God knows how soon she may) the principles on which that alliance was based. May not the ["declining if not" *interlined*] lost influence of Virginia be attributed to causes more certain than to this supposed ["self" *interlined*] seperation? causes which should excite the sympathy ["& regard" *interlined*] of the other States rather than that acerbity of feeling & tr[i]umphant exultation which has been sometimes manifested. Virginia in point of wealth (which is power) is ["now" *interlined*] poor indeed. This poverty has been ["in a great measure" *interlined*] superinduced by ["measures" *canceled and* "the policy" *interlined*] of the Gen[era]l Govt. against which her patriotism has forbid her to raise a single murmur ["of complaint" *interlined*]. The high discriminating duties ["which have been imposed" *interlined*] & the ["total" *interlined*] abolition of ["her" *canceled and* "our" *interlined*] valuable and convenient West India trade, have been continued causes of this impoverishment. To this may be added a decrease of population, owing to the ["continued" *interlined*] migration ["of her citizens" *interlined*] to the west, ["which" *canceled and* "whereby she" *interlined*] has ["been" *interlined*] drained ["as" *canceled*] of ["much wealth & nearly all her" *interlined*; "so many" *canceled*] men of spirit[,] enterprize & talents.

There can be no doubt but that on matters of mere policy many things must be done now, which ought not to have been done in the times to which I have alluded. The growing wealth[,] population & extent of the country are at stake in the pending contest. I have from its ["begining" *canceled and* "earliest commencement" *interlined*] been extremely desirous that Virginia should fold her arms & remain perfectly passive and ["in regard to the election, and ca" *canceled*] neuter in regard to the canvass, and only concern in the election so far, as to aid in perfecting the ascertained wishes of the other States. Having already given to the union 4 presidents, having no candidate now to offer & no strongly justifiable cause of preference among those presented to her, it would have been peculiarly auspicious to the resuscitation of her waning ["influence" *canceled and* "popularity" *interlined*] to have been thus courteous. In regard however to the election of Presid[en]t she has thought proper to pursue a different course, & will no doubt find herself in a minority. In regard to the other Branch of the subject ["she is not committed" *interlined*]. Such ["however" *interlined*] has been the interest in the election of a President that I am unable to say any thing of public opinion ["as" *canceled*; "in relation" *interlined and changed to* "in regard"] to that of Vice President, & can only speak my own opinions and wishes in relation to ["it" *canceled and* "that Subject" *interlined*]. What I have said above fully indicates them, but considering you as already & inevitably elected I should indeed be mortified[,] vexed & disappointed if Virg[ini]a does not give you ["a" *canceled and* "her" *interlined*] unanimous support. I ["can not" *canceled and* "am not" *interlined*] however ["say" *canceled and* "sanguine" *interlined*] that such will be the result. ["The frank if not blunt manner in which I have alredy apprized you of your standing with us forbids a sanguine hope as to the result." *interlined.*] Mr. [Albert] Gal[l]atin's withdrawal has left our electors ["free" *canceled*] to ["the" *interlined*] excercise of their own sound discretion.

If under existing circumstances Virg[ini]a should throw away her vote I do think that you ["&" *canceled*] as well as the States who have already elected you will have cause to complain. It will at least have a spiteful appearance. She will spit against the wind, or bite against a file ["instead of" *canceled*; "rather than" *interlined and then canceled*; "instead of making a virtue of necessity &" *interlined*] yielding with a good grace to the wishes of those who on similar occasions have yielded to hers. If oportunities should occur, enableing me to ["the" *canceled*] excercize to advantage the discretion given me in the P.S. of y[ou]r letter, I shall not fail to correct as far as possible all misapprehensions of your politics.

445

Thus my D[ea]r Sir have I intruded on your valuable & precious time a long letter, which cannot by possibility have presented a single Idea new to you. You will consider much of it as containing what I believe to be the sentiment of Virg[ini]a Rather than an exposition of my own, and all of it ["if you please" *canceled and* "I beg" *interlined*] as evidence of the sincere regard & esteem of y[ou]r friend, W.H. Roane.

ALS (retained copy) in ViHi, Harrison Family Papers.

From W[ILLIAM] H. ROANE, "Copy"

Council Chamber, Richmond
Dec. 1st 1824, ½ past 11 oC[l]ock

My D[ea]r Sir, I snatch a very hasty moment to acknowledge the rec[ei]pt of your favour of the 27th Ult. and to say to you that our college of Electors have this moment given ["in their vote" *canceled and* "the" *interlined*; "unanimously" *changed to* "unanimous"; "for" *canceled and* "vote of this State to" *interlined*; William H.] Crawford ["to be" *canceled and* "as" *interlined*] Pres[i]d[en]t and ["for" *canceled and* "to" *interlined*] *Nathaniel Macon* as *Vice Pres[i]d[en]t!*

I am not sufficiently master of my native language to express in ["terms of" *interlined*] suitable ["terms" *canceled and* "energy" *interlined*] my entire disapprobation of this latter vote, or my reasons for such disapproval & therefore shall not attempt it now. I am glad that you are already prepared to receive this inteligence, and will rest yourself with Philosophic composure on time and events, to devellope your political character & ["dispell" *changed to* "dispel"] the mistakes of Virg[ini]a ["in relation" *canceled and* "as" *interlined*] to your real opinions. You have *ample time* and oportunity to do so, & I ["trust" *canceled and* "hope" *interlined*] the day will ["come when it will be" *interlined*] be [*sic*] the pleasure and interest of Virginia to acknowledge her mistake ["and" *canceled*] in this respect and make you the best & amplest remuneration for whatever injury she has now done you. I beg ["that" *canceled*] you to permit no feeling whatever to attribute the vote of this day (here) to any other consideration than a supposed adherence to political principle. Had you not have been thus misunderstood your high reputation in every other particular would long since have rendered you the favorite of this State. Again I say that I have strongly disapproved the course of Virg[ini]a throughout this canvass. ["Consistency did not require her to vote

for Mr. Macon, for he was no more a candidate than (Albert) Gallatin & is not a favorite in Virg(ini)a" *interlined.*] It was one in which
she in truth felt no deep concern, & has suffered a few news-paper
editors to engender an unnatural & artificial zeal alike unbecoming
to her magnanimity of character and ["to her" *interlined*] true interest. I join in the wish that our private friendship may be far
beyound the reach of accident, & offer you the sincere benediction
of my friendship. W.H. Roane.

ALS (retained copy) in ViHi, Harrison Family Papers.

[Floride Colhoun Calhoun] to [Josiah S.] Johns[t]on, [Senator
from La.], 12/22/[1824]. "Mr. & Mrs. Calhoun, request the favour
of Mr. Johns[t]on's Company at dinner on Tuesday next at 5 OClock.
The favour of an answer is requested." LU in PHi, Josiah S. Johnston Papers.

To [JOHN QUINCY] ADAMS, [Secretary of State]

[Washington, 1824? or earlier]
D[ea]r Sir, M[a]j[o]r [Isaac] Robe[r]deau who has charge of the
mathematical instru[men]ts has left his office, and the French Killo-
grame cannot be had to day. I will transmit it tomorrow morning.
Yours &, J.C.C.

ALI in MnHi, Allyn Kellogg Ford Collection (microfilm).

To [PETER HAGNER]

[Georgetown, D.C., 1825 or earlier?]
D[ea]r Sir, We have some compa[n]y to dine with us to day and as
my cabbage are not near equal to yours, I will thank you for a few
heads. I am &, J.C.C.

ALI in NcU, Hagner Family Papers.

To [Samuel L.] Southard, "At Mrs. Hardy's," [1825 or earlier?].
"Permit me to introduce you to my friend Mr. Wiley, who informs
me that he has some business with you." ALS in NjP, Samuel L.
Southard Papers.

From C[hristopher] Vandeventer, [Washington, *ca.* 1/1825]. "Agreeably to your directions I have examined the report [of 12/15/-1824] of the Board of Tactics upon the Book entitled 'School of Cavalry &c,' by Lieut. [William Theobald Wolfe] Tone." Vandeventer feels that Tone's preface, singled out by the Board as marked by "reprehensible egotism" is, "besides its arrogance . . . used as a depository for the vanity & indiscretion of the writer." He feels, however, that the Board was too critical of Tone's work, too ready to condemn things that could be corrected. He recommends that a new board be established to compare Tone's work to the French system of cavalry and that it be ordered to report within two years the best system for adoption by the U.S. Army. ALS in DNA, RG 107 (Secretary of War), Letters Received (Unregistered Series), 1789–1860, U-1830 (M-222:28, frames 1544–1549).

[Floride Colhoun Calhoun] to [Josiah S.] Johns[t]on, [Senator from La.], 1/12/1825. "Mr. & Mrs. Calhoun request the favour of Mr. Johns[t]on's Company at dinner on Tuesday next, 5 OCl[oc]k. The favor of an answer is requested." LU in PHi, Josiah S. Johnston Papers.

From [DE WITT CLINTON, Governor of N.Y.]

Albany [N.Y.,] 4 February 1825

Sir, Mr. [Eliakim] Littell an enterprising, intelligent and respectable Citizen of Philadelphia will communicate to you a plan which he has projected for the promotion of education, literature and science, on an extensive scale. He has conferred with me on this subject. Approving its outlines and viewing you as a sincere and distinguished friend of these great interests, I have taken the liberty of recommending him and his plan to your favorable consideration. I have the honor to be with great respect Your most Ob[e]d[ien]t Se[r]v[an]t [De Witt Clinton].

Draft in NNC, De Witt Clinton Papers, Letterbooks, 6:398. NOTE: Copies of this letter were sent also to Thomas Jefferson, John Marshall, James Kent, William Wirt, and John Q[uincy] Adams.

From [THOMAS H. BENTON, Senator from Mo.]

Feb[ruar]y 7th [1825]

Mr. Benton's compliments to Mr. Calhoun—expresses to him the gratitude of Mr. John Jones for the prompt justice which has been done him—with a request from Mr. Jones to know if it would be possible to pay him [for his brick contract] in this city instead of returning him to Fort Jackson?

LU in DNA, RG 77 (Chief of Engineers), Letters Received, 1819–1825, Referred, 755.

To [THOMAS H. BENTON, Senator from Mo.]

War Department Feb[ruar]y 7th 1825

Mr. Calhoun presents his compliments to Col. Benton, and informs Col. B[enton], in answer to his note of this morning, that the course which has been pursued in regard to Mr. [John] Jones's petition is the only one that could be adopted consistently with the principles established for the accountability of the Engineer Department in reference to the monied transactions.

FC in DNA, RG 77 (Chief of Engineers), Miscellaneous Letters Sent, 1812–1848, 2:203.

From W. R. SWIFT

Alex[andri]a D.C., 10 Feb. 1825

Dear Sir, The die is indeed cast. I never was more surprised, at its [that is, the choice of John Quincy Adams for President by the House of Representatives] being effected the first ballot. I shall endeavour to submit as becomes a liege subject—in exercising a four years patience.

I trouble you with the present to request the goodness of you to remember the Washington N.C. applicants for the Military Academy as far as it is proper for you to do. They were disappointed last year but their friends encouraged them to hope for success the present, meanwhile I am assured they have been prosecuting the necessary branches of study for admission with untiring assiduity. I remain

449

with great respect & esteem Your very obed[ien]t S[ervan]t, W.R. Swift.

ALS in DNA, RG 94 (Adjutant General), Application Papers of Cadets, 1805–1866, 1824, 354 (M-688:34, frames 417–418). NOTE: Louis Quin and Alexander F. Telfair were the recommended applicants. In an ALS of 3/13/1825 to the Secretary of War, Telfair accepts the appointment proffered him on 2/21/-1825.

From DAVID BARTON, [Senator from Mo.]

Washington, 3d March 1825

Sir, Col. Nathan Boone, of Missouri, wishes the appointment of a Commissioner, or Surveyor, to mark the road to Mexico, proposed in a bill passed by Congress at the present Session.

Col. Boone is a worthy citizen, a superior woodsman, and suitably qualified for such service—he has been much employed in such duties in Missouri, and I believe would perform such service to the satisfaction of the President [James Monroe]. Very respectfully, David Barton.

ALS in DNA, RG 77 (Chief of Engineers), Letters Received, 1819–1825, Referred, 785. NOTE: An EU reads: "To be appointed."

To [CHRISTOPHER VANDEVENTER]

Washington, 11th March 1825

My dear Sir, I needed not the additional testimonial of your communication of the 2d Inst. to satisfy me of the warmth and sincerity of your friendship. During the long course of my administration of the Department, I have at all times witnessed in you the most sincere & disinterested attachment, not only to me personally, but to the reputation of the Department and the interest of the Country. I am fully aware of the character & the object of the attacks, which have been made on you. They never in any degree impaired my confidence in your integrity. For your kind wishes for my future welfare accept of my sincere acknowledgement; and permit me to avail myself of the occasion to assure you, that I never can be indifferent to your success in life, and I shall at all times be happy should it be in my power to contribute to it. Should you deem my services on any occasion important to ["it" *canceled*] you, I enjoin it on you to command them freely and without hesitation. With sincere regard I am &c. &c., J.C. Calhoun.

Ms. copy in DNA, RG 107 (Secretary of War), Letters Received (Unregistered Series), 1789–1860, H-1829 (M-222:25, frame 252). NOTE: An AES dated 8/28/1828 reads, "I have compared the within with the original & certify it to be a true copy. John S. Ball, Town Clerk of Erie, N.Y." An ALS of 3/10/1828 from J[ames] Hamilton, Jr., to Secretary of War J[ohn] H. Eaton transmits "accompanying Documents" to be placed on the War Department files, as Vandeventer requested and Eaton agreed to.

To DAN[IE]L S. HENDERSON, Secretary

Washington, March 13th 1825

Sir, I accept with pleasure the honor of membership confered on me by the Clariosophic Society [of South Carolina College], which I request you to make known to the Society with my sincere acknowledgements for the mark of approbation and esteem. I feel that an apology is due for the delay, which I must request the favour to make through you to the society. The delay is in no degree to be attributed to a want of respect to the society, but wholly to the pressure of official duties, during the late session of congress, which compelled me to suspend my correspondence. Your letter making known my election was placed on the file of my private correspondence and has shared in the common delay. With great respect I am &C, Jno. C. Calhoun.

FC in ScU, University Archives, Clariosophic Society Papers, Debate & Roll Book (No. 3), 1820–1826, pp. 204–205; PC in *The Clariosophic and Euphradian Societies, 1806–1931*, p. 23.

To [Micah Sterling?, Watertown, N.Y., *ca.* 3/1825]. In this undated fragment (the bottom half of four pages) Calhoun mentions a mutual classmate who he has recommended to the Postmaster General for a position, as well as an unnamed pension applicant whose claim has been at least partially allowed. About the recent Presidential elections, he says, "The great body of those, who sustained the administration and its measures, had but little choice between Mr. [John Quincy] Adams and G[e]n[era]l [Andrew] Jackson; and had not important principles been set at naught ["there would have been" *interlined*] a general disposition to acquiesce in the election of either. But as it has gone [*end of page; another page fragment begins*] is, that the man elected has been elected by the influence and exertions of a single individual [Henry Clay], acting against the known will of his State and constituents, and that he who has been so elected, has rewarded him by whose efforts he succeeded, ["by" *canceled and "with" interlined*] the highest" [*and here this page ends*]. ALU (fragment) in ScU-SC, John C. Calhoun Papers.

SARAH B. LOWNDES to [Floride Colhoun] Calhoun

[Charleston,] May 18th, 1825

My dear Madam, In the Year 1823 Mr. [Joel R.] Poinsett [Representative from S.C.] at my request made application for a Cadets Warrant for West Point, for my Son Edward Tilghman Lowndes. Mr. Poinsett informed me that my Son's name was entered in the Book with the names of other applicants. As yet we have heard nothing on the subject. My Son was 15 y[ea]rs old in Jan[uar]y last, and could we succeed in procuring a Warrant for him we should feel ourselves much indebted. With my very best wishes for your health and happiness, and also for all who are dear to you, I am my dear Madam with great Respect and affection Very sincerely Your's, Sarah B. Lowndes.

ALS in DNA, RG 94 (Adjutant General), Application Papers of Cadets, 1805–1866, 1823, 105 (M-688:24, frames 510–511). NOTE: An EU referred this letter to the Engineer Department. Sarah Bond I'On had married Thomas Lowndes, who served as a Representative from S.C. during 1801–1805.

From JOHN J. MORGAN

City of New York, Decem[be]r 19th 1825

Sir: Permit me to recommend to you Mr. John C[hamplin] Church of this city. He is a young gentleman of respectability: of good appearance, manners, education and connexions.

He is desirous to obtain a Lieutenancy in the Marines: and should he be appointed, I am quite persuaded will make a good officer. Very respectfully, John J. Morgan.

ALS in DNA, RG 127 (U.S. Marine Corps), Adjutant and Inspector's Department, 1798–1949, Personnel Records, Officers, Applications for Commissions, 1815–1831 and 1844–1846.

To Asbury "Dickens" [*sic*; Dickins], Secretary of the C[olumbian] Institute, [Washington], 12/20/1825. In conformity to the rules of the organization, Calhoun wishes his membership to be enrolled in "the class of Physical Science." ALS in DSI, Columbian Institute Records.

To [William] Lambert, Treasurer of the C[olumbian] Institute, 12/20/1825. "I enclose $5 the amount due on my admission as a resident member . . . ." ALS in DSI, Columbian Institute Records.

To [Richard] Rush, 1/19/[1826?]. "Mr. & Mrs. Calhoun request the favour of Mr. & Mrs. Rushe's company at dinner on Wednesday next at 5 o'clock. The favour of an answer requested." ALU in NjP, Rush Family Papers (published microfilm of The Letters and Papers of Richard Rush, reel 12, item 5788).

From JOHN CHAMPLIN CHURCH

Newyork [City,] 21 Jan[uar]y 1826
Sir, I have the honor to enclose, a letter [of 12/19/1825] in my favor from Jno. J. Morgan Esq. and have taken the liberty to annex a Copy of my application to Mr. [Samuel L.] Southard [Secretary of the Navy].

Should it be convenient for you to further my views you will confer a favor, which will be gratefully remembered—on Sir—with great respect Your Ob[edien]t Serv[an]t, Jno. Champlin Church.

ALS with En in DNA, RG 127 (U.S. Marine Corps), Adjutant and Inspector's Department, 1798–1949, Personnel Records, Officers, Applications for Commissions, 1815–1831 and 1844–1846. NOTE: A copy of Church's letter of 1/21 to Southard is enclosed. An AEI by Calhoun reads: "Submitted for the consideration of the Sec[re]t[ar]y of the Navy." An answering EU reads: "Ans[wer] Mr. Calhoun—rec[eive]d & filed—that you are acquainted with the late arrangements for filling the M[arine] C[orps] & therefore ["I" interlined] need only state to you that the chance of Mr. C[hurch] is not very flatt[er]ing."

From BOLLING HALL, [former Representative from Ga.]

Ellerslie [Ala., illegible date; "Decr" altered to "Jany"] 1826
Sir, My last letter to you, when you were Sec[retar]y of war remains unanswered: this I attribute to the frank and unreserved manner in which I expressed my sentiments on some of your official Acts, al-

though you had previously requested me to do so; but more particularly, I presume because my weight and influence in the political scale, was too ["insignificant" *canceled and* "small" *interlined*] to effect your future prospects of promotion. Why did you not recollect that the sturdiest oak in the forrest has often fallen a victim to insignificant insects, and altho humble in talents and of small influence among ten millions of people, yet when the scales were equally poised, the dust of the earth might incline the balance. I know that great men cannot bear with patience to have their faults set in array before them, & that the fri[e]nd who attempts to perform this unthankful service incurs their displeasure. I will not insult your understanding by quoting authorities from ancient or modern history to prove the truth of this position: no Sir for I still revere your talents, they are of a superior order, and when you first came into Congress there was no man in whom I had more implicit confidence, nor was this confidence impaired untill, you and Henry Clay held your secret Caucus in the Senate Chamber [in 1816?] to the exclusion of such men as N[athaniel] Macon and others whose patriotism was never doubted, and this too for the ostensable object of promoting Mr. [James] Monroes election, although you knew that [William H.] Crawford had explicitly forbid his name to be used as a candidate. I could not see, nor do I yet understand why you were so anxious to place Mr. Monroe in the executive chair, who you had frequently in my presence pronounced not capable of discharging the duties of Sec[retar]y of war. Mr. Monroe is a man who I respect, and believed him to be an honest and upright politician, when left to himself; but he was surrounded by men ["whose object" *interlined*] was their own aggrandizement—the errors which he committed serve as precedents for almost every violation which can be committed on the Constitution, and they have been improved & enlarged by the present incumbent [John Quincy Adams], ["so" *interlined*] that we have no land marks to guide our political barque (for the Constitution has become a meer nose of wax) except the few who remain firm to the old republican principles, which carried ["us" *interlined*] safe through the revolutionary struggle and guided our way to present prosperity—but those few are now in the back ground; Although they see ["us" *interlined*] toss'd by the waves and driven by the winds toward the fearful gulph of Consolidation and irresponsibility, they have not the command of the rudder, nor the power to cast the sheet anchor. Pardon me when I say I charge much of this to you? It is a great compliment, but a severe censure [*ms. torn; one or two words mutilated*] perhaps I have erred.

David B. Mitchell, former Indian agent whose life has been devoted to the service of his country, was sacraficed, not because he had violated the laws (for the federal Court has decided the right of the negroes to be in Bowen who brought ["them" *interlined*] to the agency) but because he was a friend to Crawford—while such creatures as [John] Clark and [John] Crowell were basking in the sunshine of executive favor—Crawford to whom Monroe was indebted for his elevation, and you for the office which you held under him, was sacrificed for his unyielding integrity and firmness, while the infamous Ninian Edwards, was promoted and bouyed up, by Monroe, Adams & Calhoun, at the time when it was well known that he was traducing and calumniating the character of a man whose fault was his virtue, and then labouring under the most severe affliction. Judge [William] Smith of your State fell a sacrafice for his attachment to Crawford, and many others turned out of office, much, better ["men" *canceled*] than ["those" *canceled and* "some" *interlined*] who fill'd their place. Judge Smith is again elected in despite of the opposition. When I see such old veterans taking the field, a hope is revived that we shall still be able to conquor the uncircumcis[e]d philistians; and I am not with["out" *interlined*] hope that I shall again see you in the foremost ranks defending the rights of your much injuried Country, not holding a meer sinacure office, 'tho in name the second in the nation, where your talents are buried, and you have not even the power to call a member [of the Senate] to order; if the name of office, and the salary attached to it are objects, you have them. I know you will spurn the idea. [*Ms. torn*]ation and intrigue, we have been divided and subdivided [un]till we are shorn of our strength as Sampson was of his hair by his faithless delilah. Our ey[e]s have not yet be[en] put out, tho ambition has blinded many who are still groping in the dark and the sport for their surrounding enemies. Your support of the compensation law was the first fatal stab given to the influence of the Republican party of which you know I then ["predicted the effect" *canceled and* "warned you of the consequence" *interlined*]—if my suspicions in respect to you are founded in error it would afford me great pleasure to be corrected—for it ["is" *interlined*] with great reluctance I ever abandon an old friend. Yours Respectfully, Bolling Hall.

[P.S.] I had just finished ["my" *altered to* "this"] letter when I rec[eive]d my papers from Washington in which were contained a copy of a letter said to be written by E[lijah] Mix, charging you with receiving a part of the profits of the infamous Rip Rap contract; and your prompt and pathetick call on the the [*sic*] H. of Representatives for a free and full investigation of the vile calumny. I am truly gratified to find that Mr. [John] Floyd of Virginia, a firm and decided friend of Mr. Crawford has taken an open and decided stand to repell such premeditated slander—but I regret to see that [Daniel Pope] Cook the son in law, & accomplice of N[inian] Edwards in his premeditated attack on Crawford has volunteered his service in your favor ["from" *canceled*]. What would be your feelings if the Sec[retar]y of State, the Sec[retar]y of War, & the Post master Gen[era]l, in this case were to shew the same distinguished marks of respect for Mix, as were conferred on Edwards when he was the known Calumniator of Crawford[?]

ALS (retained copy or draft) in A-Ar, Bolling Hall Papers.

To [Richard] Rush, 2/10/[1826?]. "Mr. Calhoun accepts with pleasure the invitation of Mr. & Mrs. Rush for Friday next, and regrets that the indisposition of Mrs. Calhoun prevents her acceptance." ALU in NjP, Rush Family Papers (published microfilm of The Letters and Papers of Richard Rush, reel 12, item 5842).

To [James Barbour,] Sec[retar]y of War, [*ca.* 2/15/1826]. Calhoun encloses a letter [*not found*] from [Benjamin L.] Beall [a Clerk in the War Department]. He supports the raising of Beall's salary to $1,000, an action which he intended to take "last year" but was unable to accomplish. ALS in DNA, RG 107 (Secretary of War), Letters Received (Unregistered Series), 1789–1860, C-1827 (M-222:24, frame 931).

To [James Barbour, Secretary of War, *ca.* 2/17/1826]. An entry in a register of letters received indicates that the War Dept. received a letter on this date from Calhoun "transmitting application of S[arah] B. Lowndes on behalf of her son as Cadet." The letter was referred to the Engineer Dept. Entry in DNA, RG 107 (Secretary of War), Registers of Letters Received, 1800–1870, 20:70 (M-22:20).

From [Thomas Jefferson, 3/23/1826]. An entry in Jefferson's "Epistolary Record," compiled by himself, indicates he wrote a letter of this date to Calhoun introducing Th[omas] J. R[andolph], Jefferson's grandson. Abs in DLC, Thomas Jefferson Papers, Epistolary Record (Presidential Papers Microfilm, Jefferson Papers, reel 57).

To "Editor of the New Journal," 6/6/1826. Calhoun requests "that his subscription be delivered to his Georgetown address." (The Washington, D.C., *National Journal* is probably the newspaper referred to.) From *American Book Prices Current,* 1984, vol. 90, p. 19.

Records of the Pendleton Farmers' Society, 9/14/1826–7/14/-1831. Calhoun attended a meeting of the Society on 9/14/1826, at which time he was proposed by the President, John Ewing Colhoun, as a resident member. On 10/12/1826 Calhoun again attended a meeting and was elected to membership. Calhoun attended meetings on Aug. 9, Oct. 11, and Oct. 12, 1827; Oct. 9, 1828; July 9, Sept. 10, Oct. 8 and Oct. 9, 1829; July 8, Aug. 12, and Oct. 15, 1830; and July 14, 1831. Scattered ms. entries in ScCleA, Pendleton Farmers' Society, Minutes, 1824–1833, pp. 69–144.

To Gen[era]l A[LEXANDER] McCOMB [*sic*; MACOMB] "of the War Dept."

[Washington] 8th Dec[embe]r [1826]

D[ea]r Gen[era]l, If circumstances will permit, I would be much gratified with the success of the enclosed application.

The father of the young man is an old acquaintance of mine and a very worthy man. The writer of the letter of application [John Belton O'Neall], is the Speaker of our [S.C.] House of Rep[resentati]ves and one of our most esteemed citizens. With much respect I am & &, J.C.C.

ALI in Pierre Labouchere Autograph Collection, Bibliothèque Municipale, Nantes, France. NOTE: An EU indicates that the applicant was Spencer C. Warrington.

To [MICAH STERLING, Watertown, N.Y.]

[1826 or later]

.... I am glad to hear that my namesake grows so finely and I hope that he may equal the anticipations of his parents.

Make my best respects to Mrs. [Betsey Bronson] Sterling. Sincerely, J.C. Calhoun.

Fragment of an ALS in ICHi, John C. Calhoun Papers.

To [SAMUEL L.] SOUTHARD, [Secretary of the Navy]

Pendleton, 26th March 1827

D[ea]r Sir, I will be much obliged to you, if in your power, to enable me to give a particular answer to the enclosed [*not found*]. The writer is a gentleman of talents and respectability, but has been unfortunate in his money transactions.

I had the pleasure on my arrival to find my family well; and have returned with my usual relish to agricultural pursuits, which I find much more agreeable than politicks. With great respect I am & &, J.C. Calhoun.

ALS in CtHi.

From THO[MA]S C. LEVINS

28 Green St. N. York [City], April 21st 1827

Dear Sir, By letters rec[eive]d from the University of Virginia I am informed that the present professor of mathematics in that Institution intends to resign his situation. Relatively to a professorship in this university, you had the kindness, on a former occasion [12/29/-1824], to write in my behalf to Mr. [Thomas] Jefferson. The chairs were then occupied. Allow me in the present instance to solicit y[ou]r interest by writing to Mr. [James] Madison the Rector of the College.

Thanking you for y[ou]r kind attention relatively to the Naval Acad[em]y, I remain sincerely & with regard y[ou]r ob[e]d[ien]t Serv[an]t, Thos. C. Levins.

ALS in ViU, University Archives, Chronological File. NOTE: Calhoun recommended Levins for the vacant professorship in a letter of 5/13/1827 (*The Papers of John C. Calhoun*, 10:288–289).

To E[benezer] B. Williston, [Norwich, Vt.]

Pendleton, 23d April 1827

D[ea]r Sir, When I saw you in Washington last winter, I hoped it would be in my power to obtain correct copies of my speeches, but did not succeed. They were with few exception[s] printed in pamphlet form, but I omitted to preserve any copy among my papers, and as I never corrected the proof sheets, it is more than probable, that even in that form, they are not correct.

If you can furnish me with copies ["from the Int(elligence)r" *interlined*] I will look over them, and correct such errors as may occur to me.

If you should print any, I would suggest one which you have omitted in your list, a speech delive[re]d in the session of 1815–16 in which I took a very general view of our policy, on one of the tax bills, and ["also" *interlined*] the speech on the bill making appropriation for internal improvement, ["at" *canceled*] delivered next winter.

The Speech on the N[ational] Bank was most imperfectly reported, so much so as to bear a very imperfect likeness to the original. As the views in relation to it, have been greatly misapprehended, it was my intention to write out what I said on the occasion during the course of the summer from a very distinct recollection of the argument, but I do not know whether it would be in time for your collection, or whether it would fall within your plan. With much respect I am & &, J.C. Calhoun.

ALS in VtNN, Williston Papers. NOTE: Williston was a Professor at the American Literary, Scientific and Military Academy in Norwich. He was engaged in compiling his *Eloquence of the United States,* a five-volume set of speeches that was first published in 1827 in Middletown, Conn. Calhoun's speech of 12/12/-1811 on the increase of the Army and that of 2/4/1817 on internal improvements were included in the work.

J[ohn] E[wing] Colhoun, Pendleton, to Lt. J[ames] Edward Colhoun, U.S.S. Macedonian, "Montevideo, South American Station," 5/4/1827. "The V.P. [John C. Calhoun] and family are at Clergyhall, all well and very busily engaged in Farming, building and overhauling every thing, with a view to a permanent settlement. Their furniture and other things have all arrived from Washington, and the house will soon be completed; so remodeled that you will not know it." After discussing other family news, he continues, "I offered Tickleberry (1000 acres) to J.C. C[alhoun] last fall at 7 dols. pr. acre, but he declined purchasing, not wishing to involve himself. I would prefer that it could remain in the family situated as it is, but will offer it for sale this summer . . . ." ALS in ScU-SC, James Edward Colhoun Papers.

To [VIRGIL MAXCY]

Pendleton, 24th July 1827

My dear Sir, After full consideration, I cannot come to the conclusion, that it would be either proper, or beneficial to take the excursion, which you suggest as coming from some of my friends. I am not ignorant, that I have suffered by the artful misrepresentations of the coalition in the Northern section of our country, but cannot believe, that any attempt on my part to remove the false impression as proposed, would be successful. It might possibly tend to correct error, as to the two topicks, to which you allude, but would necessarily expose me to greater and more dangerous misrepresentations. I would be held up as a mere seeker of popularity, and even as courting the coalition, who assume to themselves an exclusive attachment to the measures [to] which ["they" *canceled and* "you" *interlined*] refer. The truth is, that the real cause of the attacks on me to the North is my opposition to Mr. [John Quincy] Adams, and it is for that ["cause" *canceled and* "circumstance" *interlined*] too, that it has been in any degree successful. Let me but become his partisan, and all would be well there. I knew from the first, that my course would expose me to much loss in that quarter, and it was on this that Mr. [Henry] Clay's friend[s] calculated with so much certainty, that I would be forever prostrated. But a publick man is unworthy of the confidence of the people, who cannot steadily pursue principle through such difficulties, clamly [*sic*; calmly] looking forward to the steady operation ["of time" *interlined*] to disipate error.

I will not now enter on what you allude to, as a change in my opinion as to the doctrine of appropriation, with a view to discuss it. It may not, however, be improper to state, that I do not look on it as a change, so much as a farther developement of my habitual doctrine, on that important point. I now, as I ever have, believe that it was intended, that the first clause of enumerated powers ["should" *interlined*] not only give the power to raise a revenue, but also the power to appropriate it, and that too to provide for the common defence, and general welfare. But it is obvious, that ["the" *interlined*] question still remains, what is meant by the term general welfare as used

461

in the constitution. I had not gone farther formerly, than to say, that all objects of national importance were comprehended, and no more. But it is obvious, that the question is not precluded, but still remains, what is meant by nationally important. Now if I mistake not ["that" *canceled*] the solution of this question, by the soundest rules of construction, must lead to the conclusion, that the power of appropriation to the general welfare, or to national objects, is neither more, nor less than, the power to apply the funds of the government to the objects for which it was created.

I see that you are startled at the idea, that this conclusion will in point ["of" *interlined*] fact lead to the extreme[?] of the Virginia doctrine. But that my [*sic*] no means follows. Those who ["differ" *canceled*] agree on this point, may greatly differ in determin[in]g the extent of the powers really delegated by the constitution, and to which ["of course" *interlined*] the money power can be applied, as I have explained it. But it is not only in the above particular, that the deliberate investigation, which I bestowed on the subject last winter, modified my opinion. I formerly conceived that the power in its application required the consent of the State, and individuals ["which" *canceled and* "that" *interlined*] might be effected, but I now am thoroughly of the opinion, that it is, to the extent, which it exists, sovereign and independent, which perhaps would remove me, as far from what is considered the Virginia school, as the other may be supposed to approximate to it.

On this subject I have much to say when I see you, as it has still continued to occupy my attention. Sincerely, J.C. Calhoun.

ALS in DLC, Galloway-Maxcy-Markoe Papers, vol. 34.

From E D W A R D E V E R E T T, [Representative from Mass.]

Washington, 14 Dec[embe]r [18]27

Dear Sir, I this day re[ceive]d from my friend, Charles L. Bonaparte prince of Musigrano some grains of the Oryza Mutica L. or dry Culture rice. They are the product of three grains, procured by the prince several years ago from wh[ich] he has succeeded in raising several Ounces with which experiments are now making on a large scale in Italy. I have placed about half the quantity of grains received by me at the disposal of the Col[umbian] Institute, it having been in return for a copy of their circular, that this interesting seed was sent me, by the prince of Musigrano. I beg leave to request you to accept the remainder & to make such disposition of this specimen of Upland rices, as you may think best. I am uninformed how far it has already been subjected to experiment in this Country. I remain, dear Sir, faithfully & respectfully Yours, Edward Everett.

FC in MHi, Edward Everett Papers, 62:190–191 (published microfilm, reel 25, frame 461). NOTE: Charles L. Bonaparte (1803–1857), son of Lucien Bonaparte and nephew of Napoleon I, was a noted scientist.

To H[enry] Middleton [U.S. Minister to Russia], 5/16/1828. In this one and one-half page, quarto ALS, Calhoun introduces "a relative of mine, Lieut. J[ames] E[dward] Colhoun of the U. States Navy." ALS advertised in Catalogue 231 [1959] of the Carnegie Book Shop of New York City, p. 6, item 81.

To C[HRISTOPHER] HUGHES, [U.S. Chargé d'Affaires to the Netherlands]

Washington, 16th May 1828

Dear Sir, I take the liberty of introducing to your acquaintance Lieut. J[ames] E[dward] Colhoun of the U. States Navy a relative of mine who visits Europe with the intention of seeing its principal cities and countries. His object is to gratify his curiosity and to become more accurately acquainted with that interesting portion of the globe.

Any attention, which you may extend to him will place me under particular obligations. With great respect I am [your] Ob[edien]t, J.C. Calhoun.

ALS in NNC, General Manuscript Collection.

From S[AMUEL] L. S[OUTHARD]

Navy Dep[art]m[en]t, 14 July, 1828

Sir, I have received your letter in favor of young [Charles D.] Maxwell, for the appointment of Midshipman. I would with much pleasure gratify your wish at once, but am afraid the number of recent appointments from the State of Delaware will not allow it. His name however will be noted, and his desire to enter the service considered, when an occasion offers to gratify it. I am, respectfully, &c, S.L.S.

FC in DNA, RG 45 (Naval Records), Miscellaneous Letters Sent by the Secretary of the Navy, 1798–1886, 16:488–489 (M-209:6).

From S[AMUEL] L. S[OUTHARD]

Navy Dep[art]m[en]t, 6 Aug. 1828
Sir, I have the honor to acknowledge the receipt of your letter (without date) enclosing an application from Lieut. J.D. Knight, to be attached to the Exploring Expedition.

Lieut. Knight had, *at his own request*, and before his wishes on this subject were made known to the Department, been ordered on other service; it is now too late to relieve him, and supply his place, before the vessel will sail. I am, respectfully, &c, S.L.S.

FC in DNA, RG 45 (Naval Records), Miscellaneous Letters Sent by the Secretary of the Navy, 1798–1886, 16:508 (M-209:6).

To V[IRGIL] MAXCY

Pendleton, 24th Nov[embe]r 1828
My dear Sir, I write to acknowledge yours of the 20th Oct[obe]r last [*not found*] and to inform you, that I will set out with Mrs. Calhoun for Washington on the 26th and expect to be in the city about Christmass, where we shall be very happy to see you and Mrs. [Mary Galloway] Maxcy. I have been detained to this late period by private business, an attention to which I could not postpone, but which I fear has delayed our journey so long, that it will be rendered very unpleasant from the lateness of the season.

You have succeed[ed] well in Maryland. I had from the beg[in-n]ing great doubts, as you will recollect, whether we should be able to hold our own in a State directly under[?] the droppings[?] of the Treasury, and in which we had to encounter in addition the influence of the State Government.

Our triumph is decisive; and it only remains to make a wise and virtuous ["of" *canceled*] use of it. The next 4 years will require uncommon discretion.

I do not think the [William H.] Crawford electors in Georgia will vote for ["me" *interlined*], but I have no information on the subject. I judge from circumstances only.

Mrs. C[alhoun] desires her affectionate regards to yourself, Mrs. M[axcy] & family. Sincerely, J.C. Calhoun.

ALS in MHi, Endicott Autograph Collection.

To [WILLIAM CALHOUN, Abbeville District, S.C.]

Pendleton, 4 Sep[tember; *sic*; February?] 1829
My Dear Brother, I sincerely sympathize with you and your family under the severe dispensation of Providence which has fallen on you. It is among the heaviest that could have befallen you; yet as hard as it may be, it is your duty to bear it with resignation. The ways of Providence are indeed mysterious, and far above our comprehension; but as I believe in his wisdom and goodness, I do not in the least doubt that he orders all things for the best. To another and a better world we must look for exemption from evil and woe. This is a life of probation, and it may be in part the object of his afflictive dispensations to prepare us by such trials for the more perfect state of existence yet to come. You have at least one pure consolation, the spotless character of those who stood so near and dear to you but who are now removed. The death of the virtuous may at first be thought to be a heavier affliction than any other but when we come to reflect that the only rational object that we can assign for this our present state of existence is to form virtuous habits, they may well be said to have attained fullness of days, however young in years who have succeeded in this great object.

I feel that these or any other reflections are but a poor consolation to a breast rent with sorrow like yours and that of your family. Time only can pour the oil of consolation into a wounded heart, but you will at least receive this as a token of the sympathy of a brother who takes a lively interest in all that concerns you.

We are all well and Floride [Colhoun Calhoun] and all the family desire to join their consolation for your heavy loss. We would be happy to see you and your family if you could with convenience make us a visit. Affectionately, J.C. Calhoun.

Copy in ScU-SC, Noble Family Papers. NOTE: This letter is copied into the middle of an ALS of 6/15/1885 from W[illia]m Pinkney Starke to [Sarah Calhoun Noble]. Starke says of the letter, "It is a clipping from some newspaper and was preserved by your cousin Anna [Maria Calhoun Clemson]." Catherine Jenner de Graffenreid Calhoun, wife of John C. Calhoun's brother William, died on February 3, 1829.

To Maj. C[HRISTOPHER] VANDEVENTER, Erie [County,] N.Y.

Washington, 14th March 1829

My dear Sir, Such has been my incessant occupation, that I have been compelled to suspend my private correspondence for the last four or five weeks, which will account for my [not] acknowledging your last letters at an earlier date.

Your friends have not been unmindful of you, as you will see by the enclosed letter from Maj[o]r [James] Hamilton [Jr.]. I called to see Maj[o]r [John H.] Eaton yesterday, and he confirmed the statement of Maj[o]r Hamilton, with the addition that he had no idea that [James] Gadsden would accept. The offer had been made to him before it was publickly known that Maj[o]r Eaton would be the Secretary [of War], and consequently before your name could be brought forward.

Whether you ought to accept, must depend on all of the circumstances of the case, of which your present ["circumsta" *canceled*] prospect constitute[s] an essential point. If your prospect at present be good where you are, if you see your way clearly both as to the means of making property and the prospect of usefulness, there would be strong inducement I would suppose to remain where you are; but, if on the contrary, there be doubt on those points, particularly as to the first, it may form a conclusive reason for accepting. [Your] good sense must decide.

The formation of the Cab[ine]t does not fully meet publick ex-[pe]ctation, in several particulars. Gen[era]l [Andrew] Jackson formed it, without consulting his prominent friends. I hope it may do well. As to myself I have no reason to complain. A majority I believe to be friendly; but I placed my prospect not so much on the friendship of the members, as the general success of the administration. I think my prospect was never better.

We set out for our residence in Carolina on Wednesday, where I will be glad to hear from you. With great respect I am &, J.C. Calhoun.

[P.S.] Let me suggest as a friend, if you accept of the place to pursue a conciliatory course with all, whatever may be your present or past [rela]tion with them. I speak of those [con]nected any way with Dept. The reason will be obvious to you on a litt[le] reflection. Whether you accept [or] decline the triumph will be complete, and a course of conciliation will be ["wi(?)" *canceled*] both wise and dignified.

I have just received your last. What I have already written will I trust suffi[ci]ently explain my position. I by no means conceive it to be such as you think it. J.C.C.

ALS with En in MiU-C, Christopher Vandeventer Papers; variant PEx's with En in the Washington, D.C., *United States' Telegraph*, March 6, 1832, p. 3. NOTE: An AEI by Vandeventer reads: "These papers relate to Maj[o]r Eaton's promise to appoint me chief clerk, & his apology to Gov[erno]r Hamilton for not keeping his promise." The enclosed letter of 3/11/1829 from Hamilton to Calhoun is printed in *The Papers of John C. Calhoun*, 11:8–9.

To the Rev. [RODOLPHUS] DICKINSON

Pendleton, 24th May 1829

Dear Sir, I expected to have meet [*sic*] you at church to day and to have delivered the enclosed [*not found*] personally. I would have transmitted it to you soon after, I received the information from Mr. [Richard?] Rush, but as he expected to receive additional, which might be acceptable, I held it in the expectation of obtaining it from him, till the period of my departure from Washington, but without getting it. I hope, however, that which Mr. Rush's note furnishes, may be satisfactory. With great respect I am & &, J.C. Calhoun.

ALS in the Pocumtuck Valley Memorial Association Library, Deerfield, Mass., Dickinson Family Papers. NOTE: Dickinson (1786–1862), a native of Mass., was a scholar and Episcopal Minister with parishes in S.C. from *ca.* 1820–1832.

To "Col." C[HRISTOPHER] VANDEVENTER, [Erie County, N.Y.?]

Pendleton, 18th Aug[us]t 1829

My dear Sir, You have acted correctly in refusing the place offered you in the War Department. You could not accept of that, or any other inferior to what you formerly held, without degredation.

Maj[o]r [John H.] Eaton has offered me no explanation for the breach of promise, and I remain without any knowledge of the cause, except that, which his explanation offered to Maj[o]r [James] Hamilton [Jr.] ["offered" *or* "afforded" *interlined*], and which he has made known to you, and which I suppose to be the true one, tho' it does him no credit. I would be much gratified to see you fill the post office at Buffalo, yet under existing circumstances I do not think it would be proper for me to make a move. I believe Major [William T.] Barry to be personally, and politically my friend; but I do not think, I could make another effort without the assurance of success. To fail would be alike injurious to both. The best ["think" *canceled*] thing that could occur would be to keep it open till the meeting of Congress, when I doubt not, your many friends in Congress could bring your name forward with the assurance of success. The manner, that you were dismissed, your servi[c]es ["in th" *canceled*] & suffering in the late war, and ["your" *interlined*] bus[i]ness habits would give you strong claims. By writing to some friend in Washington, who may be well acquainted with the Post Master General your cause may be aided.

I think you have been most unkindly treated, but let me suggest a course of silence & prudence. Any expression of discontent would be attributed to mortification at defeat, which is always undignified. With your good sense and expe[rie]nce, you cannot fail, if prudent, to acquire a local popularity, and to have justice done to you finally, by those in power.

I am glad to learn, that your farming prospects are so good. Our season has been very wet, but the corn & cotton in the upper count[r]y ["looks" *altered to* "look"] very well. I [am] hoping, however, that your farming operations are much more profitable than ours, which has in a great measure ceased to give any profits. The restrictions on our commerce bear heavily on our southern Agriculture.

My family are all ["well" *interlined*]. Mrs. [Floride Colhoun] Calhoun has added, in the last few days, a fine son [William Lowndes Calhoun] to our family. She is doing well & desires to be remembered to Mrs. [Sally Birckhead] V[andeventer] & family. With sincere regard I am & &, J.C. Calhoun.

ALS in MiU-C, Christopher Vandeventer Papers.

Records of the Pendleton Farmers' Society, 10/8/1829–11/29/-1851. Calhoun paid a membership fee of $1.50 to the Society on 10/-8/1829. On 10/4[?]/1838 he paid an $18 membership fee for nine years and on 10/2/1840 he paid $4, presumably for two years. Calhoun paid $2 fees on 10/6/1841, 10/7/1842, 6/27/1844, and 10/12/-1844. A fee of $4 was paid on 10/8/1846. An entry dated 11/29/-1851 indicates that R[ansom] Colhoun "pr. J.C. Calhoun" paid a $20 fee. (William Ransom Colhoun, 1827–1862, was a son of John Ewing Colhoun and Martha Maria Davis Colhoun.) Scattered entries in ScCleA, Pendleton Farmers' Society, Treasurer's Book, 1828–1853, pp. 2–27.

To [Virgil] Maxcy, [*ca.* 1829 or later]. "We accept your invitation with pleasure. I intended to call to day but the weather is so cold and my cold so bad, that I fear I may not be able to fulfil my intention. Truly, J.C. Calhoun." ALS in DLC, Galloway-Maxcy-Markoe Papers.

To [MARY HOPKINS (Mrs. Stephen)] PLEASONTON

Washington, 21st Jan[uar]y 1830

My dear Mrs. Pleasonton, I take the liberty of enclosing an extract from Mrs. [Floride Colhoun] Calhoun's letter, which I mentioned to you the other day. She says "I wish you would request Mrs. Pleasonton to look into the band box which I left with her in order to see whether all things are safe, and to have them aired and put up again. As the feathers will become yellow, I wish she would exchange them with some of the Milliner's for a handsome cap for myself and to get lace enough to trim it in the fashion. I wish thread lace and very fine, as it is intended for a dress cap. I wish you to bring on for me a black silk dress. Have it made fashionably, and of the best quality thin silk, as I wish it for summer; and also a black velvet beed bag."

I feel assured from your habitual kind attention, that I do not take too much liberty in requesting you to execute the above commission for Mrs. Calhoun. Any time before I leave here in the spring will be sufficiently early. Sincerely, J.C. Calhoun.

ALS in ScU-SC, John C. Calhoun Papers.

To Maj. C[HRISTOPHER] VANDEVENTER, [Erie County, N.Y.?]

Washington, 10th Feb. 1830

Dear Sir, I have delayed answering you[r] letter of the 9th Jan[uar]y [*not found*], because I had little to add to my former communication. It is now appearent, that the friends of the late administration will rally, and, with the addition of some from our ranks, will constitute a settled opposition. They have been doubtless encouraged to take a stand from causes, which you will readily fix on. The contest, judging from its commencement, will turn very much on old party grounds.

I think you show a becoming sperit in declin[in]g to make application to a certain quarter under any circumstance. I spoke with Mr. [Samuel D.] Ingham in resferrence [*sic*] to the inspection of the land offices. He is perfectly well disposed towards you; and should not the law authorising the inspection be repealed, will, if he possible can, meet your wishes. I would advice you, however, to write to him directly on the subject, in a letter which can be preserved as a memorandum of your application, as in the multiplicity of his business, it might escape his memory without something to refer to.

As to my prospects, I am well satisfied. All I ask is that the administration preserve their standing by a wise and upright of [*sic*] discharge of their duty. If things go right there, I have nothing to fear. I trust they will.

My kindest respects to Mrs. [Sally Birckhead] V[andeventer] & your family. With sincere regard I am & &, J.C. Calhoun.

ALS in MiU-C, Christopher Vandeventer Papers.

To Mrs. "L. P." [*sic*; LETITIA BRECKENRIDGE] PORTER

Washington, 21st Feb. 1830

Dear Madam, Should a corps of Topographical engineers be authorized, it will afford me great pleasure to aid the application of Lieut. [John B.?] Grayson for admission into the corps. You need not apprehend, that you have taken too great a liberty in writing to me on the subject. It will always be gratifying to me to have an opportunity of serving you, and would really be mortified should you hesitate any time to put my service in requisition for yourself, or friends.

Mrs. [Floride Colhoun] Calhoun is not with me this winter. She added a fine son [William Lowndes Calhoun] to our family shortly before I left home, which prevented her from accomp[any]ing me. I will thank you to make my respects to Gen[era]l [Peter B.] Porter. With since[re] regard I am & &, J.C. Calhoun.

ALS in NBuHi, Peter B. Porter Collection (published microfilm, reel 11, frame 350).

To [JAMES P. PRESTON, Postmaster of Richmond], "Private"

Washington, 3d April 1830

Dear Sir, I am under great obligations, for your kind feelings towards me, ["and" *canceled*] which I assure you, I very highly appreciate.

You must excuse me from speaking on a subject of so much delicacy, as that included in your question, farther than to say, that the gentlemen to whom you refer and myself are personally on good terms. Our political difference has never interrupted our social intercourse.

I enclosed some time since a letter to you, for Gov[erno]r [John] Floyd, which I hope you received. With sincere regard I am & &, J.C. Calhoun.

ALS in ViHi, Preston Family Papers.

From JA[ME]S WATSON WEBB

Washington, May 27th 1830

Sir, Having understood that an editorial article written by me on the 20th Inst., and published in the Morning Courier & New York Enquirer of the 24th has been attributed to M[ordecai] M. *Noah* [former editor of the New York, N.Y., *Enquirer*], I deem it my duty to inform you, and through you the members of the Senate, that Mr. *Noah* had no agency whatever in writing that article or any other in which the course pursued by the Senate in relation to Editors, has been censured.

Mr. Noah has no control over the columns of the Courier & Enquirer, nor is he in any way responsible for what appears in that paper. I have the honor to be Very Respectfully your Ob[e]d[ien]t S[er]v[an]t, Jas. Watson Webb, Editor, Courier & Enquirer.

ALS in CtY, Sterling Library, James Watson Webb Collection. NOTE: The above letter was addressed to Calhoun as "President of the Senate." The editorial in question had attacked four Senators as "demagogues" and a "threat to the rights and privileges of freemen."

To G[EORGE] HAY, [Washington]

Pendleton, 1st July 1830

My dear Sir, I received your's and Mr. Hay's [*sic*; Monroe's?] notes by the last mail with the enclosures, and I have this day written to the Post Master General [William T. Barry] in relation to Mr. Paine, who I sincerely hope may succeed in getting employment. I would have also written to Mr. [Samuel D.] Ingham and [former] Gov-[erno]r [of N.C., John] Branch [Secretary of the Navy], but from the peculiar state of things in Washington, it seemed to me, that it would not be in their power to do any thing in his behalf.

I hope, that your health improves, and that the effects of the warmth of Summer, will be to restore you entirely to your usual State of health.

I had the pleasure to find my family well on my return home. Mrs. Calhoun desires to be affectionately remembered to you & Mrs. [Eliza Kortright Monroe] Hay. With sincere regard I am & &, J.C. Calhoun.

ALS in ViW, Monroe Papers (James Monroe Papers in Virginia Repositories, published microfilm, roll 13, frames 695–696).

To W[ADDY] THOMPSON, JR., Greenville, So[uth] Caro[lina]

Fort Hill Place, July [*ca.* 14] 1830

My dear Sir, I have read the letter of [William C.] Preston [of 7/4], which I herewith return, with much attention, and am much obliged to you for the opportunity of perusing it.

It touches on a subject, which in the present state of our affairs, is of the deepest importance, one which, tho it might be supposed calculated to excite on my part some personal feelings, I am disposed to view wholly in its political relations. It was impossible for any South Carolinian, who was present, and who understood the present posture of our affairs, to regard the course of Judge [William] Smith [Senator from S.C.] during the last session with approbation. Myself and all of my friends had done, and continued to do to the last all in our power to produce harmony and conciliation; but with very little success; but considering, that Judge Smith, was supported by a large and respectable portion of the State, who concured Zealously and ably in vindication of the rights of the South and the principles of the Constitution, ["for us" *interlined*] to take a stand against him, under such circumstances, might only make bad worse, tho it was impossible not to see, how liable the State was to distraction, and her stand in the Union lowered, by the want of harmony in our Senatorial Representation. What course those, who have heretofore supported him, ought in duty to take, is a question of vital importance, as connected with the honor and success of the State, in her present great struggle for Constitutional liberty; but whatever it may be, I mean the enlightened and patriotick portion, it appears to me our friends are bound to cooperate with them.

Preston[']s views and reflections seem to me to be very just. It has not, as far as I know, been the intention ["of my friends" *interlined*] in any event to support the individual below [Stephen D. Miller], to whom he alludes. If his course, is such as it is said to be, it would be madness. It does seem to me, if any step be taken, it ought ["to" *canceled*] not only to come from the quarter indicated, but ought to be in favour of some prominent individual, who has acted on that side in our former division. Gov[erno]r Miller's claims are certainly strong, but I entirely concur with Preston, "the thing does not press, and there is leisure to look round."

I am very desireous of seeing you, and was quite disappointed, that you did not attend the courts in this quarter. You and Preston must not fail to make me a visit, ["while" *canceled and* "when" *interlined*] he comes to Greenville. I will not excuse you, and Mrs. [Floride Colhoun] Calhoun & myself will be still more gratified, if you will bring your family, and spend some days with us. I wrote you just before I left Washington. I hope you got my letter. Sincerely, J.C. Calhoun.

[Enclosure]
W[illiam C.] Preston to [Waddy Thompson, Jr.]
[Columbia, S.C.,] July 4, 1830

[*Ms. torn; first pages missing*]ets of the Judges [*ms. torn; one or two words missing*] Calhoun [George] McDuffie & [James H.] Hammond, I have a higher admiration than for any other three men in the United States, and I regard it as every way wrong in Judge [William] Smith to attack them, not being attacked. If he will not go with us in our struggle, or hesitates or blenches for our risk—if he is not ready to sacrifice himself for its success—he won't find me by his side or in his train. I will be willing to take up any man, who is staunch and true, and to abandon any who does not go struggle onward. There is a great difficulty in selecting a substitute [for] Judge Smith if it should be[come] necessary. [Stephen D.] Miller is the most plausible suggestion but his very strict connections with Judge Smith, interpose an embarrassing difficulty, and besides between ourselves we sh[oul]d have to require strong pledges from him. He is with us practically but differs on the constitutional doctrine, which is a dangerous difference unless made up by the enthusiasm and devotion of the individual. I think him however the on[*ms. torn; three or four words missing*] martin was sho[*ms. torn; three or four words missing*]bity— but I suspect [*ms. torn; three or four words missing*] to his own strength, and merits, than for the purpose of securing my co-operation, as it was supposed that I would be ambitious to take his place in the house of Representatives. Those who make such calculations however are deceived. I would not raise my finger in that hall for any such motive—and for the present I would rather be in that hall than any where else. If we did not stand in need of [James] Hamilton for governor I sh[oul]d say he is the man. In the mean time the thing does not [pre]ss—and we have leisure to look [arou]nd. If I am not mistaken, Judge Smith upon his return from Alabama, will bring things to a crisis. Do procure from Warren Davis a certificate which I have heard is in his possession; and send me a copy. Ask for it for *yourself.* I allude to the *Armstrong* certificate. Hamilton writes [*"to me" canceled*] that he and his friends will be in a large minority. Ker Boyce tells me it will be a very small one [*ms. torn; several lines missing*].

You know [*ms. torn; one or two words missing*]thers & the [Columbia] Telescope are devoted to Judge Smith. The [Columbia] "Southern times" goes for the right & is straining in the slips to be at him. The [*several words illegible*] Telescope too, w[oul]d go at once to the times. I have held them back ever since the Judges letter to

Levy—and will do so until no better can be done. The "Times" has bought out old Dan[ie]l Faust. If you don't take [it] already I will order it to be [*ms. torn; one word missing*] to you. Hammond is the Editor is altogether [*ms. torn; one or two words missing*]tively untrammelled by any connections and fearless.

As to the Phaeton Evans went off without giving me his ultimatum. I rather think I shall have to drive some trade with you for it for my Virginia trip as I begin to think that I shall not be able to travel in my sulky. I propose to leave here about the 18th[?].

Excuse this variety of paper, I am writing on Sunday—and could not get a fellow to the first[?; *ms. torn; one word missing*] which was the only one [*ms. torn; next six lines largely missing*].

My best love to Mrs. [Emmala Butler] Thompson whom I long to see even more than you. W[m. C.] Preston.

ALS in NjP, Andre DeCoppet Collection; En (ALS, mutilated fragment) in ScU-SC, William C. Preston Papers. Note: Calhoun's letter to Thompson is tentatively dated from its postmark, "Pendleton, S.C., 15th July."

To "Gen[era]l LA FAYETTE"

Pendleton So. Caro., 23d Oct[obe]r 1830
My dear Sir, The universal desire, which all of the Americans, who visit Europe, have to be personally acquainted with you must, I fear, prove burdensome to you; but, I trust, you will find an excuse, both for those who call on you, and those, who introduce them, in the universal admiration and love, of which you are the object on this side of the Atlantick. Mr. [Donald?] Douglass, who will deliver you this, is about to visit Europe for the benefit of the health of one of his daughters, and entertain[in]g for your character the feeling common to all of his countrymen, has requested me to give him an introduction, in order to enable him to make his respects to you. I have long known Mr. Douglass, and can say with confidence, that he is a gentleman of great respectability, who by the successful pursuit of commerce, has placed himself among our oppulent merchants.

Your extraordinary & happy revolution, in which you have borne so prominent a part, has excited with us the deepest sensation, and cannot fail to give additional confidence to the friends of the rights of man and free goverments over the whole world. Indeed, the rapidity, the moderation, the wisdom and courage, with which the movement was conducted, are altogether unprecedented. It has no parallel in history, and, should, what has been done, be maintained with the same high qualities, by which it has been achieved, the happy consequence of your revolution will speedily extend over the civilized world. I fear, however, you will have great difficulties in preserving, what you have so gloriously acquired. The diversity of sentiments within, which must always follow such great political moves, & the watchful jealousy of all of the old goverments, which will be the more strongly excited, just in proportion to your wisdom and moderation, and which will not fail to resort to every [*or* "any"] species of art and corruption to distract and devide you, constitute great impediments in your way; but, I feel much confidence, that the patriotism and good sense of the French people, will surmount every obstacle, and that you will have the glory & happiness to live to see those great political principles, to which your life has been consecrated, firmly established in Europe.

Our system is progressing, but not without its difficulties. The attempt of the goverment of the Union to regulate by the Tariff the industry of the States, and to make local and unconstitutional appropriations, have excited much discontent in the South & particularly in this State. The effect has been to call back the attention of the South to the principles, on which the general goverment was formed; to secure peace at home, & a broad, and to leave the States ["to" *canceled*] in the full exercise of local authority; and to excite a strong desire to correct every aberation from those principles. In the pursuit of this great object, many imprudent and intemperate expressions, have been used, which have afforded an opportunity to those, opposed to reform, to attempt to fix the charge of disunion, but without any just foundation. I can say, with confidence, that no portion of the country is more devoted to the Union, than the South generally & particularly South Carolina, of which stronger proof cannot be offered, than the Zeal and ananimity [*sic*] with which she is contending to resist consoladation, as the most effectual mode of preserving the Union. With sentiment of sincere & profound respects I am & &, J.C. Calhoun.

ALS in NIC, Department of Rare Books.

Memorandum [by RICHARD K. CRALLÉ]
Concerning Calhoun and William H. Crawford

[Richmond, Va., *ca.* 1831]

.... exertion to cover with disgrace. The old issues were again revived—his conduct held up to public abhorrence as equally insolent, audacious and unconstitutional. The General [Andrew Jackson], however, entrenched behind his military fame, and sustained by the Administration again baffled the machinations of his restless and vindictive enemy.

Mr. Crawford, though thus twice signally defeated in Congress did not surrender the cause. His hopes of the succession depended on the overthrow both of Gen. Jackson and Mr. Calhoun. The latter he knew had sustained the former on both of the occasions referred to; and he entertained no doubt that, as between himself and General Jackson, Mr. Calhoun would not hesitate a moment. Neither of these, it appeared, could be reached through Congress; and it therefore became necessary to resort to the Press, the columns of which teemed with the bitterest diatribes against both. In the meanwhile an active correspondence was kept up by his political emmissaries; and the nefarious system of Washington Letter-writing, since so extensively practised, became a part of the ordinary machinery of partizan ["machinery" *canceled*] electioneering. And very soon after Mr. [James] Monroe's second election, the masked batteries, through these channels began to open their fires both on Gen. Jackson and Mr. Calhoun. The Crawford Press, throughout the Union, by common consent, selected these two for immolation; and the gall and bitterness with which their columns abounded had no parallel—at least at that day. Mr. Crawford, himself, it seems was not idle. At a very early day, it appears, he sought to bring on a ["personal difference" *canceled and* "controversy" *interlined*] with Mr. Calhoun, ["and to involve him in certain party disputes and personal jealousies, growing out of" *interlined and* "in relation to" *canceled*] some appointments made by the administration. On the 12th of October 1821, he addressed the following note to Mr. Calhoun:

(Here insert the note) A [*not found*]

It seems, from the subsequent correspondence, that Mr. Calhoun called at his request, that a conversation passed between them in relation to the appointment of a Commissioner from Georgia to treat with the Creek Indians, and that, on the same day, Mr. Calhoun addressed a note to him, covering certain enclosures referring to the subject.* [*Insertion*: "This note, and the accompanying papers are probably lost, as we do not find them in the correspondence."] On the day following, Mr. Crawford addressed him the following communication:

(Here insert the letter) B [*not found*]

To this Mr. Calhoun addressed him the following answer:

(Here insert the note) C [*not found*]

Note. On this letter there is endorsed, in the hand-writing of Mr. Calhoun, the following words: "Returned this and the answer to it by mutual agreement; the cause proposed by this being only on the ground that it was the supposed wish of Mr. Crawford, growing out of a conversation at his request, on the 12th Inst. [*sic*; 10/12]. In the conversation with Mr. Crawford, among other things I stated that my recollection was, that General [Thomas] Flournoy had not been named by him [to be a commissioner to the Creek Indians] till after the resignation of General [John] Floyd; and that, between him and Mr. [Eldred] Simkins, my choice would have been the latter."

It is impossible to ascertain, at this late day, (nor is the fact important,) what particular purpose Mr. Crawford had in view in opening this correspondence. The loss of the papers referred to in it, leaves us no other clue to his manoevres than his own letter. From this it is obvious that he wished to claim the credit of Genl. Flournoy's appointment, *after it was made*, without having incurred any special responsibility on account of the recommendation; while, at the same time he was not unwilling that the disappointed aspirants should attribute their failures to the interposition of Mr. Calhoun, who had declined to take any active part in the question. Advices to this effect were undoubtedly forwarded to Georgia which produced some excitement; and we have reasons to believe that, it is to the unfair use made of this correspondence, Mr. Calhoun alludes in the conclusion of his letter to Mr. Crawford of the 30th of October 1830 [see *The Papers of John C. Calhoun*, 11:249], where he says, in returning the letter of the latter:

"Having been taught by the past the necessity of taking all possible precaution, where I have anything to do with you, I deem it ["proper" *canceled*] prudent not to deprive myself of the advantage which your Paper affords me, and have accordingly taken a copy, as a precautionary measure."

This was, indeed, an act of necessary prudence; for Mr. Crawford had already, by his artful manoevreings, or something worse, won the une[n]viable distinction of the "*Giant of Intrigues.*" He was doubtless a skillful manager, and like his colleague, Mr. [Martin]

Van Buren, attached great importance to the proper use of official patronage. Plunder, according to their philosophy—and we are not disposed to controvert its correctness—is a far more powerful element in politics than patriotism. He was, therefore, always on the alert when when [*sic*] appointments were pending; and often claimed more credit in their bestowal, than he was justly entitled to. He even claimed the credit of having introduced Mr. Calhoun himself, into Mr. Monroe's Cabinet; and when, in 1824 Mr. Calhoun expressed his preference of Genl. Jackson, he had the effrontery to tax him with ingratitude. At a later day, when, with the aid of Genl. Jackson and Mr. Van Buren he had laid the foundation of one of the most infamous intrigues on record, this charge was again revived through the newspapers in his interest. Two of the leading papers in Georgia (the Milledgeville Journal and Augusta Constitutionalist) well known to be devoted to Mr. Crawford, put forth, about the same time, the two following leaders in their respective columns:

(Here insert the articles)

About the time of the appearance of these two articles, published as if by concert, Mr. Calhoun received information, or rather intimation that there was a deeply laid scheme in progress which contemplated his political destruction, and that Mr. Crawford was at the bottom of it. He also heard that a private letter from Mr. Munroe to him, had been purloined from him, and placed in the hands of Genl. Jackson; and that an active correspondence was being carried on either between these two individuals themselves or their accredited emissaries. Knowing the settled malignity of Mr. Crawford—the wily dexterity of Mr. Van Buren, who had recently paid him a *friendly* visit, and coupling this latter circumstances, with certain inquiries which had been propounded to him by ["a certain" *canceled and* "Mr." *interlined*] James A. Hamilton of New York—an intimate confidential friend of the latter—together with the appearance of these articles, and the secret of the purloined letter, Mr. Calhoun deemed it prudent to act on the warnings he had received, and take some steps to defend himself against such a scheme of midnight assassination. With this view he addressed the following communication to Mr. Monroe, enclosing the extracts above:

(Here insert the letter.)

In reply to this Mr. Monroe, answers as follows:

(Here insert the letter)

[*Interpolation at the bottom of this ms. page:*]
" * The following is a copy of the original letter of Mr. Monroe, tendering the appointment. (Here insert the letter)

†In a private letter of the same date, enclosing the above, Mr. Monroe observes:

'I may add that, with you personally, I was better acquainted than with any one whom I did appoint. We had laboured together; and I felt gratified to be able to offer you the appointment on those sound principles, on which I acted, without exposing myself to the possibility of partiality or prejudice. As to any influence being exerted on me, no one pretended to it, or would have attempted it. The act was my own in every instance.'"

Having thus fortified himself against the insidious and unmanly assaults of his enemy, his first impulse was to publish the facts contained in this correspondence in some Newspaper printed in Georgia, and thus to unmask and expose him, in his own State, to the public gaze. A little reflection, however, aided by the native forbearance and generosity of his character, in which no sentiment of revenge, no feeling of malignity could abide for a moment, he determined to forward a copy of the correspondence to Mr. Crawford himself, and leave it to his sense of duty, truth and honor to vindicate him from the false aspersions propagated, in all appearance, with his consent, if not by his express authority. With this end in view, he prepared the following communication to be sent to Mr. Crawford:

(Here insert the letter)

This letter, however, was not forwarded, and the reason speaks volumes to the credit of Mr. Calhoun. Though hated and pursued by his enemy, for many years, without the slightest pretext of personal wrong—though caluminiated, secretly and publicly, though assailed on all sides by the cabals and combinations of this man, and his emissaries—though neither his private nor public integrity, had escaped their malignant assaults, he still, with that *mens conscia sibi recti*, which belongs only to great and good men, he chose rather to bear the wrong in dignified silence, than to subject himself to the imputation of sinister motives in vindicating himself. On the letter are endorsed the following words, in the handwriting of Mr. Calhoun:

"Prepared to send to Mr. Crawford, but on consulting some friends before a final decision, Mr. C.'s nomination by the H. of R. in Georgia, in the opinion of my friends, made it improper to send at this time."

Such magnanimity is rarely found amongst political rivals. He certainly met with none such from any of his, especially from Mr. Crawford. After his nomination by the House of Representatives in Georgia, the exposure of his conduct might have injured him no little, but he preferred rather to suffer injury himself than, though in lawful defence, to incur the suspicion of gratifying personal feelings by unmasking his conduct at such a time. The letter, we believe was never sent. Indeed, Mr. Crawford left him but little time to devote to any one of the engines of destruction which he was preparing for a future and final assault. Even at the very time of which we speak, he had adroitly sapped and mined in the dark, and prepared the train for a future explosion, which, through the contrivance of others, proved, indeed, disastrous in its effects. We shall, in the next chapter give some account of these proceedings, as they will serve to throw a clear light on others of a subsequent date, of which we shall speak in the sequel.

Chapter

The Presidential election in 1824 may be ["justly" *canceled*] regarded, in its results, present and prospective, as the most important which has occurred in our history. As Mr. Monroe justly observes, in reference to it, "Our Government is undoubtedly getting into operation under new circumstances, such as will operate in future, and put to the true test, the experiment of self government. All those who, by revolutionary services, commanded the confidence of the people, have departed; and it now rests altogether on the people themselves." This was true; and he might not, perhaps, have expressed so strong a confidence in its success, had he fully considered that, possessing no influence from these[?] commanding public services, aspirants would resort to any means to supply their place, however corrupt, infamous and ignoble.

In this contest there were four Candidates, Andrew Jackson, John Q. Adams, William H. Crawford, and Henry Clay; and the Canvass was marked by all those characteristics which render individuals and nations contemptible. Ghastly falsehood, fierce invection, furious denunciation, low cunning, vulgar declamation, base intrigue[,] bribery and corruption, ushered in the portentous era; and secured their strongholds for all future time. For most of these traits, the conduct of Mr. Crawford's adherents, in the effort to crush Genl. Jackson, was by far the most distinguish[ed.] So distracted and inflamed was the public mind, that the Electoral College was unable to make a choice, and the election, of course, devolved on the House of Representatives. The votes in the College were, for Andrew Jackson, 91. John Q. Adams[,] 84. William H. Crawford, 41. and Henry Clay, 37. Had the Constitution allowed the Electors to meet in general College, or could a second vote have been taken, the Crawford vote, (at least so far as Virginia was concerned,) would have been cast, (as we were informed at the time on high authority,) would have been cast [*sic*] for Mr. Adams, so bitter were the feelings of that Party towards Gen. Jackson. Such also would have been the case in the House, had not Mr. Adams been elected on the first ballot; at least, such was our information at the time.

The Electoral College, however, though they were unable to make choice of a President, were, it seems, at no loss to make choice of a Vice President. Of the whole number of votes cast (260), Mr. Calhoun received 182; the remaining number, (78) being distributed among five other gentlemen. It is curious and instructive to see into whose hands these *waifs* fell. Georgia, (Mr. Crawford's state) gave her *nine* votes to Martin Van Buren Esq. of New York, of whom we shall have occasion to speak more fully hereafter. New York, in return (then voting by districts,) gave *seven* votes to Nathan Sandford Esq. who, (politically speaking, is well described by the greek term, *OUTIS*). New Hampshire gave *one vote* to A. Jackson Esqr. which subsequently proved to be the richest offering made at that shrine of patriotism. Connecti-[*and here this incomplete ms. ends.*]

Autograph ms. (fragment) in ViU, Richard Kenner Crallé Papers. NOTE: The pages of this ms. are numbered seven through ten. The ms. has been assigned a date according to its content. It is possibly a small part of a biography of Calhoun on which Crallé was supposedly working *ca.* 1860. For Calhoun's 1830 correspondence with James Monroe concerning this controversy, see *The Papers of John C. Calhoun*, vol. XI.

To [GEORGE] POINDEXTER, [Senator from Miss.]

Washington, 10th Jan[uar]y 1831

Dear Sir, Circumstances, to which it is unnecessary to allude, may render it proper for me to show what were my sentiment and conduct, pending the discussion of the conduct of General [Andrew] Jackson in the Seminole war; and as you bore a prominent part in his defence in the House of Representatives, and was in the habit of free intercourse with me at the time, I must request you to state any fact, or circumstance within your knowledge calculated to show, what was my conduct, or sentiment on the occasion.

I would be obliged to you for a similar statement as to Mr. [William H.] Crawford, if you have any knowledge of his conduct, or sentiment on the same occasion. With great respect I am & &, J.C. Calhoun.

ALS in MoSW.

To Maj. C[HRISTOPHER] VANDEVENTER, [Erie County, N.Y.?]

Washington, Jan[uar]y 27th 1831

Dear Sir, I have just received your favour of the 18th In[stan]t [*not found*]; and I have concluded a prompt would be more acceptable than a long reply.

I am not surprised, that you and my other friends should feel uneasy under the many & false rumours in circulation, but let me say to you, and all, be composed. I never felt more so in my life. I stand on a rock, that of truth. At the proper time, I will move, when those, who have got up the plot will be crushed. It is proper, that all of my movements should be calm, and defensive, and, therefore, I ought to move slowly and leisurely. I do not deem it necessary to say more at present.

I have taken such steps as were in my power in favour of your son [Eugene Vandeventer, being appointed a Cadet]. I sincerely hope he may be successful.

Make my best respects to Mrs. [Sally Birckhead] V[andeventer] & family. With sincere regard I am & &, J.C. Calhoun.

ALS in MiU-C, Christopher Vandeventer Papers. NOTE: Eugene Vandeventer was granted an appointment dating from 7/1/1831.

From SAM[UE]L L. SOUTHARD, [Attorney General of N.J.]

[Trenton, N.J.,] 7 Feb[ruar]y 1831

Dear Sir, I ["have" *canceled*] rec[eive]d your letter ["of the 28th Ult." *interlined*] yesterday & have to day written to Mr. [James] M[onroe] for his permission to answer it—as I should be unwilling to do so without his consent. I cannot lay my hand on my note to you or your answer in 1825 [*one letter canceled*] to which you refer. Cannot you send me a copy? It might ["possibly" *interlined*] be useful in refreshing my recollection. I have not permitted myself to doubt that your course on this subject has been correct. I am very resp[ectfull]y &c, Saml. L. Southard.

ALS (draft) in NjR.

David Crockett, [Representative from Tenn.], Washington, to A.M. Hughs, 2/13/1831. Crockett comments critically on the state of governmental affairs, especially in relation to the Post Office, under President Andrew Jackson. "There will be an explosion take place this week that will tare their party into a Sunder. Mr. Calhoun is coming out with a Circular or a publication of the Correspondance betwen him & the President that will blow their little Red fox or alious—Martin Van buren in to atoms. Then you will see Gen[era]l Duff Green come out upon them with all of his powers." Crockett feels that nothing will be done to improve the state of the country. ALS in THi, Miscellaneous Collections.

From SAM[UE]L L. SOUTHARD

Trenton [N.J.,] 5 Mar[ch] 1831
Dear Sir, Your letter of the 28 Jan[uar]y and a subsequent one, without date [*not found*] have been received. A slight indisposition—attendance on the Courts—and private business, have prevented an earlier answer. In the one of the 28th the receipt of which I have acknowledged, you ["remark" *and* "told" *canceled and* "inform me" *interlined*], "that circumstances which you need not explain, render it necessary for you, to obtain a statement from me, of the opinion which Mr. [William H.] Crawford expressed relative to the ["con" *canceled*] conduct of Gen[era]l [Andrew] Jackson in the Seminole War, when the conduct of Com[modor]e [David] Porter in the Foxardo [*sic*; Fajardo, Puerto Rico] Affair was under consideration." In your last, you add that you "wish the Statement to be placed among your confidential papers to guard against the contingencies to which life is exposed, and with it, the evidence depending on memory."

When I rec[eive]d your first Letter, I apprised you, that I ["felt I doubted the propriety of answering it," *altered to* "was unwilling (to) answer it at that time."; "But some of my objections" *interlined*] arising from causes ["one or more of which" *canceled*] have, since ["that time" *canceled and* "then" *interlined*] been removed, ["and" *interlined*] I do not now perceive that I have any sufficient reason to justify me in refusing such a statement as you request, to a fellow member of the Cabinet, who equally with myself, was present, and took part in the deliberations to which you refer. I should furnish a similar statement to any other member who should desire it.

I have no memo: written at ["or near" *canceled and* "the" *interlined*] time, ["of what" *canceled*] which details the conversations, ["remarks" *canceled*] & opinions, of the persons present at that meeting, nor shall I pretend to give the precise expressions used—but circumstances of a peculiar ["kind" *canceled*] nature, & papers ["to" *interlined*] which I can refer, enable me to recollect ["the substance of" *canceled*] what occurred, and I have no doubt ["of the" *canceled*] that the following statement is entirely accurate, in substance.

Late in Dec[embe]r 1824, immediately after the Letter of Com[modor]e Porter dated 15 Nov[embe]r 1824, and giving an account of the transactions at Foxardo, was rec[eive]d a meeting of the Cabinet was called, at which all the members attended. The conduct of Com[modore] P[orter,] his Letter & other information were considered—and there was an entire unanimity among the members, in disapproving his conduct, as detailed by himself, and also of the necessity of taking some step in relation to him, without delay. When the course to be pursued, came under consideration, there was at first some diversity of opinion, as to the proper step to be ["first" *canceled*] taken. With a view to the mildest course, I proposed that a letter should be written to him, expressing the dissatisfaction of the Executive, at the occurrence as it then appeared ["& regret that he should have considered the conduct pursued by him necessary & proper" *interlined*] and calling for further explanation of the causes which led to it, and the circumstances attending it. To this proposition, objections ["was" *canceled and* "were" *interlined*] made, and various reasons assigned for his ["immediate" *canceled*] recal. While Mr. [John Quincy] Adams was expressing his opinion upon it, Mr. [William H.] Crawford, ["who had previously said but little" *interlined and then canceled*] with apparent warmth interrupted him, by remarking that the act could not be justified, but he did not see how any man, could condemn Com[modore] P[orter] who had justified, as he (Mr. A[dams]) & the Executive had done, Gen[era]l Jackson's invasion of the Spanish territory, which was ten times worse than the conduct of Com[modore] P[orter]. Mr. A[dams] after a moment's delay, calmly ["remarked" *altered to* "replied"], that he should ["not" *interlined*] now defend his opinions respecting Gen[era]l J[ackson] as the subject did not require it—and the discussion of the immediate topic was resumed. It was eventually determined ["that a" *canceled*] with the

485

approbation of all the members, that a letter of recal should be sent. It was written on the 27 Dec[embe]r 1824. I am very respectfully &c, Saml. L. Southard.

ALS (incomplete draft) in NjR. NOTE: This transcription has not reproduced literally every cancellation and interlineation in this ms.

To S[TEPHEN] TWINING, [Treasurer of Yale College]

Washington, 8th March 1831

Dear Sir, My son [Andrew Pickens Calhoun] informs me that the bill is correct, and I enclose a draft on New York for $132.$^{39}/_{100}$, the amount due, the receipt of which you will please acknowledge. With sincere regard I am & &, J.C. Calhoun.

ALS in CtY, Sterling Library, Records of the Treasurer.

To JOHN FORBES, [Cincinnati]

Fort Hill, 19th May 1831

Dear Sir, I received your's of the 10th March [*not found*] after my return to my residence here, and have been prevented from an earlier acknowledgement by the number and extent of my domestick and other engagements.

I am much gratified to learn, that my course in reference to the correspondence, was so well received by my friends in Ohio. The subject was a very painful one to me, but I would have been wanting in duty to myself & to my constituants, had I declined meeting it as I did. Against so formidable a conspiracy, backed by the power & influence of the Executive branch of the Government, I had no other refuge but in the Virtue and intelligence of the people, and in which I have found ample protection. The Attacks, which ["has" *changed to* "have" *and* "been" *canceled*] since been made on me, and to which you refer, are intended for diversion, and is [*sic*] a conclusive evidence of the failure of the plot. I have not the least objection, that any sentiment I ever uttered, or even entertained should be known to the publick; and would be gratified to bring out fully, if a suitable occasion offered my sentiments on the all important points of the origin & true Character of the General Government, and the relative powers of it & the State Governments; on a proper understanding of which, I am of the Opinion, the Union, the liberty & prosperity of our Country depends. On these points, my opinion[s] are not novel. They are the old Republican doctrines of '98, and you will find them fully described in the Virginia report & resolutions, the Kentucky resolutions, and the decision of Chief Justice [Thomas] McKean of Pensylvania. I go to their extent, and no farther; and if by nullification they are meant, I am a nullifier, the word has never been one of my using, but, if on the contrary, it be meant a disunionist, a disorganiser, an anarchist, never was a word more misapplied. I never breathed a sentiment of the kind; and so far from it, that I have ever held the Union of these States, as the greatest blessing next to Liberty itself; and which, in my Opinion can only be maintained by defending the just rights & powers of the State to their full extent. [*A series of dashes suggests the omission of text at this point.*] With sincere regard I am &c, J.C. Calhoun.

Ms. copy (possibly incomplete) in ScC, John C. Calhoun Papers.

From HENRY BANKS "of Virginia"

Kentucky, June 21, 1831
Dear Sir. Although you have never seen me, nor have I ever had any intercourse with you, I presume that my name has been communicated to you, particularly in regard to the presidential Election [of 1828], by which General Jackson was elevated to the Presidency. At the time when I conferred with him upon his becoming a candidate, I required, and he gave a promise that he would not become a candidate for re-election; I then had in view that you should be promoted to that office. I have lately published a declaration of opposition to him. I have also written to him to resign the Presidency whereby you would become ex-officio President; and I have in regard to that event, but a single point of demurrer against you and that relates to the partiality which has been alleged against you, for nullification. So soon as that communication is made, I will afterwards devote my whole soul to your success.

During the late years I have been much afflicted by a paralysis, by which I write with difficulty; but as I believe that my name has been referred to, and will be relied on to have some influence in the approaching election, I have thought it proper to make this communication to you. I am Sir, with the greatest respect, Your most ob[edien]t servant, Henry Banks, of Virginia.

PC (reprinted from the Frankfort, Ky., *Kentuckian* of unknown date) in the Columbia, S.C., *Telescope and South Carolina State Journal*, October 25, 1831, p. 2.

To H[ENRY] BANKS

Fort Hill, 5th August, 1831

Dear Sir—When I received your letter [of 6/21], I was preparing a statement [dated 7/26] of my opinion on the subject of your inquiry, to be laid before the public, and I herewith transmit a copy in answer to the question you put. I was induced to take the step from a sense of duty both to myself and the country; and I trust that the public, whether it approves of my opinions or not, will at least think I have done no more than my duty in frankly and fearlessly expressing my opinions, through the public journals, on a subject in which they take so much interest.

You will see that my sentiments accord with those expressed in the Virginia and Kentucky resolutions and the Virginia report. I have examined the subject with the utmost care, and the most anxious desire to arrive at truth, and under every view I can take of it, I sincerely believe that the opinions I have expressed contain the true principles ut [*sic*; of] our constitution, and the only basis on which the Union and the institutions of the country can securely stand. With great respect, I am, &c., J.C. Calhoun.

PC (reprinted from the Frankfort, Ky., *Kentuckian* of unknown date) in the Columbia, S.C., *Telescope and South Carolina State Journal*, October 25, 1831, p. 2. NOTE: In publishing this letter Banks stated that he was satisfied with Calhoun's answer. He also stated that he had no preference between Calhoun and [Henry] Clay for the Presidency, but was opposed to Jackson's reelection.

To Dr. C[HARLES] EVERETT, [Albemarle County, Va.]

Fort Hill, 19th Aug[us]t 1831

My dear Sir, The last mail brought me yours of the 20th July, and I am much obliged to you for the friendly feelings, which you express and the information which you communicate. I enclose the pamphlet to which you refer, as I suppose, one copy for your[self] and one for Mr. [Thomas W.] Gilmer, which I will thank you to deliver to him with my respects. I regret to learn, that his paper will not go into operation. With his talents & character he would not have failed to make a great & salutary impression in Virginia; a State, which it is all important to the liberty & happiness of this country, should be right at this important crisis. That he would have been extensively sustained, even out of Virginia, I cannot doubt. As far as I can judge the whole South would rejoice to see Virginia take the lead in this hour of difficulty & danger. I am sure it is the feeling [of] this State. You will see, I place myself entirely on her principles, which time & reflection have convinced me are the only ones consistent with the duration of our institutions. Nor do I believe the State right & free Trade party goes one inch beyond them. They have been basely calumniated, as disunionists, and, I regret to see, even Virginia lends ["so" *canceled and* "a" *interlined*] ready a ear to the very slander heaped on her, when she step forward to resist the current of Federal encroachment in '98.

As to the Presidency I feel little interest about it. Unless there be a great & radical change in publick sentiment, let who will come in, he will come ["in" *interlined*] to be beaten & dishonored, in his turn. I have no desire to distract the party with whom I have so long acted, but as little to see it under the control [of] the most weak [&] profligate of the party. I fear Gen[era]l [Andrew] Jackson has lost all capacity to unite the party, or to render service to the country. The publick confidence in him seems to be fatally shaken. His undignified & unconstitutional interference in reference to this State has utterly prostrated him here. His quarrel with [Samuel D.] Ingham & [John M.] Berrien will certainly loose him Pennsylvania, & not improbably, Georgia. It seems as if by a strange ["destiny" *canceled and* "fortune" *interlined*], he is destined to raise Mr. [Henry] Clay, with the American system into power. I make these remarks soley for yourself, who know me too well to put a misconcention on them. Those, ["who" *interlined*] know me not, might suppose, they indicated a wish to obtrude myself on the publick. The fact is far otherwise. If I were capable of seeking power by unworthy means, the road is broad before me. I would have but to betray the cause of principle and desert to the stronger interest, and every impediment to promotion would be removed. In resisting every seduction of the kind, I claim no merit. Power has no temptation to me, except as the means of advancing the liberty & happiness of the country. With great respect I am & &, J.C. Calhoun.

ALS in ScU-SC, John C. Calhoun Papers. Note: Charles Everett, a sometime member of the Va. House of Delegates, was the family physician and confidant of James Monroe.

To Gen. R[obert] Y. Hayne, [Senator from S.C.,] Charleston

Forthill, 22d Oct[obe]r 1831

My dear Sir, I wrote you some time since, and I hope my letter came safe to hand. That it has not been answered, I attribute to that entire occupation of your time, resulting from the state of parties in your city. To your energy & prudence, with that of [James] Hamilton [Jr.] & a few other friends, we owe our success in the city. Without them, Charleston would have been a Tariff colony, and every movement, on the ["party" *changed to* "part"] of the State, rendered impossible. I do trust, however, that your labours are in a great measure through. Your double victory, the triumph in Abbeville, the growth of the cause in and out of the State, have, I think, created a current, that must carry all before it. The result of the Free trade Convention, tho not entirely satisfactory, will, I think, add to its force. I had more fear, than hope from it, and I really feel rejoiced, if it has not done all the good it might, that it has done no harm. There is an article in the enclosed Inte[lligence]r Taken from the Globe, and intended to delude in this State, that, seems to me, ought to be noticed, at least as it relates to myself, in one particular. By reading it, you will see the construction which it puts on my motives, which it traces to the alarm I felt, least [Peter] Hagner's report should throw the responsibil[ity] of not settling the claim on me. Nothing can be more absurd. I settled the claim, as Mr. Hagner states, according [to] the rules, that govern in such cases, and, if the claim of the State for interest, was not allowed by me, it was owing to a defect of power, and not, that I doubted of its justice. The want of power, on my part, laid the foundation of the application to Congress; and there was, in fact, not the least inconsistency between my rejection of the claim, for the want of power, as Secretary of War, and urging Gen[era]l [Andrew] Jackson to recommend it to the favourable notice of Congress, on account of its equity. The course is usual. The Virginia claim for interest, on the same ground, was rejected by me, & afterwards recommended to Congress by Mr. [James] Monroe & allowed and Gen[era]l Jackson recommending the South

Carolina claim, without directing it to be allowed by the Secretary of War, adopts the distinction. Yet, to those, who do not make the distinction, there might appear an inconsistency, that requires explanation, and as it is highly important to me to maintain my character, when the whole weight of the government is directed against me, and, as you are familiar with the whole affair of the claim, I must request you, as a friend, to prepare a suitable article for the Mercury, unless you should be strongly of the impression, that it ought not to be noticed. I would not give you this trouble, did I not apprehend, that any notice of it in the paper here, might be attributed to me.

I hope you expect to be in Washington at an early period. I will be there before the session, which will throw the formation of the Committees on the Senate, ["&" *interlined*] which will make your presence, with that of our friends, important. The session must be one of deep interest, & no small distinction.

Hamilton will give you the news from the interior, with my views on the various topicks, on which we conversed.

I felt myself compelled to meet the errors of [John H.] Eaton's statement; and, in doing so, I found, I could not say less, than what I have done. I hope you concur in the correctness of the step.

When at leisure, I will be happy to hear from you. Mrs. [Floride Colhoun] Calhoun joins me in best respects to yourself & Mrs. [Rebecca Alston] Hayne. Sincerely, J.C. Calhoun.

ALS in ScHi, A.C. Balzano Collection.

To Maj. C[HRISTOPHER] VANDEVENTER, [Erie County, N.Y.?]

Washington, 17th June 1832
Dear Sir, I am glad to hear of your safe arrival at home. I can well imagine how badly your farming business advanced in your absence. I have had much expe[rie]nce of the effects of the absence of the owner in the same business.

Gen[era]l [Duff] Green has taken a list of the documents, which you requested, and has promised to have them forwarded. I have no spare copies.

I doubt the propr[i]ety of your commencing a discussion at this time. I know ["how" *interlined*] ignorant the great mass at the

["North" *interlined*] are in relation to the real operation of the Tariff on us at the South and the true character of the Constitution, or the remedial ["measure" *altered to* "measures"], which the South has proposed, but, I fear, that the publick mind has not yet approached a point, at which discussion may be profitable with you, and, ["that fear" *canceled,* "th" *interlined and then canceled,* "that" *interlined*] the effects of premature discussion will, but ["serve to" *interlined*] increase prejudice, rather than to instruct, or enlighten. You, however must consider this, but as a suggestion. I am too far off to form any opinion that can be relied on.

A skilful Physician watches the ["crisis" *canceled and* "progress of a disease" *interlined*], and prescribes at the critical moment. We must imitate his example. I think nothing will be done, as to the Tariff, ["and" *canceled and* "at" *interlined*] least nothing satisfactory.

Make my best respects to Mrs. [Sally Birckhead] V[andeventer] and your family & believe me to be with since[re] respect yours & &, J.C. Calhoun.

ALS in MiU-C, Christopher Vandeventer Papers.

From J[OHN] MARSHALL, [Chief Justice of the U.S. Supreme Court]

Richmond, Aug. 27th 1832

Dear Sir, I have received your address ["making known" *canceled and* "communicating" *interlined*] to your fellow citizens your sentiments "on the relations of the States and the general government," which I have read with deep interest and attention.

My uniform devotion to the existing union—a devotion founded on a firm conviction ["of its vital importance to our" *canceled and* "that it is identical with" *interlined*] liberty and real independence as well as ["to" *canceled and* "with" *interlined*] our greatness ["insures my great" *canceled and* "is a guarantee for the" *interlined*; "most anxious solicitude respecting passing events—especially those in the south" *inadvertently not canceled and* "importance I attach to your opinions on this subject at any time, more especially at the present" *interlined*].

I thank you for this flattering mark of your recollection, and beg you to be assured that I am with great and respectful esteem, Your obed[ien]t, J. Marshall.

ALS (draft) in CtHi, Hoadly Collection.

To S[AMUEL] D. INGHAM, [New Hope, Pa.]

Fort Hill, Nov[embe]r 18, [18]32

My dear Sir, I see [Andrew] Jackson is reelected by a triumphant majority. It looks badly for our country and its institutions; but we must not dispair. He has beaten the monopolists and the anti Masons; but has not yet encountered the honest & patriotick, those who prefer the constitution and liberty of the country to all other considerations. The action of the system has thrown them out of the contest. What we behold is but the legitimate fruits of consolidation; and the remedy and only remedy is the restoration of the rights of the States, and that can only be effected by the seperate action of ["the States" *altered to* "some one State"] in the first instance. Our State has by this time, I presume acted, and if she has ["authorised" *canceled*] made it the duty of the Legislature, as I hope she has, to apply in the manner prescribed by the Constitution, for a general Convention of the States, the issue then will be between ["a" *canceled*] such a convention and force—an issue on which, I trust the sound and patriotick of every party may rally against the inclination, which I doubt not Gen[era]l Jackson and his spoilers[?] will have to resort to force. I do solemnly believe, that nothing but the meeting of the States in Convention can save the Country and its institutions. The system can go on no longer and will end in despotism, or disunion, unless ["those, who" *canceled and* "the power which" *interlined*] made it and put it in motion, be called in to repair its damages and put it anew[?] in motion; and to this point the efforts of all who love their country ought to be directed.

I see you do not entirely agree to our doctrine. You object that it is not to be found in the Constitution. We have never claimed it, as expressly provided for; on the contrary, we have ever contended, that it ought not to ["been" *canceled*; "there" *interlined and canceled*; "have" *interlined*] been, as it belongs clearly ["to" *interlined*] the mass of the reserved rights, and is therefore not unconstitutional. That such was the ["fra" *canceled*] opinion of the framers of the Constitution, we have the strongest proof in the frequent attempts made in the Convention to deprive the States of the right by conferring on the Government the right to judge of its powers, as against the States, and of coercing their obedience by force; all of which failed. My object, however, is not to argue the point; but to say to you, that you must not dispair of the Republick. We thought to arrest the disease by Presidential elections. It first began to show itself in 1816. The spoil party was then formed under the auspices of Mr. [William H.]

Crawford. A Congressional caucus was its instrument. It disclosed itself with greater power in the contest of 1824,25, under the same chief and with the same ["weapons" *altered to* "weapon"]. It was again put down; but by this time the monied action of the gover[n]-ment had become so strong, that to get possession of it Mr. [John Quincy] Adams & Mr. [Henry] Clay set aside the will of the people, in the expectation of maint[ain]ing themselves through the force ["of" *interlined*] patronage. This expectation failed; but, he whom we raised to power deserted us and our principles, and threw himself into the position, from which his opponents had been ousted; and from which they have found it impossible to dislodge him. They were not the men to put him out; and the system has in the mean time become so disordered, that no ["resource" *canceled and then interlined*] is left to save the institutions and liberty of the country, but to call in the authority of the States through a general convention, and by their high authority to remedy a disorder, which has proved too strong ["for the" *canceled*] to be remedied through the ordinary action of the system. It is to that point that our effort will be directed, and, I trust, that [*word mutilated*; we] shall ultimately have the cooperation of the wise and good every where. It is the last great effort to save the liberty of the country.

Mrs. [Floride Colhoun] Calhoun has had the misfortune of a miscarriage. She has been very dangerous, but is now, I trust, safe. She desires to be affectionately remembered to yourself, Mrs. [Deborah Kay Hall] Ingham & family. Sincerely, J.C. Calhoun.

ALS owned by Ronald E. Bridwell; copy in ScU-SC, John C. Calhoun Papers.

Land grant signed by Robert Y. Hayne, Governor of S.C., Columbia, 3/14/1833. By this document, John C. Calhoun is granted a tract of 1,000 acres of land surveyed for him on 7/30/1832, situated in Pickens District "on a branch of Toxaway Creek waters of Tugaloo River," having the shape shown on a plat certified on 1/22 by Theo-[dore] Stark, Surveyor General (recorded copy in Sc-Ar, Records of the Secretary of State, Office of the Surveyor General, State Plats, 50:164 and 165). Recorded copy in Sc-Ar, Records of the Secretary of State, Recorded Instruments, Land Grants, Columbia Series, 81:65.

Land grant signed by Robert Y. Hayne, Governor of S.C., Columbia, 3/14/1833. This document grants to John C. Calhoun a tract of 1,000 acres of land on the "branches of Toxaway creek waters of Tugaloo River," located in Pickens District and surveyed for Calhoun on 7/30/1832. (A plat certified on 1/22 by Theo[dore] Stark, Surveyor General, shows the bounds of the grant [recorded copy in Sc-Ar, Records of the Secretary of State, Office of the Surveyor General, State Plats, 50:164 and 165].) Recorded copy in Sc-Ar, Records of the Secretary of State, Recorded Instruments, Land Grants, Columbia Series, 81:66.

Land grant signed by Robert Y. Hayne, Governor of S.C., Columbia, 3/14/1833. In accordance with the provisions of S.C. law, John C. Calhoun is granted a tract of 1,000 acres of land located in Pickens District "on a branch of Coneross waters of Seneca River" surveyed for him on 10/31/1832. (A plat certified on 1/22 [recorded copy in Sc-Ar, Records of the Secretary of State, Office of the Surveyor General, State Plats, 50:166] certified by Theo[dore] Stark, Surveyor General, shows the shape and bounds of the grant.) Recorded copy in Sc-Ar, Records of the Secretary of State, Recorded Instruments, Land Grants, Columbia Series, 81:64.

Ed[ward] W. Johnston, editor of the Columbia, S.C., *Telescope,* to Richard K. Crallé, Richmond, 4/7/1833. In assessing the political struggle in South Carolina over nullification, Johnston feels that, "the people of this State will not, while this controversy for the independence of the State Governments is on foot, allow themselves to be drawn into a presidential contest." Calhoun has been informed of this opinion by Dr. Thomas Cooper and by [William C.?] Preston but has made no reply. ALS in ScCleA.

From W[illia]m Dubose

Pine Ville [S.C.,] August 6th 1833
Dear Sir, I had the pleasure of receiving your favour of the 8th June, tho some time after its date, covering the letter from Mr. [James K.] Paulding to yourself. It has been unanswered to this time, I beg you to believe, entirely in consequence of a protracted indisposition & a desire to extend my enquiries on the subject of his letter, in this neighborhood & amongst those most likely to have received & cherished authentic traditions of a character so endeared to the pride & recollections of those amongst whom he resided, as Gen[era]l [Francis] Marion. It gives me great pleasure to understand that his life

& actions are likely to employ the labours of one so competent to do them justice as Mr. Paulding. I can not doubt, that from what has already been written on the subject, sufficient materials may be collected to enable him to complete such an undertaking as he proposes. You are doubtless prepared to believe that after the long period which has elapsed since the death of Gen[era]l Marion all traditions relating to him, even upon the scene, where the actions of his life, were ["once" *interlined*] the theme of all, have become obscure & little to be relied upon. Few of his cotemporaries still live & they are widely scattered over the Southern Country. Independently of this however, there are other sources at command, which may furnish abundant materials for a history of his public life at least. Of these Mr. Paulding refers to [Mason L.] Weem[s]'s work on the subject alone & may not be aware that of the distinguished men of the Revolutionary war, it has been the fortune of few to have had more written of them, in the form of History, Biography & anecdotes than Gen[era]l Marion, or to have had their general truth & authenticity better stamped by the testimonys of Relatives, friends & compatriots. When Mr. Weems first undertook the work to which Mr. P[aulding] refers, it is well known that he recceived all the aid from the late Hon[ora]ble Rob[er]t Marion, the Nephew of the General, which the possession of all his important papers & his own knowlege derived from years of confidential & affectionate intimacy & intercourse, enabled him to supply, & from Col. [Peter] Horry, in whose name the work purports to be written, an officer in high command in Marions brigade—as well as from many other Intelligent & distinguished Compatriots & intimates of the General, then & many years after—living in this neighborhood. The work appeared in my day & recollection & during the life of his Widow [Mary Videau Marion] & Nephew & of the other individuals referred to, with all of whom I was myself intimate. However little they may have been pleased with its excentricities of style & manner the truth & accuracy of the narrative as to the facts & incidents, were always acknowleged by those who had attended him personally throughout the war, or whose intimacy with him might have enabled them to detect errors of fact. However unworthy therefore Weems life, as a literary work, may be of the fame of the General, I doubt not, that with others to which Mr. Paulding may have access, it abounds with materials in skilful hands, for a worthy biography of Marion. Some years posterior to this publication, the late Judge [William D.] James, published a vol. on the same subject entitled, I think, A history of Marion's Brigade, containing much valuable information relating to Marion himself, his brigade

& its principal officers. The Judge had himself, in very early youth joined & served with the Corps & together with a very extensive & influential family connexion in the District of Country (now Williamsburgh & Marion Districts) where the early & independent operations of the Brigade lay had shared in all its dangers & honors. His father [John James] was one of its Majors & a brave, Intelligent & efficient officer. From the character of the Judge, his intelligence & his ample means of information, full faith is certainly due to his relation.

From the year 1780 when General Henry Lee of Virginia with his legion, was detached by Gen[era]l [Nathanael] Greene to cooperate with Marion in preparing the way for his own entrance into our State, to the close of the contest, the public life of Marion is embodied in the history of the war in the southern department. During this period he served almost constantly with Lee, either at the head of a separate force, before which all the British posts between Georgetown & Granby were subdued, or under the command of Greene himself. Of this period of our southern war a very interesting & minute account has been given by Gen[era]l Lee in his Memoirs. When to these are added [David] Ramsay's history of the Revolution, [William] Moultrie's Memoirs & the anecdotes of Major [Alexander] Garden, all of them actively engaged in the scenes of the day & relating important events, in which Marion bore a part second to none, I can not doubt that only the skill & talents of Mr. Paulding are wanting to give his Countrymen, a history of Gen. Marion, worthy of his great character. I may also add to this [*ms. torn; one word missing*] of authorities Judge [William] Johnson's life of Greene—I doubt not th[*ms. torn*] papers & documents originally furnished to Gen[era]l Horry by Mr. Marion may be recovered if desired, from the Representatives of Horry or Marion. It is also not improbable that our own public officers in this State, may still supply matter important to a Biographer of Marion, tho not so to a general historian like Ramsay or Johnson. I regret that the circumstances of our Country at this season, & other causes, have not allowed me to make more extensive enquiries before I replied to yours. I have thought however, that what I have said, might enable Mr. P[aulding] to form some opinion of the sufficiency of the materials, certainly at his command. It will afford me great pleasure to forward to him all the works referred to, with such Maps as may enable him to form an opinion as to our topography in relations to Marion's operations or such of them as may not be at his command at the North. Should other materials be necessary, I shall take equal pleasure in aiding to collect them. With great respect I have the honor to be, Wm. Dubose.

ALS owned by Charles Gouverneur Paulding. NOTE: Dubose (1786–1855), a planter and lawyer of St. Stephens Parish, a legislator and later lieutenant governor of S.C., was the son of Francis Marion's staff officer Samuel Dubose.

To J[AMES] K. PAULDING, New York City

Fort Hill, 4th Sept. 1833

Dear Sir, The enclosed [of 8/6] is from a gentleman [William Dubose] of some[?] respectability to whom I wrote on the subject of your letter in reference to the life of [Francis] Marion. Should you think proper to open a correspondence with him on the subject, I am sure he will take pleasure in aiding your patriotick intention of giving the publick a more full ["au" *canceled*] authentick account of the life and actions of one of the most remarkable men who appeared in our revolution. With great resp[ec]t I am & &c, J.C. Calhoun.

ALS with En owned by Charles Gouverneur Paulding.

To Dr. [WILLIAM] CRUMP, [Chief Clerk of the Pension Office]

Washington, 7th Dec[embe]r 1833

Sir, I enclose the case of John Harris, and will be much obliged to you for an early decision of his case. There can be no doubt of his service. I have known him from ["a child" *canceled and* "my infancy" *interlined*]; and the facts of his service & wound in the cause are known to all in that region of country. He is an excellent man; sober & respectable; an elder, of long standing, in the Preysbeterian church, and a son in law of the Gallant Gen[era]l [Andrew] Pickens, whose efforts in behalf of his country in the revolution, are so well known.

I see among the papers a letter from Mr. Patrick Noble, a son of Maj. Alexander Noble, of the Revolution, which states [f]acts, that may be important in the [es]tablishment of Mr. Harris' claim. Mr. Noble is well known to me. His statement may be implicitly relied on. No man in the State stands higher for probity. He is now speaker of our House of Representatives. With great respect I am & &, J.C. Calhoun.

ALS in DNA, RG 15 (Veterans Administration), Revolutionary War Pension and Bounty-Land Warrant Application Files, 1800–1900, S21808 (M-804:1200, frames 688–689). NOTE: A Clerk's EU indicates that a certificate of pension dated 12/9/1833 was sent to Calhoun for Harris.

Report by Horace Binney of a conversation with Calhoun, [Washington, 1834]. In a letter of 1/5/1861 to Francis Lieber, Binney recalled Calhoun's words spoken in conversation in 1834: "[The poor and uneducated] are increasing; there is no power in a republican government to repress them; their number and disorderly tempers will make them in the end efficient enemies of the men of property. They have the right to vote, they will finally control your elections, and by bad laws or by violence they will invade your houses and turn you out. Education will do nothing for them; they will not give it to their children; it will do them no good if they do. They are hopelessly doomed as a mass to poverty, from generation to generation; and from the political franchise they will increase in influence and desperation until they overturn you. The institution of slavery cuts off this evil by the root. The whole body of our servants, whether in the family or in the field, are removed from all influence upon the white class by the denial of all political rights. They have no more tendency to disturb the order of society than an overstock of horses or oxen. They have neither power nor ambition to disturb it. They can be kept in order by methods which a republican government, as well as a monarchical or a military one, can apply. They have no jealousy of the other class, nor the other of them. They never stand on the same platform with the white class. They only require supervision and domestic discipline to keep them in good order; and such means are easily applied and become normal in the State. The white class is therefore left to pursue without apprehension the means they think best to elevate their own condition. Slavery is indispensable to a republican government. There cannot be a durable republican government without slavery." In describing the conversation to Lieber, Binney said, "He [Calhoun] walked with me one morning, in the year 1834, for nearly two hours on the esplanade of the Capitol; and gave his views to me, I suppose fully, as he had a full opportunity." PC in Charles C. Binney, *The Life of Horace Binney with Selections from his Letters*, pp. 313–316.

Remarks in the Senate, 3/4/1834. Amid a debate involving rival claims to a Senate seat from R.I., [Ezekiel F.] Chambers [of Md.] made reference to a possible precedent, the Senate having received a minority paper. Calhoun "said he was in the Chair on the occasion alluded to, and had a distinct recollection of it. It was submitted as a paper, and printed as a paper, not as a report." From *Register of Debates*, 23rd Cong., 1st Sess., col. 806; variant in the Washington, D.C., *United States' Telegraph*, March 6, 1834, p. 2.

Remarks in the Senate about a motion made by [Thomas H.] Benton, 4/18/1834. During a protracted debate concerning [Andrew Jackson's] protest, spectators in the galleries became disorderly for "some time." Benton "moved that the Sergeant-at-Arms be directed to take into custody those persons who disturbed the Senate." [John M.] Clayton opposed the motion on the ground that it was impracticable. Echoing that sentiment, Calhoun "suggested that there was one objection to the motion; and that was, the impossibility of executing the order which had been given. It was not possible for the Sergeant-at-Arms to execute any such order." From *Register of Debates*, 23rd Cong., 1st Sess., cols. 1387–1388. Also printed in the Washington, D.C., *Daily National Intelligencer*, April 19, 1834, p. 3; the Washington, D.C., *United States' Telegraph*, April 21, 1834, p. 3.

To N[ICHOLAS] BIDDLE, [Philadelphia]

Washington, 14th June 1834
Dear Sir, I take the liberty of introducing you to Mr. [William J.] Alexander of North Carolina, who proposes to make a short visit to your city. Mr. Alexander is speaker of the House of Representatives of that State, and ranks among her most respectable citizens. Any attention, which you may extend to him will be considered by me as a personal favour. With great respect I am & &, J.C. Calhoun.

ALS owned by Robert H. Mackintosh, Jr.

To JOHN FORBES, [Cincinnati]

Washington, 25th June 1834

Dear Sir, I have bearly time, in the midest of the pressure of business incident to the close of a session, to acknowledge your letter of the 8th Inst. [*not found*], and to express the satisfaction I have felt on its perusal.

You do not feel more confidence, than what you ought, as to the final triumph of our cause. Experience will continue to prove, as it is now daily doing, that our institutions and our liberty can be preserved on no other principles, but those for which we contend. I hold it to be susceptible of the clearest proof, that all the evils, that we now experience, have grown out of the opposite view of our System.

As to the next Presidential election, our friends every where may rest assured of one thing, that the State right party of the South, and I trust every where, hold our doctrines far higher than the Presidency, and that all of our movements ["towards" *canceled*] in relation to it, will be governed wholly in reference to them. One point, I hold to be fixed, that we ["shall" *interlined*] rally on ["none" *canceled and* "no one" *interlined*], who does not openly support our doctrines. As to myself, I feel no solicitude in relation to the subject. Should it be the desire of our friends & party generally—should they think that by bringing my name forward, that the cause would be advanced, and the interest of the country promoted, I could not object; but if otherwise, I ["would" *canceled and* "shall" *interlined*] be content. To save our institutions, and our liberty is the only object of my ambition. I am, however, of the impression, that there is ["yet" *interlined*] ample time to move on the Presidential election. The people can better decide a year hence ["on a proper selection" *interlined*] than at the present time. I write you freely, and for your own eye only.

I enclose a copy of my speech on the Protest [of President Andrew Jackson] in pamphlet form.

I expect to leave this for my residence near Pendleton on Tuesday next, where, if any thing of importance should ["occur" *interlined*], I would be glad to hear from you. With great respect I am & &, J.C. Calhoun.

Photocopy of ALS and typescript in AzTeS, Information Exchange Database Collection.

Deed executed by John C. Calhoun, Pickens District, S.C., 11/23/-1834. By this deed, Calhoun sells for $75 to J[ames] Edward Colhoun of Abbeville District 1,000 acres on "Toxaway Creek waters of Tugaloo River," 1,000 acres on "a Branch of Toxaway Creek bounding on the above mentioned tract of land," and 1,000 acres of land on the Coneross Creek. On 11/25/1834 Floride [Colhoun] Calhoun signed a renunciation of dower rights on these tracts. The deed was witnessed by Nancy Morrison. Recorded copy in Sc-Ar, Pickens County Deeds, C-1:22 (microfilm).

Deed executed by J[ames] Edward Colhoun, Pickens District, S.C., 11/23/1834. By this deed he sells to John C. Calhoun for $5 "and other legal considerations," 640 acres of land on Twenty-Six Mile Creek. Recorded copy in Sc-Ar, Anderson County Deeds, U-322:322–323.

Contract for the purchase of lands, 12/2/1834. This document records a partnership between John C. Calhoun, and Andrew P[ickens] Calhoun, on the one part, and Ker Boyce on the other, for the purchase of lands in the Red River district of La. "or elsewhere." Boyce agrees to advance $20,000 for this purpose through an agent in New Orleans. Lands will be purchased by Andrew P[ickens] Calhoun and Andrew Pickens [Jr.] and held in accordance with an agreement specified in correspondence [*not found*] previously conducted between John C. Calhoun and Boyce. Boyce is to be repaid one-half of the $20,000 "so soon as the lands which may be purchased for the firm shall have been divided," with interest at seven per cent from 11/19/1834. Pledged to Boyce for faithful fulfillment of the contract are 880 acres of land in Anderson District, S.C., and two slaves belonging to Andrew P. Calhoun and 770 acres of land in Anderson District and six slaves belonging to John C. Calhoun. The contract was signed in [Columbia] Richland District on 12/2; witnessed by John T. Chappell and John J. Chappell; recorded in Columbia on 12/-6/1834; and recorded by the Clerk of Court in Pickens District on 1/5/1835. An endorsement by Richard Anderson as attorney for Boyce, found on the second recorded copy only and dated 6/1/1835, attests that the "mortgage has been duly satisfied." Recorded copy in Sc-Ar, Records of the Secretary of State, Recorded Instruments, Miscellaneous Records (Main Series), 1671–1973, I:97–100; recorded copy (microfilm) in Sc-Ar, Pickens County Deeds, C-1:28–30.

To JOHN VANDERLYN, Charleston

Senate Chamber, 21st Dec[embe]r 1834

Dear Sir, I have just received your letter left in the care of Mr. King, and herewith enclose you a letter to my friend Gen[era]l [James] Hamilton [Jr.]. The high standing and universal acquaintance of Gen[era]l Hamilton with every class of citizens in Charleston, will I feel confident supercede the necessity of an introduction to any other friend in Charleston. I am sure he will take pleasure in forwarding the object of your visit.

I hope you may have the success your [*sic*] deserve, and I know not how to express myself more strongly for your welfare. With sincere regard I am & &, J.C. Calhoun.

ALS in Museum of the City of New York, John Vanderlyn Collection. NOTE: Vanderlyn (1775–1852), a native of N.Y., was an artist noted particularly for his portraits of prominent men.

From Samuel F.B. Morse, 1835. Morse writes a full-page inscription to Calhoun on the front end-leaf of a copy of his *Foreign Conspiracy against the Liberties of the United States*. First edition (New York: 1835). Book offered for sale by Bodley Book Shop, New York City, according to a page from an unidentified catalog.

From R[ICHARD] K. CRALLÉ and Others

Lynchburg [Va.,] Oct. 17th 1835

Sir: The undersigned ["ap"(?) *interlined*] as a Committee appointed by a number of the Citizens of Lynchburg and its neighbourhood, are charged with the duty of inviting you, and your Colleague, the Hon. W[illia]m C. Preston, in their name, to pass through this Town, on your way to Congress, and to partake of a public dinner with them, on such day as may be most convenient to you. They are informed that the route through Lynchburg is nearly as direct as any other from your residence to Washington City: and ["therefore" *interlined*] hope that by adopting it on this occasion, while you will afford them an opportunity of paying their personal respects, ["they" *canceled and* "you" *interlined*] will not ["be" *interlined*] put you [*sic*] to any inconvenience, nor interfere with ["your" *canceled and* "other" *interlined*] engagements.

It is needless to assure you that we take pleasure in ["in the performance" *interlined*; of] the duty thus devolved on us by our fellow citizens. This testimony of the estimation in which they hold your public and private character, we feel authorized to say, is cordially tendered to you by very many, who honestly differ with you in opinion on several important political questions: but we flatter ourselves, the tribute will not be less acceptable on that account. On the contrary, it may be the more gratifying, as affording the evidence that, under our free institutions, public servants who openly, and honestly and independently maintain their principles—whatever may be the differences of opinion in regard to their nature and tendency—will always find intelligent, and patriotic, and liberal interpreters of their motives[?] and conduct.

In discharging the duty assigned to us by those we represent, we take the occasion to join with them in expressing the hope that it may not be opposed to your feelings nor inconsistent with your public or private engagements to accept of the invitation we are desired to proffer—and at the same time to ["assure you" *canceled*] tender to you the assurances of our individual respect and esteem. Your ob[edien]t Ser[van]ts, ["Thos. A. Holcombe" *canceled*], Sam[ue]l J. Wiatt, W[illia]m Radford, E. Fletcher, A. McDaniel, M. Langhorne, Tho[ma]s A. Holcombe, S.H. Davis, N.H. Toler, J.M. Warwick, Dr. Latham, J.B. Cabell, Dr. Payne, Dr. Rhodes, A. Leftwich, N.J. Floyd, F.T. Bowen, C.L. Mosby, J. Saunders, R.K. Crallé.

Draft (in Crallé's handwriting) in ViU, Richard Kenner Crallé Papers. NOTE: Calhoun's name appears nowhere on this document, but the fact has been assumed from the reference to "your Colleague" Preston.

From [the Rev. NOAH WORCESTER?]

[Brighton, Mass.?,] April 26, 1837
Sir, Permit a stranger in the seventy-ninth year of his age to address to you some thoughts which have been occasioned by a just sentiment uttered by you in the Senate of the United States, near the close of the last session of Congress. I have not referred to the astounding opinion "that experience will show that slavery is a good for both races;" but to what you said in reply to Mr. [William C.] Rives, after he had expressed his belief "that slavery is an evil both moral and political." The newspapers gave your reply in the following words— "if slavery is considered to be an evil by the Senator from Virginia,

he ought to aid in getting rid of it; it is his duty to do so as a wise and good man."

Conscience and common sense readily acquiesce in your opinion that a man "ought to aid in getting rid" of what he believes to be a moral evil; and it is hoped that the sentiment will be impressed on the minds of myriads of your countrymen by all the weight of your character. Should you exert your influence for that purpose you may be the instrument of immense good, not only to slaveholders but to the people of the free States. It may do much towards exciting a candid and kind feeling between men of different opinions in different parts of the country, so that the subject of slavery may be freely and fully discussed without producing that bitterness, animosity and reviling which has too often been apparent. Hence perhaps a course may be discovered for the removal of slavery, contrary to the belief of Mr. Rives. Or if slavery is a good, as you imagine, free discussion may be the way in which that good is to be made obvious. It is not more evident that a man "ought to aid in getting rid" of what he believes to be evil, than that every man should be applauded—not reproached—who conscientiously acts on this principle. How unreasonable then is the conduct of men who defame as incendiaries those who seek the abolition of slavery firmly believing, with Mr. Rives, that it is an evil. It is in such a belief that I now write to you—and I do it in the hope that I may "aid in getting rid" of slavery, by engaging you to exert your extensive influence to promote kind feelings among men of different opinions. It will be easy for a mind so discerning as yours, to see that a general adoption of your sentiment on this point would tend greatly to suppress that bitterness which has so often appeared between men in different regions of our country.

Besides, if all "*ought* to aid in getting rid" of what they believe to be evil, may we not reasonably suppose that much might have been done before now, had the principle been adopted and reduced to practice fifty years ago? The avowed belief that slavery is an evil was for a long time common in the slave States, as well as in the free States. It was the decided opinion of Mr. [Thomas] Jefferson when he wrote his "Notes on Virginia"; and there has been abundant evidence that this opinion was very common, though not universal. I would ask you the plain question, How long have you known it to be the avowed opinion of any eminent men that "slavery is a good for both races?" How long is it since it was the common language of slave holders, "that slavery is an evil brought on us by the arbitrary government of Great Britain"—hence an evil for which we are not to be blamed? Is it as much as seven years since the latter was the common plea of the South? I first saw the doctrine "that slavery is a good" in an extract from a Charleston paper, and in that extract it was freely admitted that the Northern people had not been made acquainted with the then present views of slaveholders, "that slavery is a good." The avowal of this sentiment soon brought to my mind the following prediction—"For this cause God shall send them strong delusion that they should believe a lie, that they all might be damned"— that is, *condemned* or *punished*—"who had not believed the truth, but had pleasure in unrighteousness." From that time to the present, I do not know that I have ever seen or thought of the doctrine when the prediction did not soon occur. I shall briefly mention some things which seem to me as proof that those "believe a lie," who believe that "slavery is a good for both races."

1. In former ages slavery was the effect of war. Conquerors became slaveholders, and the conquered became slaves, whatever might be their color. Was slavery *then* "a good for both races?"

2. If I am not under a mistake there was a long period when the blacks were in the front rank of mankind, as to learning and civilization. During that period, the Israelites were enslaved by the Egyptians, who were then a black race, and before all other people of that day as to learning. These facts were fully stated several years ago in an interesting article written by A[lexander] H. Everett, and which has recently been published in "The Philanthropist" printed at Cincinnati by Mr. [James G.] Birney. Was slavery *then* "a good for both races?" If so, why were miracles wrought for the redemption of the Israelites?

3. There was a time when our English ancestors were so barbarous as to sell their children for slaves to the Irish. The custom was prohibited, says Mrs. [Sarah Kirby] Trimmer, A.D. 1014. Was slavery *then* "a good for both races?"

4. In our own age many white people have been enslaved by the Algerines—some of these were from the United States. Will you say that this slavery was "a good for both races?"

5. Mr. Jefferson in his "Notes on Virginia" endeavored to impress this awful idea on the minds of his countrymen, that it is possible, if not probable, that by the righteous providence of God the present condition of the whites and the blacks will be reversed—that the whites will become slaves, and the blacks slave-holders. Will you say that in such a reverse of conditions, slavery will still be "a good for both races?"

6. Within a century, a great part of the slavery which existed a

hundred years ago has been abolished. This is supposed to have been effected by the progress of light and truth. It must doubtless have resulted from an increase of light and civilization, or from an increase of darkness and barbarism.

7. The doctrine "that slavery is a good" has made its appearance in our country in opposition to what has been believed to be the blessed effects of light and truth. This seems to me to be a good reason for believing that your new doctrine is the effect of "strong delusion." For if we admit that your doctrine is an uncommon ray of light by which the world is to become illuminated, what are the consequences to be expected? Are they not these—that many nations who have abolished slavery, in whole or in part, will, on perceiving your new light, adopt a retrograde march, and re-establish slavery in its most barbarous forms—that the people of our country will cancel their Revolutionary creed "that all men are created equal" and that *liberty is an unalienable right*—and also revive the African slave trade, which is now piracy by the laws of the land; and that Great Britain will retrace the steps by which she abolished the slave trade and slavery—re-establish both—carry on the slave trade in her own vessels and fill her numerous islands with slaves?

Surely, Sir, such things must be expected by you, or you cannot reasonably suppose that your new doctrine will be adopted by other nations as light, but will be rejected and abhorred as one of the wildest delusions of the human mind.

Much has been said by the advocates of slavery to impress the idea, that the condition of the Southern slaves is as good if not better than the condition of the Northern servants or laborers. If those who say such things believe them to be true, why do they not perceive that there is as great danger of exciting Northern insurrections by what they say of our laborers, as there is of exciting southern insurrections by what we say against slavery? Why then do they not forbear to publish their views lest they should excite Northern insurrections? Besides, how will such reasoners account for it that Northern legislatures encourage the instruction of the laboring people, while the Southern legislatures forbid teaching the slaves under severe penalties, through fear that if the slaves should be taught to read and write, they will not be contented with their present condition? Are we to ascribe all the difference in the two cases to the greater humanity of the Northern legislatures? or to the fact that the Southern legislators know it to be falsehood when any pretend that the condition of the slaves is as good as the condition of the Northern laborers?

It is possible, Sir, that you may wish to know more about the man who has thus taken the liberty to address you with all the frankness of a friend. Had Mr. [Thomas S.] Grimké been living, I might have referred you to him for some information; but as he is dead, I can think of no one to whom I can refer you but the Rev. Mr. [Samuel] Gilman of Charleston. The writer, however, regards himself as one who on all disputed questions aims to be on the side of truth and humanity, whether that be the popular side or not; but aware of his liability to err, he aims to exercise the same candor towards those from whom he dissents, that he desires of them towards himself. He is therefore yours with great respect, [Noah Worcester?].

PC in the Boston, Mass., *Christian Register and Boston Observer*, May 27, 1837, p. 2; PC in *The Liberator*, vol. VII, no. 23 (June 2, 1837), p. 94; PC in *The Genius of Universal Emancipation and Quarterly Anti-Slavery Review*, vol. XV, no. 1 (July 1837), pp. 39–41. NOTE: In a note printed in the *Christian Register*, the editor of the newspaper stated that "the name of the writer was given in the letter sent to Mr. Calhoun; but he has thought it the better way to suppress it in the copy for publication." *The Liberator* reprinted this note but added it was "presumed" that the writer of the letter was "the venerable and excellent Noah Worcester, of Brighton, Mass."

To A[RMISTEAD] BURT, Abbeville, S.C.

Fort Hill, 5th Aug[us]t 1837

My dear Sir, I regret very much, that your engagements were such as to prevent you from making us a visit when you were up in June. We would have been very glad to see you; and I had much to say on several points, on which I would have been glad to have had your views.

I will with pleasure comply with your desire, as to my portrait when I go on to Washington.

I have not spoken to Col. [John Ewing] Colhoun yet in relation to Mr. [George] McDuffies portrait. He & his family are in the deepest affliction. Yesterday he buried his second son John Ewing. His oldest [William Ransom Colhoun], was at the same time dangerously ill of the fever, and he himself very low with the dyspepsia. As soon as his son is well enough he intends to visit the Lime Stone Springs in Spartanburgh. Before he goes, I will seek some occasion, to communicate to him Mr. McDuffie's wishes in relation to his portrait.

It is very uncertain whether, I will have an opportunity of seeing you before I go on to Washington. It will depend on the route I will take. It is my present intention to take the direct route from here by GreenVille, Linco[l]nton, Salisbury, as it will take me through a high & healthy region all the way; but if I should not, I will pass through Abbeville, when I would be very glad to see you. I will set out between the 20th & 25th, and should I take Abbeville in my way will let you know the day when you may expect me, so that you may be at home at the time.

I am very happy to hear, that my brother William [Calhoun] is better. I would have been down to see him, but my time is so short, and ["ex" *canceled*] I expected several friends here by appointment which prevented me from leaving home; and I have ["not" *canceled and* "yet" *interlined*] to make a visit to Georgia, before I leave home, on business. I hope, however, if I take the route by GreenVille, I shall have the pleasure of meeting him at the Lime Stone Springs. The stage, if I mistake not goes by. I have been looking for Mr. Mc-Duffie for some time. I hope he is not unwell.

Mrs. [Floride Colhoun] Calhoun & the family join their love to you & Mrs. [Martha Calhoun] Burt. Sincerely & affectionately, J.C. Calhoun.

ALS in ScCleA.

To B[ENJAMIN] W. LEIGH, [former Senator from Va., Norfolk]

Washington, 16th Sep[tembe]r 1837
My dear Sir, I handed over the [Richmond] Whig [of 9/13] to Mr. [Richard K.] Crallé, who will give the correspondence a place in the [Washington] Reformer. What a base old calumniator! I think this ["present" *canceled*] exposure will put an end to his power to do mischief.

I was glad to receive even so short a note from you, as that [of 9/13] which accompanied the Whig. We are now in the midest of the predicted events of 1834. What a triumph for you! How deep the degradation of your enemies! I believe the period has arrived, that the banks & Govt. should seperate. The interest of both demands it; but it ought to be done most gentlely [*sic*]. A national bank is impossible, and, if possible, in the present state of things it could do but little ["harm" *canceled*] good, and would be exceedingly dangerous. As to a reconnection with the league of [State] banks, it is out of the question. I do trust, that we agree in opinion, but if not, let me beg of you to suspend the formation of a definite opinion for the present, till you can see the whole ground. There are few men whose ["good" *interlined*] opinion, I value so highly as yours. Truely & sincerely, J.C. Calhoun.

[P.S.] Poor [Martin] Van [Buren] he had no choice. His cunning, timidity & blindness of event[s] forced [him] to a position that left him no choice.

ALS in ViU, Benjamin Watkins Leigh Papers. NOTE: Leigh's letter of 9/13, to which the above is a reply, is published in *The Papers of John C. Calhoun*, 13: 539. The "base old calumniator" referred to by Calhoun was William Smith, a former Senator from S.C.

To Gen. W[ADDY] THOMPSON, [JR., Representative from S.C.]

[Washington, 1837 or 1838?]

Mr. Calhoun's respects to Gen[era]l Thompson, and herewith returns the petition of W[illiam] Harper. In the present temper of the Senate, and especially of the Committee on pension, he fears, that there is not the least prospect of granting the prayer of the petition. As far as ["I have" *canceled and* "he has" *interlined*] observed not a petition for pension has been favourably reported on. The only prospect, he thinks, of getting the pension is to obtain the sanction of the House again in its favour, which he presumes would not be difficult, when by possibility it may be forced through the Senate.

He suggests this course for the consideration of Gen[era]l Thompson, but if he should take a different view, and return ["it" *canceled and* "the petition" *interlined*], he will cheerfully present it, and use his best efforts to ["see, that" *canceled and* "obtain" *interlined*] full justice for Mr. Harper.

ALU in ScU-SC, John C. Calhoun Papers.

From SEABORN JONES, [former Representative from Ga.]

Columbus [Ga.,] 19th Feb[ruar]y 1839

My dear Sir, I am sure you will excuse me for imposing upon you the trouble of this business in a matter in which I have a large interest. You have no doubt heard of the large contract made by Gen[era]l [J.C.] Watson and others with some Indian chiefs under the Sanction of Gen[era]l Jessup [*sic*; Thomas S. Jesup] for the purchase of all the alleged fraudulent cases from the said Chiefs. Ag[ains]t the validity of this contract I submitted an argument to the Com[missione]rs [Alfred] Balch & [T. Hartley] Crawford and those Gentlemen presented ["an"(?) *canceled*] reports to the President decidedly ag[ains]t the said Contract. With some friends I have contracts from individual Reserves which conflict with this large contract. Notwithstanding these reports of the Com[missione]rs Gen[era]l [Andrew] Jackson did so far sanction the large contract as to allow the contractors to procure the assents of the Individual Indians. These assents were obtained as the original contracts had been by procuring other Indians to personate the true Indians the owners of the lands. We have fought ag[ains]t the large contract till we are tired and have proposed to the Sec[retar]y at War to have the pattents issued to the Indians and let the Courts in Alabama determine upon the validity of the contracts under which we and our opponents claim. This has been opposed by them, because they know that the means by which they first acquired any claim (personating the right Indians & stealing the land) cannot bear investigation—that the large contract by which they sought to prop their fraudulent claims is no better and that the *assents* which they have taken under the permission of the President are in the same situation. The course we have proposed of issuing the patents to the real Indians meets the approbation of all the Alabama Delegation as I have been informed—that Mr. [Joel R.] Poinsett sees no objection to it and that it is now before the Att[orne]y Gen[era]l [Felix Grundy] for his opinion as to its legality under the treaty. Now I wish you to examine this subject and aid us, if you agree with me, in presenting the matter to the Att[orne]y-Gen[era]l in such way as to satisfy him that it can legally and ought to be done.

A short history of the transaction will aid your research. A number of persons about the beginning of 1835 commenced having the right Indians personated and getting contracts certified for $5 or $10 a half section. When these facts were bro[ugh]t to the knowledge

of the Pres[iden]t he ordered [Robert W.] McHenry to stop certify-
ing & make an examination. The result of this was a report by Mc-
Henry ag[ains]t them. The individuals who were implicated &
whose contracts were reported ag[ains]t had influence enough at
Washington, thro some of the Inferior Officers, to procure an order
for another examination. Colo[nel John B.] Hogan was directed to
make it & his report was stronger ag[ains]t them & more unsatisfactory. Then [G.D.] Anderson & [J.W.] Burney were appointed with
Hogan. They were progressing & reporting ag[ains]t the fraudulent
contracts when their operations were broken up by the Indian Hostilities. Before they closed their labors in consequence of those
hostilities Capt. [John] Page about the 9th of May 1836 reported a
talk he had held with O poth le Yoholo (perhaps a greater scoundrel
white or red does not live) in which Capt. Page says, O poth le Yoholo
proposed that the *persons holding fraudulent Claims* should come to
the towns & they & the Chief of the town (the right Indian being
produced) should each choose a man to value the land & the fraudulent purchaser should then pay the money to the proper Indian in
the person of an Ag[en]t of the government who should write on the
contract *"recertified"* & sign his name to it. Now mark this arrangement is proposed in favor of the *Land stealers* to whom a presumption is thus given. It is to be hoped this view did not present itself
to Gov. [Lewis] Cass or he would not have sanctioned the course.
About the 13th of May, Judge [Eli S.] Shorter wrote to the Sec[re-
tar]y of War that Capt. Page had informed him of this talk and as
one of *those purchasers* in his behalf & in behalf of the other purchasers he assented to this plan. The Sec[retar]y at War authorises
Capt. Page to have the plan carried into execution. The war coming
on under date of 19th May Gen[era]l Jesup is instructed to carry this
plan into effect. You will see the whole arrangement is made for the
benefit of the fraudulent purchasers, *the land stealers.* To have carried this scheme into effect, illegal and fraudulent as it was would
have required more money, than those gentlemen could then have
commanded and it was necessary to change it. This Gen. Jesup was
soon prevailed upon to do and not long after he came into the Nation,
he notified the Indians and the public that they must prepare for removal by about the middle of August. Numbers of persons went to
Tallassee where ["the" *canceled and* "numbers of" *interlined*] Indians were assembled to buy their lands and carried large amounts of
money, as it was well known very valuable tracts remained unsold &
it was expected the Indians would be then sent off & would sale before they went. When the purchasers arrived there was no persons

authorised to certify & no sales of Course. A secret negotiation was then going on for this large contract. Some how or other it got out and a larger amount offered for the land. Those ["land stealers" *canceled*] fraudulent purchasers were to have the preference. At midnight the contract was made & signed and it is pretended the money was paid to the Chiefs next day—for the acc[oun]ts on the back of the Contract were dated the next day. If any payment was made the Chiefs, it was in direct violation of one article of that contract which required the money to be paid to the *Individual Reservees.* This contract was protested—reported against—and not sanctioned by the President. The President did authorise the claimants under it to get the assents of the Individual Indians. The treaty gave him no such power. The treaty authorised the *Indian* to sell with the approbation of the *President* and did not authorise the *President* or his *Gen[era]l Commanding* to sell the land & then call on the Individual Reservee for his *consent.* Besides the treaty limited five years for the minority or tutelage of the Indian. And before the *Consent* of the Indian could be obtained, that term must expire and did expire & when it had expired, the President no longer had any right to give or withhold his consent. That contract or the *assents* afterwards procured cannot be of any legal validity and Patents ought not to issue under it to any person. It would only be to place them on higher ground in Court and compel the persons claiming adversely to file Bills in Equity or Scire facias to set those grants aside. Who then ought the Patents to issue in favor of? If a fair trial were practicable we could show that we have made fair & bona fide purchases from the proper Indians and that we are equitably entitled to them. But a fair trial cannot be had at Washington and we are willing to waive our claim for a Patent and say let the Patent issue to the Indian and we are willing to shew to the Courts in Alabama that ours [is] a good & theirs a fraudulent title. That their large contract is illegal & void & that their *assents* were obtained in the same way (by personating the right Indians) as their original fraudulent contracts were. Now Comes the question which has been submitted to the Att[orne]y General. Can these patents legally issue to the Individual Reservees under the treaty? But little reflection can be necessary upon an examination of the treaty and of the facts to bring us to the conclusion that they can.

The 2nd article gives the reservations. The 3rd gives the right of selling them with the approbation of the President—and the 3rd provides, that "At the end of five years, all the Creeks entitled to these selections, and *desirous of remaining,* shall receive *patents*

513

therefore ["from the U." *canceled*] in fee simple, from the United States."

That these Indians have not sold to the fraudulent purchasers, the Reports of McHenry, Hogan and Burney[,] Anderson & Hogan all prove. That they did not sell under the large contracts, made for the benefit of the same persons, the reports of Balch & Crawford clearly establish. There can be as little question that they were desirous of remaining and that they were compelled to remove at the point of the bayonet.

In letter of 19 May 1836 to Hogan, Anderson & Burney[,] "The object at present is to reduce them to ["subjection" *canceled*] submission, and to remove them without further delay to the Country west of the Mississippi." ["]The military commanding Officer &c to remove them by military force to the country west of the Mississippi." The instructions given to Gen[era]l Jesup on the same day are in the same spirit. Many other letters might be referred to (but I have the document not before me) to prove the same thing. ["When the Indians" *canceled*] Gen[era]l Jesup gave public notice that the Indians must be prepared for removal by a given day and when the Indians were assembled at Tallassee they were not *invited* to go—but distinctly informed they must go. There can be no doubt they were required and compelled to remove west of the Mississippi about September 1836 and that [they] were desirous of remaining and some would have remained in Alabama longer than the 22 March 1837 (at which time their tutelage expired) had they not been compelled to remove. These facts being beyond controversy, they are under the treaty entitled to [*partial word canceled*] patents for their Individual reservations.

The right of the Indians to patents being clear there can be [no] substantial reason for refusing them unless the Government is determined to ratify the large contract and confirm the claims of the fraudulent purchasers in spite of all the testimony—the law & the reports which have [been] made against by Her own officers specially charged to examine into & report upon them. If this be so we would be glad to know it and we will then cease to trouble the officers of the govt. and our selves in procuring & examining *testimony*. Indeed it can scarcely be called *testimony*. One man states that he heard another say &c and one Capt. gives his *opinion* of Indian usages directly contrary to the regulations of the President, and a Commanding Gen[era]l *deems* it best to *disobey* instructions and make[?] out a new course *agreeably to his opinions* and the benefit of those persons he wishes to serve, however contrary to the treaty and the instructions given for his government.

It is not and cannot be testimony nor can we obtain the legal testimony for any enquiry & investigation at Washington—nor can we have a fair trial.

We cannot get the legal testimony—Because we cannot *compel the persons* who *do know* the fraudulent manner in which the contracts were made to give their *voluntary* affidavits. They are friendly to those persons who have committed the frauds. They will not depose & some of them will I have no doubt leave the State or go to Jail before they will testify even in Court. Again the testimony is all taken ex parte—and there is no opportunity of Cross examination. Again it is impossible for the the [*sic*] Sec[retar]y of War or any Com[missione]r at Washington to Judge of the Credit of the Witnesses; and often many of the men engaged in the same practices if not interested in the contracts are bro[ugh]t forward to bolster them up by false testimony. It is impossible a fair investigation can be had & consequently an improper decision will most likely be the consequence.

You will find Page's letter of 9th May 1836 in Senate Document 276 of Session 1835 page 384. Gen[era]l Jesups instructions 19 May 1835 same doc. page 276. I cannot give you the page of Shorters letter 18 May 1836.

Will you allow me to ask the favor of you to examine that document and the reports made by Balch & Crawford together with the pamphlet Doc. 452 H. of Rep. 25 Cong. 2 Session and the reports made by Balch & Crawford in the fall of 1836 which are not in that document. I know I am giving you a great deal of trouble but hope my apology will be found in the belief I have that you do not fear trouble in ascertaining truth, & affording the means of rendering Justice. Please submit this long letter to the Att[orne]y Gen[era]l & Sec[retar]y at War with such remarks as you may deem proper & necessary. Believe me y[ou]rs very resp[ectfull]y, Seaborn Jones.

ALS in DNA, RG 75 (Bureau of Indian Affairs), Letters Received by the Office of Indian Affairs, 1824–1880, Creek Reserves, 1839.

From J[AMES] K. PAULDING

Navy Department, Dec[embe]r 18th 1839
Sir, Your letter [*not found*] with its enclosure from Solomon Cohen
Esq[ui]r[e], for the appointment of Mr. David Lopez as midshipman
has been received, and will be respectfully considered when the Department is furnished with his precise age, to which effect Mr. Cohen
has been written this day. I am very respectfully Your Ob[edien]t
Serv[an]t, J.K. Paulding.

FC in DNA, RG 45 (Naval Records), Miscellaneous Letters Sent by the Secretary of the Navy, 1798–1886, 26:412 (M-209:10).

To A[NDREW] P[ICKENS] CALHOUN, [Marengo County, Ala.]

Fort Hill, 16th Oct., 1846 [*sic*; 1840]
My Dear Andrew: Your letters of the 16th and 24th of last month
came by the same mail, a week since, and brought the agreeable intelligence of the continued and uninterrupted good health of the
place, to a period so late, that I hope all danger has passed. The
severe trial of the year, acknowledged to be one of the most sickly,
gives good ground to believe that you have had the good fortune of
selecting a spot, combining the rare advantages of a low latitude,
great fertility and good health. It is difficult to say how much value
it adds to the place. The continuance of the health of yourself and
family and the complete restoration of Patrick's, of which I learned
by his last letter, relieved me from much anxiety. I am glad to hear
that your prospect of a cotton crop continues so good, and that you
have suffered comparatively little by the worm, whose ravages I
hope have stopped ere this. There are some indications of them in
my cotton, and I understand they have done much mischief in the
State. If the accounts from Florida are to be trusted they have done
more damage there than any where else. Taking it altogether the
prospect is a short crop and good prices.

Our election is over. [William] Butler is elected [U.S. Represen-
tative] by a small majority (147) owing to a division of the vote between [Jesse W.] Norris and [Joseph] Powell, the latter of whom
could not be induced to withdraw. Haygood [*sic*; Benjamin Ha-
good] (Federal) beat [Bailey] Barton, Republican by 14 only for

the State Senate. It is said the election will be contested, on account of bad votes. Your Uncle John [Ewing Colhoun], who was also a candidate, got less than 200 votes. The Harrison Federal party carried in this district all their candidates except one to the [S.C.] House of Representatives, Col. [William] Hunter. In Greenville, the opposite ticket prevailed throughout by a large majority. I have not heard from the other parts of the State yet. There is no doubt, however, of almost perfect union in the State.

I am waiting according to your advice for frost before I set out. As yet we have had none though a great deal of cool weather. It is now raining and has been for the last fifteen hours with a prospect of continuing as much longer. The probability is it will be followed by cold weather and frost. If it should, I will lose no time in setting out. I cannot fix the day, as that depends on the weather. Should it turn cold enough for frost, you may send your carriage to Selma, in time for me to get there going by Dahlonega [Ga.] and allowing one or two days on the road. I will take the stage to there and thence by the nearest and quickest stage routes. You need not send before frost, as I do not think it would be prudent to venture before. John [C. Calhoun, Jr.] will probably accompany me.

As I hope it will be but a short time before we meet, I will postpone what I had to say on politics and other subjects till then. All join in sending their love to you and Margaret [Green Calhoun]. I am glad to hear that Duff [Green Calhoun] thrives so well and is so promising, I shall be quite curious to see him. Your affectionate father, John C. Calhoun.

P.S. Your Uncle William [Calhoun] was better by the last accounts from him.

PC in Alvan F. Sanborn, ed., *Reminiscences of Richard Lathers* . . . , pp. 31–33; variant typescript in DLC, Carnegie Institution of Washington Transcript Collection.

To [JAMES K.] PAULDING, [Secretary of the Navy], "Private"

Senate Chamber [*ca.* March 1841]
My dear Sir, I intended to call this morning in order to see you, but was prevented by the call of a friend & I am compelled to do, that by note, which I intended to do verbally. I understand, that the place of Naval agent at the Norfolk station is vacant, and that Dr. Collins

is among the applicants, and that his claims are well sustained in the State. I am not personally acquainted with the Doctor, but have had from my Virginia friends a very favourable account of his character & qualifications for the place. Under these impressions, I would be highly gratified, with his appointment, if it can be made with ["proprety"(?) *canceled and* "propriety" *interlined*]. If I am correctly informed, the appointment would give much satisfaction in the District and would have a salutary political effect by uniting heart[i]ly many, who have been heretofore temporarily seperated but are now ["united" *canceled*] cooperating. I shall endeavor to call at your office in relation to the contents of this note to day or tomorrow. Truly, J.C. Calhoun, Tuesday.

ALS owned by Charles Gouverneur Paulding. Note: On 3/11/1841 William Henry Harrison nominated George Loyall to be Navy Agent for the port of Norfolk, Va.

From C[ornelius] C. Baldwin

Balcony Falls, Rockbridge co[unty],
Virginia, July 12, 1841

Dear Sir: It is possible that you may have observed in the papers the proceedings of a Convention of the Iron-masters of Virginia, held in Lexington in this county on the 15th ulti[mo], for the purpose of petitioning Congress for an increased duty upon English iron. The Convention assert, in their published proceedings, that the iron trade of Virginia must go down unless increased protection is extended to it by Congress; & I have been informed, by members of the Convention, that a duty of 35 per cent. will be asked for on *English* iron. You will see from the proceedings that the cooperation of iron masters throughout the Union is earnestly invoked. The movement is no doubt a cunningly concerted thing, & the ball has been been [*sic*] in motion in the *South* for effect elsewhere. That a powerful effort ["will" *changed to* "is to"] be made to revive the tariff policy, all the signs of the times clearly indicate. It therefore becomes the South to gird on her armour & prepare for battle.

I am an anti-tariff man out & out. I concur with you heartily & entirely in your views upon this subject, & I thank you for your able & untiring efforts, in spite of all the obliquy of your enemies, in defence of the rights & interests of the South.

As this tariff movement has originated *here*, I propose to counteract it by an adverse movement *here.* I intend to call a meeting, in a few weeks, to denounce this insidious tariff movement, & to prepare a memorial to Congress, fully exposing its character. I therefore address you for the purpose of asking information on the following points:

What duty is imposed by existing laws on English iron? & what is the amount of protection actually extended to it in our sea ports?

At what price could English iron (manufactured) be imported into this country, duty free?

How much foreign iron is annually imported into this country? How much ["iron" *interlined*] is made at home?

How much will an increased duty of 35 per cent. raise the price of iron?

I would be highly gratified if you would prepare a memorial to Congress, too—roughly discussing the whole subject in all its various aspects. A document of that kind is greatly needed at the present moment, particularly in western Virginia, which is strongly infected with tariff notions. You would thus render an important service to the cause of free trade & Southern interests. If you could prepare it at any time within the next six weeks, it would be time enough for popular action upon the subject, before the next session of Congress, tho' the sooner the better. The effects of protecting duties on the agricultural interest should be clearly exhibited, & the common place arguments of the tariffit[e]s strongly [*ms. torn*]ed.

I will thank you for any documents bearing upon the subject. With great respect, your fellow citizen, C.C. Baldwin.

P.S. In [*sic*] inclose the proceedings referred to. What are the provisions of the act of [18]32? See proceedings.

ALS with En in ViHi, Hunter Family Papers. Note: An AEU by Calhoun reads "See Mr. [Robert M.T.] Hunter." The enclosed clipping is from an unidentified newspaper. The account of the tariff meeting was signed by John Jordan, Chairman, and Geo[rge] M. Payne, Secretary.

Testimonial by Calhoun, Albert Gallatin, C[aleb] Cushing, P[eter] S. Du Ponceau, and David Hoffman, Washington, [7/13]. The testimonial is for Henry R. Schoolcraft and his plan to publish a periodical, The Algic Magazine, And Annals of Indian Affairs, devoted to "topics connected with the Indian tribes of this continent." The testimonial states Schoolcraft "has enjoyed favorable opportunities of personal observation on the subjects referred to, united to apt and close habits of remark, and industrious research, as is evinced by his travels and other publications." Schoolcraft's nineteen years spent as an agent for Indian affairs provides him with "authentic sources of information" concerning the Indian race. His work will "fill an admitted chasm in the literary wants of the reading public." PC's in DLC, Henry Rowe Schoolcraft Papers.

To Maj. C[HARLES] YANCEY, Warminster, Va.

Washington, 22 July 1841

My dear Sir, I enclose a printed copy of your proceedings.

The tone and sentiments of your Resolutions gave great satisfaction to our friends, and have had a good effect in cheering and sustaining us in the ardeous struggle we are engaged in maintaining the liberty and institutions of the country.

Nothing yet is certain, as to the result of the session. [Henry] *Clay's bank* project will *probably fail*; but I fear it will only be to establish the no less objectionable project of [Thomas] Ewing [Secretary of the Treasury].

I am grateful for the honor confered on me by the Republicans of Buckingham in selecting me as the organ to present their proceedings to the Senate. With great respect I am & &, J.C. Calhoun.

ALS in ScU-SC, John C. Calhoun Papers. NOTE: Calhoun addressed this to Yancey at Buckingham Court House, Va., but it was forwarded to Warminster. The resolutions from Buckingham County were presented by Calhoun to the Senate on 7/17 and are abstracted in *The Papers of John C. Calhoun*, 15:622.

To Gov. "Grayson" [*sic*; WILLIAM GRASON of Md.]

[Washington, January 2, 1842]

.... well known to you. I have long known him, and I regard him as a citizen of great worth & possessed of a sound strong understanding.

We have the Exchequer scheme under consideration in the Senate. It receives, in its present form, no favour from any side. The Clay whigs are exceedingly bitter against it, as well against Mr. present name, nor on the measures they support. All we have to do [John] Tyler & his administration; especially Mr. [Daniel] Webster. I regard the party as utterly prostrated. The devision in their ranks can never be healed; and, if it could they can never rise under their is to see, that the fruits of our great victory be not lost. We owe it to the people and ourselves, that the ground on which we have achieved it, shall be honestly and in good faith ["be" *canceled*] carried out when we reach power. With great respect, yours truly, J.C. Calhoun.

Partial facsimile of ALS offered for sale in Remember When Auctions, Inc., Catalog No. 38, part II, 1996, p. 59.

From CHARLES H. LARRABEE

Pontotoc Mississippi, Sept. 13 1842
Sir, I have for some time past, been in expectation of seeing a sketch of your life and public services, in the columns of the Democratic press—but have been disappointed.

The object of my communication is, to ascertain whether any such sketch has ever been published, and if so, to request you to forward me a copy. I hope you will not deem me arrogant, as a private individual—an admirer of your self, in briefly stating my views as to the availibility or claims of those prominent members of the Democratic party, whose names have been mentioned in connexion with the Presidential office.

Placing your claims to that station above all others, and believing your prospects of nomination, and of course, of election—especially if the proper action is *soon* shown by your friends—to be greater than those of any other, I hope you will agree with me in believing that some measures of vigorous action must be immediately put in operation.

Under the present aspect of the political horizon, I deem Mr. [Martin] Van Buren wholly out of the question. His course upon the Tariff question has never been *decisive*; nor does that course harmonize with the antagonistic views which the Democratic party must uphold during the next canvass, and which it seems so decisively to have chosen—naturally enough, it is true, from the ultra miscalled *Protective* sentiment of [Henry] Clay & his partizans. This reason must in my opinion, alone be a decisive one, with the National nominating convention—not to mention others which must occur to yourself.

Mr. Van Buren aside, I can but think Col. [Richard M.] Johnson the next most probable person to receive the nomination. But his claims are secondary, and the proper action of your friends, will most assuredly place his name at the foot of the list. He has not been lately in active public life, nor has he ever been prominent as a statesman.

Col. [Thomas H.] Benton has placed himself without the pale, nor do I regard his avowed preference of Mr. Van Buren, as weighing much. James Buchanan I deem less likely to receive the nomination than either of the others, and less certain of election should he by chance receive it, let his friends be ever so vigilant.

Of course it is unnecessary for me to trouble you further with my peculiar views, or to further particularize. But this much—if a short sketch, adapted to the reading of the people at large—written in a popular manner, has not been prepared for the press, I hope you will allow me to urge upon you the necessity of having such sketch prepared immediately. And should it meet your views, I will undertake to write out a short history of your life, and communicate it to any paper in our State you may designate, either under my proper signature, or a fictitious one.

If you agree with me in this matter, I would prefer you to write out a general outline, furnish me with the necessary documents [*ms. torn*; or?] direct some friend so to do and I will im[me]diately prepare the sketch, and submit it to you for approval.

As I am wholly unknown to you, I will merely mention that I am a young man, just entering upon active life, & would refer you to Hon. Thomas H. Williams formerly Senator from this State, and Hon. Samuel Beardsley formerly in the House from New York.

I am happy to inform you, that in this section of country, & indeed as far as I can learn through the State—you are the first choice of the people, and I may be wrong, but I truly think a sketch of your life—properly prepared, would do much to make your claims known, and ensure your nomination. If it is convenient I would like you to send me as many of your Speeches as you can spare. Hoping Sir, my communication will meet with your favor, and renewing my assurances of partiality for yourself and admiration of your services I Remain Respectfully Your Ob[e]d[ien]t Serv[an]t, Charles H. Larrabee.

ALS in ScCleA. Note: An AEU by Calhoun reads: "Mr. Larrabee[,] Send copy of Biography when published. Answered." Larrabee (1820–1883) was a native of N.Y. living at this time in Miss. and was to serve as a Representative from Wisc. 1859–1861.

To R[OBERT] H. GOULD, "Copy"

Washington, January 26th 1843

Dear Sir, I have received your letter of December 31st and it would afford me much satisfaction to be able to advance your interests; but I am hardly in a position to do so, unless very indirectly. I entertained a profound respect for your late distinguished Father [Judge James Gould], whom I have always regarded as one of our most eminent jurists, and I should always be happy to serve any member of his family; in addition to which, my personal knowledge of you, ["would" *canceled*] gives me full confidence that you would discharge with talent and integrity the duties of such an appointment as that which you seek. I can only regret, therefore, the slight probability which exists of my having any opportunity to assist you. Yours truly, (signed) John C. Calhoun.

Ms. copy in DNA, RG 59 (State Department), Letters of Application and Recommendation during the Administrations of Franklin Pierce and James Buchanan, 1853–1861, Robert H. Gould (M-967:19, frame 722). NOTE: This copy is in Gould's handwriting. He enclosed it with copies of letters from Levi Woodbury, Duff Green, and Abel P. Upshur, in a letter to Lewis Cass, dated 4/29/1857, seeking appointment as a consul in southern Europe. The appointment sought in 1843 is not known.

From ALEXANDER WALKER

New Orleans, April 15 1843

My dear Sir, I send you a hastily drafted address of the Democratick members of our Legislature, which is a fair exponent of the general sense and feeling of the Democracy of La. I do so from an apprehension that you or your friends may be in the errour of supposing, that the sugar interest and Creole prepossessions are opposed to your claims and principles. From much observation of the part[*ms. torn*] I am decided in the conviction that yo[*ms. torn; one or two words missing*] the choice of the Louisianais for the Pr[esidency.] The Commercial class in our City begin[*ms. torn*] discover the evils of all Tariffs, imposts, B[*ms. torn*] credit systems, paper currency &c, and the beauty and advantages of free trade, cash dealings and specie currency. The rapid filling up of the vacuum created by the winding up of four fifths of our Banks, with specie, and the successful transaction of the affairs of Government through *that* medium, without the aid of Banks; the realization of what, two years ago, was deemed a wild fancy, a political *Eutopia*, though with admirable foresight and wisdom predicted by you, has attracted to yourself, your history and speeches an unusual degree of attention & curiosity. Our population is a very mixed one—more so than any of the same size in the world, but so minutely divided as to prevent anything like clanship, national or sectional divisions. A more homogeneous & united society does not exist, nor one more independent in opinion or segacious in observation. The immense conflict [*ms. torn*]tellect and skill in the competition of [*ms. torn*]tive and energetick from every quarter [*ms. torn*] world produces the most remarkable [*ms. torn*]ity and industry. Men go through no apprenticeship here, there is no biding one's time, no waiting on events, but all as soon as they arrive join in our ["grand" *interlined*] race whose goal is a fortune. Of consequence our people are intensely practical—a *matter-of-fact, to-the-point* people. The mere show & parade, the gild & glare of the politicians and orators of *the day*, are only regarded here as any other exhibition pleasing to the senses. It is only the man of sound practical wisdom, utilitarian views, [*one illegible word*] concise & forcible address who can gain the confidence & secure the support of this people. For these reasons, it is my firm belief that no statesman in our country has in La., so many & such ardent admirers and friends as yourself. But, Sir, I am taking too great a liberty with you. Some years ago on my return from the University of Virginia, I had the good fortune to happen in the same stage with you, at a time when you had taken a position which exposed you to much [*ms. torn*]umely and misconstruction, and though [*ms. torn*] parental or other influences I had acquired [*ms. torn*] prejudices against you as a man and a poli[*ms. torn*] I was so deeply impressed by your kind & courteous manner, your great knowledge, and to a youthful mind peculiarly happy style of communicating that, and your own profound thoughts, that ever since, I have cherished for you the warmest regard & highest admiration; and these must be my apology for thus addressing you. Allow me to subscribe myself—ever y[ou]r friend and servant, Alexander Walker.

ALS in ScCleA. Note: An AEU by Calhoun reads, "Mr. Walker of Louisiana[,] send copy of the Carolina address when published." A second AEU reads, "Sent with a letter." Alexander Joseph Walker (1818–1893), a native of Va., was editor of the important New Orleans, La., *Jeffersonian*. He held public offices and served in the Confederate army.

From G. M. Thompson

Stratford Connect[icut,] 9th Aug. [18]43

My d[ea]r Sir, Some time in June I travelled with our friend Col. F[ranklin H.] Elmore from Columbia to charleston, on our way down I told him I ["would" *interlined*] write him and give him the political complexion of Connect., to day I have done so, and I thought in as much as I was acquainted with you in Newberry some fifteen years ago, that I could take the liberty to write you and give you some Ideaw what was going on in the East. In the first place to be frank I was a [William H.] Harrison man in Columbia, where I reside when at home, and am still a [Henry] Clay man If there is any chance for him, and Knowing your frank and Lofty mind so well I am confident you will applaud me for being so frank myself in not disguising it.

Now Sir allow me to say that I have conversed with a great many men in New England & find first all the bar with a few exceptions in favor of you for the next president, all the men headed to the next congress are Calhoun men with one exception Doct. [Samuel] Simons of Fairfield County, who by the by is a wide mouth open [Martin] Van Buren man, & by the by I must make a little digression, he is trying his best notwithstanding his abuse of Mr. [John] Tyler and says he is not fit for President, to get my Brother Joseph out of his office as Collector in this county, because he is in favor of you. My connexions pretty much all live in this county, they are numerous, and respectable and wield a great influence & they all go for you, this you may depend on. For my character I refer you to the Hon. Jno. B[elton] ONeall who has known me from a boy in Newberry So. Ca. Now Sir if it would not be asking of you too much I should like through your influence not to have my Brother removed, and if removed to have him replaced, my object for writing this is to show you the trecherous hearts of these men towards Mr. Tyler, professing to be his friends when at the same time they are his worst enemies. I like justice, true[?]. It is nothing to me what the politicians do here, as I am a So. Carolinian, yet still I feel an interest in Brother who onced lived with me in Newberry village, and now to the point you are gaining ground daily this way. Have been prowling about the State and have seen a good many farmers and mechanics, and say to you 7 out of ten prefer you to Van Buren. Your name is mentioned in all crowds. A great many whigs say they go for you, and all say if there is no chance for Clay they go the whole figure for you, and I do most sincerely believe predicating my belief on public opinion that you can be elected president regardless of the nomination. Mr. V. Buren has his wire pullers at work and perhaps he will get the nomination. If so It will be by the lowest intriguing ways. Mark what I tell you that you are gaining ground daily. Your course is onward. Nothing can stop the ball but an overruling providence. The ball is increasing daily and hourly, men [*one illegible word*] are geting their Eyes open, and your political character is undergoing daily the scrutiny of both parties, by t[he] by your old class mate Mr. [David] Plant [former Representative from Conn.] is wide awake to your interest. My Brother Joseph hereafter will enter into a correspondence with the comitee of charleston and give them such news respecting yourself and your onward course as may occur. In a few days he says the New Haven Register will hoist her flag for you. Hoping these few lines will meet your aprobation I remain your sincere friend, G.M. Thompson.

[P.S.] I shall be travelling some time East before I leave for the South & shall try and gather all the information I can respecting your onward course, most of the whigs or at least a great many have turned[?] to be your friends.

ALS in NcD, John C. Calhoun Papers.

To [RICHARD F.] SIMPSON, [Representative from S.C.]

Fort Hill, 21st Dec[embe]r 1843

My dear Sir, I hope you had a pleasant & safe journey to Washington, & that you are by this time settled down in comfortable quarters & with a pleasant mess for the session.

To write news from Pendleton to Washington, would be like sending coals to New Castle. We have none, but what is local, all of which my son [Patrick Calhoun], who will deliver you this, will give.

My immediate ["object" *canceled and* "object in writing" *interlined*] is to request you to let Mr. [Lucius] Lyon of your House [from Mich.] have $20 on my account. It is for my neighbour, Mrs. [Placidia Mayrant] Adams, who has a mortage on some lands in Michigan, which she is about to foreclose, the expense of which, it is intended to meet. I will refund it to you, when you return. I wrote to Mr. L[yon] that you would let him have it.

I shall always be happy to hear from you. Yours truly, J.C. Calhoun.

ALS owned by Maureen and Edward Simpson. NOTE: AES's by Simpson read, "From J.C. Calhoun" and "Answered."

To R[ICHARD] F. SIMPSON, [Representative from S.C.]

Fort Hill, 1st Feb: 1844

My dear Sir, I am obliged to you for transmitting the seeds of the Osage orange, which my good friend Judge [Edward] Cross [Representative from Ark.] was so kind as to give to you, for that purpose. Please ["to" *canceled*] give him my thanks for the same, & ["to" *canceled*] tell him, that I shall be happy to hear from him.

I am, also, obliged to you for your suggestions. I am always happy to have the advice of my friends. All I have to ask of my friends in Congress is to do their duty manfully, without thinking of me. Insist sternly on the rights of the South, and above all not ["to permit themselves" *interlined*] to be betrayed again by false promises, however solemnly given, by the friends of Mr. [Martin] V[an] B[uren]. There is no faith in them, as experience has proved. Take nothing but *performance hereafter.* For 15 years they have deceived & betrayed us; & they ought to be told so to their face in Congress. If we should be betrayed again, we shall become the scorn of the whole Union. 'Till their passed pledges are redeemed, both on the Tariff & Abo[li]tion, we ought to have nothing to do with them. As it now stands, I would as leive [*sic*] go into convention with ["with" *canceled*] Geddings [*sic*; Joshua R. Giddings], or [John Quincy] Adams, as [Samuel] Beardsley or [John W.] Davis [Representatives from Ohio, Mass., N.Y., and Ind., respectively]. If I were in the House, I would tell them so. The higher the tone on the part of our friends, and the more resolutely they insist on the rights of the South, the better for all concerned. They would do great injustice to the cause & to myself, to sacrafice a particle of our just rights in reference to any future prospect of mine. I would be the last to ask it, & the first to denounce it. I have never sought office by sacraficing our rights, and my friends would do me great injustice, by making sacrafices for me, which I would not make for myself. Had I thought proper to purc[h]ase the Presidency by sacraficing the rights of the South, I might long since have filled the office. As it is, I never expect to do ["so" *interlined*], and hope never shall, if it is to be acquired by such means.

I shall at all times be happy to hear from you. Truly, J.C. Calhoun.

ALS owned by Maureen and Edward Simpson.

To R[OBERT] M. T. HUNTER, Lloyds, Essex [County], Va.

Fort Hill, 21st Feb: 1844

My dear Sir, I received Mr. [James A.] Seddon's letter [of 2/5] and answered it some days since, and now hasten ["to" *interlined*] answer yours [of 2/6], which the mail of yesterday brought me.

I am happy to be able to say to you, as I did to Mr. Seddon, that, in my opinion, my friends in the convention, taking ["into consideration" *interlined*] all the circumstances under which they acted, did the best they could. Whatever error has been committed, was committed by the central Committee of this State. It would have been a stronger & more coercing position, to have made the withdrawal, of my name depend on the fulfilment of their ["promise" *canceled and* "pledges" *interlined*] on the part of Mr. [Martin] V[an] B[uren]'s friends. I have had no satisfactory explination, why the committee acted as it did, but I apprehend, that it was caused by a pressure from Washington. I feared from the first there would be a pressure from that quarter in favour of a lower tone, than became the occasion, and to guard ag[ai]nst it, I requested the Committee, in a private letter, not to defer publication, till they could hear from Washington. This, however, is inter nos.

Your Address is excellent. It covers the ground, which I could not occupy well, and the two taken together make up the full argument ag[ai]nst the Convention, with the exception of not more than one or two points.

I have no doubt, the Baltimore Convention has been stript of all its weight, and that it will be the last of the kind, which will be ever held. But I go farther. The objections lie deeper and go ag[ai]nst any intermediate body, except that provided by the constitution, in the election, and I am inclined to think, even against that. There is no truth in the argument, that a convention is necessary to preserve harmony & union. It is more the cause of discord & division, than union & harmony. Were there no such contrivance, the only means left to preserve Union, would be adherence to principles & ["to make" *interlined*] the selection of him ["by general consent" *interlined*], who most fully represents them, and is the most capable of upholding them, a means far more effecient & safe than convention or caucus. If my friends ever should present my name again, I trust, it will be independent of either. I do not think it would be possible ["for me" *interlined*] to assent to permit my name again to go before either.

The position ["of" *interlined*] my friends in Virginia is a strong one, and yet it is a hazardeous one. There is great danger you will ["be" *interlined*] drawn into the vortex of the canvass, with such violence, as to forget the position assumed in your Address, and to go the full length of defending V[an] B[uren] in every thing, in your ["violence" *canceled and* "opposition" *interlined*] to [Henry] Clay. That danger will be greatly increased by our friends agreeing to act as electors. You acted wisely in declining, & I would have been glad, that all had followed your example. My fear is, that nothing, which ought to satisfy us will be done by the V[an] B[uren] men to redeem their p[*ms. torn*] either in reference to the Tariff or Abolition, or any thing else; and yet ["I fear" *interlined*] our friends will be so deeply committed as to be compelled to give him ardent support. Can nothing be done to prevent that? If the canvass could be kept back untill it was seen, what they intend to do, it would be very desirable. I have not the least faith in the ["V(an) B(uren)" *interlined*] party. My impression is strong, that, if compelled to choose, they will sacrifice us for the abolitionists &, not improbable, for the Tarifites. They intend to make the most of the fact, that Clay is a slave holder. It will put us in an awkward position. We ought to be on our guard.

I have resumed my treatise on government within the last few weeks. It will require thought, and I shall have to progress slowly. My time, one way and another, is much more engrossed, than I had expected, on retiring. Truly, J.C. Calhoun.

ALS in ViHi, Hunter Family Papers. Note: Hunter's "Address" mentioned in Calhoun's third paragraph appears in the Richmond, Va., *Enquirer*, February 10, 1844, pp. 1–2. It was adopted by a "Democratic Republican" meeting on 1/31 and addressed the party voters in opposition to the structure of the pending national convention.

To [RICHARD F.] SIMPSON, [Representative from S.C.]

Fort Hill, 9th March 1844

My dear Sir, I owe a Mr. [Estwick] Evans in Washington $2 on account of a subscription to a pamphlet written by him on State rights and have informed him, that if he will call on you & show my letter, that you will pay him the amount, which you will oblige me by doing.

I see the Northern Democrats continue to act badly, with a few exceptions. They seem to have but one object in view; to act so, as to get the tariff & abolition votes without offending the South. They certainly must think us very stupid, or very tame to suppose they can play it successfully. It would be, indeed, a strange spectacle to to [*sic*] see the Southern people & the tariff & abolition parties united on the same candidate.

We have nothing new. The season has been delightful. The spring is gradually approaching, & everybody busy in preparing for the next crop. Yours truly, J.C. Calhoun.

ALS owned by Maureen and Edward Simpson.

From EUSTIS PRE[SCOTT], "Confidential"

New York [City,] 20th July 1844

My Dear Sir, Since I had the pleasure of seeing you, I have had an opportunity of conversing with many of our friends in this State, and in a visit to Boston have met several from other States, all of whom speak in the most sanguine manner of the success of the democratic ticket. Mr. [George F.] Barker Att[orne]y Gen[era]l of this State assures me that it will succeed by 10,000, on a strict party vote, should no extraneous issues be made. He conceives the annexation project decidedly unpopular with all parties here. The same may be said of Massachusetts and I am informed that Pen[n]sylv[ani]a is also opposed to it, but of the latter I have no means of judging. Probably the strongest opposition to the measure is to be found in these three States.

Mr. Hall of Zanseville Ohio assures me that we shall carry that State. If so, I should consider the election of our candidates certain. I have late letters from Tenn. and the Southern part of Ky. which speak of unlooked for enthusiasm in favor of the Presidential ticket.

I am thereby convinced that had our demonstration in Louisiana been responded to by the other southern States (as it ought to have b[een)] *our* candidate would have been now b[efore?] the people, and his election would have been certain, we should have commanded every free trade vote of both parties, and altho perhaps in this State with some reluctance the strict party vote. We have committed the same error which the whigs did in 1840, *then* they could have elected their strongest man, we could have done so at this time.

The election in Louis[ian]a is no index of the strength of the annexation question. I believe 4/5ths of all the members elected are in favor of it. The result is rather a triumph of the French party over the American, in consequence of our being deprived of over 1000 votes. Still I am confident we shall have a majority on joint ballot and a large majority in the convention, and the vote of the State may be considered certain for [James K.] *Polk*. Should our opponents be successful in this campaign, I am confident that their own measures would break them down in two years. The eyes of the people are being opened and they will not much longer suffer themselves to be made tributaries to the manufacturers. At the end of that period I would not hesitate [to] meet them on the question of a Protective, [*ms. torn*] Revenue Tariff, and in many States the [*ms. torn*] will command a majority even at this time.

If we can succeed in negotiating a few more treaties for a reduction of duties on terms of reciprocity and the Senate continues to reject them, we shall arouse the entire Commercial & Agricultural interests in our favor. With Spain, Portugal, the Brazils, Belgium, Holland & other powers much yet may be done in that way, if we approach them prudently & courteously, and every treaty made with other powers strengthens the free trade party in England.

I hope our friends in South Carolina & Alabama will be a little more temperate. The word *disunion* sounds harsh, and can never be favorably received in any section. Time will remedy all the evils of which the south so justly complain, even now, abolition is compelled to hide itself in the by-ways, it will not bear exposure to the light or open way. Let us then patiently persevere in measures to produce the desired result in which all our friends can unite. Excuse my dear Sir the frankness with which I write. I mix much with the world, and know how immediately every movement in your own State effects your interest, and I am sanguine enough to believe you can become the head of a great nation—irrespective of mere party lines. I perceive movements in a little *Post Office Clique* here, which are very injurious to the Administration, and I fear are intended to throw weight into the scale of our opponents—provided the parties may see the chances on that side. I do hope we shall soon see the Administration *openly* ranged on our side [*ms. torn*] would certainly add to our strength materially. Very truly & respectfully Y[ou]r Obed[ien]t Serv[an]t, Eustis Pre[scott].

ALS in ScCleA.

From G[EORGE] M. DALLAS

[Philadelphia?] 29 July 1844
Dear Sir, Should the Surveyor Generalship of Iowa and Wisconsin become vacant, I do not think the post could be filled by any one better calculated, by capacity and moral worth, to give entire satisfaction than Mr. Martin Coryell, of this State, son of an old and valued friend of mine [Lewis S. Coryell]. His studies, pursuits, intelligence, and deportment would make him a valuable acquisition in the public service: and there are numbers who, sympathising with his family and aware of his merits, would experience great gratification in hearing of his appointment. I am very respectfully & truly Y[ou]r friend & obed[ient] Ser[vant], G.M. Dallas.

ALS in DNA, RG 45 (Naval Records), Subject File, Naval Bases (including Navy Yards and Stations): Labor and Civil Personnel (PL), Miscellaneous Correspondence concerning Labor Conditions, Memphis. NOTE: Dallas had a few weeks before been nominated for Vice-President by the Democratic national convention.

From JAMES M. CRANE[?]

Richmond Virginia, May 31st 1847
Dear Sir, Your public life has been so remarkable that all must admit that ["will admit" *canceled and* "a knowledge" *interlined*] of it is necessary to make a *perfect* history of the American Union and it will be received by posterity for what it is worth. There is no doubt but what you are anxious to ["impress on the" *interlined*] present and coming generations that you have fulfilled your part, ["&" *interlined*] are ready still to fulfill your part, as an upright statesman and patriot to the country you serve. I shall grant you sincerity and

truthfulness of purpose and I wish your life spared long. I have repeatedly differed with you and although a young man I had the right to do so whether I was right or wrong in the exercise of it. Excuse my candor.

Your opinions are valuable now and will be hereafter. I shall therefore not conceal my purpose in addressing you & will publish your reply. Whatever faults I have (and they are many) I feel that my heart is right towards the country of which I am a citizen. I desire ["for" *interlined*] her a *peaceful* progress and on that account I abhor this war, for I believe it was avoidable. War I look upon as the most terrible of national vices, and operates as a check to the spread of intelligence, enterprise and conservative principles. I dread this war, more than I do a famine, hurricane or a volcano. Its effects on our future condition to me is a most frightful picture. Ought not public sentiment to be forming[?] over the country so as to force from the next session of Congress a just and amicable termination of this war. The South have nothing to gain by its continuance, but every thing to loose [*sic*]. Not one foot of ground can ["they" *canceled and* "we" *interlined*] inherit but on such terms as the north may prescribe. Can we ["then" *interlined*] afford to pour out ["our" *interlined*] blood like water, give up our means by the millions to sack Mexican cities and towns, slaughter ["its" *canceled and* "her" *interlined*] population, and to ["hugh" *canceled and* "hew" *interlined*] and carve out territory never to be possessed. My dear Sir you owe an obligation to posterity I think at this time which you cannot and ought not to throw off. Something ought to be done to check the mad career which prevails in our national councils. It will destroy us if it is not checked. It is corrupting the young men of our country—infusing dangerous and profligate sentiments into their minds. Its withering influence is felt also very perceptibly upon the enterprise and industry of the Union. The silver and ["the" *interlined*] gold ["is" *canceled and* "are" *interlined*] all going to Mexico and what are we to gain by it? And is it to be continued?

If it is to be continued, when and where shall it end. All of our commanders ["by" *canceled*] on land and on sea, declare that ["that" *interlined*] illfated ["on"(?) *canceled and* "people" *interlined*] against whom we are making war are more irreconcilable to us than ever. They have sworn on their altars and by their spiritual advisers that they will never make ["a" *canceled*] peace while an American soldier treads upon their soil, but if we cease to pursue them they will. The officers and soldiers in the army commanded by General [Winfield] Scott and Gen[era]l [Zachary] Taylor are unanimous in the opinion that nothing can be gained by a farther prosecution of the war. None ever expect to live to see it terminate. My dear sir the country wants proper counsel. You, [Henry] Clay and [Daniel] Webster the three intellectual giants of our ["day" *interlined*] may as well lay aside all hopes ["of ever expecting" *canceled and* "that" *interlined*] the people of America in their present condition will ["seem"(?) *canceled*] place ["either" *canceled and* "any one" *interlined*] of you in that station where you can enforce better councils. They have been humbugged for the last 15 or 20 years. They are now about half crasy and fit for anything, and they will be ready ["at most any time" *interlined*] to elect the ["most" *canceled*] smallest in intellect ["and" *canceled*] littlest in soul and the most noisy and unscrupulous of ["our" *canceled*] politicians ["in preference to any great man" *interlined*]. Under present circumstances you are likely to go to your grave leaving your country in a most ["unpleasant if not" *interlined*] dreadful condition. Our people do not now look to statesmen as their political guides and from whom they are to choose their rulers. ["Now" *canceled*] Suppose this spirit increases and war will increase it, what are we naturally to expect from it. It is well for the country that Gen[era]l Taylor ["has" *canceled and* "possesses" *interlined*] the moderation and good sense that he does possess. If he was an ambitious man the day of his election would date our downfall. This election may any how[?]. Now do we want war and territory if this is to be the fruit of it. Surely not.

I have no ambition or vanity to gratify in asking your opinion. God knows I am unburdening my whole heart to you. I dread the future under present circumstances and I wish if possible to rouse public sentiment so as to demand that this war shall be prosecuted no further. Our course from the first has been harsh & overbearing with Mexico. We can settle ["our" *interlined*] difficulties *even now* with her amicably if we will. If we can then ought we not. Your position is such that your opinion will be of more weight than any other man living and I with millions would like to know it. Yours most truly, James M. Crane[?].

ALS in ScCleA.

To [FRANKLIN SMITH?, Canton, Miss.]

[Washington, January 25, 1848?]

.... I thank you for the strong expression of your desire to see me in possession of the Presidential chair; but I hope my friends will not think of bringing my name forward for the office. I have no desire for it; and if I had it would be useless. The path of duty is not in the present state of parties and condition of the country, the path of the Presidency. I took it with a full knowledge that it was not, and am neither dissatisfied nor disappointed. To present my name would be to weaken me in the performance of my duty. It would give a pretext to call the disinterestedness of my motives in question; and thereby weaken my efforts to save the country and its institutions. . . .

PEx in the Spartanburg, S.C., *Spartan*, May 2, 1850, p. 2. NOTE: The *Spartan* prefaced this extract with the following: "We make the following extract of a letter from the Hon. John C. Calhoun, to a citizen of Madison [County, Miss.], which we find in the last *Madisonian*." See Smith's letters of 12/22/1847 and 5/4/1848 to Calhoun in *The Papers of John C. Calhoun*, 25:35–37 and 390–391.

SYMBOLS

◫

The following symbols have been used in this volume as abbreviations for the forms in which documents of John C. Calhoun have been found and for the respositories in which they are preserved. (Full citations to printed sources of documents can be found in the Bibliography.)

A-Ar	—Alabama Department of Archives and History, Montgomery
Abs	—abstract (a summary)
ADS	—autograph document, signed
ADU	—autograph document, unsigned
AEI	—autograph endorsement, initialed
AES	—autograph endorsement, signed
AEU	—autograph endorsement, unsigned
ALI	—autograph letter, initialed
ALS	—autograph letter, signed
ALU	—autograph letter, unsigned
AU	—University of Alabama, Tuscaloosa
AzTeS	—Arizona State University, Tempe
CC	—clerk's copy (a secondary ms. copy)
CCEx	—partial clerk's copy
CLU	—University of California-Los Angeles
CtHi	—Connecticut Historical Society, Hartford
CtLHi	—Litchfield Historical Society, Litchfield, Conn.
CtY	—Yale University, New Haven, Conn.
DeGE	—Eleutherian Mills Historical Society, Greenville, Del.
DLC	—Library of Congress, Washington
DNA	—National Archives, Washington
DS	—document, signed
DSI	—Smithsonian Institution, Washington
DU	—document, unsigned
En	—enclosure
Ens	—enclosures
EU	—endorsement, unsigned
FC	—file copy (usually a letterbook copy retained by the sender)
FU	—University of Florida, Gainesville
Ia-HA	—State Historical Society of Iowa, Des Moines
ICHi	—Chicago Historical Society, Ill.
InHi	—Indiana Historical Society, Indianapolis
InU	—Indiana University, Bloomington
LS	—letter, signed
LU	—letter, unsigned
M-	—(followed by a number) published microcopy of the National Archives

MB	—Boston Public Library, Boston, Mass.
MdBE	—Enoch Pratt Free Library, Baltimore, Md.
MH	—Harvard University, Cambridge, Mass.
MHi	—Massachusetts Historical Society, Boston
MiU-C	—Clements Library, University of Michigan, Ann Arbor
MnHi	—Minnesota Historical Society, St. Paul
MoSHi	—Missouri Historical Society, St. Louis
MoSM	—Mercantile Library Association, St. Louis, Mo.
MoSW	—Washington University, St. Louis, Mo.
MWA	—American Antiquarian Society, Worcester, Mass.
N	—New-York Historical Society, New York City
NbHi	—Nebraska State Historical Society, Lincoln
NBuHi	—Buffalo and Erie County Historical Society, Buffalo, N.Y.
Nc-Ar	—North Carolina Department of Archives and History, Raleigh
NcD	—Duke University, Durham, N.C.
NcU	—Southern Historical Collection, University of North Carolina at Chapel Hill
NhD	—Dartmouth College, Hanover, N.H.
NhHi	—New Hampshire Historical Society, Concord
NIC	—Cornell University, Ithaca, N.Y.
NjMoN	—Morristown National Historical Park, Morristown, N.J.
NjP	—Princeton University, Princeton, N.J.
NjR	—Rutgers University, New Brunswick, N.J.
NN	—New York Public Library, New York City
NNC	—Columbia University, New York City
OFH	—Rutherford B. Hayes Library, Fremont, Ohio
OHi	—Ohio Historical Society, Columbus
PC	—printed copy
PDS	—printed document, signed
PEx	—printed extract
PHi	—Historical Society of Pennsylvania, Philadelphia
PPAmP	—American Philosophical Society, Philadelphia, Pa.
PPL	—Library Company of Philadelphia, Pa.
RG	—Record Group in the National Archives
Sc-Ar	—South Carolina Department of Archives and History, Columbia
ScC	—Charleston Library Society, Charleston, S.C.
ScCleA	—Clemson University, Clemson, S.C.
ScHi	—South Carolina Historical Society, Charleston
ScU-SC	—South Caroliniana Library, University of South Carolina, Columbia
T	—Tennessee State Library and Archives, Nashville
THi	—Tennessee Historical Society, Nashville
TU	—University of Tennessee, Knoxville
TxU	—Barker Texas History Center, University of Texas, Austin
Vi	—Library of Virginia, Richmond
ViHi	—Virginia Historical Society, Richmond
ViU	—University of Virginia, Charlottesville
ViW	—William and Mary College, Williamsburg, Va.
VtNN	—Norwich University, Northfield, Vt.

BIBLIOGRAPHY

◫

This bibliography is limited to sources of and previous printings of documents published in this volume.

Aderman, Ralph M., ed., *Letters of James Kirke Paulding.* Madison: University of Wisconsin Press, 1962.

Alexandria, Va., *Gazette,* 1808–.

Ambler, Charles Henry, ed., *Correspondence of Robert M.T. Hunter, 1826–1876,* in the *American Historical Association Annual Report* for 1916. 2 vols. Washington: U.S. Government Printing Office, 1918, vol. II.

American Farmer. Baltimore: 1819–1834.

American State Papers . . . . 38 vols. Washington: Gales & Seaton, 1832–1861.

Anderson, John M., ed., *Calhoun: Basic Documents.* State College, Pa.: Bald Eagle Press, 1952.

Annals of Congress: Debates and Proceedings in the Congress of the United States, 1789–1824. 42 vols. Washington: 1834–1856.

Baltimore, Md., *Sun,* 1837–.

Bassett, John Spencer, ed., *The Correspondence of Andrew Jackson.* 7 vols. Washington: Carnegie Institution, 1926–1935.

Benton, Thomas H., ed., *Abridgment of the Debates of Congress.* 16 vols. New York: D. Appleton & Co., 1854–1861.

Binney, Charles C., *The Life of Horace Binney with Selections from his Letters.* Philadelphia and London: J.B. Lippincott Co., 1903.

Boucher, Chauncey S., and Robert P. Brooks, eds., *Correspondence Addressed to John C. Calhoun, 1837–1849,* in the *American Historical Association Annual Report* for 1929. Washington: U.S. Government Printing Office, 1930.

Bradley, Cornelius Beach, ed., *Orations and Arguments by English and American Statesmen.* Boston and Chicago: Allyn & Bacon, 1894.

Briggs, Lilian M., ed., *Noted Speeches of Daniel Webster, Henry Clay, John C. Calhoun* . . . . New York: Moffat, Yard & Co., 1912.

Camden, S.C., *Journal,* 1826–1891?.

Carter, Clarence Edwin, and John Porter Bloom, eds., *Territorial Papers of the United States.* 28 vols. to date. Washington: 1934–.

Charleston, S.C., *City Gazette,* 1783–1840.

Charleston, S.C., *Courier,* 1803–1852.

Charleston, S.C., *Evening News,* 1845–1861.

Charleston, S.C., *Mercury,* 1822–1868.

Charleston, S.C., *Richards' Weekly Gazette,* 1850.

Christian Register. Boston: 1821–.

Clariosophic and Euphradian Societies, 1806–1931. Columbia, S.C.: Epworth Orphanage Press, [1931].

Columbia, S.C., *Palmetto State Banner,* 1846–1853?.

Columbia, S.C., *Telescope*, 1828–1839?.

Columbia, S.C., *Tri-Weekly South Carolinian*, 1849–1865.

Columbus, Ga., *Enquirer*, 1828–1873.

Congressional Globe . . . 1833–1873 . . . . 46 vols. Washington: Blair & Rives and others, 1834–1873.

Cook, Harriet Hefner, *John C. Calhoun—The Man*. Columbia, S.C.: privately printed, 1965.

Crallé, Richard K., ed., *The Works of John C. Calhoun*. 6 vols. Columbia, S.C.: A.S. Johnston, 1851, and New York: D. Appleton & Co., 1853–1857.

DeSaussure, Henry William, *Reports of Cases Argued and Determined in the Court of Chancery of the State of South Carolina . . . .* 4 vols. Columbia, S.C.: Cline & Hines, 1817–1819.

Edgefield, S.C., *Advertiser*, 1836–.

Flippin, Percy Scott, ed., "Herschel V. Johnson Correspondence," in *North Carolina Historical Review*, vol. IV, no. 2 (April, 1927), pp. 182–201.

Flippin, Percy Scott, *Herschel V. Johnson of Georgia: State Rights Unionist*. Richmond, Va.: Dietz Printing Co., 1931.

Genius of Universal Emancipation. Baltimore: 1825–1839.

Georgetown, S.C., *Winyah Observer*, 1841–1852.

Greensborough, Ala., *Alabama Beacon*, 1835–1911.

Greenville, S.C., *Mountaineer*, 1829–1901.

Hearon, Cleo, "Mississippi and the Compromise of 1850," in *Publications of the Mississippi Historical Society*, vol. XIV (1914), pp. 7–229.

Hubbell, Jay B., ed., "James Kirke Paulding's Last Letter to John C. Calhoun," in *North Carolina Historical Review*, vol. XXXII, no. 3 (July, 1955), pp. 412–414.

Huntsville, Ala., *Southern Advocate*, 1825–?.

Jackson, Miss., *Flag of the Union*, 1850–1856?.

James, Edwin, *Account of an Expedition from Pittsburgh to the Rocky Mountains . . . .* 2 vols. Philadelphia: Carey & Lea, 1823.

Jameson, J. Franklin, ed., *Correspondence of John C. Calhoun*, in the *American Historical Association Annual Report* for 1899. 2 vols. Washington: U.S. Government Printing Office, 1900, vol. II.

Jenkins, John S., *The Life of John Caldwell Calhoun*. Auburn, N.Y.: James M. Alden, 1850 and later editions.

Jervey, Theodore D., *Robert Y. Hayne and His Times*. New York: Macmillan Co., 1909.

Johnston, Alexander, ed., *American Orations. Studies in American Political History . . . .* 4 vols. New York and London: G.P. Putnam's Sons, 1896–1897.

Jones, William, *Remarks on the Proposed Breakwater at Cape Henlopen. . . .* Philadelphia: Chamber of Commerce, 1825.

Laurensville, S.C., *Herald*, 1848–1933.

Lemmon, Sarah, ed., *The Pettigrew Papers*. 2 vols. Raleigh: North Carolina Department of Archives and History, 1971, 1988.

Lence, Ross M., ed., *Union and Liberty: The Political Philosophy of John C. Calhoun*. Indianapolis: Liberty Press, 1992.

Liberator, The. Boston: 1831–1865.

Library of Southern Literature . . . . 17 vols. New Orleans, Atlanta and Dallas: Martin & Hoyt, 1907–1912.

Littell's Living Age. Boston: 1844–1896.

Lucas, John B.C., *Letters of the Hon. J.B.C. Lucas from 1815 to 1836*. St. Louis: published by John B.C. Lucas, 1905.

Lynchburg, Va., *Virginian*, 1822–1893.

McClure, Alexander K., ed., *Famous American Statesmen and Orators, Past and Present . . . .* 6 vols. New York: F.F. Lovell, 1902.

[McCord, Louisa Cheves], "Separate Secession," in *Southern Quarterly Review* (new series), vol. IV, no. 8 (October, 1851), pp. 298–317.

McGrane, Reginald C., ed., *The Correspondence of Nicholas Biddle Dealing with National Affairs, 1807–1844*. Boston and New York: Houghton Mifflin Co., 1919.

Mason, Virginia, *The Public Life and Diplomatic Correspondence of James M. Mason*. New York and Washington: Neale Publishing Co., 1906.

Miller, Lillian B., and others, eds., *The Selected Papers of Charles Willson Peale and His Family*. 4 vols. New Haven, Conn.: Yale University Press, 1983–1996.

Monroe, Haskell M., Jr., James T. McIntosh, et al., eds., *The Papers of Jefferson Davis*. 10 vols. to date. Baton Rouge: Louisiana State University Press, 1971–.

[Musson, Eugène,] *Lettre à Napoléon III sur l'esclavage aux états du Sud, par un Créole de la Louisiane*. Paris: Dentu, 1862. (English edition, London: W.S. Kirkland & Co., 1862.)

National Era. Washington: 1847–1860.

New Orleans, La., *Daily Delta*, 1845–1863.

New Orleans, La., *Daily Picayune*, 1836–1914.

New York, N.Y., *Herald*, 1835–1924.

New York, N.Y., *National Anti-Slavery Standard*, 1840–1872.

Pendleton, S.C., *Messenger*, 1807–?.

Peters, Richard, ed., *The Public Statutes at Large of the United States of America . . . .* 8 vols. Boston: Little, Brown & Co., 1846.

Philadelphia, Pa., *Pennsylvania Freeman*, 1838–1854.

Philadelphia, Pa., *Pennsylvanian*, 1832–1861.

Pickens, S.C., *Keowee Courier*, 1849–1868.

Register of Debates in Congress . . . 1824–1837 . . . . 14 vols. Washington: Gales & Seaton, 1825–1837.

Richmond, Va., *Daily Dispatch*, 1850–1883.

Richmond, Va., *Enquirer*, 1804–1877.

Richmond, Va., *Whig*, 1824–1888.

St. Louis, Mo., *Republican*, 1836–1919.

Sanborn, Alvan F., ed., *Reminiscences of Richard Lathers. . . .* New York: Grafton Press, 1907.

Spartanburg, S.C., *Spartan*, 1843–1853.

Speeches of Hon. John C. Calhoun and Hon. Daniel Webster, on the Subject of Slavery, Delivered in the Senate of the United States, March, 1850. New York: Stringer & Townsend, 1850.

Speech of Mr. Calhoun, of South Carolina, on the Slavery Question. Delivered in the Senate of the United States, March 4, 1850. [Washington: John T.] Towers, [1850]. (Another pamphlet with the same title, published by Buell & Blanchard, no place, no date.)

Speech of the Hon. Daniel Webster, in the Senate of the United States, on the Subject of Slavery. No publisher: no date.

Sumter, S.C., *Banner*, 1846–1855?.

Taylor, Frances Wallace, Catherine Taylor Matthews, and J. Tracy Power, eds., *The Leverett Letters: Correspondence of a South Carolina Family, 1851–1868*. Columbia: University of South Carolina Press, 2000.

Turner, Joseph Addison, *The Cotton Planter's Manual: Being a Compilation of Facts from the Best Authorities on the Culture of Cotton* . . . . New York: C.M. Saxton and Co., 1857.

Tuskegee, Ala., *Macon Republican*, 1845–1861?.

U.S. House of Representatives, *House Journal*, 14th Cong.

U.S. House of Representatives, *House Documents*, 15th–17th Congs.

Vicksburg, Miss., *Sentinel*, 1838–1851?.

Warner, Charles D., ed., *Library of the World's Best Literature*. 30 vols. New York: Peale & Hill, 1896–1899, and other editions.

Washington, D.C., *Daily National Intelligencer*, 1800–1870.

Washington, D.C., *Republican*, 1822–1824.

Washington, D.C., *United States' Telegraph*, 1826–1837.

Washington, D.C., *Union*, 1845–1859.

Webster, Daniel, *Writings and Speeches of Daniel Webster*. National edition. 18 vols. Boston: Little, Brown & Co., 1903.

Wilson, Clyde N., ed., *The Essential Calhoun*. New Brunswick, N.J., and London: Transaction Publishers, 1992, 1999.

INDEX

543